Armies / and / Politics / in / Latin / America

Armies / and / Politics / in / Latin / America

REVISED EDITION

Edited by

Abraham F. Lowenthal

and

J. Samuel Fitch

HM

HOLMES & MEIER
New York • London

First published in the United States of America 1986 by
Holmes & Meier Publishers, Inc.
30 Irving Place
New York, N.Y. 10003

Great Britain:
Pindar Road, Hoddesdon
Hertfordshire EN11 0HF England

Library of Congress Cataloging-in-Publication Data

Armies and politics in Latin America.

    Bibliography: p.
    Includes index.
    1. Latin America—Politics and government—1948–
2. Latin America—Armed Forces—Political activity—
History—20th century. 3. Coups d'état—Latin America—
History—20th century. 4. Military government—Latin
America—History—20th century. 5. Civil-military
relations—Latin America—History—20th century.
I. Lowenthal, Abraham F. II. Fitch, John Samuel.
F1414.2.A793 1986   322'.5'098   86-14918
ISBN 0-8419-0913-X
ISBN 0-8419-0916-4 (pbk.)

Manufactured in the United States of America

Contents

Preface to the Revised Edition

Ten years ago, when the first edition of *Armies and Politics in Latin America* was published, no one doubted that the armed forces were central to Latin American political life; they ruled directly in most nations of the hemisphere. Yet despite the military's obvious political role, there was no synthetic or comparative book to analyze the different ways in which the armed forces affected Latin America's politics. I first brought together the essays in *Armies and Politics* to illustrate diverse approaches to a subject that clearly deserved more systematic attention than it was receiving.

In the mid-1980s, as J. Samuel Fitch points out in his introductory essay, armies no longer rule directly in most countries of Latin America. Even while the armed forces have been withdrawing from outright political leadership, however, the literature analyzing the political role of the Latin American military has been greatly enriched. Increasingly sophisticated studies have been done on the political beliefs of military officers, on the military coup as a political process, on the processes of policy-making under military rule and the policy impact of military regimes, and on the problems of transition from military back to civilian rule. Research conducted during the last several years has emphasized sharp differences in the political role of the armed forces in various sociopolitical contexts. The importance of the interaction between institutional and contextual factors in shaping the military's involvement in Latin American political life has become increasingly evident.

Only seven of the eighteen articles in this substantially revised edition of *Armies and Politics* are repeated from the first version (now out of print). One essay (by David Ronfeldt) is a new essay by the same author on the same subject. Ten of the essays are reprinted in this edition for the first time. The articles have been selected because of their quality and because, taken together, they provide a useful overview of the field.

This volume would not have been possible but for the willingness of Professor Fitch to serve as coeditor. Professor Fitch took the lead in reviewing the most recent literature for new selections and prepared the introductory essay, which picks up where my 1974 review of the literature leaves off and evaluates the writing of the last decade. It has been a rare pleasure to collaborate formally with Sam Fitch on a subject we have been discussing informally since the early 1970s.

Both Professor Fitch and I are grateful to all the contributors for allowing us to republish their essays and, in many cases, for revising, editing, and updating their work. We also express thanks to the University of Southern California and the University of Colorado for the logistical support they have provided, and to Barbara Lyons of Holmes & Meier for encouraging us to undertake this project.

Abraham F. Lowenthal

I
Introduction

Abraham F. Lowenthal  *Armies and Politics in Latin America*

Introduction to the First Edition

I

Army officers rule in considerably more than half the countries of Latin America; in most of the rest, they participate actively in politics without currently occupying the presidential chair. In Brazil and Peru, military regimes with sharply different reputations appear entrenched. Ecuador's military government seems to waver uncertainly between the Brazilian and the Peruvian "models," as do officers in several other countries. In Chile, the armed forces deliberated long before finally taking over in September 1973, shattering the longest period any Latin American country in this century had experienced without military rule. The armed forces of Argentina relinquished office in 1973 but not without attempting to impose restrictive terms on their successors, and in 1976 the generals returned to power. In Uruguay, the army is taking an increasingly direct and expansive role, while in Paraguay it continues to serve as an instrument of prolonged personal rule. In Panama, nationalist reform under

From Abraham F. Lowenthal, "Armies and Politics in Latin America," *World Politics* 27, no. 1 (October 1974): 107–30. Copyright © 1974 by Princeton University Press and reprinted by permission of the publisher, Princeton University Press.

Author's Note: I express here my appreciation to several colleagues who commented on this essay in draft, and particularly to Henry Bienen, Peter Cleaves, David Collier, John Fitch III, Elizabeth Hyman, Robert Kaufman, Guillermo O'Donnell, and David Ronfeldt for their valuable suggestions.

military auspices prevails; in Santo Domingo, there is constant reshuffling; in Bolivia, renewed "stability" exists in the context of perpetual strife. Not even Cuba's revolution has ended military participation in politics; on the contrary, the armed forces may well be Cuba's strongest and most influential political institution.[1]

Why do most Latin American armed forces participate so overtly in national political processes? Why have things changed so sharply from the time, little more than a decade ago, when only one Latin American country was ruled by a military regime and the "twilight of the tyrants" was being heralded?[2] What different political roles have been performed by Latin American military institutions? What accounts for the differences? How do Latin American armies govern? How does military rule differ from civilian rule in Latin America?

As Lyle McAlister observed in his comprehensive survey in 1966, until about a decade ago the literature on what was then called "militarism" was mostly descriptive, not explanatory.[3] It concentrated on *caudillos* (personalist military leaders) rather than on military institutional development. Authors primarily concerned with the civilian political process discussed the political activities of Latin American armed forces as a peripheral matter; their treatment tended to be normative, prescriptive, and even polemical. Scholars almost invariably grounded their analyses in a "democratic-civilist" model of civil-military relations, derived from European and North American experience, which assumed that armed forces characteristically exercise limited defense and police functions of an essentially non-political nature. When military officers played an overtly political role, that was regarded as exceptional and regrettable. It was termed "intervention," implying the temporary introduction of a coherent body into a separate system; its policy consequences were assumed to be universally regressive. Most writers dealt with all military "interventions" as if they were more or less alike, the key difference among countries being whether or not "intervention" occurred. It was assumed (or at least hoped) that military involvement in Latin America politics would decline as socioeconomic modernization and mobilization occurred, as armies became more "professional," and as the influence of announced United States support for democratic regimes made itself felt.

During the early 1960s the literature began to change, particularly in four respects. First, the political activities of Latin American armies came to be regarded as a topic sufficiently important to be studied directly. Second, authors began to highlight distinctions among the political roles played by armies in different countries, though the first attempts to classify various kinds of military participation in Latin American politics were crude and unsatisfactory.[4] Third, various writers on Latin America (John Johnson foremost among them) began to question the earlier assumption that military participation in politics was invariably regressive.[5] Fourth, it was increasingly recognized that the armed forces and civilian politics were often closely intertwined, that armies were not encapsulated institutions set apart from politics except when intervening.

In evaluating the literature published through 1965, McAlister noted that it tended to be broad and general; to begin to accept the notion that "the military is an integral component of Latin American society *interacting* with other elements rather than acting against them"; to be contributed primarily by North American scholars and mainly by historians; to lack firm data and empirical support for conclusions offered; and to be almost devoid of comparative studies.[6]

II

Writings on armies and politics in Latin America published since 1965 differ sharply from those reviewed by McAlister.[7]

1. Whereas the literature before 1966 tended to be general and regional, national case studies now predominate.[8] In fact, significant books dealing comprehensively and comparatively with the differing political roles exercised by Latin American armed forces have recently been conspicuous by their absence.

2. It has by now become the established wisdom that armed forces interact continuously with the other elements in Latin American societies. Emphasis is beginning to turn, however, toward examining the educational and other institutional procedures, including recruitment and socialization, which set military forces somewhat apart from other social groups, and imbue in military officers a sense of corporate autonomy and interest.[9]

3. Some of the most insightful writing on this subject is now being done by Latin Americans.[10]

4. Historians continue to be among the most prolific writers on the political roles played by Latin American armies, but major conceptual advances have come from several political scientists.

5. Careful empirical work now characterizes this literature. For example, Robert Potash's *The Army and Politics in Argentina, 1928–1945: Yrigoyen to Perón* (Stanford 1969), draws on extensive data about the recruitment, composition, and training of Argentine officers, as well as on (almost overwhelmingly) detailed information about informal cliques within the Argentine military and their relations with civilian factions. The evidence Potash adduces—much of it from previously unavailable diplomatic records and from personal interviews—enables him to document the emergence of a highly professional, notably self-protective Argentine officer corps. The basic argument, which he spells out briefly in his conclusions (and promises to elaborate in a second book, on the Perón era), is that the Argentine army's more assertive role, reflected in Perón's rise, is attributable largely to gradual changes within the military over the preceding fifteen years. Potash emphasizes the doubling of the Argentine

officer corps between 1930 and 1945, its increasing professionalism, the establishment of the equivalent of a National War College with year-long courses for senior officers, and the creation of arsenals and factories run by the military. These changes tended to confer increasing self-confidence on the officers in their own capacity to handle national problems, and have facilitated the Argentine army's adoption of an ever more overt political role.

Alfred Stepan's *The Military in Politics: Changing Patterns in Brazil* (Princeton 1971) is also based on a wealth of data, including detailed information on the social and educational background of Brazilian officers and cadets, reports on applications to military academies, extensive interviews with Brazilian officers sympathetic to the author's research, and an imaginatively executed content analysis of several military journals and of civilian political debate. Stepan focuses mainly on explaining why the Brazilian military in 1964 turned away from what he calls a "moderator" model to its current "directive" role.

Under the "moderator" model, the military institution is repeatedly called in to preserve the political balance but is denied the right to attempt systematically to direct lasting changes within the political system. Until 1964, acceptance of this role by Brazilian officers was contingent upon their acknowledgment of the "legitimacy and feasibility of parliamentary political forms and upon their assessment that in comparison with civilians they possess a relatively low capacity for ruling" (p. 63). In 1964, however, what Stepan terms a "boundary change" occurred. Stepan stresses the confluence of developments external to the military (Brazil's macrosocial crisis and the widespread impression that the civilian political system was failing) with internal circumstances, especially the emergence of a focus on national development strategy in the Superior War College. By 1964 Brazilian officers were skeptical about the ability of civilians to solve Brazil's problems and increasingly self-confident about their own capacity to implement a reasonably coherent development strategy (which was worked out with the aid of civilian technocrats). A full-scale, long-term takeover resulted.

Stepan concludes by examining the Brazilian regime's first four years in power; he challenges the "realist" assumption that military governments are less subject than civilian regimes to the problems of policy incoherence and instability. Stepan shows how the military's preoccupation with preserving unity has made for important discontinuities, ugly repression, and consequently eventual self-isolation, from which no escape is easily imaginable. Stepan does not directly confront the question of whether the Brazilian military might have avoided its present apparent *cul de sac,* but seems to imply that the tensions between the "military as government" and the "military as institution" will inevitably undermine the effectiveness of a long-term military regime and/or drive it to repression. It took less than five years for this process to become painfully evident in Brazil.

The impressive degree to which Peru's military regime has maintained its apparent cohesion and continuity and a reputation for tolerance for more than five years raises interesting questions, therefore. Do special circumstances in Peru account for the Velasco regime's ability to preserve its unity and self-confidence? Or is the Peruvian regime's relative success to date fragile, and eventually likely to be strained by the pressures Stepan discusses?

Important background material for analyzing the Peruvian case is provided in *100 Años del Ejército Peruano: Frustraciones y Cambios* and *El CAEM y la Revolución de la Fuerza Armada,* two recent books by Victor Villanueva, a retired Peruvian Army major.[11] In *100 Años del Ejército Peruano,* Villanueva concentrates on what he sees as a century-long "process of change in the military mind which brought it, slowly but persistently, to the need to capture political power," a need based fundamentally on a series of institutionally transmitted "traumas" and "frustrations" (p. 11). Several decades of collective experience have imbued Peruvian officers with an aversion for civilians, political parties, and "politics," a "generously positive self-estimation," a "subjective need for autonomy and power," and "confidence at being better equipped than civilians to govern the country" (p. 11).

In his most recent volume, Villanueva discusses a more specific influence on the current Peruvian regime: the mid-career education Peru's officers have been receiving since 1950 at the Centro de Altos Estudios Militares (CAEM), Peru's equivalent of the National War College. Whereas other writers on the current Peruvian regime tend generally but vaguely to attribute much of the junta's reform orientation to the CAEM program (about which little concrete information had previously emerged), Villanueva provides enough data to speculate about the specific impact of CAEM. On the basis of a reasonably well-documented (though somewhat spotty) examination of the CAEM curriculum and professional staff roster for the 1950's and 1960's, Villanueva rejects the view that CAEM was significantly influenced by Marxists and other radical civilians. Rather, Villanueva argues, the CAEM doctrine emerged from a more narrowly military concern with institutional self-protection and self-assertion in the context of national development needs; most important, it "rationalized the old rejection the military felt for the civilian" (p. 170). Villanueva's work can be criticized: some of it is more polemical than profound; insufficient evidence is provided for several key assertions (for example, that civilian professors have generally been guided by the CAEM leadership regarding their approach, rather than vice versa); and the emphasis on long-term, institutional psycho-experience is sometimes farfetched. But much can be learned from a judicious reading of

Villanueva's contributions; his books are rich in detail, full of specific comments and insights, and informed by a sensitivity to personal and contextual variables that are sometimes ignored in more scholarly treatises.

6. Though excellent studies of individual countries are now available, it remains largely true that systematic comparative work is lacking on the political role of Latin American armies.

A few exceptions should be noted, however.[12] The most valuable effort so far published is Guillermo O'Donnell's *Modernization and Bureaucratic Authoritarianism: Studies in South American Politics* (Berkeley 1973), which concentrates on Argentina and Brazil. O'Donnell challenges the widely accepted notion that rising levels of modernization are conducive to democratic political arrangements. He suggests instead that there may be an "elective affinity" between situations of "high modernization" and "bureaucratic authoritarianism," which usually takes the form of a military regime that diminishes the influence of the already activated urban popular sector on national politics. O'Donnell stresses the bureaucratic and exclusionary nature of these authoritarian regimes more than their military character, implying that the latter trait may be of secondary importance or even coincidental. The key point is that technocratic elites in charge of various kinds of bureaucratic organizations try to reshape society and politics to permit more extensive application of their own expertise; in order to have their way, they cut off popular participation and even employ force.

Not all cases of "bureaucratic authoritarianism" are alike. O'Donnell distinguishes between Argentina and Brazil chiefly with regard to the degree of autonomy and organization within the "popular" (mainly labor) sector of each before the eventual turn to authoritarianism. Argentina's more highly organized and complex popular sector, O'Donnell argues, precludes thorough, long-term demobilization—short of extremely harsh repression. Brazil's lower degree of prior popular mobilization, however, has permitted the military regime to consolidate its hold. O'Donnell enriches his discussion with a brief aside on Peru, whose current regime he characterizes as "populist authoritarian," because it does not aim to exclude the present participants, but to incorporate new participants within an expansive, nationalist, and anti-oligarchical coalition like that experienced by Brazil and Argentina during the eras of Vargas and Perón.

A more extensive treatment of Peru and Brazil is provided by Luigi Einaudi and Alfred Stepan in *Latin American Institutional Development: Changing Military Perspectives in Peru and Brazil* (Santa Monica 1971).[13] They intelligently discuss why armies with essentially similar organizations, structures, and procedures, in countries with roughly comparable social and economic problems, and subject to the same kind of foreign (principally North American) doctrinal influences forged national security doctrines that eventually led them to substitute direct, long-term rule for a previously more restricted political role. But, though well worth consulting for its concise, well-informed, and clearly written analyses of the two cases, the Einaudi-Stepan volume is essentially a juxtaposition of separately conducted studies rather than the application of a comparative framework to different cases. Disciplined comparative statements are scarce, and the study's conclusions amount to little more than a restatement of the general propositions appropriately presented in the introduction. What is particularly regrettable is that Einaudi and Stepan say so little to explain why the Brazilian and Peruvian armies, similar in so many aspects detailed by the authors, now play such apparently different roles.

Stepan begins to deal with these differences, albeit still somewhat sketchily and almost exclusively in terms of factors internal to the respective armies, in his essay "The New Professionalism of Internal Warfare and Military Role Expansion," included in this volume. Contrasting the "new professionalism" exemplified in Brazil and Peru with the "old professionalism" discussed in most of the literature on armies and politics, Stepan shows how and why the more advanced Latin American armies are playing such active political roles. Contrary to what was expected, we may be in for more, and longer-lasting, military regimes.

III

The faith of a decade ago—that military involvement in Latin American politics would decline as a result of economic development, social modernization, military professionalization, and American influence—can no longer be sustained. As it appears that the military's significant role in Latin American politics is here to stay, attention has turned increasingly not only to analyzing why this is so, but also to examining the consequences of military rule for policy outputs and outcomes.

Perhaps the most interesting aspect of the recent literature on why Latin American armed forces "intervene" is that so many writers still pose the question that way. Even a cursory familiarity with Latin America might well lead one to ask instead why armies have refrained (or appear to refrain) from taking an extensive and direct political role in a handful of Latin American countries: Costa Rica, Mexico since the 1930's, Venezuela since 1958, and Chile and Uruguay until very recently. Studies of these cases are scarce, however, and generally unilluminating.

Probably the major book on the military in Chile, *Las Fuerzas Armadas en el Sistema Político Chileno,* by Alain Joxe, disputes the conventional view that the Chilean army had not recently (before 1973) involved itself much in politics.[14] Joxe asserts—plausibly, even persuasively, but by no means in a detailed or elaborated fashion—that the Chilean army has had a "latent and permanent participation" in the political process as the middle class's principal agent in shaping and protecting the social, political, and economic systems for its benefit (pp. 40–41). Although the Chilean military has not taken office directly very often—in 1891, 1924, 1931–32 (and in 1973)—Joxe argues that each military takeover in Chile counts for ten somewhere else, because the army does such a thorough and effective job each time in rearranging the system to protect vital middle-class interests. But Joxe offers scant explanation of why the Chilean middle class, in contrast to others in Latin America, needs to rely on overt military "intervention" so infrequently.

Liisa North's essay in this volume, "The Military in Chilean Politics," goes a long way toward answering this question, and toward accounting for the brutally repressive role of today's military rulers of Chile. Emphasizing the political and institutional history of Chile's armed forces, North stresses the interplay of long-term trends and immediate situational variables in helping to account for the Chilean tragedy.

For the reader interested in analyzing why some Latin American armies participate overtly in politics less often than others, Winfield Burggraaff's *The Venezuelan Armed Forces in Politics, 1935–1959* (Columbia, Mo. 1972) is disappointing, for Burggraaff deliberately cuts off his account just when the Venezuelan army stopped "intervening." Within its purview, Burggraaff's volume provides some interesting information on how the Venezuelan army evolved from a *caudillo's* personal instrument to an increasingly autonomous and coherent professional institution. But although Burggraaff asks "what motivated Venezuelan officers to intervene directly in politics between 1928 and 1958," he answers only by citing a catalogue of possible explanations among which it is "risky to assign weights" (p. 195).

Edwin Lieuwen's *Mexican Militarism: The Political Rise and Fall of the Revolutionary Army, 1910–1940* (Albuquerque 1968) deals with a fascinating series of questions: how a traditional army was destroyed and replaced by a revolutionary one, how the revolutionary army was professionalized, and then, how the professional army was practically withdrawn from politics and civilian authority was established.[15] Of particular interest in Mexico's experience was the Calles era in the mid-1920's, when the decision was made to professionalize the Mexican army from the bottom up by developing a corps of young professionals. The task of removing the generals from politics (some by purge, many others by payoff) was in most cases left to later—the presidents were generals until 1946—by which time the autonomy and continuity of the military institution were assured. The questions Lieuwen poses are considerably better than the answers he provides, however; this may be because the main answers involve post-revolutionary social, economic, and political circumstances beyond the scope of the data Lieuwen considers in focusing on the military itself.

Few writers, then, discuss why some Latin American armies usually avoid direct and active political roles; none do so satisfactorily. What about the question almost all of them face: why do most Latin American armed forces participate overtly in politics?

A wide variety of explanatory propositions has been advanced. Some writers emphasize institutional, "internal," or "push" factors: the size and firepower of armies; the size, class origins, socialization, training, cohort experience, and degree of professionalization of officers; and the effects of foreign military assistance. Others highlight social, "external," "environmental,"' or "pull" circumstances: levels of economic and political development, political culture, and social stratification systems. Not only have many variables been cited, but there has been little consensus on the effects of any of them. It has been argued that smaller, or larger, armies are more likely to "intervene"; that "professionalization" expands, or restricts, an army's political activity; that the emerging predominance of middle-class officers will promote, or restrain, their political participation and will make the army's policy impact progressively redistributive, or regressive; that foreign influence leads to "interventionism," or the contrary; that rising levels of development and modernization will promote democratic, or authoritarian, politics; that the political traditions and culture of Latin America require an apolitical stance by military officers, or that they reinforce their proclivity for politics.

Robert Putnam has attempted to test a number of these contradictory propositions for the decade preceding 1966.[16] Analyzing aggregate data, Putnam relates measures of a series of independent variables, such as socioeconomic development, political development, characteristics of particular military institutions, and foreign assistance and training, to the dependent variable, "military intervention," defined as the armed forces' veering away from the management and use of controlled violence in the service of the state, to participate in or influence other, non-military agencies and functions of the state.[17] Putnam's article is useful mainly for the doubts it casts on some of the hypotheses that have been widely discussed, particularly regarding the supposed influence of foreign military missions and of "coup contagion" (i.e., the effect of coups in neighboring countries) on the incidence of military intervention. Putnam's other major findings—that "social mobilization" is strongly and negatively related to "military intervention" but that "economic development" is positively correlated—are questionable. The statistical analysis suffers from serious problems in measuring key variables, violations of various statistical assumptions, and inappropriate inferences about processes of change from cross-sectional data. In addition to these methodological difficulties, Putnam fails to differentiate among the wide variety of armies and political roles within the phenomenon of "military intervention."[18]

The same comment applies to Martin Needler's "Political Development and Military Intervention in Latin America."[19] Needler seeks to explain the frequency and timing of coups d'état and to ascertain whether there is any overall trend with regard to their effects on social and economic policy. He concludes that coups occur more often than not when economic conditions are deteriorating; that they increasingly tend to occur against constitutional regimes, often just before or just after elections; that their redistributive effects on economic and social policy, if any, are regressive; and that, though their incidence is cyclical, the secular trend is descending (i.e., coups seem to occur less frequently now than before 1960). Needler's empirical observations do not appear to hold up well, however, for the years since 1966 have been punctuated by coups, at least some of them clearly reformist.

Even for the period he discusses, Needler's argument lacks explanatory power. Although he offers some hypotheses, particularly the "swing man" proposition (which focuses on the dynamics of coups themselves and how these affect timing and policy orientation), Needler cannot say much that will meaningfully explain such an undifferentiated class of phenomenon as Latin American coups. Essentially, his statements about trends are grounded in the view that expanded participation is inevitable and will lead to fewer coups, but this conclusion is by no means self-evident. Needler also believes that military "intervention," being self-protective of military corporate interests, is bound to restrict participation and to protect the socioeconomic status quo. However plausible these assertions, they do not necessarily hold true either; the current rash of military regimes in Latin America undermines Needler's first assertion; Peru's current experience, at least, would appear to contradict the second.

IV

Whereas Putnam and Needler lump together all types of military coups, a growing literature on specific countries underlines the great variance among examples of military participation in politics. Each case study highlights particular circumstances, but taken together they suggest four main distinctions.[20]

First, Latin American military institutions exercise their political influence either directly and overtly, as rulers, or indirectly, as a kind of specially endowed pressure group.[21] Nowhere in Latin America (with the possible exception of Costa Rica, where the officer corps is largely disbanded by each new administration) do armed forces play an insignificant political role or even one mainly limited to national defense and police functions.

Second, among those countries where direct military rule occurs, it may be personalist, factional, or institutional. A regime is personalist when a politician in uniform uses the armed forces (or part of them) to expand and protect his power, whether exercised on his own behalf or on behalf of a civilian group or groups. Personalist regimes are most common in countries with poorly institutionalized, unprofessional armed forces.[22] Factional regimes occur when a group of officers, aspiring to accomplish an institutional coup, assumes control, usually against the will of the established military hierarchy; this formulation is bound to be transitory, for the faction will soon find itself either displaced or able to transform the military institution to its liking. Institutional regimes occur, in turn, when the leadership of the armed forces rules on the basis of established procedures likely to survive the particular chief; this may happen when the armed forces' top officers take power (purging dissenters), or when a faction successfully gains dominance within established channels.[23] Although its incidence has so far been infrequent, institutional rule is relatively stable once it has been accomplished, for no other social or political group is likely to remove from office a military establishment united in its will to govern.

Third, military regimes may be distinguished on the basis of their frequency and length. Brief, intermittent coups may be personalist (when no one *caudillo* can consolidate national control) or institutional (as was the case in Peru in 1962 and in Brazil and Argentina several times before 1964). Long-term military rule may reflect the establishment of a strongman regime in the absence of mass participation or complex social and political organizations, as in Nicaragua or Paraguay; but it may also be institutional, as it is today in Brazil and Peru.

Finally, and perhaps most important, military regimes differ sharply in their programmatic aims and consequences. In some countries, particularly in Central America and the Caribbean, armies have served mainly to enrich *caudillo* leaders, their military henchmen, and their civilian accomplices. In other cases—in Peru through 1960 and in Colombia until Rojas Pinilla, for example—armed forces have protected landowning "oligarchies" against challenges to their wealth and power, even those posed by urban middle-class elements. In a few situations—in Chile in 1924–25, in Brazil during the Vargas period, in Argentina under Perón, and in contemporary Panama and Peru—military regimes have helped middle-class groups, including organized labor, to reduce the influence of entrenched ruling classes. In such cases, armies have aided in extending the franchise and/or other rights to new participants in politics, and have spurred redistributive economic and social reforms. But in still other cases—in contemporary Argentina and Brazil, and especially in Chile— the policy of the military has been to restrict political participation, to demobilize and depoliticize, and even to repress.

V

What accounts for the dramatically different policies adopted by military regimes in different countries, or even at successive points in one nation's history? What can explain not only the frequency and level of military participation in Latin American politics, but also its several forms: direct and indirect; personal, factional, and institutional; intermittent and long-term; reformist and regressive?[24]

Case studies, like those by Potash, Burggraaff, Einaudi, and Villanueva, tend to stress internal institutional factors. Discussions of the Peruvian case, for instance, underline the army's recruitment and promotion of officers from the provincial middle class; its training program, particularly the CAEM course and the experience of many officers in U.S. installations; its historic difficulties with and consequent distrust of civilians; and the experience of top-ranking officers who had to put down guerrilla uprisings in the mid-1960's. These factors are hardly irrelevant, but comparative data suggest that none, by itself, is a sufficient explanation for the Peruvian military's evolution. Most officer corps in Latin America come predominantly from the provincial middle class, but few (if any) parallel the Peruvian Army's current stance.[25] Peru's CAEM course is unusual among Latin American countries, but it is by no means unique, and most officers who have graduated from nearly equivalent institutions in Argentina and Brazil have emerged with attitudes and policy preferences very different from those declared by their Peruvian counterparts. Besides, not even the most extravagant proponents of the impact of education would argue that a nine-month course for mature professionals, or even shorter exposure to foreign training, could fundamentally affect their values and behavior. And other armies, in Latin America and elsewhere, have emerged from battles with guerrillas determined to repress them, rather than eager to foster structural change.[26]

If internal variables are insufficient to explain the variety of political roles played by Latin American armies, what about arguments that attribute the military's political behavior "not to the social and organizational characteristics of the military establishment but to the political and institutional structure of the society"?[27] José Nun argues that armies in Latin America have usually acted as representatives of changing middle-class interests, compensating for that class's "inability to establish itself as a well-integrated hegemonic group."[28] Samuel Huntington elaborates this insight, portraying armed forces across the world as "doorkeepers to the expansion of political participation in a praetorian society; their historic role is to open the door to the middle class and to close it to the lower class."[29]

The Nun-Huntington hypothesis, though it obviously tends to obscure somewhat the heterogeneous character and interests of the "middle class" in most Latin American countries and to play down the effects of international influences on their behavior, represents a major analytical advance. It clarifies how the military can be reformist in one context and reactionary in another while pursuing more or less consistent lines of action. Virgilio Rafael Beltrán's analysis of several different types of military participation in Argentina, for instance, shows that the army was never aligned with "popular" sectors against the "middle class," but several times joined middle-class groupings, first against the oligarchic minority and then against the majority.[30]

But the hypothesis relating the military's political role to levels and types of middle-class participation explains less than it seems to. That military officers of middle-class origin act—in any particular circumstance or even in many—compatibly with general middle-class interests does not prove that the officers are protecting the middle class. As Fitch argues (in the context of Ecuador), the officers' "strong corporate self-identification with the military institution, rather than their peripheral identification as members of the middle class," may account best for their political position.[31] If narrow institutional requirements and general class interests coincide, the explanation may relate to common responses to similar problems rather than to any similarity of origin or perceived interest. This point is important because there are cases—Argentina in the early 1930's, Peru in 1968—when a military group deposed an eminently middle-class regime. The Peruvian case, in which the military's "revolutionary" program appears to have gone beyond what all but a small fraction of Peru's middle class will support, raises this question most sharply. But the Nun-Huntington approach, by itself, also fails to account for other cases—for instance, the substantially changed character of military participation in Argentine politics between 1955 and 1966, from "legalists" to long-term rulers. How can such "exceptions" be explained?

The most persuasive writers stress the confluence and interaction of macrosocial factors with those internal to the military institution.[32] Stepan, for instance, maintains that although an army's political role cannot be deduced from its organizational characteristics, the latter importantly affect the military's exercise of a role structured in large part by wider social forces. O'Donnell emphasizes the interrelation of social and institutional forces in Argentina, arguing that the level of military "professionalization" is a key variable, but that its impact is conditioned by the wider sociopolitical setting. "The professionalization of the armed forces in the praetorian context raises the critical point from which military intervention becomes probable," O'Donnell argues, implying that the more "professional" the army, the less likely overt "intervention" becomes. But "once that point is reached, the military intervention takes place with more cohesion, with a comprehensive justificatory ideology, and with the purpose of achieving goals much more ambitious than those in coups undertaken by less professional armed forces."[33]

VI

Perhaps the most interesting series of questions regarding military participation in politics—little discussed until recently—relates to the effects of military rule.[34] How do military regimes differ from their civilian counterparts, predecessors, and successors? What difference does it make whether or not politicians, technicians, and bureaucrats wear uniforms?

By far the most systematic and comprehensive effort to deal with the consequences of military rule in Latin America is Philippe Schmitter's "Military Intervention, Political Competitiveness, and Public Policy in Latin America: 1950–1967."[35] Noting that the supposed impact of different types of regimes on public policy is rarely accompanied by evidence, Schmitter draws on the literature to formulate a series of "speculative contradictory hypotheses" susceptible to testing against available socioeconomic data and indicators of public policy variables. (Schmitter limits his review to analyzing expenditures; dimensions of civil liberty, for instance, are deliberately ignored.) Some of Schmitter's arguments may scare off readers unfamiliar with quantitative analytical techniques and their argot; those not so handicapped may question his eclectic application of several methods and wonder about the quality of some of the basic data.[36] But Schmitter's exercises provide a very useful start, suggesting several effects that various types of regimes may have on patterns and results of public policy. Military regimes apparently spend more than their civilian counterparts on "defense" and less on social welfare; the highest defense expenditures occur when the military is an intermittent ruler.[37] The type of regime affects "how much Latin American polities can extract from their environments (i.e., total government expenditures and revenues), upon whom the burden of this extractive process will fall (i.e., taxation), how much of these scarce resources will be plowed back into the system to develop it (i.e., public investment), and which social groups will be benefited (i.e., sectoral expenditures)." But "indicators of overall system performance *(outcomes)* are much less predictably affected by regime-type . . . than are indicators of direct governmental allocation *(outputs).* How much Latin American countries invest, industrialize, increase their GNP, raise their cost of living, increase their school enrollment and/or engage in foreign trade seems more the product of environmental or ecological factors than the willful acts of politicians grouped according to their competitiveness or civilian-military status."

Schmitter's essay, though making imaginative use of a wide variety of available data, points up the need for improved and more comprehensive data sets on specific countries. Even more, as Schmitter himself suggests, his study indicates the need for careful analysis of causality and process in individual cases or pairs of cases, conforming to or deviating from the modal patterns. To date, however, there is only one such study: Barry Ames, "Rhetoric and Reality in a Militarized Regime: Brazil since 1964" (*Sage Professional Papers in Comparative Politics* No. 1–402, H. Eckstein et al., eds), looks at how the Brazilian military government and its civilian predecessors handled a series of issue areas: housing, tax, and educational policies. He suggests that the policy-making process did not differ equally across the various issue areas from one type of regime to another; rather, it differed according to the priority given the particular issue by the military, the degree (if any) of prior policy commitments and clearly articulated goals, and the strength of clientele groups.

Ames's analysis, like Schmitter's, suggests that military regimes do affect public policies, but not as much as they claim or their critics assert. But lumping together all "military" regimes and distinguishing them from all "civilian" regimes may be profoundly misleading. As O'Donnell hints, certain social circumstances may produce regimes, whether civilian or military, that resemble each other much more than they do other civilian or military regimes under different socioeconomic circumstances.[38] The incipient literature on public policy making in Latin America should illuminate this point.

VII

The recent literature on the political role of Latin American armed forces is extensive, empirically based, and increasingly subtle conceptually. Obvious differences between the political activities and impacts of armies in countries like Brazil and Peru, the Dominican Republic and Argentina, Bolivia and Chile—indeed, the vast differences among the military institutions themselves and between the political roles played by the same army at different times in a given country's history—have dissolved easy assumptions about the nature of military involvement in Latin American politics. It becomes increasingly clear that armies participate in Latin American politics in several different ways and that no simple explanation accounts for all. More important, it becomes evident that approaches relating characteristics of the military institutions themselves to the social context in which they operate provide the most promising avenues for explaining the various political roles played by Latin American officers.

What remains to be done?

1. Additional case studies are needed to help us analyze how the political roles of armies have evolved within different national contexts, why coups sometimes occur and sometimes do not, why military regimes are sometimes brief and sometimes long, sometimes reformist and sometimes reactionary, how armies have been affected by macrosocial and institutional changes, and what effects various forms of military participation have had on national politics and policy. Research on cases where military participation has become less overt (e.g., Venezuela), or where military rule has now entrenched itself (e.g., Peru), would be of greatest interest.

2. Contextually sensitive analysis is particularly needed on how armies govern in Latin America, what coalitions they form, what clienteles they

respond to, how they make and execute decisions, and generally whether, how, and why the substance and style of military regimes differ in Latin America from those of civilian governments.

3. Research is required on pairs of cases chosen to highlight theoretically significant differences: Peru and Brazil, Argentina and Chile, Panama and Nicaragua, for example. Emphasis should be given particularly to specific institutional aspects that may vary from country to country: recruitment, socialization, and training patterns, for instance. Because it may be unrealistic to expect individual researchers to attain the necessary degree of access to military institutions in more than one country, carefully designed collaborative projects seem indicated.

4. How soldiers affect Latin American politics should be compared with what we know of their role elsewhere, particularly in other third world regions. "Neo-realist" writings on the Middle East and Asia distorted North American perceptions of the Latin American military in the 1960's.[39] Writings on Latin America, in turn, are said to have misled scholars when they turned to analyzing sub-Saharan armies.[40] Recent "revisionist" writings on the military role in African and Arab polities, together with those here reviewed on Latin America, should provide for a mutual correction of focus.[41]

5. The most exciting task is to synthesize and integrate within an inclusive theoretical formulation the by now abundant literature on the political roles armies play in Latin America and in other regions.

It is not possible in this brief essay to take up that final challenge. It may be appropriate, however, to advance one central proposition suggested by the literature reviewed here: that the relation between the level of military institutionalization and the institutionalization of civilian political procedures may be a key determinant of the varying political roles army officers play.[42]

As Huntington argues, the single most important variable affecting military participation in politics is the ratio between the scope of political participation and the strength (autonomy, coherence, complexity, and adaptability) of civilian political institutions. Whenever popular participation exceeds the capacity of political institutions to channel it in a routinized, stable manner, "praetorianism" of one kind or another results, no matter what the absolute level of popular participation. Extensive and unmediated political activity takes place, not only by soldiers but also by priests, students, and labor leaders.

Important variations mark the spectrum of "praetorian" cases, however. Some armies "moderate" or "arbitrate"; others "direct" or "rule." Some act overtly for brief periods only; others take power for an extended time. Some push progressive, redistributive policies; others are conservative, if not reactionary.

Huntington postulates that the policy impact of military rule varies with the level of civilian political participation. In the "oligarchic" phase of limited participation, military *caudillos* (like civilian leaders) do not challenge the structure of power and rewards; they merely seek to assure themselves that they will benefit from it. Armies entering politics during a period of expanding middle-class participation in a previously aristocratic society are likely to play a "radical" role, opening the system and distributing resources and rewards more equitably than was previously done. But the impact of military involvement in an already highly participant polity (i.e., at the "mass praetorian" phase) is bound to be restrictive and repressive, Huntington argues, for the popular majority now threatens the prerogatives of the middle class, including the armed forces.

Huntington's persuasive argument does not fully explain, however, why military participation in different "praetorian" societies varies so much in duration, intensity, and style. Why do officers in Peru and Panama seem to go way beyond middle-class civilian politicians in their reformist zeal, for instance? Or, why is military involvement in the politics of Santo Domingo, Haiti, or Nicaragua so much closer to gang plunder than to institutional exercise of national responsibility?[43]

A study of the differing levels of institutional strength among Latin American armies and the comparative strengths of civilian and military organizations in specific countries might be most illuminating in this connection.

An army's institutional strength may be measured, at least roughly, with reference to: (1) its resources (e.g., percentage of GNP and of national budget spent on defense, percentage of eligible men under arms, expenditure per soldier); (2) its professional level (e.g., years of schooling required of senior officers, number of military journals published, extent to which academic achievement and other "objective" measures affect promotions); and (3) its institutional cohesion and coherence, reflected also by its autonomy in such spheres as recruitment, assignments, and promotion.

If we were to rank the institutional strength of past and present Latin American armies, I suspect we would discover that military involvement in politics changes in a curvilinear fashion as armies gain in organizational strength and coherence.[44] At the lowest level of military institutionalization, officers participate in politics overtly, frequently, on a personalist basis, and often for long periods. At the intermediate level of military institutionalization, after "professionalization" has been emphasized, officers tend to participate less overtly (and if overtly, for briefer periods) than at an earlier stage, perhaps because they are protecting their still fragile corporate autonomy. At this intermediate stage, tensions are common between personalist leadership and institutional considerations; it is not unusual for the most professional officers (the best educated, least dependent on political ties for their previous promotions, etc.) eventually to displace the *caudillo* and restore civilian life. At a still higher stage of military institutionalization, in turn, armies are again more likely to play an overt role, this time long-term and directive, as officers achieve a self-confident sense of corporate autonomy and even superiority. At this stage, "intervention" may be reluctant, but when it comes it will probably be intensive and long-lasting.

Analyzing the relation between the strength of military institutions, the strength of civilian institutions, and the level of civilian political participation would also be of interest. If military institutionalization outpaces the evolution of parties and other civilian institutions, long-term, directive, and institutional rule by the armed forces is likely. The policy impact of military involvement will vary, however, with the level of mobilization and participation. At an intermediate stage, officers may self-confidently help to expand participation and even redistribute rewards, assured by their predominant strength that their own corporate interests are unendangered. At a high level of participation, rule by a well-institutionalized army may be equally overt, directive, and extended. But as military rule is occasioned precisely because mass participation was deemed threatening to the armed forces, its impact will be restrictive and regressive.

Conversely, when military institutionalization lags behind, as it does in most of Central America and the Caribbean at the intermediate level of civilian participation, or perhaps in Uruguay at a higher level, the consequences are also predictable. At the intermediate level of participation, officers are more likely to participate overtly, as personalist instruments, and for more extended periods than are the more professional units characteristic of other such polities. At a high level of participation, officers will participate less overtly and directively than would the highly institutionalized armies usually associated with high-participation situations.

The foregoing argument obviously needs elaboration and testing. No doubt it needs to be further qualified as well—particularly with regard to the impact of the specific previous experience of each country on participation of the military in politics, and of the relative timing of each country's economic growth and social mobilization.[45] It is offered in this preliminary form, however, as one contribution to the theory-building process that the extensive literature on armies and politics in Latin America now clearly invites.

Notes

1. More than half the members of the Central Committee of Cuba's Communist Party are army officers. See Jorge Domínguez, "The Civic Soldier in Cuba," reprinted in this volume. See also Eduardo Gonzalez, "The New Role of the

Revolutionary Armed Forces in Cuba," paper presented at the Conference on the Latin American Military, University of California, Riverside, April 1970; and Gonzalez, "Political Succession in Cuba: After Fidel . . . ?" paper presented to the 1973 Annual Meeting of the American Political Science Association, New Orleans, September 1973.

2. Late in 1961, Paraguay's was the only military government in all of South America. See Tad Szulc, *Twilight of the Tyrants* (New York 1959), and Edwin Lieuwen, *Arms and Politics in Latin America* (New York 1961), for the view that military participation in Latin American politics was declining.

3. See Lyle McAlister, "Recent Research and Writing on the Role of the Military in Latin America," *Latin American Research Review,* ii (Fall 1966), 5–36.

4. Lieuwen (n. 2), for instance, distinguished among three groups of countries: those in which the military dominated politics, those in which armies were in transition from political to non-political bodies, and those in which they were non-political. At least six of the seven cases in the supposedly transitional category, however, have since then moved in the direction contrary to Lieuwen's argument, and some of his "non-political" armies have taken an active political role. In any case, Lieuwen's three descriptive categories lacked explanatory power; little was said to indicate why particular countries fell into one category or another. Essentially similar criticism may be made of Theodore Wyckoff's "The Role of the Military in Latin American Politics," *Western Political Quarterly,* xiii (September 1960), 745–63.

5. They suggested that the military's institutional characteristics—its coherence and continuity, its technical orientation, its national perspective, and particularly its recruitment of officers from the upwardly mobile lower middle class—might dispose officers to support economic development, expanded participation, democratic procedures, and progressive redistribution. See John Johnson, ed., *The Role of the Military in Underdeveloped Countries* (Princeton 1962), and *The Military and Society in Latin America* (Stanford 1964).

6. See McAlister (n. 3), 32–36.

7. See Elizabeth Hyman, "Soldiers in Politics: New Insights on Latin American Armed Forces," *Political Science Quarterly,* lxxxvii (September 1972), 401–18; and David Ronfeldt, "Patterns of Civil-Military Rule," in Luigi Einaudi, ed., *Beyond Cuba: Latin America Takes Charge of Its Future* (New York 1974), 107–28. A comprehensive bibliography is provided by Klaus Lindenberg, *Fuerzas Armadas y Política en América Latina: Bibliografía Selecta* (Santiago 1972).

8. Among the major country studies published since 1966, other than those published in this volume or mentioned elsewhere in his article, are: on Argentina, Darío Cantón, *La Política de los Militares Argentinos, 1900–1971* (Buenos Aires 1971); Marvin Goldwert, *Democracy, Militarism and Nationalism in Argentina, 1930–1966: An Interpretation* (Austin 1972); Carlos Astiz, "The Argentine Armed Forces: Their Role and Political Involvement," *Western Political Quarterly,* xxii (December 1969), 862–78; Virgilio Rafael Beltrán, "The Army and Structural Changes in 20th Century Argentina," in Jacques Van Doorn, ed., *Military Profession and Military Regimes: Commitments and Conflicts* (The Hague 1969), 317–41; on Bolivia, William H. Brill, *Military Intervention in Bolivia: The Overthrow of Paz Estenssoro and the MNR* (ICOPS, Washington, D.C. 1967); on Brazil, Georges-André Fiechter, *Le Régime Modernisateur du Brésil, 1964–1972* (Geneva 1972); Ronald Schneider, *The Political System of Brazil: Emergence of a "Modernizing" Authoritarian Regime, 1964–1970* (New York 1971); Frederick M. Nunn, "Military Professionalism and Professional Militarism in Brazil, 1870–1970: Histor-

ical Perspectives and Political Implications," *Journal of Latin American Studies,* IV, No. 1 (1972), 29–54; Riordan Roett, "A Praetorian Army in Politics: The Changing Role of the Brazilian Military" in Roett, ed., *Brazil in the Sixties* (Nashville 1972), 3–50; on Chile, Frederick M. Nunn, *Chilean Politics, 1920–1931: The Honorable Mission of the Armed Forces* (Albuquerque 1970); Roy A. Hansen, "Military Culture and Organizational Decline: A Study of the Chilean Army," Ph.D. diss. in sociology (University of California, Los Angeles 1967); on Colombia, Richard Maullin, *Soldiers, Guerrillas, and Politics in Colombia* (Lexington, Mass. 1973); Francisco Leal Buitrago, "Política e intervención militar en Colombia," *Revista Mexicana de Sociología,* XXXII, No. 3 (1970), 491–538; Anthony Maingot, "Colombia," in Lyle McAlister and others, *The Military in Latin American Socio-political Evolution: Four Case Studies* (Washington, D.C. 1970); on Ecuador, John S. Fitch III, "Toward a Model of Coups D'Etat as a Political Process in Latin America: Ecuador, 1948–1966," Ph.D. diss. in political science (Yale University 1973); on Guatemala, Richard Adams, "The Development of the Military" in Adams, ed., *Crucifixion by Power: Essays on Guatemalan National Social Structure, 1944–1966* (Austin 1970), 238–77; Jerry Weaver, "Political Style of the Guatemalan Military Elite," *Studies in Comparative International Development,* V (1969–70), 63-81; on Mexico, Jorge Alberto Lozoya, *El ejército mexicano (1911–1965)* (Mexico 1970); on Panama, Steve Ropp, "Military Reformism in Panama: New Directions or Old Inclinations," *Caribbean Studies,* XII (October 1972), 45–63; on Peru, Carlos Astiz and Jose Garcia, "The Peruvian Military: Achievement Orientation, Training, and Political Tendencies," *Western Political Quarterly,* XXV (December 1972), 667-85; François Bourricaud, "Los militares: por qué y para qué?" *Aportes* (April 1970), 13–55; Bourricaud, "Voluntarismo y experimentación: los militares peruanos: manos a la obra," *Mundo Nuevo* (December 1970), 4–16; Julio Cotler, "Crisis política y populismo militar," in José Matos Mar and others, *Perú: Hoy* (Mexico 1971), 87–174, and "Bases del corporativismo en el Peru," *Sociedad y Política,* No. 2 (November 1972), 3–11; Jane Jaquette, "Revolution by Fiat: The Context of Policy-making in Peru," *Western Political Quarterly,* XXV (December 1972), 648–66.

9. Cf. Robin Luckham, *The Nigerian Military: A Sociological Analysis of Authority and Revolt, 1960–67* (Cambridge 1971).

10. In addition to the works by Nun and O'Donnell reprinted in this volume and the works cited above, see Oscar Cuellar, "Notas sobre la participación de los militares en América Latina," *Aportes* (January 1971), 6–41; Liliana de Riz, "Ejército y política en Uruguay," *Revista Latinoamericana de Sociología,* No. 3 (September–December 1970), 420–42; and Alberto Sepulveda, "El Militarismo Desarrollista en América Latina," *Foro Internacional,* XIII (July–September 1972), 45–65.

11. For further discussion of Villanueva, see James M. Malloy, "Dissecting the Peruvian Military," *Journal of Inter-American Studies and World Affairs,* XV (August 1973), 375–82.

12. Four additional comparative efforts deserve mention. McAlister and others (n. 8), contains competent but not closely related studies of Peru, Argentina, Colombia, and Mexico, with a useful final attempt by McAlister to derive comparative generalizations. Brady Tyson's "The Emerging Role of the Military as National Modernizers in Latin America: The Cases of Brazil and Peru," in David Pollock and Arch Ritter, eds., *Latin American Prospects for the 1970's: What Kind of Revolution?* (New York 1973), 107–30, presents insightful but inconclusive speculation on the possibility that Peru's regime will eventually evolve in a direction similar to Brazil's. James Malloy's "Popu-

lismo militar en el Perú y Bolivia: Antecedentes y posibilidades futuras,"
Estudios Andinos, II (1971–72), 113–36, strains somewhat to fit limited data on
the Peruvian regime's first three years into a framework Malloy had developed
in his earlier work on Bolivia. Charles Corbett's *The Latin American Military
as a Sociopolitical Force: Case Studies of Argentina and Bolivia* (University
of Miami, Center of Advanced International Studies 1972), brings together two
very unlikely objects of comparison, apparently chosen simply because the
author (formerly a U.S. military attaché) had firsthand familiarity with each.

13. See also Einaudi's *The Peruvian Military: A Summary Political Analysis*
(Rand, Santa Monica 1969), "U.S. Relations with the Peruvian Military," in
Daniel Sharp, ed., *U.S. Foreign Policy and Peru* (Austin 1972), 15–56, and
"Revolution from Within—Military Rule in Peru Since 1968," *Studies in
Comparative International Development,* VII (Spring 1973), 71–87.

14. The Joxe volume was published in 1970 in Santiago, Chile, by Editorial
Universitaria. There is, interestingly, no book-length study in English of the
Chilean military which deals with the post–World War II period.

15. For knowledgeable skepticism regarding the degree to which the Mexican
army has actually withdrawn from politics, see David Ronfeldt, "The Modern
Mexican Military," reprinted in this volume. See also Franklin Margiotta,
"Changing Patterns of Political Influence: The Mexican Military and Politics,"
paper presented at the 1973 Convention of the American Political Science
Association, New Orleans.

16. See Robert D. Putnam, "Toward Explaining Military Intervention in Latin
American Politics," *World Politics,* XX, 1 (1967), 83–110.

17. *Ibid.* The definition is paraphrased from Robert L. Gilmore, *Caudillism and
Militarism in Venezuela* (Athens, Ohio 1964), 4–5.

18. See Edward Tufte, "Improving Data Analysis in Political Science," *World
Politics,* XXI (July 1969), 654; and Jerry L. Weaver, "Assessing the Impact of
Military Rule: Alternative Approaches," in Philippe C. Schmitter, ed., *Military Rule in Latin America: Functions, Consequences, and Perspectives*
(Beverly Hills 1973), 83–86, 96–98. I am indebted to John S. Fitch III and
Jeffrey Hart for help on this point.

19. *American Political Science Review,* LX (September 1966), 616–26.

20. Cf. Manfred Kossok, "The Armed Forces in Latin America: Potential for
Changes in Political and Social Functions," *Journal of Inter-American Studies and World Affairs,* XIV (November 1972), 375–98.

21. On the limitations of the "pressure group" concept for analyzing the political
role of Latin American armies, see Hyman (n. 7), 410–11.

22. Cf. Samuel Decalo, "Military Coups and Military Regimes in Africa," *Journal
of Modern African Studies,* II, No. 1 (1973), 105–27.

23. For an interpretation of the current Peruvian regime (generally regarded as
eminently institutional), as deriving primarily from the dominance of one
army faction, see Abraham F. Lowenthal, "Peru's Ambiguous Revolution" in
Lowenthal, ed., *The Peruvian Experiment: Continuity and Change Under
Military Rule* (Princeton 1975).

24. Amos Perlmutter, in an article based primarily on Middle Eastern and Asian
cases but explicitly generalized to Africa and Latin America as well, distinguishes between two subtypes of institutional military regimes: "arbitrator-types" and "ruler-types." Arbitrator-types are only briefly direct, if at all; they
are "professionally oriented," and are little interested in political ideology or
organization. "Ruler-types" are more likely to be long-term and direct, to
submerge professional considerations to others, and are much concerned
about ideology and organization. But Perlmutter's observation about professional orientation does not appear to apply in the Latin American context

(e.g., Peru and Brazil) unless one defines "professional orientation" as excluding long-term civilian responsibility, in which case Perlmutter's point is somewhat circular. See Perlmutter, "The Praetorian State and the Praetorian Army: Toward a Taxonomy of Civil-Military Relations in Developing Polities," *Comparative Politics,* I (April 1969), 382–404.

25. Fitch shows that Ecuadorean officers come from socioeconomic origins very similar to those of their Peruvian colleagues, for instance. See Fitch (n. 8), 248–49.
26. This seems to have been the case, for instance, in the Dominican Republic and Bolivia. For another case where counterinsurgent activities have apparently stimulated military interest in structural reform, however, see Maullin (n. 8).
27. Samuel P. Huntington, *Political Order in Changing Societies* (New Haven 1968), 194. For an earlier, still useful formulation, see Gino Germani and Kalman Silvert, "Politics, Social Structure and Military Intervention in Latin America," *European Journal of Sociology,* II (1961), 62–81.
28. See "The Middle-Class Military Coup Revisited," reprinted in this volume.
29. Huntington (n. 27), 222.
30. Beltrán (n. 8).
31. Fitch (n. 8), 331–32.
32. The best recent literature on the political roles of African armies shares this emphasis. See, for instance, Claude E. Welch, "Radical and Conservative Military Regimes: A Typology and Analysis of Post-Coup Governments in Tropical Africa," paper presented at the 1973 Convention of the American Political Science Association, New Orleans; and Henry Bienen, "Military and Society in East Africa: Thinking Again about Praetorianism," *Comparative Politics,* VI (July 1974), 489–517.
33. See O'Donnell, "Modernization and Military Coups: Theory, Comparisons, and the Argentine Case," reprinted in this volume.
34. The volume Schmitter has edited (n. 18) contributes much less than its title promises on this point. Only Weaver's essay deals systematically with the effects of military rule.
35. In Morris Janowitz and Jacques van Doorn, eds., *On Military Intervention* (Rotterdam: Rotterdam University Press, 1971). Cf. Eric Nordlinger, "Soldiers in Mufti: The Impact of Military Rule Upon Economic and Social Change in the Non-Western States," *American Political Science Review,* LXIV (December 1970), 1131–48.
36. For a critique of Schmitter's methodology, see Barry Ames and Edward Goff, "A Longitudinal Approach to Latin American Public Expenditures," paper presented at the 1973 Convention of the American Political Science Association, New Orleans, 9–11. See also Weaver (n. 18), 93 ff.
37. On military spending, however, cf. G. E. Heare, *Latin American Military Expenditures, 1967–1971* (U.S. Department of State, Washington, D.C. 1973) for an argument that "[t]here is actually little direct correlation between military spending and the degree of military power in government."
38. David Ronfeldt (n. 7), points out, indeed, that the line between "civilian" and "military" regimes is often hazy, and that most Latin American countries are usually governed by civil-military coalitions.
39. Johnson's writings (n. 5) were influenced by the then expanding literature on military participation in the politics of the Middle East and Asia, a literature which tended to exaggerate the progressive impact of military intervention, even in Asia, by inferring too much from the armies' formal characteristics. See Robert M. Price, "A Theoretical Approach to Military Rule in New States: Reference-Group Theory and the Ghanaian Case," *World Politics,* XXIII (April 1971), 399–430. By the 1970's, revisionist writers were generally

skeptical about the supposed progressive impact of military participation, particularly in African politics. See Claude Welch, ed., *Soldier and State in Africa: A Comparative Analysis of Military Intervention and Political Change* (Evanston, Ill. 1970); and Anton Bebler, *Military Rule in Africa: Dahomey, Ghana, Sierra Leone, and Mali* (New York 1973).

40. See Welch (n. 32), 2.
41. Aside from the works previously cited, I have in mind particularly the books reviewed in Decalo (n. 22), in Amos Perlmutter, "The Arab Military Elite," *World Politics,* xxii (January 1970), 269–300, and in Aristide Zolberg, "The Military Decade in Africa," *World Politics,* xxv (January 1973), 309–31.
42. For comparable formulations, see A. R. Luckham, "A Comparative Typology of Civil-Military Relations," *Government and Opposition,* vi (Winter 1971), 5–36; and Claude Welch, Jr., and Arthur Smith, *Military Role and Rule* (N. Scituate, Mass. 1974).
43. My own writings on the Dominican military make this point. See, for example, Lowenthal, "The Political Role of the Dominican Armed Forces," reprinted in this volume.
44. See, for instance, the suggestive data discussed by Fitch (n. 8), 106, 112.
45. See David Collier, "Timing of Economic Growth and Regime Characteristics in Latin America," *Comparative Politics,* vii, No. 3 (April 1975), 331–59.

J. Samuel Fitch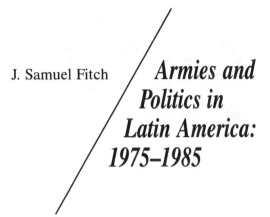
Armies and
Politics in
Latin America:
1975–1985

The political map of Latin America has changed remarkably in the period since Abraham Lowenthal's 1974 essay on armies and politics. In 1974 Brazil was ruled by an entrenched military dictatorship. In Chile and Uruguay, military officers consolidated newly installed authoritarian regimes. Peru's military government introduced a new worker-controlled sector of the economy. Military governments in Ecuador and Panama promised to promote social and economic reforms. Military regimes ruled most of Latin America for most of the decade.

In the mid-1980s, all but four Latin American countries have civilian governments. Though the transition process is incomplete, Brazil now has its first civilian president in twenty-one years. In Peru and Ecuador, civilian governments that came to power five years ago have completed their term of office and handed over power to elected successors. In Uruguay, after voters refused to approve a military-sponsored constitution, military leaders were forced to call presidential elections, which resulted in an opposition victory and installation of a new civilian government. A civilian president is still in office in Bolivia, despite four-digit inflation and at least one attempted coup. In Argentina, leaders of the former military junta are on trial for crimes committed during the military government.

The tide of military takeovers that swept Latin America in the 1960s and early 70s has been followed by an equally strong tide of military failures. Slowly but steadily military regimes have given way to civilian replacements. In Central America the outcome is less certain than in South

America. Although civilian governments have been installed in Honduras, El Salvador, Nicaragua and Guatemala, the growing militarization of the region may reverse the trend away from military rule.

For students of civil-military relations in Latin America, these trends raise many of the classic questions about the military and politics as well as new questions about the nature and limits of military rule:

1. Why do the armed forces overthrow established governments? Are recent coups against military governments different from earlier coups against civilian regimes?
2. How do military governments differ from civilian governments? To what extent are military governments alike or different? How do recent military governments differ from those of previous decades?
3. Why have both conservative and reformist military governments failed in Latin America? Why did military regimes that seemed solidly in control a decade ago subsequently collapse?
4. What accounts for the liberalization of military regimes and the restoration of civilian government? Under what circumstances are military coups likely to occur again?
5. What explains the obvious differences in patterns of civil-military relations within and between different subregions? Why did direct military intervention *not* occur in Mexico, Colombia, and Venezuela, despite the economic problems and political tensions of the last decade? Are civil-military relations in Central America different from those in South America? Why?

This essay attempts to summarize what has been learned about these questions in the period since Lowenthal's 1974 review. It provides an overview of the sections in this volume, by drawing from both the chapters here and the broader research literature on the Latin American military in politics.

Military Coups

A growing consensus has emerged regarding the preconditions for military coups. Coups occur when military officers believe a crisis situation exists. Public disorders and public opinion hostile to the government, threats to the military's institutional interests, violations of the constitution by civilian presidents, evident inability of the incumbent administration to manage a serious economic crisis, or a significant "Communist threat" will

Note: This listing covers the period since Lowenthal's 1974 essay, excluding works appearing in this volume. Individual chapters in edited volumes included in this bibliography are not listed separately, unless cited above.

increase the military's sense of crisis. Personal ambitions and personal ties may influence individual officers, but the decision to stage a military coup is generally an institutional decision, reflecting the collective evaluation of government performance within the upper ranks of the armed forces as a whole. In most cases coup decisions do *not* include any detailed discussion of the policies to be followed after the coup.[1]

Military officers use similar criteria to evaluate the performance of military governments.[2] Economic failures and public hostility and demonstrations against military governments contribute to a growing perception that military rule has failed. When the policy failures of military governments threaten military unity, prestige, or legitimacy, continued military rule becomes a threat to the military's institutional interests. Senior officers not directly involved in the government withdraw their support. The result is typically a palace coup, installing a new set of military leaders who promise an eventual return to civilian rule. The decision to initiate a process of withdrawal does not signify intramilitary agreement on a program specifying the pace of the transition, the conditions under which liberalization will proceed, or to whom power will be transferred.

Despite the agreement on the situational preconditions for military coups, there is no agreement on *why* these conditions are important to the officers making these decisions. In whose interests do military officers act in installing or overthrowing military regimes? Radical analysts have generally followed Nun's argument linking the middle-class origins of most Latin American officers and the military's occasionally anti-oligarchical but general conservative political actions.[3] Non-Marxist writers, on the other hand, including several with access to interview data, have generally stressed the weak class identification of most officers and their strong identification with the military as an institution.[4]

These opposing views stem in part from the different levels of analysis used by Marxist and non-Marxist scholars and in part from differences in the coups being analyzed. As Martin Needler points out, at the systemic level military actions may objectively serve middle-class or elite interests in maintaining order and preserving the status quo. This does not imply that these actions were taken *in order* to serve those interests.[5] On the other hand, the existence of a psychological identification with the military as an institution does not exclude the existence of other identifications, including class. Class issues are poorly defined or secondary in most political crises, hence the military's strong identification with its institutional interests tends to predominate. When the antecedent crises are marked by a high level of ideological polarization and class conflict, the military's class affiliations provide *additional* motivation for conservative behavior and political alliances.[6] The concept of multiple identifications of varying intensity and relevance to particular crises is consistent with the available individual-level data. It also explains the importance of several issues in the 1973 Chilean coup and the 1975 Peruvian coup[7] which cannot be accommodated within institutional interests explanations. Still missing in this debate is any detailed analysis of the Central American militaries where close linkages to local elites are still common, in some cases amounting to outside penetration of, if not control over, military forces.

Research on military officers' beliefs about the role of the armed forces in politics has highlighted the spread of the "national security and development" doctrine.[8] Stepan and others have stressed the expansion in the scope of legitimate military concerns implicit in the shift from a focus on national defense to the broader concept of national security. Together with the post-1959 fear of revolutionary insurgency, this new mission definition effectively erased the boundary between military and non-military concerns. Still, much of the substantive content of the doctrine was merely a reformulation of earlier geopolitical writings and corporatist doctrines from the 1930s.[9]

Although recent writings have challenged the attempts of Wolpin and others to link the emergence of national security doctrine to ideological indoctrination via U.S. military assistance programs,[10] U.S. preoccupation with guerrilla warfare and support for "civic action" undoubtedly helped legitimate this redefinition of military roles. Cross-national differences in the timing of the spread of the security and development doctrine from specialized training centers like Brazil's Superior War College to the rest of the military indicate the doctrinal shift resulted largely from changes in the domestic environment which discredited competing role beliefs, particularly constitutionalist doctrines. Growing economic and political instability provided empirical support for the claim that development was not possible without national security (i.e., suppression of the left and creation of a strong state). Once the national security doctrine emerged as the dominant role belief, it was easy for the military to conclude that security and development could be achieved only through long-term military rule to restructure that environment.

The Peruvian experience demonstrates the wide variations in substantive interpretation of the national security doctrine. In Peru a professionalized and politically active military found itself in the 1960s confronted with a significant rural insurgency, an unevenly developed economy dominated by foreign interests, and a weak civilian government seemingly incapable of enacting a backlog of badly needed reforms.[11] The result was the emergence of a radical military faction for whom the principal threat to national security and development lay in Peru's exploitation by the oligarchy and its foreign accomplices.[12] In Peru, as in Brazil, the general acceptance of the national security doctrine did not prevent serious internal splits over specific policies and the duration of military rule.[13]

Consensus is also emerging on the structural conditions that lead to military coups. Increasingly the traditional focus of North American political scientists on weak political institutions, rising mass participation, and the inability of populist governments to manage a rising level of class conflict is combined with an economic and class analysis derived from dependency theory.[14] Both the political problems of the area and its economic crises have important roots in the particular patterns of disarticulated development characteristic of dependent capitalist societies. In the 1960s and 1970s, economic crises linked to balance-of-payments deficits played an important role in heightening political conflict, raising class tensions, and undermining public support for civilian governments that seemed incapable of stopping inflation and promoting economic growth.[15] Increasing modernization without political or economic integration of the majority of the population led to a growing crisis of hegemony. The left criticized the inegalitarian and non-autonomous character of dependent development; technocratic elites complained about their inability to function in a politically and economically unstable and uncertain environment. Military regimes offered the latter an opportunity to use their skills to promote growth within the existing order by eliminating the threat posed by the former. The need to maintain the support of external actors in economies still heavily dependent on export earnings, foreign capital, and foreign technology further enhanced the attractiveness of a military crackdown on the left and "irresponsible" unions.[16]

The emphasis here on the structural causes of military coups does not imply a mechanistic concept of causation or economic determinism. Several countries weathered these crises without coups. Especially in crisis situations, individual leadership and policy choices make a difference. Nevertheless, under both civilian and military regimes, political and economic crises are typically rooted in larger social forces and economic and political structures. These structures constrain the range of leadership options, condemning some policies to failure, and making other choices credible and attractive to key participants, including the military. Coups are rarely just the result of poor leadership or bad policy choices.

Military Rule

The rise of institutional military governments in the 1960s and 1970s has led to new research on military rule. Cross-national statistical studies of the differences between civilian and military government have produced conflicting results, depending on the time period and the countries included in the analysis.[17] As Remmer points out in her review of the statistical literature, this only confirms the obvious: not all military governments are alike. At a minimum, different *types* of military regimes must be distinguished.[18]

Recent military governments which have ruled in the name of the armed forces as a whole are easily differentiated from personalist military regimes like those of Batista or Somoza. While such regimes continue to dominate in many African countries, the Stroessner regime in Paraguay is now Latin America's only surviving example. There are also transitional military governments such as those governing Ecuador from 1976 to 1980 and Argentina from 1955 to 1958. These regimes are characterized by their commitment to return to civilian government and their preoccupation with the problem of negotiating the military withdrawal from direct rule, often in the face of severe economic crises. Their limited time-horizon clearly differentiates them from long-term conservative military-bureaucratic regimes like that in Brazil or reformist military regimes like the one in Peru.

Within each type of military government, significant differences exist between the policy orientations of military governments and their civilian predecessors. Although policies often change slowly even in military regimes, from a longitudinal perspective the changes in particular countries are readily apparent,[19] especially in areas like urban wages and income distribution, which are typically omitted in cross-national statistical studies. Virtually every study of military government agrees, however, that the most striking differences are political: the reduced scope for political participation by non-elites, restrictions in civil liberties, and the frequent use of violence against real or imagined opposition.[20]

The differences between military and civilian rule are readily apparent in recent conservative military regimes in Argentina, Brazil, and Chile. Several key features characterize this new form of military rule.[21] First, within these regimes policy-making has generally been tightly controlled by high-ranking officers and a select nucleus of civilian technocrats drawn largely from the civilian bureaucracy and, to a lesser extent, the transnational sector of the economy. Civilian political leaders and civilian elites have generally been excluded from direct participation in policy decisions.[22] Second, these regimes have generally pursued an economic model emphasizing "opening" the economy to foreign capital in order to promote efficiency and increase export earnings. The stabilization policies imposed to reduce inflation and attract foreign capital have in almost every case forced a sharp drop in urban real wages and an equally dramatic increase in income inequality. The chief beneficiaries of this economic model have been those in the top 5 percent of an already inegalitarian distribution of income. The political corollary of the economic emphasis on stabilization and investment-driven growth has been the political exclusion of the working class through the closure of the electoral arena and the imposition of regressive labor codes severely limiting political activity and the right to strike. Third, despite the heavy social costs of these policies to the poor, conservative military regimes have had only fleeting success in promoting growth or controlling inflation.[23] Brazil was more successful in attracting foreign investment and promoting rapid growth than Chile, Argentina, or Uruguay, but this was also true under previous civilian administrations.[24] Fourth, denationalization of the economy, growing inequalities, and the closing of democratic channels of participation and protest contributed to the rise of revolutionary opposition movements. In each case, the guerrillas were defeated through the systematic use of torture, death squads, and disappearances. Domestic intelligence agencies were expanded to function both as instruments of repression and mechanisms for exercising policy control over state agencies.[25]

Finally, these regimes were plagued by a systematic crisis of legitimacy. Neither the national security doctrine nor corporatist doctrines resurrected from the 1930s found any significant civilian acceptance.[26] Over time, public support for the military's claim to have saved the country, whether from "communism" or economic disaster, faded as the military's own failures became more evident. Human rights violations deepened the legitimacy crisis.[27] Internal splits within the military multiplied. Increasing numbers of officers began to look for a safe exit, leaving behind a legacy of external debt, ideological polarization, and political de-institutionalization.

The prevailing characterization of these regimes as bureaucratic-authoritarianism highlights the core alliance between military and civilian techno-bureaucratic elites and draws attention to the growing importance of the state as a political and economic actor. At the same time it underplays the key role of the military as the dominant component within the state and understates the importance of factional divisions within the military with respect to state policy and presidential succession.[28] It also ignores the political limitations imposed by the military's opposition to open political conflict and the limited appeal of military ideology and doctrine even among civilian groups who benefited from its policies.[29] The inability of these regimes to legitimize themselves over the long term clearly stems in part from the fact that they are perceived as *military* dictatorships. Civilian regimes pursuing similar economic policies and/or similar alignments with foreign capital have generally experienced less severe legitimacy problems. Despite the demonstrated willingness of virtually every civilian sector to acquiesce in or support military coups that protect or advance their particular interests, the *norm* of popular democracy appears deeply entrenched in Latin American culture. That norm constitutes an intrinsic barrier to the long-term institutionalization of military regimes, particularly conservative regimes dedicated to the political and economic exclusion of the popular sectors.

Most of the recent research on reformist military regimes has focused on Peru. More than a dozen books[30] and scores of articles have traced in detail the rise and fall of the Revolutionary Government of the Armed Forces headed by General Juan Velasco Alvarado. Taking advantage of widespread frustration with the ineffectiveness of the Belaúnde government, the military government moved quickly to nationalize the International Petroleum Company and impose a major land reform. The military strengthened the economic role of the state, eventually asserting state control over most sources of foreign exchange. These reforms were followed by a controversial industrial profit-sharing law, nationalization of the press, and an abortive attempt to create a worker-controlled social property sector of the economy. After Velasco was overthrown in 1975, the regime took a sharp turn to the right, ending with the return of Belaúnde in 1980.

The failure of the military radicals in Peru resulted in part from the economic crisis which began in 1974. The development model adopted by the Velasco government led to a sharp increase in public investment and other expenditures without any equivalent increase in revenues to finance the greatly expanded state role in the economy. Adverse changes in world commodity prices and the failure to find significant petroleum deposits account for part of the problem. Other revenue sources were available, but the government was unwilling to raise taxes on corporate profits or middle- and upper-class incomes.[31] Despite the regime's radical rhetoric, income redistribution was largely limited to workers already within the upper 25 percent of the income distribution. The agrarian reform affected less than 30 percent of Peru's agricultural families.[32] The principal winners were the military and sectors of the middle class who benefited from the enormous expansion of the state bureaucracy. The limited scope of the reforms restricted the regime's potential political base. Popular support was alienated by the bureaucratic and military-dominated character of SINAMOS, the agency created in 1971 to serve as the regime's principal political vehicle.[33] As the radical faction headed by Velasco pushed beyond the initial reform consensus, it found itself attacked from the right by economic elites fearful that the regime was abandoning capitalism altogether and from the left by peasant and union organizations demanding deeper reforms. The inability of the regime to secure the economic cooperation of the private sector *or* control the rising mobilization from below finally led to an alliance of conservative and technocratic factions that overthrew Velasco in 1975 and subsequently ousted most of his supporters.[34] Under Morales Bermúdez, many of the key reforms of the previous government were scrapped. Orthodox stabilization policies were imposed and worker and peasant organizations repressed. Real wages and salaries fell sharply.[35] After 1975 the attempt to define a distinctly Peruvian model of development was largely abandoned.

The Peruvian experience and the even less successful "revolutionary military government" in Ecuador (1972–1976) suggest several important limitations of reform-oriented military governments.[36] Even when the progressives control the government, most officers have only limited ideological commitments to structural change.[37] The factional balance within the military is therefore highly sensitive to changes in economic conditions and to the balance of civilian forces supporting or opposing reform. The internal contradictions of the military's reform program, the rapid exhaustion of easy reforms, and the growth of elite opposition inevitably shift that balance of forces, leaving the progressive faction increasingly isolated from the rest of the military. The fact that military reformers share the conservatives' fear of autonomous political mobilization of the popular sectors leaves the regime vulnerable to the inevitable pressures for a return to more orthodox economic policies, especially in the face of economic difficulties. As noted by Cleaves and Pease García, the lack of class alliances that contributes to the regime's initial autonomy also contributes to its ultimate collapse.[38]

Regardless of their policy orientations, the military regimes of the last two decades share a number of common features. First, the initial appearance of military unity and proclamations of military solidarity typically mask very real divisions within the military over the direction of government policy and the wisdom of continuing direct military rule. Only a small fraction of the officer corps holds positions within the government at any given time. Hence conflicts inevitably emerge between the faction in power and those who perform normal military functions. Military governments have not proven to be more cohesive or coherent than their civilian counterparts.[39] Nor have they proven to be more successful in dealing with the structural problems of Latin American societies. Indeed, in the political realm, they have proven to be less successful, in part because of the technocratic antipolitical mentality characteristic of the more professionalized militaries.[40] Where open or semi-open elections have been held, candidates and/or parties identified with military regimes have been overwhelmingly rejected.[41]

Notwithstanding these common features, the record of the last decade also demonstrates the wide variations in military governments, even within similar types of regimes. The Velasco government in Peru was considerably more radical in its policies and more successful in implementing its reforms than its Ecuadorian counterpart, but less successful politically than the Torrijos government in Panama. Similar variations are evident among the bureaucratic-authoritarian military regimes. The personalist nature of the Pinochet government and the military's limited institutional participation in the Chilean regime[42] are similar in some respects to the Onganía government (1966–1970) in Argentina, but very different from the post-1964 military governments in Brazil or the second Argentine bureaucratic-authoritarian regime (1976–1983). What accounts for the differences in economic policies of these regimes—the monetarist emphasis of "los Chicago boys" in Chile and Delfim Neto's statist policies in Brazil?[43] The only generic similarities appear to be the common antipathy toward unions, lack of concern for distributional issues, and the desire for foreign investment.

The wide variation in policies even among ideologically similar military governments suggests the need to recast the typology of military regimes in terms of structure and class alliances, rather than policy orientations.[44] In this view, the policies of individual military governments are best analyzed as an outcome of the interaction between the type of regime and its particular historical and sociopolitical environment. Given the weak class-identifications of officers in the more professionalized militaries, military governments generally enjoy relative autonomy in the initial choice of class alliances. Over time that autonomy is diminished by the lack of mass support and the need for elite and/or external cooperation in its economic program.[45] From this perspective it is easier to understand the similarities in the Peruvian and Brazilian regimes, e.g., the closed style of decision-making, the reluctance to allow autonomous political participation, and the expansion of the state role in the economy. The differences in the pattern of class alliances implied in the project of the dominant military faction helps account for the initially different orientations toward agrarian reform and foreign capital as well as the shift toward more orthodox policies in Peru after 1975.

Extrication from Military Rule

The political and economic failures of military regimes normally lead to the overthrow of the incumbent military faction and the installation of new leaders committed to a negotiated withdrawal from direct military rule. Despite important differences stemming from (a) the degree of failure of the military regime, (b) the degree of polarization and repression involved in the original coup, and (c) the extent of continuity or discontinuity in civilian institutions during the military government,[46] certain common features mark this extrication process. First, withdrawal is unlikely without successful suppression of the revolutionary opposition as well as guarantees that human rights abuses and other crimes committed during the previous government will not be prosecuted.[47] Second, given the military's claim to rule by virtue of its superior performance, the withdrawal process is often spurred by economic crises.[48] Partly as a result of these economic failures and partly as a result of opposition to expansion of the state role in the economy, as Chalmers and Robinson point out, over time key power groups typically reevaluate their initial support of the military regime. The exercise of state autonomy vis-a-vis local elites leads to the formation of a powerful coalition favoring liberalization and an end to direct military rule. Once the original set of leaders has been overthrown, their successors in the new transitional military regime are forced to seek political alliances with the moderate opposition to secure acquiescence in the imposition of stabilization and austerity policies and to provide a controlled withdrawal process.[49] By a similar logic, hard-line military officers opposed to a return to civilian rule will look for civilian allies fearful of a return to the status quo ante. Although these alliances open up a limited political space and promote re-politicization of civilian life, they also make it more difficult to fully demilitarize politics in the long run.[50] Nevertheless, the withdrawal process typically achieves a momentum of its own.[51] The re-creation of a political space and the diminished threat of violent repression encourage the re-politicization of previously demobilized sectors more rapidly and explosively than anticipated by the regime.[52] Despite the efforts of military leaders to control the selection of their civilian successors, the return to elections typically produces unwanted results which then cannot be repudiated. In the late 1970s, external support from the United States and Europe provided an additional impetus for honoring election results and reestablishing constitutional regimes.[53]

Civil-Military Relations

The experience of the last decade confirms Lowenthal's hypothesis that a key determinant of the different patterns of civil-military relations in Latin America is the relative level of institutionalization of civilian political versus military organizations. In the smaller, less professionalized military institutions of Central America, the corporate identity and solidarity of the officer corps are relatively weak.[54] Personal cliques, factionalism, and individual gain play a larger role in military behavior.[55] Reflecting the lower level of professional socialization, military thinking appears to be less technocratic and antipolitical than in the South American militaries, leading to greater willingness to enter into partisan political alliances with civilian factions as, for example, in Guatemala. Lower levels of professionalization also facilitate civilian political penetration of military and paramilitary forces, like the Salvadorean Treasury Police. Despite the weaker military institutions of these countries, the lower level of modernization in export-dependent, often mono-crop economies and the legacy of various episodes of direct U.S. intervention have inhibited the development of even moderately institutionalized civilian parties. In relative terms the military is still the most coherent national political institution.[56] The result has been a history of personalist military regimes alternating with weak attempts at military populism and reform. Neither has been able to come to grips with the socioeconomic changes of the last two decades which have undermined old patterns of political domination and given rise to new forms of political organization of the poor. The increasingly heavy reliance on death squads, disappearances, and intimidation have only deepened the crisis.

The relative institutionalization hypothesis also helps explain why Chile and Uruguay were the last of the more modernized countries in South America to fall to bureaucratic-authoritarianism, despite their high levels of political mobilization and early problems with import-substitution development. The relative weakness of Ecuador's attempt to emulate Peru's reform military government similarly in part reflects the lower level of professionalization of the military in Ecuador. The ability of Mexico to maintain civilian control during a period of growing military professionalization owes largely to the institutional strength of the Institutional Revolutionary Party (PRI) and the growing professionalization of the Mexican state apparatus.

As the Mexican example suggests, the relative institutionalization of civilian and military organizations must be analyzed in dynamic rather than static terms. In the 1960s and 1970s, economic crises and ideological polarization systematically undermined even strong civilian institutions, especially legislatures and center-left parties. At the same time, military professionalization increased as part of the general strengthening of state structures throughout the region. This combination produced growing military self-confidence, growing frustration with weak civilian leaders, and growing willingness to apply military concepts and methods to political, economic, and social problems.[57] On the other hand, involvement in direct military rule had the counter-effect of disrupting institutional solidarity within the military, weakening professional norms for promotion and assignment, and promoting civilian penetration and politicization of intramilitary cleavages. Thus the balance between military and civilian institutionalization still varies significantly from country to country. The result is divergent patterns of civil-military relations which continue to evolve according to the specific conditions and historical experiences of individual nations.

In both Central and South America, external military assistance programs have aggravated the imbalance between civilian and military institutions. Although postwar U.S. military transfers of training and technology contributed to the rise of more professionalized militaries in the 1950s and 1960s[58], the United States has been far less important in recent years as a source of training or arms. Indeed, the most advanced Latin American militaries—Brazil and Argentina in particular—have become major arms exporters[59] and training centers for officers from other countries, including those excluded from U.S. training because of human rights violations. The United States remains an important supplier of credit arms sales and training for many of the smaller militaries. It also maintains an active program of contacts and cooperation with the more advanced and more clearly autonomous militaries like Peru and Argentina. The political impact of these contacts is still a matter of controversy. Most neo-Marxist writers see the U.S. role as critical; non-Marxists generally see the U.S. role as *reinforcing* existing ideological predispositions.[60] There seems little doubt, however, that external military assistance programs have the general effect of assisting military professionalization and thus worsening the existing imbalance in the relative institutionalization of civilian and military organizations.

Prospects for the Future

Despite the recent trend away from direct military rule, the future of civil-military relations in the region remains highly uncertain. New civilian governments face an enormous burden of foreign debt, which requires them to adopt orthodox austerity and stabilization policies in order to meet IMF and creditor banks' conditions for debt re-negotiation. In the short term, such policies seem inescapable, given the central role of foreign trade in the region's economies. In the longer term, such policies will inevitably frustrate the aspirations of the popular majorities. Civilian regimes are unlikely to achieve enduring legitimacy solely by holding elections. If the substantive policy outcomes of civilian rule turn out to be no different from those of military rule, political unrest and revolutionary violence will return. The Sendero Luminoso movement in Peru is an ominous reminder that the internal security threat which led to military intervention in the 1960s and 1970s has not disappeared.

The critical question is whether extrication will lead to democratization or simply to another cycle of weak civilian governments followed by a new wave of military coups. Can civilian rule be institutionalized, especially under present conditions? The limited duration of previous cycles of military withdrawal in the late 1940s and late 1950s indicates the magnitude of the task. The installation of a civilian president does not change the structural conditions that led to the installation of military regimes in the first place. Depending on the duration and degree of repression of civilian organizations during the military dictatorship, the successor governments must also adjust to complex changes in political alignments and allegiances.[61] As long as key civilian groups remain only semi-committed to democratic norms, military intervention is likely to recur.[62]

The immediate prospects vary significantly from country to country. In Brazil, the withdrawal process has been very gradual and controlled from above. The military has less need to intervene directly against the new civilian president, but is in a strong position to do so if it chooses. In Argentina, the collapse of the military regime following the British victory in the Malvinas/Falklands has prevented the military from controlling the transition process. Public discussion of the scope and brutality of the repression during the military government has seriously weakened the legitimacy of the armed forces in the eyes of civil society, making renewed military intervention unlikely, at least in the short term. In Ecuador and Peru, where military regimes were unsuccessful but less traumatic, the military appear to be reluctant to intervene again directly, but neither country has effectively institutionalized civilian control.

As Barros and Coelho point out, specification of a new role for the military is one important prerequisite for institutionalizing civilian government. It is not clear whether the withdrawal from direct military rule signifies the resurgence of traditional military role beliefs, a real or partial repudiation of the security and development doctrine, or the emergence of new doctrines. At least in the more professionalized militaries, one possibility may be the re-specification of the national security doctrine in external defense terms similar to that of the European and North American militaries. Provided civilian leaders agree to avoid recourse to the military to arbitrate their disputes, the experiences of Cuba, Mexico, and Venezuela suggest that it is possible to develop stable forms of civilian control.[63] Yet in all these cases, the establishment of a more professionalized military came *after* the development of mechanisms of political control and after the development of strong civilian institutions. In contemporary South America, the task appears far more complex and the outcome much more uncertain.

Finally, there is the question of the impact of the military buildup in Central America. The revolutionary government in Nicaragua seems likely to follow the Cuban "civic soldier" model as it moves to create a larger, more professional military to combat the U.S.-backed military opposition. In Honduras and El Salvador, relatively new and inexperienced civilian governments are faced with increasingly well-equipped, U.S.-trained militaries. The Reagan administration has also renewed military training and arms aid to Guatemala. In a region which has traditionally been dominated by the armed forces, the sharp increase in external military assistance seems likely to reinforce the historic imbalance between civilian and military institutions.[64] The recent history of the larger Latin American countries suggests that the short-term military advantages gained through that assistance are likely to be accompanied by serious long-term political costs.

The Research Agenda

Over the last decade the research literature on the Latin American militaries in politics has continued to grow. Studies of bureaucratic authoritarian rule and military radicalism in Peru have made an important contribution to correcting the earlier overemphasis on military coups. Comparative analyses of the breakdowns of democracy[65] and transitions from authoritarian to constitutional regimes[66] have provided important theoretical insights and a more comprehensive understanding of the process of military intervention and withdrawal.

In other respects, however, the rate of progress in understanding the Latin American militaries has been disappointing. Country-oriented case studies still predominate, despite the need for more explicit comparative analysis. Millet, Sereseres, and others have provided useful analyses of several Central American militaries, but there is still a serious imbalance between the increasing depth of detail about the military in Brazil, Argentina, Chile, and Peru and the limited number of studies devoted to countries like Bolivia, Panama, or Paraguay. Lowenthal's 1974 call for more attention to the study of military nonintervention seems to have been disregarded. More rapid progress in the decade ahead will require changes in research methods and in the selection of topics and countries to be studied.

The first requirement is more field research. Critical controversies over the relative importance of class identifications or the ideological effects of foreign military training cannot be resolved on the basis of indirect inference from the behavior of the military as a whole. Individual-level data on military officers' perceptions, beliefs, backgrounds, and actions are necessary to test competing explanations of military behavior.[67] Interview data are needed to improve our understanding of ideological differences within and between Latin American militaries and to develop better explanations of the dynamics involved in changing attitudes toward the role of the military in politics. Given the obvious difficulties in interviewing active duty officers, more attention needs to be given to retired officers, who are both more accessible and more willing to discuss politically sensitive subjects. Explanations of military behavior have become increasingly sophisticated and complex without corresponding improvements in the quantity or quality of the data available to test competing arguments. As long as the bulk of the writing on the Latin American military is done from afar, mostly by North Americans, progress will continue to be slow.

Second, there is a clear need for more comparative research. Systematic analysis of the political significance of differences in the institutional characteristics of Latin American armed forces will require a shift away from country-specific case studies toward paired cases and multi-country studies. Comparative studies of *similar* military institutions are likewise needed to assess the effects of the military's interaction with different class alignments, political structures, economic contexts, and international environments. The wide variations in policies and performance within and between different types of military government provide numerous opportunities for contextually sensitive comparative analysis. Longitudinal studies[68] of carefully selected comparable cases offer one alternative for reconciling the theoretical advantages of multi-country studies with the sensitivity to context found in single-country studies.

Finally, given the slow pace of scholarly research and the enormous number of unanswered questions about military politics and military rule, more research needs to be directed to theoretical issues with direct policy consequences. The worldwide expansion of U.S. military aid and training programs under the Reagan administration raises again many unresolved questions about the ideological and institutional effects of external military assistance, particularly for the Central American countries. The return to civilian governments in much of the region poses the question of how these governments can increase the odds that extrication will lead to democratization, rather than just a temporary military withdrawal. What do the experiences of Mexico, Colombia, or the Dominican Republic suggest as strategies for the institutionalization of at least limited civilian control? What conditions encourage military allegiance to less interventionist doctrines about its role in politics? What changes in civilian behavior are required to lessen the risk of future coups? The Latin American experience provides clear evidence of the heavy human costs of coups and military rule. Individuals and scholars committed to democratization must devote more research to the issues facing those struggling to institutionalize more humane patterns of civil-military relations.

Notes

1. As a result, most military governments spend at least a year consolidating power and trying to reconcile internal differences in order to define a policy program. In Peru most observers have expressed doubt that the Plan Inca, supposedly the blueprint for the "Peruvian revolution," actually predated the coup, at least in the form in which it was later published. (McClintock, "Velasco, Officers, and Citizens," p. 280.) Neither the Plan Inca nor the *Filosofía y plan de acción del gobierno revolucionario y nacionalista del Ecuador* published shortly after the 1972 coup in Ecuador provides a very reliable guide to the policies actually pursued by these governments. (Fitch, "Radical Military Regimes in Latin America," pp. 4–15.)
2. Needler, "The Military Withdrawal from Power," p. 622. However, the "communist threat" criterion works in reverse. The threat must be removed in order to permit the emergence of military factions favoring a return to civilian rule.
3. The military has also been identified in neo-Marxist writings as an arm of the national bourgeoisie or a "comprador elite" indoctrinated with the conservative anticommunist values and ideology of the U.S. military. In principle, the question of self-identification is distinct from the question of ideological orientations. Military officers may share ideological positions with or be influenced by groups with whom they do not identify.
4. In addition to the chapters by Lowenthal, O'Donnell, Stepan, Fitch, and North in this volume, see Nunn, "New Thoughts on Military Intervention," pp. 288–291, and Barros, *The Brazilian Military*, pp. 10–17, 51–79.
5. Martin Needler, "Military Motivations," p. 68; Wynia, "Militarism Revisited," p. 109.
6. "In a capitalist [social] formation, the orientations of officers are determined simultaneously, but in differing degrees depending on the context, by (a) class origin; (b) class position; (c) their existence as a specific social category; and (d) their specific position within the state apparatuses." North and Nun, "A Military Coup," p. 172. In certain contexts, the military's class identifications and institutional interests may lead to actions contrary to middle-class or elite values and interests. See Miles Wolpin, "Military Radicalism in Latin America," pp. 399–405.
7. E.g., the reaction against the introduction of mandatory "ideological" texts in religious schools in Chile and opposition to nationalization of the press and legalization of Quechua as a national language in Peru.
8. And see Calvo, "The Church and the Doctrine of National Security" and Crahan, "National Security Ideology and Human Rights" for useful summaries of the basic doctrine.

9. Arriagada, "Ideology and Politics," pp. 15–17, and *El pensamiento político de los militares*, pp. 71–168; Nunn, *Yesterday's Soldiers*, pp. 250–296; McCann, "Origins of the 'New Professionalism'," pp. 505–522.

10. Horowitz, "From Dependency to Determinism," pp. 230–234; Smith, "U.S.–Latin American Military Relations" p. 272. Cf. Wolpin, *Militarism and Social Revolution*, p. 29.

11. Lowenthal, "Peru's Ambiguous Revolution," pp. 26–30.

12. North, "Ideological Orientations of Peru's Military Leaders," pp. 254–259. Recent research disputes earlier assertions about the role of the Centro de Altos Estudios Militares (CAEM) in the development of this radical variant of the security and development doctrine. According to Stepan (*State and Society*, pp. 145–146), and Philip ("The Military Institution Revisited," pp. 428–429), the key figures in the most progressive faction in Peru never attended CAEM, though many had served in the intelligence agencies which investigated several corruption cases linking local and foreign elites during the Belaúnde administration. CAEM graduates were prominent in the technocratic faction that supported reform from above but opposed mass mobilization in support of those reforms.

13. Markoff and Baretta, "Professional Ideology and Military Activism," pp. 180–181.

14. Guillermo O'Donnell's work on bureaucratic authoritarianism is still the leading example of this kind of synthesis.

15. See, however, the criticism of O'Donnell's argument that the 1964 coup in Brazil and the 1966 coup in Argentina were "necessary" in order to shift from horizontal to vertical import-substitution industrialization. Hirschman, "The Turn to Authoritarianism," pp. 68–81; Serra, "Three Mistaken Theses," pp. 111–128; and Wallerstein, "The Collapse of Democracy in Brazil," pp. 3–40.

16. Although the historical particulars vary significantly, similar structural problems can be found in the earlier stages of dependent development.

17. Tannahill, "The Performance of Military and Civilian Governments," pp. 233–244; Ames and Goff, "Education and Defense Expenditures," pp. 175–197; Jackman, "Politicians in Uniform," pp. 1078–1097; McKinlay and Cohan, "A Comparative Analysis of Political and Economic Performance," pp. 1–30, and "Performance and Instability," pp. 850–864. See also Ayres, "Political Regimes, Explanatory Variables, and Public Policy," pp. 15–35.

18. However, there seems to be no agreement on how many different types of military governments there are or on the appropriate criteria for constructing such a classification.

19. See Hayes, "Policy Consequences of Military Participation," pp. 21–52. Unfortunately this study covers only the initial years of the military regime in Brazil.

20. Tannahill, "Performance," pp. 238–242.

21. On the bureaucratic authoritarian regime, see O'Donnell, *Modernization and Bureaucratic-Authoritarianism*, "Reflections on the Patterns of Change in the Bureaucratic Authoritarian State," "Corporatism and the Question of the State," and "Tensions in the Bureaucratic-Authoritarian State." See also the critical reviews of O'Donnell's work in Collier, *The New Authoritarianism in Latin America*, and Remmer and Merkx, "Bureaucratic-Authoritarianism Revisited," pp. 3–40, and O'Donnell's "Reply," pp. 41–50.

22. Barros, however, notes a sharp increase in the number of sectoral consultative councils in Brazil between 1964 and 1969. (*The Brazilian Military*, pp. 254–264.) See also Pion-Berlin's chapter in this volume on the role of the *gremios* in Chile.

23. Edward Epstein, "Legitimacy, Institutionalization, and Opposition," pp. 40–45. Cf. Cohen, "The Impact of Bureaucratic-Authoritarian Rule," pp. 132–134.
24. Kaufman, "Industrial Change and Authoritarian Rule," pp. 217–244.
25. Angell, "The Soldier as Politician," pp. 116–117 and 131–132; Barros, *The Brazilian Military*, pp. 210–217.
26. Angell, "The Soldier as Politician," pp. 129–130. See also Calvo, "The Church and the Doctrine of National Security," pp. 80–84.
27. On the political costs of repression, see Philip, "Military Authoritarianism in South America," pp. 17–18; and Remmer, "Political Demobilization in Chile," pp. 294–297.
28. Philip, "The Military Institution Revisited," pp. 421–436; Fontana, "Fuerzas armadas, partidos políticos y transición a la democracia," pp. 29–31.
29. Angell, "The Soldier as Politician," p. 125.
30. See in particular Booth and Sor; (eds.), *Military Reformism and Social Classes;* Cleaves and Scurrah, *Agriculture, Bureaucracy, and Military Government;* Collier, *Squatters and Oligarchs;* Cotler, *Clases, estado, y nación en el Perú;* Fitzgerald, *The Political Economy of Peru;* Lowenthal (ed.), *The Peruvian Experiment;* McClintock, *Peasant Cooperatives and Political Change;* McClintock and Lowenthal (eds.), *The Peruvian Experiment Reconsidered;* Middlebrook and Palmer, *Military Government and Political Development;* Pease García, *El ocaso del poder oligárquico;* Philip, *The Rise and Fall of the Peruvian Military Radicals;* Stepan, *State and Society;* Stephens, *The Politics of Workers' Participation;* and Webb, *Government Policy and the Distribution of Income.*
31. Fitzgerald, "State Capitalism in Peru," pp. 77–78.
32. Eckstein, "Revolution and Redistribution," p. 357. Domestic producers who received land still suffered from the government's policy of holding down agricultural prices.
33. McClintock, "Velasco, Officers, and Citizens," pp. 300–306. Cotler ("Democracy and National Integration," p. 33) notes that it "very rapidly became clear that what the officers and their experts understood by 'participation' was a military parade." See also Erwin Epstein, "Peasant Consciousness under Peruvian Military Rule," pp. 280–300. Similar policies toward mass participation were adopted by the Torrijos government in Panama (Priestly, *Military Government and Popular Participation*, pp. 90–123, 205–382).
34. North, "Ideological Orientations," pp. 251–270.
35. Thorp, "The Evolution of Peru's Economy," p. 49.
36. Fitch, "Radical Military Regimes," pp. 27–32.
37. Hence radical military regimes lack the ideological underpinnings that typically give some coherence and stability to radical civilian regimes, especially Marxist-Leninist systems.
38. See also Stepan, *State and Society*, pp. 301–311.
39. See Villanueva, "Peru's 'New' Military Professionalism," pp. 157–178.
40. Loveman and Davies, *The Politics of Antipolitics*, pp. 3–13.
41. The Pinochet regime's success in managing two government-controlled referenda and ARENA/PSD victories in the more traditional areas of Brazil are important exceptions.
42. See especially Varas, "Fuerzas armadas y gobierno militar," pp. 401–408; and Garretón, "Modelo y proyecto político del régimen militar chileno," pp. 355–396.
43. Angell ("The Soldier as Politician," pp. 120–121) argues that conservative military regimes are generically predisposed toward monetarism. Conversely, Barros ("The Changing Role of the State," pp. 23–26) argues that in the more

professionalized militaries, officers live outside the market economy and hence tend not to share the free-market doctrines espoused by economic elites opposed to expansion of the state role in the economy. The observed differences in economic doctrine may in fact be largely situational, depending on the relative availability of foreign finance and direct investment capital, the magnitude of the foreign debt (and therefore the influence of the IMF), and changes in intellectual fashion in the international community of economists.

44. See Cardoso, "On the Characterization of Authoritarian Regimes," pp. 38–39, 49–53.
45. The autonomy of military regimes is also constrained by the fact that military officers, despite their weak class consciousness, nevertheless have concrete class interests derived from their relatively high placement within the existing structure of social stratification.
46. O'Donnell, "Tensions," pp. 315–318; O'Donnell and Schmitter, "Transitions from Authoritarian Rule," pp. 41–57.
47. Argentina is the obvious exception. Without the military's humiliating defeat in the Malvinas/Falklands war, the policies of the Alfonsín administration toward members of the previous government would not have been possible.
48. Edward Epstein, "Legitimacy," pp. 37–54.
49. O'Donnell and Schmitter, "Transitions from Authoritarian Rule," pp. 61–74; Needler, "The Military Withdrawal from Power," p. 622.
50. See Rouquié's chapter in this volume.
51. This does not mean the process is irreversible or the outcome predictable. See Fontana, "Fuerzas armadas," pp. 7–14.
52. More attention should be given to the analysis of psychological dynamics under military rule. O'Donnell's analysis of the privatization of daily life under the second Argentine bureaucratic authoritarian regime offers a number of provocative suggestions for future research ("Democracía en la Argentina"). Cohen's analysis of a 1972 Brazilian survey showing high levels of satisfaction with and trust in the military government *at all socioeconomic levels* (*Popular Support,* p. 185), raises important questions about the claims above regarding the inherent lack of support for military regimes and the persistence of the norm of popular democracy. Cohen estimates that no more than 10 to 20 percent of the sample had been "depoliticized" since 1964, but it is doubtful whether standard survey techniques are capable of capturing the kind of phenomena described by O'Donnell. In state elections two years after this survey, pro-government candidates were overwhelmingly defeated.
53. Needler, "Military Withdrawal," p. 623.
54. In addition to Richard Millett's chapter in this volume, see also Millett, *Guardians of the Dynasty;* Sereseres, "The Guatemalan Armed Forces"; Priestly, *Military Government and Popular Participation in Panama;* Garcia, "Political Conflict Within the Salvadorean Armed Forces"; and Etchison, *The United States and Militarism in Central America.*
55. Cf. Lowenthal's analysis of the Dominican military in this volume.
56. Sereseres, "The Guatemalan Armed Forces," p. 24.
57. See Barros's detailed description of the strengthening of the military socialization process over time in Brazil, to which he juxtaposes the growing incoherence and disorganization of civilian elites. (*The Brazilian Military,* pp. 51–191.)
58. See Nunn, *Yesterday's Soldiers,* on the contribution of earlier European military assistance programs to the early stages of professionalization in various South American countries and the subsequent rise in "professional militarism." Nunn notes that professionalization had adverse political effects in these countries, precisely because civilian institutions were in turmoil.

Although the development of professional military organizations and a professional military mentality also led to civil-military tensions in Western Europe, civilian institutions were able to cope with those tensions and sustain the subordination of the military to civilian control.

59. Herrera, "Crecimiento económico," pp. 251–265.
60. Fitch, "The Political Impact of U.S. Military Aid," pp. 365–369; Smith, "U.S.–Latin American Military Relations," pp. 283–284. Cf. Wolpin, "Military Radicalism," pp. 405–410.
61. Remmer, "Redemocratization and the Impact of Authoritarian Rule," pp. 253–275.
62. Viola and Mainwaring, "Transitions to Democracy," p. 13. Potash, *The Army and Politics in Argentina,* p. 381.
63. In addition to the chapters by Dominguez and Ronfeldt in this volume, see Ruhl, "Civil-Military Relations in Colombia," pp. 123–146, and Gene Bigler, "Professional Soldiers and Restrained Politics in Venezuela," pp. 175–196.
64. See Jenkins and Sereseres, "U.S. Military Assistance and the Guatemalan Armed Forces," p. 587, on the impact of earlier military-assistance programs in Guatemala.
65. Juan Linz and Alfred Stepan (eds.), *The Breakdown of Democratic Regimes.*
66. O'Donnell, Schmitter, and Whitehead (eds.), *Transitions from Authoritarian Rule.*
67. See Manwaring, "Career Patterns and Attitudes," pp. 235–250, for an example of the creative use (and limitations) of secondary data for this kind of analysis.
68. Cross-sectional statistical analyses of aggregate data for all or most of Latin America have not been very productive. In addition to serious problems with data quality, specification error, and multi-collinearity, these efforts are theoretically inappropriate, given the basic assumption that military behavior reflects a complex interaction of institutional and societal variables over time. See Thompson, "Systematic Change," pp. 441–459, and Ruhl, "Social Mobilization," pp. 574–586, for two instructive attempts to replicate the results of earlier statistical studies.

References

Ames, Barry, and Ed Goff. "Education and Defense Expenditures in Latin America: 1948–1968." In Craig Liske et al. (eds.), *Comparative Public Policy: Issues, Theories, and Methods,* pp. 175–197. Beverly Hills, Cal.: Sage Publications, 1975.

Angell, Alan. "Chile After Five Years of Military Rule." *Current History* 76, 444 (1979), 58–61, 88–89.

Angell, Alan. "The Soldier as Politician: Military Authoritarianism in Latin America." In Dennis Kavanagh and Gillian Peele, (eds.), *Comparative Government and Politics: Essays in Honor of S.E. Finer,* pp. 116–143. Boulder, Col.: Westview Press, 1984.

Arriagada Herrera, Genaro. "Ideology and Politics in the South American Military." Paper presented to the Woodrow Wilson International Center for Scholars, Washington, 1979.

Arriagada Herrera, Genaro. "National Security Doctrine in Latin America." *Peace and Change* 6, 1–2 (1980), 49–60.

Arriagada Herrera, Genaro. *El pensamiento político de los militares (Estudios sobre Chile, Argentina, Brasil, y Uruguay)*. Santiago: CISEC, n.d.

Ayres, Robert. "Political Regimes, Explanatory Variables and Public Policy in Latin America." *Journal of the Developing Areas* 10, 1 (1975), 15–35.

Barros, Alexandre de S.C. *The Brazilian Military: Professional Socialization, Political Performance, and State Building.* A dissertation submitted to the Department of Social Sciences, University of Chicago, 1978.

Barros, Alexandre de S.C. "The Changing Role of the State in Brasil: The Technocratic Military Alliance." Paper presented to the Latin American Studies Association, Atlanta, March 1976.

Becker, David. " 'Bonanza Development' and the 'New Bourgeoisie': Peru under Military Rule." *Comparative Political Studies* 15, 3 (1982), 243–288.

Bigler, Gene. "Professional Soldiers and Restrained Politics in Venezuela." In Robert Wesson (ed.), *New Military Politics in Latin America,* pp. 175–196. New York: Praeger, 1982.

Black, Jan Knippers. "The Military and Political Decompression in Brazil." *Armed Forces and Society* 6, 4 (1980), 625–638.

Booth, David, and Bernardo Sorj (eds.). *Military Reformism and Social Classes: The Peruvian Experience 1968–1980.* New York: St. Martin's Press, 1983.

Calvo, Roberto. "The Church and the Doctrine of National Security." *Journal of Interamerican Studies* 21, 1 (1979), 69–88.

Cardoso, Fernando Henrique. "On the Characterization of Authoritarian Regimes in Latin America." In David Collier (ed.), *The New Authoritarianism in Latin America,* pp. 33–57. Princeton, N.J.: Princeton University Press, 1979.

Child, John. *Unequal Alliance: The Inter-American Military System, 1938–1978.* Boulder, Col.: Westview Press, 1980.

Cleaves, Peter, and Martin Scurrah. *Agriculture, Bureaucracy, and Military Government in Peru.* Ithaca, N.Y.: Cornell University Press, 1980.

Cochrane, James. "Tendencia del gasto militar y del tamaño de las fuerzas armadas en América Latina." *Foro Internacional* XVI, 3 (1976), 380–400.

Cohen, Youssef. "The Impact of Bureaucratic-Authoritarian Rule on Economic Growth." *Comparative Political Studies* 18, 1 (1985), 123–136.

Cohen, Youssef. *Popular Support for Authoritarian Governments: Brazil Under Medici.* A dissertation presented to the Department of Political Science, University of Michigan, 1979.

Collier, David (ed.). *The New Authoritarianism in Latin America.* Princeton, N.J.: Princeton University Press, 1979.

Collier, David. *Squatters and Oligarchs: Authoritarian Rule and Policy Change in Peru.* Baltimore, Md.: Johns Hopkins University Press, 1976.

Corbett, Charles. "Politics and Professionalism: The South American Military." In Brian Loveman and Thomas Davies (eds.), *The Politics of Antipolitics,* pp. 14–22. Lincoln: University of Nebraska Press, 1978.

Cotler, Julio. *Clases, estado, y nación en el Perú.* Lima: Instituto de Estudios Peruanos, 1978.

Cotler, Julio. "Democracy and National Integration in Peru." In Cynthia McClintock and Abraham Lowenthal (eds.), *The Peruvian Experiment Reconsidered,* pp. 3–38. Princeton, N.J.: Princeton University Press, 1983.

Crahan, Margaret. "The Evolution of the Military in Brazil, Chile, Peru, Venezuela, and Mexico: Implications for Human Rights." In Margaret Crahan (ed.), *Human Rights and Basic Needs in the Americas,* pp. 46–99. Washington: Georgetown University Press, 1982.

Crahan, Margaret. "National Security Ideology and Human Rights." In Margaret Crahan (ed.), *Human Rights and Basic Needs in the Americas,* pp. 100–127. Washington: Georgetown University Press, 1982.

del Solar, Francisco José. *El militarismo en el Perú.* Caracas: Solartre Libros, 1976.

Dietz, Henry. "Political Participation by the Urban Poor in an Authoritarian Context: The Case of Lima, Peru." *Journal of Political and Military Sociology* 5 (Spring 1977), 67–77.

Dietz, Henry, and David Scott Palmer. "Citizen Participation under Innovative Military Corporatism in Peru." In John Booth and Mitchell Seligson (eds.), *Political Participation in Latin America: Citizen and State,* pp. 172–188. New York: Holmes & Meier, 1978.

Eckstein, Susan. "Revolution and Redistribution in Latin America." In Cynthia McClintock and Abraham Lowenthal (eds.), *The Peruvian Experiment Reconsidered,* pp. 347–386. Princeton, N.J.: Princeton University Press, 1983.

Epstein, Edward. "Legitimacy, Institutionalization, and Opposition in Exclusionary Bureaucratic-Authoritarian Regimes." *Comparative Politics* 17, 1 (1984), 37–54.

Epstein, Erwin. "Peasant Consciousness Under Peruvian Military Rule." *Harvard Educational Review* 52, 3 (1982), 280–300.

Etchison, Don. *The United States and Militarism in Central America.* New York: Praeger, 1975.

Feldman, David. "Argentina, 1945–1971: Military Assistance, Military

Spending, and the Political Activity of the Armed Forces." *Journal of Interamerican Studies and World Affairs* 24, 3 (1982), 321–336.

Fishel, John. "Attitudes of Peruvian Highland Village Leaders Toward Military Intervention." *Journal of Interamerican Studies and World Affairs* 18, 2 (1976), 155–178.

Fitch, John Samuel. *The Military Coup d'Etat as a Political Process: Ecuador 1948–1966.* Baltimore, Md.: John Hopkins University Press, 1977.

Fitch, John Samuel. "The Political Impact of U.S. Military Aid to Latin America: Institutional and Individual Effects." *Armed Forces and Society* 5, 3 (1979), 360–386.

Fitch, John Samuel. "Radical Military Regimes in Latin America: Revolution, Rhetoric, and Reality in Peru and Ecuador." Paper presented to the Latin American Studies Association, Washington, 1977.

Fitzgerald, E. V. K. *The Political Economy of Peru, 1956–78: Economic Development and the Restructuring of Capital.* Cambridge: Cambridge University Press, 1979.

Fitzgerald, E. V. K. "State Capitalism in Peru: A Model of Economic Development and Its Limitations." In Cynthia McClintock and Abraham Lowenthal (eds.), *The Peruvian Experiment Reconsidered,* pp. 65–93. Princeton, N.J.: Princeton University Press, 1983.

Fontana, Andrés. "Fuerzas armadas, partidos políticos y transición a la democracia en Argentina: 1981–1982." Kellogg Institute Working Paper no. 28, University of Notre Dame, 1984.

Fruhling, Hugo, Carlos Portales, and Augusto Varas. *Estado y fuerzas armadas.* Santiago: FLASCO, 1982.

Garcia, Jose. "Political Conflict Within the Salvadorean Armed Forces: Origins and Consequences." Paper presented to the Inter-University Seminar on Armed Forces and Society, Chicago, 1983.

Garretón, Manuel Antonio. "Modelo y proyecto político del régimen militar chileno." *Revista Mexicana de Sociología* 44, 2 (1982), 355–396.

Geller, Daniel. "Economic Modernization and Political Instability in Latin America: A Causal Analysis of Bureaucratic Authoritarianism." *Western Political Quarterly* 35, 1 (1982), 33–49.

Gorman, Stephen. "The Peruvian Revolution in Historical Perspective." In Stephen Gorman (ed.), *Post-Revolutionary Peru: The Politics of Transformation,* pp. 1–32. Boulder, Co.: Westview Press, 1982.

Handelman, Howard, and Thomas Sanders (eds). *Military Government and the Movement Toward Democracy in South America.* Bloomington: Indiana University Press, 1981.

Hayes, Margaret Daly. "Policy Consequences of Military Participation in

Politics: An Analysis of Tradeoffs in Brazilian Federal Expenditures." In Craig Liske et al. (eds.), *Comparative Public Policy: Issues, Theories, and Methods,* pp. 21–52. Beverly Hills, Cal.: Sage Publications, 1975.

Herrera Lasso, Luis. "Crecimiento económico, gasto militar, industria armamentista y transferencia de armas en América Latina." *Foro Internacional* 23, 3 (1983), 242–265.

Hirschman, Albert. "The Turn to Authoritarianism in Latin America and the Search for Its Economic Determinants." In David Collier (ed.), *The New Authoritarianism in Latin America,* pp. 61–98. Princeton, N.J. Princeton University Press, 1979.

Horowitz, Irving Louis. "Castrology Revised: Further Observations on the Militarization of Cuba." *Armed Forces and Society* 3, 4 (1977), 617–631.

Horowitz, Irving Louis. "From Dependency to Determinism: The New Structure of Latin American Militarism." *Journal of Political and Military Sociology* 5, 2 (1977), 217–238.

Horowitz, Irving Louis. "Military Origins of the Cuban Revolution." *Armed Forces and Society* 1, 4 (1975), 402–418.

Horowitz, Irving Louis, and Ellen Kay Trimberger. "State Power and Military Nationalism in Latin America." *Comparative Politics* 8 (January 1976), 223–244.

Jackman, Robert. "Politicians in Uniform: Military Governments and Social Change in the Third World." *American Political Science Review* 70, 4 (1976), 1078–1097.

Jenkins, Brian, and Caesar Sereseres. "U.S. Military Assistance and the Guatemalan Armed Forces." *Armed Forces and Society* 3, 4 (1977), 575–594.

Kaufman, Robert. "Industrial Change and Authoritarian Rule in Latin America: A Concrete Review of the Bureaucratic-Authoritarian Model." In David Collier (ed.), *The New Authoritarianism in Latin America,* pp. 165–254. Princeton, N.J.: Princeton University Press, 1979.

Leogrande, William. "The Demilitarization of the Cuban Revolution: A Rejoinder to Irving Louis Horowitz." *Armed Forces and Society* 3, 4 (1977), 609–616.

Linz, Juan, and Alfred Stepan (eds.). *The Breakdown of Democratic Regimes.* Baltimore, Md.: Johns Hopkins University Press, 1978.

Loveman, Brian, and Thomas Davies (eds.). *The Politics of Antipolitics: The Military in Latin America.* Lincoln: University of Nebraska Press, 1978.

Lowenthal, Abraham. "Peru's Ambiguous Revolution." In Abraham

Lowenthal (ed.), *The Peruvian Experiment: Continuity and Change Under Military Rule,* pp. 3–43. Princeton, N.J.: Princeton University Press, 1975.

McCann, Frank, Jr. "The Brazilian Army and the Problem of Mission, 1939–1964." *Journal of Latin American Studies* 12, 1 (1980), 107–216.

McCann, Frank, Jr. "The Brazilian General Staff and Brazil's Military Situation, 1900–1945." *Journal of Interamerican Studies and World Affairs* 25, 3 (1983), 299–324.

McCann, Frank, Jr. "Origins of the 'New Professionalism' of the Brazilian Military." *Journal of Interamerican Studies and World Afairs* 21, 4 (1979), 505–522.

McClintock, Cynthia. *Peasant Cooperatives and Political Change in Peru.* Princeton, N.J.: Princeton University Press, 1981.

McClintock, Cynthia. "Velasco, Officers, and Citizens: The Politics of Stealth." In Cynthia McClintock and Abraham Lowenthal (eds.), *The Peruvian Experiment Reconsidered,* pp. 275–308. Princeton, N.J.: Princeton University Press, 1983.

McClintock, Cynthia, and Abraham Lowenthal (eds.). *The Peruvian Experiment Reconsidered.* Princeton, N.J.: Princeton University Press, 1983.

McDonald, Ronald. "The Rise of Military Politics in Uruguay." *Inter-American Economic Affairs* 28 (Spring 1975), 25–43.

McKinlay, R. D., and A. S. Cohan. "A Comparative Analysis of the Political and Economic Performance of Military and Civilian Regimes." *Comparative Politics* 8, 1 (1975), 1–30.

McKinlay, R. D., and A. S. Cohan. "Performance and Instability in Military and Nonmilitary Regime Systems." *American Political Science Review* 70, 3 (1976), 850–864.

Makin, Guillermo. "The Military in Argentine Politics, 1880–1982." *Journal of International Studies* 12, 1 (1983), 49–68.

Manwaring, Max. "Career Patterns and Attitudes of Military-Political Elites in Brazil: Similarity and Continuity, 1964–1975." *International Journal of Comparative Sociology* 19, 3–4 (1978), 235–250.

Marcella, Gabriel. "The Chilean Military Government and the Prospects for Transition to Democracy." *Inter-American Economic Affairs* 33, 2 (1979), 3–20.

Margiotta, Frank. "Civilian Control and the Mexican Military: Changing Patterns of Political Influence." In Claude Welch (ed.), *Civilian Control of the Military,* pp. 213–253. Albany: State University of New York Press, 1976.

Markoff, John, and Silvio Duncan Baretta. "Professional Ideology and Military Activism in Brazil: Critique of a Thesis of Alfred Stepan." *Comparative Politics* 17, 2 (January 1985), 175–191.

Mendes, Candido. "The Post-1964 Brazilian Regime: Outward Redemocratization and Inner Institutionalization." *Government and Opposition* 15 (Winter 1980), 48–74.

Michaels, Albert. "Background to a Coup: Civil-Military Relations in Twentieth-Century Chile and the Overthrow of Allende." In Claude Welch (ed.), *Civilian Control of the Military,* pp. 283–311. Albany: State University of New York Press, 1976.

Middlebrook, Kevin, and David Scott Palmer. *Military Government and Political Development: Lessons From Peru.* Beverly Hills, Cal.: Sage Publications, 1975.

Milenky, Edward. "Arms Production and National Security in Argentina." *Journal of Interamerican Studies and World Affairs* 22, 3 (1980), 267–288.

Millett, Richard. *Guardians of the Dynasty.* Maryknoll, N.Y.: Orbis Books, 1977.

Moore, Richard. *Soldiers, Politics, and Reaction: The Etiology of Military Rule in Uruguay.* A dissertation presented to the Department of Political Science, University of Arizona, 1978.

Needler, Martin. "The Logic of Conspiracy: The Latin American Military Coup as a Problem in the Social Sciences." *Studies in Comparative International Development* 13, 3 (1978), 28–40.

Needler, Martin. "Military Motivations in the Seizure of Power." *Latin American Research Review* 10, 3 (1975), 63–80.

Needler, Martin. "The Military Withdrawal from Power in South America." *Armed Forces and Society* 6, 4 (1980), 614–624.

North, Liisa. "Ideological Orientations of Peru's Military Leaders." In Cynthia McClintock and Abraham Lowenthal (eds.), *The Peruvian Experiment Reconsidered,* pp. 245–274. Princeton, N.J.: Princeton University Press, 1983.

North, Liisa, and José Nun. "A Military Coup is a Military Coup . . . or is it?" *Canadian Journal of Political Science* 11, 1 (1978), 165–174.

North, Liisa, and Tanya Korovkin. *The Peruvian Revolution and the Officers in Power, 1967–1976.* Montreal: McGill University Center for Developing-Area Studies, 1981.

Nunn, Frederick. *The Chilean Military in Politics: Essays on Civil-Military Relations, 1810–1973.* Albuquerque: University of New Mexico Press, 1976.

Nunn, Frederick. "Military Professionalism and Professional Militarism in Brazil, 1870–1970: Historical Perspectives and Political Implications." *Journal of Latin American Studies* 4, 1 (1972), 29–54.

Nunn, Frederick. "New Thoughts on Military Intervention in Latin American Politics: The Chilean Case, 1973." *Journal of Latin American Studies* 7, 2 (1975), 271–304.

Nunn, Frederick. *Yesterday's Soldiers: European Military Professionalism in South America, 1890–1940*. Lincoln: University of Nebraska Press, 1983.

O'Donnell, Guillermo. "Corporatism and the Question of the State." In James Malloy (ed.), *Authoritarianism and Corporatism in Latin America*, pp. 47–87. Pittsburgh, Pa.: University of Pittsburgh Press, 1977.

O'Donnell, Guillermo. "Democracia en la Argentina: *micro y macro*." Kellogg Institute Working Paper no. 2, University of Notre Dame, 1983.

O'Donnell, Guillermo. *Modernization and Bureaucratic-Authoritarianism: Studies in South American Politics*. Berkeley: University of California Press, 1973.

O'Donnell, Guillermo. "Reflections on the Patterns of Change in the Bureaucratic Authoritarian State." *Latin American Research Review* 13, 1 (1978), 3–38.

O'Donnell, Guillermo. "Reply to Remmer and Merkx." *Latin American Research Review* 17, 2 (1982), 41–50.

O'Donnell, Guillermo. "Tensions in the Bureaucratic-Authoritarian State and the Question of Democracy." In David Collier (ed.), *The New Authoritarianism in Latin America*, pp. 285–318. Princeton, N.J.: Princeton University Press, 1979.

O'Donnell, Guillermo, and Philippe Schmitter. "Transitions from Authoritarian Rule." In Guillermo O'Donnell, Philippe Schmitter, and Lawrence Whitehead (eds.), *Transitions from Authoritarian Rule*. Baltimore, Md.: Johns Hopkins University Press, forthcoming.

Palmer, David Scott. "Political Participation Under Military Rule." *Plural Societies* 9 (Spring 1978), 59–74.

Pease-García, Henry. *El ocaso del poder oligárquico: Lucha política en la escena oficial, 1968–1975*. Lima: DESCO, 1977.

Perez, Louis, Jr. "Army Politics in Socialist Cuba." *Journal of Latin American Studies* 8, 2 (1976), 251–272.

Philip, George. "Military Authoritarianism in South America: Brazil, Chile, Uruguay, and Argentina." *Political Studies* 32, 1 (1984), 1–20.

Philip, George. "The Military Institution Revisited: Some Notes on Corporatism and Military Rule in Latin America." *Journal of Latin American Studies* 12, 2 (1980), 421–436.

Philip, George. *The Rise and Fall of the Peruvian Military Radicals, 1968–1976*. London: Aldene Press, 1978.

Potash, Robert. *The Army and Politics in Argentina 1945–1962: Peron to Frondizi*. Stanford, Cal.: Stanford University Press, 1980.

Priestly, George. *Military Government and Popular Participation in Pan-*

ama: The Torrijos Regime 1968–1975. A dissertation presented to the Graduate School of Arts and Sciences, Columbia University, 1981.

Reif, Linda. "Seizing Control: Latin American Military Motives, Capabilities, and Risks." *Armed Forces and Society* 10, 4 (1984), 563–582.

Remmer, Karen. "Political Demobilization in Chile, 1973–1978." *Comparative Politics* 12, 3 (1980), 275–301.

Remmer, Karen. "Redemocratization and the Impact of Authoritarian Rule in Latin America." *Comparative Politics* 17, 3 (1985), 253–275.

Remmer, Karen, and Gilbert Merkx. "Bureaucratic-Authoritarianism Revisited." *Latin American Research Review* 17, 2 (1982), 3–40.

Rosenberg, Mark B. "Nicaragua and Honduras: Toward Garrison States?" *Current History* 83, 490 (1984), 59–62.

Rouquié, Alain. "Argentina: The Departure of the Military—End of a Political Cycle or Just Another Episode." *International Affairs* (Great Britain) 59, 4 (1983), 575–86.

Rouquié, Alain. "Hegemonía militar, estado y dominación social." In Alain Rouquié (ed.), *Argentina, hoy,* pp. 11–50. Buenos Aires: Siglo XXI, 1982.

Ruhl, J. Mark. "Civil-Military Relations in Colombia: A Societal Explanation." *Journal of Interamerican Studies and World Affairs* 23, 2 (1981), 123–146.

Ruhl, J. Mark. "Social Mobilization, Military Tradition, and Current Patterns of Civil-Military Relations in Latin America: Testing Putnam's Major Conclusions." *Western Political Quarterly* 35, 4 (1982), 574–586.

Salinas Bascur, Raquel. "Chilean Communications Under the Military Regime: 1973–1979." *Current Research on Peace and Violence* 2 (1979), 80–95.

Schulgasser, Daniel. *Military Professionalization, Political Power, and Public Policy Making in Turkey, Brazil, and the People's Republic of China.* A dissertation presented to the Graduate School of Rutgers, the State University of New Jersey, 1982.

Sereseres, Caesar. "The Guatemalan Armed Forces: Military Development and National Politics." Paper presented to the Latin American Studies Association, Atlanta, March 1976.

Serra, José. "Three Mistaken Theses Regarding the Connection Between Industrialization and Authoritarian Regimes." In David Collier (ed.), *The New Authoritarianism in Latin America,* pp. 99–164. Princeton, N.J.: Princeton University Press, 1979.

Smith, Brian. "U.S.–Latin American Military Relations Since World War II: Implications for Human Rights." In Margaret Crahan (ed.),

Human Rights and Basic Needs in the Americas, pp. 263–300. Washington: Georgetown University Press, 1982.

Soares, Glaucio Dillon. "Military Authoritarianism and Executive Absolutism in Brazil." *Studies in Comparative International Development* 14, 3–4 (1979), 104–126.

Stepan, Alfred. *State and Society: Peru in Comparative Perspective.* Princeton, N.J.: Princeton University Press, 1980.

Stephens, Evelyne Huber. "The Peruvian Military Government, Labor Mobilization, and the Political Strength of the Left." *Latin American Research Review* 18, 2 (1983), 57–94.

Stephens, Evelyne Huber. *The Politics of Workers' Participation: The Peruvian Approach in Comparative Perspective.* New York: Academic Press, 1980.

Tannahill, Neal. "The Performance of Military and Civilian Governments in South America, 1948–1967." *Journal of Political and Military Sociology* 4 (Fall 1976), 233–244.

Thompson, William. "A Multivariate Analysis of Regime Vulnerability and Proneness to the Military Coup." *Journal of Political and Military Sociology* 7 (Fall 1979), 283–289.

Thompson, William. "Organizational Cohesion and Military Coup Outcomes." *Comparative Political Studies* 9, 3 (1976), 255–276.

Thompson, William. "Regime Vulnerability and the Military Coup." *Comparative Politics* 7, 4 (1975), 459–487.

Thompson, William. "Systematic Change and the Latin American Military Coup." *Comparative Political Studies* 7, 4 (1975), 441–459.

Thorp, Rosemary. "The Evolution of Peru's Economy." In Cynthia McClintock and Abraham Lowenthal (eds.), *The Peruvian Experiment Reconsidered,* pp. 39–61.

Urriza, Manuel. *Perú: Cuando los militares se van.* Caracas: Ediciones CIDAL, 1978.

Varas, Augusto. "Fuerzas armadas y gobierno militar: corporativización y politización castrense." *Revista Mexicana de Sociología* 44, 2 (1982), 397–411.

Varas, Augusto, and Felipe Aguero. *El proyecto político militar.* Santiago: FLASCO, 1984.

Varas, Augusto, and Fernando Bustamonte. *Fuerzas armadas y política en Ecuador.* Quito: Universidad Central del Ecuador, 1978.

Varas, Augusto, Carlos Portales, and Felipe Aguero. "The National and International Dynamics of South American Armamentism." *Current Research on Peace and Violence* 3, 1 (1980), 1–23.

Vellinga, M. L. "The Military and the Dynamics of the Cuban Revolutionary Process." *Comparative Politics* 8, 2 (1976), 245–271.

Villanueva, Victor. "Peru's 'New' Military Professionalism: The Failure of the Technocratic Approach." In Stephen Gorman (ed.), *Post-Revolutionary Peru: The Politics of Transformation*, pp. 157–178. Boulder, Co.: Westview Press, 1982.

Viola, Eduardo, and Scott Mainwaring. "Transitions to Democracy: Brazil and Argentina in the 1980s." Kellogg Institute Working Paper no. 21, University of Notre Dame, 1984.

Waldmann, Peter, and Ernesto Garzón Valdés (eds.). *El poder militar en la Argentina (1976–1981)*. Frankfurt: Verlag Klaus Dieter Vervuert, 1982.

Wallerstein, Michael. "The Collapse of Democracy in Brazil: Its Economic Determinants." *Latin American Research Review* 15, 3 (1980), 3–40.

Wayman, Frank. *Military Involvement in Politics: A Causal Model*. Beverly Hills, Cal.: Sage Publications, 1975.

Webb, Richard. *Government Policy and the Distribution of Income in Peru, 1963–1973*. Cambridge, Mass.: Harvard University Press, 1977.

Wesson, Robert. *New Military Politics in Latin America*. New York: Praeger, 1982.

Williams, Edward. "Mexico's Modern Military." *Caribbean Review* 10, 4 (1981), 12–13, 45.

Wolpin, Miles. *Militarism and Social Revolution in the Third World*. Totowa, N.J.: Allanheld, Osmun and Co., 1982.

Wolpin, Miles. "Military Radicalism in Latin America." *Journal of Interamerican Studies and World Affairs* 23 (November 1981), 395–428.

Wynia, Gary. "Militarism Revisited." *Journal of Interamerican Studies and World Affairs* 25, 1 (1983), 105–119.

II
General Approaches to the Analysis of the Military in Politics

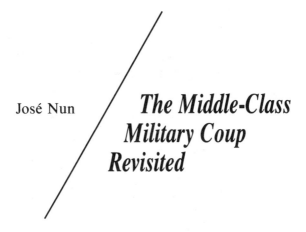

José Nun

The Middle-Class Military Coup Revisited

Unless a distinction is made between the structural and the circumstantial factors of military intervention in Latin American politics, important differences between countries are apt to be ignored. Table 1, for instance, shows that the number of successful coups varies independently of the degree of economic development: there were as many in Argentina as in El Salvador and fewer in Honduras than in Brazil. Evidently the intervention of the military in politics represents a different phenomenon in a country with an income per capita of $500, 70 percent of its population living in cities, and with a large middle class, than in one where less than one-third of the population lives in cities, income per capita is only $150, and scarcely 8 percent of the population can be classified as belonging to the upper and middle classes.[1]

Interpretations which tend to ignore these differences have generally been influenced either by traditional liberal antimilitarism or by the advocacy of militarism as a dynamic force for economic development.[2]

The *liberal model,* based on the experience of Europe in the eighteenth

From José Nun, "The Middle-Class Military Coup," in *The Politics of Conformity in Latin America,* ed. Claudio Veliz (London: Oxford University Press, 1967). Reprinted by permission of the author and the Royal Institute of International Affairs, London, U.K. [This article should not be confused with another version of the essay published in 1964. It should be noted that the article was written in 1966 and does not, consequently, incorporate subsequent events into its analysis. Ellipsis points indicate deleted text.—Ed.]

Table 1. Armed Forces in Latin America

	(a) % of urban population (1960)	(b) % of illiterates (1961)	(c) % of labour force engaged in manufacturing & construction (1960)	(d) % of upper & middle classes in total population (c. 1950)	(e) % of urban upper & middle classes in total urban population (c. 1950)	(f) GNP distributed per capita (US $ 1960)	(g) Total regular armed forces	(h) Ratio of armed forces to population	(i) % military budget of total budget	(j) No. successful military coups (1920–1966)
Argentina	68	14	29	36	38	466	108·500 (1963)	0·51	13·2	7
Uruguay	82	15	28	(33)			13·110 (1963)	0·49	1·0	2
Chile	63	20	24	22	30	439	45·710 (1965)	0·62	18·0	4
Cuba	55	22	18	22	36		79·000 (1963)	1·21		4
Venezuela	62	48	15	18	27	885	22·240 (1962)	0·33	8·0	4
Costa Rica	38	21	15	22	31	310	1·230 (1964)	0·09	1·0	1
Panama	41	30	10	15	32	363	3·439 (1964)	0·32		3
Mexico	54	43	15	17	37	272	52·850 (1964)	0·15	1·0	
Brazil	39	51	17	15	35	168	263·100 (1960)	0·37	11·4	5
Colombia	46	38	17	22	28	250	22·900 (1964)	0·15		2
Ecuador	35	44	25	10	21	161	13·280 (1963)	0·30		9
Peru	36	53	18			190	44·940 (1963)	0·41	18·0	4
Bolivia	30	68	13	8	26	86	11·010 (1960)	0·31	11·0	9
Paraguay	34	34	17	14	27	129	9·100 (1962)	0·50		7
El Salvador	33	61	14	10	25	200	6·650 (1961)	0·25	12·0	6
Nicaragua	34	62	13		23	229	4·100 (1963)	0·25		1
Dominican Rep.	29	57	11			207	17·200 (1963)	0·57	26·0	4
Honduras	22	65	9	4	25	186	4·200 (1965)	0·21	7·0	2
Guatemala	31	71	10	8	16	156	8·500 (1965)	0·22	23·0	6
Haiti	13	89	7	3	14	98				5

and nineteenth centuries, envisaged the army as the bastion of traditional and feudal values. Its officer corps was drawn from the aristocracy, and was antagonistic to the liberal bourgeois state. From 1815, with the Pax Britannica contributing to a decrease of militarism and the state taking deliberate measures to ensure civilian control over the armed forces, there ensued a professional revolution which reached its peak by the end of the nineteenth century. The developmentalist model conceives of the army as an intelligentsia in uniform, dedicated to progress and development and peculiarly suited to achieving them. It is based on the experience of the Afro-Asian countries, where the officer corps was mostly drawn from the popular sectors. There is a Nasserist version of this model which will be discussed later. Finally, the socialist model, which, from a rejection of militarism similar to that espoused by the liberals, has progressed to an acceptance of the integration of the military in the body politic as a means both of strengthening it and of lending additional prestige to the civilian leadership.

These three ways of approaching the problem imply that the armed forces are an independent sector, or at least that they are hardly at all integrated with the rest of society. Thus, according to one such theory, the traditional army is a step behind the modern society which is forming around it; according to another, the modern army is a step ahead of the traditional society which is disintegrating. In fact both these theories presuppose an inverse relationship between militarism and the consolidation of the diversified social structure typical of a developed country. As one writer asserts: "Army officers in politics are typical of pre-industrial nations lacking a strong middle class."[3] How then is one to explain the military coups in countries such as Argentina or Brazil, which have strong middle-class sectors, and such a high degree of industrial growth that in the former country one-third of the labour force is employed in manufacturing industry or construction, while in the second domestic production accounts for two-thirds of the capital goods the country requires?[4]

An objective analysis shows that Latin America is lacking in two of the basic elements of the liberal model: in the first place, its armies were generally formed after the professional revolution; and, secondly, the greater part of their officers are recruited from the middle class and not from the aristocracy.

Merle Kling has proposed an interesting modification of this model. His argument may be summarized as follows: in Latin America, the oligarchy and foreign capital maintain a rigid control over the conventional bases of economic power and prevent the rise of other social groups; the government therefore appears as the only base of economic power, the ownership of which can change; and from this situation there arises the privileged position of the military in the ruthless struggle to take possession of this coveted source of potential power; instability is therefore "a function of the contradiction between the realities of a colonial economy and the political requirements of legal sovereignty among the Latin American states."[5]

Even if one ignores the economic emphasis of this theory and concedes that the personal ambition of military leaders is the basic driving force behind military interventions, it is obvious that this interpretation is only valid for very undeveloped countries, characterized by a bi-polar social structure (oligarchy/masses), and a very low degree of mobility and institutional differentiation—conditions which can hardly be said to be prevalent in the more advanced countries of Latin America.

Similar objections can be raised to the "developmentalist" model—largely based on the experience of the Afro-Asian countries—which analyses "the political implications of the army as a modern institution that has been somewhat artificially introduced into disorganized traditional societies."[6] It is applicable, in other words, to countries of very recent formation, where the civil and military bureaucracies are the only alternatives, in almost entire absence of modern institutions. It is unnecessary to emphasize the difference between such societies and those of Argentina or Brazil.

This lends added interest to an examination of instability in the more-developed countries of Latin America. In the two already mentioned—Argentina and Brazil—military coups are features of the present-day situation. In the other three[7]—Uruguay, Chile, and Mexico—the last quarter-century has been marked by political stability. Is it possible, by means of an analysis of the experience of these countries, to isolate structural factors capable of explaining interventionism in situations remote from those envisaged in the traditional models? Over twenty years ago it was observed that "a government which cannot rely upon its middle classes will, almost certainly, be unable to rely upon the unbroken loyalty of its army."[8] Is this the situation? And, if so, why?

This essay attempts to analyse certain structural elements that have not generally been considered in previous interpretations of this phenomenon. For at least two reasons it makes no claim to be exhaustive; first, it excludes the very important circumstantial factors, which cannot be dealt with here; and, secondly, because a model of this nature does not claim to be an exact reflection of reality, but only to place some emphasis on certain important aspects that are not immediately obvious.

The Middle-Class Professional Army

To understand the problem of political instability, one must look behind the military façade (just as, to understand Latin American inflation, one had to look behind the monetary façade). With this end in view, both the social basis of the officer corps and some of the consequences of its recent professionalization must be considered.

Social Basis

Although statistical information on this subject is still scarce, most authorities are agreed in admitting that, since the end of the nineteenth century, the majority of Latin American officers have been recruited from the middle class.[9]

In his study of generals, brigadiers, and admirals in Argentina, José Luis de Imaz found that only 23 percent of the sample examined were descended from the traditional families. He estimated that 73 percent of the brigadiers and generals interviewed came from families belonging to the wealthy bourgeoisie, 25 percent from the lower middle class, and only 2 percent from the working class.[10] Although the category "upper middle class or wealthy bourgeoisie" is excessively large, and includes everybody from landowners to professional men, and even supposing that all the fathers concerned who were landowners, businessmen, or industrialists belonged to the upper class—which is certainly an exaggeration—this survey does indicate that two-thirds of the officer corps is of middle-class origin. Moreover, contrary to what is generally believed, the data provided by Imaz indicate that "[Argentine] generals, today just as much as formerly, come from an urban background, half of them the capital and the Greater Buenos Aires area."[11]

John Johnson reached similar conclusions with regard to the middle-class origin of Brazilian officers,[12] even though in this case the greater part came from the small towns in the interior. . . .

In Chile, where the officer corps represents a more typical cross-section of the urban population as a whole,[13] there has been, ever since the war of 1879, a continuous penetration of the military profession by the sons of middle-class families.[14] A similar trend has been evident in Uruguay and Mexico since the turn of the century. In the case of Mexico, it is possible that recruitment has taken place from even lower social strata: for example, an examination of the applications for admission to the Military College in 1955 reveals that 14.64 percent of the candidates were the sons of workers and 2.98 percent the sons of peasants.[15]

This description does not imply that the class situation of the officer corps entirely explains its political behaviour. It does, however, restrict the field of investigation, and makes possible an assessment of the importance and relative autonomy of outside factors inhibiting or determining the behaviour of this group.[16] It is, after all, not entirely fortuitous that the liberal model which prevailed in the nineteenth century should have paid particular attention to the basis of recruitment of those destined for military command: "After all, their origins constitute the source of the 'non-Armed Force' opinions of the armed force organizations."[17]

In the countries under discussion, there are other factors which presumably tend to strengthen this class affiliation, owing to continual contact between the civil and military spheres. Among these are the lack of a tradition of active warfare, which diminishes the separation between the daily life of the officers and that of the rest of the population. Another factor that has still not been investigated is the mediating role fulfilled by retired officers: the available data do, in fact, indicate a tendency towards "rejuvenation" among the higher ranks of the armed forces,[18] which means that the retirement—voluntary or enforced—of the officer occurs when he is still fully active and capable of embarking on a civilian career, while at the same time keeping in touch with his old comrades in arms. Moreover, whereas in technologically backward societies the increasing technical specialization of the army tends to link the officer more closely to foreign sources, in societies of a higher cultural development, such as those we are analyzing, the same phenomenon leads to increased contacts between the officer and his civilian colleagues.

Finally, it is worth pointing out an obvious fact which is too often forgotten, namely the "civilianization" of the officers that is a direct consequence of their continual political activity. Although one should not exaggerate the importance of such contacts, which in any case are limited to certain social sectors, this is nevertheless an argument against the traditional conception of the army as an institution completely isolated from its social context, and the consequent exaggeration of the uniqueness of the armed forces' attitudes and behaviour. It would, of course, be absurd to deny the existence of characteristics peculiar to the army as such but so far no attempt has been made to determine how important these are in determining an officer's behaviour.[19] Several studies devoted to this question apply to the military establishment the concept of the "total institution" formulated by Goffman.[20] However, such studies pay less attention to the distinctions drawn by the same writer with regard to methods of recruitment and the permeability of the institution to the influences surrounding it,[21] and ignore his assertion that "total institutions do not really look for cultural victory,"[22] which explains the relative ease with which its members are able to become reintegrated into the society outside the institution.[23]

Organization

While it is true, on the one hand, that the greater part of the officer corps comes from the middle class, the military establishment can, on the other hand, count on a degree of cohesion and institutional solidity which is entirely lacking in the Latin American middle class.

The tendency to consider social phenomena in isolation and in the abstract has led some writers to suppose that professionalization *per se* induces officers to withdraw from politics, by placing a barrier between them and the rest of society. Oddly enough, Mosca argued with equal conviction, and for well-founded reasons, that the contrary was true and, more recently, Finer has supported his arguments.[24] With regard to the Latin American armed forces, one observer asserts: "On the contrary, in those countries in which they have been most highly professionalized, they seem to have become even more closely linked with the rest of society than formerly."[25]

What happens in reality is that every system of domination attempts to internalize violence by the means most suited to its values and interests. Thus professionalism became generally accepted in European armies only at the end of the nineteenth century and as a result of deliberate government policy. The bourgeois state had experimented with various formulae for the control of the armed forces—examples of which are the unsuccessful French and American attempts to have the highest posts of command submitted to popular election—until the logic of capitalist society eventually dictated the solution. In the framework of a general tendency towards fragmentation and division of labour, the exercise of violence was also converted into a specialized field calling for high professional qualifications, and became part of a series of particular sub-systems enjoying a relative degree of autonomy. In this way "military institutions have taken on more and more the characteristics common to civilian large-scale organizations."[26] Professionalization is therefore the means by which the armed forces are incorporated into a determined place in the structuralization of society as a whole, and it is this, and not professionalism as such, that explains the apparent political neutrality of the army in the Western democracies.

This process of professionalization was bound to produce different results in Latin America, since it not only took place in armies at different stages of development but did so in the context of pre-industrial societies with structures based on the hegemony of the oligarchy and not that of the bourgeoisie.

In Europe "military organization had established its form centuries before professionalization definitely began."[27] This explains in part the successful establishment of organizational controls designed to counteract the possible centrifugal tendencies which might result from increased professionalization. In Latin America organization and professionalization take place almost simultaneously, increasing the probability of discrepancies leading to open conflict.[28]

This early professionalization had two important social consequences: first, as has been indicated above, the middle class was admitted to the career of arms through the creation of military academies; and secondly, in contrast to its own organizational weakness,[29] this class was now allied to a sector with a remarkable degree of institutional cohesion and articulateness. In other words the armed forces became one of the few important institutions controlled by the middle class.[30]

This relationship partly explains political instability due to military intervention but it is open to two important criticisms: first, from those who consider that the profession of arms conditions its followers so thoroughly that one may ignore any other variable in seeking for explanations of their behaviour; and, secondly, from those who maintain that the middle class, by its very nature, is dedicated to the support of political stability and democratic institutions.

I have already given some of the reasons why I consider the first objection to be valid only in a relative sense. With regard to the second, it will be necessary to touch briefly on some of the factors that lead the middle class to associate with military intervention in politics.

Middle Class and Bourgeoisie

Hitherto I have deliberately used the expression "middle class" rather than "bourgeoisie." G. D. H. Cole has drawn the distinction:

> Bourgeois, to any historically-minded person, calls up at once the image of a body of citizens asserting their collective, as well as their individual, independence of a social system dominated by feudal power based on landholding and on the services attached to it; whereas the words "middle class" call up the quite different image of a body of persons who are placed between two other bodies—or perhaps more than two—in some sort of stratified social order.[31]

The same writer goes on to say that the bourgeoisie as such is not in the middle of anything, at least not consciously so.

At this point it is necessary to consider the degree of relative independence of the rural and urban sectors of the same national society; it is on this supposed independence that the hypothesis of structural dualism, so frequently met with in studies concerned with Latin America, is based. The concept of a middle class implies, by definition, a system of unified vertical stratification. But the application of the hypothesis of dualism to the Latin American situation admits of two different interpretations; in the first, the traditional and modern "poles" are analysed as if they were relatively independent entities, with the result that some writers speak of "two countries within the same territory." Hence the tendency to transfer mechanically to the Latin American situation a technologically determinist hypothesis like Ogburn's "cultural lag." The observer "isolates" São Paulo from the North-East, for example, and assumes that for the latter to attain the level of development of the former, all that is required is to transform the North-East without considering whether a transformation would involve equally profound changes in São Paulo. On the other hand, the dialectic interpretation finds the key to the situation in the internal unity of a historically determined system of domination. This is the unity explaining the frustration of a middle class which is prevented from fulfilling the role of a bourgeoisie. In order to analyse such an interpretation, it is necessary to distinguish between two principal stages in the evolution of the system: that of the unity of the oligarchy and that of its crisis.

The Hegemony of the Oligarchy

[Due to] characteristics associated with the process of colonization, in the case of the urbanization of Latin America, . . . there was never any real dissension between the urban centres and the nascent landowning aristocracy. "Colonization was in large part an urban venture, carried out by urban-minded people"[32] and the city represented both the point of departure and the residence of the owners of land. . . .

This initial "unitary" characteristic becomes even more pronounced in the second half of the nineteenth century, with the rapid integration of the Latin American national economies into the world market. As Celso Furtado has observed, "the entrepreneurial attitude that made the rapid development of lines of export possible had its origin within the merchant groups which operated from the urban centers."[33] Instead of a divergence developing between the interests of the dominant groups in the cities and those in the rural areas, the urban mercantile sector consolidated its position as a landowning and capitalist oligarchy.[34]

[Generally speaking,] it was thus that the great Latin American capitals became the places of residence of the privileged sectors during the era of "outward" economic growth. Beside them there developed the middle class, of the primary-products export model, composed of the exporters and importers, small industrialists, professional men, and civil servants, all integrated into the hegemonic system of the oligarchy.

This did not mean that the state was simply the expression of the subjective will of one social class, as if the underlying unity of the hegemonic structure were given by the ideology of the dominant group. On the contrary, this unity must be sought in the total structure of society, in which this ideology was only one element among many. The function fulfilled by the state—providing a framework for the oligarchy—must not be obscured by being forced into the nineteenth-century liberal model imported from Europe. In Latin America there was no question of the *status quo* being challenged; *laissez-faire* was in practice the political instrument which consolidated the economic system, and its application constituted "a deliberate measure consciously designed to achieve specific ends and not the spontaneous and automatic expression of an economic situation."[35] Structure and super-structure thus became fused into an extremely solid historical block, and found their expression in an advanced juridical and institutional system. Marx asserts that a particular class can only maintain its supremacy by exercising it in the name of the general rights of society. On the basis of a particular economic system, this "conquérante" oligarchy was able to evolve a systematic justification of its dominant position by means of a normative structure which defined those general rights in terms which applied to the existing internal relationships among social groups. The fundamental reason for its success was undoubtedly the high degree of efficacy of the system itself: the bonanza arising from the export of raw materials convinced all its beneficiaries—direct and indirect—that Argentine meat, Brazilian coffee, Uruguayan wool, and Chilean minerals guaranteed permanent economic expansion. To be optimistic, it was enough to conceive of the future as an extension of the present, and the middle class enthusiastically adopted that conservative outlook which takes no account of the future or the vicissitudes it may bring. It was members of the oligarchy, not of the middle class, who were responsible for the first industrial expansion of any importance, and it was they who organized the new industrial and commercial enterprises, in which the middle class participated only as a second-rate but acquiescent partner. . . . Since the basic principles of the system were never called into question, commercial or industrial collapse was regarded as a problem affecting only the individual concerned, or, at most, held to be the result of corruption of a system that, in its uncorrupt state, was considered unsurpassable.

The expanding middle class made no attempt to change the system as a whole: it merely demanded recognition of its legitimate right to play a part in it. Its aspirations were limited to a desire for participation in political affairs and for revendication of its moral status.[36] The most interesting features of this process were the speed with which these aspirations were satisfied and the instrumental role of the military.

This process began in Uruguay, with the election in 1903 of José Batlle y Ordóñez. This chronological priority undoubtedly reflects the very early development of the Uruguayan middle class: at the turn of the century, it already constituted between 25 and 30 per cent of the population of the Republic, and *Batllismo* was "the political movement which most exactly reflects [its] rise."[37] The great leader of the *Colorados* came to power in the middle of a civil war fought against the landowning groups connected with the Blanco Party. Whereas the armed forces of the latter were basically composed of peons recruited from the big estates, the regular army gave its support to *Batllismo* and made it possible for Batlle to establish himself in power.[38]

In Argentina, a military lodge was formed as early as 1890, under the influence of the *Unión Cívica,* the immediate predecessor of the *Unión Cívica Radical,* the middle-class party which carried Hipólito Yrigoyen into the presidency in 1916. In the intervening period there were increased contacts between the Radicals and the officer corps—some of the officers played an active part in the 1893 and 1905 rebellions—and this was one of the factors which eventually induced the oligarchy to allow free elections. As Puiggrós observes: "They feared the democratic revolution, and at the same time they realized that they could not continue to monopolize political power with the immense majority of the people against them and with Radicalism increasingly influencing the army, the police and the civil service."[39] This also explains the failure of the coup planned at the last minute by the oligarchy-dominated Senate, designed to force the resignation of President Sáenz Peña, suspend the elections, and return to the system of restricted suffrage.

In Chile, the aspirations of the middle class found expression in the *Alianza Liberal* which, in 1920, put Arturo Alessandri in the presidency. "The 'revolution of 1920' was never envisioned by most of its instigators as anything more than a program of mild palliatives; but it was unable to furnish even the palliatives."[40] Among the most obvious reasons for its failure was the systematic opposition of the Senate, still controlled by the oligarchy. As Gil observes, "the majority of the Chilean armed forces, composed of middle-class members in the officer corps and of men of proletarian origin in the rank and file, were sympathetic to the national cry for reform."[41] When, after the parliamentary elections of 1924, even the new Congress—in which Alessandri already commanded a majority—postponed the implementation of the President's programme, the army took action, overthrew the ministerial cabinet and "in an hour and without debate, the 'suggestive rattling of army sabres in the congressional galleries' obtained approval of a complete program of social legislation which had been pending for years in the Congress."[42] Although the movement was initially commanded by a group of officers identified with the upper class, "the majority of the armed forces' officers opposed the restoration to power of a discredited oligarchy."[43] Thus in January 1925 another coup, this time engineered by young officers led by Carlos Ibáñez and Marmaduke Grove, eliminated the conservative faction, brought Alessandri back to the country, and drew up a new constitution which, in the words of a liberal commentator, "although it was the work of a *de facto* government and was imposed by force of arms, has stood the test of time, and has lasted with minor modifications until our own day."[44] Thus the armed forces ensured the establishment in power of the middle class, whose programme was put into practice by Colonel Ibáñez who, as a result of military pressure, became president in 1927. One should not forget, therefore, in considering the subsequent political stability of Chile, that "the institutional structure that has governed Chile down to the present day was fashioned by Ibáñez between 1927 and 1931."[45]

In Brazil, the continuous expansion of the armed forces since 1864 made them a stronghold of the incipient middle class, to which the Empire offered few occupational opportunities. "That middle-class army, which to a certain extent formed a body outside the organizational structure of the Imperial state, would eventually overthrow it."[46] "Florianismo," however, marked the failure of the premature attempt of this sector to establish control over the state.[47] Although the solidarity of the Old Republic

(*Republica velha*), rendered the process slower in the case of Brazil, events subsequently followed a path similar to those in Argentina and Chile: "The middle-class revolutions that took place between 1922 and 1937 represented the efforts made by that class to achieve, by military means, a power that always eluded it."[48] The first step towards the final achievement of this objective was the revolution of 1930, which brought Getulio Vargas to power, thanks to the decisive part played by the *tenentismo* movement. The support of the military for the regime was reaffirmed in 1932, with the defeat of the attempt to restore the oligarchy. The new groups soon realized, however, that adherence to the 1934 constitution and the effective implementation of the basic principle for which they had struggled—universal and secret suffrage—would result in their defeat at the hands of the paternalistic ballot-rigging practised by the landowners.

> Thus the middle class found itself in the peculiar position of wishing to control the state without altering the existing social and economic structure, and of being compelled by considerations of *Realpolitik* to jettison its political principles with the anti-democratic coup of 1937 and the setting up of the *Estado nôvo*.[49]

Although several circumstantial factors make it exceptional, the case of Mexico nevertheless partially confirms the pattern outlined above. The limited nature of the political aspirations of the middle class was summed up in the well-known *Maderista* slogan, "Effective suffrage and no re-election." The emphasis was, above all, political: "Madero wanted wider participation and more democratic processes in politics in an effort to end the *continuismo* of the Díaz régime."[50] This explains the timidity of the agrarian measures contemplated in Article 3 of the Plan of San Luis Potosí, which nevertheless was enough to mobilize Emiliano Zapata and his followers:

> He and his men soon threw themselves into the Revolution, not because they were excited by the magic words "effective suffrage and no re-election," as this political document [the Plan of San Luis Potosí] suggests, but because they believed in the agrarian measures promised in Article 3.[51]

The complete ineffectiveness in this respect of the thirteen and a half months of Madero's government provoked the insurrection of the Southern leader and his proclamation of the Plan of Ayala, which gave contemporary expression to the slogan of Flores Magón: "Land and Liberty." It was this peasant unrest that forced the middle class to support the reforms which, albeit with great hesitation, Venustiano Carranza was introducing; so much so that the domination of the oligarchy was in fact broken only in the following decade, under the government of Obregón, whose work was completed by Lázaro Cárdenas. As for the army, its situation was slightly different from that described in the countries discussed above. In his successful attempts to establish control, Porfirio Díaz had considerably weakened it. Gradually he forced the retirement of a quarter of the hundred generals in the army, and dismissed about four hundred more junior officers.[52] Also the professionalization of the armed forces was much slower than in the other cases quoted: "Although there was a perceptible French influence and part of the equipment was German, Mexico did not invite any foreign military mission, and rarely sent officers to study abroad. Consequently, the army was backward in both military techniques and equipment."[53] For this reason, as Edwin Lieuwen points out, the army was no more than a "fragile shell" when the 1910 revolution broke out. Nevertheless as soon as the revolution began, a number of officers, steadily increasing, "deserted the regime and joined the revolutionary forces, impressed by their power and popular support."[54] In other words, in Mexico too a sizeable part of the regular army supported the attempts of the middle class to seize power.

All this highlights the relative speed with which the middle class achieved the satisfaction of its claims; and the decisive role played by the armed forces in this process. But what must be emphasized above all is the limited nature of those claims. Except in the case of Mexico, the political events did not constitute one of those "cathartic" movements when the ascent to power of a new social group leads to profound structural changes. It was the very reverse of that process: the middle class had no need of time to develop a characteristic outlook, because it merely adopted that of the oligarchy. It accepted its heroes, its symbols, its culture, and its laws. (It is significant that both Yrigoyen and Alessandri decided to play with "loaded dice," assuming the presidency at a time when the parliamentary majority was in the hands of the oligarchy.) The middle class did not question the economic basis of the system, but formulated the conflict in terms of "equality of opportunity," that is to say equality of access to the alternatives defined by that system; for this reason the two sides eventually agreed on the socialization of the political conflict, leaving the economic one on a purely private plane. In contrast to this, the exceptional merit of the Mexican Revolution lay in its handling of the agrarian problem.

Two points are worth making. First, a description of the integration of the middle class into a historical situation dominated by the oligarchic hegemony need not be interpreted as a moral accusation levelled against that class, on the grounds that it failed in its historic mission, since in fact its behaviour was governed by the limited framework of its "possible consciousness," bearing in mind the conditions surrounding its formation. Secondly, this is a process and not a static phenomenon. Important political changes such as these cannot be explained simply in quantitative terms. The very expansion that was the result of the ascent and social integration of the middle class began, in fact, to weaken the hegemony of the oligarchy, making it especially vulnerable to the vicissitudes of the period that followed and leading it towards its definitive crisis.

The Hegemonic Crisis

After the 1929 depression, exports in the countries under discussion ceased to constitute the axis of the economic system, and internal investment replaced the external sector as the dynamic growth factor.

In the favourable conditions of a highly protected internal market—as an indirect consequence of measures taken to prevent catastrophe for the exporting groups—there took place a process of totally unplanned industrial development. The peculiar characteristic of this process of substitution of imports[55] was that it made possible industrialization without an industrial revolution, and without necessarily antagonizing the landowning oligarchy. These considerations are of the utmost importance in the interpretation of the behaviour of the new middle-class groups[56] that emerged during this period because the aspirations of these groups found expression within the framework of the hegemony of the oligarchy; the conditions of their development did not result in a fundamental conflict with that system. This is the reason for the essentially conservative nature of its political consciousness, insofar as it never transcended the limits of a corporative-economic interest and was incapable of reaching the level of "universality" attained by this oligarchical system.[57]

This makes it easier to understand, in the first place, the apparent ambiguity of outlook manifested by these new sectors, which caused so many unfounded speculations about the emergence of a national bourgeoisie: its reformist impulses have invariably originated and exhausted themselves on the level of immediate economic interests. It is therefore quite logical, for example, to assert that "the state that helps 'my industry' has nothing to do with the more abstract state which, legislating and acting, participates in the economic life and becomes the eternal symbol of the anti-enterprise."[58] In the same way an industrialist can be protectionist in outlook with regard to his own products, and an advocate of free trade with regard to the materials that such production requires.[59]

Moreover, it would be erroneous to consider as a lack what is a negation. The particularism of this class consciousness really means that the new group finds appropriate, or rather that it appropriates, the existing normative structure. The repeated failure of the developmental theorists, who have eventually become convinced of the sociological weakness and artificiality of their hypotheses,[60] shows that it is not just a question of supplying what is lacking but of contending with something actually in existence.

It would be wrong to suppose, however, that the factors in this situation have remained invariable: on the contrary, the very emergence of those sectors and the growth of the urban proletariat have undermined the hegemony of the oligarchy, as happened in Brazil and Argentina after the second world war. It is interesting to examine both cases because they represent two typical variants of the model of industrialization based on import-substitution, and also because these countries have continued to be potentially Bonapartist, in so far as the crisis of the domination of the oligarchy has resulted from the action of social groups without a vocation for exercising hegemony. In such conditions there exists a basic tendency to instability, which the Roman-style[61] military coup tries unsuccessfully to correct.

The Brazilian Variant

During the *Republica velha,* federalism and parliamentarism were the principal expressions of the oligarchic political formula, which established the Federal States as the exclusive domains of various landowning groups. . . . The middle class came into power in 1930: there followed an intensive campaign to integrate the political life of Brazil at the national level, accompanied by an increasing utilization of the urban masses as an element of manoeuvre in the confrontations that ensued. The old agrarian sectors were, however, successful in preserving the federal and parliamentary structure. . . .[62] As Brandão Lopes asserts,

> the essential point to remember is that during this period (1945–64), Brazil became a composite state in which differing types of interests (instead of the almost unchallenged domination exercised by the agrarian interests in the past) develop agreements and compromises; and in which the "people," in the sense of the lower and middle urban sectors (though still lacking in a definable class-consciousness and ideological outlook) must be taken into consideration, even though it in no way participates in the power structure.[63]

The Bonapartist content of the *Estado nôvo* consisted, in precise terms, of the replacement of the traditional hegemonic system by an "adaptation of the formula of socialization of losses and division of profits to the terms of the new social reality emerging in the country and, simultaneously, its institutionalization."[64] It is worthwhile emphasizing that there was no question of the middle class ingenuously falling into an ideological trap. In the first place, as I have already pointed out, the suspension of the system of political representation, caused by the establishment of the *Estado nôvo,* served its interests. In the second place, *cartorialismo* appeared to be the functional solution of the problem of its lack of occupational opportunities. Above all, however, as far as the industrial sector was concerned, there were no basic causes of conflict between it and the oligarchy. . . .

"[T]he success that Brazil had in the substitution process is the counterpart of the fact that it was in this country that development benefited a smaller number of people and begot the sharpest social tensions."[65] The correlative of a high level of capital accumulation in the framework of a highly protected but limited market was a constant tendency "to find oneself unexpectedly with idle capacity and to divert investment into new channels, a situation which resulted in the dilemma expressed by the slogan: 'Grow rapidly or perish!' "[66] The first of these alternatives was possible as long as the dynamic impulses underlying the import-substitution process were maintained, but these have exhausted themselves without the country being able to find a pattern of self-sustained development. The result is the tendency to stagnation.

In one sense, this might lead one to suppose that the foundations have been laid for an agrarian-industrial conflict that would transform the middle class into a genuine bourgeoisie. Such a hypothesis is now more plausible than formerly; but the course of events so far makes it necessary to introduce at this juncture two considerations.

One is the extreme heterogeneity of this middle class. I am not referring solely to the fact that in Brazil, as everywhere else, it constitutes the "occupational salad" of which Mills wrote, but also to the already mentioned particularism of its outlook which has prevented it from transcending that heterogeneity and achieving a more general consciousness of solidarity, and which has also made it especially vulnerable to the influence of the upper class.

The other factor—intimately connected with the preceding one—has been the entry of the urban proletariat into the political arena. *Varguismo* was instrumental in establishing control over the explosive character of the first stage of this process, and Brazil's prosperity made it possible to gratify the aspirations of the new working class, a process undoubtedly facilitated by the low level of expectations resulting from the pre-capitalist background of the labour force. But what is happening now is a curiously regressive development: as the maturity of the working class increases— leaving out of consideration its evidently reformist outlook—the rate of economic growth of the country is diminishing for the reasons outlined above, and there is also a steadily diminishing possibility of gratifying its demands without a structural transformation of the system.

It was much to Vargas's credit that in his later years he partially realized that this situation had developed, and tried to redefine the power system of the country. But although the army had allowed him to take over the presidency in 1930 as the representative of the middle class, and to reaffirm the establishment of the latter in the government by means of the 1937 coup, that same army, in October 1945 and August 1954, expressed the fears of that same class in the face of the more popular orientation the regime was beginning to acquire.

> In both cases, Getulio Vargas was overthrown by the armed forces, who acted on both occasions as the spokesmen and instruments of the Brazilian middle class. In both cases the middle class, which could no longer impose its own orientation on the politico-social development of the country, took a reactionary stand in the face of the government's looking to the proletariat for support and moving towards a Left-Wing solution.[67]

This is also the principal characteristic of the most recent military coup, which was preceded by an intensive press campaign and street demonstrations by middle-class groups demanding the intervention of the armed forces. Goulart had consolidated his position in the government thanks to the general strike of September 1962, and the labour movement "for the first time organized for independent action, became more conscious of its power."[68] Moreover the organization of peasant forces was progressing in the North-East. At the same time, the rate of growth of the economy was slowing down, in the midst of galloping inflation. Unable to identify the structural basis of this process and to give articulate expression to a programme capable of mobilizing the popular sectors, the middle class opted for the radical Right and, frightened by the populist measures of the government, allied itself with the traditional defenders of the *status quo* and gave encouragement to the coup.

> The movement of April 1964 thus united all the property-owning classes of society: the agrarian sectors out of fear of land reform, the industrial sectors out of fear of losing their mechanisms of security, the middle classes panicked at the prospect of a closing of the social distance separating them from the masses, and all of these sectors were moved by the even greater fear of the emergence of a process of development diverging from the classical pattern of American democracy, to which they are all culturally linked.[69]

The Argentine Variant

A fundamental characteristic of the Argentine case—as well as of the Uruguayan—is the early absorption of the agrarian pre-capitalist sector and the consequent unification of the domestic labour market. For this reason, and viewing the problem in comparative terms, it makes less sense to refer to a dualistic structure. Another consequence of this is that the process of industrialization took place in a context of a limited supply of labour, which constituted a permanent threat to the profit margins of the rural producers, in contrast to the position in Brazil, "making difficult their recovery when favourable conditions appear in the export markets."[70] Despite this, and notwithstanding the presence of peculiar factors, here too the middle class has shown itself unable to break away from its tacit agreement with the landowning sector.

In order to understand the situation, it is necessary to insist on the great efficacy of the system during the era of the hegemony of the oligarchy. At the end of the last century Argentina was already predominantly urban and was undergoing a rapid process of modernization, in which immigration played an important part. The future of the land of cattle and wheat appeared definitely assured: "A powerful tide carried everything upwards and everyone thought that the ascent would never stop until it reached the clouds, that it would never stop at all."[71] For this reason, the principal task of Yrigoyen consisted in ensuring the participation of the middle class in the project inaugurated by the generation of 1880, not of changing that project.

So true was this that when setbacks occurred in the 1920s, it was not the middle class which blamed the raw-material-exporting system established by the oligarchy, but the oligarchy which condemned the system of parliamentary democracy defended by the middle class: "The Yrigoyen government was a proof, in the eyes of many people, of the definitive failure of universal suffrage."[72]

This remarkable subordination of the middle class—combined with the fact that it was their representatives who were in power during the 1929 crisis (in contrast to the situation in Brazil)—partly explains the oligarchical character of the coup of 6 September 1930. As Dardo Cúneo observes:

> If the military rebellion was in fact just a walk through the city, this was not due to the ability of the army conspirators; it was principally due to the weakness of the middle class, to its forgetting its historic role as a class. So great was its inactivity in this respect that, although the army was officered by members of that same middle class, it served the interests of the oligarchy against theirs. The Radical government was incapable of expressing any inspiring message or of rallying its supporters.[73]

In 1928 Yrigoyen had failed to seize the opportunity of liquidating the San Martín Lodge, the nucleus of the movement that would overthrow him two years later; once the coup had occurred, the *Unión Cívica Radical,* controlled by Alvear, refused to assume the political leadership of the officers who were prepared to rise against the oligarchical restoration.[74] Although these circumstances do not alter the fact that—to a certain extent—the 1930 coup was an exception to the pattern that I have been describing,[75] they at least serve to emphasize the fact that the military coup was not carried out against the opposition of the middle class, and the representatives of the latter did little or nothing to modify its course.

Thus, in a political climate the most salient characteristic of which is "the weakness of all the political attitudes that are not the expression of the interests of the traditional privileged classes,"[76] Argentina carried out the first stage of the process of industrialization based on import-substitution. By the middle of the 1940s the contribution of the manufacturing sector to the national product was already greater than that of the agricultural sector. After the end of the war Perón not only consolidated this industrial growth, but also gave concrete satisfaction to the political rights of the urban and rural workers. The coup of June 1943 thus led to the adoption of populist measures, to the direct benefit of the new middle-class groups, whose partial opposition to the regime revealed, nevertheless, the persistence of traditional ideological tendencies.

Peronismo marked the definitive crisis of the hegemony of the oligarchy; but in Argentina, as in Brazil, it was not succeeded by the setting up of the hegemony of the bourgeoisie, but by a series of alliances and compromises which constituted the essence of a Bonapartist system.

The prosperity of the early post-war years made it possible for the regime to concede considerable benefits to the popular sectors without doing too much damage to other social groups. Perón once said that an adversary must either be forgiven or eliminated: nothing is more dangerous than a wounded enemy. The experience of his government confirms the truth of the aphorism and reveals him as a poor follower of his own precepts. The nationalization of foreign trade and bank deposits were basically measures designed to transfer revenue from the rural sector to industrial expansion. But, in addition to being limited in scope,[77] these measures were not accompanied by a proper agrarian policy. In this respect, the ambiguity appears especially negative, in so far as the government disrupted the traditional system of production—especially through legislation protecting tenants—without imposing the solutions required to supersede it; a wounded enemy, the oligarchy would wreak its revenge on a country which no longer accepted its exclusive tutelage. . . .

As a result, not only was there paralysis in a sector vital to Argentina's development, but the effects were felt on the standards of living of the popular sectors whose expectations had been raised by the experience of the Perón regime. The maintenance of the situation, however, is a current proof of the principle stated by Gramsci: " 'Civil society' has become an extremely complex structure capable of resisting the catastrophic 'incursions' of immediate economic factors (crises, depressions, etc.): the superstructures of the civil society are similar to the trench system in modern warfare."[78] Frightened by the possibility of the country's political development taking a radical turn, the middle-class prefers to take refuge in those same trenches. The process is thus a "self-fulfilling prophecy": the middle class is unable to assume the leadership of the popular movement and becomes increasingly separated from it, while the movement continues to be Peronist, and, what is more, addicted to a form of Peronism from which certain middle-class groups originally sympathizing with it have deserted,[79] and which tends, therefore, to become more closely identified with Perón's first presidency than with his second.

In these circumstances, the free elections which were once the dream of the middle class have become its nightmare. Established in the ideological camp proper to the oligarchy, it can interpret the stagnation only as a political problem; it therefore exercises constant pressure on the military to intervene, prevent the triumph of Peronism, and overthrow the government of the day which is failing precisely because it represents that middle class. This is the background of the March 1962 and June 1966 coups. It was no coincidence that, two days after the second coup, the Buenos Aires Stock Exchange showed the most spectacular rises in four years.[80] One of the *civilian* theorists supporting the movement observed with satisfaction that "instead of electing, the people will now have the right of consenting and participating in political decisions. . . . Such consent may be either 'implicit'—a passive acceptance of the new order—or 'explicit,' in cases where the new régime evolves towards plebiscitary forms."[81]

The Middle Class and Democracy

It is commonplace to compare the rapid expansion of the Latin American political arena with the very gradual evolution of the British electoral system.[82] Without underestimating the undoubted interest of this kind of analysis, it is fair to say that "it conveys the impression that England became a democracy primarily as a result of statutory changes in the electoral system, whereas in fact the historical process involved was a good deal more complex."[83]

One of the decisive elements in that process was precisely the efficacy of the Victorian bourgeoisie in articulating the popular consensus. For this purpose, it skillfully utilized the deferential attitudes still persisting in the working class; it ceaselessly diffused the values associated with its capitalist, liberal and Christian ethical system; it gave enthusiastic encouragement to a complex of institutions "devoted to self-improvement and self-help,"[84] and, above all, it proved able, from the middle of the last century, to effect a considerable improvement in the economic position of a labour aristocracy which responded eagerly to such encouragement.[85] Without this intermediate process, which made possible the ending of the original identification of the "labouring classes" with the "dangerous classes," the electoral reform of 1867 would be incomprehensible: the workers only began to be accepted as citizens when their conformism had extinguished the old Chartist fervour.[86] It was for that reason that the suffrage lost its disruptive character, and was able to fulfil in the political sphere the legitimizing function that the contract fulfilled in the economic sphere. In other words, the validity of the classical Marxist proposition according to which representative democracy is the form of government which most closely corresponds to the interests of the bourgeoisie depends on the previous consolidation by the latter of its hegemonic supremacy, its development of a metaphysical justification of its leading role, and its demonstration of its efficacy as a ruling class.

In the course of the above analysis, we have tried to point out some of the reasons for the failure of the Latin American middle class to achieve this position. The central nucleus of its problem is that, when it has still not succeeded in working out a stable political compromise with the oligarchy, it is already having to face the problem which Disraeli formulated a century ago: "The Working Class Question is the real question, and that is the thing that demands to be settled."[87]

Electoral data provide only an approximate indication of the magnitude of the problem. At the outbreak of the first world war, in a somewhat similar stage of industrial development, only 10 to 15 percent of the population of Europe took part in elections;[88] in the countries we are considering, however, the proportion is often three or four times as great, e.g.: Argentina, 43.9 percent (1963); Uruguay, 36.4 percent (1958); Chile, 30.5 percent (1964). These figures are close to the most recent ones for the United States, e.g., 38 percent in 1964.

Unable to consolidate themselves as a bourgeoisie, the most that the progressive sectors of the Latin American middle classes have been able to do has been to offer the popular sectors programmes based on fundamentally quantitative goals, mobilizing them to seek the satisfaction of their demands within the existing structural framework. This is the essential ingredient in the populism of Perón, Vargas, and Ibáñez; and it provides one of the clues to its unique character: whereas elsewhere—e.g., the United States or Canada—populist movements have had an agrarian basis and arose in periods of depression, in Latin America these movements were fundamentally urban and were associated with periods of prosperity.

For this reason economic stagnation fixes the limits of such movements, as is shown by the change of orientation of Perón's regime around 1950, and the swing of Ibáñez to conservatism which coincided with the falling-off of the Korean War boom.[89]

It has often been alleged that the Latin American middle class was progressive as long as it needed popular support to achieve power and, once established there, became reactionary.[90] Although this observation is more or less valid as a mere description of actual events, the formula is dangerous on account of the class-subjectivism to which it may lead: it can tempt the observer too easily to make a metaphorical association with a psychological "vertigo" supposedly felt by that class when it reaches the heights of power.

If this analysis is correct, it is its internal composition and the manner in which it has achieved power within the framework of the hegemony of the oligarchy which is beginning to disintegrate that explains the behaviour of this middle class. Moreover, if we employ for a moment the hypothetical representation of history recommended by Weber, it is probable that if the process of import-substitution had been accompanied by opportunities of exploiting an external colonial market, these countries would have achieved self-sustained growth without radical internal changes and with a Fabian-style working-class participation in political affairs.

What actually happens is quite different, and tends to aggravate the instability of the middle class. In the first place, it lacks the internal cohesion of the upper class, which not only still dominates strategic sectors of the economy but has firm control over the symbols of prestige.

Secondly, it can no longer fulfil the only promises it is able to formulate to the masses whose organization is now increasing dangerously, in contrast to the middle class's own institutional weakness.

It is necessary at this point to introduce a word of warning—even though this is not the place to go more fully into the matter—in view of the tendency of many interpreters to refer to the *"massification"* of the Latin American societies which we are considering;[91] one must be careful to distinguish between the points of view of the observer and the person observed, even though they may use similar terminology. It is in this case that the observation of Raymond Williams is particularly appropriate: "There are in fact no masses; there are only ways of seeing people as masses."[92] To the oligarchies at the turn of the century, the "masses" were the rising middle classes, just as for the latter the "masses" are now the rural and urban workers: "If you disapprove of the changes you can, it seems, avoid open opposition to democracy as such by inventing a new category, mass-democracy, which is not such a good thing at all."[93]

In these conditions, and in spite of the objective indicators of "massification" that the observer may detect, the concept of the masses does not express a general tendency towards levelling but merely identifies the proletariat, conceived as such by the propertied classes regardless of the degree of internal solidarity that those masses have been able to achieve.

If we concentrate our attention on the low level of class-consciousness of the new working class, we are apt to forget that an essential ingredient in a social class, as T. H. Marshall has emphasized, is the way in which a man is treated by his neighbour. I do not mean by this that the Latin American political struggle will assume the form of the nineteenth-century conflicts: both the context and the protagonists have changed greatly. Nevertheless, as the populist atmosphere wears off, the central contradiction takes visible shape in somewhat similar terms. For this reason, even though Furtado may be right in emphasizing the differences in revolutionary potential between the urban and the rural workers,[94] it is worth remembering that the continued existence of such differences is a function of the ideological vigour of the dualistic structure as a confusing form assumed by Latin American capitalist development. On the economic plane, the underlying unity of the process is increasingly revealed by the chronic tendency to stagnation; on the political plane, it is the alliance of the middle class with the oligarchy that fully reveals that unity.

The Middle-Class Military Coup

Schumpeter maintained that "without protection by some non-bourgeois group, the bourgeoisie is politically helpless and unable not only to lead its nation but even to take care of its particular class interest. Which amounts to saying that it needs a master."[95] He was obviously referring to Great

Britain, in view of the "protective" flexibility with which the aristocracy managed to adapt itself to the rise of the bourgeoisie. Moreover, in the case of France, the disintegration at the time of the Revolution of the traditional "protecting strata" was responsible for the high degree of instability that characterized the nineteenth century. However, in order to understand the peculiar synthesis achieved by the Third Republic—which "was throughout, in spirit and operation, middle class rather than either aristocratic or peasant or proletarian"[96]—it must be borne in mind that in France too there existed a "protecting stratum," namely, the civil service, the pre-revolutionary organization of which was maintained almost intact, and which established an element of continuity which has lasted through five republics and two empires.[97]

If Schumpeter's proposition is valid for a *"bourgeoisie conquérante,"* it must be even more so in the case of a class fragmented by the particularism of its outlook and formed in a context of bargaining and compromises. For this reason, translated into the terms of this theory, my thesis is that in the Latin American countries we are considering, owing to the absence of an English-style adaptation facilitated by a remarkable economic development, and also of a French-style bureaucracy capable of absorbing the shocks originating from political conflict, it is the armed forces which assume the responsibility of protecting the middle class. It was with their support that the middle class achieved, at the beginning of the century, political recognition from the oligarchy; it was with their protection that it later consolidated itself in power; and now it is with their intervention that it seeks to ward off the threat posed by the popular sectors that it is incapable of leading.

This explains the continuous civilian pressure in favour of military intervention, which a mere chronicle of the events rarely reveals.[98] Although he does not draw all the possible conclusions from his assertion, Imaz observes:

> Thus, the appeal to the armed forces as a source of legitimation—quite apart from all the other explanations given—has become a tacit rule of the Argentine political game. It is a rule that no one explicitly invokes, but from which all political groups have benefited at least once. Publicly they would all deny the existence of such a rule, but in reality it can never be ignored by Argentine politicians, who, at one time or another during this quarter of a century, have all gone to knock on the door of the barracks.[99]

The oligarchy, of course, has recourse to this expedient, and attempts to influence the military in its favour. However, the history of the coups that have taken place in the twentieth century shows that the military have only exceptionally shown a tendency to act as the representatives of the oligarchy. In other words, if the connexion between the upper class and military interventionism serves to explain an exceptional case such as the overthrow of Yrigoyen advocated also by the middle class, nevertheless, it is the connexion between the army and the interests and values of the middle class which explains most of remaining interventions.

Thus, failure to emphasize and distinguish between the structural factors that cause the chronic instability of this class and its *penchant* for interventionism can be doubly misleading; first, because it prevents a full understanding of the peculiar characteristics of Latin American political development, and thus fails to relate to their historical context the very concepts of parliamentary democracy and of the middle class;[100] and, secondly, because it leads the observer to treat the armed forces as external factors, who interfere with the supposed normal evolution of a political process, either through personal ambition or because they have been beguiled by the upper class into serving its interests. The problem is inevitably reduced to psychological terms, and the political development of Latin America comes to be interpreted as depending less on social transformation than on a change of mentality on the part of the army officers.

Provisional Stability

We must now make brief reference to the cases of Uruguay, Chile, and Mexico. Although, as I pointed out above, the army in these countries supported the rise to power of the middle class, their apparent political neutrality since that event seems to constitute an objection to my main argument, which up to now has been principally illustrated by reference to the cases of Argentina and Brazil. I believe, however, that it can be seen to corroborate my argument, if we identify certain peculiar characteristics on which this apolitical behavior is based.

In Uruguay, the civil war at the beginning of the century resulted in the triumph of the middle class through a tacit pact with the oligarchy. . . . In this context, most middle-class aspirations have been connected with the obtaining of better government employment, and the patronage system of the political parties and state paternalism have been appropriate instruments for the satisfaction of these demands.

These and other factors which have helped to make the case of Uruguay exceptional have become less operative in recent years. First, the reduced size of the internal market resulted in a rapid exhaustion of the process of import-substitution; and, secondly, as in the case of Argentina, the persistence of an agrarian structure based on big estates has caused a fall in productivity in the rural sector, to such an extent that since 1943 there has been no increase in the volume of the essential exports of meat and wool. The result is complete economic stagnation, and the gross product per capita has remained practically stationary for the last twenty years. This has coincided with a period of intense rural migration, accompanied by the familiar "revolution of rising expectations." Once again the public sector has tried to canalize these pressures: the numbers of people employed by it grew between 1955 and 1961 at a rate of 2.6 percent per year, and the private sector by only 0.9 percent. As Solari observes, "It is now a question of how long the state can continue to fulfill this function."[101] One of the first symptoms of the disintegration of Uruguay's *aurea mediocritas* was the victory in 1958 of the *Blanco* Party, which replaced the *Colorados* who had enjoyed ninety-three consecutive years of power.[102] In this decade, industrial conflicts have become more frequent, and some civilian sectors have significantly begun to urge a military intervention to thwart the "Communist menace."

In the case of Chile, the expansion of the foreign-owned nitrate and copper concerns resulted in a rapid increase in the public sector, since owing to the system of taxation "it was the government and not the native owners of the exporting sector which was the agent administering, spending and distributing a considerable proportion of the revenue generated by foreign trade."[103] To these elements—which lend the Chilean case some of the characteristics previously mentioned of the French and British cases—there were added two circumstances that are especially relevant to this discussion: first, the reduced size of the Chilean political arena—until 1946, the number of voters never exceeded 8–9 percent of the population;[104] secondly, and for this very reason, the fact that the system made it possible to pass on the benefits derived from mining and the first stage of industrialization to those popular sectors which participated in political life, thus facilitating their acceptance of the rules of the game. It is worth noting, for instance, that "Chile is probably the only country in the world that instituted a legal minimum salary long before a minimum wage."[105] In other words, the military interventions of the 1920s consolidated the power of the middle class *vis-à-vis* a particularly flexible oligarchy; this régime integrated a limited proportion of the population into the national political system ("probably about a fifth to a quarter of all Chileans live in what we think of as a modern society")[106] and, at the same time, gave it access to its benefits.

It is not necessary to emphasize that I have pointed out only a few of the factors that explain Chile's stability: despite everything, it may be noted that every broadening of the political framework has been accompanied by the threat of its complete breakdown: between 1946 and 1952 the number of voters increased by 75 percent, and in the latter year, in a context of open rejection of the parties of the establishment, Carlos Ibáñez was elected; between 1958 and 1964 the electorate increased by a further 78 percent, the entire political spectrum was displaced leftwards, and the Christian Democrats were elected on a platform which can certainly be described as populist. Moreover, the Chilean economy has been virtually stagnant since 1954. In these circumstances, it seems safe to assume that, in the short term, stability will be maintained as long as the government succeeds in preserving a compromise with the higher levels of the urban wage-earning sector. However, the political significance of these groups as spokesmen for the working class as a whole has . . . been small and has probably been decreasing, especially since the stagnation of the Chilean economy during the last decade began to reduce the opportunities of employment and to endanger the standards of living which these groups had gained for themselves. [107]

It is, therefore, probable that the pressures exercised by the lower strata of the urban and rural proletariat will become stronger in the future and—if the government fails to satisfy their demands—may cause breakdown of the stability which a limited degree of democracy has made possible in Chile. Thus conditions would again favour a middle-class military coup, the possibility of which was widely rumoured when an electoral triumph of the *Frente de Acción Popular* was feared.

Finally, with regard to Mexico, as we have already observed: "Apart from the important peasant group of Zapata's followers which remained politically marginal until the assassination of Carranza, the Mexican Revolution from the outset had middle-class leanings." [108] The historical importance of the movement—and what made it exceptional in the Latin American context until the Bolivian and Cuban revolutions occurred—lies in its elimination of the landowning oligarchy. It thus opened the way to the formation of an authentic bourgeoisie, with an original normative structure and a collective sense of direction capable of mobilizing the politically active part of the population. As a further illustration of the difference between the form and the content of social institutions, in this case it was not a liberal state but an interventionist one that organized the hegemony of the bourgeoisie, while at the same time the atmosphere of the revolution lent a "universality" to its particularist aspirations. This explains the misgivings expressed by a decided supporter of the movement:

> This bourgeoisie has realized its potential, has become strong and becomes stronger with every day that passes, not only in the national sphere but in the international as well . . . and, like every bourgeoisie, it tends not only to become independent of the force that created it, the government, but to convert the latter into a mere instrument of its interests; the government thus ceases to be a mediator, capable of balancing the interests of the bourgeoisie against those of the rest of the nation. [109]

In this process, the armed forces played a decisive role, and their present neutrality is in fact a function of the consolidation of the hegemony of the bourgeoisie: "The military element is the permanent reserve of order; it is a force which acts 'in a public way' when 'legality' is threatened." [110] The greatest problem facing this "legality" is the fact that at least 50 percent of the population has been denied the benefits of development: [111] "The self-same people who made the agrarian revolution, or their descendants, have little but poverty for their reward now that the revolution has passed into the industrial stage because it has been channelled through the capitalist system."[112] The stability of Mexico, therefore, depends much less on the good humour of its generals than on the ability of its bourgeoisie to incorporate these internal colonies into the life of the nation.

The External Factor

Up to this point I have avoided referring to external pressures in favour of military intervention because it is these internal factors that determine the efficacy of any external pressure that may be brought to bear.

I mean by this that the density of social relationships in the countries under discussion is such as to make highly improbable a military coup pure and simple, in the sense that a group officers supported by the United States Embassy seizes control of the government at midnight. The size and complexity of the military establishment, combined with the frequent divergences of opinion among the officers themselves, tend to make relatively impracticable a *putsch* that does not enjoy a relatively high degree of consensus.

With this consideration in mind,[113] two points must now be emphasized. The first directly concerns the armed forces: namely, the extent to which their outlook is influenced by the strategic revolution closely linked to the development of the Cold War and the rise of national-liberation-front movements. It is in this sense that Horowitz is right when he affirms that "United States policies of military globalism tend to make obsolete earlier efforts at a standard typology of Latin American military styles and forms based exclusively on internal political affairs."[114] Here we are not only considering the greatly expanded programmes of military aid, but the fact that, since 1961, the United States has reappraised the basic policy underlying such aid, replacing the principle of hemispheric defence—for which it assumes sole responsibility—by that of internal security.[115]

What is most important to remember is that, by definition, the counter-insurgency operational projects blur the distinction between the military and the political spheres of action. In the context of the *guerre dans la foule*—a permanent war, which need not be declared—there is no longer any sense in the classical distinction according to which the civil power was responsible for the direction of the war and the military power for the conduct of military operations. In such a war, since the enemy is not immediately recognizable, his identification depends on the military operations themselves; this limits considerably the sphere of civilian decision.

In other words, political intervention has now become, for the Latin American officer, a matter of professional interest. In this connection, it would be interesting to study the probable increase of the potential conflict of loyalties already mentioned: to the organization and to their profession. The tactics of imperialism may affect one more than the other, insofar as it may concentrate on the sending of missions to the country concerned, or on inviting selected officers for training in its own establishments. One may hazard a conjecture that the second alternative will be preferred in the case of the more advanced countries of the continent, where direct manipulation of the military establishment as such would not be so easy. This accounts for the increased importance attributed by the United States military academies to the political indoctrination of their Latin American guests.

I said above that I would draw the reader's attention to two points. The second of these is, in fact, essential to an understanding of the first. I refer to the particular vulnerability of the Latin American middle class in the face of the strategies used during the Cold War. This corresponds exactly to the worsening of its relations with the popular sectors, and thus systematic anticommunism appears as the kind of rationalization most appropriate to its interests. Moreover as a correlative of the absence of any vocation for hegemony among its various component fractions, the middle class only achieves a precarious unity on the basis of negative principles. It is opposed to corruption and to communism, without realizing that the former is a function of the irrationality of the system that the middle class helps to perpetuate, while the latter is merely the name that its own fears give to the aspirations of the popular sectors. This sufficiently explains why, in the five countries under discussion, it is in those where the middle class is least stable and feels most threatened that this type of outlook most flourishes. It was a Brazilian officer, General Golbery do Couto e Silva, who formulated the "ideological frontiers" doctrine, and an Argentine officer, General Onganía, who demonstrated enthusiastic adherence to it.

Some Conclusions

Precisely because the military establishment is inseparable from the society surrounding it, it is legitimate to infer in these cases a different pattern of civil-military relations from those described at the beginning of this essay. Military interventionism does not threaten the middle class (as in the liberal model), nor is it a substitute for its absence (as in the developmentalist model); it tends to represent that class and compensate for its inability to establish itself as a well-integrated hegemonic group.

Several consequences follow from this interpretation.

1. The ideologists of the middle class—whose interests, according to one partisan observer, coincide not only with those of Latin America but also with those of humanity in general[116]—would be wrong to interpret my analysis as a justification of interventionism; I have, on the contrary, tried to demonstrate why the middle class is not in a position to contribute to the development of these countries. Moreover, in its present form military interventionism tends to prevent rather than favour the possibility of

certain sectors of that class ever transcending their profoundly traditional outlook.

In this connexion, the observation of Gramsci is perfectly valid when he distinguishes between "progressive" and "regressive" varieties of Caesarism.[117] Despite its compromising and its limitations, the first variety does assist the consolidation of new social groups, whereas the second tries to preserve the elements of a social order that has exhausted its possibilities of development. This is the fundamental difference between a Vargas and a Castello Branco.

Just at the moment when the loss of the dynamic impulse of the import-substitution model is creating the objective conditions for ending the agrarian-industrial pact, free elections are becoming an essential instrument of political bargaining, which makes possible the gradual union of the progressive groups. This possibility is, however, eliminated by the fears of the upper and middle classes; it is for this reason that both the Brazilian and the Argentine military governments have lost no time in suspending the electoral process, and are tending to search for forms of functional representation which avoid the risk inherent in normal elections.

We are not concerned here with advocating territorial representation in the abstract, nor must corporativism in general be identified with one of its manifestations, i.e. fascism. However, given the present degree of development of the societies I am considering, the danger inherent in projects of this kind is that they constitute an institutional "freezing" of a system of relationships which must be changed. For this reason, the price that is paid for reducing the electoral influence of the popular sectors is the maintenance of the self-same structure that has led to the crisis. Therefore, not only is this a transitory solution, since it does not deal with the fundamental causes of the problem, but it already reveals what it leads to in the long term: as the tendency to stagnation increases, so will popular discontent, and the corporativist system will develop an increasingly rightwards bias. This will happen even though, in the short term, fortuitous movements of economic expansion—due, for instance, to a temporary fluctuation in the foreign market—may favour compromises with trade union organizations of a reformist outlook.

2. The other point worth mentioning is the possibility of a "Nasserist" variant; this is a frequent theme in present-day Latin American writing.

There are, of course, two possible meanings of the term Nasserism. One of them, on an extremely vague and theoretical level, applies the term to any military group whose objectives are "a mixture of radical independence, the reconquest of national identity and emphasis on social progress."[118] According to this interpretation, Kemal Ataturk and Perón were Nasserists *"avant la lettre."* Obviously, this greatly reduces the scientific usefulness of the concept, because what it gains in general applicability it loses in precision.

The other meaning, however, is specific, and refers to one prototype of national development—the Egyptian—and is the only one that appears relevant to a concrete analysis. From this point of view, I believe that the Nasserist variant as such is inapplicable in the context of these countries. I will give briefly some of the reasons on which I base this assertion, leaving out of account obvious ethnic and religious differences between the two contexts.

In the first place—as in the Afro-Asian model in general—the degree of integration of the Egyptian army into the society around it was considerably less than in the case of Latin America. . . . In addition to this lack of integration of the Egyptian officer into the context of the influential sectors in the country, there was also the impact of the immediate colonial situation and, later, the "experience of the concrete Fatherland"[119] as a result of the disastrous Palestine campaign.

In addition to these peculiar characteristics, it is necessary to take into account the circumstances of the country. In 1952 Egypt was an essentially agricultural country, with nearly 70 percent of the population consisting of *fellahs*,[120] a per capita income of under \$120, nearly 80 percent illiteracy, and an industry contributing only 10 percent of the gross national product.[121] At the same time, as a consequence of underdevelopment and foreign control over important sectors of the economy, there was an absence of national bureaucratic and entrepreneurial cadres.

Finally, the degree of popular participation in the system was extremely low. . . .

It will be observed that we have here the characteristics peculiar to the developmentalist model, with the addition of the colonial factor, which tended to increase the nationalism of this first generation of Egyptian officers drawn from the popular sectors. Given this context, it is understandable that, after the 1952 movement, the army should become, in theory and in practice, "the real backbone of the state,"[122] and that the degree of mobilization of the urban and rural workers should be very limited. At the same time it explains the extreme economic liberalism which characterized the first phase of the Revolution (1952–56), when desperate efforts were made to attract foreign capital and thus encourage the incipient industrialization process.

. . . In other words: the previous absence of popular participation, to which I referred above, and an especially favourable international situation—due, above all, to Soviet support—made it possible to liquidate the aristocracy and the foreign interests " 'from above,' bureaucratically, without the bourgeois revolution being obliged to resolve the problem of democracy and that of the rural sector."[123] It is this specific development of Nasserism that establishes the limits of the movement. . . .

It is obvious, even from this brief outline, that there is a great difference between the Egyptian case and that of the Latin American countries under discussion, as regards the integration of the military into civilian society, a much higher degree of popular participation, and the absence of an immediate colonial experience. The most important factor, however, is the greatly superior level of development as compared with Egypt in 1952; in the Latin American countries under discussion, therefore, the chief problem is not that of introducing technical innovations but of organizing rationally and establishing social control over those that already exist. . . .

At the risk of over-simplifying the problem, it can, therefore, be asserted that these countries have already passed the Nasserist stage as far as their industrial expansion is concerned—and also as regards the degree of popular mobilization—though not as regards the confrontation with the oligarchy and the foreign interests. The immediate task facing the continent is the appropriation for social ends of the potential economic excedent, through a radical transformation of its existing structures.[124] However, both the level of development and of institutional complexity, and the vulnerability of various sectors of the army to pressures exercised by the beneficiaries of the *status quo* would appear to condemn to failure a revolution "from above" directed by the armed forces. It must be remembered that, in order to succeed, such a movement would have to acquire a populist character; and the stagnation of the economy, the fears of the propertied classes, and the increased maturity of the urban and rural proletariat all militate against such a development.

Even if there are in Latin America groups of officers of a Nasserist outlook—which seems doubtful—and supposing that the present character of the groups in the higher command remains unchanged, their position would necessarily be very weak; and to imagine that, in the countries we have considered, such officers could come into power by means of a coup, would be to transfer into the military sphere the Utopianism that underlies advocacy of the "Cuban way" in the civilian sphere.

It is precisely the potential existence of such a fraction among the army officers—I am now referring to the more general meaning attached to the term Nasserism—that can encourage confidence in an alternative to violent revolution, which both the international situation and internal factors (among them, the very strength of the armed forces) render, for the moment, impracticable. In Latin America, however, the efficacy of such a progressive group cannot make itself felt *before*—as in the Egyptian case—but only *after* an intensive mobilization of the popular sectors. It is on this, and not in any *appel au soldat*—which, thus, introduces an element of confusion—that the success of a coalition based on a programme of revolutionary reforms will depend.[125] And it is the struggle to achieve such a programme that can lead to the organization, from below, of a new hegemonic consciousness capable of putting an end to the crisis.

De Tocqueville once said that "it is not in the army that one can find the remedy for the ills of the army, but in the country."[126] In this study I have tried to give a contemporary twist to this proposition in the context under discussion; the concluding reflection would be that "neither is it in the army that one can find the remedy for the ills of the country."

Notes

1. Intentionally, the data given in this example correspond approximately to those of Argentina and Guatemala. In a recent study of Latin American militarism, the case of the latter country was considered as a paradigm of events in the rest of the continent. See Fedro Guillén, "Militarismo y golpes de estado en América Latina," *Cuadernos americanos*, 140/3 (1965), pp. 12–16. Lieuwen makes equally far-sweeping generalizations in his examination of the coups that occurred between 1962 and 1964. See Edwin Lieuwen, *Generals vs. Presidents—Neo-Militarism in Latin America* (New York, 1964).
2. For a critical commentary on the literature dealing with this subject, see Lyle N. McAlister, "Changing Concepts of the Role of the Military in Latin America," *The Annals,* 360 (July 1965), pp. 85–98; and my study "A Latin American Phenomenon: The Middle Class Military Coup," in *Trends in Social Science Research in Latin American Studies* (Berkeley), Mar. 1965, pp. 55–99. For a typical expression of the liberal theory, see Edwin Lieuwen, *Arms and Politics in Latin America* (New York, 1961); the best exposition of the developmentalist theory is John J. Johnson, *The Military and Society in Latin America* (Stanford, 1964).
3. James H. Meisel, *The Fall of the Republic—Military Revolt in France* (Michigan, 1962), p. vi.
4. Cf. ECLA, *Problemas y perspectivas del desarrollo industrial latinoamericano* (Buenos Aires, 1964), p. 21.
5. Merle Kling, "Towards a Theory of Power and Political Instability in Latin America," in John H. Kautsky, ed., *Political Change in Underdeveloped Countries* (New York, 1962), p. 201.
6. Lucian W. Pye, *Aspects of Political Development* (Boston, 1966), p. 173.
7. I have omitted Cuba from this analysis both because of the incongruence of its indicators of development and because of the exceptional situation resulting from the Revolution. Together with Mexico—as we shall see later—and Bolivia, it provides the only case in Latin America illustrating the socialist model of civilian-cum-military rebellions. Thus, Article 6 of the law establishing the new Bolivian army lays it down that "military academies must be constituted fundamentally of elements of the middle class, working class and peasantry, which in addition to the technical training relating to the military art, will be educated to respect and protect the national sovereignty and the aspirations of the people, and to defend the riches of the country against the ambitions of the oligarchy." See McAlister, "The Military," in J. J. Johnson, ed., *Continuity and Change in Latin America* (Stanford, 1964), p. 146.
8. Katharine Chorley, *Armies and the Art of Revolution* (London, 1943), p. 78.
9. Cf. McAlister, in Johnson, *The Military & Society,* p. 145; Johnson, ibid. pp. 102 ff. For a discussion of the same tendency in Europe, see Morris Janowitz, "Armed Forces in Western Europe: Uniformity and Diversity," *European J. of Sociology,* 6 (1965), p. 232.
10. José Luis de Imaz, *Los que mandan* (Buenos Aires, 1964), p. 58.
11. Ibid. p. 56.
12. Johnson, *The Military & Society,* pp. 235–38. Also Charles Wagley, *An Introduction to Brazil* (New York, 1963), pp. 253–54.
13. Johnson, *The Military & Society,* p. 108.

14. Cf. Liisa North, *Civil-Military Relations in Argentina, Chile and Peru* (Berkeley, 1966), pp. 17–20.
15. Javier Romero, *Aspectos psicobiométricos y sociales de una muestra de la juventud mexicana* (Mexico City, 1956), quoted in McAlister (Johnson, *The Military & Society,* p. 147).
16. Cf. Louis Althusser, *Pour Marx* (Paris, 1966), pp. 85–128.
17. Marion J. Levy, Jr., *Modernization and the Structure of Societies—a Setting for International Affairs* (Princeton, 1966), ii, p. 595. . . .
18. Imaz, p. 68.
19. As far as Latin America is concerned, the only study I know that compares attitudes of cadets before and after their military training is Mario Monteforte Toledo, *Guatemala—monografía sociológica* (Mexico City, 1959), pp. 367 ff.
20. Erving Goffman, *Asylums—Essays on the Social Situation of Mental Patients and Other Inmates* (New York, 1961), *passim.*
21. Ibid. pp. 118–19.
22. Ibid. p. 13.
23. Ibid. p. 73.
24. See Gaetano Mosca in A. Livingston, ed., *The Ruling Class* (New York, 1939), ch. 9, and S. E. Finer, *The Man on Horseback: the Role of the Military in Politics* (New York, 1962), pp. 26–30. See also Stanislav Andreski, "Conservatism and Radicalism of the Military," *European J. of Sociology,* 2 (1961), pp. 55–58, and Philip Abrams, "The Late Profession of Arms: Ambiguous Goals and Deteriorating Means in Britain," ibid. 6 (1965), pp. 241–42.
25. Arthur Whitaker, "Nationalism and Social Change in Latin America," p. 99, in J. Maier and R. W. Weatherhead, eds, *Politics of Change in Latin America* (New York, 1964), pp. 85–100.
26. Janowitz, *European J. of Sociology,* 6 (1965), p. 226.
27. Jacques Van Doorn, "The Officer Corps: A Fusion of Profession and Organization," ibid. p. 270.
28. One example of this tension was provided in 1965 by the resignation of General Juan Carlos Onganía from the post of commander-in-chief of the Argentine army because of the government's failure to take account of professional perquisites in the appointment of the secretary for war.
29. See below.
30. I believe it would be fruitful to reinterpret from this point of view the hypotheses of Merle Kling mentioned above, even though I would insist that I only consider them to be applicable to the less-developed countries of Latin America, which I am not dealing with in this study.
31. *Studies in Class Structure* (London, 1955), pp. 90–91.
32. Richard Morse, "Urbanization in Latin America," *Latin American Research R.,* 1/1 (1965), p. 38.
33. Celso Furtado, *Development and Stagnation in Latin-America: a Structuralist Approach* (Yale, mimeo, 1966), p. 13.
34. I am, of course, giving a general outline of a long-term process. In the short term, however, there are conflicts which derive precisely from the activities of the urban mercantile sectors in their attempts to displace the pre-capitalist landowning sector.
35. Antonio Gramsci, *Notas sobre Maquiavelo, sobre política y sobre el estado moderno,* tr. J. M. Arico (Buenos Aires, 1962), p. 54.
36. On the moral outlook of the middle class—possibly a constant in Latin American political life—see, in general, Svend Ranulf, *Moral Indignation and Middle Class Psychology* (New York, 1964) and, more specifically, IBESP, "O moralismo e a alienação das classes medias," *Cadernos do nosso tempo,* 2 (1954), pp. 150–59.

37. Aldo E. Solari, *Estudios sobre la sociedad uruguaya* (Montevideo, 1964), i, 119. According to the estimates of this writer—to whom I owe the figures quoted in the text—the 1908 census data make it possible to classify as middle class about 40 percent of the active population of Montevideo, "which is a very high percentage for that time."

38. Cf. Milton Vanger, *José Batlle y Ordóñez of Uruguay* (Harvard UP, 1963), p. 167.

39. Rodolfo Puiggrós, *Historia crítica de los partidos políticos argentinos* (Buenos Aires, 1956), p. 111. See also North, pp. 26–27.

40. Frederick B. Pike, *Chile and the United States—1880–1962* (Notre Dame, Ind., 1963), p. 177.

41. Federico G. Gil, *The Political System of Chile* (Boston, 1966), p. 58.

42. Ibid. Gil's quotation is from John Reese Stevenson, *The Chilean Popular Front* (Philadelphia, 1942), p. 37.

43. Pike, p. 179.

44. Ricardo Donoso, *Breve historia de Chile* (Buenos Aires, 1963), p. 101.

45. Pike, p. 188.

46. Helio Jaguaribe, *Desarrollo económico y desarrollo político,* tr. I. Sáenz, (Buenos Aires, 1962), p. 167.

47. "With Floriano Peixoto, the middle class, through its elite of army officers and doctors, makes it first attempt to radicalize the petty-bourgeois revolution, installing in power a revolutionary government, infused with the ideology of that class and the possession of power by its leaders" (ibid. pp. 167–68).

48. IBESP, "O golpe de Agosto," *Cadernos do nosso tempo,* 3 (1955), p. 6.

49. Jaguaribe, "The Dynamics of Brazilian Nationalism," in Claudio Veliz, ed., *Obstacles to Change in Latin America* (London, 1965), p. 170.

50. L. Vincent Padgett, *The Mexican Political System* (Boston, 1966), p. 22.

51. Jesús Silva Herzog, *Trayectoria ideológica de la Revolución Mexicana* (Mexico City, 1963), p. 28.

52. Lieuwen, *Arms and Politics in Latin America* (New York, 1961), p. 104.

53. Ibid. p. 105.

54. Ibid. p. 106.

55. See Maria Conceição Tavares and others, "The Growth and Decline of Import Substitution in Brazil," *Economic B. for Latin America,* 9/1 (Mar. 1964), pp. 1–60.

56. Although in the context of this study I keep using the term "middle class," it is obvious that, in these circumstances, the real phenomenon implies something much wider than the concept. However, it is sufficient for the time being to draw the reader's attention to this broad group of interests delimited by the oligarchy on the one hand, and the rural and urban proletariat on the other.

57. For an analysis of the various manifestations of the collective political consciousness, see Gramsci, *Notas sobre Maquiavelo,* pp. 71–74. As this writer points out: "Already [at the time of the extended economico-corporative solidarity] the question of the State arises, but only in the sphere of obtaining equality with the dominant groups, claiming the right to participate in legislation and administration and even to modify it, or reform it; but to do all this within the existing basic structure" (p. 71).

58. Fernando H. Cardoso, *O empresario industrial e o desenvolvimento econômico do Brasil* (São Paulo, Tese, 1963), p. 164.

59. Cf. Gustavo Polit, "Rasgos biográficos de la famosa burguesía industrial argentina," *Fichas de investigación económica y social,* 1/1 (1964), p. 66.

60. For a detailed analysis of the different variants of the Brazilian developmentalist ideology, see Michel Debrun, "Nationalisme et politiques du dévelop-

pement au Brésil," *Sociologie du travail,* 6/3 (1964), pp. 235–57, and 6/4, pp. 351–80. The particular interest of the Brazilian case lies in the fact that rarely has an ideology been self-conscious: an example of this is the objectives and work of the Instituto Superior de Estudos Brasileiros. See Frank Bonilla, "A National Ideology for Development: Brazil," in Kalman H. Silvert, *Expectant Peoples—Nationalism and Development* (New York, 1963), pp. 232–64.

61. I am referring to temporary military dictatorship, acting as an interregnum between two civilian governments. In Argentina and Brazil, the last decade has seen a number of coups of this type; the two most recent military movements have the declared aim of ending this situation.

62. For a perceptive analysis of this point, see Furtado, in Veliz, pp. 154 ff., and Glaucio A. Dillon Soares, "El sistema electoral y la reforma agraria en Brasil," *Ciencias políticas y sociales,* 8/29, 431–44.

63. Juarez R. Brandão Lopes, "Étude de quelques changements fondamentaux dans la politique et al société brésiliennes," *Sociologie du travail,* 2 (1965), p. 245.

64. Luciano Martins, "Aspectos políticos de la Revolución brasileña," *Revista latinoamericana de sociología* (1965), p. 398.

65. Furtado, *Development & Stagnation,* p. 36.

66. Ignacio Rangel, *A inflação brasileira* (Rio, 1963), pp. 35–36.

67. IBESP, *Cadernos do nosso tempo,* 3 (1955), p. 4.

68. Neuma Aguiar Walker, "The Organization and Ideology of Brazilian Labor," in Irving L. Horowitz, ed., *Revolution in Brazil* (New York, 1964), p. 252.

69. Martins, p. 410.

70. Furtado, *Development & Stagnation,* p. 36.

71. Francisco Romero, *Sobre la filosofía en América* (Buenos Aires, 1952), p. 25.

72. Tulio Halperín Donghi, *Argentina en el callejón* (Montevideo, 1964), p. 23.

73. Dardo Cúneo, *El desencuentro argentino 1930–1955* (Buenos Aires, 1965), p. 168.

74. For an account by one of the protagonists, see Teniente Coronel Atilio Cattáneo, *Plan 1932—Las conspiraciones radicales contra el General Justo* (Buenos Aires, 1959), especially pp. 25 ff., 228 ff. Also Puiggrós, p. 321.

75. For an analysis of the institutional antecedents of the 1930 coup, see Darío Cantón, "Notas sobre las Fuerzas Armadas argentinas," *Revista latinoamericana de sociología,* 3 (1965), pp. 290–313.

76. Halperín Donghi, p. 32.

77. Compare Juan Carlos Esteban, *Imperialismo y desarrollo económico* (Buenos Aires, 1961), pp. 44–50.

78. Gramsci, *Notas sobre Maquiavelo,* p. 94.

79. Cf. Torcuato S. Di Tella, *El sistema político argentino y la clase obrera* (Buenos Aires, 1964), p. 90.

80. See *Confirmado,* 2/55 (7 July 1966), p. 65.

81. Mariano Grondona, "Definiciones," *Primera plana,* 4/184 (July 1966), p. 11. The "superstructural emphasis" of the coup becomes evident when, on the one hand, its representatives insist on the thoroughgoing renewal that it implies, and, on the other, the economic team selected by the "new" government is formed by the same people who have exercised these functions for the last decade or others closely connected with them.

82. See, for example, Gino Germani, *Política y sociedad en una época de transición* (Buenos Aires, 1962), pp. 153 f.

83. Trygve R. Tholfson, "The Transition to Democracy in Victorian England," *International R. of Social History,* 6/2 (1961), p. 226.

84. Ibid., p. 232.

85. For an excellent analysis of this subject, see E. J. Hobsbawm, *Labouring Men—Studies in the History of Labour* (London, 1964), pp. 272–315.
86. Cf. Royden Harrison, "The 10th April of Spencer Walpole: The Problem of Revolution in Relation to Reform, 1865–1867," *International R. of Social History,* 7/3 (1962), pp. 351–97.
87. R. A. J. Walling, ed., *The Diaries of John Bright* (New York, 1931), p. 297.
88. Cf. Stein Rokkan, "Mass Suffrage, Secret Voting and Political Participation," *European J. of Sociology,* 2/2 (1961), 132–52. Even in Great Britain it has been estimated that around 1913 no more than 17 percent of the population had the right to vote.
89. In the case of Brazil, observers have recently noted the tendency towards the adoption of an ideology on the part of the politician operating the patronage system, as his possibilities of immediately satisfying the demands of the electorate become increasingly restricted. It is obvious that this transition from being "Saviour of the Poor" to being "Saviour of the Fatherland" implies, eventually, the negation of the patronage system and as such represents a risk that the dominant groups do not seem prepared to take. See Carlos Alberto de Medina, *A favela e o demagogo* (São Paulo, 1964), pp. 95–96.
90. See, for example, ECLA, *The Social Development of Latin America in the Post-War Period* (Santiago, 1963).
91. Thus, Torcuato S. Di Tella and others, eds., *Argentina, sociedad de masas* (Buenos Aires, 1965).
92. Raymond Williams, *Culture and Society* (London, 1958), p. 300.
93. Ibid., p. 299.
94. Cf. Furtado, "Reflections on the Brazilian Pre-Revolution," in Horowitz, pp. 62–73.
95. Joseph A. Schumpeter, *Capitalism, Socialism and Democracy* (London, 1947), p. 138.
96. David Thomson, *Democracy in France* (London, 1958), p. 58.
97. Compare Charles Frankel, "Bureaucracy and Democracy in the New Europe," in Stephen R. Graubard, ed., *A New Europe?* (Cambridge, Mass., 1964), p. 541. See also Stanley Hoffman, "Paradoxes of the French Political Community," in Hoffman and others, *In Search of France* (Cambridge, Mass., 1963), p. 1–117.
98. The reader has only to glance at the Argentine or Brazilian press in the months before the recent military coups. An analysis of the contents of such publications as *Confirmado, Primera Plana,* or *Estado de São Paulo* would be extremely revealing.
99. Imaz, p. 84.
100. This is the fundamental mistake made by studies which attempt to describe in the abstract the developmentalist strategy of a middle-class elite. Compare Clark Kerr and others, *Industrialism and Industrial Man* (Cambridge, Mass., 1960), ch. iii. One thus loses sight of the essentially relational nature of the notion of social class. Compare Stanislaw Ossowski, *Class Structure in the Social Consciousness,* tr. S. Patterson (London, 1963), p. 133.
101. Solari, p. 156.
102. See Carlos M. Rama, "La crisis política uruguaya," *Ciencias políticas y sociales,* 5/16 (1959), pp. 233–42.
103. Aníbal Pinto, *Chile, una economía difícil* (Mexico City, 1964), p. 160.
104. See Gil, p. 213.
105. Albert O. Hirschman, *Journeys towards Progress* (New York, 1965), p. 264. The law establishing minimum salaries for employees was passed in 1937, whereas this measure was extended to the workers only in 1955.

106. Silvert, "Some Propositions on Chile," in Robert D. Tomasek, ed., *Latin American Politics* (New York, 1966), p. 387.
107. Osvaldo Sunkel, "Change and Frustration in Chile," in Veliz, p. 129.
108. Moisés González Navarro, "Mexico: The Lop-Sided Revolution," in Veliz, p. 226.
109. Leopoldo Zea, "La Revolución, el gobierno y la democracia," *Ciencias políticas y sociales,* 5/18 (1959), p. 543.
110. Gramsci, *Notas sobre Maquiavelo,* p. 81.
111. Cf. Pablo González Casanova, *La democracia en México* (Mexico City, 1965), p. 81.
112. González Navarro, in Veliz, p. 228.
113. It is important to relate this consideration to the new forms assumed by imperialist activities, especially the growing tendency to replace direct investment by various types of association with local concerns. This is even more valid in the case of the relatively advanced countries such as those we have been describing, and it is symptomatic of the internalization of the external influence to which I have referred in the text. See Hamza Alavi, "Imperialism, Old and New," in John Saville and Ralph Miliband, eds., *The Socialist Register* (London, 1964), pp. 116 ff.
114. Irving L. Horowitz, *The Military of Latin America* (mimeo) p. 45. Horowitz analyses in detail the incidence of the external factor, and I therefore refer the reader to his work "The Military Elites," in S. M. Lipset and Aldo Solari, eds., *Elites in Latin America* (London, 1967), pp. 146–189.
115. Cf. Lieuwen, *Generals vs. Presidents,* pp. 114 ff.
116. Víctor Alba, "La nouvelle classe moyenne latinoaméricaine," *La Revue socialiste,* 133 (1960), p. 468.
117. Gramsci, *Notas sobre Maquiavelo,* pp. 84 ff.
118. Anuar Abdel Malek, "Nasserismo y socialismo," in R. García Lupo, ed. 1, *Nasserismo y marxismo* (Buenos Aires, 1965), p. 186.
119. Jean Ziegler, *Sociologie de la nouvelle Afrique* (Paris, 1964), p. 294.
120. Abdel Malek, *Égypte—société militaire* (Paris, 1962), p. 26.
121. Charles Issawi, *Egypt in Revolution* (London, 1963), pp. 46–47.
122. Ziegler, p. 347.
123. Hassan Riad, "Las tres edades de la sociedad egipcia," in García Lupo, pp. 38–107.
124. For an analysis of the concept of "potential economic excedent," see Paul A. Baran, *The Political Economy of Growth* (New York, 1957). . . .
125. The idea of "revolutionary reformism" is discussed by, among others, André Gorz, *Stratégie ouvrière et néo-capitalisme* (Paris, 1965), and Lucio Magri, "Le modèle de développement capitaliste et le problème de 'l'alternative' prolétarienne," *Les Temps modernes,* nos. 196–197 (1962), pp. 583–626.
126. Alexis de Tocqueville, *De la démocratie en Amérique* (Paris, 1963), Bk. ii, ch. 26, p. 349.

Guillermo A. O'Donnell

Modernization and Military Coups: Theory, Comparisons, and the Argentine Case

I examine here one aspect of the political behavior of the Argentine military: the formulation of demands backed by the threat of the use of force, and especially the execution of coups d'état against national authorities. I deal with a brief period of Argentine history (1955–66). This, therefore, is not a general study of the "role of the military in developing countries," nor an analysis of "civic-military relationships in underdeveloped countries." I will attempt to demonstrate that these topics are too broad in scope to allow for more than shallow and empty generalizations. The study of the political behavior of the military[1] requires at a minimum the specification of two structural levels and their analysis along a temporal dimension: the condition of the larger national society to which the military belongs (including the so-called "external factors") and the state of the military organization itself. Each of these affects the other, both change over time, and both have an important but changing impact on the political behavior of the military. And, in turn, both can be substantially affected by the consequences of that behavior. Neither of these factors can be adequately specified when the referent is as general as "the military in underdeveloped countries," nor can they be incorporated at

From Guillermo O'Donnell, "Modernización y Golpes Militares: Teoría, Comparaciones y el Caso Argentino," *Desarrollo Económico* (October–December 1972). Edited and reprinted in translation by permission of the author and original publisher. English translation copyright © 1976 by Holmes & Meier Publishers, Inc.

this level of generalization into an analytical framework capable of examining their complex interactions through time.

In the first section of this study I consider briefly some characteristics of the Argentine social structure during the 1955–66 period. The second section focuses on the changes effected within the military organization during this period. The third section presents propositions to explain the behavior analyzed in the first two sections; it also explores the consequences of this behavior for the two structural levels—societal and organizational—which are treated as independent variables in the first stage of analysis. Additionally, these propositions provide a basis for critically analyzing certain theoretical conceptions about the political role of the military in countries characterized by "high modernization." The fourth and final section formulates more specifically important aspects of the analysis.

First Structural Level: The Argentine Social Context, 1955–66

The period 1955–66 marked the worsening of a crisis which embraced—and embraces—numerous facets of Argentine society. The complex manifestations of this crisis make it impossible to attempt a satisfactory summary within the confines of this study. I will limit myself to stating briefly those factors which appear to have exerted the most significant and direct influence on the political behavior of the military. Thus, the criterion used is somewhat arbitrary, and this summary does not pretend to substitute for a detailed study of the Argentine social context during the 1955–66 period.[2]

Argentina does not fit the stereotype of the "underdeveloped country."[3] The Argentine case is one of high modernization.[4] Argentina is a dependent society, marked by an imbalanced productive structure and spatial configuration. It is subject to many social rigidities, a high concentration of economic and political power, and a low level of creativity directly applicable to productive processes. The great influence of more economically advanced societies on institutions, roles, and social practices, particularly in the more modernized sectors (especially the large urban centers), is reflected in patterns of dependence. These are linked to other structural characteristics of high modernization: a high degree of industrialization, high urban concentration, a high level of social differentiation and of political activity, and a relatively solid and autonomous organizational base (especially among trade unions) in the popular sector.[5]

Argentine industry operates at high cost, with multiple inefficiencies, a combination of high oligopolistic concentration and numerous small producers, and a growing need for raw material imports, capital goods, and technological know-how. These characteristics, combined with stagnant agricultural production, produced a chronic balance of payments deficit which contributed to the limited economic growth and high inflation of the 1955–66 period. After the overthrow of Perón, the prevailing viewpoint was that controlling inflation and increasing exports were requisites for Argentine economic growth. To attain these objectives, it seemed indispensable to contain demands for goods and services in order to transfer income to the producers of agricultural exports. Because it was felt that excess demand originated in the consumption expectations of the popular sector, these socioeconomic policies tended to worsen the situation of the very same sector which maintained a strong loyalty to Peronism. Consequently, the socioeconomic cleavage between the "popular sector" and the "rest of society" tended to coincide with the political cleavage between "Peronists" and "anti-Peronists." This situation was accentuated by the vindictiveness of numerous public decisions during the period 1955–58, and by the various attempts to destroy and to weaken the unions. It was inevitably consolidated by the exclusion of Peronism from the electoral process, whether by direct and open proscription, or through the annulment of elections of Peronist candidates.

It is necessary to mention some aspects of the economic situation during the 1955–66 period. Per capita income grew at an annual rate of only 1.3 percent and from year to year great fluctuations occurred within this low average.[6] The annual inflation during the period was 32.67 percent, but the average inflation in the negative growth years was 39.68 percent.[7] Deflated wages surpassed the level of 1947 only in 1958 and 1965, declining again the following year. After reaching a maximum of 46.9 in 1952, the percentage of the gross national product represented by wages and salaries had fallen to 39.8 in 1965, despite the fact that as early as 1961 productivity per worker exceeded the rate in 1953 by 23 percent.[8] The low productivity of the agrarian sector and the deficient structure of the industrial sector generated a massive demand for imported goods in years of resurgent economic activity. This further worsened the economic strangulation which originated in the balance of payments deficits.[9] This led to drastic devaluations, generally accompanied by measures to reduce internal demand, to eliminate "marginal" producers, and to transfer income to agrarian producers.[10] The devaluations fed inflation by raising the price of imports and exportable foodstuffs intended for domestic consumption, while the associated recessive policies markedly diminished production and demand. This resulted in negative growth, inflation, and a large negative redistribution of income.

The devaluations were supposed to provide relief in the balance of payments through controls on internal demand and through the relative price improvement of agricultural exports. Another intended long-term effect of these measures was to improve agricultural productivity, and with that to obtain a definitive solution to external economic strangulation. But these policies meant severe losses for the urban-industrial sector, which in response actively promoted the high levels of conflict characteristic of the

1955–66 period. As a result of this opposition, the recessive policies were soon relaxed and their expected benefits were never forthcoming. The dynamics of the situation can be summarized as follows: The devaluations benefited the agrarian producers and, to a large extent, the financial sector. But as inflation continued, as new devaluations failed to occur, and as the pressure from the urban sector intensified, the urban sector began to recoup its losses.[11] In one swift blow the recessive economic effects were quashed, the incurred inflation compensated for the effects of devaluation, and domestic, non-agrarian economic activity increased again. This generated a new balance of payments crisis and a new devaluation.

It is difficult to exaggerate the political consequences of these processes, especially in a context of (1) prior hostility of important sectors of the population toward the regime and the ruling officials, (2) the exclusion of the first plurality within the electorate from all real possibility of access to governmental positions, and (3) the importance of the organizational support of the social sectors ultimately destined to suffer the consequences of the economic policies already mentioned. It should be pointed out that the combination of constantly high inflation, drastic devaluations and limited economic growth meant that the maintenance of a steady income in monetary terms was equivalent to a real loss of that income of approximately one-third per year. Moreover, since the rate of inflation was higher in the negative growth years, this real loss tended to be greater in the years in which competition between social sectors was closer to conditions of zero sum. Each "player" was forced to run a race not only against inflation but also against other "players," because the zero-sum conditions dictated that any benefits gained by one player had to be "paid for" by the other players who were then left in the dust in the race against inflation.

Inflation and zero-sum conditions also determined that for each sector the time spent "catching" inflation was of critical importance. As time passed, real losses increased and it became more unlikely that one would attain sufficient new monetary income to compensate for that already lost through inflation. This situation produced strong politicization and concentration of socioeconomic demands. Politicization occurred for three reasons. First, the most efficient means for the competitors to effect a reallocation of resources was to influence the choice and implementation of public policies. Second, the coercive apparatus of the state represented the means necessary to impose these reallocations on the sectors that would have to "pay" for them with a real decline in their income levels. Third, it was impossible to channel demands through governmental institutions (such as Parliament, the political parties, or the provincial and municipal governments) because they played a very secondary role in the allocation of socioeconomic resources. It also became increasingly improbable that other institutions would achieve any real influence in the expression and resolution of conflicts.

This situation maximized the importance of channels of political access which allowed one to exercise power over the presidency directly.[12] Since the armed forces were the most effective channel for exercising power over the presidency, competing civilians tried to persuade military factions to articulate sectoral demands. These patterns of demand formulation implied for governments the explicit threat of being overthrown. The credibility of this threat was reinforced by numerous *planteos*[13] and by various coups d'etat (successful and unsuccessful) during the period 1955–66. This gave an obvious advantage in the race against inflation to those sectors that could initiate threats of coups d'etat by the armed forces.

The better organized urban workers counted on a strategy which, although more indirect and costly, could produce similar results. The promotion of high levels of social protest, such as paralyzing production by means of strikes and occupying buildings, placed governments in the position of being unable to maintain "law and order," and for that reason, in imminent danger of being toppled. With this base, the better organized workers could aspire (although at a cost sometimes high in terms of repression) to obtain an improvement in wages and working conditions from governments already chronically pressured by military factions and their civilian allies who saw in the persistence of high levels of social protest the best justification for the overthrow of the government.

The threats of a coup d'etat were very real, and any government which valued its survival could not afford to ignore them. Therefore, governments tended to adopt the public policies demanded by the most threatening sector at a given moment.[14] The conditions of zero sum, however, meant that these same decisions created new threats from other sectors that possessed direct or indirect means of exerting power over the government. Frequent and apparently erratic changes of public policies resulted from these circumstances.

The resulting situation is related to the concept of "mass praetorianism" proposed by Samuel Huntington.[15] Accentuating a notable historical tendency, the norms for political behavior and for the implementation of demands became farther and farther removed from those institutionally prescribed. Norms tended to be transformed into naked power strategies. All those sectors that were capable of using the strategy of formulating threats against the government did so, for to be more threatening than the other sectors was the most effective means available to each sector for the attainment of its demands. This resulted in a marked tendency to escalate the level of threats and to convert the presidency into the focal point of a veritable agglomeration of demands, which existing conditions made particularly urgent and hardly compatible.

Meanwhile those sectors and regions, lacking the organizational power to threaten the government effectively, became increasingly marginalized in the allocation of resources. In addition, the government's resources markedly diminished during the period.[16] Under these conditions, government personnel were limited in their ability to make and implement decisions other than those demanded by the most threatening sectors at any given moment. In turn, this incapacitation of the government and its steadily declining political resources worsened the larger social situation and consolidated the zero-sum conditions.

In the previously mentioned "race," all sectors pursued the goal of adjusting their incomes to meet the rate of inflation. For this purpose, they rationally used the most effective strategies at their disposal. But these strategies were mutually exclusive, for each was biased toward the social context in which it operated and on which it depended for the fulfillment of its demands. It was unlikely, therefore, that the sectors by themselves could find some means of channeling their competition in less prejudicial ways. This should have been facilitated by governmental action, but the government's increasing weakness, its loss of resources, and its dubious legitimacy, resulting from the proscription of the first plurality within the electorate, impeded any serious attempt along these lines. Consequently, in the context of high modernization and mass praetorianism, the aggregation of individual rationalities easily led to profound irrationality and a crisis of the entire system.[17]

The continuous crisis generated by this dilemma voided a substantial proportion of the sectoral gains. It became evident that almost everyone was losing and only a few winning—and then only to see part of their winnings annulled shortly thereafter. This perception of the situation led to the questioning of the very rules of the "game" and of the political institutions which had been unable to guide the game more efficiently. This generalized perception of the sterility of the "political game" corresponded to a similar perception of the inadequacy of the socioeconomic criteria which had shaped both the ostensible content of demands and the implementation of policies. Increasingly, participants from very different ideological viewpoints proposed drastic changes in the existing distribution of political power and socioeconomic resources and the introduction of a new political regime, presumably capable of carrying out and institutionalizing the changes.

Toward the end of the period 1955–66, the majority of the participants reached what might be termed a "consensus of termination": the existing political regime had exhausted its resources and had to be replaced. Naturally, the "consensus" was strictly limited to the replacement of the existing regime. The participants remained in disagreement regarding the new rules to be introduced and the new distribution of power and resources they should reflect. But despite this, the "consensus of termination" eliminated the few points of support remaining to the existing regime.[18] From this point on, the principal question became how long it would take for a winning coalition to form among the participants that had arrived at the so-called termination consensus.[19] A question of equal importance to the theme of this study was the time which would elapse before the advent of military intervention, an intervention which would represent a radical change from the existing political regime.

Second Structural Level: The Argentine Armed Forces 1955–66

The Argentine armed forces have a long-standing tradition of coups d'état and intense participation in national politics.[20] Following the overthrow of Juan Perón in a climate of intense social protest, the armed forces and the Peronist unions became the most visible opponents in an intense conflict. The reconstruction of the national government and the ascent of Frondizi to the presidency after an electoral "pact" with Perón produced vehement dissatisfaction in the military. Also, as expressed by the commander-in-chief of the army, General C. Toranzo Montero, the armed forces felt they were charged with the protection of "the Republican way of life against all extremism or totalitarianism," and were ultimately responsible, due to the "failure of the civil authorities," to "restore the values of national unity and of public order," for resolving the problems "caused" by Peronism.[21] This "custodial function" of the military opened the way for a long series of plots and coups.

This definition of the armed forces' role left to their unilateral interpretation the meaning of the "values" to be protected and the conditions under which they would be threatened. On this basis they opted for the electoral exclusion of the supposedly "totalitarian" Peronism. In addition, since it could be argued that those "values" were compromised by practically any governmental decision, their custodial function permitted the armed forces to become a channel for numerous and changing sectoral demands. The armed forces became a reflection of the praetorian competition of the non-Peronist sectors of Argentine society. This situation, together with the frequent coup threats in support of sectoral demands, resulted in the severe factionalization of the armed forces. This factionalization, in turn, resulted in several internal *putsches,* the destruction of vertical patterns of authority, and the abrupt end of careers for numerous officers.

When Frondizi was overthrown in 1962, the *golpista* officers attempted to reestablish a prolonged dictatorship to restore "order and an authentic democracy." However, by this time, an important reaction had taken shape within the army and the air force. Many officers argued convincingly of the disastrous effects—for both military organization and their own careers—of the intense politicization and the resultant factionalization of the military. These officers argued for a return to their "specific duties" and opposed political participation including any installation of a prolonged military dictatorship. Today it appears evident that this argument was fostered by an acute concern for the survival of the organization itself, which seemed threatened by internal division and by growing levels of social protest.[22] This argument favoring organizational survival and the preservation of careers had great impact within the military. Likewise, its obvious implication (a "return to the barracks") found immediate support among the numerous civil sectors frightened by the possibility of a *golpista* dictatorship.

The organizational motivation for the "return to the barracks" policy was the conflict between the dictatorial *golpistas* and a new breed of legalist, professional officers.[23] These groups confronted each other twice, in September 1962 and April 1963, resulting in a decisive victory for the "legalists." This "legalist" victory did not benefit the first plurality of the electorate, however; in spite of their professed support for professional "apolitical" armed forces, after some internal debate the "legalists" decided to continue the electoral exclusion of the Peronists.

After the "legalists" attained firm control of the armed forces, a series of important organizational changes took place. Under the direction of General Onganía, "legalists" conducted a successful process of professionalization[24] which merits detailed examination. First, they reestablished patterns of authority more in keeping with vertical lines of command.[25] Second, they established new methods of military training which emphasized the study of modern technology and "contemporary social problems."[26] Third, in 1964 a "program of military assistance" was signed with the United States which played an important role in armaments modernization and adaptation to the type of warfare foreseen by the new "Doctrine of National Security."[27] Fourth, a clear sense emerged of the distinction between belonging to the military organization and belonging to the rest of society.[28] In summary, these occurrences produced a marked advance in the professionalization of, and in U.S. influence over, the Argentine armed forces. These factors, in turn, generated consequences of great importance.

The first and perhaps most important of these consequences was a clear recognition of the organizational achievements of the military and the need to preserve them through a high degree of internal cohesion. Still fresh was the memory of the organizational damage wrought by the type of political participation characteristic of the *golpista* period, particularly the internal factionalization resulting from the channeling of sectoral demands through the military in the praetorian game. Consequently, the "legalist" officers insisted on adopting a position supposedly "above politics," which among other things meant that the political plots, which were so commonplace in previous years, disappeared in the period 1963–66.[29] Of course, a position "above politics" did not indicate disinterest in national politics, nor did it signify that the new military leaders entirely dismissed the possibility of new coups d'état. Rather, as General Onganía stated repeatedly, the armed forces should not interfere with the normal official activities of civilian authorities, but should and could intervene in "cases of extreme seriousness," as determined by the armed forces in each concrete case.

A second and closely related consequence was the redefinition of the position and functions of the armed forces in Argentine society. To quote General Onganía,

> [The armed forces] exist to guarantee the sovereignty and territorial integrity of the Nation, to preserve the moral and spiritual values of Western and Christian civilization, to maintain public order and domestic peace, to promote the general welfare, to sustain the enforcement of the Constitution, of its rights and essential guarantees, and to maintain the republican institutions in which they are established legally.[30]

The functions of the armed forces became much broader than those postulated by the *golpista* officers, who tended to define their role as preventing "totalitarian parties" from attaining governmental power. But more importantly, for the armed forces to fulfill their vast "mission," their organizational power and Argentine socioeconomic development were postulated as necessary conditions. Therefore, any problem that would hinder establishment of these conditions could be interpreted as an impediment to the fulfillment of the armed forces' mission. According to this concept, the functions of the armed forces are so extensive and essential that any problem affecting these conditions has to be interpreted as an attack on the most "vital" interests of the nationa. Since by action or inaction governments can impede the fulfillment of the "fundamental premises," it is obvious that within this conception governmental authorities can receive only conditional loyalty.

This conception should be understood from the perspective of a third consequence: the armed forces' adoption of the so-called "Doctrine of National Security." U.S. authorities supported the adoption of this "doctrine" by the Latin American armed forces as the best safeguard against the impact of the Cuban Revolution and the revolutionary potential of the area.[31] According to this "doctrine," the local armed forces, in addition to the "traditional aim" of preparing for foreign wars, must include among their "specific duties" the execution of "internal warfare" against "subversive" agents who attempt to wrest the "underdeveloped" nations from the sphere of "Western civilization" and to bring them under "communist" control.[32] Since the "enemy" is multifaceted, "internal warfare" can be "ideological, economic, or political."[33] Consequently, multiple strategies are needed to fight him. In addition, the description and definition of the enemy are not always clear. "Here is where the combat experience of the armed forces and their special preparation for warfare make them indispensable in the securing of the objective—in the characterization of the enemy, in the determination of his capabilities and modes of operation, in the selection of strategy and in assuring that the appropriate course of action is taken to achieve desired ends."[34] "Victory" in this "war" will mean the attainment of a satisfactory state of "national security"—defined as "the situation, certainly classifiable, in which the vital interests of the nation are safe from interferences or disturbances—internal or external, violent or nonviolent, open or surreptitious—that can neutralize or delay development and consequently weaken the very existence of the Nation or its sovereignty."[35]

"Subversion" flourishes "in an underdeveloped socioeconomic environment." Therefore, without a prosperous, highly integrated society with a low level of conflict, "national security" will not be attained and the armed forces will not have accomplished one of their fundamental goals. From this it naturally follows "that development is the very essence of national security."[36] It also follows that "there consequently does not exist a doctrine or a strategy of the armed forces which differs from that of the entire society."[37] "Security" is confused with "development," and both become part of the "specific functions" of the armed forces. This ideology permits, at least potentially, the militarization of any social problem which for whatever reason is considered important by the officers of the armed forces.

The persistence of the social processes alluded to in the first section of this study could be interpreted as an indication that the "fundamental premise" of "socioeconomic development" was not being fulfilled. In addition, the combination of this with high levels of social protest led to the diagnosis of the growing probability of an extensive diffusion and final victory of "subversion." According to the national security conception, poor government management and the strangulation of development interacted to facilitate "subversion." Therefore, the underlying logic of the national security conception indicated that it was part of the "specific duty" of the armed forces to eliminate these two "authentic causes" of "subversion."

But these conclusions are only valid if a fourth consequence has also resulted from the efforts at professionalization: the military officers must be convinced that their capabilities are clearly superior to those of the civil sectors, and that these capabilities are sufficient to solve a wide range of social problems. That conviction resulted, in part, from the continuation of socioeconomic problems and the persistence of mass praetorianism. However, it is my impression that it resulted principally from the very success of the attempt at military professionalization. As the military officers saw it, they had resolved "their" problem while the civil sectors and the government continued in a state of total crisis. This feeling of organizational accomplishment led to the belief, however illogical, that the military possessed a superior capacity to confront the social problems which the civil authorities evidently could not solve.[38] But in my opinion, the military's perception and evaluation of the social structure and of its own role were not consciously justificatory pretexts for taking over the government. The majority of these officers were acutely aware of their organizational accomplishments and were sincerely convinced of their superior ability to attain "socioeconomic development" and to eliminate "subversion." The armed forces were not only the "last hope" for a situation viewed as bordering on acute social crisis—as the *golpista* officers had also claimed—but they were also an organization which had acquired technical skill, training in "social problems," and sufficient internal unity to involve themselves directly and successfully on the socioeconomic battlefront.

Another factor of great importance to the military's renewed political activities should be added to those previously mentioned. Many officials believed that their corporate interest in maintaining professionalism and cohesion would be seriously endangered if they persisted in their decision to suspend direct political participation. The state of society threatened the reintroduction of internal factionalization. In a praetorian environment military officers, motivated by their own perception of corporate interest, can fall into a period of organizational introspection. But this same interest will lead the military officers to intervene once again as praetorianism persists, to avoid the risk of internal division and decline in the level of professionalization. But—and this is an extremely important point for the theme of this study—this new intervention has the characteristics, purposes, and social effects which reflect the changes within the military organization.

By 1965, indications were abundant that numerous civil sectors had reached the "consensus of termination" and were pressing strongly for a new military intervention. The high level of social protest, marked by strikes and the occupying of businesses, seriously worried the more established sectors. In addition, President Illía was noted for his lassitude and his ineffectiveness in making decisions, and the Parliament seemed reduced to a forum for personal quarrels. Given this stimulus, the internal evolution of the military, and the continuation of the processes mentioned in the first section of this study, it is no exaggeration to say that in 1965 the major question was simply the date of the new coup d'etat.[39] The choice of the date seems to have been largely determined by an attempt to limit the risk of reintroducing military factionalization over what attitude to adopt toward the elections coming in 1967. The military continued to be divided over the electoral participation of the Peronists who still retained a plurality within the electorate. To deal with this problem effectively, the "legalist" officers had to execute the coup late enough for the risk to be clearly perceived in the military, but no so late that the electoral campaign of 1967 had already begun. In this way the "legalist" leaders optimized the probability of strong military cohesion in support of the coup d'état and minimized the possibility of civil opposition.[40]

On June 28, 1966, a revolutionary junta, made up of the commanders-in-chief of the three branches of the armed forces, deposed President Illía and designated General Onganía as president. The new government dissolved the institutions of the former political regime, enunciated the wide-ranging "goals of the Revolution," and stated their willingness to stay in power for the indefinite (but doubtless long) period of time required to achieve these goals. With very few exceptions the social sectors and public opinion expressed their support for the coup.[41]

The ideology of "national security" permitted the transformation of a conception of organizational interests into an argument justifying a coup d'état which attempted the indefinite displacement of the civil government personnel. The state of society had to be improved, not only because it implied "underdevelopment" and fed "subversion," but because it threatened to reintroduce military factionalization. From the point of view of this ideology, a return to the *golpista* period would mean that the "highest interests of the nation" would suffer, due to the inevitable deterioration of the organization which had claimed for itself total obligation and responsibility for the protection of those interests. Under the "national security" doctrine, on the other hand, not only would all the visible and important social problems remain subject to military control, but, in addition, the corporate military goals, especially the attainment of conditions considered vital for the survival and expansion of the organization, would remain indistinguishably linked to the "highest interests of the nation"—as defined by the military.

The real advance in military professionalism, the feeling of organizational accomplishment and of superior capability, the high degree of corporate identification, and the ideology of "national security," characterized a military process which produced enough objective capacity and subjective confidence to execute a coup d'état which sought a drastic and definitive change from the existing political regime. In order to do this, and despite the fact that various civil sectors had reached the termination consensus well before June 1966, it was necessary for the armed forces to have completed the process of professionalization (with four consequences already indicated) and for the social structure to have presented new dangers of factionalization in the armed forces. The *golpista* military officers intervened several times, but with much more specific demands and with the expressed purpose of restoring governmental power to "appropriate" civilian rule. When in 1962, the *golpistas* tried to take over the government directly and for an extended period of time, they failed because of their precarious control of the seriously divided military and the absence of a justifying ideology. In contrast, the new "legalist" military leaders did not intervene until, strongly united, they could take direct control of the government with the intention of maintaining power indefinitely to accomplish much more ambitious goals. For what occured in 1966, two necessary conditions had to exist which were absent in 1962: (1) variables in the social structure which were expressed in the termination consensus, and (2) variables within the military organization resulting from its process of professionalization. The professionalization of the armed forces in a praetorian context raises the critical point for military intervention. But once the critical point is reached, military intervention takes place with more internal cohesion, with a comprehensive justificatory ideology, and with the purpose of achieving goals much more ambitious than those of the coups undertaken by less professional armed forces. Contrary to what many governing officials and experts have supposed, professionalization of the armed forces does not resolve the endemic problem of militarism. All it does is exchange a higher critical point for the probability of a much more comprehensive military intervention directed toward the establishment of much more complete domination.

What has been said up to this point permits us to propose generalizations which available information suggests should be applicable to other nations whose social structures have similar characteristics of high modernization and mass praetorianism. The next section will be devoted to comparing these propositions with prevailing interpretations in political sociology, with which they differ in several important respects.

Comparative Theoretical Focuses on the Political Behavior of the Military

The social and organizational processes described in the preceding sections support propositions[42] applicable to the political behavior of the military in social contexts of high modernization.[43]

Proposition 1: The "highly modernized" nations have distinct characteristics which tend to generate equally distinctive patterns of political behavior. Specifically, (a) a prolonged process of industrialization that fails to acquire either a sufficient level of vertical integration or a scientific-technological structure capable of generating innovations and of applying them continuously to the uneven productive processes typical of this form of industrialization; and (b) the existence of large and complex urban centers with a politically active and highly organized popular sector. Furthermore, high modernization tends to consolidate historically inherited problems (particularly external dependence and inequitable distribution of resources) and to generate high rates of inflation, irregular economic growth and limited governmental capability.

Proposition 2: If this historical legacy also includes a high level of popular alienation from the political regime and its authorities, as well as little conformity between real and institutionally prescribed behavior, it is highly probable that nations experiencing situations of high modernization will undergo prolonged periods of mass praetorianism.[44] In a situation of high modernization and mass praetorianism, political competition tends to establish inter-sectoral violence and threats against the government as the most effective means of formulating and articulating demands. This leads to a decline in the role played by formally democratic institutions, to an even greater diminution of governmental capability for resolving social problems, and to the consolidation of conditions of zero-sum competition between sectors. These consequences reverberate, aggravating mass praetorianism.

The logic of the situation of high modernization and mass praetorianism leads to diminishing socioeconomic returns and to growing political activity on the part of the urban popular sector. In turn, this heightened political activity is perceived by a substantial part of the more established sectors as a serious threat to their control. This perception provokes defensive reactions aimed at closing direct access to the political process for the popular sector and its leaders as a requisite for the implementation of public policies which, by favoring an even greater concentration of resources in large public and private organizations, will supposedly generate higher and more stable rates of economic growth. But the form the defensive reaction will take depends in great measure on changes in the military organization.[45]

Proposition 3: Given the conditions specified in the previous propositions, there exists a strong probability of frequent interventions by the armed forces, as much by threats of force *(planteos)* as by taking over governmental power. The motivation and a fundamental effect of these interventions was the closing of direct political access to the popular sector and the denial of its public policy demands. In these interventions, the armed forces express and execute the defensive reaction of the more established sectors to the growing levels of political activism by the popular sector, to the conditions of zero sum which characterize the competition for the distribution of resources, and to mass praetorianism generally.

The preceding proposition coincides with an important current in the study of the political behavior of the military.[46] José Nun has argued that in contemporary Latin America, political interventions by the military were expressions of the ambiguities and fears aroused in the middle class (from which a good part of the army officers are drawn) by processes of social change which had mobilized the working class and had placed in question the viability of capitalist development in the more economically advanced nations of the continent.[47] Much later, Samuel Huntington continued this line of argument in more general terms: the armed forces tend to fulfill a "progressive" role in promoting the entry of the middle class into a political arena previously monopolized by traditional oligarchies; but once this objective is reached, its principal preoccupation is to impede the political participation of what Huntington calls "the lower class."[48]

With certain reservations, it seems clear that the Latin American case supports the interpretation of these two authors. In those cases (such as

Argentina and Brazil) in which, through an extended period of industrialization, a substantial part of the middle sectors has secured various agreements with the traditionally dominant sectors, the motivation and effects of military interventions have been in the direction implied by this structuralist focus. In other cases—Argentina during the Perón era, Brazil under Vargas, and modern-day Peru—where the aspirations of numerous middle sectors were to a large extent blocked by still dominant traditional sectors, and where industrialization, density of urban concentration, and the degree of political activism of the urban popular sectors were considerably lower, the armed forces fulfilled the more "progressive" role also foreseen by these authors. But, although the structuralist focus points in the correct direction, it leaves various outstanding problems which should be carefully considered.

First, it pays little or purely circumstantial attention to the consequences which military organizational factors can have on the political behavior of the military.[49] Accordingly, this focus refrains from studying over time empirical variations in the form and degree of the closure of political access for the popular sector which military interventions may produce. As the Argentine case illustrates, these different forms of military intervention hold different consequences for the society and for the political regime.

Second, this conception may be sufficient as a generic description of military behavior under different kinds of social structures, but it cannot in reality explain variations in this behavior in similar kinds of societies. One possible solution to this problem, which is utilized by these authors, is to postulate that the middle-class background of the majority of the armed forces officers leads them to "express" or to "represent" the attitudes and interests of the middle class. But the presumption of this linkage as the principal factor explaining the political behavior of the military ignores the factor of military organization itself. It also overlooks the ambiguity of the terms "express" and "represent," and above all, the extreme heterogeneity of the so-called "middle class" in highly modernized societies.[50]

> *Proposition 4:* The different ways in which the armed forces close political access to the popular sector, and reject its public policy demands, depend to an important extent on the nature of the military organization. The state of the military oganization is a variable, whose empirical changes should be studied over time because they are a fundamental factor for explaining and predicting the political behavior of the armed forces.

This proposition should be stressed strongly. It is the basis for important differences in the interpretation of military behavior that I am proposing from those that come from the "structuralist" focus and from the "neorealist" focus, which I will analyze next. One important difference with the "structuralist" authors is the emphasis on the explanatory role of the level of organization. A second and more important difference is on the level of military organization as a variable which should be studied empirically over time. One can apply the term "army" to the forces in nineteenth-century Prussia, in nineteenth-century Argentina, and in present-day Argentina, but it is deceptive to imply that the concept "army" has the same meaning in these various applications. To mention only two very basic matters: for most of the nineteenth century the Argentine army had no clear supremacy in the control of the means of violence inside the national territory, and most of its members did not dress in a way that distinguished them from the civilian population.[51] It makes no sense to designate as "army" entities which differ in fundamental respects, nor to hope that by some magic effect of names they will conduct themselves in similar ways. The state of the military organization varies from one national unit to another and within the same national unit over time. And these variations should be empirically determined and theoretically weighed for the purpose of explaining or predicting the political behavior of the military.

"Neo-realist"[52] interpretations of military behavior are derived from characteristics of "the military in the developing countries" inferred from the probable consequences of transferring the organizational forms of the military in Western countries to transitional societies.[53] On the basis of these presumed characteristics, "neo-realists" deduce that the capabilities of the military are significantly superior to those of the civilian sectors in terms of technological qualification, efficient and rational decision-making and implementation, of "modernizing" motivations. In turn, this presumed superiority endows the military with special abilities, markedly superior to those of the civilian sectors, to conduct and attain the "development" of their nations.[54] From this conception, it follows easily (although not always in an explicit way) that not only is it probable that the military will directly assume governmental power in the "underdeveloped countries" but also that they should assume it for the sake of "development."[55] The least that can be said about the evidence this interpretation offers in support of its arguments is that it is completely unsatisfactory.[56] But it is worth the effort to analyze some of its aspects and implications.

First, the "neo-realist" focus is a salient example of a futile search for the political actor endowed with the abilities and attitudes most suitable for directing the processes that would culminate in "socioeconomic development," with political stability and with a strong affiliation with the "Western" sphere.[57] But the simplistic conception of the social structure and of the processes of change implied by the search for the great "actor" is not of utmost importance for the thesis of this work. Rather, it is more relevant to emphasize the conceptual mechanisms that permit attributing such a role to the armed forces in the "underdeveloped" nations.

Disregarding historical contexts, different actors in different social structures have received the same names. This nominal identity permits postulating an incorrect analogy regarding the real attributes of different historical actors. In turn, that analogy carries the hope that those different actors will exhibit similar political and social behavior.[58] The risk of committing this erroneous extrapolation from one actor or well-known sector (generally the existing one is some "developed" nation) toward an actor or sector nominally identical, but almost completely unknown (the one existing in the "underdeveloped world") is particularly great in the case of the military. In almost all underdeveloped nations, the military has tried to imitate the formal organizational characteristics of the military in more highly developed countries. If one departs from an impression (which one suspects is highly idealized) of what the "developmental" role of the armed forces of the more "developed" countries would be and if one is also disposed to believe that the resemblance in formal characteristics of military organization is indicative of resemblance in real characteristics, it is then possible to postulate, with some validity and without need of empirical testing, that the military in the "underdeveloped" countries have the special abilities which "neo-realist" authors attribute to them.

Second, only if one is disposed to believe that the formal characteristics of the military organization correspond to a high degree with its real characteristics is it possible to affirm, as the "neo-realist" authors typically do, that the military has a high degree of internal cohesion and possesses vertical patterns of authority which allow it to make efficient and expedient decisions. Further, when this is contrasted with the impression of the inefficiency, confusion and dislocation of the civilian sectors—also typical of these authors—it is possible to postulate the special "developmental" capabilities of the armed forces. But the internal cohesion of the military in the "underdeveloped" countries is one of the more persistent unfounded myths of contemporary social science. All the empirical studies show that the internal cohesion of the military is, in the best of cases, a difficult and precarious achievement; more typical are very frequent and very prolonged periods of profound factionalization.[59] The Argentine case and, in general, all of Latin American history, illustrates this statement quite well.

Third, the attribution of internal cohesion, of superior technological and decision-making capability, and of a modernizing ethos lacking in the civilian sectors implies more than the previously mentioned extrapolation from an (idealized) image of the characteristics of the military in the more "developed" countries. It also implies ignoring a point upon which the "structuralist" authors have correctly insisted: no study of the political behavior of the military can ignore differences and changes in the state of its social context. Nations may have in common their "underdevelopment" and the fact that their militaries exist in an "underdeveloped" society. But beyond this hardly useful level of generalization,[60] it is essential to take into account important differences in the societies to which the military belong, as much from one country to another as within a single country over a length of time. Failure to do so will result in erroneous generalizations based upon the extrapolation from the experience of the more "developed" countries or upon the unjustified extension of the findings in one "underdeveloped" nation to the large and heterogenous whole formed by all "underdeveloped" countries.

Fourth, even if the attribution to the military of high internal cohesion and superior technological and decision-making ability were empirically valid, these characteristics are neither necessary nor sufficient conditions for explaining political intervention by the military. As the Argentine case (1955–63) shows, intervention can occur in their absence. To execute a coup successfully, it is sufficient for a civilian-military coalition to over-come the resistance of other civilian-military coalitions. Neither the mili-tary's internal cohesiveness nor its superior ability to the civilian sectors (except in the control of the means of violence) is required. Further, by the logic of the "neo-realist" conception, it is after the coup that the military could actually put its internal cohesion and its superior technological and decision-making capability to the service of its country's "socioeconomic development."[61] But although there is a high probability of internal cohe-sion when the military is dedicated to a strictly professional conception of its function, this probability is bound to diminish as the military assumes and exercises governmental power. Consequently, it is precisely at the moment in which the military could begin to discharge the privileged role postulated by the "neo-realists" that an essential part of its presumed superior ability—internal cohesion—is likely to diminish or rapidly disap-pear. Again the Argentine case (1955–63 and 1966–72) illustrates this point very well.

Fifth, although a high degree of internal cohesion can exist during the exercise of governmental power by the armed forces, the "neo-realist" focus postulates that such cohesion favors the promotion of national "socioeconomic development."[62] The presumed connection between the internal cohesion of the armed forces and propitious governmental man-agement, however, is far from obvious. A high degree of cohesion may be a necessary condition for "preserving internal order," a perceived requisite for future economic growth, but one should not confuse the fulfillment of this "function" with the attainment of "socioeconomic development."

The following propositions explore in more detail the explanatory con-tribution of variations in the state of the military organization.

Proposition 5: In a praetorian context, the armed forces will tend ini-tially toward a low level of professionalism. Under such conditions they will participate directly in the praetorian game, channeling the demands and threats posed by the civilian sectors and maintaining a low critical threshold for attempting the overthrow of the government (civilian or military). In this way the armed forces become important factors contributing to the high political instability (from cabinet crises to coups) which characterizes the praetorian periods. The weak professionalism of the armed forces (especially their weak internal cohesion) prevents them from espousing important goals or from effecting significant changes in the state of the social context. Political interventions by scarcely professional armed forces tend to hand over or return governmental power to their civilian allies after short periods of direct governmental control. Although some military factions may wish to attain more ambitious and comprehensive objectives, the weak internal cohesion and the lack of a justificatory ideology generally accepted among the members of the armed forces impede the realization of these designs.[63]

Proposition 6: The persistence of praetorianism at the societal level and of factionalization at the military organizational level implies great costs for the military officers including threats to the survival of their organization, uncertainty in their personal careers and the severe reduction of their possibilities of power over the national political processes. Furthermore, the high levels of social conflict and the high degree of political activism by the urban popular sector (both characteristics of mass praetorianism in high modernization) induce well-established sectors and actors (including foreign interests) to view the armed forces as an indispensable guarantee for the preservation of the country's existing social structure and its international alliances. The perception of corporate interest on the part of the military officers, together with civilian persuasions to strengthen the military organization, generate a military reaction directed at rapidly and drastically raising existing levels of professionalism. One condition necessary for achieving this goal is a temporary military retreat from its direct and immediate participation in the praetorian game.

Proposition 7: The professionalist reaction enjoys a good probability of success either by completely displacing those officers most compromised in the praetorian game (the Argentine case) or by attaining control over the military academies, elite units, and contacts with the military in the more developed nations by the officers that concern themselves with the process of professionalization (the Brazilian and Greek cases). In both instances marked progress occurred in internal cohesion, combat capabilities, and corporate identification. At the same time, the withdrawal from direct political participation by the armed forces does not impede the continuation of mass praetorianism among the civilian contenders.

Proposition 8: The organizational gain involved in the significantly higher level of professionalization tends to be contrasted by part of the military to the continuation of the social crisis. This contrast foments a very low opinion of the capability and the motivations of the civilian sectors, and a feeling of superior military ability for resolving not only its present organizational problems but also the wide range of salient societal problems.

The military tends to see itself as the only sector that has been able to provide a solution to "its" problem.[64] Simultaneously, the greater internal cohesion, technical capabilities and corporate identification attained by the military allow it to act more effectively within a certain range of problems (internal conduct of its organization, training for various forms of combat, and use of armaments). This superior ability does not imply a similar progress in the military aptitude for solving problems external to its organization as "neo-realists" argue, but it does seem to have a marked influence on the military officers' extrapolation from one context to the other. This is a crucial point in the evolution of the political attitudes of the military officers.

During the period in which the professionalization of the armed forces is weak, it is not credible to view the military officers as possessing the superior capabilities necessary to resolve the social problems of high modernization. For that reason, the officers of the scarcely professionalized armed forces tend to divide themselves into coalitions in which the civilians play a decisive role, and in their interventions they do not pretend to do much more than to hand governmental power over to their civilian allies. Further, in the period of low professionalization, it is improbable that an ideology justifying military interventions guided by much more ambitious and comprehensive goals will emerge and be generally accepted. But the situation changes radically with the successful professionalization of the armed forces. The old allies are looked upon with resentment, new civilian contacts are established, and the level of the military's corporate identity rises rapidly. In turn, this heightened identity stimulates further growth of the military's perception of its marked superiority over the civilian sectors.

Proposition 9: The consequences of military professionalization (in particular, of greater internal cohesion and corporate identification), combined with the feeling of superiority with respect to the civilian sectors, facilitate and, in turn, are facilitated by, military adoption of political ideologies which will potentially militarize all of society's salient social problems. Adoption of such ideologies also places the preservation of the achieved professionalization (especially the high degree of internal cohesion) at the level of the highest national interest—as defined and interpreted by the military.

In the nations located within the United States' sphere of influence, the "doctrine of national security" fulfills this role. As mentioned previously, this ideology (or any "functional equivalent") legitimizes a military political intervention aimed at a much more ambitious and comprehensive domination than that which the officers of factionalized and scarcely professional armed forces could formulate.[65] One fundamental aspect of this ideology is the preeminence it gives to the corporate interest of the armed forces. Military cohesion is a prerequisite for "victory" in the "internal wars." Therefore, everything should be subordinated to the preservation and augmentation of the internal cohesion of the armed forces. In addition, the structural position of the armed forces, especially its control over the means of organized violence, permits—if and when the professionalist impulse has been successful—the elaboration or adoption of an ideological justification for political domination in which the corporative interest is identified with "the highest interests of the Nation."

The change in the political ideology of the military officers and its close connection with the organizational changes encompassed in the shift from a low state to a relatively high state of professionalism is of utmost importance. The content of the military officers' political ideology, its changes and connections with the organizational changes, should be contrasted with a third component of the "neo-realist" attitude, which attributes a particular *ethos* to the military, resulting from education in military institutions. This *ethos* is composed of a strong devotion to duty, intense national identity, a certain indifference toward civilian sectoral interests, a "puritan" attitude, and a tendency toward corruption weaker than that of the civilian sectors. This "neo-realist" attribution implies taking at face value another ostensible aspect of the military organization—the self-image of the military officers. It is worth mentioning some aspects of this new problem.

First, since empirical data which could verify or disprove the attribution are lacking, it is impossible to know at what point the self-image coincides with real attitudes. The least one can suspect is that the degree of correspondence has important variations from one country to another and over a length of time in the same country.

Second, who holds these attitudes or predispositions? Do all military officers at all hierarchical levels? If not, who ought to hold them in order for it to be possible to affirm that such predispositions permit (together with the attributed characteristics already discussed) military officers to play a privileged "developmental" role? In this sense one can formulate a likely hypothesis: the real existence of the mentioned *ethos* is an inverse function of the degree of political participation by the military. When a group of officers attempts a takeover of governmental power (and more so when it exercises power) it must dedicate a substantial part of its energies, preparation and time to achieving developmental goals. Such activities are scarcely military ones.[66] They place the military in daily contact with sectors, problems, and rules for decision-making which probably cause important adjustments in the predispositions or attitudes (presumably) acquired during the interval in which they were more circumscribed by the military's internal organizational life.

Third, these supposedly "functional" attitudes are not the only ones that one might attribute to military officers. Others are strong prejudice against what is political, mental rigidity, bureaucratization, and a predominant preoccupation with order and stability. Additional attitudes could be mentioned that do not seem very adequate for carrying out the complex tasks of governing and promoting "socioeconomic development."[67] This mixture of favorable and unfavorable attitudes (presumably) would imply attribution of a complex group of predispositions. Without empirical data—almost wholly nonexistent—it is impossible to know how each one of these presumed predispositions interacts with the others to generate the attitudinal climate which presumably influences the political behavior of the military.[68]

Fourth, Proposition 9 suggests that it may be more useful to locate certain factors of the military's behavior at a more specifically political level. The expressed ideologies of the armed forces define their role in society, outline their relations with other sectors, and legitimize their domination of governmental power. The degree of possible variations in the military's political behavior emerging from an adequate study of these ideologies will usually be much lower than that corresponding to (presumed) attitudes whose empirical reference is much more vague and isolated from political issues.[69]

Proposition 10: Given the conditions stipulated in the preceding propositions, internal cohesion of the armed forces is converted into the most highly valued organizational achievement, and its preservation into the dominant preoccupation of its members. The persistence of mass praetorianism implies an inevitable risk for the preservation of internal cohesion and/or for the very survival of the military institution. The corporate interest in guaranteeing the preservation of cohesion raises the critical point at which military intervention and the assumption of governmental power become probable. But, insofar as praetorianism is perceived as (and effectively is) a grave menace to cohesion and survival, it creates strong impulses in favor of new military intervention. In contrast to the previous ones, the coups executed by professional armed forces aim at a radical transformation of the social context, in ways which would supposedly eliminate threats to the military organization and to its professional achievements.

This proposition underscores the importance of the perception of corporate military interest as an explanatory factor in the promotion of new coups and in the ends to which they are directed.[70] The professional interests of the military officers (including involvement with their own careers), the expansion of potential political power implied by professionalism, and the emergence of justificatory ideologies cause the preservation of internal cohesion and the survival of the organization to predominate the thoughts of the military leaders. In praetorian conditions, civilians quickly recognize the efficacy of the armed forces as a channel for their demands and seek from them limited actions to satisfy these demands. But for the professional military leaders it is clear that to continue taking frequent part in civilian conflicts fatally reintroduces factionalization.[71] This results in a temporary withdrawal by the military from political participation, creating a "political vacuum" in the last stages of mass praetorianism and high modernization. Praetorianism continues in full force, aggravated by the persistence of social problems and by the increase in the rates of political activity of movements and sectors (particularly the popular sector) which are no longer contained by military interventions.[72] But eventually praetorianism, as well as the characteristics of growing conflict which tend to accompany the "withdrawal" of the military, ends by being perceived as the most serious threat to internal cohesion and to the survival of the military organization. Whether by means of national problems on which the armed forces cannot avoid taking positions which will divide them (the case of the electoral participation of the Peronists in Argentina) or by means of the emergence of mass movements that seem resolved to eliminate the armed forces or at least reconstruct them profoundly (the Brazilian and Greek cases), a context of mass praetorianism cannot fail to generate strong inducements in favor of a coup on the part of the professional armed forces.

Some Suggestions and Projections

Organizations try to reduce uncertainty perceived as affecting the internal state and/or viability of the organization. With this objective they attempt to negotiate, with those who appear to control the factors underlying the uncertainty, "solutions" which will stabilize the "context" relevant to the organization.[73] In other cases, instead of negotiating, organizations may attempt a more ambitious strategy: if there is no satisfactory way to regulate the context, an organization "tries to move its boundaries—to incorporate or encircle unreliable units."[74] In both negotiation and incorporation, the organization's directors operate through concepts and strategies which reflect their bias in perception and evaluation, as well as the patterns of decision-making which result from organizational specialization in certain types of activity.[75]

There is a striking parallel between these characteristics of organizations and the military behavior studied in this paper. The military's "withdrawal" from direct participation in the praetorian political game is in good part determined by the concern to assure the survival and eventual consolidation of its organization. But, although this "withdrawal" doubtless improves the state of the organization, it resolves neither the uncertainty provoked by its praetorian context, nor the risks which that context presents for military organization. In fact, it would seem to accentuate them. The period of organizational introspection required by the transition from a low to a high level of professionalization isolates the military from its social context. But this isolation is precarious and temporary. It soon becomes evident to military leaders that if they attempt to maintain this isolation for a prolonged period, internal cohesion will be broken, and the very survival of the organization will be threatened. The social context is a source of risks which the military cannot control unless it succeeds in converting the social context into a form which (presumably) will assure that these risks will be definitively eliminated. The uncertainty emanating from the social context compounds the feeling of organizational accomplishment and superior aptitude for completing a utopian political project designed to obtain a perfectly integrated and harmonized society (that is, one which is no longer a source of uncertainty).[76] In accordance with what has been said thus far, the ways in which relevant aspects of the social context are perceived and evaluated closely correspond to the military organization's biases: the "actors" in the context are "enemies" to be defeated on various "fronts"; the solution to social problems implies "battles" to be won, "operations" to complete. An essentially hostile conception of the social context and its actors, and of the means suitable for confronting them, contributes[77] to the military's implantation of authoritarian political forms, regardless of the "progressive" or "conservative" content of its projected public policies.

These analogies do not seem spurious. Their validation will permit us to subsume several aspects of the military's political behavior, until now unexplained or seemingly paradoxical, under the genus of organizational behavior oriented toward the reduction of uncertainty in the social context. In addition, these analogies serve to place in proper perspective two fundamental differences between the behavioral patterns of private organizations and those of the armed forces. First, the latter can utilize means which are only rarely at the disposal of private organizations. On the basis of its control over the instruments of organized violence and its high degree of internal cohesion, professionalized armed forces need not *negotiate* with other actors a "satisfactory" stabilization of the social context (negotiation which praetorianism suggests would be hardly successful). The armed forces can *impose* upon other political actors, through force or explicit threats of force, its own conception of the ways in which the social context should be stabilized. The second and fundamental difference is that, due to the structural position of the armed forces, their relevant social context can only be the entire national entity of which they are a part. The result is the expansion of the real and ideological "borders" of the military organization, aimed at absorbing or incorporating into the orbit of its decisions all of the social problems which seem important to military leaders. The national character of the context relevant to the military also implies that any attempt at stabilization will center on the attainment of direct control of the national government. It represents the focal point of power and legality from which the social context can most efficiently and definitively be modified.

Armed forces which are minimally professionalized tend to be a nominal aggregate of civil-military coalitions, lacking a strong sense of corporate identity. In contrast, professionalized armed forces are acutely conscious of their distinctiveness and convinced of their superior capabilities in comparison with those of civilian sectors. This contributes to the military officers' self-image as members of an organization clearly differentiated from anything civilian and also to the adjustment of their political behavior to their perception of their corporate interests. Because of their professionalism, not in spite of it, professionalized armed forces manifest a high probability of taking upon themselves the responsibility for overcoming recurring civil-military crises by way of the installation of a new political regime. They consider the potential militarization of all salient social problems and their resolution in the direction of consensus, integration, and harmony as ideologically justified.

The political utopia of professionalized armed forces is a defensive reaction against the multiple tensions of high modernization and its probable concomitant, mass praetorianism.[78] Once the government has been taken over, however, the results fall far short of the expectations of that utopian vision. In addition, as with all predominantly defensive ideologies, the mobilization content[79] of the professionalized military's political utopia is weak, and its real influence over behavior tends to diminish after a relatively brief exercise of governmental power. Once the armed forces are in power, the realities of national government begin to blunt the simplistic angles of their ideology, especially when, as in the case of Argentina, the new regime fails to suppress expressions of social protest and fails to implement a technocratic conception of "development." The ideology's loss of effective force spells the reemergence of mass praetorianism, zero-sum conditions in the social context, and military factionalism.

Proposition 11: Once they are in direct control of the national government, leaders of professionalized armed forces remain preoccupied with the preservation of internal cohesion. This preoccupation permeates their criteria for decision-making and is hardly congruent with the attribution to the military of superior capabilities for rapid and efficient decision-making.

The sharing of an ideology of "national security" (or its equivalent) and a social utopia of harmony and integration does not prevent daily dissension on problems as fundamental as the criteria by which public and private goods should be allocated among diverse regions and sectors. The military's concern not to carry these disagreements to the point of provoking internal factionalism leads to dysfunctional consequences: a marked slowness in decision-making; an inhibition of initiative in governmental decision-making due to the veto power of various military strata;[80] the application of criteria of military seniority in assignments to governmental positions (including president of the nation),[81] the arbitrary allocation of certain governmental functions and areas of competence to particular service branches; immense difficulties in coordinating the actions of functionaries who are, in reality, responsible to their respective branches.[82] The classic discovery is made that governmental problems are much more complex than had been imagined and much less amenable to resolution through vertical patterns of decision-making and command.[83]

> *Proposition 12:* Government by professionalized armed forces once again generates the serious risk of rupturing their internal cohesion. If their governance is "successful," this risk can be temporarily controlled but at the cost of high levels of repression and a marked isolation of the military government from many political actors. If their governance "fails," internal cohesion is inevitably ruptured. The principal cleavage within the military organization emerges between those who maintain that an even more right-wing radicalization is necessary ("deepening the Revolution") and those who maintain that a quick "exit" from the most salient position of power would be the lesser of evils given the circumstances.

In the case of Argentina, real social explosions demonstrated that the government had failed to politically deactivate the popular sector and its most important organizational support, the unions. The government also "failed" to guarantee "order and authority," raise and stabilize rates of economic growth, diminish inflation, alleviate balance of payments problems, and carry out other measures required by the technocratic conception of "development" which it attempted to implement and which its civilian allies demanded. General Onganía was succeeded by General Levingston, who seemed inclined to "deepen the Revolution." A short time later he was deposed by General Lanusse, on the basis of the argument favoring a rapid "exit."

In 1971, a new coup, promoted by officers who saw in "exit" a "betrayal" of the "Revolution" and the promises made by the armed forces, failed. It was not yet clear, in June of 1972, whether a "continuist" position or the attempt to find an exit via elections would prevail within the armed forces. In other words, military factionalism reappeared, simultaneous with mass praetorianism and the zero-sum socioeconomic processes alluded to in the first section of this paper. The expectations built around the political utopia delineated by the military in 1966 had to be adjusted to the recognition that the regime inaugurated by that coup d'état had failed in even the most narrowly technocratic norms of performance.

Although the basis for my opinions on this matter is highly speculative, it seems clear that the principal component of the new internal cleavage remains the perception of corporate interest. But whereas in the past the effort at professionalization and coup d'état seemed the most "obvious" means of protecting the interest, today it is far from obvious which side of the option between "continuism" and "exit" can best serve it. "Exiting" implies elections—mass praetorianism has reemerged, the government is clearly unpopular and cannot obtain enough guarantees that the "appropriate" candidate will be elected. On the other hand, the indefinite continuation of the current regime presupposes a degree of military cohesion currently nonexistent. Governmental failure has eroded the military's confidence in the authority of its "developmentalist" aptitudes, and an enormous degree of governmental coercion, probably too disruptive to the interests under protection, would have to be exercised.[84]

This paper has focused on one aspect of the political behavior of military institutions: their formulation of demands via "threat" tactics and more especially, their execution of coups d'état against national governments.[85] This is also the focus of most of the literature on the military in politics, but I hope to have demonstrated the flaws in the currently prevailing emphases and the potential for alternative foci. The Argentinian armed forces of 1960, 1965, and 1970 were nominally the same. Nevertheless, their political behavior differed in many very fundamental ways. Processes of change of the larger social context and within the organizations themselves determined and were influenced by differences in the militaries' political behavior—their objectives, their political ideologies, the means and aptitudes at their disposal (and those which they thought they had) for the attainment of objectives, the public policies which they proclaimed and, later the public policies which they constructed and attempted to implement.

The resulting framework is one of complex interactions over time, between two structural levels, the larger social level and the organizational level, and between those levels and the military's political behavior. Simplifying, one can affirm that a high level of modernization tends, on one hand, to result in mass praetorianism, and on another, to introduce "professionalizing" changes in military organization. These, in turn, effect critical changes in the means and objectives with which militaries attempt to affect the social context of which they are a part. In a first stage, concerns centered on the military organization itself induce a successful attempt at professionalization. In a second stage, that same motivation contributes toward the execution of a new coup d'état, which inaugurates a "bureaucratic" type of political authoritarianism. This coup d'état implies a level of political participation by the military and a militarization of social problems which greatly exceed what could have been attempted by officers of a less professionalized institution. Therefore in conditions of high modernization, a relatively high level of military professionalization is achieved which in short order induces the most intense and comprehensive type of military politicization. This is a paradox built into the very logic of the situation, to which a second paradox is added: the high probability that this politicization will destroy a fundamental component of military professionalization, whose preservation powerfully contributed to the decision to assume governmental power—the internal cohesion of the armed forces. Therefore, mass praetorianism and military factionalism can easily emerge in the political regime which the military implanted precisely in the hope of eliminating both. Should this occur, "the politicians" may return to the scene, but it would be risky to guarantee them an incumbency longer than that required for the concretizing of a new professionalist attempt by the armed forces.

Notes

1. When referring to the "military" in this study, I am referring to the "officers of the armed forces." When I refer to any of the branches of the armed forces, I will specify which one I am referring to, "army," "navy," or "air force."
2. For a development of this section's theme, I recommend my book *Modernization and Bureaucratic Authoritarianism: Studies in South American Politics* (Berkeley: Univ. of California Press, 1973).
3. I am placing the terms "development" and "underdevelopment" in quotation marks. In doing this I want to register my disagreement with the concepts underlying these terms, concepts which I will discuss below.
4. In using the concept of "modernization" and its related term "high modernization," I follow David E. Apter, *The Politics of Modernization* (Chicago: Univ. of Chicago Press, 1965), and *Choice and the Politics of Allocation,* (New Haven: Yale University Press, 1971).
5. For the purpose of this study, I am designating as the popular (urban) sector that sector composed of the working class and of segments of the middle class (principally consisting of unionized workers).
6. Statistics from Banco Central, *Boletín Estadístico,* various issues.
7. C. Díaz Alejandro, *Essays on the Economic History of the Argentine Republic* (Yale University Press, 1971).
8. CEPAL, *El Desarrollo Económico y la Distribución del Ingreso en la Argentina,* 1968. This is a work of primary importance for the study of the sociopolitical dynamics of the period.
9. C. Díaz Alejandro (*Essays on the Economic History of the Argentine Republic,* Yale University Press, 1970, p. 356) estimates that the income elasticity of the demand for imported goods was 2.6. (In other words, each unit of growth of national income caused an increase of demand of 2.6 units of imported goods.)
10. For economic analysis of these policies, see A. Ferrer et al., *Los Planes de Estabilazación en la Argentina* (Paidos, 1968).
11. Without considering yet how the gains of this "sector" were distributed between workers and entrepreneurs.
12. Defined here in the sense of H. Lasswell and A. Kaplan (*Power and Society,* Yale University Press, 1950) as the capacity to submit to severe limitations and sanctions.
13. By *planteos* I mean demands formulated by officers of the armed forces, which are accompanied by the threat of the use of force in the event they are not satisfied by the national government.
14. The observation is not strictly true for the period 1963–66. During this period the national government made a clear effort to diminish the degree to which

public decisions were subjected to the game of sectoral threats. But apart from the fact that it is difficult—and unnecessary for the purposes of this study—to discover to what degree this was achieved, it would seem that this aided the overthrow in which all the participants of the praetorian game—losers and winners—played a part.

15. According to this author, "praetorianism" emerges when the levels of political participation and mobilization markedly exceed the levels of political institutionalization. "Mass praetorianism" tends to occur when this disjunction occurs in highly modernized and politically mobilized societies where large socio-political movements and complex organizations play an important role. In various sections this author describes the principal aspects and consequences of mass praetorianism. "In all societies, specialized social groups engage in politics. What makes such groups seem more 'politicized' in a praetorian society is the absence of effective political institutions capable of mediating, refining, and moderating group political action. In a praetorian system social forces confront each other nakedly; no political institutions, no corps of professional political leaders are recognized or accepted as legitimate intermediaries to moderate group conflict. Equally important, no agreement exists among the groups as to the legitimate and authoritative methods for resolving conflicts. . . . In a praetorian society, however, not only are the actors varied, but so also are the methods used to decide upon office and policy. Each group employs means which reflect its particular nature and capabilities. The wealthy bribe; students riot; workers strike; and the military coup." Samuel Huntington, *Political Order in Changing Societies* (New Haven: Yale Univ. Press, 1968), p. 196.

16. I mean by "resources" all of the human and economic means available to the government for decision-making and implementation of public policies. For data on this question and others previously mentioned, see my *Modernization and Bureaucratic Authoritarianism*.

17. Expressed in its most general terms, this potential dilemma has always challenged political theory. But the probability of its emergence is particularly high in conditions of high modernization, where the persistence of several bottlenecks to development, of dependence and of social rigidities, all historically inherited, interact with high levels of political activity and organizational support within the complex group of political actors created by the high level of social differentiation characteristic of the more modernized "centers" of these nations. By "emergence" of the dilemma, I am indicating not only its detection by the observer, but also its perception by the contending actors and the resulting adjustment of their strategies to that perception.

18. The situation described in these pages agrees very well with David Apter's analysis of the unfolding of what he calls "reconciliation systems" in situations of high modernization.

19. Naturally in this type of situation the formation of coalitions follows well-defined patterns. In my *Modernization and Bureaucratic Authoritarianism*, I argue that, in a context of high modernization and mass praetorianism, the tendency is toward the formation of a winning coalition supported by large private and public organizations (including the armed forces in the latter). The personnel who occupy the top positions in these organizations tend to perceive the "solutions" to the state of the social structure as requiring a high concentration of economic and political resources which would benefit the organizations they control. This project, in turn, implies the political elimination of the popular sector, which must pay a good portion of the cost of the public decisions which further this high concentration. The forced political exclusion of the popular sector underlines the crucial importance of govern-

mental enforcement of the public policies of the "bureaucratic-authoritarian" regime which this coalition tends to inaugurate. This, in turn, emphasizes the important role that the military sector plays within the coalition. But as I will point out further on, important changes in the structure of the military organization itself must occur so that it can play such a role, and, consequently, that the new political regime can be installed.

20. This and the following section are based on the analysis of publications and on interviews with military officers which were carried on intermittently since 1957–58. Until 1963–64 I spoke with them more as a participant than as an observer of the processes which are being examined here.

21. Taken from *La Prensa,* April 9, 1959.

22. J. M. Saravia argues that these organizational preoccupations, and not democratic convictions, were the determining factor in the "anti-coup" position of these officers (*Hacia la Salida,* Emece, 1968). This interpretation is supported by the prologue to his book, written by one of the more influential military officials, General López Aufranc. The crucial significance of this organizational preoccupation was also evident in the conversations I had with military officials before and after the emergence of this internal conflict.

23. These officials were soon designated by names with positive connotations, such as "professionalists" or "legalists," which should be compared with the derogatory implications of the names given to their rivals.

24. By "professionalism-professionalization" I mean a condition of the military organization characterized by: (1) technical and organizational capacity for the management of those means of violence overwhelmingly superior to those available to civilians; (2) internal cohesion, expressed in regular obedience to the formally established lines of comand; (3) corporate self-identification, expressed in "a sense of organic unity and consciousness of themselves as a group apart from laymen." This last is taken from Samuel Huntington (*The Soldier and the State,* A. Knopf and Random House, 1957, p. 10), whose definition of professionalism inspired this study.

25. After 1963 the incidents of open military disobedience to hierarchical superiors disappeared. In addition, even the *golpista* officials whom I've interviewed since 1963 agreed that the organizational changes implemented by the "legalists" included (and to a large extent were based on) a notable improvement in operating patterns of authority.

26. For more information on this point see Robert Potash, "Argentina," in L. McAlister et al., *The Military in Latin American Socio-Political Evolution: Four Case Studies* (American University, Washington, D.C., 1970), pp. 85–126.

27. On this point and other related aspects see L. Veneroni, *Estados Unidos y las Fuerzas Armadas de América Latina* (Ediciones Periferia, 1971).

28. In my conversations with "legalist" officials, a theme which appeared time after time was that the *golpistas* had turned into slaves of civil groups and "politicians," without benefit to the state of the social structure and with serious damage to the military organization. I also have the impression that after the "legalist" victory, there was an important change in the type of personal contact which the military leaders maintained. This contact tended to be progressively concentrated on technocrats and "apolitical" civilians in such a way that personal and institutional links with people in control of large organizations (above all private) were consolidated; this alliance constituted the nucleus of the coalition which executed the coup d'état of 1966. But, and also in contrast with the previous period, the civilian contacts during the "legalist" period tended to be defined within the framework of a subordinate relationship in which the armed forces, as an organization and according to

the hierarchical lines of command, received "technical" information over a wide range of social problems offered by those contacts.

29. For an orthodox example of the "legalist" position (and its numerous ambiguities), see General B. Rattenbach, *El Sector Militar de la Sociedad,* (Biblioteca del Círculo Militar Argentino, 1966). P. Beltran and J. Ochoa de Eguilar (*Las Fuerzas Armadas Hablan,* Paidós, 1969) analyze the content of a number of military statements, among them those corresponding to the "legalist" period.

30. In this speech, General Onganía spoke in his capacity as commander-in-chief of the army with the specific purpose of outlining the armed forces' conception of its place and function in Argentine society. The complete text of this speech can be found in *La Prensa,* August 6, 1964.

31. With respect to this particular motive, consult L. Veneroni, *op. cit.;* R. Barber and E. Ronning, *Internal Security and Military Power* (Ohio University Press, 1966); W. Just, "Soldiers," *Atlantic* (October–November, 1970); and R. P. Case, "El Entrenamiento de los Militares Latinoamericanos en los EEUU," *Aportes,* no. 6 (October 1967), pp. 44–56.

32. The phrases in quotations correspond to the definition of "internal warfare" according to the official doctrine of the Argentine army: "Conducción para las Fuerzas Terrestres," Anexo I, inciso F, número 37 (El Instituto Geográfico Militar, 1968).

33. The quotations are from an article by General J. Guglialmelli, "Función de las Fuerzas Armadas en la Actual Etapa del Proceso Histórico Argentino," *Estrategia,* no. 1 (May–June, 1969), pp. 8–19. For a similar vein of thought consult General O. Villegas, *Guerra Revolucionaria Comunista* (Pleamar, 1963), and *Políticas y Estrategias para el Desarrollo y la Seguridad Nacional* (Pleamar, 1969).

34. General J. Guglialmelli, *op. cit.;* the same conception is obvious in a number of speeches and statements by leaders of the armed forces from 1963–64 to the present.

35. The quote is from the definition of "national security" found in a document of the Superior War College, "La Seguridad Nacional. Un Concepto de Palpitante Actualidad," *Estrategia,* no. 4 (November–December, 1969), pp. 132–34. For a similar definition see the "Ley de Seguridad Nacional," no. 16.970. Also see General O. Villegas, *ops. cits.*

36. J. Guglialmelli, who points out that "development as an essential factor of national security constitutes a basic part of our military doctrine"; "Fuerzas Armadas y Subversión Interior," *Estrategia,* no. 2 (July–August, 1969), pp. 7–14. Also see General O. Villegas, *op. cit.,* 1969 and the Superior War College, *op. cit.*

37. J. Guglialmelli, *op. cit.,* July–August, 1969.

38. For a typical example of this feeling of superior capability, see Colonel M. Orsolini, *Ejército Argentino y Crecimiento Nacional* (Arayü, 1965). Also, works by the military authors already cited.

39. Carlos Astiz ("The Argentine Armed Forces: Their Role and Political Involvement," *The Western Political Quarterly,* 22, no. 4, pp. 862–78, 1969) has compiled publications which openly discussed the coup d'état before its actual occurrence.

40. This interpretation of the choice of the date of coup d'état and of the reasons which led to that decision is taken from the primary information which came from interviews with "legalist" officials, in Robert Potash, *op. cit.*

41. For data on this and other matters alluded to in this section, consult my *Modernization and Bureaucratic Authoritarianism,* chapter 2; see also Carlos Astiz, *op. cit.*

42. Each of those processes is connected with a number of the propositions. The propositions group and organize them for easier comprehension.
43. For another South American example of high modernization, Brazil, consult Alfred Stepan, *The Military in Politics: Changing Patterns in Brazil* (Princeton University Press, 1971). This book and my conversations with its author have greatly influenced the present study.
44. The necessity for the qualification introduced in this paragraph is made evident by a third Latin American case of high modernization, Mexico. In spite of the fact that this country displays the structural characteristics of high modernization (including an increasing concentration of resources in large organizations in which private owners of foreign property predominate; see among others, M. Singer, *Growth, Equality and the Mexican Experience,* The University of Texas Press, 1969, and P. Gonzalez Casanova, *La Democracia en México,* México D. F., 1965), the legitimacy of the regime, of its institutions, and of its governmental personnel—resulting from a still fresh revolutionary past—has impeded, until now at least, the emergence of mass praetorianism.
45. Propositions 1 and 2 are a synthesis of a theory of the emergence of bureaucratic authoritarian regimes in cases of high modernization. In my previously cited book, I have attempted a first statement of that theory in relation to contemporary South America and its two countries with the most highly modernized centers, Argentina and Brazil. The strong tendency toward mass praetorianism and authoritarianism in situations of high modernization suggests similarities to other, non-South American cases. Contemporary Greece, and various central European countries between the two world wars, merit detailed study in this direction. See especially K. Legg, *Politics in Modern Greece* (Stanford University Press, 1969), and A. Janos, "The One-Party State and Social Mobilization: East Europe Between the Wars," in S. Huntington and C. Moore, *Authoritarian Politics in Modern Societies: The Dynamics of Established One-Party Systems,* pp. 204–35 (Basic Books, 1970). Although the processes which preceded its inauguration registered a level of violence significantly greater than those already mentioned, contemporary Spain's authoritarian regime exhibits the characteristics associated with high modernization. See especially the study by J. Linz, "An Authoritarian Regime: Spain," recently reprinted in S. Rokkan and E. Allardt, eds., *Mass Politics* (Free Press, 1970). I have proposed designating these regimes "bureaucratic" because of two of their more fundamental and distinctive characteristics: large public and private organizations on which they base their domination and the typical patterns of personal careers for most of their governmental personnel. These authoritarian regimes are certainly very different from the "traditional" authoritarian ones that correspond to societies predominantly agrarian, scarcely differentiated, and endowed with only a small nucleus of political activism. They are also very different from the "populist" authoritarian regimes. These latter regimes, of which the present Peruvian one seems to be a good example, include an attempt to expand popular political participation and activity, together with the adoption of measures to channel and limit this activity by means of rigid governmental controls. In these efforts the "populist" regimes should be contrasted with the bureaucratic-authoritarian regimes, which attempt the radical elimination of political participation by the popular sector, its political deactivation and its domination by a coalition of large organizations in which the role of foreign-owned firms which produce for the domestic market is increasingly important. On the bureaucratic regimes one can find more detailed accounts in F. Cardoso and E. Faleto, *Dependencia y Desarrollo en America Latina,* Siglo XXI, 1969, and in my work, *op. cit.*

46. This trend has been a healthy reaction against the "neo-realist" (or "militarist") focus which I will criticize later in this study. For a good examination of the various interpretations of the problem of military intervention see O. Cuellar, "Notas Sobre la Participación Política de los Militares en América Latina," *Aportes,* no. 19, pp. 7–41.
47. See J. Nun, "The Middle Class Military Coup," in C. Veliz, ed., *The Politics of Conformity in Latin America* (Oxford University Press, 1967), pp. 66–118. There is a slightly different Spanish version in *Desarrollo Económico,* "Crisis Hegemónica y Golpe Militar de Clase Media," no. 22–23. [An edited reprint of this article appears in this volume—Ed.]
48. S. Huntington, *op. cit.,* 1968. This focus, which will be called "structuralist" for its emphasis on ordered factors situated at the global social structural level, is synthesized clearly in the following passage from the cited work: "[The military] become the guardians of the existing middle-class order. They are thus, in a sense, the door-keepers in the expansion of political participation in a praetorian society: their historical role is to open the door to the middle class and to close it to the lower class" (p. 222). Other authors have expressed similar points of view, either on Latin America (M. Needler, *Political Development in Latin America: Instability, Violence and Revolutionary Change,* Random House, 1968) or on "underdeveloped" countries (E. Nordlinger, "Soldiers in Mufti: the Impact of Military Rule upon Economics and Social Change in Non-Western States," *The American Political Science Review,* 64, no. 4, pp. 1112–30, 1970). Nordlinger's article contains a good critique of the "neo-realist" or "militarist" conception, which I will analyze.
49. Again S. Huntington eloquently expresses this point of view: "The effort to answer the question, 'What characteristics of the military establishment of a new nation facilitate its involvement in domestic politics?' is misdirected because the most important causes of military intervention in politics are not military but political and reflect not the social and organizational characteristics of the military establishment but the political and institutional structure of the society." *Op. cit.,* 1968, p. 194. The position is embellished further in the descriptive parts of the works by J. Nun and E. Nordlinger, but it is characteristic of the view which I have called "structuralist" that the explanatory arguments are centered on the level of the global social structure.
50. The "middle class" tends to be no more than an immense residual category consisting of those that are neither particularly rich nor particularly poor. Therefore, especially in the context of high modernization where social differentiation had increased enormously (especially in the large urban centers), this category includes such sectors as public functionaries, students, intellectuals, small businessmen, employees, and others, whose political behavior usually differs in many and very important respects. Which of these sectors is "represented" or "expressed" in the political behavior of the military? And although this question may have an answer, in what form does the link between the "middle class" and the political behavior of the military operate, especially with regard to the mediation of the organizational level of the military? For a similar critique, see A. Stepan, *op. cit.,* pp. 45–46. Of course, with these reflections I do not pretend to do justice to the works which represent a formidable advance with respect to those that I will analyze later on.
51. The situation of various countries of the third world and the memoirs of military chiefs cited by R. Price (n. 53) suggest that not even these two characteristics of the military can yet be really taken for granted.
52. I am using the designation proposed by A. Stepan, *op. cit.* Possibly it would be

more precise to give the name "militarist" to this conception, not only because of its kind evaluation of the "developmental" capabilities and potentialities of the military, but also because of its tacit prescription that the military should take over governmental power directly.

53. The quotation is from R. Price, "A Theoretical Approach to Military Rule in New States: Reference Group Theory and the Ghanaian Case." *World Politics* 23, no. 3, pp. 399–430 (1971). This author adds some interesting alternatives to his critique of the "neo-realist" focus. See also A. Stepan, *op. cit.*, pp. 7, 253.

54. In the future when I refer to the attribution of "special abilities" to the military, it should be understood in the sense expressed here.

55. For additional works formulating this point of view, one can read G. Pauker, "Southeast Asia as a Problem Area in the Next Decade," *World Politics* 11, pp. 325–345 (1959); L. Pye, *Aspects of Political Development,* pp. 172–87 (Little Brown, 1966); H. Daadler, *The Role of the Military in Developing Countries* (Mouton, 1962) and, with specific reference to the Latin American case, J. J. Johnson, *The Military and Society in Latin America* (Stanford Univ. Press, 1964). Other authors recognize a similar function by the military sector, but stop short of coming to the conclusion that those (presumed) characteristics allow the military to play a privileged role in "development." See, for example, S. Finer, *The Man on Horseback: the Role of the Military in Politics* (Praeger, 1962); M. Janowitz, *The Military in the Political Development of New Nations: An Essay in Comparative Analysis* (The University of Chicago Press, 1962); E. Shils, "The Military in the Political Development of New States," in J. Johnson, ed., *The Role of the Military in Underdeveloped Countries,* pp. 7–68 (Princeton University Press, 1962); and E. Lieuwen, *Arms and Politics in Latin America* (Praeger, 1960).

56. On the basis of their case studies, A. Stepan and R. Price, *op. cits.,* also argue that the position criticized here lacks all empirical substance. See, in the same sense, E. Nordlinger, *op. cit.*

57. This change of expectations and of tone, as well as their consequences on the analysis and recommendations that one derives, is particularly visible in the case of an author who has written influential works on Latin America. In his book published in 1958 *(Political Change in Latin America: The Emergence of the Middle Sectors),* J. J. Johnson attributes a privileged developmental role to the "middle sectors," and conceives of development politically in terms of the emergence and consolidation of democratic political regimes. In his later book (published in 1964), the optimism of the previous work has disappeared, his emphasis on order and stability is greater, and the military has displaced the "middle sectors" as the principal depository of the author's hopes. For a good analysis of the strong emphasis on political stability underlying a good part of the literature on "political development," see M. Blackman, "Latin American Political Development: the View from the U.S.," paper presented at the Seminario sobre Indicadoras de Desarrollo Nacional, Río de Janeiro, 1972.

58. This critique not only ignores the underlying differences between identical names, but also ignores the differences which, even between really similar sectors, would result from their insertion in different global social contexts (national units in this case).

59. For similar affirmations based on their own data see A. Stepan and R. Price, *op. cits.* See also D. Rapoport, "The Political Dimensions of Military Usurpation," *Political Science Quarterly,* 83, pp. 551–73 (1968), and W. C. McWilliams, "Introductions," in W. C. McWilliams, ed., *Garrisons and Government* (Chandler Publishing Co., 1967).

60. Or, to be more exact: this level of vagueness.

61. It could be argued that the armed forces can play its supposedly decisive or privileged role as vanguard or principal executor of "development" without the necessity of directly controlling the national government. But, to my knowledge, not even the most openly militaristic authors have attempted this argument. One apparent exception could be seen to derive from the arguments for implanting the doctrines of "civic action" among the Latin American armed forces. But no one seems to believe fully in the developmental consequences of activities oriented explicitly toward preventing "subversion" in particularly depressed areas and/or toward keeping busy officers who, it is feared, would otherwise conspire against the national authorities. For this explicit motivation, consult L. Veneroni, R. Barber and E. Ronning, and W. Just, *op. cits.*

62. This position is particularly visible in J. J. Johnson when he writes: "Social upheavals will keep societies [Latin American ones] in disequilibrium and will bring to the surface people who in their restlessness and insecurity will welcome ideologies requiring total commitment. . . . In any event, since the armed forces will probably remain for some time the only agency capable of countermanding rampant demagoguery, they will appear different to the states of Latin America than they do to states with great national cohesion. . . . Furthermore, for the next decade or more, they will on occasion be the most reliable institution to ensure political continuity in these countries. They will, in certain instances, stand as a bulwark of order and security in otherwise anarchical societies; at other times, if they were to follow a policy of non-intervention in the civilian area, it would remain the preservation of an unsatisfactory status quo" (*op. cit.,* 1964, pp. 260–61). Although from a different angle, the same proposition is expressed by L. Pye when he concludes that one positive characteristic of military governments is that it is more probable that they will be better allies of the "West" than civilian governments (L. Pye, *op. cit.,* pp. 185–86). In a very fundamental sense the premises of the "neo-realist" focus come to their logical conclusion with this: Some internally cohesive armed forces are capable of preserving "internal order" against "subversion" or "anarchy," but the "developmental" role that had been originally attibuted to them disappears—except as the distant and less than likely result of the fulfillment of the role which remains really of interest, the preservation of the existing social structure.

63. The content of this proposition coincides closely with the model of the "moderating role" proposed by Stepan as typical of the Brazilian armed forces prior to the coup of 1964; see A. Stepan, *op. cit.,* especially p. 172.

64. Of course, neglecting to consider that the military has means for resolving internal conflicts (from purges to simple combat) usually not available to the civilian sectors.

65. For analysis of the importance of this ideology in other South American countries see P. V. Beltran, ed., *Las Fuerzas Armadas Hablan* (Paidós, 1969); A. Stepan, *op. cit.,* especially p. 172; L. Einaudi, "The Peruvian Military: A Summary Political Analysis" (The Rand Corporation, 1969); and A. Quijano Obregón, *Nacionalismo, Neoimperialismo y Militarismo en el Perú* (Ediciones Periferia, 1971).

66. Unless, of course, one believes that the "doctrine of national security" is substantially correct.

67. An intuitive combination of attitudes to the military underlies the conclusions of authors such as S. Finer, M. Janowitz and E. Lieuwen (*ops. cits.*) who, although they avoid most of the failings criticized here, vacillate in their arguments, eventually concluding that military attitudes permit the armed forces to play a privileged "developmental" role.

68. That is to say, what is really important is not a list of presumed attitudes but the form in which these attitudes come together finally in each concrete case. To isolate them one from another is an intellectual exercise which permits arriving at conclusions previously anticipated by the value preferences of the author. For example, if one chooses to stress the dominant preoccupation with order and stability, one comes to conclusions of the type proposed by E. Nordlinger, which are clearly opposed to the ones postulated by the "neo-realist" authors: "The vision [of the military officers] of political stability hinders social and economic change insofar as such changes are a product of governmental responsiveness to articulated and forcefully promoted demands; repressing these demands largely rules out their fulfillment." Nordlinger, *op. cit.,* pp. 1137–38.

69. This argument should be understood in the sense of promoting a level of facts and of analysis which seems analytically more useful than the one implied by the attribution of attitudes just examined. Naturally, it does not imply that a choice must be made between the two levels of inquiry. Political ideologies and a presumed *ethos* are levels of analysis of different attitudinal "depths" and, as such, are both legitimate material for study. Moreover, one could imagine investigations at a level of even greater psychological "depth," such as trying to determine what type of personal characteristics (if any) can influence choice of the military profession and what effect educational experience in the military organization can have on these characteristics. All of these are interesting possibilities, but it would seem that the "deeper" the psychological factors analyzed, the greater the possible variation in the dependent variable of interest (political behavior), the more numerous the intervening variables and—perhaps above all, the more improbable it is that one could locate reliable, pertinent data. This last problem is far from being trivial, above all in a subdiscipline which, like that of the political sociology of the armed forces, is characterized by a paucity of the available information and by a scarcity of reasonably confirmed theoretical propositions.

70. This tends to confirm the hypothesis that the influence of corporate interest (in other words, of the perception of such interest) will increase as the degree of professionalization increases. Although within different overall conceptions, various authors have emphasized the importance of the corporate interest of the armed forces; see S. Finer, A. Stepan, E. Lieuwen, *ops. cits.;* E. Lieuwen, *Generals vs. Presidents—Neo-Militarism in Latin America* (New York, 1964); M. Needler, "Anatomy of a Coup d'Etat: Ecuador 1963," (Institute for the Comparative Study of Political Systems, Washington, D.C., 1964).

71. As has been indicated in the previous sections, this is the real meaning of affirmations of the type made by General Onganía in the period 1963–66, in the sense that the armed forces must refrain from intervening except in the case of "extreme circumstances." For a similar position taken by General Castello Branco prior to the Brazilian coup of 1964, see A. Stepan, *op. cit.* and T. Skidmore, *Politics in Brazil, 1930–1964* (Oxford University Press, 1967).

72. On the growing levels of political activity and of social protest in the period which closely preceded the Greek coup, see K. Legg, *op. cit.;* for the Brazilian case, see A. Stepan, *op. cit.,* T. Skidmore, *op. cit.* and O. Ianni, *O Colapso de Populismo no Brasil* (Editorial Civilizacao Brasileira, 1968). For a more detailed analysis of the Argentine case and a more complete bibliography of the Brazilian example, consult my *Modernization and Bureaucratic Authoritarianism.*

73. An example of this is the concerted agreement on sale prices among "competitive" firms in a given market.

74. The quote is from J. Thompson, *Organizations in Action* (McGraw Hill, 1967),

p. 160. An example of this is the attempt to eliminate competition and establish a monopoly.

75. Any successful career in a large organization requires large "investment" in terms of specialization in matters considered highly "functional" to the activities of the organization. This, in turn, implies a high degree of "trained incapacity" to perceive, evaluate, and make decisions according to patterns different from those learned in the course of that career—although the problem to be faced may bear little relation to those typically confronted in the area of specialization. On the learning of these biases and "programs" of decision-making, see, above all, J. Cyert and J. March, *A Behavioral Theory of the Firm* (Prentice-Hall, 1963).

76. As can be expected from what has already been said, this utopian view is particularly visible in the intervals immediately following the seizure of governmental power by professionalized militaries. The cases of presidents Organía and Castello Branco are sufficiently illustrative.

77. I reiterate that the above-mentioned matter "contributes" to this implantation, because a complete explanation cannot exclude the critical independent effect of factors in the larger social context, alluded to in section 1 of this paper and studied in greater detail in my book *Modernization and Bureaucratic Authoritarianism*.

78. In accordance with David Apter (*op. cit.,* 1971) this would be a case of "right-wing radicalization." The purpose (and to a large extent the effects) of the implantation of the new political regime is the introduction of a fundamental change in the allocation of social resources. There is a tendency to qualify these attempts as "reactionary" or "conservative," minimizing implicitly their effect in introducing important social changes. The content of these changes may be subjectively disagreeable (it is for me), but that is a question which differs from its detection and study. For a discussion of this matter in a vein similar to the one indicated here, see F. Cardoso's article, "El Modelo Político Brasileno," *Desarrollo Económico,* 11, no. 42, pp. 218–47, (1972).

79. On these concepts see David Apter, *op. cit.,* 1965.

80. More than a few functionaries at the highest level of the regime inaugurated in Argentina in 1966 have complained publicly of the slowness and the vetoes to which decision-making initiatives have been subjected. It seems safe to affirm that in this respect, a serious problem of the regime deposed in 1966 and one on which the first military proclamations placed great emphasis, has not been solved.

81. On the application of criteria of seniority in military command in deciding presidential designations in Brazil, and its close connection with the desire to avoid what would otherwise threaten division in the armed forces, see A. Stepan, *op. cit.,* pp. 253–66. In Argentina, the presidential designation of General Lanusse seems to have been dominated by similar factors.

82. In Argentina, the provinces, public enterprises, and autarchic entities which have been assigned to particular branches are numerous. It should be evident that this phenomenon, as well as those already indicated, are hardly congruent with the probability of regularly "hitting the mark" in the designation of governmental personnel and in the coordination of their actions.

83. Although these characteristics of military rule are derived from the Argentine case, A. Stepan notes similar ones in the apparently more "successful" case of Brazil: A. Stepan, *op. cit.*

84. If I may be permitted a personal note, it may be, if a truly open electoral option finally prevails, and if the bureaucratic-authoritarian experience has taught a substantial proportion of the civil sector that is in their interest to formulate their demands in a more regulated manner, a future government might be able

to count on sufficient political time to institutionalize non-praetorian norms of competition and to resolve some of the more severe socioeconomic bottlenecks. These are big "ifs," but in the type of learning process involved in what we are discussing, a possibility might be found for the political democratization of highly modernized nations.

85. Insisting here upon something which emerges from all that has been said thus far, I hope it remains clear that in this article I do not attempt to explain coups d'état (a task undertaken in my book, already cited numerous times), but rather, the military's contribution to those coups. It pays to insist on this point because serious errors of analysis tend to originate from the confusion of these two matters.

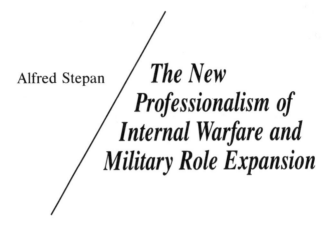

Alfred Stepan / *The New Professionalism of Internal Warfare and Military Role Expansion*

Since 1964 the Brazilian military establishment has steadily assumed control over a widening area of the country's social and political life. Indeed, there exists the possibility that what we are witnessing in Brazil is the creation of a new political and economic model of authoritarian development. Others [have examined] the internal workings, policy outputs, and institutionalization possibilities of this model. My focus is on how changing military ideology contributed to the events leading up to the the military coup of 1964 and the emergence of the military-bureaucratic and authoritarian-developmentalist components of the model.

In this [essay] I argue that what happened in Brazil was, to a significant extent, part of the wider military phenomenon of what I call the "new professionalism of internal security and national development." In analyzing how the ideology of new professionalism arose and how it contributed to the expansion of the military's role in politics, I also endeavor to identify some of the institutional and political variables that are peculiar to Brazil and that help account for some of the special characteristics of the military regime.

From Alfred Stepan, ed., *Authoritarian Brazil* (New Haven: Yale University Press, 1973), pp. 47–65. Copyright © 1973 by Yale University Press and reprinted by permission of the author and publisher.

Conflicting Paradigms: New Professionalism vs. Old Professionalism

In the 1960s, the political roles of the Brazilian and Peruvian military establishments underwent a great expansion. Yet, as measured by a number of indicators, these military establishments are probably the two most professional in Latin America.[1] They have relatively universalistic procedures for the recruitment and promotion of officers, highly structured military schooling programs that prepare officers for passage to the next stage of their careers, highly articulated and well-disseminated military doctrines and well-programmed military-unit training cycles, all coordinated by extensive general staff systems. If there is one central concept of modern civil-military relations, it is the concept of "professionalism." According to this concept, as the professionalism of a military establishment increases along the lines indicated above, the military tends to become less political in its activities. In the case of Brazil, however, professional standards coexisted with increasing politicization in the years leading up to 1964. Thus, either Brazil must be considered a deviant case, or one must suggest an alternative framework that is capable of incorporating Brazil, Peru (where a similar process of professionalization and politicization has been at work), and, I suspect, a number of other countries, such as Indonesia, as the predictable outcome of the new paradigm.

It is the argument of this essay that the highly bureaucratized, highly schooled, and yet highly politicized armies of Brazil and Peru are best viewed not as lapses from the paradigm of the "old" professionalism, but as one of the logical consequences of the "new" professionalism. To clarify the theoretical and empirical aspects of this assertion, I briefly consider first the components of the old professionalism. Though many aspects of the argument are widely reproduced by writers who have not studied his work, the classic formulation of the argument about military professionalism and its relation to the political activity of the military is Samuel Huntington's. As quoted or paraphrased from his own writings,[2] his argument is as follows:

1. *On the nature of modern warfare and the requisite skills.* Modern warfare demands a highly specialized military; the military cannot master the new skills needed to carry out their tasks while at the same time "remaining competent in many other fields" as well (*The Soldier*, p. 32).

2. *On the impact of professionalism.* As a result of this specialization, "the vocation of officership absorbs all their energies and furnishes them with all their occupational satisfactions. Officership, in short, is an exclusive role, incompatible with any other significant social or political roles" ("Civilian Control," p. 381).

3. *On the relationship between political and military spheres.* The functional specialization needed for external defense means that "it be-

came impossible to be an expert in the management of violence for external defense and at the same time to be skilled in either politics or statecraft or the use of force for the maintenance of internal order. The functions of the officer became distinct from those of the politician and policeman" (*The Soldier,* p. 32).

4. *On the scope of military concern.* "At the broadest level of the relation of the military order to society, the military function is presumed to be a highly specialized one. . . . A clear distinction in role and function exists between military and civilian leaders" ("Civilian Control," pp. 380–81).

5. *On the impact of professionalism on military attitudes to politics.* "Civilian control is thus achieved not because the military groups share in the social values and political ideologies of society, but because they are indifferent to such values and ideologies" ("Civilian Control," p. 381).

6. *On the impact of professionalism on civil-military relations.* "The one prime essential for any system of civilian control is the minimizing of military power. Objective civilian control achieves this reduction by professionalizing the military" and by "confining it to a restricted sphere and rendering it politically sterile and neutral on all issues outside that sphere" (*The Soldier,* p. 84; "Civilian Control," p. 381).

This argument runs through a large part of American military writing and appears frequently in congressional discussions of the rationale for United Stated military assistance policies to developing countries. The argument that assistance policies should be given in order to professionalize the military has been rationalized on the grounds that in doing so the United States could help convert traditional, politicized armies into modern, apolitical ones. However, as the extensive quotations from Huntington illustrate, the professionalization thesis was rooted in the assumption that armies develop their professional skills for conventional warfare against foreign armies. In his later writing Huntington has stated that if the focus shifts from interstate conflict to domestic war it will encourage a different pattern of civil-military relations than that expounded in the passages quoted above.[3] Since many later writers have failed to note this qualification, the concept of military professionalism is still widely misunderstood, and it is useful to formulate explicitly the differences between the old professionalism of external warfare and the new professionalism of internal security and national development.

In reality, by the late 1950s and early 1960s, the success of revolutionary warfare techniques against conventional armies in China, Indochina, Algeria, and Cuba led the conventional armies in both the developed and underdeveloped world to turn more attention to devising military and political strategies to combat or prevent domestic revolutionary warfare. In fact, by 1961, the United States military assistance programs to Latin America were largely devoted to exporting doctrines concerned with the military's role in counterinsurgency, civic action and nation building.[4] In Latin America the process by which the military came to define its mission primarily in terms of dealing with threats to internal security was accelerated by the defeat and destruction of the conventional army in Cuba by Castro's guerrilla force. In Brazil and Peru, where the military was highly institutionalized, the perception of the threat to the internal security of the nation and the security of the military itself led to a focusing of energies on the "professionalization" of their approach to internal security. The military institutions began to study such questions as the social and political conditions facilitating the growth of revolutionary protest and to develop doctrines and training techniques to prevent or crush insurgent movements. As a result, these highly professionalized armies became much more concerned with political problems.

Thus there was a dual process at work. Because of their preoccupation with subversion and internal security, many military establishments in Latin America attempted to undertake institutional professionalization and development and were given extensive United States military assistance in doing so. Yet, given the changed political climate, the formulators of United States military assistance programs and the chiefs of many Latin American military establishments now believed that professional military expertise was required in a broader range of fields. Instead of increasing functional specialization, the military began to train their officers to acquire expertise in internal security matters that were defined as embracing all aspects of social, economic, and political life. Instead of the gap between the military and political spheres widening, the new professionalism led to a belief that there was a fundamental interrelationship between the two spheres, with the military playing a key role in interpreting and dealing with domestic political problems owing to its greater technical and professional skills in handling internal security issues.[5] The scope of military concern for, and study of, politics became unrestricted, so that the "new professional" military man was highly politicized.

The new professionalism of internal security and national development almost inevitably led to some degree of military role expansion. However, variables stemming from the larger political system in addition to those associated with the military subsystem affect the degree of this role expansion. The weaker the civilian government's own legitimacy and ability to supervise a "peaceful" process of development, the greater the tendency will be for the new professionals to assume control of the government to impose their own view of development on the state.

The old professionalism of external security and the new professionalism of internal security and national development share many external characteristics, especially those of highly developed military schooling systems and elaborate military doctrines. However, the *content* and *consequences* of the two forms of professionalism are quite distinct, as is

Table 1. Contrasting Paradigms: The Old Professionalism of External Defense
The New Professionalism of Internal Security and National Development

	Old Professionalism	*New Professionalism*
Function of military	External security	Internal security
Civilian attitudes toward government	Civilians accept legitimacy of government	Segments of society challenge government legitimacy
Military skills required	Highly specialized skills incompatible with political skills	Highly interrelated political and military skills
Scope of military professional action	Restricted	Unrestricted
Impact of professional socialization	Renders the military politically neutral	Politicizes the military
Impact on civil-military relations	Contributes to an apolitical military and civilian control	Contributes to military-political managerialism and role expansion

shown schematically in Table 1. It is useful to distinguish the two types of
military professionalism for reasons of policy as well as theory. Since 1961,
United States military policy toward Latin America has been to encourage
the Latin American militaries to assume as their primary role counterinsurgency programs, civic-action and nation-building tasks. This policy has
often been defended, in the name of helping to create a professional army,
and by implication, an apolitical force in the nation. However, in terms of
the schema presented in the table, technical and professional specialization of the military in conjunction with doctrines and ideologies of internal
security will tend to lead toward military role expansion and "managerialism" in the political sphere.[6]

It also seems useful to point out for reasons of politics as well as theory
that the new professionalism is not only a phenomenon of the developing
countries. Some of the key ingredients of the new professionalism were
observed in France in the 1950s and played a major role in the civil-
military crises there in 1958 and 1961. Even in the United States, the
military's development of the new professionalism in the fields of counterinsurgency and civic action has resulted in the development of skills
that, though originally developed for export to the developing countries
such as Brazil in the early 1960s, were by the late 1960s increasingly called
upon within this country. Huntington's view of the old professionalism,
where the military was functionally specific and unconcerned with domestic political events, is now less meaningful for this country. The United
States Army has increasingly been used to quell riots and given the
function of maintaining internal order. Once given this function, the inter-

nal logic of the new professionalism comes into play, and the military sets about in a "professional" way to train to perform this function. In the late 1960s, many units such as the crack 82nd Airborne Division spent an increasing amount of their time training how to occupy American cities in case of domestic riots. The next "new professional" question for the United States was to inquire into the nature of the enemy. This involved the military in a surveillance and intelligence-gathering role within the United States.[7]

New Professionalism in the Brazilian Political Crisis

The processes leading toward the development of the new professionalism were evident in Brazil before 1964. In Brazil, many of the external standards of the old professionalism had greatly increased before this date. The military schooling system was highly evolved. To be eligible for promotion to the rank of general an army line officer was required to graduate from Military Academy (Academia Militar das Agulhas Negras, AMAN), the Junior Officer's School (Escola de Aperfeiçoamento de Oficiais, EsAO), and the three-year General Staff School (Escola de Comando e Estado Maior do Exército, ECEME), whose written entrance examination is passed by less than a quarter of the applicants. In terms of rank structure, the rank distribution was roughly similar to that of the United States. According to Janowitz, 21.7 percent of officers in the United States Army were colonels or generals in 1950. In 1964, the figure for Brazil was only 14.9 percent.[8]

At the same time, new military institutions were developing in Brazil that were to become centers of the new professionalism. Of prime importance was the Superior War College (Escola Superior de Guerra, ESG) which was formally established by presidential decree under Dutra in 1949. At the time of its founding, the United States played a key role through a military advisory mission that stayed in Brazil from 1948 to 1960. By 1963, the ESG decreed its mission as that of preparing "civilians and the military to perform executive and advisory functions especially in those organs responsible for the formulation, development, planning, and execution of the policies of national security."[9] That the new professionalism of national security as developed at the ESG was very different in conception from that of the old professionalism, which in theory confines military activity to a more restricted sphere, is clear from an examination of the seven academic divisions of the college. These were (1) political affairs, (2) psychological-social affairs, (3) economic affairs, (4) military affairs, (5) logistical and mobilization affairs, (6) intelligence and counter-intelligence, and (7) doctrine coordination.[10]

One interesting aspect of the new professionalism was its relation with civilians. In the 1950s in Brazil, the participation of civilians became a key aspect of the college's program. Precisely because the military viewed the situation in Brazil as going beyond questions handled by the old professionalism, and because the ESG was to be connected with all phases of development and national security, it was felt the Brazilian military needed to socialize civilians from such fields as education, industry, communications, and banking into the correct national security perspective. By 1966, in fact, the ESG had graduated men from many of the key sectors of the political and economic power structure in Brazil: by this date, 599 graduates were military officers, 224 were from private industry and commerce, 200 from the major government ministries, 97 from decentralized government agencies, 39 from the federal Congress, 23 federal or state judges, and 107 were various professionals, such as professors, economists, writers, medical doctors, and Catholic clergy.[11]

By the late 1950s and early 1960s, the ESG had developed its key ideological tenet: the close interrelationship between national security and national development. The doctrines taught at the college emphasized that modern warfare, either conventional or revolutionary, involved the unity, will, and productive capacity of the entire nation.

The low-mobilization, high-control policies of the military governments since 1964 had their intellectual roots in the ESG's doctrine that an effective policy of national security demands a strong government that can rationally maximize the outputs of the economy and effectively contain manifestations of disunity in the country. The new professionalism contributed to an all-embracing attitude of military managerialism in regard to Brazil's political system. The ideas and suggestions aired at the ESG at least five years before the coup of 1964 ranged from redrawing state boundaries (to eliminate old political forces and restructure the federation along "natural" economic boundaries) to the enforcement of a two-party system.[12] The language in the 1956 ESG lecture quoted below foreshadowed the tone, substance, and rationale of later military government attempts to impose a hierarchical, semicorporatist unity on the Brazilian political system.

> We live in a climate of world-wide war that will decide the destiny of Western civilization.
>
> A decentralized system is fundamentally weak in periods of war, which demand a centralized and hierarchic structure. As total war absorbs all people, institutions, wealth, and human and national resources for the attainment of the objectives, it seems certain that centralization and concentration will increase the efficiency and ability of the political and national power.[13]

Though the ESG always concerned itself to some extent with conventional warfare, it became the center of ideological thought concerning counterrevolutionary strategy in Brazil. In early 1959 the chief ideologue of the school, Colonel Golbery, argued that indirect attack from within was a much more real threat to Latin America than direct attack from without:

> What is certain is that the greater probability today is limited warfare, localized conflict, and above all indirect Communist aggression, which capitalizes on local discontents, the frustrations of misery and hunger, and just nationalist anxieties. . . . Latin America now faces threats more real than at any other time, threats which could result in insurrection, outbursts attempting (though not openly) to implant . . . a government favorable to the Communist ideology and constituting a grave and urgent danger to the unity and security of the Americas and the Western world.[14]

It was this perception of threat, in conjunction with the ESG's underlying preference for "ordered politics," that led to their advocacy of the primacy of the politics of national security (implicitly directed by the military) over competitive politics. Golbery contended that in times of severe crises,

> the area of politics is permeated . . . by adverse pressures, creating a form of universalization of the factors of security, enlarging the area of the politics of national security to a point where it almost absorbs all the national activities.[15]

It was from this perspective of the relation between internal security and national development that the ESG set about studying all problems viewed as relating to the security issue. Its civil-military, national security elites studied inflation, agrarian reform, banking reform, voting systems, transportation, and education, as well as guerrilla warfare and conventional warfare. In many of these studies, some of the fundamental aspects of Brazilian social and economic organization were depicted as needing change if Brazil were to maintain its internal security.

Initially, these critiques of Brazilian society by military intellectuals seemed academic, and the influence of the ESG's doctrine was not pervasive within the military in the mid-1950s. But by the early 1960s, as the military perceived a deepening crisis in Brazil, the ESG's emphasis on the need for a total development strategy to combat internal subversion found an increasingly receptive audience in the military. Through the military's highly structured and well-developed publication and education systems, the ideology of internal warfare was widely disseminated throughout the officer corps. The ECEME, one of the major institutions of the old professionalism, became a central vehicle for socializing an entire generation of military officers in the internal-warfare doctrines. The training program is three years long, and entrance is highly competitive. Unless an army line officer is graduated from the ECEME, he is ineligible for promotion to general, for appointment to the teaching staff of any military school, or to the general staff of any senior command. Thus the ECEME is the central recruitment and socialization institution of the senior army officer corps of the Brazilian army.

An examination of the curriculum of the ECEME shows that, like the ESG, it increasingly became devoted to the doctrines of the new professionalism, with its emphasis on the expanded political, economic, and social roles of a modern army in times of internal-security threats. In the 1956 curriculum, for instance, there were no class hours scheduled on counterguerrilla warfare, internal security, or communism. By 1966, however, the curriculum contained 222 hours on internal security, 129 on irregular warfare, and only 24 hours on the "old" professional military topic of territorial warfare.[16] Through military publications, such as the newsletter *Boletim de Informações,* sent from the Estado Maior to key troop commanders, the content of the new professionalism was systematically disseminated to all army units.[17]

In their studies of the Brazilian political system the new professionals had, since the early 1960s, moved toward the position that (1) numerous aspects of the economic and political structures had to be altered if Brazil were to have internal security and rational economic growth and (2) the civilian politicians were either unable or unwilling to make these changes. By early 1964, through the prism of internal-warfare doctrines of the new professionalism, a substantial part of the Brazilian military establishment perceived the rising strike levels, the inflation rate of over 75 percent, the declining economy, the demands of the Left for a constituent assembly, and the growing indiscipline of the enlisted men as signs that Brazil was entering a stage of subversive warfare.

Moreover, the new professionals had come to believe that, in comparison to the civilian politicians, they now had constructed the correct doctrines of national security and development, possessed the trained cadres to implement these doctrines, and had the institutional force to impose their solution to the crisis in Brazil. Thus, after overthrowing the civilian president in 1964, the Brazilian military did not return power to new civilian groups, as they had in 1930, 1945, 1954, and 1955, but assumed political power themselves for the first time in the century.

Since 1964, the military has frequently been internally divided over specific policies and the problems of succession. Nevertheless, one must not lose sight of the important point that many of the doctrines of internal warfare, formulated originally at the ESG and later institutionalized in the ESG-influenced government of Castello Branco, permeated almost all major military groups in Brazil and were accepted as a basic new fact of political and military life. The central idea developed at the ESG was that development and security issues are inseparable. Even when differences over policies developed between the Castello Branco government and the Costa e Silva government, almost all military officers agreed that since labor, fiscal, educational, and other problems were intrinsic to the security of the nation, it was legitimate and necessary for military men to concern themselves with these areas. From this basic premise came the steady broadening of military jurisdiction over Brazilian life after the military assumed power in 1964, despite the fact that an important faction of the military had hoped to eventually allow the inauguration of liberal political forms.

Even within the military government itself, security matters have been given special prominence. A new agency, the National Information Service (Serviço Nacional de Informações, SNI), combining the functions of the FBI and CIA in the United States, has been created, and its director has been granted cabinet rank. In 1968 and 1969, national security laws were passed that have greatly increased the role of SNI and other intelligence units. Since 1969, every ministry has had an SNI representative, responsible for ensuring that all policy decisions of the ministry give full consideration to national security issues. Thus the new professionalism of internal warfare and national development contributed to the expansion of the military's role in Brazil that led ultimately to the military's assumption of power in 1964, and afterward to a widening of military control over those aspects of Brazilian life perceived in any way as threatening to the executors of the national security state—that is, the military.

New Professionalism in Peru

The argument that the internal logic of the new professionalism tends to contribute to an extension of the role of the military in politics receives support from a study of the only other country in Latin America to have developed fully an ideology relating internal security to national development and to have institutionalized that ideology within the military. This country is Peru.[18] The grouping of Peru with Brazil may at first seem incongruous because the policies of their military governments have been very different. However, the two countries are strikingly similar when analyzed from the perspective of the central part played by their respective war colleges in the process of military role expansion. In both countries the staffs and students at the war colleges attempted to systematically diagnose their nation's security-development situation. In the end both colleges had forged a doctrine that implicitly "legitimated" long-term military supervision of the development process. Furthermore, in both military establishments there was the belief that the war colleges and general staff schools had trained the cadres capable of administering this military-directed process. Both, in short, are examples of the new professionalism.

In Peru, as in Brazil, reasonably developed standards for the professional officer's education, promotion, and training exist. In Peru, educational performance is central to any officer's advancement. Eighty percent of all division generals on active duty between 1940 and 1965, for instance, had graduated in the top quarter of their military academy class.[19] A comparable figure for generals in the United States Army in Morris Janowitz's 1950 sample was 36.4 percent.[20]

In 1950, the Peruvian military established it own superior war college, called the Center for Higher Military Studies (Centro de Altos Estudios Militares, CAEM). By the late 1950s, CAEM had largely turned its energies to analyzing the nexus between internal security and national development. As in Brazil, the military's assessment of the development process led the Peruvian military officers into political diagnosis, but in the case of Peru their orientation was markedly more nationalistic and anti-oligarchical in tone. Five years before the Peruvian military assumed power, a CAEM document stated:

> So long as Peru does not have programmatic and well organized political parties, the country will continue to be ungovernable. . . . The sad and desperate truth is that in Peru, the real powers are not the Executive, the Legislature, the Judiciary, or the Electorate, but the latifundists, the exporters, the bankers, and the American [United States] investors.[21]

CAEM studies in the late 1950s and early 1960s diagnosed a number of problems of Peruvian society. Against a background of growing social tensions and political paralysis, the organization of peasants by Hugo Blanco and later the guerrilla outbreak of 1965–66 served to broaden the consensus within the military that direct action was necessary. Though the military defeated the guerrillas in six months, they intensified their investigations of the causes of insurgency. They concluded that rural conditions in Peru were so archaic and unjust that, unless there was a profound change in the rural structure of the country, more guerrilla outbreaks could be expected. The military concluded from their studies that Peru was in a state of "latent insurgency," which could only be corrected, in their view, by a "general policy of economic and social development."[22] In Einaudi's words, "elimination of the latent state of subversion became the primary objective of military action."[23]

The military's analysis of the factors contributing to latent insurgency included elite intransigence, fiscal and technical inefficiencies, and a wide variety of administrative weaknesses traceable to the weakness of the government and the underlying contradictions of the social structure.[24] As in Brazil, the military educational system in Peru had produced a whole cadre of officers with a highly articulated ideology of internal security and national development, and with a new confidence as to the utility of their technocratic and managerial education. These officers feared that the country could evolve into a dangerous state of insecurity if fundamental changes in the polity and economy were not brought about. Like the Brazilian military officers schooled at the ESG, the Peruvian officers trained at CAEM came to the conclusion that civilian governments were incapable of bringing about these changes, and that their own CAEM training in the new professionalism gave them the trained cadres and correct ideology for the task of restructuring the country. This attitude strongly influenced the military's decision to assume and retain political control of the country.

Significantly, in Einaudi's interviews with key Peruvian generals, implicit reference was made to the impact the new professional training has had on military confidence to rule. A former minister of war commented that in the past the military felt culturally inferior and that "when a general met an ambassador, he turned red in the face and trembled." But a leading general in the current regime argued that whereas past military attempts to induce change, such as the regime of Colonel Sánchez Cerro, were doomed to failure because military men were not adequately trained in matters of national development, the present military officers possessed the correct training to be successful. He commented: "Sánchez Cerro was alone. I am but one of forty. And behind us comes a generation of still better trained officers ready to carry on should we falter."[25]

Brazil and Peru: Their Contrasting Policies

Peru is relevant for our analysis of Brazil not only because it is an example of the new professionalism, but also because it illustrates that the new professionalism contributes more to the military's general attitude to political action than to specific policies. In the two countries, the new professional military men have chosen quite different paths. Why has this occurred, and what are the chances that the military in Brazil might take a Peruvian turn?

This is not the place for an extensive comparative analysis of the two regimes, but some of the factors contributing to the different policies of the two military regimes should be stated. First was the impact of World War II. During the war, Brazil sent a combat division, the Fôrça Expedicionária Brasileira (FEB), to fight in Italy as allies of the United States. My extensive interviews with many of the key leaders of the 1964 military government in Brazil indicate that some of the distinctive characteristics of the Castello Branco government—its pro-Americanism, its favorable attitude toward foreign capital, its distaste for "excessive" nationalism— had their roots in this experience. The ally relationship also prepared the way for close personal and institutional ties between the United States and the Brazilian military establishment.[26] In this area, Peru has no comparable experience.

A second area of divergence between the two countries involves their superior war colleges. The Brazilian war college was established and largely dominated by veterans of World War II, who saw the college as the place to "institutionalize the learning experience of World War II." When officers training at the ESG were sent abroad, they were normally sent to

United States military schools, and this experience reinforced the security emphasis, which had found a place in United States schools. Some of the officers associated with CAEM, however, had direct contacts with French-Catholic reformist priest Lebret or attended United Nations civilian-directed schools in Chile. These experiences reinforced CAEM's emphasis on development and helped cast the school's concern for development in a nationalistic light. At the Brazilian ESG, many of those attending the courses were private businessmen, and undoubtedly this contributed to the ESG's bias in favor of capitalism and efficiency. The private civilian industrial sector has never been as heavily represented at CAEM.

A third factor influencing the direction and content of the military regimes in Brazil and Peru is the size of the private industrial sector. The much larger and more powerful private industrial sector in Brazil conditioned military attitudes by inhibiting the adoption of the Peruvian approach, because the private sector is considered so large, dynamic, and advanced that the military doubts its own ability to run the industrial sector efficiently. Industrialists are therefore viewed as allies in the low-mobilization, high-coercion development model in Brazil. In Peru, on the other hand, the industrial sector is smaller and less dynamic. It appears that in the less developed economy, the scope for military Nasserism is greater and the working-class groups far more amenable to the military nationalist-statist approach.

A final factor to be considered in this [essay] is the way in which the nexus between security and development issues were viewed by military officers at the time they seized power. In 1964, military officers in Brazil were primarily concerned with what they viewed as the immediate security threat. In Peru, on the other hand, the defeat of the guerrillas in 1966 gave military officers time to focus almost exclusively on the long-term development aspects of security. The initial acts of the Brazilian military regime after 1964 were consequently largely concerned with repression, which by 1968 had become institutionalized coercion. In Peru, the military government has been largely concerned with nationalism and development and this has meant that significant internal opposition from the Left is absent.

Even this cursory analysis of some of the different historical, institutional, and economic legacies in the two countries helps clarify why the "Peruvian wing" within the Brazilian military has not been able to assume control in Brazil and why it is unlikely to do so in the future. What in fact is the future of the new professionalism in Brazil?

One factor that must be taken into consideration is that in a number of ways the Brazilian military in the 1950s and 1960s was for the first time moving toward becoming a professional *caste*. In the period 1941–43, for instance, sons of military families represented 21.3 percent of all cadets admitted to the military academy. This figure had increased to 34.9 percent by 1962–66. More startling is the fact that, as the military professionalized its educational system, it expanded its military high schools in order to ensure the entry into the military school system of a sufficient number of attractive officer candidates. In 1939, 61.6 percent of all cadets at the military academy had attended civilian high schools. By 1963–66, only 7.6 percent of all cadets had attended civilian high schools. Thus, probably about 90 percent of the present army officers in Brazil entered the military educational system when they were about twelve years old.[27]

Once the military assumed power, the movement toward professional homogeneity was accelerated. About 20 percent of the field grade officers have now been purged from the military for ideological deviation. Possession of the "correct" revolutionary mentality is now indispensable for promotion or assignment to a key command. The purging of a significant group of senior officers, together with the purging of politicans, has created an "Argentine" extrication dilemma. The military fears leaving office because of the threat posed by the return to power of previously purged officers and politicians. Institutional factors such as these must be borne in mind in any assessment of the possibility of military rule ending in Brazil.

On the other hand, despite the new professionals' agreement on the inseparability of internal security and national development, the contrast between Peru and Brazil has helped point out that the ideology itself leaves unspecified most concrete policy decisions. Nor can the particular ideological unity of the military help resolve succession crises. In fact, the nine years of Brazilian military rule have gravely injured military unity. The military experienced major internal crises in October 1965, November 1968, and September 1969. "Defense of the military institution" was one of the keys to the new professionals' entry into national politics. If, however, internal disunity increases over policy or succession problems, "defense of the institution" may well be one of the keys to extrication, via a caretaker junta. The military leaders are attempting to institutionalize the system so that levels of coercion and dissent diminish and support rises. The Mexican model of institutionalization is often mentioned by the military. However, the absence of a revolutionary myth in Brazil and the much more advanced state of both the economy and, more importantly, social groups would seem to rule out this possibility.

Notes

1. See Alfred Stepan, *The Military in Politics: Changing Patterns in Brazil* (Princeton: Princeton University Press, 1971), chap. 3; and Luigi Einaudi, *The Peruvian Military: A Summary Political Analysis* (Santa Monica: RAND Corporation, RM-6048-RC, May 1969).
2. Samuel P. Huntington, *The Soldier and the State: The Theory and Politics of Civil-Military Relations* (New York: Vintage Books, 1964); idem, "Civilian Control of the Military: A Theoretical Statement," in *Political Behavior: A*

Reader in Theory and Research, ed. H. Eulau, S. Eldersveld, and M. Janowitz (New York: Free Press, 1956).

3. See in particular his "Patterns of Violence in World Politics," in *Changing Patterns of Military Politics,* ed. Samuel P. Huntington (New York: Free Press, 1962), pp. 19–22.

4. This shift has been well documented. For an overview and a guide to the United States government programs and publications see W. F. Barber and C. N. Ronning, eds., *Internal Security and Military Power: Counter-insurgency and Civic Action in Latin America* (Columbus: Ohio State University Press, 1966). See also M. Francis, "Military Aid to Latin America in the United States Congress," *Journal of Inter-American Studies* 6 (July 1964): 389–401. A strong criticism of this policy from the Latin American perspective is John Saxe-Fernández, *Proyecciones hemisféricas de la pax Americana* (Lima: IEP ediciones y CAMPODÓNICO ediciones, 1971).

5. A thorough and brilliant analysis of some psychological and political implications of this type of military ideology of total counterrevolutionary warfare (especially in the context of a weak political system) is Raoul Girardet's discussion of the French army. See his "Problèmes idéologiques et moraux," and "Essai d'interprétation," in *La Crise militaire française, 1945–1962: Aspects sociologiques et idéologiques,* ed. Raoul Girardet (Paris: Librairie Armand Colin, 1964), pp. 151–229.
   In the early 1960s the Indonesian army's Staff and Command School formulated a development and security doctrine that was later implemented in large part when the military assumed power in 1965. For the doctrine and an insightful analysis, see Guy J. Pauker, *The Indonesian Doctrine of Territorial Warfare and Territorial Management* (Santa Monica: RAND Corporation, RM-3312-PR, November 1963).

6. I develop this argument at greater length in my congressional testimony; see U.S. Congress, House of Representatives, *Hearings before the Subcommittee on National Security Policy and Scientific Developments of the Committee on Foreign Affairs on Military Assistance Training,* 91st Cong., 2nd sess., October 6, 7, 8, December 8, 15, 1970, pp. 105–11, 117–29 passim.

7. For a more detailed discussion of these themes, see Bruce Russett and Alfred Stepan, eds., *Military Force and American Society* (New York: Harper & Row, Torchbook, 1973).

8. For documentation see Stepan, *The Military in Politics,* chap. 3.

9. Decreto No. 53,080, December 4, 1963.

10. Ibid.

11. For a short official history of the ESG, see the heavily documented essay by General Augusto Fragoso, written while he was commandant of the school, "A Escola Superior de Guerra (Origen—Finalidade—Evolução)," *Segurança & Desenvolvimento: Revista da Associação dos Diplomados da Escola Superior de Guerra,* año 18, no. 132 (1969), pp. 7–40. The figures on occupations of graduates were provided by the ESG and reprinted by Glauco Carneiro, "A guerra de 'Sorbonne,' " *O Cruzeiro,* June 24, 1967, p. 20.

12. See, for example, Christovão L. Barros Falção-de, Capitão-mar-e-guerra, *Mobilização no campo econômico,* Curso de Mobilização Nacional, Escola Superior de Guerra, C-03-59; and David Carneiro, *Organização política do Brasil,* Escola Superior de Guerra, Departmento de Estudos, C-47-59. These and all subsequent ESG documents that I cite I found either in the archive of Castello Branco located in the library of ECEME or in the Biblioteca Nacional. Most ESG documents are still classified by the Brazilian government.

13. Ildefonso Mascarenhas de Silva, *O poder nacional e seus tipos de estructura,* Escola Superior de Guerra, C-20-56, pp. 32–34.

14. Golbery do Couto e Silva, *Geopolítica do Brasil* (Rio de Janeiro: José Olympio, 1967), pp. 198–99 (from a chapter originally written in 1959). This book is based on ESG lectures. The developments in the Cuban revolution in late 1960 and 1961 intensified the ESG fear of the "communist threat."
15. Golbery do Couto e Silva, *Planejamento estratégico* (Rio de Janeiro: Biblioteca do Exército Editôra, 1955), pp. 38–39. Most of this book had its origin in lectures originally given at the ESG. The book is one of the major sources for the ideology of the ESG.
16. Based upon my examination of the curriculum of ECEME on file at their library.
17. Ministério da Guerra, Estado Maior do Exército, *Boletim de Informações.* Copies of this are on open file at the Biblioteca do Exército in Rio de Janeiro. Before October 1961 the format was that of a very straightforward review of professional topics and routine surveys of international news. From October 1961 on, the format changed to one much closer to the framework and terminology of the ESG and, most significantly, began to deal with the question of the threat to internal security presented by communism.
18. Argentina, which I would rank highest after Brazil and Peru among the countries of Latin America on a rough scale of new professionalism, experienced a military coup in 1966. Analysts specifically pointed to the evolution of a military ideology concerned with internal security and national development as an important factor in the inauguration of the authoritarian military regime. This would be in keeping with the thesis of the present essay. See Guillermo A. O'Donnell, "Modernización y golpes militares: Teoría, comparaciones y el caso Argentino," (Buenos Aires: Instituto Torcuato Di Tella, Documento de Trabajo, September 1972). [A translation appears in this volume.—Ed.]
19. Luigi Einaudi, *The Peruvian Military,* p. 7. The analysis of Peru owes much to my discussions with Einaudi. We coauthored the monograph *Latin American Institutional Development: Changing Military Perspectives in Peru and Brazil* (Santa Monica: RAND Corporation, R-586-DOS, April 1971), in which Einaudi is primarily responsible for Peru and I am primarily responsible for Brazil.
    In 1972, while on a SSRC-ACLS grant I carried out research in Peru and visited CAEM. Although the discussion in this essay reflects some of the results of this research, extensive analysis and documentation of the material must await a later publication. One particularly relevant finding is based on my study with Jorge Rodríguez of the University of York, England. Of the 404 articles to appear in the *Revista de la Escuela Superior de Guerra* (Peru) from 1954 to 1967, the percentage of articles whose content met our criteria of "new professionalism" increased from virtually zero in 1954–55 to well over 50 percent by 1964.
20. Morris Janowitz, *The Professional Soldier: A Social and Political Portrait* (New York: Free Press, 1960), pp. 134–35.
21. CAEM, *El estado y la política general* (1963), pp. 89, 92, cited in Einaudi and Stepan, *Latin American Institutional Development.*Víctor Villanueva, in his important book, *El CAEM y la revolución de la fuerza armada* (Lima: IEP ediciones y CAMPODÓNICO ediciones, 1972), pp. 85–88, notes that while this document was initially released with the approval of the director of CAEM, it was withdrawn due to pressure. Villnueva argues that this document is considerably more nationalistic and concerned with structural change than most CAEM studies in this period. Nonetheless for purposes of our comparison the document reveals a set of concerns very different from those found at the ESG in Brazil.

22. See Peru, Ministerio de Guerra, *Las guerrillas en el Perú y su represión* (Lima, 1966), p. 80. Articles in this vein had been appearing in Peruvian military journals even before the guerrilla movement of 1965–66. See in particular Lieutenant Colonel Enrique Gallegos Venero, "Problemas de la guerra contrarrevolucionaria," *Revista de la Escuela Superior de Guerra,* año 11, no. 2 (1964), pp. 97–106.

23. In Einaudi and Stepan, *Latin American Institutional Development.* A civilian social scientist who has been on the faculty at CAEM since 1959 told the author that from 1959 to 1962 CAEM experienced a phase of radicalization aimed at bureaucratic and organizational reform in Peru and that many of these policies were implemented by the 1962–63 military government. From 1964 to 1968 CAEM underwent a new phase of radicalization, but this time the studies explored and advocated much deeper social and structural changes because of the realization that organizational changes alone had been insufficient to resolve Peru's security and development crisis. Interview with Jorge Bravo Bresani, Lima, June 22, 1972.

24. See Brigadier General E. P. Edgardo Mercado Jarrín, "La Política y estrategia militar en la guerra contrasubversiva en la América Latina," *Revista Militar del Perú* (Chorrillos), November–December 1967, pp. 4–33. In many ways this article is a classic example of new professionalism.

25. Einaudi and Stepan, *Latin American Institutional Development,* p. 59.

26. For a more detailed discussion and documentation, see Stepan, *The Military in Politics,* pp. 239–44.

27. The data on social origins and educational background of cadets at the Academia Militar das Agulhas Negras were obtained at the academy by the author.

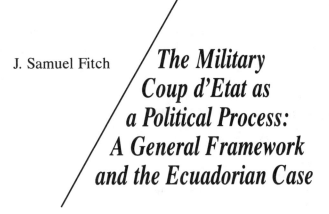

J. Samuel Fitch

The Military
Coup d'Etat as
a Political Process:
A General Framework
and the Ecuadorian Case

In most Latin American countries the military coup d'état is an integral part of the political system, rather than an aberrant event. Yet, despite the rather extensive literature on the military in politics, there has been little progress toward development of a coherent theoretical model of the coup d'état as a political process. In part this stems from the obvious difficulties in obtaining empirical data on the military, particularly data on individual officers. Given these data limitations, it has been difficult to confirm or disconfirm the many different hypotheses that have been offered to explain military behavior.

The development of better theory has also been hampered by the absence of a conceptual framework capable of integrating the various partial perspectives that abound in the literature. Coup participants and historians, for example, tend to explain coups in terms of antecedent events. Social scientists—particularly Latin Americans—tend to focus on the structural determinants of military behavior. Political scientists—particularly Americans—tend to be equally, if not more, interested in the institutional sources of that behavior. All these are essential components. The framework presented here attempts to clarify the relationships among

Author's note: I am indebted to Alfred Stepan, Juan Linz, Abraham Lowenthal, Ron Brunner, Bill Ascher, and many others for their criticism and assistance in the development of this analysis, which originally appeared in *The Military Coup d'Etat as a Political Process: Ecuador 1948–1966* (Baltimore, Md.: Johns Hopkins University Press, 1977).

the several different levels of analysis that must be included in any comprehensive theory of the coup d'état. At the individual level the model must specify how individual officers decide to support or oppose the overthrow of the existing government. Second, the actions and attitudes of individual officers have to be translated into a collective decision, into success or failure for that particular coup. Finally, the particular events to which individual officers are responding have to be linked back to the structural changes and characteristics that generate these crises. The analysis must also specify how the behavior of the armed forces is shaped by its institutional characteristics and how the actions of the individual officers and the military institution serve to sustain or transform the larger structural environment in which they are embedded.

Ecuador serves as a useful focus for this analysis because its postwar history includes both successful and unsuccessful military coups and periods of minimal military intervention (1948–1960) as well as periods of military government (1963–1966, 1972–1980). As one of the smaller, poorer South American countries, Ecuador shares many characteristics in common with other Latin American nations—sharp urban-rural and class inequalities, a rapidly changing social structure, rising levels of political participation, and a high level of economic dependence on international trade as the primary engine of economic growth and government finance. Even though in some respects Ecuador is not a typical Latin American country, we will argue that our analysis applies quite broadly to the military in other countries. Even where the particulars differ, the analytical framework proposed here provides a systematic way of identifying what the key intraregional and interregional variations in military behavior are.

Decision Criteria for Military Coups

Logically the first problem is to specify the criteria by which individual officers decide to support or oppose the overthrow of the government currently in power. On numerous occasions during the last thirty-five years Ecuadorian officers have had to make that choice, deciding in 1961, 1963, and 1972 to oust civilian governments and in 1966 and 1976 to overthrow military regimes. In 1970 they backed the President's seizure of extraconstitutional powers and in 1954 and 1975 the majority rejected attempted coups. Based on extensive interviews with many of the key participants in four of these coups,[1] it is clear that most Ecuadorian officers evaluate the government's performance in terms of a reasonably well-understood set of criteria that identify the particular elements of the political and/or socioeconomic context which are relevant to the decision to support or oppose any given government. In the 1961 coup against J. M. Velasco Ibarra, for example, a majority of officers cited Velasco's violation

Table 1: Factors Entering Coup Decisions of Individual Officers
(Uncued, open-ended explanations of four civil-military crises)

Factors	1954	1961	1963	1966
Constitutionality of government	68% (47%)	92% (52%)	40% (0%)	14% (0%)
Public disorders	0% (0%)	56% (16%)	9% (0%)	49% (0%)
Public hostility to government	0% (0%)	48% (0%)	40% (0%)	59% (18%)
Threat of communism	0% (0%)	0% (0%)	86% (34%)	0% (0%)
Institutional interests	42% (11%)	8% (4%)	11% (0%)	59% (23%)
President's personal behavior	5% (0%)	4% (0%)	94% (51%)	0% (0%)
Socioeconomic problems	5% (0%)	16% (0%)	20% (9%)	54% (32%)
Personal ties/antagonisms	68% (42%)	40% (12%)	20% (3%)	36% (9%)
Miscellaneous	0% (0%)	8% (0%)	11% (0%)	9% (0%)
	N = 19	N = 25	N = 35	N = 22

NOTE: Figures indicate the percentage of each sample citing that factor, with multiple responses permitted. The figures in parentheses indicate the percentage of each sample stressing that factor as the most important element in that coup.

of the Constitution in ordering the arrest of opposition leaders including the vice-president, the strong tide of public opinion against the government, and opposition to the use of the army troops to suppress antigovernment riots and disorders. In 1963, the most prominent and nearly universal military complaints against President Arosemena were his personal conduct in several drinking incidents, his failure to crack down on the "communist threat," and heavy lobbying by influential civilian groups and most of the national press for Arosemena's overthrow. In all four of the coups studied, individual officers were also strongly influenced by considerations of personal self-interest and by personal ties and antipathies to the President and his key supporters and opponents. Although the salience of the issue varied, in each case the government was also judged in terms of the impact of its policies on the military's institutional interests. In each of Velasco's presidencies, for example, officers were torn between gratitude for his generosity in granting pay increases and equipment purchases and outrage over his utter disregard for professional norms in military promotions and assignments. Finally, in 1963 and 1966, a few officers voiced their concern over the failure of the government's economic and social programs. If we combine each officer's evaluation of government performance in terms of these seven criteria, we find a strong correlation with the positions taken by these officers in both the successful and unsuccessful coups.[2] There is also strong evidence of change over time in the composition of the set of decision criteria used by the Ecuadorian military, in particular the virtual disappearance after 1961 of the constitutionality criterion as a major concern.

The criteria used by Ecuadorian officers to decide whether to overthrow the government closely parallel the criteria used by other Latin American militaries in making coup decisions. In Brazil, for example, in 1961 a majority of the officer corps rejected the attempted coup against Goulart, citing his constitutional right to the presidency, the lack of public support for the attempted coup, and concern for their institutional interests, in particular the fear of intramilitary bloodshed if Goulart's enemies in the military persisted in their efforts to prevent Goulart's accession to the presidency. Three years later, however, the majority decided against Goulart, given his failure to curtail the activities of the radical left, his

Table 2: Correlations between Ratings of Government Performance on Seven Decision Criteria and Positions Taken in Coup

Coup Sample	Outcome of Coup	Kendall's Tau	Pearson r	N
1954	Unsuccessful	.79	.91	18
1961	Successful	.57	.73	20
1963	Successful	.83	.85	29
1966	Successful	.86	.92	19

support for attempts to unionize noncommissioned officers and enlisted men which they interpreted as a direct attack on the military institution, and strong "public", i.e., middle-class and elite, support for military action against Goulart. In Argentina, Chile, Colombia, Peru, Bolivia, and Venezuela, we find evidence of similar criteria being invoked to decide for or against a military coup.[3] Despite Velasco's multiple presidencies, one criterion not encountered in the Ecuadorian interviews was the prohibition against the return to power of individuals or parties deposed in previous coups. This suggests a need for caution in attributing electoral motives to coups that happen to occur near election time and a need for further research to specify the particular conditions that led to repeated veto coups against the Aprista party in Peru and against Peronistas in Argentina.[4]

Military Role Beliefs

An officer's decision to support or oppose a coup is not solely a function of his evaluation of government performance according to these criteria; that decision also depends on his beliefs about the proper role of the armed forces in dealing with these kinds of situations. In Ecuador, we find four distinct doctrines about the role of the military in politics, each of which provides a different prescription for responding to political crises.

The first type of role belief is the classical professionalist doctrine, according to which the military officer is an expert in the art/science of war. Political questions are outside the military's sphere of expertise; hence military involvement in political questions is illegitimate, a distraction from if not a violation of his professional responsibilities. In this view, the duty of the military is to uphold "the constituted order." In Ecuador, there were few exponents of the classical professionalist doctrine, but those officers who embraced these beliefs typically backed the incumbent government, even in circumstances which most of their fellow officers considered more than sufficient justification for a coup.

A much larger group of officers accepted the definition of the military's role given in the Ecuadorian constitution, which authorized the creation of the armed forces to provide external defense, maintenance of public order, and defense of the Constitution. In this view, the military should refrain from involvement in political questions except insofar as necessary to ensure that the government and its opponents remain within the general limits of the Constitution. Thus most Ecuadorian officers rejected the minister of defense's attempt to overthrow Velasco in 1954 as contrary to their duty to uphold the Constitution. In 1961, when Velasco overstepped the constitutional boundaries in his dispute with the opposition-controlled Congress, the military immediately moved to overthrow Velasco and replace him with Vice-President Arosemena.

In the early 1960s, a growing number of officers began to argue that the political role of the military could not be limited to defending the Constitution. According to this view, the military had an inescapable duty to act as the ultimate arbiter of the political game, intervening whenever it was necessary to safeguard national interests in times of crisis. Since the "arbiter" doctrine left it to the military to define what constituted a national crisis without any precise guidelines as to how to decide when military action was legitimately called for, in practice advocates of this view tended to favor intervention whenever there was clear evidence of an elite and middle-class consensus that the current situation was indeed a crisis.

In recent years, particularly since 1970, many officers have opted for a new conception of the military's role based on the doctrine of national security. In this view, the military officer has a professional responsibility to safeguard national security, defined broadly to include not only military capabilities, but also the country's economic base, popular morale, international alliances, and the quality of national leadership. Since the primary threat to national security is perceived to be revolutionary insurgency, the military is legitimately involved in all aspects of economic and social development which might affect popular support for present or future guerrilla forces. Although a sharp split emerged in the late 1960s between followers of the Peruvian and Brazilian variants of the security and development doctrine, both factions agreed on a greatly expanded role for the military in politics, including direct military rule whenever necessary to ensure national security or promote development.

The proportion of officers subscribing to each of these role beliefs varies widely over time and between different countries in accordance with the military's perceptions of its own competence to rule in relation to its confidence in civilian leadership. In Ecuador, the generation of officers who held high rank in the 1950s generally felt educationally and socially inferior to members of the political elite like Galo Plaza or Camilo Ponce. As the banana boom faded and the level of political conflict and disorder began to rise, increasing numbers of officers felt that the military was far more honest and disciplined and at least as competent as most civilians. By 1963 only a handful of officers opposed the creation of a military

Table 3: Trends in Definition of Military's Role in Politics: Ecuador 1954–1966

Coup Sample	Classical Professionalist	Constitutionalist	Arbiter	Developmentalist	N
1954	16%	63%	16%	5%	19
1961	13%	44%	30%	13%	25
1963	0%	19%	48%	32%	35
1966	0%	13%	63%	22%	23

government following the overthrow of Arosemena. Although the level of military schooling in non-military topics was not as advanced as in the more developed Latin American militaries, many officers, especially those trained in Brazil, Argentina, and Mediterranean Europe, began to see themselves as better equipped to govern than populists like Velasco or Asaad Bucaram. This developmentalist faction generally gained adherents during civilian administrations, but the failure of recent attempts at military rule has strengthened the argument of the arbiter faction that the military should limit itself to temporary intervention in times of crisis and then return to the barracks once the crisis is resolved.

Both the particular types of role beliefs encountered among Ecuadorian officers and the dynamics underlying the changing factional balance between them seem quite general. Alfred Stepan and Guillermo O'Donnell in chapters in the present volume and others have described in detail the emergence of the security and development doctrine in a number of different Latin American militaries.[5] In Argentina the split in the early 1960s between the *legalistas* and the *gorillas* parallels the constitutionalist/arbiter split in Ecuador. The shift away from the constitutionalist doctrine in favor of the security and development doctrine under Allende in Chile as well as the corresponding doctrinal shifts that occurred in Brazil and Argentina in the 1960s in each case reflected a sharp loss of faith in the ability of the civilian leadership to manage the problems facing the country and a rising confidence in the technical and managerial abilities of the armed forces, not just to restore political order but also to plan and promote economic growth and development. In Ecuador and elsewhere, the failure of various military governments to achieve these goals has led to military withdrawals from power. Most often, this turns out to be only a temporary withdrawal, since the loss of military self-confidence is generally not accompanied by any real increase in military confidence in the civilian alternative. Generally the next period of civilian rule convinces many officers that the failures of the previous military government were not so bad after all. As a result, "redemocratization" is typically an uncertain, often temporary phase in the long-term cycle of alternating military and civilian regimes.[6]

Institutional Characteristics

It is now widely accepted that the military's political behavior reflects both the institutional characteristics of the military and the particular sociopolitical environment in which that military exists. In Ecuador, postwar increases in the size of the armed forces and in the level of military professionalization both had important impacts on the military's response to its political environment. If we define professionalization in terms of the level of development and complexity of the military career, it is clear that the Ecuadorian armed forces are considerably less professionalized than the larger South American militaries. The Ecuadorian military did not achieve a level of professionalization clearly superior to that of the Central American and African militaries until after the Second World War. During the first half of the twentieth century, promotions from the ranks were fairly common and specialized training was not required as a prerequisite for advancement. As a result, the military lacked a strong sense of corporate identity or solidarity. Even though individual officers were often coopted into the political struggles among various elite factions, the military as an institution was politically quite weak. The army in particular was subjected to constant government interference in its internal affairs, which the military was unable to resist despite the high level of factional division and instability among the civilians.

By the mid-1950s, partly as a result of U.S. military assistance programs, partly as a result of internal reforms following Ecuador's defeat in the 1941 war with Peru, the overall level of professionalization improved significantly. Although there was no equivalent of Brazil's Superior War College or Peru's CAEM until 1972, the typical officer was a graduate of his respective service academy, with one or more advanced courses, including in most cases two years at the command and general staff college. In addition, most senior officers had at least some foreign training.

As a result of this higher level of professional socialization, most officers came to identify more strongly with the *institución armada* and less with various civilian groupings, including class and region of origin. The emergence of a predominant identification with the armed forces directly affected the military's response to political crises, since it is this psychological tie to the military which underlies the set of coup decision criteria described earlier. The military disliked public disorders because the use of army troops to quell antigovernment disturbances typically damaged the prestige and public image of the armed forces. During the 1950s many officers held strongly to the norm of constitutionality, because they believed the failure to adhere to that norm was one of the causes of Ecuador's defeat in 1941, for which the military received much of the blame. Even the military's obsessive concern with the threat of communism rests less on ideological or class considerations than on the belief that the radical left would destroy the regular armed forces.[7] As a result, then, of the higher level of professionalization in the postwar period, the military began to articulate and enforce *its own* criteria for determining whether or not to sustain any particular government in power.

The increase in the size of the Ecuadorian military to roughly twenty thousand men facilitated the growing autonomy of the armed forces during the postwar period.[8] Given the substantial increase in the number of officers, in particular the proliferation of staff and technical positions, the weight of any individual unit or officer was correspondingly diminished. Buying off key commanders or appointing one's friends to strategic posts no longer afforded the government much protection. Conspiracies among various handfuls of active-duty and retired officers continued to be commonplace, but the decision to stage a coup increasingly became a collective military decision, arrived at in open military caucuses following some triggering event like Arosemena's banquet speech or Acosta Velasco's decision to fire the head of the War Academy in 1971. In these deliberations the government can generally count on a small group of loyalists and a group of diehard opponents, both motivated largely by personal antagonisms and loyalties. The outcome of the collective decision thus depends on the consensus of opinion among the middle and upper ranks, responding both to the political situation as they perceive it and to their beliefs about the proper role of the military in such situations. In this respect the Ecuadorian military clearly differs from many of the African and Caribbean militaries where the military often becomes the captive of a particular leader (or family) like Somoza or Batista and where personal interests, secret conspiracies, and lightning attempts to seize the Presidential Palace all play a much more significant role in the politics of military coups.[9]

Structural Causes

Given the previous analysis of coup decision criteria, we can now pose the question of why some countries recurrently experience the kinds of political events—extensive public disorders, loss of public support, constitutional crises, perceived threats of revolutionary insurgency, personal and institutional conflicts between the President and top military leaders—that lead to military coups. In Ecuador this analysis is facilitated by the sharp contrast in military behavior during the 1948–1960 period and the years following. Despite the high level of instability prior to 1948, in 1952 Galo Plaza completed his full four-year term of office, the first freely elected Ecuadorian President ever to do so. Each of the succeeding elections brought a new government to power and in each case the transition was managed without incident. A minor coup attempt in 1950 and a more serious attempt in 1954 were both repudiated by the majority of the officer corps. In contrast, the military intervened three times in the sixties to overturn the incumbent government. After a temporary respite in the late sixties, the military intervened in 1970 and again in 1972, assuming direct military control of the government for the remainder of the decade.

In retrospect, the higher level of stability during the 1948–1960 period appears to have been largely a result of the combination of particularly favorable economic conditions and the relatively low level of political participation. After several decades of severe recession following the collapse of cacao exports in 1922, Ecuador took advantage of a favorable market in the late 1940s to quickly become the world's largest producer of bananas. Exports and gross national product (GNP) increased rapidly; inflation was almost nonexistent. The lion's share of the new prosperity went to a small number of landowning and commercial families on the coast, but sierra landowners also benefited through the growing demand for domestic agricultural products. The middle class found new job opportunities in the rapidly expanding bureaucracy. Expansion of coastal plantations provided additional jobs and income for the rural proletariat and migrant laborers from the interior. In a political system suffering from a severe hegemonic crisis since the 1920s, where neither the elites nor other classes held strong convictions of the legitimacy of constitutional politics,[10] the satisfaction of economic demands was clearly the principal determinant of political stability. During the banana boom most of the politically active public was simply indifferent to the conflicts between the incumbent government and various opposition factions. The coup attempt in 1954 failed, largely because it was almost entirely an intramilitary affair in which the dissident officers found almost no support for their cause among significant elements of the civilian leadership. The stability of this period was also a reflection of the disenfranchisement of illiterates and the comparatively low level of politicization of the urban and rural workers in Ecuador and hence the low level of demands the government was being called upon to satisfy.

By the late 1950s, the situation had begun to change. With the recovery of Central American banana production and United Fruit's success in marketing its Chiquita banana in the United States, Ecuadorian exports fell, GNP declined, and government budget deficits soared. Unemployment increased, and inflation, though still low by international standards, was sharply higher than in previous years. In 1959 there were major urban riots in Guayaquil, comparable to the American urban explosions in Watts and Detroit. The economic crisis coincided with a period of growing political mobilization, especially among the urban subproletariat in Quito and Guayaquil. In the 1960 presidential elections, 34 percent of the adult population voted, double the rate of participation in the elections of 1948. The result was a sharply higher level of demands on the government for urban services to the *barrios suburbanos*, for urban and rural development projects, and for social programs that the government was both financially and administratively unable to provide. Moreover, for the first time the political agenda now included such divisive issues as a reform of the country's inegalitarian agrarian structures and the question of Ecuador's relationship to foreign corporations and the whole system of international capitalism.

The country's historically feeble political institutions were unable to channel the rising level of political participation or to manage the higher level of conflict which emerged in the 1960s. The traditional parties, including the Socialists and Communists, were ideologically and organizationally ill-prepared to respond effectively to the growing politicization of the urban masses. As in other Latin American countries at more or less the same time, the electoral arena was increasingly dominated by populist leaders, first Velasco Ibarra and later Asaad Bucaram. With a party organization that scarcely existed six months before the 1960 elections, Velasco thoroughly trounced three rival coalitions. Though his margin was smaller in the 1968 elections, Velasco again waged a successful campaign against the traditional parties. On both occasions, his populism soon led to budget crises, major confrontations with Congress, and in 1961 a military decision to oust Velasco in favor of the Vice-President. In 1970 the military tried the opposite tack, backing Velasco's decision to close Congress and rule by decree until the military decided to take over shortly before the elections scheduled for 1972. Both Velasco and Bucaram appealed effectively to the specific discontents and needs of newly enfranchised working-class voters, but neither had a coherent ideology or program to address the problems facing their constituents. Like most populist leaders in other countries, once in power Velasco pursued policies that were mostly advantageous to elite interests.[11] As a result, popular support for Velasco's populism was as ephemeral as Velasco's respect for constitutional limits on his powers as President.

Arosemena and the military governments that followed the 1963 and 1972 coups offered a variety of basically reformist solutions to Ecuador's development problems. Arosemena was stymied from the very beginning by the absence of a political base for his reform program. His allies in the Liberal party opposed most of his reforms and his own National Revolutionary party was largely a personal vehicle with only limited support, even among Ecuador's relatively minuscule organized labor and student groups. The elite-dominated Congress easily blocked passage of his reform legislation and the armed forces and the conservative press allied to force an end to his attempt to steer a neutralist course in the conflict between the United States and Fidel Castro. Unable to deliver on his reform promises, Arosemena increasingly abdicated his responsibilities, making him an easy target for the coup that overthrew him in 1963.

The Military Junta (1963–1966) and particularly the military regime headed by General Rafael Rodríguez Lara (1972–1976), which claimed to be a nationalist revolutionary regime *a la peruana,* both had the advantage of being able to bypass elite resistance to reforms in Congress and in the courts, but both suffered from the lack of an organized mass base with which to counter the determined resistance of the elites, even to measures explicitly designed to undercut the demand for more radical reforms. Neither government possessed a coherent reformist ideology and neither was willing to sustain a reform program against strong elite opposition. Although oil revenues and a rapidly expanding government budget helped keep Rodríguez Lara in power slightly longer than the Military Junta, both were eventually overthrown by an alliance of dissident officers, right-wing elites, and civilian politicians. Despite their occasionally radical rhetoric, neither military government had much long-term impact, giving way in both cases to interim governments that called new elections leading back to another round of civilian leadership.

Structural Consequences

The institutionalization of the military coup d'état as an integral part of the political process has had a profoundly conservative influence on postwar Ecuadorian politics, not only in the obvious sense of eliminating leftist or potentially leftist governments like Arosemena, but also in terms of building a general crisis-management process into the political system. Despite the high level of discontent generated by Ecuador's archaic and inegalitarian socioeconomic structures, whenever those discontents erupt in a political crisis the result is generally a military coup to install a new government. Not only leftist governments, but any government that proves unusually repressive or corrupt or simply incompetent, any government that lacks a base of public support, is likely to be overthrown. Once the offending government is ousted, a new government is installed to the applause of all those offended by its predecessor, and the crisis dissipates. If a new crisis erupts—as it invariably does, given the debility of the country's political institutions and an economy dependent on foreign markets over which Ecuador has no control—the result is another coup and another new government, perhaps a military regime this time, but not a government likely to change any of the basic structures of Ecuadorian society. Over time cynicism and apathy may grow but not to the point of endangering "the system."

Thus, underneath the high level of surface political instability—six coups and eleven presidents in the last twenty-five years—Ecuadorian politics is in one sense ultrastable. The institutionalized coup d'état prevents the accumulation of discontents generated by rapid social change and unjust social structures. The coup prevents the transformation of these discontents into revolutionary convictions of the illegitimacy of the status quo.[12] In Ecuador and in Latin America generally, the military coup satisfies mass (and elite) demands for change at a relatively superficial level, thereby reducing the intensity of demands for more fundamental changes. In Cuba and in Nicaragua, the inability of the army to overcome the personal control of Batista and Somoza, respectively, in order to stage a coup transferring power to the nonrevolutionary opposition was a critical factor in preventing the premature termination of the anti-dictatorial struggle. The coup d'état is therefore more than just a symptom of political decay. It has become a major barrier to basic changes in social and economic structures without which political legitimacy and the development of new political institutions will be difficult to achieve.

Notes

1. The interview sample consisted of a total of eighty officers, mostly drawn from the army and from the ranks of colonels and generals. The sample includes from two-thirds to three-fourths of the key participants in each coup studied, and roughly one-fifth of all officers with the rank of lieutenant colonel or above who were in the country at the time of the coup.
2. This procedure implicitly assigns equal importance to each criterion. In practice, personal interests and in 1954 and 1961 the constitutionality norm are the best predictors of individual officers' positions. The level of public disorders and lack of progress toward socioeconomic reforms appear to be the least important criteria, although the salience of public disorders may be obscured by its high correlation with public opinion. The lower correlation in 1961 stems largely from the fact that differences in positions taken in the coup resulted less from different evaluations of government performance than from divergent conceptions of how the military ought to respond. See *The Military Coup d'Etat*, pp. 83–87.
3. Alfred Stepan, *The Military in Politics: Changing Patterns in Brazil* (Princeton, N.J.: Princeton University Press, 1971), pp. 67–121, 153–71, 188–212; Robert Potash, *The Army and Politics in Argentina: 1945–1962* (Stanford, Cal.: Stanford University Press, 1980), pp. 170–214, 332–76; Guillermo O'Donnell, *Modernization and Bureaucratic Authoritarianism* (Berkeley, Cal.: University of California Institute of International Studies, 1973), pp. 115–65; Arturo Valenzuela, *The Breakdown of Democratic Regimes: Chile* (Baltimore, Md.: Johns Hopkins University Press, 1978), pp. 81–110; Paul Sigmund, "The Military in Chile," in Robert Wesson (ed.), *The New Military Politics in Latin America* (New York: Praeger, 1982), pp. 97–116; Liisa North, *Civil-Military Relations in Argentina, Chile, and Peru* (Berkeley, Cal.: University of California Institute of International Studies, 1966); Richard Maullin, *Soldiers, Guerrillas, and Politics in Colombia* (Lexington, Mass.: D. C. Heath, 1973), pp. 111–18; Lyle McAlister, Anthony Maingot, and Robert Potash, *The Military in Latin American Socio-Political Evolution* (Washington, D.C.: Center for Research on Social System, 1970); Gene Bigler, "Professional Soldiers and Restrained Politics in Venezuela," in Wesson, *New Military*, pp. 175–96; Luigi Einaudi, *The Peruvian Military: A Summary Political Analysis* (Santa Monica, Cal.: Rand Corporation, 1969); and William Brill, *Military Intervention in Bolivia: The Overthrow of Paz Estenssoro* (Washington, D.C.: Institute for the Comparative Study of Political Systems, 1967). See also the speeches of various Latin American military leaders in Brian Loveman and Thomas Davies (eds.), *The Politics of Anti-Politics: The Military in Latin America* (Lincoln, Neb.: University of Nebraska Press, 1978), pp. 173–219.
4. Cf. Martin Needler, "Political Development and Military Intervention in Latin America," *American Political Science Review* 60, 3 (1966): 620, and William Thompson, *The Grievances of Military Coup-Makers* (Beverly Hills, Cal.: Sage Publications, Comparative Politics Series 01-047), pp. 37–39.
5. Margaret Crahan, "The Evolution of the Military in Brazil, Chile, Peru, Venezuela, and Mexico" and "National Security Ideology and Human Rights," in Margaret Crahan (ed.), *Human Rights and Basic Needs in Latin America* (Washington, D.C.: Georgetown University Press, 1982), pp. 46–127; and Luigi Einaudi and Alfred Stepan, *Latin American Institutional Development: Changing Military Perspectives in Peru and Brazil* (Santa Monica, Cal.: Rand Corporation, 1971), pp. 16–40, 58–70, 73–85, 123–32.
6. Eric Nordlinger, *Soldiers in Politics: Military Coups and Governments* (En-

glewood Cliffs, N.J.: Prentice-Hall, 1977), pp. 207–10.

7. See Martin Needler, "Military Motivations in the Seizure of Power," *Latin American Research Review* 10, 3 (1975): 62–78.

8. This analysis should not be taken to imply any simple relationship between the size of the military and the frequency of military intervention. See Stepan, *Military in Politics,* pp. 21–29.

9. Cf. Samuel Decalo, *Coups and Army Rule in Africa* (New Haven, Conn.: Yale University Press, 1976) and Ruth First, *Power in Africa: Political Power in Africa and the Coup d'Etat* (Harmondsworth, England: Penguin Books, 1971).

10. Augustín Cueva, *The Process of Political Domination in Ecuador* (New Brunswick, N.J.: Transaction Books, 1982), pp. 1–61, and Oswaldo Hurtado, *Political Power in Ecuador* (Albuquerque, N.M.: University of New Mexico Press, 1980), pp. 167–362.

11. Cueva, *Political Domination,* pp. 63–96; Rafael Quintero, *El mito del populismo en el Ecuador* (Quito, Ecuador: FLASCO Editores, 1980); and James Malloy, "Authoritarianism and Corporatism in Latin America (Pittsburgh: University of Pittsburgh Press, 1977), pp. 3–19.

12. Harold Lasswell and Abraham Kaplan, *Power and Society: A Framework for Political Inquiry* (New Haven, Conn.: Yale University Press, 1950), pp. 276–77.

III
Case Studies
in Civil-Military
Relations

Liisa North /*The Military in Chilean Politics*

On September 11, 1973, the attempt to create a democratic socialist society in Chile was brought to a violent end by a coup d'état. Contrary to the expectation of Allende and the Unidad Popular (U.P.) leadership and mass base, organization of the coup did not precipitate a division in the armed forces significant enough to provoke a civil war. Since the coup, an increasingly large number of analyses have appeared probing the fundamental causes and reasons for U.P.'s inability to remain in power. Those analyses have documented (1) the role of the United States in damaging the Chilean economy through credit boycotts, dumping of copper reserves, etc.; (2) the economic chaos created by the lockouts, black markets, and speculation organized by entrepreneurial associations (the *gremios*); (3) the attenuation of the government's power to contain ever increasing economic and social disorder as a consequence of Christian Democratic and National party obstructionism in Parliament; and (4) the internal division within the U.P. coalition itself which made it difficult for the government to act consistently and decisively.[1] Certainly the fundamental causes of the coup are not to be found in the armed forces.

From Liisa North, "The Military in Chilean Politics," *Studies in Comparative International Development* 11, no. 2, copyright © 1976, by Transaction, Inc. Reprinted by permission of the author and Transaction, Inc.

Author's note: Many thanks to Antonio Bandeira, Claudio Duran, J. P. Farrell, Steve Hellman, Abraham Lowenthal, and Herbet de Souza, who provided me with invaluable criticism and comment on the first draft of this paper.

However, to the extent that the analyses of the coup have been made in a lacunae of information concerning those institutions and their interaction with the U.P. government, Allende and his advisors have been faulted with a generally weak and naive policy vis-à-vis the armed forces.

Errors were obviously made by the U.P. government in formulating a general strategy that would have permitted it to remain in power and accomplish the transition to socialism. And errors were made in the tactics pursued vis-à-vis the armed forces. Suggestions concerning the organization of popular militias and dismissal of officers suspected of disloyalty, however, ignore the realities of the Chilean military organizations: their capacity, organization, and zealously guarded professional autonomy concerning promotions, assignments, and dismissals, as well as their monopoly over arms.[2] The formulation of a strategy to prevent professional military organizations from successfully intervening to end a revolutionary process was and is extremely difficult.

The U.P.'s strategy vis-à-vis the armed forces was, of course, part and parcel of its overall strategy to maintain power and implement the transition to socialism. It was generally premised on the possibility of working through the existing institutional structures of the state, given their strength and relative autonomy within the democratic political system of Chile. According to the analysis of Allende's personal political advisor, Joan Garcés, it was more specifically premised on the U.P. government's adherence to constitutional norms, and its capacity to maintain public order and a reasonable amount of economic stability, if not actual growth (Garcés, 1972: 27–50; Martner, 1972:P 135–47). The maintenance of these conditions, along with the broad guarantees and numerous benefits promised to the country's large middle class in the U.P. program,[3] were perceived as necessary for winning over or at least neutralizing that powerful and well-organized sector of the population. Neutralization, of course, signified the prevention of an alliance of the middle class with the large landowners and bourgeois industrialists, who would be spearheading an aggressive opposition in their attempt to maintain control over the means of production. This strategy, heavily dependent on a supportive or neutral middle class, implied the necessity of controlled and disciplined working-class and peasant mobilization in support of the government. Spontaneous and "illegal" mass action would threaten public order and, at a minimum, provide material for powerful antigovernment propaganda to which both the middle class and the armed forces would be very responsive.

Garcés's analysis and the U.P. literature in general demonstrated an acute awareness of the instruments of control available to the state, and the importance of the middle class in the political system. While these issues were extensively and carefully examined, the forms that a disciplined working-class and peasant mobilization would have to take were rather sparsely elaborated. In fact, Garcés limited "social pressure from the bottom" to "specific cases or very concrete objectives" (Garcés, 1972:

35). This suggests that the mobilization of the mass base for a socialist transformation was not perceived as a continuous process that had to be initiated from the moment that the U.P. ascended to power.[4] The implications of this orientation will be taken up after the analysis of the U.P.'s strategy vis-à-vis the military has been completed.

The conditions identified as necessary for obtaining the support or neutrality of significant sectors of the middle class were also those considered necessary for maintaining the loyalty of the officer corps of the armed forces, or at least a large enough number of officers to prevent a successful right-wing coup. In addition, the armed forces shared certain institutional norms and problems which the U.P. government could attempt to utilize for maintaining their loyalty. In any event, a policy of direct confrontation was to be avoided. Although the possibilities of gaining some support within the officer corps and neutralizing the majority were fundamentally dependent on the success of the overall strategy, my primary objective here is to analyze the U.P. strategy vis-à-vis the armed forces.

In order to carry this out, it is necessary to review the known facts concerning the history, officer recruitment patterns, and capacity of Chile's armed forces, among which I include the Carabineros (a militarized national police force), as well as the army, navy, and air force.[5] Given the tradition of nonintervention enjoyed by Chile's armed forces, none has been the object of extensive study. There are only two major works available on their contemporary structure, both limited in scope and information (Joxe, 1970; Hansen, 1967), and many of the key events in the Allende government's interaction with the armed forces remain to be clarified. Of necessity therefore, the analysis presented here is tentative.

Political History of the Chilean Military

Unlike most Latin American military institutions, the Chilean armed forces have had a historical tradition of nonintervention in the political process. Or more precisely, interventions had been infrequent enough to permit the development of a myth, shared by both the military and civilian populations, concerning the neutrality and apoliticism of the armed forces. The last coup prior to September 11, 1973, occurred on September 13, 1932; its goal was the organization of elections to reestablish normal democratic procedures following a period of instability, dictatorship and military conspiracies and interventions which had begun in 1919.

The armed forces' overt political involvement during the period extending from 1919 to 1932 was basically related to the acute economic problems and intense and frequently violent social conflicts which Chile was experiencing at that time. With the spectacular expansion of the nitrate export industry in territories conquered from Peru and Bolivia in the War of the Pacific (1879–83), and the growth of the copper export industry following the turn of the century, Chile experienced a rapid process of social change and capitalist economic development. Domestic industries were established, the size of the state bureaucracy grew quickly, and people moved into cities. By 1920, 46.4 percent of the population lived in urban centres of 2,000 or more; 28 percent lived in cities of 20,000 or more (Germani, 1971; Rouma, 1948). Concurrently, both a significantly large middle class and a working class came into being. Particularly during the second decade of the twentieth century, both classes began to organize (often in conflict and independent of each other) and demand social and political reforms from what were extremely corrupt governments, governments which represented the interests of an oligarchy composed of large landowners, wealthy financiers, merchants, and native mining entrepreneurs allied with foreign investors. The workers' struggle was particularly bitter: in December of 1907, 2,000 men, women, and children were gunned down by the army during a nitrate miners' demonstration at Santa Maria de Iquique; between 1911 and 1920, there were 293 strikes, many of them violently repressed. In addition, the struggle for reform, particularly after World War I, took place in an increasingly deteriorating economic situation, a consequence of the development of synthetic nitrate production elsewhere and the postwar slump.

In this situation, the military organizations (the army in particular) began to conspire seriously in 1919 and finally intervened on September 5, 1924, to support reform programs backed by the middle class and important sectors of the working class.[6] The situation, in a number of superficial respects, paralleled that of the Allende years. The reform candidate who had won the presidency in 1920 was unable to obtain the passage of his program in a Parliament controlled by an oligarchic opposition. Unlike 1973, 1924 saw young army officers intervene to force passage of the reform proposals of the president.[7]

The effect of the military intervention of 1924 and its sequels was to advance the process of middle-class participation and increase representation of its interests in the state apparatus. For the protagonist of the political process which began with the presidential election of 1920 was the middle class; the working class participated in a subordinate role. As middle-class demands were at least minimally satisfied, the governments of the late twenties and early thirties engaged in the repression of working-class organizations and of the Communist party in particular. It was not until the mid-thirties that the working-class organizations began to gain full freedom of operation.

Significantly, the interventionist military institutions of 1919–32 already enjoyed a tradition of apolitical professionalism. And indeed the officers intervened in the political process in 1924 only at the point when a significant number were convinced that civilian politicians were incapable of resolving the crisis. Army officers were particularly concerned about the effects on discipline and morale of the repression in which their institution was repeatedly called to engage. In 1924, these officers therefore requested Parliament to "dispatch the laws demanded by the working class in order to end their anguish which . . . affects the troops who should not be brought into contact with popular agitation" (Bicheno, 1972: 106). Shortly after this intervention, the Carabineros (a part of the army cavalry) were reorganized "into a national police force by integrating the old Carabineros with city police forces" (Hansen, 1967: 88).[8] The army was thereby relieved of duties related to the maintenance of internal order except in major emergencies.

The military conspiracies and interventions of the period extending from 1919 to 1932 were, therefore, fundamentally a response to acute economic, social, and political conflicts. The younger army officers in particular, who since the 1880s had been recruited to an increasing extent from the middle class, intervened to back up the reform demands of the class of their origin in order to establish social peace.

A secondary but nevertheless significant reason for at least the 1919 conspiracy and the open intervention of 1924 related to a number of problems specific to the military institutions. Many officers were mobilized into political action primarily on the basis of professional complaints. These included: the violation of professional military principles of merit and seniority on the part of politicians and members of the elite who had maneuvered to obtain promotions and privileged assignments for their friends and relatives; neglect on the part of politicians in providing funds for equipment; and low salaries as well as the nonpayment of salaries during the months immediately preceding the 1924 coup (Nunn, 1963: 145; Saez Morales, 1934: 19).[9]

Between 1932 and 1970 social conflict in Chile never became acute enough to elicit military intervention. The middle class was fully integrated into the state apparatus during the thirties and forties. The left organizations of the working class (the Communist party, the Socialist party, and the labor organizations) lacked unity until the fifties and engaged primarily in electoral politics, never seriously threatening the power and privileges of the upper and middle classes. In this situation of orderly political competition, some economic growth, and relatively attenuated social conflict, the tradition of military professionalism and apoliticism, of respect for the constitution and democratic process, could be reinstituted and fortified.

During the 41 years prior to Allende's election, the Chilean armed forces did reestablish a strong professional culture which was apolitical to the extent that officers subordinated their own political views to the professional norms of the military institutions, which were legally bound to respect the constitution. According to Hansen, summarizing the statements of 37 retired army generals, "Any breach of the norm of nonparticipation in partisan politics resulted in early retirement. The officer had not only to have no contacts with organized political groups but also had to present an image of political neutrality" (Hansen, 1967: 191). Toleration of deviance from the norm varied, however, depending on whether the deviance was toward the left or the right. While a "strong manifest commitment to any political philosophy . . . endangered an officer's career," overt "radical left" commitments were particularly frowned upon (Hansen, 1967: 191).

The reestablishment of a strong professional culture within the military institutions and the application of sanctions against officers with overt political commitment were, in fact, given particular impetus by three coups which took place in 1932 (North, 1967: 34–37, 74–75; Bicheno, 1972: 115–20). The application of political criteria in promotions and assignments, an unavoidable concomitant of interventions, naturally destabilized career expectations and created resentments. Furthermore, one of the 1932 coups was particularly offensive to the upper and middle-class public: on June 4, Air Force Colonel Marmaduke Grove led a coup which established the "Socialist Republic of Chile." Although Grove and his associates were quickly deposed in another coup (June 16), even his ephemeral success appeared a shocking threat to the propertied classes. By late 1932, the officer corps wanted re-isolation from politics as institutional chaos approached an all time high, and prestige descended to an all time low: "For a matter of weeks, officers were socially ostracized and openly taunted by the public. Large numbers of officers were retired and the military budget for 1933 was drastically cut. In addition, to insure against further intervention, a civilian militia was organized and remained active until 1936" (Hansen, 1967: 59). This militia was formed by the sons of the upper and middle classes, and it was designed to keep officers with radical political perspectives as well as the civilian left in line.

Fundamentally, it was the exercise of strong civilian leadership, capable of moderating social conflict by meeting the major demands of the middle class and by making limited concessions to the working class, that precluded military interventions between 1932 and 1973. However, the internalization of professional norms of political neutrality on the part of officers was also important. It can be argued that the officer corps' ideology during this period was primarily constitutional and professional, although that is a relatively fragile ideology in any society experiencing acute class conflict. Nevertheless, a professional military culture was a reality, i.e., it had significant behavioral consequences.

Although there were no open military interventions into politics between 1932 and the election of Allende, there were a number of conspiracies within the military organizations, primarily in the army. Significantly, those conspiracies were largely based on institutional grievances, which is not to say that the conspiracy leaders (in contrast to most supporters) were lacking in political motivation. A conspiracy in 1939 was definitely fascist oriented, being directed against the Popular Front government, which was supported by the Socialist and Communist parties and led by the Radical party (Bicheno, 1972: 126–27; Joxe, 1970: 78). An incipient conspiracy in 1946 was inspired by Peronism and included some type of participation by a number of Socialist political leaders (Joxe, 1970: 79). A conspiracy in 1948 was inspired by a mixture of corporatist-type claims and Peronist nationalism (Joxe, 1970: 79–80). Peronist ideology again surfaced in conspiracies organized in 1951 and 1955.[10] (The 1955 conspirators were court-martialed in 1956, "accused of conspiracy, lack of discipline and violation of the principle of hierarchy as well as of the principle of apoliticism of the Army" [Joxe, 1970: 81]). The leader of a conspiracy which concluded with a rebellion in 1969, Army General Roberto Viaux, manifested his extreme right-wing political position later; however, in 1969 the support and considerable sympathy that he received within the armed forces was largely based on institutional professional claims (Bicheno, 1972: 133).[11] The numbers of officers involved in most of these conspiracies were apparently small, and upon discovery, the military organizations themselves administered punishment.

The institutional complaints which surfaced in these conspiracies, and particularly in the army, were not mere fabrications to camouflage political goals. After the Second World War, the percentage of the national budget devoted to the armed forces continued to decline, with few interruptions. While all branches of the armed forces felt the squeeze, the army apparently suffered the most as its share of the defense budget dropped from 41–42 percent to 35 percent. "As a result of this double squeeze, the Army's portion of the 1964 budget was only about 40 percent of the prewar level" (Hansen, 1967: 196). This trend had an obvious negative impact on the capacity to maintain equipment and train recruits, as well as on officers' salaries. In the mid-sixties, in comparison to other professional groups, the salaries of army officers

> were extremely low, and were perceived so, not only by officers, but also by middle and upper class civilians. . . . The salary of sub-Lieutenant was as low as that of common laborers. The wives of lieutenants, captains and majors without independent means were generally forced to work to supplement the family income. Often wives employed as secretaries earned more than their officer husbands. The economic difficulties faced by the officer, especially in the lower ranks, were not a question of luxuries, but of decent housing, clothing and an education for their children (Hansen: 1967: 200).[12]

The situation of Carabineros officers was substantially the same, while air force and navy officers' salaries may have been somewhat higher (Duran, 1974).[13]

In 1970, what generalizations might be drawn from this history about the possibilities of military intervention? First, acute economic problems coupled with social and political conflict could very likely set the stage for a military intervention. Second, the major part of the officer corps was apparently constitutionalist, and therefore it could be expected that before the armed forces could agree to intervene, social and political conflict would have to reach crisis proportions. Third, military conspirators, historically, were able to recruit support for themselves not only on the basis of political claims, but also on the basis of institutional professional claims. Fourth, conspiring officers had been "progressives" as frequently as they had been right-wingers. The rationale for calling Peronist-nationalist conspirators "progressive" lies in the fact that significant sectors of Chilean Socialism passed through a Peronist ideological period in the forties and fifties, and as was indicated earlier, Socialist leaders were in contact with Peronist officers.

These generalizations did not apply equally to all branches of the armed forces. Progressive tendencies were significant in the army and the Carabineros; but for reasons to be developed later, they were weak in the air force and almost absent in the navy. Nevertheless, the history of the Chilean armed forces provided a cogent foundation for the U. P. leaders' belief that nationalist and progressive elements existed within the officer corps, and that it would be difficult to provoke the constitutionalist majority into intervention, particularly if U. P. policies responded to the major institutional problems of the armed forces. In other words, there was room for maneuver.

Social Recruitment and Social Relations of the Officer Corps

From the last decade of the nineteenth century, the officer corps of the Chilean army was increasingly recruited from the middle class. By the forties, middle-class dominance in the corps was complete, and during the fifties and sixties, given the declining prestige of the institution, cadets began to be recruited from the lower-middle class also (Hansen, 1967: 210).[14] The only survey data on the social recruitment of army officers, however, are limited to 37 generals retired between 1952 and 1964. Their fathers were businessmen (20 percent), professionals and managers (26 percent), military officers (26 percent), farmers (20 percent), and white collar employees (9 percent) (Hansen, 1967: 172). If the occupations of the fathers of these generals are at all representative of the army officer corps as a whole, the majority were recruited precisely from those social categories which by late 1972 were inviting military intervention to depose Allende, through actions such as their participation in, or support for, the October "bosses' strike."

The officer's class origin, of course, is not the only class factor in his experience. He, as an officer, occupies a middle-class position, and he most frequently marries into his own class or higher. In Chile, as elsewhere, the typical first assignments of officers are in the provinces.

> *Most of the officers' informal contacts . . . were with members of the rural upper class:* landowners, professionals, businessmen and those people in

the provincial towns with "means." . . . Officers in the provinces were accepted as members of the set. They were invited to their social functions and were looked upon (and looked upon themselves) as potential husbands for their daughters.

[Since] the great majority of military posts were located in the provinces [and] as all officers were required to spend a specified period in each rank in a command position, *periodic contacts with the rural upper class were maintained throughout their career.* This continuing association was reflected in the relatively high percentage of the . . . [generals'] in-laws . . . who were engaged in occupational pursuits typical of the rural upper class: agriculture and business (Hansen, 1967: 170, italics added).[15]

More precisely, it was particularly in southern Chile that officers established contacts with the rural upper class, or in other words, members of the country's landowning aristocracy. In the desert north, the professional and business classes with whom the officers interacted, although upper class in local terms, formed part of the middle class in national terms.[16] At the higher ranks an officer spent more time in and around Santiago, where the advanced schools, key garrisons, and headquarters of the army are located. There his civilian social contacts and friendships were established primarily among members of "the new urban middle class: professionals, managers, and bureaucrats" (Hansen, 1967: 177).[17]

In summary, the typical army officer is a member of the middle class in terms of his own occupation and his father's occupation. His close civilian social contacts include the middle class and, to the extent that the data summarized above are representative, the provincial upper class. Even limited systematic information on the social origins of the officer corps of the Carabineros, air force, and navy is lacking. However, observers familiar with Chilean political history and social structure tend to agree that Carabineros officers, to a greater extent than army officers, are the sons of lower-middle-class families, and even working-class families, while the air force and the navy recruit more officers from the upper-middle class. These two latter branches of the armed forces apparently enjoy more prestige, given their more advanced technology, the possible transferability of the technical training to attractive civilian occupations, and perhaps greater possibilities for travel. The navy, in particular, has an aristocratic tradition, and even today recruits quite a few of its officers from the upper class.

While the differences in the social origins of the officers in the four branches of the Chilean armed forces are not dramatic (all essentially recruit from the middle class), they may be significant enough to produce variations in fundamental social and political attitudes, especially if parallel differences in marriage patterns and civilian social contacts also exist. It is probably not pure coincidence that Allende found least support among navy and air force officers, although class alone may not provide a complete explanation.

With increasing political tension, social conflict, and economic chaos, especially after the October 1972 "bosses' strike," both the Unidad Popular and the opposition began to identify the struggle taking place in Chile as a class war (De Souza, 1973a: 61–82: 1973b: *passim*).[18] In this situation, the conflict within the officer corps between fundamental social and political orientations (which, of course, correspond with the predominant orientations of the officer's class of origin and social contact) and professional norms of nonintervention was bound to become acute. Thus the U.P. strategy of wagering on the constitutionalism of the armed forces, of attempting to neutralize and/or win over the officer corps to permit the dismantling of the capitalist system, was problematic.

However, to argue that the September 11 coup was inevitable due to the class nature of the officer corps is precisely to ignore the acuteness of the conflict which did take place inside the armed forces. Professional norms of nonintervention were strongly established, and despite the significance of the social-class relationships described, most officers spent most of their time with other officers and/or recruits. Among the 37 retired generals studied by Hansen, friendships with other officers far outnumbered those with civilians. Asked to identify the occupations of their five best friends during their final years of active service, they named 192 fellow officers compared to 36 civilians (Hansen, 1967: 178). While the friendship pattern indicates relative isolation from civilian social contacts, it did not imply isolation from the general, or even a particular, ideological environment: officers were not constrained in their choice of reading material, but until sometime in the sixties, only *El Mercurio,* the newspaper which articulated the position of Chile's landowning and industrial elite, was available in the officers' clubs. Subsequently the Radical Democratic *La Tercera,* popularly identified as a "minor *Mercurio,*" was ordered (Duran, 1974). The friendship pattern did, however, imply the officers' relative isolation within a particular type of institution with its own traditions and norms, and therefore the possibility of maintaining some distance between a unique professional culture and civilian social conflict and debate.

Furthermore, during their careers officers experienced significant contradictions which could attenuate class loyalties. In the army, the first assignments in the provinces

> placed young officers in intimate and continuous social relations with members of the lower class. . . . Often the conscripts looked upon him as a patron or father, and strong interpersonal ties developed. The young officer noted that in many cases *the new conscripts had been badly treated.* Many were *undernourished, unkempt and ill. Most had little education.* . . . Contact with conscripts and other lower class personnel continued throughout the career, although generally on a progressively less direct and intimate basis (Hansen, 1967: 170, italics added).

These experiences, of course, could produce within the officer merely a sense of superiority and contempt for the lower classes. However, in the context of underdevelopment, coupled with increasing political debate concerning problems of "modernization" and reform, they could also lead to some questioning of a system which brought into the army recruits who could hardly be expected to perform well as soldiers.

Military participation in national development programs also brought army officers into direct contact with problems of economic growth, manpower training, social problems, etc. Military civic action programs were controversial within the army officer corps. At least a significant minority was opposed to them on the grounds of their incompatability with the military's unique defense functions. However, a majority of the retired generals interviewed by Hansen favored increasing the army's participation in national development programs, and almost half of those in favor could be described as politically progressive (Hansen, 1967: 236).[19]

The contradictions and both real and potential divisions within the army were therefore significant. A similar situation apparently existed within the Carabineros, whose officers, often as a function of their repressive role, were also in frequent contact with the day-to-day problems of the poorer sectors of the population. The air force and the navy, with their greater isolation from the social and economic problems of the country, experienced fewer internal conflicts. (The officer corps of the navy, in particular, was practically united in its opposition to Unidad Popular.)

Thus the cumulative impact of a number of relatively minor differences in social origins, civilian social contacts, and career experiences apparently created significant differences in sociopolitical attitudes among the officer corps of the four branches of the armed forces and within each branch.[20] The Unidad Popular leaders were aware of these differences, as were the officers themselves. The U. P. strategy of attempting to neutralize and/or win over the officer corps was therefore not only based on reliance on the armed forces' constitutionalism. It was also based on an analysis of the actual and potential cleavages within and among the armed forces.

Military Preparedness and U.S. Military Aid

There are some discrepancies in the data concerning the size of the Chilean armed forces, which may result from differences in the base years used. According to two reports published in 1967 and 1968, the number of men and officers integrated into the army, navy, and air force totalled 46,000. According to two other reports published in 1967 and 1973, the total for the three services reached 60,000 (Joxe, 1970: 95; IDOC, 1973: 12). The strength of the Carabineros is variously reported as 24,000 and 30,000 (Joxe, 1970, 97; IDOC, 1973: 12). Whether the 46,000 or 60,000 figure is taken as the correct one, the ratio of military personnel to total population in Chile is among the highest the Latin America, second or third to Cuba (Joxe, 1970: 95). If the Carabineros are included in the calculation, Chile definitely ranks second (Joxe, 1970: 98). Given the professional military training and organization, as well as the level of armament of this national police force, there are legitimate grounds for their inclusion, although it must be remembered that a part of Carabineros personnel are engaged in activities such as traffic control. Whatever the precise figures and ratios may be, the evidence argues for a relatively high level of military strength, particularly in view of the fact that Chile (unlike Cuba) has not been faced with a foreign threat in recent times, or (unlike her continental neighbors) with a domestic guerilla problem.

In addition to the relatively high manpower strength, the military institutions of Chile are well organized, well trained and well disciplined. Those institutions, for example, could hardly be compared to the corrupt, disorganized, and demoralized armed forces of Batista's Cuba (Gonzalez, 1974: 89–90).[21] And despite the institutional complaints of the army officers, the military organizations as a whole are quite well equipped, having a strong counterinsurgency power and high degree of mobility. For example, the air force is well equipped with troop and materiel transport craft, and its light bomber squadron of B-26 Invaders is particularly suited for low-level tight-pattern bombing, in urban areas if necessary (IDOC, 1973: 12).[22]

The high level of training and equipment was to a significant extent maintained through the United States Military Assistance Program (MAP). In 1952, Chile signed a bilateral mutual defense assistance pact with the United States, thereby becoming eligible for MAP aid under the Mutual Security Act of 1951 (Klare, 1972: 276–77). Until the Cuban Revolution, MAP aid, in the logic of the cold war, was "made available for the modernization of Latin American armies in order to strengthen the hemisphere's defenses against external aggression" (Klare, 1972: 276). With the review of U.S. military strategy following Castro's victory and the radicalization of the Cuban revolutionary government, "funds for counterinsurgency training and equipment were first made available to Latin American armies in . . . 1963" (Klare, 1972: 279). Thus in 1968, for example, 76 percent of the military aid the Department of Defense requested for Latin America was to be spent "on hardware and services related to counterinsurgency" (Klare, 1972: 279). Between 1953 and 1966 Chile, a peaceful country, ranked "second only to Brazil among Latin American countries as a recipient of U.S. military aid . . . both in terms of military grants and delivery of surplus stocks" (*Monthly Review,* 1971: 10; NACLA, 1972: 53; Joxe, 1970: 99–110). And on a per capita basis, Chile received more U.S. military assistance than any other Latin American country. During the same period, this aid amounted to 9.7 percent of Chile's total defense expenditures (Joxe, 1970: 103, Klare, 1972: 281).[23] After 1963, although precise figures are lacking, it can be assumed that most of this aid, in line with the general pattern of military aid to Latin

America, was directed toward increasing the counterinsurgency potential of the Chilean armed forces.

The United States has also invested heavily in the training of Chilean military personnel, primarily officers.[24] Between 1950 and 1968, 2,064 Chileans were trained in the United States and 549 on Canal Zone bases (Joxe, 1970: 101),[25] and during the sixties, the U.S. maintained an annual average of 48 military personnel in Chile (NACLA, 1972: 53). In line with the post-Cuban Revolution U.S. military strategy, the "training programs [were] designed . . . to emphasize the importance of counterguerilla operations" (Klare, 1972: 298).

There were variations in the amount of U.S. aid and training provided to the different branches of the armed forces. During a five-year period in the sixties, the favored aid recipients were the navy and the air force (Hansen, 1967: 203). From 1959 to 1969, the average annual percent of total armed forces personnel programmed for training on U.S. bases was .3 for the army, 1.1 for the navy and 1.4 for the air force (Kemp, 1970: 4). Although "during the 1960s the proportional amount of army training given to Chile by the United States [was] one of the lowest in Latin America" (Kemp, 1970: 29) and considerably lower than air force and navy training, the Chilean army benefited from the presence of a large number of U.S. Mobile Training Teams (MTTs). In fact, from 1961 to 1967 "the levels of MTTs remained considerably higher by overall Latin American standards than the levels of direct training" (Kemp, 1970: 29).[26] Also, the number of army personnel programmed for training in the United States rose steeply in 1968, and although it declined somewhat in 1969, that year's figure remained above the levels of 1959–67 (Kemp, 1970: 29, 31).

What is the significance of these trends in U.S. training and assistance? Over the decade 1959–69 the greatest continuous impact of U.S. aid and training was apparently felt by the air force and the navy. Since this was the case, the already-identified antipathy toward the U.P. and the reactionary attitudes of navy officers, in particular, as well as sectors of the air force officer corps, could easily have been fortified by more extensive interaction with their U.S. counterparts.[27] The steep rise in the training of army personnel during 1968 and 1969, which was also accompanied by the purchase of helicopters,[28] may well have been based on a political calculation on the part of U.S. military advisors as well as Chilean officers. For by 1968 it was becoming clear that the 1970 presidential elections might produce a left-wing victory, given the increasing conflict between the Christian Democratic and National parties, and the consequent improbability of their unity behind a single candidate. And after all, it was primarily the ground forces that would have to deal with a popular revolt. (In this respect, the United States also had helped to prepare the Carabineros. During the sixties, the United States began to provide significant amounts of aid to this militarized police force, which received 2.4 million dollars between 1961 and 1970 through the Public Safety Program

[NACLA, 1972: 53; Joxe, 1970:98]. The Carabineros, of course, had been the main instrument of internal repression since the 1920s.)

The rather impressive level of preparedness of the Chilean armed forces has led several observers to argue that the hybrid middle-class/elite Chilean governments of the last decades have maintained a particularly large, and well-equipped and trained military apparatus as the last line of defense against a revolutionary threat, a threat based on the increasing electoral and organizational power of the working class. The same reasoning, the argument continues, underlies U.S. policy (*Monthly Review,* 1971: 12; Joxe, 1970: 110–11). There is little doubt concerning the validity of this argument vis-à-vis the United States. However, the argument is somewhat problematic vis-à-vis the post World War II governments of Chile.

Certainly the middle class and elites expected the armed forces to defend them in the case of a revolutionary threat. But apparently they felt secure enough in their capacity to control the political process and the state to reduce military spending, and not to respond to the institutional complaints concerning salaries and equipment which kept emerging from the army, in particular. In terms of manpower, since the forties, "the long-term growth of the military has not even kept pace with that of the general population" (Hansen, 1967: 198).[29] The share of defense (army, navy, and air force) in the national budget went down from 18 percent in 1948 to 9 percent in 1968 (Joxe, 1970: 87–88). Joxe presents a table on military spending over a five-year period which covers four years of the Conservative Alessandri administration and one year of the Christian Democratic Frei administration. (See Table 1.) Although military spending as a share of the national budget continued its downward trend, given the rapidly increasing amount of state spending (particularly under the Christian Democratic administration), Frei, at least during the first year of his government, significantly increased the absolute amounts of military expenditure. The Carabineros and police were particularly favored, the army least so. During the last year of his government, Frei was, in fact, confronted with a mutiny over salaries in the army. As late as May of 1973, Joxe still argued that the evolution of the military budget prior to 1970 had "certainly not contributed to aligning [at least] the army strongly to the forces of the traditional right" (Joxe, 1973: 20, 22).[30]

The U.P. was thus faced with highly professional armed forces with an impressive capability for internal repression. Their ideological formation throughout the sixties had been strongly influenced by U.S. counterinsurgency training. In general, this training no doubt reinforced anticommunist and antisocialist attitudes within the officer corps. However, the constitutionalist tradition was also strong; the majority of officers, like the civilian population, believed and took pride in Chile's uniquely democratic history in Latin America. In addition, there was dissatisfaction with the manner in which both the Conservative Alessandri and Christian Democratic Frei administrations had dealt not only with the internal problems of

Table 1. Military Spending 1961–1965 (base 100:1961)

	1961	1962	1963	1964	1965
Police and Carabineros	100	103.7	90.4	90.6	109.2
Defense (total)	100	97.3	89.0	87.4	97.8
Army	100	96.3	83.0	82.1	82.9
Navy	100	98.5	97.1	92.3	107.1
Air Force	100	96.3	79.2	84.2	99.3

Source: Joxe, 1970:97.

the military institutions, but also with the social and economic problems of the country (Farrell, 1974).[31]

The U.P. Strategy vis-à-vis the Armed Forces in Theory

Summarizing from the information presented above, it is possible to identify the factors that allowed U.P. strategists to believe that a rightist military intervention might be prevented. They were: (1) the constitutionalist professional norms of the majority of the officer corps (to repeat, this is not to say that the officers were apolitical, but to emphasize that historically they had tended to subordinate, and perhaps would continue to subordinate, their political predilections to principles of constitutionalism and nonintervention); (2) the presence of nationalist and progressive officers, particularly within the army, and therefore the difficulty of organizing a right-wing coup without precipitating a split in the armed forces; (3) the possibility of using the satisfaction of institutional demands as a tactic for reducing pressure for intervention.

Operating against the above were the following factors: (1) the middle-class social affiliations and fundamentally conservative or centrist political attitudes of the majority of officers, which acute social and economic conflict had historically brought to the surface; (2) the ideological implications of professional military training and education with their emphases on order, hierarchy, and authority; (3) the presence of clearly reactionary elements in the officer corps; (4) the ideological influence of U.S. training and continued association of Chilean officers with their U.S. counterparts.

In terms of the general political analysis of the military, Allende and his advisors were also convinced (and I believe correctly so) that any attempt on the part of the government to organize armed militias of workers and peasants, or otherwise clearly step outside the bounds of legality, would have quickly resulted in giving the upper hand to the reactionaries in the officer corps. For it must be stressed that the progressive officers who supported and cooperated with Allende were also constitutionalist, and it was on the basis of *legalistic and professional arguments* that they could influence officers with no sympathy for the U.P. government to remain neutral. This fact had another implication: any abnormal interference by the executive in military promotion and assignment patterns would also redound to the benefit of reactionaries, for such interference could easily be identified as an assault on the professional integrity of the military. Within normal accepted routine, however, Allende could exert limited influence on promotions; generals were nominated by the president and "political reliability was thus an important [and accepted] criterion at this level" (Hansen, 1967: 191).

Respect for the legality of the existing system and the internal autonomy of the military institutions were identified as a fundamental, but by no means sufficient condition for maintaining the loyalty of the armed forces. Public order and a modicum of economic stability were also required, as the strategy vis-à-vis the military was part and parcel of the strategy toward the middle class. The officer corps could hardly be expected to repress middle-class protest (no matter what forms it took) over a sustained period. And neither the middle classes nor the officer corps could be expected to easily countenance a lengthy economic crisis or repeated disturbance of the public order through illegal takeovers of land or factories, or for that matter, mass demonstrations calling for the destruction of the existing legal order. Therefore, the necessity of controlled and orderly mass mobilization, and the discouragement of spontaneity (Garcés, 1972, *passim*).[32] Thus, among the reasons for not encouraging continued mobilization on the basis of the popular organizations which spontaneously emerged as a response to the October 1972 "bosses' strike," military pressure figured.

The holding of mass mobilization in check, for which the U.P. has come under severe scrutiny by its critics on the left, formed an integral part of the strategy. It was a part of the attempt to retain the support of progressive officers, to hold the effective allegiance of the professional constitutionalist majority, and to isolate the interventionist right. The U.P. wanted to avoid engaging in any action that might throw the majority constitutionalist center of the officer corps into the arms of the reactionary right. Conversely, the Allende government expected to be able to maintain the loyalty of the constitutionalists if illegal or violent action was instigated by reactionary officers and political leaders.

In general terms I believe that U.P. analysis of the situation within the armed forces was sound. It required a great degree of flexibility and decisiveness in its implementation, rapid adjustment in response to the quickly deteriorating social, political, and economic situations, particularly after the October 1972 crisis and the attempted coup of June 29. Unfortunately, U.P. policy manifested a certain "inflexibility" and a serious lack of decisiveness: as it became clear that most of the middle class had moved into opposition, the U.P. was not able to agree on an alternative strategy that faced up to this fact.

The U.P. Policy vis-à-vis the Armed Forces in Practice

The analysis of the military made by U.P. strategists and Allende led them to take action to satisfy the institutional demands of the armed forces (including the retention of close ties with the U.S. military establishment), to respect the internal promotions and assignment patterns, and to integrate the armed forces (the army in particular) not only into a few national development projects, but into the day-to-day operations of vital sectors of the public administration and the economy.

The U.P. government approved salary increases for the armed forces, the largest for the lower and middle ranks. The armed forces also benefitted from new housing projects and the acquisition of new equipment, and top-ranking officers acquired cars specially imported for them (*Latin America*, 1972b: 386; Joxe, 1973: 2029). Figures on military spending under Allende are not available. However, there is no doubt that it went up. In addition, the Chilean armed forces continued to receive grants, equipment, and training from the United States. Military aid was, in fact, the only type of aid that the United States gave to Chile during Allende's presidency. In 1971, for example, the United States granted the air force five million dollars for the acquisition of transport aircraft and paratroop equipment (NACLA, 1972: 53). The United States also continued to participate in various joint maneuvers with the Chilean armed forces and attend their celebrations. This policy of building up the armed forces, of course, involved serious risks, since increased strength could be used to destroy the U.P. government as well as uphold it.

While respecting formal regulations concerning promotions, Allende had "safe generals" as commanders of all the branches of the military by the beginning of 1972 (Joxe, 1973: 2029). Joxe describes them rather intriguingly as "favorable to the U.P., or rather to the class alliance which attempts to restore an essential role to the non-monopolistic bourgeoisie" (Joxe, 1973: 2029). The meaning and implications of this characterization of "safe generals" are not entirely clear in Joxe's analysis; in fact, some of these generals supported the September 11 coup, while others opposed it.

Finally, the U.P. government integrated members of the armed forces into the planning and management of key sectors of the economy.

> For the first time in Chilean history, representatives of the military participate[d] directly in the production of goods and services. Brigadier General Pedro Palacios Cameron was named (December, 1970) director of the Chuquicamata Copper Company, and representatives of the Army, Navy and Air Force [were] on the national production boards of the copper, iron and nitrate companies. Military representatives [were] part of Odeplan, the National Planning Organization, which . . . [had] cabinet status. Further, the U.P. . . . included the military in its development activities in the four southern provinces of Cautin, Malleco, Valdivia and Osorno. Military men

participate[d] in the distribution in the "one-half liter of milk" program; in the planning of the Third U.N. Conference on Trade and Development, which [was] held in April 1972 in Santiago; and in the government agency responsible for developing national sports (NACLA, 1972: 52).[33]

This account of military participation in economic management and administration in general could be much extended.

What were the consequences of this policy? Little accurate information is available. However, some observers have argued that on the whole it had a positive effect on the armed forces' support for U.P. Officers involved in the food distribution program, for example, became acutely aware of the ways in which the black market operations of the middle class and the political right were sabotaging the economy. In one exceptional case, a young officer who had been involved in the government's economic programs resigned from the army in order to better aid in the achievement of U.P. goals by helping to organize the *cordones industriales* (Bandeira, 1974). The overall effects of officer integration into economic management and public administration, however, were contradictory. Certainly some progressive officers already favorable to expanding military civic-action programs responded positively, but officers adamantly opposed to expanding military participation outside very narrowly defined limits were not lacking, even in the army. Their reaction was highly negative. In particular, "stories of army officers being actively engaged in the mass mobilization movement" were seen "as an attempt by the extreme left wing of the Allende government to seriously violate . . . professional norms" (Farrell, 1974). Anxiety concerning the U.P. government's capacity and commitment to maintaining the professional integrity of the armed forces even affected "officers who were neutral or, indeed, supporters of Allende" (Farrell, 1974). Furthermore, the participation of officers in public administration and economic management not only acquainted them with the negative consequences of the black market, U.S. actions, etc.; it also brought them into immediate touch with the "administrative inefficiencies and ineptitudes" (Farrell, 1974) of the government. Finally, it remains to be clarified whether it was not primarily the progressive officers who were incorporated into national development programs, thereby leaving officers neutral or opposed to U.P. in command of troops.

Whatever the effect on officers were in terms of increased support or withdrawal of support from Allende, it is certain that the incorporation policy gave control, or partial control, of important enterprises and activities to military personnel, and provided them with experience that would make the future institution of a military government easier. Thus, this policy also had its double edge.

Military penetration into the state apparatus also took forms not foreseen in the original strategy. As conflict between the U.P. and various opposition groups reached crisis proportions, becoming violent in various provinces (e.g., over land reform), those provinces were declared Emergency Zones (De Souza, 1974). According to Chilean law an Emergency Zone was a virtual mini-military dictatorship: the military commander of the area took over all normal civilian political functions and could name military personnel to manage critical sectors of the local administration. As the number and duration of the Emergency Zones increased in the course of Allende's presidency, more and more officers had to confront and deal with the entire range of economic, social, and political problems and conflicts in their areas of operation. The military takeovers in the Emergency Zones were "qualitatively similar to a coup" (De Souza, 1974): the military could use all means necessary to maintain public order.

Furthermore, whereas the president could choose the officers to be appointed to nationalized industries, planning agencies, etc., the commanders of units in particular provinces were designated by the military, and the executive's control over their manner of operation was severely limited. Thus the military in many areas became increasingly autonomous in the exercise of power. It should also be remembered that there were extensive social contacts between officers and members of the landed rural upper class in the southern provinces, and between officers and members of the business and professional middle class in the northern provinces as well as Santiago. As landowners in particular, and business and professional groups to a lesser extent, became increasingly threatened by U.P.'s reform measures, to act within the confines and spirit of U.P. policies must, of necessity, have become increasingly problematic for large numbers of officers; in fact, they increasingly acted in contradiction to those policies, particularly in the south, where the postcoup repression was especially harsh (*Latin America,* 1974: 149).

In addition to the military presence in the national bureaucracy and in the Emergency Zones, following the October 1972 "bosses' strike," the military entered the cabinet. In fact, "the key . . . which . . . ended the strike that . . . brought the country to the brink of paralysis, was the appointment to . . . [the] cabinet of senior officers from the three branches of the armed services" (*Latin America,* 1972a: 353). Officers, although not the same ones in all ministries, remained in the cabinet until the parliamentary elections of March. They again reentered the cabinet in August with the second middle-class/entrepreneurs' strike, which was begun by the truck owners on July 26.

Thus by September 1973, the Allende government was virtually a captive of the armed forces, which were or had been involved at all levels in the country's crisis as managers of enterprises, as bureaucrats in the national administration, and as political leaders in the Emergency Zones and in the cabinet. By September political debate in the officer corps had been open for months, and divisions were profound. Allende and the U.P. leadership still calculated on a split within the armed forces if a right-wing coup were attempted. They expected support from army and Carabineros officers in particular.

The Strategy of the Opposition vis-à-vis the Armed Forces and the Breakdown of the Constitutionalist Majority

The extreme right had been attempting to provoke a military coup from the moment that Allende was elected. Before Allende's inauguration, extreme right-wing elements kidnapped and, through a blunder, assassinated the army's commander-in-chief, General René Schneider, in the expectation that the left would be blamed for the attack and that the officer corps would unite to prevent Allende's ascension to power. Despite the participation of the commander-in-chief of the navy and the air force, the commander of the Santiago division of the army and the director of the Carabineros, the plot failed. Although General Schneider's personally strong constitutionalist commitment, well known as the "Schneider Doctrine," was important in defusing the plot, his views would not have prevented an extension of the conspiracy if the majority of the officer corps had not shared his position (Garcés, 1974a: 20–23). The conditions for a successful right-wing coup did not yet exist within the armed forces or within the civilian political arena. In terms of the objectives of the right, the assassination backfired. For the moment at least, it solidified the majority of the officer corps' resolve to respect the election mandate, for military investigators were able to ascertain the culpability of the extreme right. It also allowed the government to eliminate a few militant reactionaries from the officer corps, although by no means all. Several other conspiracies were were discovered during Allende's presidency.

With the failure of the initial attempts to provide a coup, the opposition to the U.P. turned to all forms of parliamentary and legal obstructionism to prevent the implementation of the U.P. program. It also turned to the systematic organization of economic chaos, a task in which it was aided by U.S. policy, to prepare the ground for an eventual coup. The "bosses' strike" of October 1972 had the overthrow of the government as its ultimate objective. However, with the entrance of the military into the cabinet, opposition tactics were toned down as both the National party and the Christian Democrats began to prepare for the March parliamentary elections. They expected to obtain a two-thirds majority, which would have allowed them to impeach Allende. Instead, the U.P. gained seats in Congress, its popular vote (despite the extremely difficult economic situation) reaching 44 percent, an increase of approximately 8 percent over the 1970 vote for Allende. With the possibility of electorally defeating the government eliminated, the opposition turned again to tactics intended to provoke a coup, of which the strikes beginning on July 26 were the last major and successful act.

Prior to this last assault on the U.P., a premature coup took place on June 29. It was premature in the sense that its right-wing organizers in the armed forces were not yet fully prepared; they did not have enough officers from the increasingly diminishing and wavering constitutionalist sector willing to support them, and (probably most important) Allende supporters still remained in key positions in the military hierarchy, particularly in Santiago. Most prominent and respected among them was General Carlos Prats, commander-in-chief of the army. However, by that time the officer corps was rapidly becoming more and more willing to support a right-wing coup, or at least not to oppose one.

The attitude changes taking place in the officer corps were fundamentally related to the general intensification of class conflict following the March elections. A total stalemate had been reached. Within the existing parliamentary system, the U.P. could not fully implement and rationalize its social and economic reforms without non-U.P. support. The opposition could not legally remove the president, but it could continue to maintain a chaotic situation in which class polarization would become more and more acute as the economy, already in a critical state for more than a year, continued to deteriorate. Furthermore, U.P. reforms in the process of implementation or discussion were seriously menacing the economic and social status of petit bourgeois sectors: agricultural marketing and purchasing cooperatives of necessity implied the elimination of middle men— small and medium as well as large merchandising operations; a state-operated trucking corporation implied the elimination of significant numbers of private operators. Those sectors of the middle class not adversely affected by U.P. reforms were ready to be convinced that they would be in the near future. In the logic of this process, the Christian Democratic party, the most important middle-class political organization, which had already been calling for and organizing "civil disobedience" since early 1972, redoubled its opposition with, of course, the aid of the United States. Thus by May and June of 1973 not only the landowners and the bourgeoisie, but also most of the middle class were neither supportive nor neutral; they were in strident opposition to the government. This, of course, had a profound impact on the officer corps.

In addition to the intensification of class conflict, the officer corps was particularly agitated by two phenomena which, although manifestations of the basic class conflict, were not intrinsic to it. One, the U.P.-proposed educational reform, was also agitating the middle class. The other, MIR (Movimiento de Izquierda Revolucionaria) and left Socialist proselytization among soldiers, was specific to the military institutions. The educational reform was identified by the opposition as a totalitarian move to control the minds of *their* children: the text of the proposal, with its avowed commitment to the creation of a new man, fed and inflamed the fears of the upper and middle classes, and along with them, the officer corps (Farrell, 1974).[34] The opposition press (*El Mercurio* in particular) organized a veritable propaganda war against the U.P. government on this issue. However, it was left-wing attempts at the penetration of the armed forces that produced reactions among officers that "ranged from extreme unease over to substantial anger, if not outright fear" (Farrell, 1974).[35]

Since not only the MIR but left-wing Socialists, who formed part of the U.P. coalition, were identified by the military as responsible for proselytizing among conscripts, by extension the president was also held responsible. But neither the impact of the educational reform nor left-wing proselytizing should be isolated as "explanations" for the coup (Alexander, 1974: 4).[36] They must be analyzed in the context of the generalized and increasingly violent class conflict that permeated Chilean society by mid-1973, and the lack of coherent and unified political direction on the part of the U.P. government and leadership. Officers were not only becoming convinced that Allende would or could not maintain the professional integrity of the armed forces, but also that he could no longer control the political, social, and economic process underway.

A Reactionary Coup: Was It Inevitable?

Despite the already weak position of the government within the officer corps at the time of the June 29 attempted coup, its failure created a situation in which the U.P. could possibly have taken the type of offensive action that would either have preserved and solidified the government, or provoked a split within the armed forces leading to the civil war, but not to the massacre of the left which has taken place. For high-ranking officers within the progressive group then argued that the moment was appropriate for purging the active right-wing elements from the military institutions. In addition, the attempted coup had provoked a resurgence of popular mobilization and organization. The U.P. masses were demanding, and willing to support forceful action on the part of the president. Progressive officers, for their part, were willing to receive support from the unions: although a workers' military *organization* hardly existed, many workers were, in fact, armed by June (De Souza, 1974; Garcés, 1974a: 31–54; 1974b).

The September 11 coup organizers themselves have indicated that the situation following the June 29 uprising was critical for them (Kandell, 1973: 24). During the coup attempt, hundreds of officers indicated their willingness to support the government. And within the U.P.'s strategic analysis of military policy, the purge would have been appropriate; i.e., the attempted coup was an illegal, unconstitutional act on the part of the right and as such provided grounds for offensive action.[37]

The events following the June 29 revolt, and the reasons for not attempting a purge are not entirely clear. Allende's own politically cautious attitude and his profound fear of civil war were certainly a factor. Divisions within the U.P. coalition also played their role. Apparently, for some time before the June 29 uprising, Allende and his advisors had been considering the necessity of developing structures that would have allowed loyal officers to coordinate their actions with workers' organizations. However, this required a tactical unity which did not exist in the U.P.

(Garcés, 1974a: 43). In particular, the left in the coalition distrusted the officers and argued for relying on armed workers. Thus the lack of structures for coordinated action that would have channeled effective and directed mass support to loyal officers may have inhibited Allende from taking the risks of forceful action against what was by then a fairly large group of officers involved in conspiracy.

The lack of forceful action at that time, however, gave the initiative to the right, both inside and outside the armed forces. As a consequence, both the military and civilian supporters of the U.P. were demoralized. And the demoralization became worse in the following weeks as both groups were essentially left without political direction (Touraine, 1973; *passim*). Some factories were converted to the production of armaments, and Communist party members, at least, were directed to obtain arms.[38] However, U.P. action during the months of July and August, on the basis of available descriptions, appears to have been particularly uncoordinated, indeed, even chaotic.

Meanwhile, the actions of the military and civilian right were increasingly well coordinated. Key U.P. supporters in the armed forces, General Prats most important among them, were maneuvered into resignations and retirements (Garcés, 1974a: 48–51). The military searched factories and working class districts for arms—apparently well informed about where to find them. The coup organizers coordinated their actions with civilian fascist and right-wing groups, while the economy was brought to virtual chaos through strikes organized by businessmen's associations and by hundreds of violent acts of sabotage. Finally, Christian Democratic leaders began to openly invite military intervention.

At the end of August, Allende personally decided to implement his earlier proposals involving structures to coordinate the actions of loyal officers and workers' organizations (Garcés, 1974a: 44). But it was too late. The U.P. no longer had control over the situation, the group of officers involved in the organization of coordination with workers was infiltrated, and the majority of the officer corps could now be convinced to support the coup, or at least not to oppose it.

Miliband has summarized well the military dynamic following the June 29 coup:

> People who are thus and thus at one time, who are or are not willing to do this or that, *change* under the impact of rapidly moving events. . . . Thus conservative but constitutionally-minded army men, in certain situations, become just this much more conservative-minded; and this means that they cease to be constitutionally-minded. The obvious question is what it is that brings about the shift. In part, no doubt, it lies in the worsening "objective" situation; in part also, in the pressure generated by conservative forces. But to a very large extent, it lies in the position adopted, and seen to be adopted, by the government of the day. . . . The Allende administration's weak response to the attempted coup of June 29, its steady retreat before the

conservative forces (and the military) in the ensuing weeks . . . all this must have had a lot to do with the fact that the enemies of the regime in the armed forces . . . grew "more and more numerous." In these matters, there is one law which holds: the weaker the government, the bolder its enemies, *and* the more numerous they become day by day (Miliband, 1974: 463).

Even in the crisis situation of August, it was apparently not an easy task to convince officers to support the coup. According to officers engaged in the plotting,

The greatest obstacle . . . was the armed forces' 40-year tradition of political neutrality: "I would have pulled my hair out for teaching my students for all those years that the armed forces must never rebel against the constitutional government," said an officer who formerly taught history at a military academy. "It took a long time to convince officers that there was no other way out" (Kandell, 1973: 23–24).

In fact, many officers were never convinced. During the day and night before the coup, the right-wing officers carried out their own purge within the armed forces. According to their initial declarations, only 50 officers were arrested (Kandell, 1973: 24), a statement belied by the fact that 57 air force officers alone have been tried for resisting the coup. And the air force officer corps had fewer U.P. supporters within it than the army. According to other sources, "several hundred" officers were executed or arrested in the purge; "some sources speak of between 2,000 and 3,000 members of the armed forces and police losing their lives in the coup before the coup" (*Latin America,* 1973: 357).

In summary, military involvement in the process set into motion with the election of Allende was unavoidable, but a successful reactionary coup on September 11 was by no means inevitable. In the light of the history of the Chilean armed forces and factors related to their organization and strength, the strategy vis-à-vis the military of those within the U.P. who most consistently supported Allende was certainly problematic but basically sound; the conditions for a civilian armed uprising simply did not exist in Chile, and the government therefore had to maintain significant support and neutrality within the officer corps in order to maintain itself in power. While the strategy vis-à-vis the military was basically sound, it was tied to an overly inflexible general strategic orientation, involving the maintenance of middle class support and a lack of emphasis on mass organization. Because the necessity of forceful and continuous mass organization was not recognized by important sectors within the U.P. coalition, the coalition was incapable of arriving at a tactical unity that would have permitted it to counter the right-wing and fascist offensive. Allende's proposals concerning the coordination of loyal officers with workers' organizations could have been a step in the right direction. But in order to be successful, it needed forceful parallel action in the civilian political arena. In this respect, Miliband's critique concerning the lack of "a network of organs of power, parallel to and complementing the state power, and constituting a solid infrastructure for the *timely* 'mobilization of the masses' and the effective direction of its actions" is apropos (Miliband, 1974: 472).

In order to have effective structures of parallel power when the system reached a crisis, it was necessary to consistently pursue their organization from the moment that the government was inaugurated. I believe that this could have been done in ways that would not have precipitated a coup. In other words, a somewhat different overall strategy did not necessarily imply abandoning the policies identified as necessary for maintaining a maximum of military support. Mass organization did not have to involve unconstitutional action, disturbance of public order, or immediate arming of workers, the conditions identified by Allende and his advisors as the precipitators of a coup by a united officer corps. The actions of loyal officers after June 29 also indicate that when a crisis was reached, they were willing to act with and arm workers' organizations *to defend the system as it was legally constituted*. The possibility of pursuing this strategy, however, was made difficult by the divisions within the U.P. For the left in the coalition it would have involved abandoning unrealistic assumptions about soldiers with arms deserting en masse, and accepting the necessity of close cooperation with the progressive sector of the officer corps, as well as the fact that the armed forces could not be confronted by a mass insurrection in the conditions that prevailed in Chile (Garcés, 1974a: *passim*). For the moderates it would have involved an acceptance of the fact that in the long run a major portion of the middle class would *not* remain neutral—the logic of U.P. reforms in favor of the working classes, both urban and rural, of necessity involved a negation of the interests of significant sectors of the middle class, which would not be willing to compromise on what they identified as the sine qua nons for maintaining their social and economic status. If this had been recognized, the need for structures of parallel power would have appeared more urgent.

Of course, it can also be argued that the U.P. made serious political and propaganda errors which unnecessarily alarmed the middle class and the officer corps (e.g., the proposed educational reform), and that these relatively marginal factors were crucial in tipping the scales against the U.P. in a situation where the balance of forces was about even; that the fundamental causes of the coup inhere in Chile's status as a dependent nation and the international policy of the United States in particular; that Allende personally could not provide the kind of leadership that the situation demanded. Mistakes were certainly made and the international situation was clearly unfavorable. Both problems, as well as Allende's leadership, need to be more thoroughly analyzed and evaluated. However, the analysis of problems related to the role of the middle class and mass organizations, and strategy vis-à-vis highly professional and capable military institutions, remain fundamental for any discussion of socialist transformation not only in Chile, but anywhere in the "Western democracies."[39]

Notes

1. Among the best analyses of the fundamental causes for the success of the fascist coup of September 11 are Miliband (1974: 451–73) and Garcés (1974a: 11–54). For an insightful day-to-day account and analysis of the events preceding the coup, see Touraine (1973).
2. For analyses critical of the U.P. policy vis-à-vis the armed forces, see Sweezy (1973) and Plotke (1973).
3. The Popular Unity's "Program of Government" is available in a large number of publications; among them are NACLA (1972: 130–42) and Allende (1973: 23–51).
4. Garcés argued that this strategy did not "exclude the thought of resorting to social pressure—from the bottom—in specific cases or for very concrete objectives." However, for him, it was "the opposite of political realism and a deformed vision of the political process to affirm: 'We suggest to the Unidad Popular and to the Government that to rely on the *real protagonists* of the social process underway would have been more serious and more courageous on their part: between February and October of this year (1971) 345,000 industrial workers, peasants, settlers and students have participated in strikes and illegal take-overs. . . .' The maintenance of public order is not only a requirement of every government; it always favours whoever controls the government" (Garcés, 1972: 35).
5. Since the coup, the Carabineros have been formally recognized as the fourth branch of the armed forces—they were integrated into the Ministry of Defense whereas formerly they formed part of the Ministry of the Interior.
6. The reforms proposed included social security legislation, state control of banks and insurance companies, the separation of church and state, and direct election of the president. For more information on this period, as well as on Chilean political history in general, see Gil (1966) and Petras (1970).
7. For a very good brief discussion of this period, see Bicheno (1972: 97–134). Although the progressive officers gained control of the situation in the armed forces, there was also a strong reactionary sector in the officer corps, particularly in the navy (Pike, 1963: 178–81).
8. The effects of internal repression were also demoralizing for the army officer corps, who had directed two successful international wars during the nineteenth century, and thought of themselves as the protectors of the nation against external aggression.
9. General Saez Morales, who lived through these events, discusses favoritism particularly bitterly in his memoirs (Saez Morales, 1934: 19).
10. The name the 1951 conspirators gave their group was "Por Una Mañana Auspiciosa" or PUMA. The 1955 group was known as the "Linea Recta," and it was a reconstituted version of the PUMA (Joxe, 1970: 80).
11. Already a year before Viaux's rebellion, there was considerable disturbance within the army concerning salaries and other institutional problems: the minister of defense was removed and replaced by a general who was supposed to deal with the institutional problems. His inaction provoked further resentment and therefore sympathy among officers for Viaux's movement, which received considerable support from the navy and air force as well as the army.

Viaux obtained the removal of the minister of defense as well as salary increases and new equipment for the army from Frei's government. No serious charges were brought against Viaux: he was simply dismissed. Viaux was probably already involved with civilian right-wing political groups, but the full political implications of his 1969 rebellion remain to be clarified (Duran: 1974).

A good summary of the conspiratorial activities of Chilean officers by Nef (1974: 59–63) has come to my attention since the completion of this summary analysis. Nef stresses the conservative and reactionary tendencies within the Chilean armed forces. There is no doubt that those tendencies existed. However, my reading of the available evidence convinces me that the political situation in the armed forces was more contradictory and complex than Nef's analysis suggests. Nef, for example, points out (1974: 62) that Viaux attempted to present himself as a "peruanista," i.e., a progressive. To me, this indicates that Viaux was convinced that he could not obtain widespread support within the officer corps on the basis of a right-wing position.

12. Hansen (1967: 295) also reports widespread dissatisfaction with the military as a career choice for their sons among upper- and upper-middle-class respondents in Santiago.

13. Professor Duran, for example, indicated that his uncle, who was an army officer, gave up his military career in 1968 for economic reasons. Duran also remembers meeting an officer's wife who was driving a taxi to supplement the family income.

14. Hansen (1967: 211) writes: "The basis of the present trend toward incorporation of lower middle class elements appeared to rest upon the decline in the prestige of the career. Talented youth from the upper and middle class were no longer attracted to the military as a career. As a result, the base of recruitment had been broadened in order to provide sufficient officer candidates." Hansen writes broadly of the military; however, he provides data only on the army. Therefore, in using his thesis, I take all references to the military (unless he specifies air force, etc.) as limited to the army.

15. The fathers of the 37 officers' wives were businessmen (31%), professionals and managers (17%), military officers (14%), farmers (31%), and white collar employees (6%) (Hansen: 1967: 172).

16. These regional variations were pointed out to me by Duran (1974).

17. Concerning the 37 retired generals' organizational affiliations, Hansen (1967: 177, 179) writes: "All retired generals interviewed had belonged to at least one military association, and over a third to only military associations. Of civilian affiliations, middle class organizations such as Rotary, Masons, various historical societies, and sporting clubs predominated. Only one general belonged to Santiago's elitist Club de Union, and another four to various provincial equestrian clubs which were likely to have a large proportion of their members drawn from the traditional elites."

18. On September 2, 1973, Eduardo Cruz Mena, president of the striking College of Physicians said: "It is certain many people will die as a result of the lack of medical attention; in wartime one has to kill." Quoted in *Last Post* (1973: 26).

19. Hansen (1967: 248) writes: "In general, our data suggested a close connection between political views and an officer's orientation toward military participation in civic action programs. Officers who held leftist political sentiments were more favorable to civic action than rightists. Eighty-nine percent (N = 9) of those who identified themselves as 'leftists' favored an increase in civic action programs as compared to 52% (N = 21) of 'somewhat leftist' and 17% (N = 6) of 'rightists' and 'somewhat rightist.'" Hansen indicates that "somewhat leftist" could be considered a basically "centrist" position (p. 301) and

therefore I have chosen to consider the "leftists" only as politically progressive.

20. Given air force and navy recruitment of their officers from the better-off sectors of the middle class, and even the upper class in the case of the navy, the professional political culture of the two institutions may include more elitist values than those to be found in the army and Carabineros.

21. Gonzalez (1974: 89–90) has described the Cuban army thus: "To begin with, the Cuban army had a low level of professionalism. Staffed in large part with Batista's cronies who had joined him in the 'Sergeants' Revolt' of 1933, the army was shot through with senior officers who had distinguished themselves only by their personal corruption and attachment to the dictator. The top leadership, therefore, was generally deficient in many of the hallmarks of military professionalism—strong constitutional commitment as opposed to personal attachments, career advancement on the basis of military merit rather than political criteria, adherence to military doctrine, and a distinct sense of military mission. . . . Such an army was capable of an internal police function, of quashing Moncada-like assaults. But it was incapable of sustaining a counterinsurgency campaign. . . . Corrupt at its very core, the Batista army was susceptible to bribery by the *fidelistas,* who were sometimes able to buy their way through enemy lines. . . ."

22. The potential military use of the B-26 Invaders was pointed out to me by an ex-officer of the U.S. army who was involved in training Latin American officers at Fort Sill, Oklahoma, in 1967.

23. It is not clear whether the figures used by Joxe (1970: 103) and Klare (1972: 281) include the cost of training Chilean officers on U.S. bases.

24. For a discussion of U.S. military training programs and institutions for Latin America, see Klare (1972: 295–307). Enlisted men as well as officers are trained at U.S. bases. For example, courses on "aircraft maintenance, electronics, radio, instrument training and repair," etc., are available for enlisted personnel at the Inter-American Air Force Academy in the Canal Zone (Klare, 1972: 302).

25. Between 1959 and 1969, the "average annual number of Chilean military personnel programmed for training" for the U.S. and Canal Zone bases was 370. (Klare, 1972: 298).

26. There were also air force and navy MTTs in Chile (Kemp, 1970).

27. It would also be interesting to know at which ranks of the Chilean officer corps U.S. training had been most extensive, and whether or not there were significant differences in strongly anti-U.P. attitudes from rank to rank.

28. Between 1965 and 1969, the Chilean army purchased 26 helicopters from the U.S. (Kemp, 1970: 32).

29. Since Chile in the 1960's still had one of the highest ratios of military personnel to civilian population, this indicates that the level of militarization in Chile before the forties must have been remarkably high.

30. In his earlier work, Joxe (1970: 113) also discussed the possibilities of "military populism"; but that he considered a possibility only in a situation in which middle-class living standards were not threatened by the left.

31. Farrell (1974) became acquainted with a group of air force officers in Santiago while he was acting as a consultant to the Ministry of Education from January 1970 to July 1971. He paraphrased the officers' attitudes: "Well, in '58, we tried Alessandri, and nothing important happened to the country. In '64, we tried Frei, and he couldn't get things moving either. We might as well try this fellow Allende, and see if maybe he can get something going. If he doesn't do anything, we can try someone else six years from now."

32. Of course, there were important differences within the U.P., but the above summary reflects what I perceive as the position of Allende and those politically closest to him.
33. See also issues of *Latin America* for 1972 and 1973. For Allende's views on the question of military participation, see Allende (1973: 135–37).
34. Farrell (1974) wrote: "To explain their reaction, I should note a very general feeling about the Allende regime which I observed amongst many middle class Chileans who were either supporters of Allende or at least neutral, i.e., prepared to tolerate him. It could be characterized by a comment I heard one friend make at a party, which comment was roundly seconded by all of those others who heard him make it. 'They can play around with the economy if they like; they can fiddle about with the political and social systems if they like; but they had better keep their damned hands off my kids.' "
35. The negative impact of proselytization among conscripts was also noted by Bandeira (1974) and Duran (1974).
36. Alexander emphasizes the proselytization and "provocation" by left-wing elements inside and outside the U.P. as "decisive" in provoking the September 11 coup (1974: 4–5). He fails to refer to the destabilization campaign coordinated by the civilian right (including sectors of the Christian Democratic party) in collaboration with the United States. That is, he does not situate left-wing "provocation" in the overall context of class conflict, and the limitations under which the U.P. government was operating.
37. Nef has pointed out that one of the factors inhibiting intervention by professional bureaucratic military organizations is "the fear or uncertainty on the part of the officer corps that intervention may not be successful and therefore harmful to the institution" (1974: 67). He also emphasizes the importance of institutional leadership. These two factors in fact could have redounded to the benefit of the U.P. government in the days immediately following the aborted June 29 uprising. Given the support of the commander-in-chief of the army, General Prats, as well as of other high-ranking officers (particularly in the army and the Carabineros), a rapid purge of right-wing officers could have produced the "uncertainty" that would have inhibited another right-wing attempt. Nef's analysis tends to overdetermine the success of a right-wing military movement, and to leave almost no room for maneuver on the part of the U.P. government vis-à-vis the military. In this respect, it would be interesting to compare the Chilean situation with the recent events in Portugal.
38. Information provided by Chilean refugees who prefer to remain anonymous.
39. For a more general analysis of the development of Chilean society, with a focus on persistent and underlying historical "authoritarian corporatist" tendencies, see Kaufman (1974).

References

Alexander, Robert J. 1974. "Chile a Year After the Military Coup." *Freedom at Issue* (no. 28): 4–19.

Allende, Salvador. 1973. *Chile's Road to Socialism*. Middlesex: Penguin Books Ltd.

Bandeira, Antonio. 1974. Series of interviews and discussions. Ph.D. candidate, Department of Political Science, York University. Formerly a student at FLACSO, Santiago, Chile.

Bicheno, H. E. 1972. "Anti-Parliamentary themes in Chilean History." In *Allende's Chile,* ed. Kenneth Medhurst. London: Hart-Davis Mac-Gibbon.

De Souza, Herbet. 1973a. *Acerca del problema del doble poder en Chile.* Santiago: FLACSO.

———. 1973b. *Las elecciones parlamentarias de Marzo de 1973.* Santiago: FLACSO.

———. 1974. Series of interviews and discussions. Ph.D. candidate, Department of Political Science, York University. Formerly at the Planning Office of the President (ODEPLAN), Santiago, Chile.

Duran, Claudio. 1973. "Chile: Revolution and Counter-Revolution." *Social Praxis* 1 (no. 4): 337–58.

———. 1974. Series of interviews and discussions. Lecturer, Division of Social Sciences, York University. Formerly of the University of Chile.

Farrell, J. P. 1974. Letter (June 25). Chairman, Department of Educational Planning, The Ontario Institute for Studies in Education, Toronto. Consultant to the Ministry of Education, Chile, January 1970 to July 1971.

Garcés, Joan E. 1972. "Chile 1971: a Revolutionary Government within a Welfare State." In *Allende's Chile,* ed. Kenneth Medhurst. London: Hart-Davis MacGibbon.

———. 1974a. *El Estado y los Problemas Tácticos en el Gobierno de Allende.* Madrid: Siglo XXI.

———. 1974b. "Chile: how they killed a democratic revolution." *Manchester Guardian Weekly* 110 (no. 1): 15.

Germani, Gino. 1971. *Sociologia della Modernizazione.* Barri: Editori Laterza.

Gil, Federico G. 1966. *The Political System of Chile.* Boston: Houghton Mifflin Company.

Gonzalez, Edward. 1974. *Cuba Under Castro: The Limits of Charisma.* Boston: Houghton Mifflin Company.

Hansen, Roy Allen. 1967. "Military Culture and Organizational Decline: A Study of the Chilean Army." U.C.L.A.: Ph.D. dissertation.

IDOC (International Documentation on the Contemporary Church). 1973. *Chile: The Allende Years, The Coup, Under the Junta.* New York: IDOC.

Joxe, Alain. 1970. *Las Fuerzas Armadas en el Sistema Político Chileno.* Santiago: Editorial Universitaria, S.A.

———. 1973 "L'Armée Chilienne." *Les Temps Modernes* 29 (no. 323): 2006–36.

Kandell, Jonathan. 1973. "Plotting the Coup." In *Chile: The Allende Years, The Coup, Under the Junta.* New York: IDOC.

Kaufman, Robert R. 1974. "Transitions to Stable Authoritarian Corporate Regimes: The Chilean Case" presented at the Inter-University Seminar on the Armed Forces & Society, at the annual meeting of the American Political Science Association, Chicago, Illinois, August 29–Sept. 2, 1974.

Kemp, Geoffrey. 1970. *Some Relationships Between U.S. Military Training in Latin America and Weapons Acquisition Patterns: 1959–1969.* Cambridge, Mass.: Center for International Studies, M.I.T.

Klare, Michael T. 1972. *War Without End: American Planning for the Next Vietnams.* New York: Vintage Books.

Last Post Staff and Latin American Working Group. 1973. "Chile Report" *Last Post* 3 (no. 6): 19–34.

Latin America, A Weekly Political and Economic Report. 1972a. "Chile: military alliance." Vol. 6 (no. 45).

———. 1972b. "Chile: military influence." Vol. 6 (no. 49).

———. 1973. "Chile: enemies within." Vol. 7 (no. 45).

———. 1974. "Chile: general power." Vol. 8 (no. 19).

Martner, Gonzalo. 1972. "The Economic Aspects of Allende's Government: Problems and Prospects." In *Allende's Chile,* ed. Kenneth Medhurst. London: Hart-Davis MacGibbon.

Miliband, Ralph. 1974. "The Coup in Chile." In *The Socialist Register,* ed. Ralph Miliband and John Saville. London: The Merlin Press.

Monthly Review. 1971. "Review of the Month: Peaceful Transition to Socialism?" 22 (no. 8): 1–18.

NACLA (North American Congress on Latin America). 1972. *New Chile,* Berkeley: NACLA.

Nef, Jorge. 1974. "The Politics of Repression: The Social Pathology of the Chilean Military." *Latin American Perspectives* 1 (2): 58–77.

North, Liisa. 1967. *Civil-Military Relations in Argentina, Chile and Peru.* Berkeley: Institute of International Relations, University of California.

Nunn, Frederick M. 1963. *Civil-Military Relations in Chile, 1891–1938.* University of New Mexico: Ph.D. Dissertation.

Petras, James. 1970. *Politics and Social Forces in Chilean Development.* Berkeley and Los Angeles: University of California Press.

Pike, Frederick B. 1963. *Chile and the United States 1880–1962.* Notre Dame, Indiana: University of Notre Dame Press.

Plotke, David. 1973. "Coup in Chile." *Socialist Revolution* 3 (no. 4): 99–124.

Rouma, Georges. 1948. *L'Amérique Latine,* vol. 1. Bruxelles: Renaissance du Livre.

Saez Morales, Carlos. 1934. *Recuerdos de un soldado: el ejército y la política,* vol. I. Santiago: Biblioteca Ercilla.

Sweezy, Paul M. 1973. "Chile: The Question of Power." *Monthly Review* 25 (no. 2): 1–11.

Touraine, Alain. 1973. *Vie et Mort du Chili Populaire.* Paris: Editions du Seuil.

Abraham F. Lowenthal

The Political Role of the Dominican Armed Forces

A Note on the 1963 Overthrow of Juan Bosch and on the 1965 Dominican "Revolution"

Several years ago, in a general essay on Dominican politics, I wrote a few pages about the political role of the Dominican Armed Forces. I argued that "the history of the past few years in the Dominican Republic may best be viewed as a constant struggle among changing alliances, not in terms of confrontation between civilian authority and the military establishment" (Lowenthal, 1969: 40). I suggested that "far from being a professional institution dedicated to certain principles that impel its occasional entry into politics, the Dominican Armed Forces have never had any significant function beyond politics, except for plunder" (Lowenthal, 1969: 40). Painting a picture of constant struggle within the Dominican Armed Forces, for power and a chance at the spoils, I played down the importance, for understanding the political role of Dominican military officers, of institutional and ideological considerations. Perhaps my most controversial proposition was that both the 1963 overthrow of Juan Bosch (the elected social democratic president) and the 1965 "constitutionalist" attempt to restore Bosch to the presidency owed less to ideology than to intramilitary

From Abraham F. Lowenthal, "The Political Role of the Dominican Armed Forces: A Note on the 1963 Overthrow of Juan Bosch and on the 1965 Dominican 'Revolution,'" *Journal of Interamerican Studies and World Affairs,* 15, no. 3 (August 1973): 355–61. Copyright © 1973 by Sage Publications, Inc. and reprinted by permission of the publisher, Sage Publications, Inc. [A table has been omitted from this edition.—Ed.]

Author's Note: I express here my appreciation to Christopher Mitchell, Peter Smith, and Peter Winn for their comments on a draft of this note.

struggles among competing cliques and to rival civilian efforts to enlist the support of various military factions. I asserted that "there does not seem to have been any appreciable difference . . . between the top military leadership of the two sides" in 1965 "with respect to previous ideology or degree of honesty. . . . The major distinction between the military leaders on either side . . . was that of age and rank: the established leaders were of higher rank precisely because they had prevailed in previous struggles to reach the top" (Lowenthal, 1969: 41–42).

My view has been considered exaggerated by several other observers (see Slater, 1970). The 1963 coup against Bosch is still often treated in the general literature on Latin American politics as a classic example of institutional military opposition to reform (Lieuwen, 1964; Needler, 1966). A specific case study of the 1963 coup interprets it as the coherent institutional response of the Dominican army to perceived threats to its status and prerogatives (Chung, 1966). And a major study of the 1965 "revolution" distinguishes the "rebels" from the "loyalists" on two grounds, one of which is that "the rebels had an ideology which advocated greater participation of all classes of people in the cultural life of the nation, together with some specific ideas on means to achieve this goal" (Moreno, 1971).

Conclusive demonstration of my view is perhaps impossible to achieve; it is certainly beyond my present capacity given available time and materials. I do wish, however, to support my interpretation, and to provide further material for others, by providing previously unpublished data that I submit as an extensive "footnote" to the work I have previously presented on Dominican politics.[1]

When the Bosch government was toppled on September 25, 1963, its demise was marked by an official *communicado* signed by twenty-five high-ranking Dominican military officers, all of them united at that moment in their agreement that Bosch should be replaced. The *communicado,* later republished in an official Dominican military "white paper" on the overthrow of Bosch, is often cited as an indication of the supposed institutional view of the Dominican military establishment (Centro de Enseñanza, 1964: 90–95).

Still skeptical about the attribution to the Dominican Armed Forces of the qualities of institutional coherence and ideological unity others have posited (extrapolating from their intepretations of the Dominican officers' role in ousting Bosch), I decided recently to compare the political role played by these same twenty-five officers just seventeen months later, when the next Dominican government (headed by Donald Reid Cabral) was being ousted by a coup aimed at returning Bosch to the presidency.

. . . No information is available to me on one of the officers. Four of the remaining twenty-four were out of the country in April 1965, sent abroad because they were out of favor with the Reid Cabral regime; in at least two cases, and perhaps in all, this disfavor resulted from the officers having plotted to overthrow Reid. Of the remaining twenty, eight supported the pro-Bosch movement on April 25, despite the stance they had adopted in 1963; in at least half the cases the officers had been fired, usually for plotting, during the Reid government. Six of the remaining twelve were busy on April 25 trying to set up their own juntas, supporting neither the Reid government nor the pro-Bosch coup. The remaining six officers, whose actions on April 25 may be interpreted as having supported the Reid government, comprised the core of the faction the United States government represented in 1965 as the loyalists, as if they were the established governmental authority. Even among these six, however, most were really members of General Elias Wessin's clique; they actually failed to support Reid Cabral during the crucial first hours of the coup, thus assuring his regime's fall, and did not become loyalists until late in the day!

What these data suggest is simply that the political behavior of Dominican military officers during the 1965 crisis cannot easily be reconciled with a view of the Dominican Armed Forces as an autonomous and coherent professional institution, or with a view of Dominican officers as primarily or even importantly motivated by ideological considerations. The fact that virtually all Dominican officers were anti-Reid by April 1965 might suggest an institutional and conceivably even ideological rejection of that regime, were it not for the chaotic pattern of individual actions. . . . Individual conversions to the pro-Bosch cause, for instance, might be attributed to belated ideological commitment, but the overall pattern— clusters of officers seeking to prevail through a variety of quickly changing alignments—may be more easily explained in cruder terms.

Showing that the Dominican Armed Forces was composed of struggling cliques in 1965 does not prove, of course, that the same was the case when Juan Bosch was overthrown, though whoever posits the institutional integrity and ideological concern of the Dominican military in 1963 might be asked to explain its apparently complete transformation in 1965. (I would attribute the apparent unanimity of the Dominican officers' cliques at the moment of Bosch's overthrow primarily to the fact that his power bases, including United States support, had so obviously crumbled that nothing was to be gained by staying off the bandwagon. There were other reasons, too, including the way Bosch handled his relations with key officers and perhaps even some "institutional" fear of Bosch, his colleagues, and their [probably falsely] reported intent to establish a civilian militia. But however genuine the Dominican officers' statement on September 25, their *communicado* only temporarily obscured the existence of competing cliques that had been struggling for predominance ever since Trujillo's death and were still at it in 1965.)

I do not mean to indicate that there were no differences between the followers of the two sides in the 1965 crisis. "The crisis certainly divided Dominican society, bringing together a coalition of the aggrieved in support of the constitutionalist cause and organizing on the anticonstitutionalist side some of the country's most retrograde elements" (Lowenthal, 1969: 41). Nor do I mean to suggest that none of the constitutional leaders was motivated by the ideologically based desire to reinstate the elected government (nor, for that matter, that none of those who opposed the coup in 1965 was acting out of loyalty to the incumbent regime). Motivations are far too complicated to exclude any from possibly important influence, or to treat them without full reference to the changing context in which they come into play.

What I do mean to argue, emphatically, is that a view of the Dominican Armed Forces in the 1960s as basically comprised of competing factions of officers concerned more about spoils than about ideology is more helpful than one that treats the Dominican Armed Forces as fundamentally a professional military institution comparable to those in many other countries in Latin America. Assuming that similar labels necessarily identify comparable phenomena is a dangerous practice—for political scientists as much as for policy officials.

What I believe but cannot show on the basis of material in hand is that a specific focus on the various intramilitary rivalries in Santo Domingo would immeasurably enhance our understanding of Dominican politics since Trujillo's death. A good dissertation, or book, is waiting to be written.

Note

1. I collected the material here summarized in the course of my research on the 1965 Dominican crisis, drawing on an extensive number of interviews, access to restricted documents, and review of the public record. My sources are detailed in the preface and appendices of *The Dominican Intervention* (1972).

References

Centro de Enseñanza de la Fuerza Armada (1964) *Libro Blanco de las Fuerzas Armadas y de la Policía Nacional de la República Dominicana.* Santo Domingo: Editora del Caribe.

Chung, H. M. (1966) "The case of the muffed mission: the 1963 coup d'état in the Dominican Republic." Caribbean Project, Foreign Policy Research Institute, University of Pennsylvania.

Lieuwen, E. (1964) *Generals versus Presidents.* New York: Praeger.

Lowenthal, A. F. (1972) *The Dominican Intervention.* Cambridge: Harvard Univ. Press.

———. (1969) "The Dominican Republic: the politics of chaos," pp. 34–58 in A. Van Lazar and R. R. Kaufman (eds.) *Reform and Revolution: Readings in Latin American Politics.* Boston: Allyn & Bacon.

Moreno, J. A. (1971) *Barrios in Arms: Revolution in Santo Domingo.* Pittsburgh: Pittsburgh University.

Needler, M. (1966) "Political development and military intervention in Latin America." *Amer. Pol. Sci. Rev.* 60 (September): 616–26.

Slater, J. (1970) *Intervention and Negotiation: The United States and the Dominican Revolution.* New York: Harper & Row.

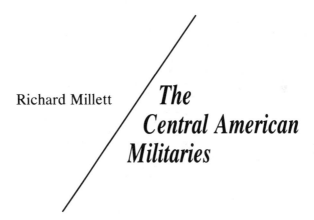

Richard Millett / *The Central American Militaries*

The Central American militaries have contributed significantly to the region's violence, and their current political power complicates efforts to end the crisis. They are plagued by conflicting and often contradictory trends, a situation which consistently frustrates the efforts of external forces, domestic elites and even their own officers to control the power which they possess. The armies are a bulwark against communism but, at the same time, their corruption and abuses of human rights provide invaluable propaganda and recruits for the radical left. Deeply rooted in regional history and tradition, the military is also one of the most modern institutions in each nation. Highly dependent on external support, it is also strongly nationalist and even xenophobic.

The Heritage of Central America's Armed Forces

The regular military institutions of Guatemala, El Salvador and Honduras have all been shaped by Spanish colonialism, their domestic political,

From Richard Millett, "The Central American Military: Predators or Patriots," in *Central America: Anatomy of a Conflict*, ed. Robert Leiken (New York: Pergamon Press, 1984). Copyright © 1984 by Pergamon Press. Revised and updated and reprinted with the permission of the author and Pergamon Press.

social and economic environments, and the impact of foreign contacts, notably those with the United States.

Although actual military forces were rather weak in Spanish Central America, one enduring colonial concept has been that of the military as a special, privileged class, exempt from the jurisdiction of the rest of society. This was embodied in the Spanish *fuero militar,* the exemption of members of the armed forces from the jurisdiction of civil courts and their elevation to the status of a privileged class. In the words of historian Lyle McAlister, the military was:

> a class apart and so regarded itself. The possession of special privileges enhanced its sense of uniqueness and superiority, and at the same time rendered it virtually immune from civil authority. Unfortunately, power and privilege were not accompanied by a commensurate sense of responsibility. A large proportion of officers and men regarded military service as an opportunity for the advancement of personal interests rather than as a civil obligation.[1]

The colonial emphasis on class also helped create the immense gap between officers and enlisted men which still characterizes Central American armed forces. The gap between the military and civilians was even wider: those abused by military personnel had little opportunity for redress. The lower classes, especially Indians, suffered most. Soldiers frequently seized what they wanted from Indian communities without compensation.[2] Military corruption also has roots in the eighteenth century. Many officers habitually used their positions to engage in contraband trade, a further example of the abuses of the *fuero militar.*[3]

The military's ability to abuse its power grew after independence due to a patron-client relationship between officers and enlisted men. Troops gave their loyalty not to elected officials nor even to the nation itself, but to their immediate commander. This system even operated within the officer corps, where officers addressed superiors as *mi general* or *mi coronel* (my general or my colonel). Local commanders' absolute control over pay, discipline, and promotion reinforced this pattern, enabling officers who revolted against the central authority to count on the support of their troops. Thus, in order to win military allegiance governments had to negotiate with individual officers. Leading officers, frequently from prominent families, were little more than the armed partisans of the party in power. The real struggle was between elite sectors who viewed the coup (or *golpe*) as the normal means of transferring power. As Professor John J. Johnson observed, "Liberty, equality and fraternity gave way to infantry, cavalry and artillery," and "the rule of force became more meaningful than the rule of law."[4]

This endemic conflict facilitated foreign intervention and exploitation and hampered development, although changes were sought in the last third of the nineteenth century. Military academies were established in 1868 in

El Salvador and in 1873 in Guatemala.[5] Similar efforts in Nicaragua in the 1890s and in Honduras at the start of the twentieth century failed, but nonetheless indicated a desire for greater military professionalism. These initial efforts leaned heavily on the services of foreign instructors, usually Chilean or German; since then, dependence on external training and support has caused tension.

Previously little more than an extension of semi-feudal elite factions or traditional political parties, the twentieth century military began to develop a separate identity as it became more professionalized. Officers rose to power because of their ability to manipulate politics within the military rather than because they came from prominent families. Graduates of the new military academies increasingly resented the power of amateur generals. The advent of new technology—notably the machine gun and later the airplane—also made the career of a military officer increasingly a full-time profession. Political elites continued to have to negotiate with the military as a separate force, for losing its support meant loss of power and could even place life and property at risk.

The military did not become an opponent of the ruling class, but rather a vital ally of that class. The military's allegiance had to be assured through financial support, co-optation into the elite by marriage or other means and expansion of its role in politics. The officers themselves now decided assignments and promotions and selected the army's commander and military cabinet members. Civilians could influence these decisions but no longer had the final say. External forces, especially the United States, sought to influence the emerging military institutions, adding to their power but further complicating the political equation. In the twentieth century, the United States tried to create a rural constabulary in Panama and to improve the professional level of Nicaragua's armed forces. In the 1920s, Secretary of State Charles Evans Hughes promoted arms limitations and military reorganization in the region. A 1923 conference of Central American states in Washington adopted a Treaty of Arms Limitation and considered establishing non-partisan constabularies trained by American instructors. A leading State Department official noted that:

> The old armies were or seemed to be one of the principal causes of disorder and financial disorganization. They consumed most of the government's revenue, chiefly in graft, and they gave nothing but oppression and disorder in return. We thought that a disciplined force, trained by Americans, would do away with the petty local oppression that was responsible for much of the disorder that occurred and would be an important step toward better financial administration and economic progress generally.[6]

Washington also feared that the weakness and corruption of existing armies might make those nations susceptible to other foreign influences. During World War I, U.S. efforts focused on eliminating German influences. In the 1920s, especially during the tenure of Secretary of State

Frank Kellogg, the Mexican government was imagined to be the source of "Bolshevik influences."

Only in Nicaragua were U.S. efforts to reshape the military effective before World War II. Armed factions were forced to disband and the *Guardia Nacional* was created and initially officered and equipped by U.S. Marines.[7] One unforeseen result of this was that enemies of the Nicaraguan regime became, ipso facto, enemies of the United States. The United States was thus drawn into five and one-half years of inconclusive guerrilla warfare against the forces of General Augusto César Sandino. This conflict later came back to haunt Washington policymakers.

Elsewhere U.S. influence grew slowly. During World War II many Central American officers received American training, either in their own nations or in the United States. The Lend-Lease programs considerably upgraded the equipment of regional militaries, especially the air forces. Exposure to North American ideas and training increased discontent among many junior officers and contributed to the overthrow of long-lasting dictatorships in Guatemala and El Salvador in 1944. As Guatemala's new rulers moved to the left, Washington became increasingly concerned over possible communist influence and rushed military supplies to neighboring countries. These arms were used by the CIA in 1954 to help topple the Guatemalan government. Shortly thereafter, the U.S. signed mutual assistance pacts with most Central American nations and sent military training missions. In 1961 the United States ambassador to El Salvador noted that the advisory group in that nation had grown so large that "there were more men in the Air Force Mission than El Salvador had either pilots or planes."[8]

Fidel Castro's rise to power and the expanding guerrilla conflicts, notably in Guatemala and Nicaragua, led to further U.S. involvement in the 1960s. The Kennedy administration promoted military reforms and civic action programs, but in later years the emphasis was increasingly on internal stability and counterinsurgency.

Though direct United States aid and training diminished steadily during the 1970s, both Central Americans and North American policymakers continued to believe that the United States could easily dictate the actions of Central America's armed forces. In reality, the military establishments were becoming less dependent on the United States and more responsive to the institutional interests of the officer corps. The 1969 Honduras–El Salvador–War left both nations' military leaders feeling let down by the United States. As the 1970s progressed, Central American nations sought other markets for military equipment. Honduras acquired combat aircraft from Israel, while El Salvador began to buy supplies from a wide variety of nations. Congress prohibited U.S. training of Central American police forces, but the impact of the United States continued to be important. Partly due to American influence, many officers became militant anti-communists. Civic action programs, prevailing counterinsurgency doctrines and the structure for regional military cooperation also reflected U.S. influence. Many officers had received at least part of their training in U.S. schools, and most uniforms were modeled on North American styles. Both the traditional right and the radical left cultivated the belief that the United States exercised significant influence over the military. That belief also endured in Washington, creating more problems than benefits in the 1980s.

El Salvador

Today the most crucial and difficult U.S. military relationship is with El Salvador. It has generated strong criticism of American policies at home and abroad, and few successes within El Salvador.

El Salvador's armed forces have expanded rapidly in recent years. In 1976 total military personnel numbered approximately 8,000, over half of which were assigned to the security forces (National Guard, National Police and Treasury Police). Only about 200 were assigned to the air force. By 1983 the army had expanded to 22,000, the air force to 2,350 and the security forces to 9,500.[9] The budget had grown from $50 million in 1978 to $139 million in 1982, plus an additional $82 million in United States military assistance.[10]

The National Guard is a 3,500-man rural constabulary, created in the 1920s on the model of the Spanish *Guardia Civil*. The National Police, the only urban police force, has nearly 4,000 members; the Treasury Police, a body formally charged with controlling customs, borders, alcohol production and related tax matters, has nearly 2,000 individuals. These "security forces" are currently all under the control of the Ministry of Defense and are largely commanded by army officer graduates of the military academy. These forces, notably the National Guard and the Treasury Police, have been the principal perpetrators of indiscriminate violence against dissidents. They have been used by the traditional rural elite against peasant organizations, agrarian reform and potential "trouble-makers." The Treasury Police also maintains an extensive network of rural informers. These security forces do much of the "dirty work" of maintaining control and eliminating "subversives" leaving the army free to concentrate on national defense, national politics and self-enrichment. Before 1980 the army suppressed only extreme dissent; for example, after the fraudulent elections of 1972 and 1977.

The one-man military rule of pre-1944 El Salvador has given way to a trend toward corporate control by the armed forces, signaled in the 1950s by the rise to power of military academy graduates.[11] While generally united in their determination to control the country, they are divided by ideology, personal loyalties and, most importantly, graduating classes from the *Escuela Militar.* Each year well over a hundred cadets are admitted to this institution, but just 10 percent graduate four years later. Brutal discipline, at times verging on sadism, weeds out those lacking strength, determination and ambition. The school admits boys of fifteen to eighteen years of age and graduates hardened men, bound by lifelong loyalty to their classmates. Each class, known as a *tanda,* strives to protect and advance its members' fortunes. Success for one member means success for all and failure for any weakens the entire group. Hence they protect the less competent, more blatantly dishonest among them, viewing those outside the *tanda* system as unfit to judge the officer corps.

To advance their ambitions, *tandas* form alliances with other *tandas,* though rarely with the class one year ahead of them in *Escuela Militar* (which had brutalized them during their plebe year), nor with the class a year behind (which they had brutalized). Under this system, loyalty becomes incestuous, and group advancement, rather than defense of the national interest, becomes the ultimate goal.[12] Officers in the security forces are bound to officers in the army through these *tanda* bonds, a tie which makes it virtually impossible to discipline an officer for crimes against civilians. In 1982 El Salvador's defense minister admitted to two United States senators that "there is no formal system of punishment for abuses by members of the Salvadoran armed forces."[13]

For this reason, the United States probably had less influence over El Salvador's military than over that of any other Central American nation. This *tanda* system made the military resistant to foreign influences. By law, Salvadoran army officers had to attend their own service schools, including the Command and Staff College. Given the post-1969 cutoff of arms sales and training of police forces it was not that difficult for El Salvador to respond to Carter administration human rights pressures in 1977 by abrogating the military-assistance agreement.

During the 1970s, increased social pressures and the growing strength of the left made a major outbreak of domestic violence increasingly likely. The military's control was weakened by corruption and growing factionalism. The Sandinista victory in Nicaragua further encouraged the left and increased the military's fears and internal divisions.

When junior officers ousted General Carlos Humberto Romero's weak and corrupt administration, the Carter administration leaped at the chance to improve contacts with the military. A small amount of training funds (IMET) and authorization for $5.7 million in foreign military sales (FMS) were hurriedly included in a supplement to the fiscal year (FY) 1980 budget. Throughout 1980, however, civil conflict mounted and the military drifted back into the control of traditional senior officers. Human rights abuses escalated steadily, culminating in charges of military involvement in the December murder of four American churchwomen and two American agricultural advisers. Shortly thereafter, Colonel Adolfo Majano, leader of the "reformist" element within the armed forces, was dropped from the ruling junta. U.S. hopes for a moderate civil-military coalition were rapidly falling apart.

U.S.–Salvadoran military relations dramatically changed in January 1981. Military assistance, suspended following the December murders, was hurriedly reinstated when guerrilla forces launched a major offensive. In addition, emergency appropriations, ultimately totaling $25 million, were added to provide equipment and supplies for the army. This was the first direct grant program for military hardware appropriated for Central America in several years. Even greater changes followed President Reagan's inauguration later that month.

The Carter administration's objectives were to persuade the army to curb human rights abuses, make basic reforms and ultimately permit civilian rule. The internal realities of military politics and the intransigent nature of the armed right confounded these efforts. The Reagan administration's priority was defeating the guerrillas. Restoring domestic order required creating a more effective military. Military assistance was raised to $82 million for FY 1982, and scores of U.S. military advisers were dispatched to El Salvador on missions lasting from a few weeks to a full year.[14] This policy assumed that defeating the guerrillas was the Salvadoran military's top priority too, and that U.S. aid would increase military professionalism, which would decrease human rights abuses and enhance the military's public image. All of these assumptions proved mistaken because, as those dealing directly with the Salvadoran military soon realized, the armed forces had their own agenda. Their top priority was *protecting* the military institutions from radical guerrillas, civilian politicians and foreign reformers. Next was promoting one's own *tanda* and excluding from the system those who had not passed through the *Escuela Militar*. Political ideology was a low priority except for officers such as those linked to the extreme right of former Major Roberto d'Aubuisson.

Under such circumstances, U.S. involvement with the military produced endless frustrations. It proved impossible to convict officers for human rights abuses, including those involving U.S. citizens. The war with the guerrillas was stagnating; economic and political costs rose steadily. To fill the expanding army's need for company-level officers, the United States began training Salvadoran noncommissioned officers in Panama. But the Salvadoran military refused to give graduates of this program regular commissions, keeping their status inferior to the *Escuela Militar* graduates'. U.S.-trained enlisted men often performed reasonably well, but a combination of high casualties and low reenlistment rates meant that the majority were out of the military a year after they were trained.

The January 1983 conflict between Defense Minister José Guillermo García and Colonel Sigifredo Ochoa disrupted the military command, paralyzed the war effort and resulted in the removal of the defense minister and the colonel's departure for Washington. Part of this conflict stemmed from differences over strategy, with Ochoa and his supporters advocating a more sophisticated approach to counterinsurgency, emphasizing aggressive small unit actions and patrolling combined with political pacification. Traditional military rivalries, however, were at the heart of the conflict, with General García striving to maintain his supporters in key positions, despite their incompetence.

By 1985, in part due to a change in defense ministers in 1983, the Salvadoran military was finally demonstrating improved command and combat capabilities. Many of the more incompetent older officers had been retired or transferred to desk or attaché posts and their replacements demonstrated a greater willingness to seek out and engage the insurgents. The army and air force had expanded to over thirty thousand while an additional ten thousand remained in the security forces. The United States had provided $128,300,000 in military assistance in fiscal year (FY) 1985 and was requesting $132,600,000 for FY 1986. Increasing use of air power had helped the army make some progress in its fight against the guerrillas, but had also led to growing charges of indiscriminate attacks on civilians and to the specter of the insurgents countering this increased firepower and mobility by acquiring SAMs.

Human rights abuses have declined somewhat but the extent and permanence of this decline and the actual ability of the Duarte administration to exercise effective control over the military remain subjects of ongoing disputes. No officer has yet been tried, let alone convicted for any crime committed against a civilian. The sacrifice of the National Guard enlisted men in the case of the nuns did not touch the officer corps, and the most determined efforts of the United States to bring to trial the officers involved in the killing of the U.S. AID employees ultimately failed. The guerrillas are now clearly on the defensive, but the military's ability to win the war is still very much in doubt. El Salvador has made progress, but there is still far to go and the progress which has been made is extremely fragile. The fear of the loss of U.S. support and the danger of defeat at the hands of the FMLN have forced significant changes on the armed forces. But it has not changed their basic loyalties nor made them believers in Western-style democracy or effective civilian control over the military. Until the Duarte administration can demonstrate that officers will be held accountable for their actions against civilians, the military will remain the dominant institution in El Salvador. And as long as that situation continues, the prospects for restoring peace remain dim at best.

Guatemala

U.S.–Guatemalan military relations over the past five years have been at least as frustrating (although considerably less publicized and less extensive) as those with El Salvador's military. Two military coups in less than a year and a half have intensified U.S.–Guatemala problems. Like its neighbor in El Salvador, the Guatemalan officer corps is a proud, largely self-trained body, but there are also important differences.

Long considered the strongest and most professional military force in Central America, Guatemala's army today numbers approximately 22,000, and is steadily growing.[15] Security forces and other paramilitary groups are both smaller and less significant in Guatemala than in El Salvador.

The Guatemalan officer corps today is a contradictory mixture of nationalists and opportunists, professionals and partisans, reformers and upholders of the status quo. It is dominated by graduates of the *Escuela Politécnica,* Guatemala's military academy, but non-graduates can rise within the officer corps. Graduating-class loyalties are less binding than in El Salvador.[16] Though the military has dominated politics for the past half-century, it has permitted civilians to occupy the top government positions. It has, however, placed strict limits on their actual power.

Politécnica graduates played a major role in the 1944 revolution which overthrew long-time dictator General Jorge Ubico and inaugurated basic reforms. President Jacobo Arbenz, overthrown by the 1954 CIA-sponsored coup, was a *Politécnica* graduate, as was the man who replaced him. Though most officers opposed drift to the left, they resented heavy-handed U.S. involvement in the fall of Arbenz and the U.S. ambassador's dominant role in installing a successor regime.[17] U.S. use of Guatemalan territory to train Cuban exiles for the 1961 Bay of Pigs invasion of Cuba further aroused nationalist sentiments, leading some young officers to leave the military and form guerrilla groups in the early 1960s.[18] Later in the decade, other Guatemalan officers turned on these insurgents. In the 1970s, yet others sought to apply the Peruvian military reform model to their nation while others converted their rank into personal gain.

U.S. problems with Guatemala's military have worsened since 1976. That year's presidential election was won, amid widespread charges of fraud, by General Romeo Lucas Garcia, who was known chiefly for his unimaginative hard line and his blood ties to one of Guatemala's richest families. President Lucas, like his Salvadoran counterpart, responded to Carter administration protests over mounting human rights abuses by abrogating the military assistance pact with the United States.

On May 29, 1978, a group of protesting Indians massacred government troops at the town of Panzos, signaling a new wave of government-supported, right-wing terrorism. Victims included two leaders of the democratic left, Alberto Fuentes Mohra and Manuel Colón Argueta, and scores of moderate politicians, labor leaders, university officials, students and journalists. The left responded with selective assassinations of government officials; more important, the guerrillas steadily gained strength in rural areas.

Conditions deteriorated further in 1980. Especially in rural areas, army units, the police and right-wing death squads were increasingly charged with atrocities. In September Guatemala's civilian vice-president resigned and fled the nation to avoid being killed by the president's supporters.

The army and far-right groups such as the National Liberation Movement (MLN) were forging an alliance. The right's private armed units took on the fight against "subversive elements," as did the *comisionados militares,* civilian recruiting and intelligence agents of the army in rural areas. The extreme right also told the military that the Carter administration wanted to install a Marxist regime in Guatemala, citing as evidence both its human rights campaign and its acceptance of the Sandinista victory in Nicaragua. Finally, the right played on the military's growing economic stake in the status quo, which included one of the nation's largest banks, a cement factory and individual officers' huge land holdings for cattle and timber production.[19]

Carter administration efforts to break this alliance were ineffective, if not counterproductive. When the United States tried to change ambassadors in 1980, the Guatemalan government refused to accept the nominated successor. Ronald Reagan's victory was celebrated by the right and the military as signaling an end to human rights pressures and a resumption of badly needed military assistance.

But the anticipated rapprochement between the United States and the Lucas García regime did not occur in 1981. The Reagan administration's low-key human rights efforts proved no more effective than the Carter administration's public ones. Political murders averaged two-hundred fifty to three hundred per month in 1981, three times the level of 1980.[20] Meanwhile, the insurgency spread and the economy began to deteriorate rapidly. The military took greater casualties, found its resources spread ever thinner and began to experience severe equipment problems. All of this produced growing dissent within the military, especially among junior officers. One lieutenant colonel observed in late 1981:

> The government has no strategy to deal with the guerrillas. It has used the tactic of disorganizing society, labeling any vocal leaderships as subversive [and] attempted to use brute force against a political problem. The guerrillas would not be a serious military problem if not for the corruption, inability to govern, exploitation and violence that provides the guerrillas recruits and legitimacy.[21]

It was not surprising that junior officers installed a new regime after the incumbent rigged elections in March 1982. The Reagan administration welcomed the change and offered assistance to the new government headed by General Efrain Ríos Montt.

The 1982 coup reflected a consensus among junior officers that internal corruption and international isolation not only hampered the fight against the insurgents, but jeopardized the army's very survival. The junior officers were, however, divided over the solution. As a compromise, they installed a three-member junta of Ríos Montt, General Horacio Maldonado Schaad and Colonel Francisco Luis Gordillo. But considerable power was retained by an advisory council of junior officers because most feared a plot by the extreme right and wanted to keep civilian politicians on the sidelines, at least for the moment. Elections were projected, but there was no agreement on the date. There was considerable support for social and economic reforms, but wide disagreement as to their exact nature.

Under the new regime, murders of civilian intellectuals, politicians and labor leaders dramatically declined. A few officers who had committed crimes under the previous government were retired, or placed in inactive status; some individuals even fled into exile, but no officers or other high officials were actually tried or imprisoned. Guatemala's new rulers feared that prosecution might further divide the officer corps, weakening the army in its fight against the guerrillas. Ríos Montt issued verbal and written orders for officers to respect civilian rights, abstain from partisan politics and end corrupt practices, but did not enforce them. The officers hoped for external support, notably from the United States, from Israel and others, but feared being linked with U.S. interests. Ríos Montt claimed that he could obtain major funds from evangelical church groups, but received only small amounts of private and U.S. government aid.

The new regime did successfully combat some rural insurgency. Following an unsuccessful amnesty program, the military embarked on a pacification program combining heavy and often indiscriminate use of force with rural resettlement. It organized often with considerable coercion, local civilian defense forces (CDF) and provided food and work for rural inhabitants, usually Indians, who came under government control.[22] Known as "fusiles y frijoles" (rifles and beans), this program decimated the guerrillas' rural support network (along with much of the rural population). By 1983, it had significantly reduced insurgent-controlled areas and the level of combat. But the tactics used roused opposition abroad, especially in the U.S. Congress, which blocked most economic and military assistance. A small amount of training (IMET) funds was provided in FY83 and $10 million in Foreign Military Sales credits were included in the FY84 budget.[23] But Guatemala could not afford to take advantage of U.S.–authorized military sales, and Ríos Montt's requests for small arms and for equipment for an engineer battallion remained unfulfilled.

In June, 1982, Ríos Montt forced his two fellow junta members to resign and installed himself as president. But his evangelical religious fervor antagonized the dominant Roman Catholic church; his erratic style offended broad elements of society; his reform proposals, including one for agrarian reform, upset the established oligarchy; and his ties with the junior officers were resented by senior commanders. By mid-1983, even many of Ríos Montt's original supporters were losing their enthusiasm for his regime. His independence in foreign policy had created growing problems with the United States and, as opposition to him mounted, Washington feared he was more a source of instability than of stability. Reports of direct U.S. involvement in the August 1983 coup which finally toppled his regime seem exaggerated, but the Reagan administration did nothing to discourage such action. Defense Minister General Oscar Humberto Mejía Victores justified his leading the coup by the need to "preserve and fortify the unity of the Army and maintain the principle of hierarchy and command."[24] While many officers were not happy to see Mejía Victores take power, the coup encountered only limited resistance.

The new president was a career military officer with a reputation as a hard-liner. Mejía Victores had earlier gained notoriety in a sharp clash with U.S. Congressman Clarence Long. But once in power he pledged to hold prompt elections and gave strong support to U.S. policy. He cooperated with Honduras and El Salvador in dealing with the Contadora Group and took a leading role in reviving the Central American Defense Council (CONDECA). Internally, he dissolved the Council of State, which under Ríos Montt had provided some limited Indian participation in the government, and quickly discarded all plans for agrarian reform. By fall, both guerrilla activities and internal repression were apparently again on the rise.

The Reagan administration at first sought aid for President Mejía Victores, but without success in the U.S. Congress. Relations cooled further in November 1983 after Indians working under a U.S. AID contract were killed. The Guatemalan government failed to take action against those responsible and the Reagan administration suspended efforts to increase assistance. Meanwhile, guerrilla activities increased as government efforts to pacify the countryside suffered from lack of funds, lack of direction, rising human rights violations and continued dissension within the officer corps. The new president's control over the military seems limited and his hold on power tenuous. Another coup is possible, but so are elections for a constituent assembly. Increased guerrilla activity seems likely, but the chances that the insurgents will seize power in the next two or three years are still remote. The key to Guatemala's future remains the army, yet the army remains divided. The Reagan administration wants to support a strong, tough military which can defeat the guerrillas, but does not want a return to the conditions of 1981 and 1982 with the accompanying slaughter of noncombatants and murders of moderate politicians. There are military elements which share these goals, but no effective means has been found to support them without strengthening the hard-liners at the same time.

The Guatemalan military evidently determined to allow a civilian to win the presidential elections in 1985, but it remains quite unclear just how much power they will permit the new government to exercise. Many army officers harbor deep suspicions of the Christian Democratic party's supposed "leftist tendencies," referring to its presidential candidate, Vinicio Cerezo, as "Vinicio Alfonsín." The military has begun to break its ties with the extreme right, but is not about to give up any control over military affairs to civilians nor is it likely to permit civilian interference in its efforts to subdue the guerrillas. Meanwhile, internal political violence continues at a high level with regular reports of political assassinations, clashes with guerrillas and forced recruitment of Indians into civil defense units. Guatemala continues to offer more frustrations than hopes for U.S. policies in the region, largely because of the ongoing lack of effective influence over that nation's dominant institution, the Guatemalan Army.

Honduras

The Honduran military differs from its Guatemalan and Salvadoran counterparts, but it shares the region's heritage and its current conflicts. As the most developed institution in the region's least developed nation, it will play a key part in Honduras's future. Long neglected, it is now the focus of intense U.S. involvement, a development which offers major risks as well as opportunities.

The Honduran security forces (FUSEP) play a smaller role than they do in either El Salvador or Guatemala. Honduras lacks powerful, private, right-wing armies but it does have the strongest, most independent air force in Central America and a small but growing navy. Army strength is over 13,500 and increasing and an additional 1,200 men serve in the air force.[25]

The composition of the Honduran officer corps differs from its counterparts. Both the army and the air force run military academies, but some officers receive their education abroad and others are promoted from the ranks. When the United States trained a group of noncommissioned officers for Honduras as company grade officers for the expanding army, the graduates were commissioned immediately by the army commander, a sharp contrast to the Salvadoran approach. Honduran officers often come from rural areas and from families of lower social class standing. They are less likely than their Guatemalan counterparts to come from career military families.

The Honduran military, lacking the Guatemalan and Salvadoran history of ruthlessness in combating insurgencies, is less isolated and alienated from the civil population. Nothing in Honduran history compares with the 1932 peasant massacre in El Salvador or the Guatemalan counterinsurgency actions of the late 1960s and early 1980s. In addition, while the Honduran military openly ruled the nation from 1963 through 1981, it always allowed civilian politicians some power and never served as an instrument for eliminating political rivals. The military also lacks extremely close ties to the rural oligarchy; in the 1980s they actually implemented limited agrarian reforms.

There have been considerable corruption and some instances of brutality and other crimes against dissenters, peasant and labor groups. But on occasion, members of the military, including officers, have been disciplined for such actions. Imprisonment is exceptional but nevertheless sets a precedent.

The differences in the Honduran military reflect the different social structure and national history. By Central American standards, Honduras is large, very poor and underdeveloped and somewhat isolated. Since independence it has been the victim of its neighbors' ambitions and fears, suffering more invasions than any other Latin American nation, the last by El Salvador in 1969. Honduran society and especially the military hold an attitude of rational paranoia and assume that neighboring nations holding strongly divergent ideologies will support Honduran insurgents. And Hondurans who express sympathy for an opposed ideology held by a neighboring nation are suspected of conspiring to subvert the government. The military believes that Guatemala did this in the 1950s and that Nicaragua is doing this today. Their recourse has been to seek foreign support against foreign enemies. The British helped counter William Walker in the nineteenth century, and the United States opposed Nicaraguan efforts to dominate in the early twentieth century.

This history and national psychology have given the Honduran military a genuine national defense mission with some popular support. When El Salvador attacked in 1969, thousands of peasants rushed to defend the nation, a fact which may have influenced the military's later decision to support agrarian reform. But facing a history of credible external threats can lead to equating all dissent with subversion and relying more on force than on diplomacy for protection. The Honduran military still views El Salvador as no less a long-range threat than Nicaragua. Salvadoran refugees are barely tolerated and important territorial disputes with El Salvador still exist.

Strong U.S. ties with the Honduran military date back to the 1930s. The Honduran military helped support the 1954 CIA-backed Guatemalan invasion, the 1961 Bay of Pigs operation and the 1965 intervention in the Dominican Republic. Involvement increased greatly in 1980 after the Sandinista victory in Nicaragua and the spread of civil conflict in El Salvador. Military assistance for FY80 was under $4 million, but approached $9 million in FY81, and exceeded $31 million in FY82.[26] The number of U.S. military advisers in Honduras also expanded steadily, reaching three hundred at one point in 1983. Ten helicopters were loaned to Honduras, U.S. Army engineers began improving roads and airports and a U.S.–operated radar station was set up.

There were numerous reasons for this increased involvement. The United States hoped to use the Honduran military to interdict supplies destined for Salvadoran insurgents and to prevent them from establishing bases along the Honduran border. In addition, it was assumed that a strengthened military would deter a resurgence of Honduran guerrillas, and that military aid would symbolize U.S. support for Honduras. But as time passed, stability in Honduras was increasingly subordinated to the desire to use Honduras as a base for the U.S. confrontation with Nicaragua.

Honduran motives for accepting U.S. military involvement are less clear. The Honduran military believes that the civil conflict in El Salvador and the Sandinista regime in Nicaragua threaten Honduran national security. The U.S. buildup of El Salvador's armed forces produced pressures within the Honduran military for substantial external assistance. The military also found evidence linking domestic terrorists with El Salvador's guerrillas and Nicaragua's government. Some support was obtained from Argentina and Israel (the Israeli Defense Minister even visited Tegucigalpa), but the Honduran military felt that only the United States could provide minimum security requirements. But past U.S. support had been neither constant nor reliable. To ensure that it would be this time, some Hondurans felt they must support virtually any U.S. regional project, adopt an extremely hard line in dealing with the Sandinistas, support Nicaraguan counterrevolutionaries and even let the United States train Salvadoran troops in Honduras. The latter was particularly objectionable, but was accepted as necessary. All of this risked escalating internal conflicts, straining civil-military relations, reducing Honduran international prestige by giving it the image of a U.S. client state, and could ultimately lead to war with Nicaragua.

The alignment has resulted in a series of large-scale, joint maneuvers with U.S. forces and a large, semi-permanent U.S. military presence in the country. Military assistance and economic aid have also increased steadily, with the latter reaching $37.3 million in FY83 and $41 million requested for FY84.[27]

For Honduras, the risks in this arrangement include increasing guerrilla activity linked to Nicaragua and military repression within Honduras. A war with Nicaragua could bring down both the civilian and military leadership. A change of U.S. administrations could leave Honduras with no effective external support against hostile neighbors. Recognition of these risks has produced some nervousness and dissent within the military and more discontent among civilian politicians, but the civilians have limited capacity to alter the situation because the Honduran Constitution leaves effective control of the military in military hands. Basic decisions are made by the commander of the armed forces and the superior council of the armed forces, a body of senior officers chosen by the officer corps. The commander can be removed by a two-thirds vote of the Congress but in reality, the armed forces commander is much more capable of removing the president than vice versa.

For the United States, the risk is that its policies are militarizing Honduras, undermining its fragile democracy and increasing internal conflict. The attempt to promote stability could actually create instability. This policy also risks a regional war and exacerbates disputes within the United States over the entire region.

The 1985 political crisis demonstrated the continued determination of the military to keep the government in civilian hands. It reaffirmed the high command's role as the ultimate arbiters of political power as the agreement ending the political crisis was worked out through military mediation and was actually negotiated in the Air Force Officers Club. But it also showed that deep divisions persist within the military. The 1984 ouster of General Alvarez restored a degree of collegiate rule to the armed forces, but also intensified divisions among the graduating classes from the army academy and weakened somewhat the authority of the high command. The President's efforts to cultivate the loyalties of one such faction, including the reported direct payment of large sums to officers of the Honor Guard, revealed the dangers inherent in this situation. Most officers want a functioning, relatively democratic civilian government, but they remain divided on such issues as relations with the contras, the degree of dependency on the United States, the methods used to promote internal security and the necessity of basic economic and social reforms in order to avoid internal conflicts. The situation in Honduras offers some elements of hope, but it also contains a clear and growing danger of division, polarization and greater domestic conflict in the not too distant future.

Conclusion

Central American armed forces differ from their counterparts in the larger nations of Latin America in numerous significant ways other than their obvious smaller size. With the exception of the Honduran Air Force, none of the air or naval components of these militaries have achieved separate service status in Central America. They are all branches of the army, with their officers graduating from the same military academy as army officers and with their top commanders often having served much of their career in other branches of the military. This provides greater unity and increases the power of those at the top of the military hierarchy, but it is also a source of growing friction, especially on the part of air force pilots who increasingly want separate service status.

Another characteristic of Central America's armed forces is their tendency to include police and other paramilitary forces within the structure of the army. In Costa Rica and, until recently, in Panama, the armed forces were, in fact, little more than militarized national police forces whose prime task was the maintenance of internal order. The Nicaraguan National Guard, which for so many decades served as the defender of the Somoza dynasty, was a hybrid military-police force with the majority of its members exercising police and other internal security functions. In El Salvador the National Police, Treasury Police and National Guard are all under army control and staffed largely by graduates on the nation's only military academy. In Honduras the National Police (FUSEP) are also a part of the armed forces, and in Guatemala such groups as the Mobile Military Police (PMA) are an integral part of the armed forces.

This combination of military and police functions gives the armed forces a greatly enhanced ability to manipulate national politics and to exercise effective internal control. It forces aspirants for political power to constantly seek at least the benevolent neutrality if not the active support of the military high command if they are to have any chance to organize and campaign, let alone actually take power. But this arrangement also greatly increases the opportunities for corruption and brutality within the military. Since the merger of police and military functions frequently includes control over immigration, customs, ports and airports and even tax collections, the scale and scope of corruption in Central America's armed forces is often astonishing. The direct involvement in everyday police functions also produces increased friction with much of the public, contributes to the generally low image of the military and adds to both domestic and international accusations of military complicity in human-rights abuses. On the whole, this close melding of military and police functions has been one of the most negative aspects of Central American militarism.

There are numerous other characteristics which Central America's armed forces share with similar institutions in the smaller nations of the rest of the hemisphere and those in many other parts of the world. The noncommissioned officer corps is normally quite weak, ill-trained and separated from the commissioned officers by an immense and virtually unbridgeable social gap. Equipment is frequently obsolete, arms standardization is a constant problem and budget limitations make it virtually impossible to maintain a spare-parts inventory. Related to this is the generally low level of equipment maintenance. As in many smaller, poorer nations, there is a lack of other modern, developed national institutions such as labor unions, institutionalized political parties, and interest groups which can compete with the military for national power. While this situation is changing, in part because of external support for such institutions, it has been a major contributor to the tradition of military dominance of political power.

Like most small nation militaries, those in Central America are highly dependent on external sources of arms and training. In Central America this has traditionally meant an overwhelming dependence on the United States. For years the senior classes of most of the region's military academies were sent en masse to the School of the Americas in Panama for training. U.S. military missions were an active and visible part of the domestic military scene and most higher officers had at least some advanced training in the United States. Equipment was overwhelmingly of U.S. origin. This pattern began to change in the late 1960s and throughout the 1970s as reductions in military sales and the size of military advisory groups, the rising cost of U.S. training and the growing pressures for human rights all combined to force Central Americans to look elsewhere for equipment and training. In the 1980s this trend has been reversed and the United States is again clearly dominant in El Salvador, Honduras and Costa Rica. In Nicaragua dependence on the United States has been replaced by dependence on Cuba and the Soviet Union, while Guatemala remains the odd man out in the Central American scenario, seeking equipment and training from such diverse sources as Israel, Taiwan, Argentina and even Switzerland.

Personal, family and, especially, military academy graduating class ties are a vital factor in the internal organization and officer career patterns of Central American armies. This is most evident in El Salvador, but is also important in Guatemala and is becoming more important in Honduras. The officer corps are still small enough that everyone knows everyone. Internal alliances, the tendency of senior officers to take junior officers as protégés and even regional ties all help determine the complex web of military politics which, in turn, exercises such a dominant influence on the national scene.

Finally, there are some aspects of the peculiar regional history of Central America which help differentiate these armed forces from those of the rest of the hemisphere. Central America has a long history of using force as the ultimate arbiter of political disputes. Armies were originally little more than the armed partisans of the political faction in power. Although the regular armed forces have developed an increasingly autonomous identity, political parties and factions continue to maintain their own armed bands, frequently using them to supplement the armed forces efforts to maintain internal control, on occasion involving them in open clashes with rival political factions, and in general contributing to the high levels of internal violence and the lack of national unity and stability. In a sense, the proliferation of guerrilla forces and their internal divisions is simply a further reflection of this long and destructive tradition. So, too, is the tendency of armed forces to become involved in training, equipping and protecting armed exile forces from other nations in the region, especially when such nations have sharply differing political ideology from that prevailing in the armed forces. Honduran support of the contras and Nicaragua's aid to El Salvador's insurgents clearly fall within this category.

In summary, Central America's armed forces have become the dominant political institution within most of their nations for a variety of reasons, most of which are firmly rooted in the region's tumultuous history. The ways in which this dominance is expressed, including the marked tendencies toward brutality, corruption and internal military rivalries also stem from this heritage, as does the close identification of most of these institutions with the United States. The conflicts of the past seven years have produced major changes throughout the region and the military has not been immune to the effects of these changes. The armed forces are becoming more modernized and institutionalized and are losing some of their ability to totally dominate the domestic scene. But, outside of Costa Rica, they remain the ultimate arbiters of power, a position which they believe they have a right to hold and which they remain determined to defend, no matter what the cost to the nation as a whole.

Notes

1. Lyle McAlister, *The* Fuero Militar *in New Spain,* Gainesville: University of Florida Press, 1957, p. 15.
2. Christon I. Archer, *The Army in Bourbon Mexico,* Albuquerque: University of New Mexico Press, 1977, p. 257.
3. *Ibid.,* p. 219.
4. John J. Johnson, *The Military and Society in Latin America,* Stanford: Stanford University Press, 1964, p. 37.
5. Gabriel Aguilera Peralta, *La integración en centroamerica,* n.p.: INCEP, n.d., p. 14.
6. Letter from Dr. Dana G. Munro to Richard Millet, February 14, 1965. For details on the 1923 conference see Thomas Leonard, *United States Policy and Arms Limitations in Central America. The Washington Conference of 1923,* Los Angeles: California State University at Los Angeles, 1982.
7. For details on this see Richard Millett, *Guardians of the Dynasty,* Maryknoll, N.Y.: Orbis Books, 1977.
8. *Washington Post,* March 15, 1980, p. A1.
9. International Institute for Strategic Studies, *The Military Balance, 1983–1984,* London: International Institute for Strategic Studies, 1983, p. 110.
10. *Ibid.,* p. 127. *El Salvador Military and Economic Reprogramming.* Hearing before a subcommittee of the Committee on Appropriations, U.S. Senate, 98th Congress, 1st Session, March 22, 1983, p. 76.
11. Robert V. Elam, "Appeal to Arms: The Army and Politics in El Salvador, 1931–1964," unpublished Ph.D. dissertation, University of New Mexico, 1968, pp. 176–77.
12. Carolyn Forché and Leonel Gomez, "The Military's Web of Corruption," *The Nation,* October 23, 1982, p. 391.
13. *El Salvador: The United States in the Midst of a Maelstorm. A Report to the Committee on Foreign Relations and the Committee on Appropriations, U.S. Senate,* 97th Congress, 2nd Session, 1982, p. 6.
14. *Foreign Assistance and Related Program Appropriations for 1984.* Hearings before a subcommittee of the Committee on Appropriations, House of Representatives, 98th Congress, 1st Session, March 1983, pp. 326–27.
15. Institute for Strategic Studies, *op. cit.,* pp. 110–11.
16. This is due in part to the fact that the *Politécnica,* while extremely rigorous, usually manages to graduate up to half of those who enter.
17. For details of this operation see Richard H. Immerman, *The CIA in Guatemala,* Austin: University of Texas Press, 1982, and Stephen Schlesinger and Stephen Kinser, *Bitter Fruit,* Garden City, N.Y.: Doubleday, 1981.

18. Richard N. Adams, *Crucifixion by Power,* Austin: University of Texas Press, 1970, p. 261.
19. Thomas P. Anderson, *Politics in Central America,* New York: Praeger, 1982, pp. 52–53. Gabriel Aguilera Peralta, "The Militarization of the Guatemalan State," *Guatemala in Rebellion,* Johnathan L. Fried *et. al.,* eds., New York: Grove Press, 1983, p. 118.
20. *U.S. Policy Towards Guatemala,* Hearing before a subcommittee of the Committee on Foreign Affairs, House of Representatives, 98th Congress, 1st Session, March 1983, p. 37.
21. *Ibid.,* pp. 43–44.
22. *Ibid.,* pp. 56–59.
23. *Foreign Assistance and Related Programs for FY1984,* p. 72.
24. *Central American Report* (Guatemala) 10, August 12, 1983, p. 241.
25. Institute for Strategic Studies, p. 111. The Air Force operates a squadron of *Super Mystere* B2 fighters and hopes to acquire U.S. F5Es in the near future.
26. *Foreign Assistance and Related Programs for FY1984,* p. 73.
27. *Ibid.*

David Ronfeldt / *The Modern*
Mexican Military

A Time for Reassessment

The military remains one of the great mysteries of modern Mexico. The more U.S. analysts know about it, the better it fits the best generalization we have about almost everything else in Mexico: unique, special, exceptional, a product of the Mexican Revolution, a case unlike anything else in Latin America. Yet the paucity of information about this hermetic institution has left policymakers and analysts, certainly in Washington and probably also in Mexico City, without sound answers to many basic questions: What is the military's effect on Mexico's domestic and foreign policies? Is it adequately prepared to assure Mexico's stability and security? How would it behave in the event of a serious political or foreign policy crisis?

In ordinary, tranquil times these questions can be neglected. But when turns of events arouse U.S. concerns about Mexico's stability, security, and

This chapter is slightly abridged from the author's study, "The Modern Mexican Military: Implications for Mexico's Political Stability and National Security" (The Rand Corporation, Santa Monica, N-2288-FF/RC, March 1985), which in turn derives from the author's lead chapter in the anthology he edited, *The Modern Mexican Military: A Reassessment,* Research Monograph 15, Center for U.S.–Mexican Studies, University of California at San Diego, 1984.

The author wishes to thank Wayne Cornelius, Director of the Center, for his support in producing that anthology. Published with the permission of the Rand Corporation.

policy behavior—as has been the case for some time now—it becomes important to update and reassess our meager knowledge about the Mexican military.

It is well known that Mexico's political and military leaders had removed the revolutionary army from political participation and committed it to professional pursuits by the 1940s.[1] Afterwards, the military's size, budget, and inventory remained quite small, and the armed forces studiously avoided the public limelight except for ceremonial occasions. Troop units were still mobilized to control some electoral, student, labor, or agrarian disturbances—but this was viewed as a police, not a partisan political function. The army's sudden visibility in subduing the massive domestic violence of 1968, however, jarred the conventional wisdom of the 1950s and 1960s that Mexico had depoliticized the military and institutionalized a stable civilian system.

Revisionist studies of the 1970s thus found that the army—largely because it could operate behind the scenes to facilitate political communication and conflict resolution in favor of the governing elites—had continued to fulfill "residual political roles," which may be essential for preserving Mexico's political system.[2] These studies are still useful, but many changes have occurred since they appeared. A new military is in the making, and its roles require a new analysis.

Long sheltered from public scrutiny, always receiving brief praise in the President's annual state-of-the-union speech, but otherwise mainly the topic of rumors and uninformed speculation, the military is now becoming a more visible, respected, and modernized partner of Mexico's ruling institutions. No single motive or reason explains this quiet but historic change; it has been set in motion, after decades of consensus that the military could be neglected, because a series of unusual events has raised an array of issues—domestic and foreign, political and military, economic and security—that Mexico's civilian establishment cannot manage alone.

The resolve to modernize and strengthen the military, most observers agree, derives from the experience of the Tlatelolco showdown in October 1968. Confronting what it perceived to be the most serious challenge to internal security in decades, the army opened fire on thousands of protestors assembled in Mexico City's Tlatelolco plaza, putting a violent end to the student-led protest movement begun several months earlier. Subsequent requirements to assure internal security during the early and mid-1970s—particularly the large counterinsurgency and anti-narcotics campaigns conducted in Guerrero and other provincial areas—reinforced the military's and the government's determination to increase the army's size, improve its organization, modernize its equipment and doctrine, better educate its officer corps, and enhance its image.[3]

In the early 1980s, the conflicts in Central America obliged Mexico's political and military leaders to face the possibility that threats could arise to the south, including along the border with Guatemala. Because of this, they reportedly began to examine, for the first time in memory, how regional and domestic conflicts could coalesce, whether Mexico should develop a comprehensive approach to national security, and what new roles the military might have to play in guaranteeing Mexico's stability and security.

Various events thus brought both the internal and external security roles of the military to the fore between the 1960s and the 1980s. To confuse the issues, unusual government crises in 1968, 1976, and 1982 led to wild, unwarranted rumors that a military coup was possible in Mexico. But even if the times had been tranquil, substantial military modernization would surely have occurred as a result of the military's opportunities to help develop and protect Mexico's new oil fields, spend earnings from the oil bonanza, and participate in the state's dramatic expansion.[4]

The reassessment presented here addresses a set of basic issues that are frequently raised in policy-oriented discussions about the Mexican military:[5]

- the modernization of the military;
- the military's place in Mexico's changing political system;
- the prospects for political instability that are of military import;
- the implications of Mexico's approach to national security.

In brief, the study argues that a new, close civil-military partnership may result from the modernization of the military and a transformation that is taking place in the composition of Mexico's political elites and the structure of its state institutions. Despite recent concerns about Mexico's stability, political unrest terrible enough to provoke a military coup or some other usurpation of civilian authority seems unlikely to occur, at least in the near future. But the military may, with civilian agreement, play expanded roles in determining how to resolve the new agenda of domestic and foreign security issues confronting Mexico.

The Modernization of the Military

The Mexican military is making impressive progress, after several decades as an institution "whose development has not kept pace with the country as a whole."[6] A comprehensive military modernization program has been adopted, the first in decades. Improvements are occurring at all levels and in all services, gradually fulfilling the principle that Mexico should have a military of quality, not quantity. The modernization program is most noticeable in the following areas:[7]

- growth in the size of the military—in both personnel and budget;
- changes in the army's organization and deployment;

- improvements in the military education system;
- the acquisition of new equipment by all services.

The Size of the Military—Personnel and Budget

The military has grown substantially in recent years, but not out of proportion to other indices of Mexico's growth. Keeping rough pace with the growth of Mexico's population, military personnel presently number about 120,000, up from 80,000 ten years ago, and a little over 60,000 twenty years ago. All this time, the number of military personnel per thousand of population has remained under 2.0, which is very low compared to other nations. Although ambitious plans reportedly exist for an eventual increase to 220,000, Mexico's recent economic recession has slowed the expansion of the military's budget and manpower.

In absolute terms, that budget has increased manyfold since 1960. But as a percentage of Mexico's gross national product (GNP), it has generally remained under 1 percent (0.7 percent in 1960 and 1970, dropping to 0.5 percent by 1980). Military expenditures as a percentage of total government expenditures have also remained low, declining from about 7 percent in 1960, to 5 percent in 1970, to 3 percent in 1980.[8]

Organization and Deployment

The cabinet-level structure of the Mexican military remains the same, with a secretary of national defense over the army and the air force, and the navy having a separate secretary. The air force remains under the army. Suggestions that the air force be made an independent service, and/or that a unified secretary of defense be created to cover all three service branches have not taken hold. The army (excluding the air force) remains the largest service branch and has the lion's share of the total military personnel and budget.

The biggest changes have occurred in the army's force structure and regional command structure.[9] The number of brigades and battalions has increased, with the new brigades formed out of battalions that were created earlier. In 1960, the army consisted of two brigades: the Presidential Guard, and the regular infantry. In 1970, there were three brigades: one mechanized (the Presidential Guard), and two infantry. By 1980, there were five: one mechanized and two infantry, plus one airborne, and one of military police. There has been speculation that a sixth brigade, armored, will eventually be formed. At the same time, the independent infantry battalions, which apparently are part of the regional zone commands rather than the aforementioned brigades, have also increased in number. Sources vary, but at least twenty new independent battalions have been created since 1970, making a total of about seventy-five such battalions. At the other end of the scale of force structure, small mobile detachments (called *partidas*) are being distributed more widely throughout the nation, especially in provincial areas where the army needs to maintain constant contact with the local populace and improve the security of strategic installations, such as hydroelectric complexes. Meanwhile, the regional command structure has also expanded to create a new military zone (the thirty-sixth) in Chiapas along Mexico's border with Guatemala, making Chiapas the fourth Mexican state to contain more than one military zone.[10] In addition, the thirty-six zones have recently been organized into nine military regions.[11]

Education

After several decades of retaining a World War II type of curriculum, the military school system is being extensively modernized, and the officer corps as a whole is receiving a much better and broader education. After introducing a prototype course in advanced military and security studies in the late 1970s, the military opened a new school in 1981, the National Defense College, to provide senior officers with advanced studies in a range of security and geopolitical subjects as well as traditional military and administrative ones. In addition, the curriculum on military strategy, tactics, and related subjects has been updated and expanded at the army's Superior War College (the ESG, the highest educational institution before 1981), which mainly trains junior and middle-grade ranks to become staff officers.[12] No information is readily available about changes in the curriculum at the Heroic Military College, the army academy that trains officer candidates for their first commission as a second lieutenant, but the government provided it with dramatic new facilities (sometimes called the Military Academy) in 1976. Overall, an effort is apparently being made to improve the military's technical education for resource and infrastructure management; this may prove useful in the event of a national emergency, for example, one affecting transportation, communications, or the production of a strategic material such as petroleum.

Equipment

All three services have expanded their inventories. The expansion has been modest, but compared to the condition of the previous inventories, the changes add up to a substantial modernization. Largely because of Mexico's interests in patrolling its new two-hundred-mile offshore economic zone as well as the offshore oil fields, the navy was the first service to expand its inventory substantially. This expansion included a domestic shipbuilding program for patrol craft. Before 1970, the navy had no destroyers, five aging U.S.-built frigates, and few large patrol craft. Since 1970, the navy has obtained two Fletcher- and two Gearing-class destroyers from the United States, six Halcon-class frigates from Spain, and thirty-one Azteca- and six Olmeca-class patrol craft, built in Mexico and the United Kingdom.[13] The numbers of inventory items acquired by the army and the air force are also modest, but the effect is substantial. During the last ten years, the army has acquired about forty Panhard ERC-90 Lynx armored vehicles from France, DN III armored personnel carriers built in Mexico, and G-3 automatic rifles made in Mexico under license from West Germany. The air force has received twelve Northrop F-5 fighters from the United States and fifty-seven Pilatus PC-7 turbo-trainers (which may be armed for counterinsurgency operations) from Switzerland.

Most of these acquisitions replace equipment that had become antiquated, even unsafe. For example, the air force's new squadrons of F-5s and PC-7s replace very old squadrons of Northrop AT-33s and T-28s, respectively (not to mention some inoperable British-made Vampires). The army's acquisitions upgrade an inventory that had emphasized light and medium tanks obtained from the United States after World War II. Nonetheless, continued progress at modernizing the army and the air force and building indigenous military industries will probably result in a measured expansion of their weaponry and capabilities. Air defense and air transport, for example, may need future attention.

This far-reaching effort to modernize and strengthen Mexico's armed forces surely improves their technical proficiency for the internal and external defense of Mexico's interests. Military power to meet potential threats is not the only purpose served, however; and it may be secondary to political, symbolic, and motivational purposes. National honor, pride, and prestige are at stake. These improvements strengthen the institutional dignity of the military, thereby probably enhancing respect for the military's roles at home (always important), for Mexico's image as an emerging medium power and world oil producer (mainly the 1970s), and for Mexico's diplomacy to resolve regional conflicts (the 1980s). Weapons may be valuable diplomatic symbols; by enabling Mexico to look stronger and more important, they may help it to influence its Central American neighbors to behave more peacefully.[14] As Mexico's defense minister, General Félix Galván López, stated succinctly in 1980 while justifying the military's modernization program, "The strong are respected more than the weak."

Will progress at further professionalizing and modernizing the military help keep it out of politics, as was the case in the past?[15] The military's capabilities to fulfill the various military, socioeconomic, and politico-administrative roles assigned to it have increased greatly since 1968. And these capabilities will continue to grow, especially as the members of the officer corps acquire advanced education. This does not mean that the military may become a "threat" or a "danger" to the political system, however, for its identity and its interests are solidly tied to supporting the Constitution of 1917 and serving as an institutional partner of the state.

The State, the Elite, and the Military

The "residual political roles" observed in the 1970s mainly concerned the army's ability to facilitate political communication from the bottom up and political control from the top down, usually in helping government leaders settle small-scale electoral, student, labor, and agrarian disturbances. At the time, there was no evidence that the military influenced national policy-making, or that officers (on leave) filled more than a few administrative and political posts (e.g., as congressional deputies or occasionally as state governors). The army's roles were thus largely instrumental, but they seemed to make a significant difference for the performance and preservation of Mexico's political system:

> Had the army behaved as a strictly professional and apolitical military that was mobilized only in case of major domestic disturbance, the president would have lost considerable capacity to control state governors. Both the president and the governor would have lost considerable control over isolated rural areas. And, in general, government and political elites would most likely have had to increase their dependence upon police and paramilitary forces, whose conduct would be much less professional and politically more manipulable in contrast to the contemporary Mexican army. Although the comparison is difficult to draw, I would even suggest that the army has had greater political impact than any opposition party, including PAN.[16]

These observations still seem to apply, and there is no evidence that the military's political roles have expanded significantly since the early 1970s. This earlier analysis is no longer sufficient, however. The roles the army may play reflect broader conditions and trends, and that broader context has changed fundamentally in Mexico and to its south—as analyzed in this and later sections.

A dual transformation has occurred in Mexico's political system since the late 1960s. A new governing elite has emerged as the successor to the old *familia revolucionaria*. And the state has grown enormously in power and scale, thereby lessening the traditional centrality of the Institutional Revolutionary Party (PRI). These elite and institutional changes have affected the military; and it in turn has participated in making the changes happen.

The Governing Elite: Advent of the Institutional Family

For decades, the concept of the *familia revolucionaria* has been used to describe Mexico's governing elite and explain its continuity over time. This elite was broad and cohesive. It included public- and private-sector leaders, and it incorporated conservative and leftist ideological leanings. In Frank Brandenburg's classic formulation, it had three levels: a top level consisting of the president and his inner council, a second level consisting of important interest group leaders, and a third level corresponding to the government bureaucracy and related organizations.[17]

Although the term *familia revolucionaria* remains in daily use in Mexico, it is assuming the status of a myth, a symbol of continuity, when in reality substantial change has occurred in the composition and structure of Mexico's governing elites.[18] This change is associated with the recent growth of the state and the public sector and is manifested in the following ways:

- The key element is the advent of a young, well-educated, interconnected generation of post-revolutionary elites in high administrative offices. This new generation is much more technocratic and statist in its nationalism and more dependent on the state for career and influence than were the old-style party-line politicians. Whereas the old generation looked to the unifying experiences of 1910, the new generation is marked by the divisive experiences of 1968.
- The new governing family seems to be narrower. It does not span the public and private sectors as widely as it used to. It does not reflect regional interests and elites as much as it used to. And it avows a nationalism that adheres more closely to staying "left within the Constitution." Thus the standard formula used for describing the revolutionary family during the 1940s to 1960s—in terms of the Cardenista (left) and Alemanista (right) wings—no longer applies, although the new elite may develop its own left (Echeverrista?) and right wings.
- The state's administrative leaders seem to be surpassing the interest-group leaders in policymaking influence. In other words, the second and third levels in Brandenburg's description have traded places. The new generation has provided the government (and its informal advisory staffs) with unusual continuity across the Echeverría, López Portillo, and de la Madrid administrations.

It appears therefore that the governing family of today is not the same as the revolutionary family of yesterday. Because the new elite is so dedicated to developing the state and its institutional interests, it seems appropriate to call it by a new name: the institutional family *(familia institucional)*.

This institutional family has not fully supplanted the old revolutionary family. The two tendencies coexist, uneasily; but the transition seems to be advanced and irreversible unless conservative political and business elements from the old family promote a confrontation. Barring some kind of upheaval in Mexico, the new governing elite will be able to consolidate its hold when, in addition to proving its technocratic capabilities, it generates a new set of party-type politicians.[19]

The military officer corps has undergone related changes.[20] The older generation of generals has been rapidly retired during the last ten years, and a new generation of increasingly well-educated officers is taking charge. This new generation is much more the product of the military institution per se. It probably has fewer links to private economic (or political) interests; hence it seems less disposed to engage in factional politics or to favor private-sector interests and overtures. It seems well prepared to support managerial and technocratic approaches to problem solving. Its convictions appear to be fundamentally "institutional."

How these developments may affect civil-military relations is largely a matter of speculation, given the lack of data. Yet the emergence of the *familia institucional* seems to portend closer civil-military relations in three respects: (1) There may be increasing contact between military officers and government officials. This is already noticeable in the military school system, which formerly isolated the formation of the officer corps from civilian contacts in order to mold a uniform institutional identity while eradicating any class, regional, and political identities. At the same time, the course work did not depart from standard military subjects and implanted a strong sense of civil-military separation. Now, however, the National Defense College and the Superior War College are cautiously incorporating limited exposure to civilian officials, lecturers, and topics. (2) The new generation of military officers, though its educational level lags behind that of the top civilian elites, may gradually demonstrate—and the civilian elites may learn—that it is acquiring the education and the administrative, managerial, and technocratic skill to help the government address a broad range of development and security issues. This could undo the long-standing perception, held in military as well as civilian circles, that the officer corps is educationally inferior (and should be kept that way). (3) The officer corps may develop a greater affinity with the civilian administrative technocrats than with the PRI party politicians, partly because the changes taking place in the military educational system may dispose the officer corps to define national problems in much the same way as does the new generation of civilians in the institutional family.[21]

The Institutional Architecture: Rise of the State

Traditional descriptions of Mexico's political system have emphasized the power of the President (not the *presidency*, but the President) and the PRI, with the latter seen as the pillar supporting virtually the entire institutional architecture. By comparison, the state, the government, and the bureaucracy were considered less developed and less central to understanding the Mexican system. The military was always thought to be available to uphold the system should the PRI fail to control a conflict; but the military was never placed in the same class with the PRI as an institutional pillar.

The overall picture seems to have changed, because the state has expanded enormously since the early 1970s.[22] The President and the PRI remain powerful and central to the Mexican political system, but it is no longer a one-pillar system. And the Cabinet, especially the subset of ministers comprising the "economic cabinet" *(gabinete económico)*, may now wield considerable influence over the President's decisions. Therefore, a revised, updated description of Mexico's institutional architecture should emphasize the state (with the President at the top, the Cabinet and bureaucracy below) and show it resting on three pillars:

- a political party pillar (the PRI);
- a military pillar (the modernizing army, or what its leaders sometimes broadly term *el Instituto Armado*);
- an economic pillar (the now vast set of state enterprises, most recently including the nationalized banks).

These pillars are not separate from the state; they are integrated into its architecture.[23]

In the past, the PRI would have been regarded as the strongest pillar of the state, and the state enterprises as the weakest. This is not the case any more. All three have undergone major changes during the past ten years. The PRI appears to be a bit weaker in comparison and the military a bit stronger, while the state enterprises have become much stronger.[24]

Whereas it is relatively easy to document changes in the relative strength and role of the PRI and the state enterprises, which are publicly more visible, it is difficult to do so for the military. But although strong evidence is lacking, it appears that the top political (and military) leadership of the transformed political system has recognized an increasing need for stronger military support in performing a broad range of domestic and foreign-policy activities. In the latter area, for example, the three "pillars" have given Mexico's government greater flexibility for attempting to influence the course of events in Central America. The PRI helped establish a regional mechanism loosely identified with the Social Democratic positions, the Permanent Conference of Latin American Political Parties (COPPPAL), and used it to support the Sandinista movement in Nicaragua and the FMLN-FDR struggle in El Salvador. At times, this helped Mexico to promote its foreign policy without directly involving Mexico's President or the Foreign Ministry. The expansion of Mexico's oil production through the state petroleum industry, Pemex, enabled Mexico, at Venezuela's invitation, to enter into the San Jose Accord (the Oil Facility Agreement) to provide oil on preferential terms to Central America. By comparison, the Mexican military has had little to do with Mexico's policy toward Central America. But additional military attachés and officers have been sent to the area as a new, unusual way for the Mexican government, especially the President, to acquire information independently of the Foreign Ministry and the PRI. And the program to modernize and expand Mexico's armed forces may help, albeit indirectly, to strengthen respect in Central America for Mexican diplomacy. By now, COPPPAL and the Oil Facility Agreement have lost importance as instruments of Mexico's policies; the strengthening of the military's information-gathering capabilities may thus prove to be the more durable innovation.

A New Civil-Military Partnership?

Outside observers, accustomed to the powerful roles the military plays in other nations, may be unimpressed by these examples and speculations about the slightly increased activities of the Mexican military. However, seasoned observers of Mexican politics and society generally agree that something new and important is evolving. Although it may have only subtle public manifestations, it may still affect who gets to rule Mexico and how it is ruled in the decades ahead.

In general—and this must be stated cautiously because our knowledge about the Mexican military remains so sparse, anecdotal, and unclear— this systemic transformation may mean that the military is moving beyond its "residual political roles" to having a more integrated, central place in Mexico's political system. A broader civil-military partnership may be developing wherein it will be more appropriate to talk about the military's role in the state rather than in "politics." A role in politics typically implies that the military is intervening or interfering in a political system, to some extent usurping civilian authority. That is not what is happening in Mexico; nor does it seem likely to happen. As discussed in the next section, a military coup seems unlikely; even a gradualist term like "creeping militarism" may represent a harsh judgment of current trends.[25]

The military is more visibly active as an instrument and symbol of the state's authority and, behind the scenes, as an information gatherer for policymakers. Evidence is lacking to claim that military officers have significant influence in policy-making, even in the area of national security. But the military is gradually being prepared, through officer education and technical modernization, to play enlarged roles in support of the state, should its civilian leadership falter and civil-military leadership be required. Exactly what offices and issues might be affected is uncertain; but if the military's administrative roles expand, they might touch the formulation of some national security and development policies. The Interior

Ministry would be the likely place for this to occur. The possible establishment of a national security council or a "political cabinet" *(gabinete político)* including the military might be the culmination of such an institutional transformation.[26]

Political Stability and Military Behavior

Discussions and rumors about the Mexican army's political roles all too often start with speculation about the possibility of a military coup. This syndrome may occur partly because analysts know so little about the Mexican military and hence fall back on patterns of thinking derived from analyses of military behavior elsewhere. In most Latin American political systems, there is little "distance" from crisis to instability to a coup. If you have the former, you're not far from also having the latter. Mexico is different: Time after time, its political system has demonstrated a profound capacity to absorb internal conflicts and crises without becoming unstable. Even in moments of apparent instability—for example, during October 1968—a military coup has turned out to be unlikely.

The new state-based political system produces tensions and conflicts that may be interpreted as signs of looming instability but that may instead reflect only the change to the new system.[27]

- Regional tensions may be more noticeable as the state expands its regional influence and promotes new regional economic development programs, especially if traditional regional politicians have less say in Mexico City's policy.
- There may be greater public-private tensions, with private-sector elites now subordinate, rather than of equal status, in the ruling coalition. This may affect foreign as well as domestic policy-making.
- U.S.–Mexican relations may seem less stable and more tense, partly because the policy postures of the new institutional family and the new state will seem more nationalistic and more independent of the United States.

In the face of these tensions, the Mexican military seems likely to remain more solidly than ever in support of the transformed political system.

Institutional Solidity Despite Economic Tensions

Recent economic crises stemming from presidential behavior have shaken Mexico's political system far more than have guerrillas and terrorists. In the context of broader debt and devaluation crises, President Luis Echeverría's effort to expropriate rich agricultural lands in Sonora at the close of his administration in 1976 and the bank nationalization at the close of President José López Portillo's administration in 1982 injured traditional working relations between the government and private sector elites. Both episodes gave rise to rumors of a possible military coup. There were no outbreaks of violence requiring military action in either case, however, and tensions eased with the change of administration and renewed assurances of goodwill toward the private sector.[28]

The evolution of the state since 1968 has wrought a restructuring of Mexico's mixed public-private economy. The balance has shifted: The private sector's former institutional weight has declined and the public sector's has grown, with considerable friction occurring between them. In the aftermath of the bank nationalization, it has been said that as much as 60 percent of Mexico's economy has fallen under state control—a figure that has led some observers to voice concern that a quiet socialization of Mexico's economy may be under way.[29] Mexico's government leaders have explained that the changes amount only to the growth of state capitalism. And the recent decisions of the de la Madrid administration to return many nationalized banking assets and to sell some nonpriority state-owned industries to the private sector provide reassurance that a mixed economy will be preserved as it is enlarged. This still does not tell us whether the growth of the state will change the nature of Mexico's economy—a question that is outside the scope of this study.[30] But the deliberate, dramatic expansion of these enterprises has at least enabled the state to consolidate its grip on the national economy, marginalize elements of the private sector, expand the state's opportunities for patronage, and acquire new instruments for political control and cooptation.[31]

The military does not appear to have any objections to this strengthening of the state's role in the economy, as long as it is accomplished according to the Constitution, reflects Mexican nationalism, preserves the mixed economy, and does not involve violent mass actions. Indeed, far from suggesting the possibility of a military coup, the army's visibility during the early months of the de la Madrid administration probably helped assure the government's survival.[32]

A Matrix of Political Violence

The institutional reliability of the army is partly a function of its capability to enforce internal security. The few cases on which data are available suggest that the army's response to political violence may depend largely on how widely instability and unrest are distributed within Mexico. The army is quite capable of handling isolated conflicts. What would strain its capabilities is a widely dispersed conflict implying that the government, or indeed the nation as a whole, may be falling apart. Two dimensions in particular are crucial to observe:

- *Mexico City vis-à-vis the provinces:* The army can handle disturbances in Mexico City as long as the provinces are peaceful. Likewise, it can handle disturbances or a temporary loss of central control in a provincial capital as long as Mexico City is peaceful. The army's manpower and other resources may be strained to the breaking point, however, if it must mobilize in both the capital and provincial areas simultaneously.
- *The elites vis-à-vis the masses:* Splits within the governing elite are unlikely to destabilize Mexico as long as "the masses" are orderly. Likewise, occasional mass-level disturbances are unlikely to destabilize Mexico as long as the governing elite remains cohesive and disciplined.[33] The simultaneous occurrence of massive public unrest and a major split within the government's upper ranks, however, would magnify the possibility of the military taking matters into its own hands, albeit with some civilian political allies.

Conflicts distributed across both dimensions at the same time—in the national capital and the provinces, at both elite and mass levels—would undoubtedly mean that the central government/PRI leadership was losing control and Mexico's political system was on the verge of collapse and in danger of a revolution or a coup.[34]

These dimensions may help illuminate why the army finally resorted to brute force at Tlatelolco in October 1968 to end the massive student-based protest movement that began in July. Dealing with the movement required the army to pull numerous units out of the provinces for use in Mexico City. The provincial capitals were initially calm, but soon before Tlatelolco the protest movement appeared increasingly likely to spread to the provinces. If this had occurred, the army (and the government) would probably have lost control of the situation. The Tlatelolco repression, by forestalling this prospect, may thus have been motivated more by domestic military and political requirements than by the oft-cited need to safeguard the holding of the Olympic Games a few weeks later.[35]

By comparison, the guerrilla movements of Genaro Vásquez Rojas and Lucio Cabañas and the 23 September League, the urban terrorist group that operated during the 1970s, never threatened Mexico's stability or raised the possibility of a military coup. Despite media attention, the two guerrilla movements had little effect outside Guerrero. The army poured thousands of soldiers into counterinsurgency operations there but did not have to deal with serious problems elsewhere. The league was tracked down and disposed of by other security forces.

In the future, political instability of military import is unlikely to develop in the absence of much sharper elite/mass and capital/provincial conflicts. And such conflicts—or at least the more widely discussed possibilities—seem unlikely to materialize.

One set of possibilities concerns potential regional conflicts. In particular, the recent unrest in southern Mexico, the settlement of refugees from Guatemala and other Central American nations, the use of Chiapas as a sanctuary by Guatemalan guerrillas, and alleged border incursions by Guatemalan army units pursuing guerrillas all raise security issues for Mexico's government and may require increasing military attention. Leftist critics within Mexico, notably Heberto Castillo, have argued that the "revolutionary osmosis" and the "Central Americanization" of political life in the southeast may generate popular violence as early as the final years of the de la Madrid administration.[36] Conservative analysts elsewhere have sounded early warnings that low-intensity conflict spreading northward from Central America and fueled by leftist sympathizers within Mexico could turn Mexico into the last "domino."[37] However, the rhetoric from Mexico City and elsewhere seems overblown: Evidence is lacking that popular discontent and radical sentiments are widespread in Chiapas, Oaxaca, or other sections of the south. And the Guatemalan military is reportedly finally winning its prolonged internal war against Guatemala's guerrilla movements. Thus Mexico's stability should not be affected as long as the southern region's troubles remain isolated within the region, the federal government continues to provide the local residents with needed services and development assistance, a large army presence is not required, and the Guatemalan insurgency continues to decline.

A somewhat dated scenario which draws on events in 1976–1977 suggests that massive unrest could occur in northern Mexico if the United States were to impose a highly restrictive immigration policy, effectively "closing the border" and repatriating apprehended aliens to Mexico, at the same time that other jobless Mexican workers are heading north to escape the effects of a peso devaluation and economic recession in Mexico. In this scenario, the intersection of the two flows, one moving south and the other north, would create an explosive social situation in Mexico's border cities, requiring the Mexican government to mobilize troops to repress disturbances. Spillover into the United States would cause violent clashes between Mexico and the United States and require the mobilization of the U.S. National Guard to restore order on the U.S. side of the border. In the end, the scenario proposes, the Mexican army would gain a strong voice in Mexican politics and government.[38] However, this scenario—the most explicit postulation I have seen of a U.S. policy toward a bilateral issue inducing the militarization of Mexican politics—is unrealistic. Despite the continuing U.S. need to improve its immigration policy and better manage the border, the United States is extremely unlikely to close this "safety valve" and thus endanger Mexico's traditional stability.[39]

Mexico City may be potentially the most unstable place in the nation. The city is well on its way to demographic, ecological, and economic disaster. Once the healthy heart of the national economy, it is now an economic burden, demanding ever higher subsidies to keep functioning.[40] It is a decaying symbol of Mexico's unfortunate enchantment with the overcentralization and overconcentration of political and economic power.

And it is trapped in a vicious circle: Too many people are trying to live there; but making it more hospitable (at great expense) would only attract more people. Although the city has large police and other security forces to attend to the growing problems of crime and congestion, it may be only a matter of time before some incident provokes large-scale civil disorder that requires the government to call out the army. Recovery of the national economy and the creation of other economic growth poles to attract and employ people would alleviate the city's problems, but these are unlikely to happen in the near future.

Institutional and sectoral criteria provide another way of looking at the possibilities for political instability involving elite/mass and capital/provincial conflicts. The PRI is having difficulty controlling pent-up demands in its labor sector, has suffered from a few local election debacles, and no longer has a clear ability to cope with the growing strength of the National Action Party (PAN) in Mexico's northern regions.[41] Many of the PRI's problems spring from its traditional practice of appointing gubernatorial, congressional, and even municipal candidates who are well connected in Mexico City, but who have not resided and built personal constituencies in the localities where they are to be elected. Were the PRI to nominate local candidates for local offices, it might have fewer local problems; but the PRI's ability to wield central control and overcome regional interests has depended for decades on imposing outside candidates.

As has often been noted, these are the kinds of problems that could eventually severely erode PRI control and might even generate government/PRI requirements for the army to enforce political stability in some instances. For the first time, the PAN may even have enough popular support to claim a governorship, in Sonora in July 1985; if so, Mexico's leaders might prefer to let the army temporarily take hold of the governor's office. However, government and PRI leaders (and probably military leaders as well) are aware of the problems the PRI faces, and a national debate is getting under way on how to reform and improve the PRI and the party system in general. This should ease public tensions, as long as the reform movement does not open an ideological breach within the governing elite.[42] A recovery of the Mexican economy would also help the PRI, especially in the north.

If organized labor (meaning mainly the unions affiliated with the Mexican Workers Confederation, CTM) engaged in a major work stoppage affecting strategic sectors of the national economy—e.g., the transportation and communications infrastructure and/or the production of a vital resource, such as petroleum—the army might be obliged to take control of some operations while compelling workers to return to their jobs. The reference point for this possibility is the railroad strike of 1959:

> Army troops mounted guard over all railroad installations in the country, and army telegraphers took over wire communications, replacing union

telegraphers who were sympathetic to the railroad men's cause. Soldiers accompanied by police and secret service men broke into strikers' homes and, at gunpoint, forced them to return to work. Engineers flanked by soldiers began moving trains out of the stations.[43]

Nothing similar has affected the energy sector, but in 1978 in Tamaulipas, army engineers laid a portion of the large-diameter gas pipeline that Pemex constructed from Tabasco toward the U.S. border so that the army would have experience in repairing, operating, and guarding the pipeline in the event of threats to it.[44] More generally, the Superior War College and the new National Defense College have increased requirements for course work on resource management; these courses are helpful in preparing officers to seek employment after retirement from the military, and they also improve the military's capability to operate a national enterprise in an emergency.

While the army is thus fairly well prepared to deal with a major labor-union work stoppage, none seems likely to occur in the near future. Organized labor has remained quite disciplined in meeting recent economic hardships, due largely to the strong leadership of aging CTM chieftain Fidel Velásquez. As is often noted, his death may diminish the government's and the PRI's hold on organized labor and may enable independent labor-union movements to emerge. Mexico produces so many surprises, however, that no one should assume that Velásquez's death will necessarily lead to unmanageable labor strife or to a "Polandization" of Mexico.

The elite/mass and city/provincial dimensions further suggest that middle-class, professional, and intellectual unrest may jeopardize political stability, even more than lower-class worker and peasant unrest. The former, once mobilized, may be more difficult to isolate than the latter. Middle-class leaders and movements tend to campaign for nationwide support and foment cleavages within the governing elite. Mexico City and the northern border cities harbor the greatest concentrations of economically and politically discontented middle-class elements who are dissatisfied with the performance of the government and the PRI. To date, however, they have endured the economic crisis with marvelous patience, and they seem likely to continue doing so if Mexico's economy and standard of living show signs of recovery.

Conclusions

In brief, Mexico's military is likely to remain constantly active in assisting the government (and the PRI) to manage episodic, small-scale conflicts throughout the nation.[45] At least in the near term, large-scale, violent domestic political unrest that is sufficiently distributed across elite/mass and city/provincial sectors to provoke the military into initiating a coup or some lesser usurpation of civilian authority seems unlikely to occur. The military's roles in government are more likely to expand (if at all) with civilian agreement, as a result of the kind of national security doctrine that the nation's political, intellectual, and military leaders may evolve.

This assessment presumes, of course, that the civilian political elites remain responsible and capable of dealing with the episodic conflicts that may occur, without engaging in divisive political infighting that could invite military intervention.[46] Broader Latin American experiences indicate that the military is usually unlikely to take the political initiative; the military response to civilian disorder is rarely determined by the military acting alone. Overtures for a military intervention in government during unstable times are far more likely to come from affected civilian politicians and private sector leaders than from army officers.[47] A special—indeed, crucial—feature of Mexico's political system has been the solidarity and discipline of the civilians comprising the revolutionary (institutional) family.

Toward a Mexican Concept of National Security

Mexico's military has always had a national defense mission and a national defense doctrine. The mission, written into the Constitution, is to defend Mexico's sovereignty and independence, maintain the Constitution and its laws, and preserve internal order. This broadly authorizes the military to fulfill both external and internal roles. Though the military has not had to face a real external threat for decades, its external defense doctrine has reflected historical experience: In the event of an attack, confine the invader to coastal areas (where decades ago disease would have weakened him), and wherever he moves inland, oppose his progress and cut his lines with mobile small-unit warfare. Whether the army has a separate doctrine for operating against internal threats is not known, even though internal security and civic action have occupied most of its time and resources since the Revolution. Its behavior in dealing with internal conflicts has been mainly tactical and police-like, applying a local force presence as the President ordains and collaborating with federal and state police agencies to end the problem at hand.[48]

Whereas national defense is an essential concern of the military, national security is regarded as a much broader, more political concern, and the military has not been encouraged to develop a national security doctrine. Indeed, Mexico's political leaders have long resisted even thinking in such terms. In their view, national security is a dangerous language that has been nurtured by the great powers and that has led armed forces elsewhere (notably South America in the 1960s and 1970s) to commit the sins of militarism: exaggerating local threats, criticizing civilian authority, seizing the government, repressing the public, and indulging in arms races.

Moreover, Mexico's leaders feared that their growing oil-export potential in the late 1970s could lead the great powers to invoke security to justify exploiting Mexico's resources and meddling in its domestic affairs, as they have done before.[49] Whereas Mexico's leaders have a history of skill at using the language of political stability to play upon U.S. interests in Mexico, they believe that U.S. officials are much more experienced at manipulating the language of national and international security.

The irregular, indigenous use of the word "security" that has occurred in recent decades suggests that Mexico's civilian leaders are predisposed to favor a form of the concept that would be primarily economic. In domestic matters, for example, they have never deliberately voiced concern about "security" conditions, but they have occasionally acknowledged "insecurity" in a socioeconomic sense when describing the living conditions of peasants and workers.[50] In the mid-1970s, "economic security" briefly gained currency as a foreign-policy slogan in Mexico when the Echeverría administration helped promote a broad movement in the United Nations and Latin America to restrain the United States from emphasizing the military dimensions of security, control the political influence of U.S. and transnational corporations, and demand more favorable U.S. trade and investment policies.[51] But these were isolated civilian tendencies; in no way did they add up to a Mexican concept of security.

As noted earlier, the long series of events since 1968—including the Tlatelolco showdown, development of the southern oil fields, revolution in Central America, and issues along the border with Guatemala—has finally resulted in an unprecedented public dialogue about Mexico's national security.[52] Foreign Minister Bernardo Sepúlveda Amor is reportedly the first civilian official in decades to use that taboo term publicly in regard to Mexico's foreign policy. And President de la Madrid incorporated several bland, but still unprecedented references to national security in his state-of-the-union address in 1984.[53] Perhaps the most revealing of the military's perspectives was cautiously disclosed by Secretary of Defense Félix Galván in a widely quoted interview in 1980: "I understand by national security the maintenance of social, economic, and political equilibrium, guaranteed by the armed forces."[54] Because Mexico has not had to grapple with a genuine threat in decades and does not now perceive one to exist, this restrained public dialogue has mainly revolved around abstract principles (such as nonintervention and respect for sovereignty) and side issues like Guatemalan refugees. Very little is known about the nature of the dialogue inside the government.[55]

The most vocal and publicly visible view comes from a set of political and intellectual leaders who would prefer not to see a national security concept developed, but if one must be developed, they want it defined in terms of defending the social and economic objectives of Mexican nationalism. These include sovereignty over natural resources, the state's dominion over key economic sectors (e.g., petroleum, electricity, communications), and the equitable distribution of income—all objectives that are enshrined in the Constitution of 1917 and reasserted in the 1976 Law to Control Foreign Investment and Stimulate Domestic Investment. By thus emphasizing the social and economic dimensions of security, this view implicitly reinforces the nationalist goals of strengthening the economic role of the state and constraining U.S. investment in Mexico. Sensitivity to issues of national sovereignty and independence means that some adherents of this view might even regard the United States as a kind of potential "threat" to Mexico's sovereignty and development.[56] In contrast, there is little concern that threats to Mexico may arise because of Soviet-Cuban activities or revolutionary change in Central America; the overriding concern is to resolve the socioeconomic inequities that breed violent conflict in the region.[57] The *gabinete económico* and the Foreign Ministry are thus viewed as the appropriate mechanisms for deciding Mexico's security policies; there is no need to create a national security council or expand the military's influence in national security decision-making.

Does this view dominate the thinking of Mexico's political and military elites? A good answer to this question is lacking and may depend largely on the course of events. The nationalist security view just described apparently emerged from a small circle of political and intellectual elites who determined the response of the López Portillo administration to the Sandinista revolution in Nicaragua. Up to now, the de la Madrid administration has not deviated much from this view (though specific aspects of its policies toward Nicaragua are less supportive, and those toward Guatemala, more cooperative).

If it seemed likely that Nicaragua would follow the Cuban model, that El Salvador would fall to the guerrillas, and that civil war would worsen in Guatemala, then broader, more conservative elements of Mexico's elite would probably demand a voice in decision-making so as to prevent spillover from the south, break the potential links between domestic and regional security conditions, and redefine Central America as a potential threat to Mexico's interests.[58] A year or two ago, that indeed seemed likely. It seems less likely today, however, because conditions have changed substantially in Central America: Nicaragua still seems to be engaged in a camouflaged Cubanization, but in Guatemala the military is prevailing against the guerrillas, and in El Salvador the guerrillas are on the defensive.

Conservative threat perceptions and ideological reactions in Mexico may yet alter the dominant nationalist security view. Meanwhile, bureaucratization appears to be affecting it as much as anything. Until very recently, the president, the foreign minister, and their selected advisers could make foreign policy, certainly toward Central America, with free hands. But the expansion of Mexico's activities in Central America and the elevation of national security thinking, especially the concern with preventing spillover from the south, have required greater attention to the links between domestic and foreign policy and have brought a great variety of government agencies into the decision-making process. For example, decisions regarding Chiapas and Guatemala have variously involved, in addition to Foreign Relations, the Ministries of Defense, Interior, Treasury, Commerce, Labor, Communications and Transportation, and Programming and Budgeting. As a result, a wide range of domestic and foreign-policy interests get consulted, and decisions are subjected to a slower, more deliberate, less personalized process.[59] This gradual bureaucratization, some Mexican analysts believe, will favor conservative tendencies in Mexico's national security thinking and behavior.

For the time being, national security thinking is progressing very cautiously in Mexico. Little is known about how it may be affecting the military, or what the military may be contributing. One well-known change, however, is that high-ranking officers now study national security concepts as an academic subject at the new National Defense College. Operational repercussions are less visible, but they too have occurred:[60] The military has strengthened the attaché system and has sent officers on special missions to improve its information from Central America. It has increased its interagency coordination with other parts of the government, including the Secretariats of Government and Foreign Relations, the attorney general's office, and the Directorate of Federal Security.[61] And it has created a new military zone in Chiapas and deployed new units to southern Mexico and along the border with Guatemala. While none of this amounts to a militarization of Mexico's policies, it all indicates that the military is being challenged to deal with an expanding agenda of security issues, problems, and even potential threats.

Special Challenges for Enhancing Security

Southern Mexico and Guatemala may ultimately raise the crucial issues concerning how Mexico's security perspectives evolve and what roles the military plays, because the border with Guatemala is where Mexico's domestic and regional policies intersect and reveal their inherent inconsistency. Mexico's policy toward Central America has sided with the forces of revolutionary change (albeit partly to moderate and coopt those forces). Mexico has decried the militarization of the antirevolutionary struggles, and it has promoted international diplomatic negotiations to resolve the area's conflicts, in ways that would protect the Sandinista regime and might achieve power-sharing for the FMLN-FDR in El Salvador. At the same time, Mexico's policy toward its "domestic Central America"— Chiapas, Oaxaca, and Guerrero—has been quick to suppress radical unrest and occasional guerrilla activity. It has resorted to heavy-handed measures, sometimes including a strong military presence, to enforce government/PRI decisions. And it has not wanted international attention to focus on issues in this, perhaps the most underdeveloped, poverty-stricken, and Indian area of Mexico.[62]

Against this background, two specific themes involving southern Mexico and Guatemala seem particularly important:

1. the military's potential roles in fostering regional economic development in Mexico;
2. the implications of the internationalization of Central America's conflicts for Mexico's security policies and for the military's influence in determining those policies.

Regional Development in Mexico

Mexico's population and industry are heavily overconcentrated, primarily around Mexico City and secondarily around Guadalajara and Monterrey. It seems evident that the integration of the nation and its political and economic stability will require a deconcentration and the development of new regional poles. This was an important objective of the National Industrial Development Plan (1979), which read as much like a document about internal geopolitics as about industrial development per se.

The governing elite has recognized a long-range need to promote regional economic development. This is a natural activity for an expanding state. However, little progress has been made, as other urgent objectives keep taking priority. Mexico's private-sector leaders still prefer to locate their investments in Mexico City and other already industrialized areas. Bureaucrats living in Mexico City resist plans to relocate some government agencies and government-operated industries to other parts of the country. Elites representing regional interests, a strong element of the old *familia revolucionaria,* have little voice in today's *familia institucional.* In addition, traditional regional elites may not want much attention from the new elites in Mexico City.[63] Thus there is no civilian political consensus and no coalition of established interests that clearly advocates economic deconcentration and rapid regional development.[64]

The crux of the problem, from a political and administrative standpoint, may be in the distinction that Mexico's leaders make between "deconcentration" and "decentralization." Ideally, they want the former without the latter. Even while recognizing the need for regional economic development, no one in the governing elite really wants to reduce the centralized power and authority of Mexico's federal government. In particular, the elites in Mexico City do not want to enable state governors to act independently of the President and the PRI.[65] Nor do they want to let the state and municipal governments control a larger share of tax revenues. Deconcentration should benefit Mexico's stability over the long run, but it is also possible that the process of creating new regional development poles and regional economic and political elites would create unwelcome, potentially destabilizing challenges to central authority.

Though the suggestion must be broached cautiously, perhaps the military could help raise the importance of promoting regional development by urging the federal government to devote more attention and resources to this objective. The military certainly has the capability to be helpful in this respect. The army, especially the zone commander, is in a good position to become an important element of the regional power elites, and it is acquiring the experience and education to do so.[66] The army has always assisted regional economic development with its growing capabilities for civic action and resource management. Army officers often gain political experience early in their careers through provincial assignments where they must deal with municipal and state officials.[67] It is said that "intellectual officers" (those who have shown a capacity for critical thinking in the military schools) are often given regional assignments. And an education in geopolitical thinking may help make the future officer corps newly sensitive to the ways in which the regional distribution (and maldistribution) of population, production capacity, infrastructure, and resources may affect Mexico's national development.[68]

Southern Mexico should be of keen interest in this regard, since Mexico has strategic assets there: its highly developed oil fields and production facilities, and the much less developed "land bridge" across the Isthmus of Tehuantepec, including the railroad, pipeline, and port facilities.[69]

While the army might thus play increasingly useful roles in promoting regional economic development and what might be called the "humanization of geopolitics," Mexico City would need to proceed with great care and cautious steps, especially in the south. Mexico's security and military policymakers would have to remain cognizant of the fact that in Latin America, insurgency often develops in previously isolated regions that have just been opened up to greater connection with the national marketplace and infrastructure and subjected to a strengthening of the state's presence and authority. In other words, southern Mexico could become increasingly conflict-ridden not simply because of spillover from Guatemala, but because of the ancillary effects of Mexico City's efforts to integrate Chiapas politically and economically into the nation.[70] Although, as discussed above, the region is unlikely to generate conflicts affecting Mexico's overall stability, its once-isolated population is now being buffeted and penetrated by forces from many directions, including domestic political and religious activists and the international media.

Internationalization of Conflict in Central America

The Mexican military is already fulfilling new roles, e.g., gathering information and intelligence about the course of events in Central America. If the military is also to play more active roles in the formulation of Mexico's security and military policies, one of the most important questions it may have to address is how to limit the internationalization of conflict in southern Mexico and Guatemala.

As Mario Ojeda and René Herrera have observed, Mexico's interests and policies in Central America are guided by "the need to eliminate a tension spot that might lead to an international conflict close to its own borders, that sooner or later would drive the country to involve itself more directly and in turn alter its until now insignificant policy of national defense.[71] Seeking to restore political stability while accommodating necessary political, economic, and social changes in the conflict-ridden nations, Mexico has developed a strategy that seems to rely largely on two elements:

- an international campaign, notably in Western Europe, to promote political negotiations and detente in Central America and prevent a regionalization of the violence;
- parallel efforts in the area to promote moderate, pluralist outcomes to the struggles and to restrain the most radical elements.

This preventive approach sounds good, but it may not adequately address the internationalization of the area's conflicts.

There has been a prolonged policy debate, especially in the United States but also in Central America, Mexico, and Western Europe, about whether the sources of violence in Central America are primarily *external* to the area (e.g., Cuban and Soviet subversion), or essentially *internal* to each nation (i.e., chronic underdevelopment, poverty, exploitation, corruption, dictatorship). For years, Mexico has argued the latter side and has criticized U.S. policy as converting an essentially local conflict into an East-West issue.

This debate is artificial and misleading. The internal and external sources of violence are virtually inseparable, and the current internationalization of conflict conforms to a neglected historical pattern: For almost two centuries, Central American elites have fought their indigenous conflicts by seeking foreign allies and resources. It is the sensible thing for contending elites to do in small countries that have weak political institutions and poor export-oriented economies, that can use external support to help compensate for the absence of domestic support, and that have a geopolitical position which attracts foreign interests. Thus even though Central America's elites may respond mainly to local conditions, their conflicts normally invite international connections.

Partly because of its historic role in the area, the weaker U.S. power and presence seem to be, the more likely are local protagonists to entertain extrahemispheric entanglements. Indeed, the relative decline of U.S. power and presence in Central America during the mid- and late 1970s, though sometimes hailed as spelling an end to U.S. hegemonic presumptions, may have contributed to the domestic and international destabilization that subsequently occurred there. The perceived U.S. decline seems to have prompted extreme elements—both left-wing and right-wing—to become newly aggressive, and it has weakened and victimized moderates who were typically associated with European-oriented Christian Democracy and Social Democracy and who quickly got caught in the cross fires of polarized conflict.[72] The U.S. decline also created a "power vacuum" for foreign entry and aroused local protagonists to seek foreign support to compensate for or take advantage of the decline. In particular, the diplomatic and economic resurgence of Western Europe and the international activism of its Christian Democratic and Social Democratic parties offered new sources of support for Central American nationalists.

In many respects, we are witnessing the development of a new pattern of low-intensity violence, whose key characteristic is its extreme internationalization. More than ever before, the revolutionaries' strategy is to promote the internationalization of ostensibly local conflicts. They have helped turn Central America into the world's most internationalized laboratory for revolutionary (and counterrevolutionary) conflict, with extrahemispheric intrusions coming from various directions. Thus, the traditional U.S.–Soviet struggle is now crisscrossed by the intrusion from Western Europe of political rivalries between Christian Democracy and Social Democracy (most evident in El Salvador). Though less significant, Israel and radical Arabs also support opposing sides in some countries. Central America has been fractured by more outside East-West struggles than any other third area of vital strategic interest to the United States.[73]

This latest pattern of internationalized, low-intensity conflict first emerged in Nicaragua during the Sandinista struggle to topple the Somoza dictatorship in the late 1970s. Within the Sandinista National Liberation Front (FSLN), the "tercerista tendency" in particular sought the involvement of moderate Latin American and West European governments in order to gain international recognition, resources, and legitimacy for the FSLN, and to isolate the United States. The political leadership of the guerrilla forces in El Salvador, particularly the Revolutionary Democratic Front (FDR) associated with the Farabundo Martí Liberation Front (FMLN), has also sought broad international support, though with less success.

Mexico has participated in bringing about this internationalization of conflict, beginning with its support for the Sandinista victory in Nicaragua, later with the Franco-Mexican communiqué supporting the FMLN-FDR forces in El Salvador, and more recently in connection with the regionwide activities of the Contadora group (Colombia, Mexico, Panama, Venezuela). In many respects, Mexico's stature, influence, and maneuvering ability in Central America have probably benefited from the strategy of internationalization; and there has been merit to the Contadora initiatives.

In the case of Guatemala, however, it seems doubtful that this kind of strategy would benefit Mexico's interests. When he was Mexico's foreign minister, Jorge Castañeda remarked that in Guatemala "the situation has not become internationalized and thus does not merit or permit actions like those taken by Mexico in other cases (Nicaragua and El Salvador). The situations are different."[74] An internationalized revolutionary struggle there would probably increase the prospects for spillover into southern Mexico, creating undesirable political and military problems for Mexico City.

Though the story remains to be told, it appears that during the last year or two the Mexican government has made a special effort to cooperate with the Guatemalan government to bring their shared border under control. For example, Mexico has moved the refugee camps away from the border, partly to keep them from serving as sanctuaries for Guatemalan guerrillas. Other measures have been taken to hinder Mexican leftist support for the Guatemalan guerrilla organizations; and, as noted previously, the Mexican army's presence has been strengthened along the border.[75]

Virtually nothing is known about the Mexican military's views on these matters. But it may turn out that unusual cooperation between it and the Guatemalan military has contributed greatly to the overall improvement in the two neighbors' relations. Most important, of course, to the prevention of an internationalized struggle here is the fact that the Guatemalan army is finally winning its prolonged war against the country's three main guerrilla groups, whose territorial strongholds and corridors of operation had all abutted the Mexican border.

Avoiding Hubris and Nemesis: A Final Comment

With so many new forces and factors in the picture, will the modern Mexican military continue to fulfill its security and development roles responsibly and in subordination to civilian authority? That, in the final analysis, is the question that keeps rising to the top. According to this study, the new military may play cautiously expanded roles not only as an instrument of domestic and foreign policy, but also as a well-institutionalized partner in the formulation of some national security and development policies. Yet the best answers that this and other studies can offer at this time still amount only to speculations based on little information.

That being the case, I choose to conclude with an observation derived from Greek mythology: the Mexican army has avoided the *hubris* that has impelled other Latin American militaries to seize power, and it has not played the role of *Nemesis* in dealing with perceived threats and evils. The dynamics of hubris and vengeance go to the heart of key concerns for both military and civilian behavior in Mexico.

As long as the modern Mexican military avoids both hubris and vengeance, it is likely to help maintain the "equilibrium" (to use General Galván's word) that lies at the core of Mexico's stability and security. In general, the military has a good record in this regard. Although the army played the role of avenger briefly at Tlatelolco in 1968, it did not continue in this role, and it avoided the hubris of seizing power from President Díaz Ordaz. The military is proud of its achievements and contributions to Mexico's development and security. It seeks institutional dignity as well as public respect and recognition. It wants its just due from a system that has let its modernization lag behind that of other institutions. And it stands ready to use force, if necessary, to defend the Constitution, the Revolution, and the government. At the same time, the military has not exhibited arrogance toward the government or the Mexican public; it has not pressed for a heavy expansion of the armed forces, military equipment, and budget resources; and it has not claimed that it could run things better than the civilians or do a better job of correcting social evils.

As long as these patterns remain ingrained within the military, the prospects for Mexico's equilibrium will depend mainly on the behavior of the civilian authorities, in particular, on their not creating political troubles because of their own hubris, and then calling on the army to rescue them and crack heads. Far from falling victim to hubris or Nemesis, the military wants to remain dedicated to fulfilling the symbolic import of its leading emblem, the Aztec eagle's knight head *(Tlacatecuhtli)*, which stands for dignity, loyalty, and duty.

Notes

1. The standard reference is Edwin Lieuwen, *Mexican Militarism: The Political Rise and Fall of the Revolutionary Army, 1910–1940,* The University of New Mexico Press, Albuquerque, 1968.
2. David Ronfeldt, "The Mexican Army and Political Order Since 1940," Rand P-5089-1, August 1975, reprinted in Abraham F. Lowenthal (ed.), *Armies and Politics in Latin America,* Holmes & Meier, New York, 1976. Other oft-cited studies from this period are Franklin D. Margiotta, "Civilian Control and the Mexican Military: Changing Patterns of Political Influence," in Claude E. Welch, Jr. (ed.), *Civilian Control of the Military,* State University of New York Press, Albany, 1976; and Lyle N. McAlister, "Mexico," in Lyle N. McAlister, Anthony P. Maingot, and Robert A. Potash (eds.), *The Military in Latin American Sociopolitical Evolution: Four Case Studies,* American University Center for Research in Social Systems, Washington, D.C., 1970, pp. 197–258. Key studies by Mexican researchers are Guillermo Boils, *Los Militares y La Política en México (1915–1974),* Ediciones El Caballito, Mexico City, 1975;

and Jorge Alberto Lozoya, *El Ejército Mexicano (1911–1965),* Jornadas 65, El Colegio de México, Mexico City, 1970.

3. Though the Tlatelolco experience created the ferment for military modernization, it should be pointed out that the results were not immediate. Sources vary, but one view holds that the first priority after Tlatelolco was to strengthen Mexico's police forces. In this view, modernization and professionalization of the army did not gain priority until after the army conducted the rural counterinsurgency operations of the 1970s.

4. Former President José López Portillo also took a personal interest in modernizing the army because of his father's association with that institution. While the present discussion emphasizes the army, it should also be pointed out that Mexico's declaration of a 200-miles offshore economic zone led to the expansion and modernization of the navy's patrol capabilities in the 1970s.

5. This chapter draws from discussions at a research workshop on "The Role of the Military in Mexican Politics and Society: A Reassessment," held at the Center for U.S.–Mexican Studies, University of California at San Diego, March 18–19, 1984—hereafter referred to as the research workshop.

6. From Major Stephen Wager, "The Modernization of the Mexican Military and Its Significance for Mexico's Central American Policy," unpublished draft, October 27, 1982, p. 1.

7. For a more thorough survey of institutional development and modernization, see Major Stephen J. Wager, "Basic Characteristics of the Modern Mexican Military," Lieutenant Colonel Alden Cunningham, "Mexico's National Security in the 1980s–1990s," and Roderic A. Camp, "Generals and Politicians in Mexico: A Preliminary Comparison," in Ronfeldt (ed.), 1984. For additional information, see Wager, "The Mexican Military," in Robert Wesson (ed.), *The Latin American Military Institution,* Praeger, New York, forthcoming.

8. Although these figures are taken from standard sources, they should all be regarded as rough estimates, provided only to indicate general trends in the modest proportions of the Mexican military. For example, military expenditures as a percentage of total government expenditures could be calculated several different ways, each providing answers somewhat different from those given here. The standard of living, especially the pay scales, provided to the military has improved substantially in recent years. Although high-ranking officers have always enjoyed generous amenities and benefits, military personnel now receive generally better housing and social security for themselves and their families. The military even has its own Social Security Institute for the Mexican Armed Forces (ISSFAM) and its own bank.

9. Although information is scarce, the navy has expanded its base structure on both coasts in order to patrol and protect the recently enlarged territorial waters as well as the offshore oil fields. Patrolling the Gulf of Campeche (site of the offshore oil fields) has apparently been emphasized, but another major goal has been the construction of a naval air station on Socorro Island in the Pacific.

10. Chronically violent Guerrero and Oaxaca each contain two zones, while oil-rich Veracruz overlaps three zones.

11. For example, the First Region includes the Federal District and adjoining areas in the state of Mexico, long considered the strategic heart of the nation. This apparently corresponds to the First Military Zone. The other military regions incorporate several military zones and cut across several states. The announcement of these military regions initially looked like an organizational innovation, but Lieuwen, 1968, says that the "army is divided into ten military regions and thirty four command zones" (p. 148).

12. This training includes military staff coordination that may apply to duties involving the state enterprises and the foreign service.
13. A deal to order four frigates built in Brazil was discussed but not closed.
14. There is no real evidence that a stronger, more visible military is helping Mexico deal with Cuba and Nicaragua, promote the demilitarization of Central America's conflicts via the Contadora process, and/or restrain Guatemala's behavior along the border with Mexico. This speculation comes from David Ronsfeldt and Caesar Sereseres, "U.S. Arms Transfers, Diplomacy, and Security in Latin America and Beyond," The Rand Corporation, P-6005, October 1977, which observes (p. 37) that "arms transfers are diplomacy by other means. Having arms, especially prestigious arms, appears to be essential for the conduct of traditional diplomacy. Indeed, arms have often been more important for their diplomatic symbolism than for their military capabilities. The acquisition and display of advanced weapons have seemed useful not so much to prepare for war, as to gain effective diplomatic instruments for negotiating and resolving conflicts short of war."
15. Lieuwen's assertion that professionalization helped depoliticize the Mexican army by the 1940s (Lieuwen, 1968, and his summary, "Depoliticization of the Mexican Revolutionary Army, 1915–1940," in Ronfeldt (ed.), 1984) is largely accepted. However, in addressing current trends, experts on Mexico and on Latin American military institutions sustain more disagreements than agreements about (1) how military professionalism should be defined, (2) whether the existing level of professionalization is high or low in the case of Mexico, (3) whether further professionalization would expand or contract political concerns among Mexico's officer corps, and (4) whether the military is marginally or intricately involved in Mexico's politics and government. These specific questions are difficult to answer, partly because research is so lacking on the Mexican military. Yet, notwithstanding the importance of learning more about the political effects of military modernization and professionalization, the answer to the broader question posed here turns ultimately on the ability of Mexico's civilian leadership to govern the nation (and coopt the military) no matter how professional the military may be.
16. Ronfeldt, 1975, p. 13, reprinted in Ronfeldt (ed.), 1984, pp. 71–72. The acronym PAN refers to the National Action Party.
17. Frank R. Brandenburg, The Making of Modern Mexico, Prentice-Hall, Englewood Cliffs, 1964, esp. pp. 4–5. A related view, using the terms "revolutionary coalition," appeared in L. Vincent Padgett, The Mexican Political System, 2d ed., Houghton Mifflin Co., Boston, 1976, p. 37n.
18. The best research on Mexico's elites is found in Camp, in Ronfeldt (ed.), 1984 (and his other research cited there); Camp, "The Political Technocrat in Mexico and the Survival of the Political System," Latin American Research Review, XX (1983), pp. 97–118; and Peter H. Smith, Labyrinths of Power: Political Recruitment in Twentieth Century Mexico, Princeton University Press, Princeton, 1979.
19. As many analysts have observed, the changeover reflects the rise of political technocrats through administrative positions, and the decline of the old-style party-type politicians. According to Camp (1985), the changeover gained momentum when President Echeverría virtually skipped a generation in recruiting elites for his administration, bringing young technocratic specialists to the fore while sidelining old-style politicians. It would appear, however, that we still have a lot to learn about relations between technocrats and politicians. At present, analysts tend to focus on the differences and tensions between them. Yet it may be that earlier, in the 1960s, some politicians competing for power deliberately sought to recruit emerging technocrats into their camarillas,

while those early technocrats were also seeking connections to established politicians. It may also be that, in the future, political technocrats competing for power will want to foster and attract new-style politicians, particularly in provincial areas, to counterbalance the technocratic tendencies of Mexico City. If so, the evolutionary change from the revolutionary family to the institutional family will reflect not just a rise of technocratic elites and a decline of old-style politicians, but more broadly, an evolution in the nature of the symbiosis between younger and older, more technocratic and more political elites.

20. The best source on changes in the officer corps, Camp, in Ronfeldt (ed.), 1984, pp. 114–115, observes one important attribute in which the officer corps has not changed so much: Whereas the civilian elites come increasingly from middle-class origins and decreasingly from working-class origins, a substantial portion of the military officer corps still had working-class origins. "If this pattern continues, it suggests an important divergence in leadership characteristics between civilians and the military. For a society in which the vast majority are from the working class, a leadership institution having roots in that class and allowing upward mobility for that group may be important to the stability of the political system as a whole, complementing a recruitment weakness in the political structure" (p. 152).

21. A newspaper report by Jesús M. Lozano, "Garantizada la Seguridad del País, Dijo Galván López a JLP," *Excelsior,* July 25, 1980, states (my translation): "For the first time in the military history of Mexico, a President went to the Secretary of National Defense accompanied by almost all the members of his cabinet to listen to the opinions of not only the Secretary but also more than twenty zone commanders and other high commanders of the Army."

22. For a broadly illuminating view, see Steven E. Sanderson, "Presidential Succession and Political Rationality in Mexico," *World Politics,* April 1984, pp. 315–334. On the development of a key ministry, see John J. Bailey, "Presidency, Bureaucracy, and Administrative Reform in Mexico: The Secretariat of Programming and Budget," *Inter-American Economic Affairs,* Summer 1980, pp. 27–59.

23. Bailey, "Political Bureaucracy and Decision-Making in Mexico," presented at the research workshop, 1984, observes that "the bureaucracy and party are structurally merged and interact in complicated ways" (p. 5). My own observation is that each pillar, and perhaps the state as a whole, is designed as a dual structure that combines central functional directorates and regional zone managements, both reporting to the top administration and each providing the top with different, separate means of command, control, and communication. At the risk of mixing metaphors, I would suggest that each pillar might thus be viewed as containing a large, central pyramid surrounded and linked with smaller outlying pyramids. In the case of the military, for example, the Secretariat of National Defense has grown in power, compared with the zone commanders. Petróleos Mexicanos (Pemex) was evidently reorganized in the mid-1960s by then-Director-General Jesús Heroles (who may be a key intellectual and political leader of the dual-structure approach), so that the regional zone managements, which used to fall largely under the jurisdiction of the functional directorates in Mexico City, reported directly to the top. The experiment in 1984 in Nayarit to create primary-type elections for selecting mayors was conducted partly to strengthen the regional bases of the PRI's own dual structure.

24. The relative weakening of the PRI may be related to the rise of the new governing elites through the state apparatus. According to reports about a survey the PRI conducted in 1983, 42 percent of the 3,500 highest-level

officials in Mexico claimed they did not belong to any political party. Only 25 percent said they were PRI members. No information is available about PRI preferences within the military. It is unlikely that the military sector of the government party, which was eliminated when the Party of the Mexican Revolution (PMR) was transformed into the PRI in 1945, will ever be revived. During the research workshop, however, Lorenzo Meyer observed that the military sector may have continued to exist informally these past forty years as a behind-the-scenes mechanism for occasional political-military consultation and for the selection of officers to appoint to congressional and other political positions.

25. The term "creeping militarism" comes from a comment by Wayne Cornelius at the aforementioned research workshop.

26. According to Cunningham, in Ronfeldt (ed.), 1984, p. 176, "This organization would consist of the president, the secretary of national defense, the secretary of government, the attorney general, the secretary of programming and budgeting, the secretary of the navy, and the secretary of foreign relations."

27. James Wilkie has suggested that Mexico's political stability may even *depend* on having periodic systemic crises: "Since each president holds power for six years and can never be reelected, at the end of six years political innovation has died out as the outgoing president seeks only to implement his 'solutions' to problems identified when he took office. To renew the political system, younger generations compete to identify crises and thus determine Mexico's course for the following six-year presidency. New leaders, then, push themselves to the top by successfully identifying a crisis and convincing enough Mexicans that theirs is indeed the most serious crisis. Viewed from outside, this political system seems unstable; from inside, this system works rather smoothly to maintain the party of permanent revolution in power. In this process the problem Mexico faces is that of distinguishing between real and apparent crises." (Wilkie, "Conflicting 'National Interests' Between and Within Mexico and the United States," in Carlos Vásquez and Manuel García y Griego (eds.), *Mexican–U.S. Relations: Conflict and Convergence,* UCLA Chicano Studies Research Center and UCLA Latin American Center, Los Angeles, 1983, p. 37.)

28. This is not to deny that some serious tensions still exist. For example, some private-sector leaders in Mexico reportedly believe, in the words of Jorge Chapa, president of the Entrepreneurial Coordinating Council (CCE) that " 'infiltration of Marxist elements in the instruments of public power, the anti-business currents that have filtered into public education at all levels, as well as an excessive growth in bureaucracy' is responsible for 'the precarious situation suffered by private businesses in Mexico today.' " From an article in *Newsletter,* U.S.–Mexico Chamber of Commerce (Pacific Chapter), December 1984, p. 2, which quotes from an interview with Chapa published in the newspaper *El Sol de México.*

29. The 60 percent figure has also been applied to Nicaragua to support claims that the Sandinista regime is attempting to install a Cuban-style economy. There has never been a real fear that Mexico's Communist Party (the PCM) might gain power in Mexico (although it has sparked controversy, for example, by proposing in 1977 that military officers and priests should be allowed to join political parties, campaign for political offices, and in the case of priests, vote). The episodic fear has instead been that the leftists among Mexico's political and intellectual elites might manage to convert Mexico, gradually, secretively, and through a series of *faits accomplis,* into a socialist or communist nation. An early expression of this view is found in Ernst Halperin, *Communism in Mexico,* Center for International Studies, Massachusetts Insti-

tute of Technology, January 12, 1963, C/63-3, which concludes that "if there is any Communist danger at all in Mexico, it would therefore appear to lie in the possibility of the Communists capturing the government by stealth and then carrying out a 'revolution from above.' Yet the ruling group of PRI politicos appear to be so tough, astute, and possessed of such a fine instinct for power that this does not appear likely in the appreciable future" (p. 23).

30. For background, see Wayne Cornelius, "The Political Economy of Mexico under De La Madrid: Austerity, Routinized Crisis, and Nascent Recovery," *Mexican Studies/Estudios Mexicanos,* Winter 1985, pp. 83–123.

31. I would hypothesize, albeit as a non-economist, that Mexico's economic system resembles "franchise capitalism": The private as well as public enterprises operate as though they had privileges and protections obtained from a higher corporation—Spain long ago, and today the state. Mexico's economic system looks as though it combines aspects of feudalism, capitalism, and socialism; yet it also defies those Anglo-European standards. Over time, the state has become the strongest force determining who gets what franchise to do what—for example, creating *ejidos* and agricultural collectives out of old haciendas and land grants after the Revolution. This process is still going on, and although leftists and rightists see in it the potential for transforming Mexico into a socialist country, the central historical tendency is to restore equilibrium to public-private relations by periodically taking a franchise away from one group (especially if the group has become noncompetitive or does not support national interests) and subsequently bestowing the franchise on a new private group.

32. The newspaper *Excelsior,* February 20, 1984, p. 1-A ff, as translated in *Latin American Report,* JPRS-LAM-84-046, April 10, 1984, p. 41, reported: " 'During the period of uncertainty observed at the start of the present administration when strict discipline had to be imposed, the Mexican army was the cornerstone of our contemporary history, since it kept intact our vital concept of a free and sovereign nation, the free play of our democratic system and, fundamentally, social peace,' President Miguel de la Madrid told the military yesterday in a message issued in connection with the day dedicated to the armed forces. The message . . . also said: 'The republic is strengthened when we call attention to the work being done by an institution which is the pillar of our country's institutional life.' " In an extraordinary speech whose significance remains unclear to me, published in *El Día,* May 16, 1982, p. 3., as translated in *Latin American Report,* JPRS 81114, June 23, 1982, No. 2527, then secretary of national defense General Félix Galván López observed: "Those who in their sad grumbling, in their pretended solemn gravity, in their historical error or in their confused intimacy dream about or mention to themselves the possibility of military participation. . . . But they should not count on us soldiers—not on any of us! The economic difficulties—however great they may be, and to whatever degree they are nurtured from whatever source—far from destroying Mexico, will make it better understand the value of its principles and the force of its constitutional outline. They may delay our objective, but they will not be able to turn aside our course or hinder our arrival. Perhaps they will show us our deficiencies and weak points, but they will be unable to alienate us from the commitments that we Mexicans have made to our flag and our country. They lack vision, perspective, reason, and valid justification. Family members do not abandon one another or voluntarily disband because of financial reasons."

33. Susan Kaufman Purcell and John Purcell, "State and Society in Mexico: Must a Stable Polity Be Institutionalized?" *World Politics,* January 1980, pp. 194–227, elaborates an important idea (p. 195): "The system is held together not by

institutions, but by the rigid discipline of the elites in not overstepping the bounds of the bargain."

34. A similar view appears in Octavio Paz, *The Other Mexico: Critique of the Pyramid,* Evergreen Black Cat Edition, Grove Press, New York, 1972, pp. 59–61, where he concludes (p. 61) that "if a rural uprising is to prosper, it is indispensable that it coincide with a profound power crisis in the cities. In Mexico this conjunction has not come about—not yet."

35. This hypothesis about the Tlatelolco showdown, which I owe to an informal conversation with a British historian, remains unverified. Other considerations would need to be taken into account in a full explanation of the showdown, including the Mexican army's concern about the appearance of armed individuals dressed in Mexican army uniforms who were not members of the Mexican army.

36. From "Leftist party figures see political radicalization in Southeast," *Excelsior,* February 24, 1984, p. 23Aff, as translated in *Latin America Report,* Foreign Broadcast Information Service, JPRS-LAM-84-049, pp. 47–49.

37. For example, Constantine Menges, "Central America and Its Enemies," *Commentary,* August 1981, pp. 32–38.

38. Jorge A. Bustamante, "Las propuestas de política migratoria en los Estados Unidos y sus repercusiones en México," *Foro Internacional* 71, enero–marzo, 1978, pp. 522–530, which concerns legislation proposed by President Jimmy Carter in 1977. An earlier version in English is Bustamante, "Toward the Analysis and Prognosis of the Political Implications of the Mexican Undocumented Migration," paper prepared for the Seventh National Meeting of the Latin American Studies Association held in Houston, Texas, November 2–5, 1977. The scenario is in keeping with a Mexican practice of raising U.S. fears about Mexico's stability in order to dissuade U.S. policymakers from pursuing measures that Mexico's leaders disapprove of.

39. One unusual idea that never gained support was proposed in 1977 by George Deukmejian, then California's State Senate minority leader, who suggested creating a U.S. military reservation fourteen miles long, from the Pacific coast to Otay Mesa southeast of San Diego, that would serve as a barrier to illegal immigration and could be used by the State Police, the National Guard, and the U.S. military, as well as for training the Mexican military.

40. Political and intellectual leaders in Mexico City often lament that the northern border region is insufficiently integrated into Mexico's national economy. I think a case could now be made that Mexico City is not well integrated into the national economy.

41. The relatively conservative, pro-business, middle-class-oriented PAN tends to be strongest in the north, while leftist parties currying peasant and labor support tend to be stronger in the south. For example, the army was called out to restore order in Piedras Negras, Coahuila, in December 1984, after PAN supporters, insisting they had really won the local mayoralty election, rioted to protest fraud by the PRI, which claimed victory. In December 1983 in Juchitán, Oaxaca, the army was called on to help the PRI and the Mexican government oust a local leftist group (affiliated with the Unified Socialist Party of Mexico, PSUM) which, claiming victory in a municipal election, had occupied the municipal offices. Outsiders observing such incidents for the first time tend to treat them as a sign of potentially serious instability in Mexico. Yet analysts with years of experience in observing Mexico know that such incidents are rather common over time, even though each may create a special media flurry when it occurs. Past incidents of the government using the army to restore order during electoral disturbances are noted in Ronfeldt, 1975, p. 2, reprinted in Ronfeldt (ed.), 1984, p. 64.

42. Cogent appraisals of the problems facing the PRI and the government are presented in Cornelius, "Mexico: The Politics of Austerity and the Electoral Challenges of 1985," paper presented to a conference of journalists, Center for U.S.–Mexican Studies, Institute of the Americas, January 25–27, 1985, and Steven E. Sanderson, "Political Tensions in the Mexican Party System," *Current History*, December 1983, pp. 401–405, 436–437.

43. From Evelyn P. Stevens, *Protest and Response in Mexico*, The MIT Press, Cambridge, Massachusetts, 1974, pp. 122–123.

44. However, this was motivated more by the prospect of a terrorist threat to the pipeline than by the possibility of labor unrest.

45. General Luis Garfias Magaña pointed out at the research workshop that the military dislikes performing political police functions, and that the government knows the military does not want to be used in this way. According to a report in *Excelsior,* January 19, 1984, p. 1-A, as translated in *Latin American Report,* JPRS-LAM-84-037, March 23, 1984, p. 27, Mexico's secretary of national defense, General Juan Arévalo Gardoqui, declared that the army, though dedicated to safeguarding the institutions, was not interested in playing either political or policing roles. According to the politically explosive (and unverified) stories related in José González González, *Lo Negro del Negro Durazo,* Editorial Posada, Mexico City, 1983, the army's high command was incensed that President López Portillo let his corrupt friend, Arturo Durazo Moreno, whom he had named head of the powerful Transit Police of the Federal District (the DGPT), wear the insignia of a three-star general, the army's highest rank. General Garfias, acting in his capacity as a congressional deputy, on temporary leave from the military, has initiated legislation that will prohibit Mexico's police forces from ever again using the military's ranks, insignias, or uniforms.

46. This assessment also assumes that outside forces such as the Soviet Union, Cuba, or radical Arab actors do not promote unrest, insurgency, and terrorism in Mexico. If this worst-case possibility is introduced, it becomes quite easy to imagine conditions of political and social unrest so extreme that the Mexican military might eventually take matters into its own hands.

47. Cornelius, 1985, articulates the strongest case for concern that "the real threat to system stability in Mexico comes from the right" (p. 12), particularly from powerful businessmen and ideological extremists who wish to challenge the PRI's preeminence via the PAN. A politically more conservative U.S. analyst, R. Bruce McColm, in "Mexico: The Coming Crisis," *Journal of Contemporary Studies,* Summer 1984, pp. 3–26, includes a timely analysis of potential threats from the left, but he also finds (p. 20) that "the major threat to Mexico's security comes less from the radical left . . . than from the economic situation and from the deteriorating image of the PRI as the guardian of the Great Revolution." Whether the rightists or the leftists represent the greater threat, elite cohesion and political stability may depend as much on external as on internal conditions, and possibly more. The continued recovery of the U.S. economy, the restoration of stable, moderate politics in Central America, and good prices for Mexico's exports (unlikely in the case of oil) could do wonders for the manageability of Mexico's chronic, cumulative domestic problems.

48. The army's sensitivities about being used as a police force initially hindered the commitment of some zone commanders and officers to engage in the massive antidrug operations of the 1970s under the direction of the Procuraduría (attorney general) and its Federal Judicial Police, according to Richard B. Craig, "La Campaña Permanente: Mexico's Antidrug Campaign," *Journal of Interamerican Studies and World Affairs,* May 1978, pp. 107–131, esp. pp. 117 and 124. Later, however, in "Operation Condor: Mexico's Anti-

drug Campaign Enters a New Era," *Journal of Interamerican Studies and World Affairs,* August 1980, pp. 345–364, Craig praises the level of coordination and cooperation that the army achieved with the attorney general's office and the police agency. To the army's benefit, troops operating in violent drug-cultivation areas, notably Sinaloa, acquired new light infantry weapons and access to transport helicopters. In a similar manner, the army also objected in 1980 that impeding the illegal entry of Central American refugees into southern Mexico was not a proper function of the army, but by 1982–1983 it was working closely with the Ministry of Interior and other government agencies to strengthen control of Mexico's border with Guatemala. Perhaps this initial resistance to performing the lesser military tasks is not unusual: For example, the U.S. military has resisted involvement in third-world conflicts (once termed the lesser-included cases) that might interfere with its preparations for fighting a possible major war in Europe.

49. This fear is reflected in Richard Fagan, "Mexican Petroleum and U.S. Security," in Vásquez and García y Griego (eds.), 1983, pp. 215–231. A moderate perspective on U.S. interests and objectives appears in David Ronfeldt, Richard Nehring, and Arturo Gandara, *Mexico's Petroleum and U.S. Policy: Implications for the 1980s,* The Rand Corporation, R-2510-DOE, June 1980.

50. The term *seguridad pública* ("public security," better translated as "public safety") has a limited, technical usage that refers to law-enforcement activities, including those of the military.

51. Mexico expressed its defense of economic security by proposing the U.N. Charter on the Economic Rights and Duties of Nations, helping to create the Latin American Economic System (SELA), generally advocating the creation of a so-called "new international economic order," and at home, promulgating the Law to Control Foreign Investment and Stimulate Domestic Investment.

52. Mario Ojeda suggested at the research workshop that Mexico's behavior in the face of adversity is sometimes driven more by the kind of international attention focused on Mexico than by Mexico's domestic reality. For example, if there had been less international attention focused on Mexico in 1968, the Tlatelolco showdown might have been avoided; and if the international press had given less credence to pessimistic rumors about Mexico's economy in 1981, the private sector might not have engaged in such massive capital flight. Though Ojeda did not say so, a national security dialogue may be emerging in Mexico partly because so many foreign observers and analysts have said that it should.

53. For example, "Strict adherence to the principles of our foreign policy will guarantee our national security and independent development" (de la Madrid, *Second State of the Nation Report,* Presidencia de la República, Mexico, September 1984, p. 25).

54. From the magazine *Proceso,* September 22, 1980, p. 6.

55. An early manifestation of the emerging debate was an interview with political analyst Isidro Sepúlveda, "México necesita crear un organismo de velar por la seguridad nacional," *El Universal,* October 23, 1981, first section, second part, p. 19.

56. An irony here is that some Mexican analysts may believe U.S. capital, technology, and information flows into Mexico jeopardize their nation's sovereignty, independence, and culture; yet these same analysts deny that Mexican immigration into the United States may have similar adverse consequences for the politics, culture, and economy of the United States. In a similar fashion, some U.S. analysts hold one set of views about the effects of Mexican immigration on the United States and quite contrary views about the effects of U.S. capital, technology, and information flows on Mexico. See

Kevin F. McCarthy and David F. Ronfeldt, *U.S. Immigration Policy and Global Interdependence,* The Rand Corporation, R-2887-FF/RF/RC/NICHD, June 1982, or McCarthy and Ronfeldt, "Immigration as an Intrusive Global Flow: A New Perspective," in Mary M. Kritz, (ed.), *U.S. Immigration and Refugee Policy: Global and Domestic Issues,* Lexington Books, D. C. Heath and Co., Lexington, Mass., 1983, pp. 381–400.

57. These points are advocated in Olga Pellicer, "National Security in Mexico: Traditional Notions and New Preoccupations," in Clark Reynolds and Carlos Tello (eds.), *U.S.–Mexico Relations: Economic and Social Aspects,* Stanford University Press, Stanford, 1983, pp. 181–192. She quotes (p. 188) a revealing editorial from the newspaper *Uno más Uno,* September 13, 1980: "For Mexicans, national security begins with, and is grounded in, social security in its widest sense. Security is the fulfillment of the basic constitutional mandates emerging from the revolutionary pact of 1917, it is the resolute defense of natural resources, the generation of wealth, the equitable distribution of income. . . . It is the certainty that, even if inequalities have not been suppressed, the possibility of opening a space for real action permitting progress in that direction has not been closed off. Insecurity comes about with the jettisoning of the concepts of sovereignty and social interest." In a brief, conservative U.S. analysis of Mexico's situation, Thomas H. Moorer and Georges A. Fuariol, *Caribbean Basin Security,* The Washington Papers/104, The Center for International and Strategic Studies and Praeger Publishers, 1984, esp. pp. 53–62 and 76–78, agree that Mexico does not yet face "a clear-cut threat to the south. What the nation does face is a latent security problem related to political and ideological turbulence in Central America" (p. 57). They reflect a U.S. concern, however, that "Mexico remains an important platform for Cuban and Soviet-related activities in the Caribbean Basin" (p. 78).

58. Writing just prior to the de la Madrid administration, Olga Pellicer, "Mexico in Central America: The Difficult Exercise of Regional Power," in Richard R. Fagen and Olga Pellicer (eds.), *The Future of Central America: Policy Choices for the U.S. and Mexico,* Stanford University Press, Stanford, 1983, pp. 119–133, observed that "various indicators, among them the limited support afforded to the Franco-Mexican communiqué and reluctance to continue sending aid to Nicaragua in the face of Mexico's own grave economic problems, suggest that in recent years the official Central American policy has not fully taken hold of the Mexican political elite's imagination. Support for the policy has come mainly from the chief executive, the foreign minister, and certain sectors of the Partido Revolucionario Institucional (PRI). Their enthusiasm is not shared by the defense minister and other sectors of the government" (p. 132).

59. See Humberto Garza and René Herrera, "Notas sobre la Formulación de Decisiones en la Política Exterior de Mexico: Su Applicación en Centroamérica," Occasional Papers Series, Dialogue #39, Latin American and Caribbean Center, Florida International University, Tamiami, September 1984.

60. See Sereseres, "The Military Looks South," in Ronfeldt (ed.), 1984, pp. 201–13.

61. In October 1982, the Secretariats of National Defense and Government and the attorney general's office apparently organized a joint commission to investigate problems along the southern border and to avoid provocations with Guatemala.

62. Carlos Rico commented at the research workshop that in contrast to the case of Mexico's policy toward other Central American countries, domestic policy

agencies are becoming increasingly involved in Mexico's decision-making toward Guatemala as its internal conflict sharpens and threatens to spill into Mexico. The policy choices for Mexico tend to get framed in extreme terms, he noted, because of the absence of a strong political center in Guatemala. Adolfo Aguilar Zinser, "Mexico and the Guatemalan Crisis," in Fagen and Pellicer (eds.), 1983, pp. 161–186, says that "a debate has accordingly developed, in which various information media, ecclesiastical groups, and organizations representing the intellectual and political left denounce Guatemala's repressive regime and urge the state to repudiate it, while business organizations and rightist political groups express distaste for the Guatemalan revolutionary movement and characterize the Guatemalan refugees as a threat to the social peace of Mexico" (p. 186). For another view, see Sereseres, in Ronfeldt (ed.), 1984.

63. See the earlier discussion about changes in Mexico's elite.
64. The *Time* magazine cover story about "A Proud Capital's Distress," August 6, 1984, reports, "Decentralization . . . is an idea that wins nods of approval but very little action. The current crowding fills Mexico City with not only 28% of all Mexicans but two-thirds of the nation's students. More than half of the country's industry is concentrated there, and seven out of ten banking transactions occur there. Yet every new plan to spur the transfer of business and government out of the capital is largely a recycling of some previous unfulfilled plan. 'There have been about five decentralization programs in the past 20 years, and all of them failed because there was no political will to carry them out'" (pp. 35–36). This appears to be one of the most important issue areas for U.S.–Mexican relations, and potentially for U.S. policy, in this decade and the next.
65. For example, see "Decreto de descentralización," *Análisis Político,* July 15, 1984, p. 48.
66. A strong statement to this effect appears in Lozoya, 1970, pp. 73–75. Yet it should also be noted that the zone commanders are regularly rotated, a practice instituted in the 1930s to prevent them from establishing local power bases that could be used to challenge central authority.
67. Lorenzo Meyer and General Luis Garfias Magaña contributed this point at the research workshop. Too little is known about the command structure of the military regions to suppose that this may provide another approach, above the zone commander, to influencing regional development priorities.
68. Geopolitical thinking is fundamentally concerned with the significance of geographic positions, including the spatial distribution and control of physical assets, resources, and lines of communication. Whereas dependency analysis, which is common among civilian intellectuals, often treats class structure as the central cause of economic underdevelopment and political instability, geopolitical analysis may emphasize the spatial maladjustment of resources, economic infrastructure, and population.
69. The Mexican "land bridge" or "land canal," originally code-named the Alpha-Omega project, was supposed to become an international alternative to shipping freight through the Panama Canal or across the United States. Elements were constructed during the López Portillo administration, but the project was never completed. Its operations initially came under the Sistema Multimodal Transístmico (SMT), which moved Mexican products for about two years but did not succeed in convincing international shippers to use the system for moving freight between Europe, the Far East, and the U.S. coasts. The SMT has recently been dissolved and replaced by a modest operation, Servicios Portuários del Istmo de Tehuantepec (Semultra), which will service container traffic between Mexico's coasts ("SMT To Begin Moving Cargo," *Journal of*

Commerce, April 17, 1984, as reprinted in *ISLA,* Vol. 28, No. 4, p. 16, and "Mexican land canal is downgraded: Unfulfilled contracts, no funds," *Latin American Regional Reports: Mexico and Central America,* RM-84-06, July 13, 1984, p. 4).

70. For example, the construction of a new dam in the region has upset local farmers and peasants and enabled radical political movements to stage protest demonstrations.

71. René Herrera and Mario Ojeda, *La Política de México Hacia Centroamérica 1979–1982,* Jornadas 103, El Colegio de México, Mexico City, 1983, p. 36.

72. Indeed, it has been in the strategic interests of both the extreme right and the extreme left to use violence to accentuate polarization and to destroy (or force into exile) moderate leaders, their parties, and their followers, in order to leave little choice but one extreme or the other.

73. This discussion of the internationalization of conflict is adapted from Ronfeldt, *Geopolitics, Security, and U.S. Strategy in the Caribbean Basin,* The Rand Corporation, R-2997-Af/RC, November 1983. See also Edward Gonzalez, Brian Michael Jenkins, David Ronfeldt, and Caesar Sereseres, *U.S. Policy for Central America: A Briefing,* The Rand Corporation, Santa Monica, R-3150-RC, March 1984; and Ronfeldt, "Rethinking the Monroe Doctrine," *Orbis,* Winter 1985, pp. 684–696.

74. Cited in Aguilar Zinser, in Fagen and Pellicer (eds.), 1983, p. 176.

75. See Sereseres, in Ronfeldt (ed.), 1984.

Jorge Domínguez

The Civic Soldier in Cuba

Two major patterns of civilian control over the military can be identified. Samuel P. Huntington calls one "subjective" civilian control;[1] it ensures control over the military by increasing the authority of a governmental institution such as a parliament, of a social class such as the bourgeoisie, or of a political party such as the Communist party, over military institutions. The other, which Huntington calls "objective" civilian control, emphasizes a professional army, separate from politics, in command of military expertise and responsibility, and corporately autonomous.

Civilian control is far from being worldwide. Among economically underdeveloped countries, particularly new states with relatively weak political institutions, military control over civilian institutions is common. This control assumes two different forms.[2] One, the military acting as arbitrator, has no independent political organization or ideology; it is often content merely to supervise the leading civilian officals. When the army does take over directly, it oftens does so for a stated and limited period, handing the government back as soon as "acceptable" civilians are found to lead it. This variety of controlling military finds nothing wrong with the social and economic status quo and prefers a civilian government. The

Portions of this chapter previously appeared in Jorge Domínguez, *Cuba: Order and Revolution* (Cambridge: Harvard University Press, 1978), and *Cuba: Internal and International Affairs* (Beverly Hills, Calif.: Sage Publications, 1982). Pp. 53–59 of the latter work reprinted by permission of the copyright holder, Sage Publications, Inc.

military acting as ruler, in contrast, has little confidence in civilian rule, rejects the existing social order, and expects to stay in power, to construct its own ideology, and perhaps develop a political organization to support its regime.

All these characterzations, and others like them,[3] are based on the assumption that there is always a firm distinction between civilians and military, that the two are at least potentially in conflict, that civilians are always capable of governing, and that military activity can be so strictly defined that taking over governments or performing normally civilian functions can readily be identified and analyzed as "unmilitary." Thus arise such terms as a "praetorian" polity, a "militarized" society, or a "politicized" army.

The facts in revolutionary Cuba contradict this dichotomy. Cuba has been ruled in large part by military men who govern large segments of both military and civilian life, who are held up as paragons to both soldiers and civilians, who are the bearers of the revolutionary tradition and ideology, who have politicized themselves by absorbing the norms and organization of the Communist party, and who have educated themselves to become professional in political, economic, managerial, engineering, and educational as well as military affairs. Their civilian and their military lives are fused. In this situation, at least until recently, one could not speak of either civilian control over the military or military control over civilians. But in the mid-1970s some new trends have appeared that may herald yet another change in the future.

The "civic soldier" has been a key political role in Cuba for a long time. Approximately two-thirds of the high-ranking officials have had civic-soldier careers; most of them learned this role during the uprising against Batista in the 1950s and the suppression of the anti-Communists in the early 1960s. Civil war, more than any other form of conflict, tends to integrate military and political roles. Civic soldiers head both military and civilian agencies in Cuba and, just as military agencies have had civilian tasks, civilian agencies have had military tasks and have used military forms of organization. The civic-soldier role includes not only former soldiers heading government organizations but also soldiers on active duty engaged in political, economic, or other nonmilitary activities.

Roles are defined in part by the expectations of others. When the characteristics of a role are defined by superiors and acknowledged by subordinates, the result is what some sociologists call the "sent role." The sent role of the civic soldier has included both military and civilian aspects. Thus a military commander's sent role includes nonmilitary duties, just as the sent roles of the minister of education or of a sugar-harvest administrator have included military duties. A renewal of specialization in the armed forces after 1973 reduced somewhat the fusion of civilian and military roles, but the armed forces have continued to perform at least some civilian functions.

This coexistence of military and civilian aspects of the civic-soldier role has implications for political conflict. There is relatively little evidence that any conflict that does occur takes place between civilians and military. When conflicts arise, civic soldiers are just as likely to split among themselves as the purely civilian minority. Nor have there been issues from which civic soldiers have stood aloof; they are involved in all public-policy issue areas. When the defense budget is debated, for example, civic soldiers are found on both sides of many issues; thus even on military subjects civic soldiers' opinions can divide, although no doubt pressures on their organizational loyalties are more difficult to reconcile than those felt by civilians.

Individuals whose roles have been defined by their superiors to include civilian and military aspects may experience objective role conflict, of which there are two kinds. "Intersender" conflict occurs when different superiors who share authority over a subordinate define the latter's role in different ways. Should the officer in charge of a motorized brigade, for example, emphasize training for combat or for a mechanized harvest? This officer is receiving different role definitions from the army and from sugar-harvest authorities. Another type of role conflict, called "intersender" conflict, occurs when one superior defines different roles for the same subordinate. For example, the party prescribes that resources be committed both to defense and to industrial investments: how is a middle-ranking official to decide when to divert resources from one activity to the other?[4]

The leaders in the 1960s addressed themselves to the problem of conflicting expectations by trying to avoid extreme specialization within and between organizations and by relying on long-standing friendships from the guerrilla-warfare days. The Ministry of the Armed Forces demanded both economic and military performance but neglected to lay down rules for apportioning time. The problem led in 1973 to a reorganization of the armed forces that required greater specialization within the military. While the armed forces as a whole continued to perform both military and economic functions, specific units were assigned to one or the other. The military tasks of civilian agencies, however, increased in the early 1970s. The Ministry of Education and the Ministry of Light Industry still required their staffs to teach, produce, and prepare for war in schools and factories. Military specialization had different consequences for military personnel and civilians. Within the armed forces, specialization simplified the definitions of the roles of most military commanders and their subordinates. Superiors mandated either military or nonmilitary roles most of the time; because the same superior was no longer defining roles in quite different ways, intrasender role conflict declined. Within the civilian agencies, most plant managers, school principals, workers, and students continued to suffer from intrasender role conflict. These civilian agencies continued to receive role definitions from the party and government leadership that included both civilian and military aspects; subordinates had to perform many different, often conflicting tasks.

The increase in the military content of civilian organizations brought many more civilians under the partial authority of the Armed Forces Ministry, a change that also increased role conflicts. Individuals were faced more directly with conflict among different superiors—some emphasizing civilian and some military activities and together creating a serious intersender conflict. But the specialization of some military units exclusively on military tasks eliminated intersender role conflict for them, since no civilian agency defined a role for them in conflict with the armed forces ministry. The military units engaged in production still had to coordinate their work closely with civilian agencies, and thus intersender role conflict could still result. The 1973 reforms may have succeeded in reducing role conflicts only within the armed forces units specializing in military tasks.

Because the civilian and military aspects of the civic-soldier role are regarded as equally legitimate, organizations are flexible. The defense budget is not cut when threats to the state decline; rather, it is simply directed to the nondefense apsects of the civic-soldier role. Military elements were stressed again after the intervention in Angola. Since loyalty to the organization will often lead to changes in emphasis for the sake of its survival or growth, the legitimacy of the civic-soldier role has facilitated these shifts.[5]

Cuban civilian-military relations fall into three distinct periods. The first, from qualified independence in 1902 until the revolution that overthrew Machado in 1933, was one of subjective civilian control. The military often served as a presidential political machine, ensuring the victory of the President's party at the polls in return for participation in a system of widespread and institutionalized graft. The military also put down the insurrections that often followed elections; these uprisings were usually minor and designed to provoke United States interference to annul the election results. No military coups were attempted during this period.[6]

The armed forces acted as arbitrators from 1933 until the overthrow of Batista in 1958. There were two successful coups, in September 1933 and March 1952, but no sustained military rule. Instead, the military placed its chosen civilians in power, among them a thoroughly civilianized Senator Batista in 1952. In 1936 the military forced the Congress to impeach the President and replace him with the Vice President. From 1933 to 1940 effective political power was held by the commander-in-chief of the army, Colonel Fulgencio Batista, who often removed civilian presidents. But a military officer on active duty never served as President of the republic. Military coups were attempted after 1940, but they all failed.

Batista relied on the existing political parties and borrowed their ideas both in 1933–44 and in 1952–58. Although he eventually developed a political organization, it was not a military one, but one of his own devising. As army chief in the 1930s, Batista toyed with corporatist political ideology but soon abandoned it. He expanded the role of the military into civilian areas, especially in education and public health, but he kept the military out of the economy. He emphasized a more effective distribution of such resources as education and public health that did not require directly taking from some to give to others. In early primary education and public health, the military supplanted civilians, but it brought to these tasks no skills that could not just as well have been provided by civilians. A technically or managerially competent military that stressed development was not the result, for the military was simply being used as "cheap labor."[7]

In the 1940s nonmilitary army activities were sharply restricted, as many educational and health functions were transferred to civilian agencies. When the Batista government sought in the 1950s to repress the opposition, they did not militarize the social system; the president chose to risk defeat rather than disrupt the economy. He deployed troops to protect private enterprises and to guarantee production, rather than to ensure the success of a military offensive. At the end of the Batista regime, therefore, the scope of military activities had been much restricted, the influence of the military on national life was limited, and attitudes toward the armed forces had become very negative.

During the third period, from 1959 until the present, the rule of Castro's government has fit none of the usual categories. While one can identify a ruling elite and some purely civilian leaders, it is not so easy to identify purely military ones. The vast majority of Cuba's ruling elite have held military rank, and no identifiable purely civilian elite has been available to take their place. There is little evidence of civilian-military conflict, not only because the purely civilian share of the elite is small, but also because the military's decisive political role is great, and the scope of its legitimate activity has never been clearly defined.

The Military Mission of the Armed Forces

The military mission of the Cuban armed forces was originally to provide for national defense and to suppress internal challenges to the authority of the government. More recently Cuba's participation in the Angolan civil war has added a third task—overseas combat. Since 1960 the Soviet nuclear shield has been one factor deterring a United States attack on Cuba, somewhat shakily in 1960 and more firmly after 1970. The Cuban armed forces, however, are responsible for their own subnuclear defense. Its major challenge thus far has been the Bay of Pigs invasion in April 1961. Since then, though with declining frequency, various exile groups have launched hit-and-run attacks on the island or have landed small parties, but they have all been quickly captured.

Cuba faced insurrections off and on, from December 1956 through 1965. Since then, episodes of internal resistance have been few and rapidly suppressed. From December 1956 to January 1959 Batista's government forces fought against Castro and his allies. During the second half of 1960 insurgents rose against Castro's government, particularly in the Escambray mountains of Las Villas province in central Cuba, an episode soon followed by the Bay of Pigs. In addition to that invasion, there were thirty-four infiltrations from abroad in 1960–61. The Bay of Pigs and the abortive Escambray uprising discouraged insurrections briefly, but they resumed in 1962, when from March to September the number of bands in the Escambray rose from forty-two to seventy-nine. By July the government had created a special corps to fight the "bandits": the Lucha Contra Bandidos, or LCB. Although the LCB units undoubtedly fought some genuine bandits, their clear targets were counterrevolutionaries.[8]

From 1960 to 1965 counterrevolutionaries rose up against the Castro government in all six provinces. At one time the country had as many as 179 insurrectionary bands. The revolutionary government estimated the number of armed oppositionists killed or captured at 3,591; about 500 combat deaths in the LCB forces were reported, apart from deaths from other military actions and terrorism, along with losses of 1,000 million pesos from all three. Antigovernment forces numbered no more than a thousand at their peak strength. The total number of deaths in the 1960s was in the same range—roughly 2,000–2,500—as in the 1950s. The number of regular troops committed by the Cuban government to defending the regime against insurrection was ten times greater under Castro than it had been under Batista; the reserve forces under Castro were ten to fifteen times greater than under Batista; the amount of actual fighting was probably the same. The difference was that Batista's government lost and Castro's won. Revolutionary government in Cuba could not have survived without effective armed forces.[9]

Military expenditures were greatest in prerevolutionary Cuba through 1940, when the Batista forces were active outside of their strictly military responsibilities; such burdens reached their ebb just before Batista staged his coup in March 1952. Among the first measures after the takeover were pay raises for the military. Although the military budget grew during the Batista regime, its proportion of national income remained constant because the economy was growing as well. Even in 1958, when it was threatened with widespread insurrection, the Batista government was still committing only a small proportion of national income to arms; the share Castro has allocated to the military is at least two or three times larger (table 1). Castro has noted that at their peak in the early 1960s Cuban military expenditures totaled "close to" 500 million pesos. Thus the statis-

Table 1. Military expenditures, 1940–1974

Year	Total expenditures (in millions of current pesos)	Total expenditures (in millions of current dollars)	Expenditures (computed from current prices) % of GNP[a]	Expenditures (computed from current prices) % of GMP[b]
1940	19	—	4.5	—
1949–50	40	—	2.6	—
1951–52	42	—	2.2	—
1958	50	—	2.3	—
1961	—	175	7.6	—
1962	—	200	8.0	—
1963	213	213	5.6	—
1964	223	221	5.2	5.3
1965	214	213	4.4	5.1
1966	—	213	4.5	5.3
1967	—	250	4.8	6.1
1968	—	300	5.8	6.9
1969	—	250	4.5	6.0
1970	—	290	5.1	—
1971	—	290	5.2	—
1972	365	319	5.1	—
1974	400	—	—	—

Sources: Computed from Cuban Economic Research Project, *A Study on Cuba* (Coral Gables, Fla.: University of Miami Press, 1965), pp. 455, 461, 621; Dirección Central de Estadística, *Compendio estadístico de Cuba, 1966* (Havana: Junta Central de Planificación, 1966), p. 13; Carmelo Mesa-Lago, "Economic Policies and Growth," in *Revolutionary Change in Cuba,* ed. Carmelo Mesa-Lago (Pittsburgh: University of Pittsburgh Press, 1971), p. 319; *Granma Weekly Review,* August 6, 1972, p. 4; Frank Mankiewiez and Kirby Jones, *With Fidel* (Chicago: Playboy Press, 1975), pp. 118–119; U.S., Arms Control and Disarmament Agency, *World Military Expenditures, 1971* (Washington, D.C.: Government Printing Office, 1972), pp. 19, 27 (hereafter cited as *ACDA*); *ACDA, 1963–1973,* p. 28; *Boletín 1970,* p. 30.

[a] National-income data, rather than gross national product, are used for 1940–1958. In constant prices, referring to national income, 6.5 percent in 1963, 5.6 percent in 1964, and 5.5 percent in 1965.

[b] In constant prices, 8.2 percent in 1963; 7.1 percent in 1964; 6.6 percent in 1965; 6.6 percent in 1966.

tics in table 1 seriously underestimate actual military expenditures. All available data, however, point to a decline in the proportion of national income devoted to military expenditure after the early 1960s, as counter-revolutionary activity declined and the economy recovered from its near-collapse of 1962–63. This decline was interrupted in 1968; military expenditure then remained at a constant, high level as a result of the expansion of the military into the economic sphere. In addition to Cuba's own resources, the Soviet Union, according to Castro himself, supplied Cuba free of charge with weapons worth several thousand million pesos between 1960 and 1975.[10]

Size and Structure

Cuba's regular armed forces grew from 24,797 when Batista took over in 1952 to 29,270 on the day he fell from power in 1958. In addition, Batista had army and navy reserves numbering 18,542 by December 1958.[11] According to Prime Minister Castro, the Revolutionary Armed Forces numbered about 300,000 at their peak in the early 1960s. By 1970 they had declined to 250,000, and by late 1974, to about 100,000. According to Raúl Castro, the Army of Working Youth had another 100,000. A large number of reserve forces were also available at various levels of readiness. The number of civilian workers under direct military command increased 23 percent between 1971 and 1975. Foreign sources have estimated the size of the professional, regular Cuban armed forces at approximately 100,000 to 120,000 from the late 1960s on. The Institute for Strategic Studies estimated that Cuba's regular armed forces amounted to 117,000 in 1975 and that the ready reserves, which could be mobilized within a maximum of seventy-two hours, numbered about 90,000 (inactive reserves were not estimated). Therefore, the change in the Cuban armed forces from 1970 to 1974 represents a shift of personnel from semiprofessional, full-time soldiers to reserve status. The size of the truly professional forces has apparently remained constant.

In practice, Cuba's external defense rests with the navy, which is equipped to intercept landings and attacks by exiles and to prevent hit-and-run raids with its air and antiaircraft defense forces, and with the Frontier Corps, a unit under the Ministry of the Interior rather than a regular part of the armed forces, which serves as the first line of defense against landings while regular army units are being called up. Cuba's other military resources are not necessary for routine defense. Estimates of the number of naval personnel have varied from 6,000 to 7,500 between 1970 and 1975; the variation is explained by the practice of shifting officers and crew back and forth between the navy and the merchant marine. The size of the air force, including the antiaircraft defense forces, has risen from about 12,000 in 1970 to 20,000 in 1975. The size of the regular army has held steady for several years at no less than 90,000—not including the reserves and the Army of Working Youth. In addition, the Frontier Corps has about 3,000 troops, and internal security units of the Ministry of the Interior, about 10,000.

Cuba also has an elite force under the jurisdiction of the Interior Ministry that is not part of the regular armed forces. This Special Forces Battalion of about 650 people was the group sent to Angola in the fall of

1975 to fight the South Africans, pending the arrival of reinforcements, while other Cuban units fought against the enemy Angolan units. Thus most of Cuba's professional forces are not engaged in routine defense, which is handled primarily by the navy, the Frontier Corps, and, to a lesser degree, the air force.[12] Altogether about 30,000 troops are concerned principally with external defense, although the air force is also available for overseas combat. An additional 10,000 are concerned solely with internal security; another 100,000 in the Army of Working Youth are mainly engaged in agricultural production, but have some nominal military training. Approximately 180,000 regular army and ready reserve troops are available either for internal security, external defense, or overseas combat, reinforced by the Special Forces Battalion; more than five hundred thousand reservists at various levels of readiness are available for combat in emergencies, and several tens of thousands of civilian workers provide logistical support under direct commands of the Ministry of the Armed Forces and the Interior Ministry. The total number of troops under the command of these two ministries, excluding the inactive reserves, and civilian workers under direct military command, was no fewer than 321,150 in the mid-1970s—the so-called order of battle. Within this number, however, there is substantial variation in the level of combat preparedness.

The force structure of the Cuban armed forces has remained stable since 1968, the pivotal date in Soviet-Cuban relations. Cuban-Soviet collaboration since that time, so important to the economy and internal stability, has produced only marginal changes in Cuba's force structure. By 1968, Cuba already had 300 heavy and medium-weight tanks; the introduction of lighter tanks increased the number to 600 by the mid-1970s and added flexibility to the corps. By 1968 the army had 200 armored personnel carriers, 100 assault guns, and 30 Frog-4 surface-to-surface missiles. The navy had between fifteen and eighteen submarine chasers and eighteen Komar patrol boats equipped with Styx surface-to-surface missiles. Five Osa patrol boats with Styx missiles, which have an effective radius of only fifteen miles, were added by the mid-1970s. The Samlet-missile coastal defense was also in place by 1968; since 1968 the navy has added only some helicopters. By 1968 the air force had twenty-four battalions, organized in 144 units, with about 600 surface-to-surface missiles. It was also equipped with a full complement of helicopters and transport planes; the number of training planes was increased from sixty to eighty-five.

From 1968 to 1974 the number of MiG-15s fell from sixty to fifteen and of MiG-17s from seventy-five to seventy; but at the same time the number of MiG-19s rose from twenty to forty, and of MiG-21s from forty-five to eighty. This shift represents both strengthening and modernization, since the MiG-15s are 1948 planes. The addition of the MiG-21s in 1965 made

Cuba the first Latin American country with supersonic aircraft. The increase in their number and the introduction of thirty more modern MiG-21Fs were responses to the spread of supersonic aircraft in the rest of Latin America. The replacement of MiG-15 and MiG-17 planes by MiG-19s and MiG-21s also reflects a policy change: interceptors replaced fighter bombers. Because fighter bombers have a much wider range, they could easily have hit the United States or other American countries. Interceptors cannot. The fighter bombers, however old, are offensive weapons: the interceptors have a shorter flight radius. After the Angolan war in 1975, Cuba also added at least fifteen T-62 tanks, and several BM-21 multiple rocket launchers.[13]

Cuba's military doctrine was matured by 1967, once the survival of the revolution had been assured. It has remained essentially unchanged since, except for the air force's shift to defensive weapons, just mentioned. In the early 1960s, Cuba had a large standing force with limited competence; it could defeat an insurrection or withstand landings by exiles, but it would have had to rely on the Soviets in the event of a major attack. By the late 1960s and early 1970s, the desire for greater strategic autonomy reinforced the government's wish to reduce the personnel burden of the military on the Cuban economy; the result was a new emphasis on a modern, professional, "small" standing force combined with an easily mobilized reserve.[14] Policy emphasized that the national defense rested first with self-reliant Cuban forces. Soviet assistance would be used only to modernize weapons inventories, to assure a continued supply of munitions and spare parts, and to provide a nuclear-weapons shield.

The standing force was reduced by divesting the armed forces of its least professional units; total force size, as well as the size of the regular, professional units, remains the same. The funds spent on the military remain large and have even risen in the early 1970s as a result of this emphasis on professional forces and modern equipment (see table 1). The military share of the gross product is lower than it was in the counterrevolutionary period, but it is higher than it was in the mid-1960s.

With the new emphasis on reserves that can be mobilized efficiently, the militia disappeared altogether. Its political functions were taken over by the Committees for the Defense of the Revolution; its other functions passed to civil defense, which operates in every work center and trains citizens to cope with war and other disasters such as the frequent hurricanes. Its more militarized successor, the reserves, also replaced other nonprofessional units of the old armed forces.[15]

All men under fifty and all women under forty have a military-reserve classification according to age, skill, and prior military experience, which governs the length of time that an individual can be called up every year for military training. The shortest period is twelve days a year; the longest, three months. All civilian organizations must defer to the military when reserves are called up for training, and they must plan to do without the people involved, whether they are needed or not; still, being called up for two or three months at a time can seriously disrupt an individual's job, not to mention private life. The draft is run by a system of military registration that operates through work centers and schools and keeps records of the skills, rank, level of combat training, and political persuasion of every potential draftee. Once drafted, reservists participate in war games. For example, 70 percent of the personnel involved in the war games of the Eastern Army in Camagüey province in the fall of 1974 were reservists; the 3,940 reservists mobilized for from twenty to thirty days who participated in the Western Army's July 1975 war games made up more than half of the troops involved. Reservists accounted for 70 percent of the Cuban troops who fought in Angola in 1975–76.[16]

Professionalizing the Military

The level of competence of the army has consequently improved by the mid-1970s. In 1971 only one of the units of the Western Army achieved a grade of better than 75 percent in marksmanship; other indicators among both officers and troops were equally low, resulting in an effort to "replace defects of instruction with enthusiasm." By the end of 1973 all the units of the Western Army were receiving grades above 75 percent.[17]

The professionalization of the armed forces can also be seen in changes in the military-school system. In 1959–60 the dropout rate in officers' school was 55 percent; by 1961–62, it had been reduced to 25 percent. The school for militia officers (the Ignacio Agramonte School in Matanzas) became the general officers' school in 1961; a school for political instructors in the armed forces (the Osvaldo Sánchez School) was established in May 1961 (both were closed in 1971 and their students transferred elsewhere). A nationwide system of cadet schools, including schools for navy, communications, infantry, artillery, tank corps, and air force personnel, was set up, and the Máximo Gómez War College for training for the top commands had been established by 1963. The first military junior and senior high schools for children between eleven and seventeen (the Camilo Cienfuegos Schools) were established in 1966. Graduates of the Camilo Cienfuegos senior high schools did not receive commissions immediately, but they had priority in admission to cadet schools. A technological institute was founded in 1966 to train military technicians and engineers. A school for administrators of military-equipment maintenance was set up in 1970. In 1969, 11.2 percent of the 214 students at the University of Havana's National Center for Scientific Research came from the armed forces or the Ministry of the Interior; 2.6 percent of the 307 papers presented in 1972 at the first national scientific conference of university students, and 2.6 percent of the 311 papers at the second, came from the military technological institute. The Naval Academy in Mariel, founded before the revolution, graduated 1,200 officers between 1959 and 1974; in 1974, it had 600 students and 170 faculty members and prepared officers for both the navy and the merchant marine.

In 1968 there were 10,000 military students enrolled in cadet schools in Cuba. A complete system of military schools included high schools; four basic-training cadet schools for the navy, artillery, air force, and other services (the Antonio Maceo Inter-Armas School, the Cuban equivalent of West Point, but with lower academic standards, had absorbed the training schools for infantry and communications and tank specialists); an advanced-training cadet school, the military technological institute, which included specialized research facilities; and a national war college. Continuing-education programs for alumni of the military technological institute were begun in 1975. This military-school system allowed admissions standards to be raised and programs of study to be lengthened. The 1,579 officers who graduated in 1970 had attended officers' school for between three and five years.

In 1976 the best-educated Cuban officers in the Angolan war were found among the military engineers and the air force. The engineers had completed senior high school and studied at the technical institute for five years. Air force officers had been trained in the Soviet Union after a year of basic training in Cuba; they, too, needed a high-school diploma to qualify for admission. Artillery officers, naval officers, and other specialized army officers had to have completed the tenth grade before being admitted to the appropriate military school. Once admitted, artillery officers went through a three-year program; the others, a four-year program. All other officers with command responsibilities were trained at the Antonio Maceo Inter-Armas School, where a ninth-grade education qualified them for admission to a three-year course of study; thus most Cuban officers were only senior-high-school graduates. The school for administrators required only an eighth-grade education and a course of thirty months.

The improved military-school system contributed greatly to the ideological coherence of the armed forces, for the lower schools fed into the higher schools, eliminating the need to recruit untrained civilians who would require more extensive training. By 1971, 74 percent of the students admitted to the military technological institute were graduates of the Camilo Cienfuegos military high schools; by 1975, 63 percent of all graduating cadets from the naval academy, the artillery and general-officer schools, and the military technological institute had previously graduated from the military high schools. Although the fifty-eight comandantes (the highest rank at the time) and the 109 officers who received the title of military "vanguard" officer in 1973 were only twenty-nine years old on the average, they had served in the armed forces for an average of eleven years; 41 percent of the 151 "vanguard" officers had served for thirteen or fourteen years.[18]

At the end of 1973 and again at the end of 1976, military ranks and armed-forces hierarchy were reorganized to approximate the system most common in the rest of the world. Until 1973 the highest rank, comandante, had no clear equivalent elsewhere. Ranks within the armed forces were poorly differentiated. Since 1976 Fidel Castro remained as commander-in-chief; a rank below him was Raúl Castro as general of the army; the chiefs of the three main armies became division generals. Everyone along the line received a new rank corresponding to the universal system. Since 1973 former officers in civilian jobs had no longer been addressed by their military titles; inactive personnel are also discouraged from wearing uniforms and insignia.[19] The change is partly symbolic, but it also serves to draw a clear line between civilian and military roles and provides an incentive for officers attracted to the military life to stay in it and work for promotion there.

Clear definitions of rank led to a new consciousness within the officer corps that was soon reflected in a system of military clubs, which clearly separated commissioned officers from noncommissioned officers and troops. The clubs are intended to provide both recreation and cultural and political education. A military unit is entitled to a so-called Lenin-Martí salon; a battalion, to a club for noncommissioned officers and troops; a division, to an officers' club. A national officers' club was established in 1975. In practice, however, club facilities are not always so readily available. The major air force base at San Antonio de los Baños had six Lenin-Martí salons by the early spring of 1976, when the entire Army of Working Youth had only begun to start one. Since the air force was regarded as an elite branch of the service and the Army of Working Youth as a very plebeian one, the availability of recreational facilities seemed contingent on rank and status.[20]

The professionalization of the armed forces and the stability of its doctrine and force structure are evidence of a high degree of military institutionalization; in fact, the process was well under way even during the 1960s. The long terms of service characteristic of the best officers, the integrated military-school system, and the autonomy of military organizations from civilian organizations for military recruitment have all since added to their stability and ideological coherence and have promoted officer loyalty to the armed forces. These factors would also have led to a military oligarchy had they been left unchecked by the Communist party. Professionalization has increased military autonomy because civilian technicians are less necessary, and it has added to the organizational complexity of the armed forces. The institutionalized armed forces, however, also need a larger share of the national budget. An added cost to civilians—and a gain for the military—was the expansion of military training and military control into the lives of many people. Another trend appeared in the mid-1960s, when the armed forces adopted social, economic, and political missions as well as purely military functions. From one point of view, civilians were militarized; from another, the military was civilianized. The result was the flourishing of the civic soldier at least through the mid-1970s.

The Angolan War

Although Cuba supported revolutionary movements in many countries since 1959, until recently that support had never been a part of the role and purpose of its armed forces. Cubans who had fought abroad had, at least officially, done so on their own, though not without open backing from their government. Che Guevara, for example, had resigned from all his positions in Cuba—under pressure to do so from Fidel Castro—before embarking on his career as an international revolutionary. Never before the Angolan war had the Cuban armed forces been committed to front-line overseas combat as part of their mission.

The Angolan war altered that pattern. Cuban military doctrine added a new mission for its armed forces; they would no longer be limited to the defense of the homeland but would also be ready to take the offensive overseas. The Cuban-Angolan agreement of 1976 committed Cuba to the unlimited defense of Angola against hostile neighbors, apparently including counterinsurgents within Angola itself. Although the treaty only requires Cuba to supply "military units and weapons necessary to support the People's Republic of Angola in case of aggression from outside," the Cuban government has chosen to categorize guerrillas opposed to the Luanda government as agents of outside forces.[21]

This change in doctrine was reflected in changes in war games, which began to include not only the defense of positions but long marches, the occupation of large areas, and the simultaneous deployment of large numbers and varieties of troops. The first of these new war games were held in July 1975, just as Angola prepared for independence. Motorized infantry maneuvers in Camagüey province in November emphasized techniques for seizing territory and for long marches. In early December, as the Angolan war reached its peak intensity, such exercises became even more complex—the largest and most complicated maneuvers ever held in Cuba.[22]

Cuba's victory in Angola proved the effectiveness of its military reforms. Approximately 20,000 Cuban troops were in Angola at any one time; the total number involved through troop rotation was probably much larger. The Angolan war also demonstrated the close military ties between the Soviet Union and Cuba: Cubans were carried over equipped only with light weapons; heavier weapons were supplied on the spot by the Soviets, so that Cuban weapons inventories were hardly touched by the war. Cuban civil air transports and merchant marine took Cuban troops to Angola. Apart from the Interior Ministry's Special Forces, Cuban troops included artillery, motorized, tank, rocketry, air force, and infantry units.[23]

The Angolan operation also indicated some of the organizational versatility of the Cuban armed forces. It showed, for instance, that troops could be mobilized by racial category. Half the Cuban troops in Angola were black, well above the black share of the armed forces and about double their representation in the general population. This disproportionate mobilization of blacks was meant to reduce the racial differences between the Cubans and their Angolan allies. Normally, however, racial distribution is carefully maintained in the divisions that constitute the Cuban army. Although the proportion of blacks in the population is twice as high in eastern Cuba as it is in the rest of the country, for instance, there are no significant differences in the racial composition of Cuba's three main armies—Eastern, Central, and Western; troops are rotated throughout the country so that each reflects the makeup of the population as a whole. To increase the proportion of blacks among the Cuban units in Angola, then, special procedures had to be followed to select black troops from all three armies.[24]

Another organizational achievement was the joint operation of the army in Angola and in Cuba. Sometime between August 20 and September 5, 1975, the chairman of the Joint Chiefs of Staff, the chiefs of the three armies and of the air force, and other vice ministers of the Armed Forces Ministry were temporarily relieved of their posts. In October, as Cuba has acknowledged, military instructors began arriving in Angola; in fact, as many as 320 were there as early as May. In November the first regular troops arrived. By spring the war was over; by July 1976 the chiefs and vice ministers were back at their posts;[25] the commanders who had replaced them were reassigned overseas. The Cuban armed forces had managed to develop two sets of officers with experience in top command posts who could alternate responsibilites between the domestic and the overseas armed forces. The permanent chiefs had the rank of division general; the second-echelon chiefs, the rank of colonel or lieutenant colonel.

Wars, however, have a price in human lives, resources, and opportunity costs. The long-range cost of the Angolan war and the apparently endless Angolan-Cuban defense pact that followed cannot yet be assessed, but at least five kinds of obvious costs were incurred. First was the demand by the armed forces for more trained military personnel. The number of reservists trained doubled from 1974 to 1975. Second, there was evidence of civilian resistance to the war, at least among the elite. Managers did not want to part with skilled manpower; loopholes in the law allowed them to keep skilled personnel from being inducted by claiming that they were indispensable, leading Prime Minister Castro to remark that it was necessary "to combat the occasionally exaggerated criteria as to who cannot be dispensed with in production."[26] Civilian resistance to military exigency had not been seen in Cuba since the 1960s.

Third, there was apparently insubordination among some troops, although its extent cannot be determined and was probably limited; the military press discussed what disciplinary procedures should be employed to combat it. The first discussion of these appeared in late November 1975 as the Cuban intervention in Angola was rapidly escalating. Orders had to be obeyed, the government stressed, even if a formal complaint was in order, provided the command was not a breach of revolutionary constitutional and legal standards. A fourth cost of the war—widespread unhappiness among the Cuban people concerning compulsory military service—was equally obvious; up to this time, the revolutionary leadership had sought to give the impression that only religious fanatics opposed the draft. Now it became clear that even ordinary people found it disagreeable and thought it coercive. Finally, the regular procedures of political control by the Communist Youth Union broke down and the number of cadets joining it declined. A gap between military professionals and politicians was forming that was far wider than any experienced in the past, partly because of the very military professionalism required by the Angolan war.[27]

Notwithstanding these real costs, there is no reliable evidence of substantial opposition to the government's decision to send troops to Angola. Neither the general principle of committing troops for the sake of "internationalist solidarity" nor the specific decision to apply that principal to Angola can be seen to have been challenged in Cuba. Most Cubans probably supported the Angolan policy in 1975–76. The war apparently exacerbated problems within the Cuban armed forces, however, and took its toll in popular acceptance of the military. Parents and spouses did not like to have their loved ones taken off to a distant war. The protracted nature of the 1977 war in Angola—where counterrevolutionary Angolan guerrillas have inflicted casualties on Cuban troops there—also appears to have presented new difficulties for the Cuban government.

The Angolan war in 1975–76 demonstrated the improvements in Cuba's armed forces and military reserves, but it also caused a strain in civilian-military relations. If this tension continues in the years ahead, and if the demands for more military professionalization to cope with protracted war in Angola remain pressing, it will spell the demise of the civic soldier; the lines of conflict between civilian and military interests will then be too clearly drawn to permit continuing fusion of those roles.

The redefinition of the military mission of the Cuban armed forces in the mid-1970s was further evident in their active participation in Cuba's foreign-aid program. At the end of 1977, Cuba had about ten foreign military-assistance programs in Africa and the middle East, of which the one in

Angola was by far the largest. In addition, some Cuban military personnel performing civilian tasks were involved in other Cuban foreign-aid programs in another half dozen countries in Africa, Asia, and Latin America.[28]

The Socioeconomic Mission of the Armed Forces

In the years between the suppression of insurgency and the Angolan war in 1975 the military had to find something to do to justify their existence. They emphasized the nondefense objectives of the civic-soldier role to promote the growth of the military. One task they set for themselves was the supervision and rehabilitation of social deviants; another was the promotion of economic growth. These tasks had been anticipated for some time.

In 1963, when the law requiring compulsory military service was being discussed, Raúl Castro argued that a three-year tour of duty was justified because it would allow the military to perform missions other than those involving national defense and domestic order. "If we emphasize military training alone," he said, "if we only want an army, we can have [the draftees] for two years . . . [but] because we believe that the armed forces should help the nation's economy . . . [we intend to make] the burden of military expenditures on our people a bit lighter; in other words, we must work as part of our service, especially in the sugar harvest."[29] In addition, the lazy, the corrupt, homosexuals, religious proselytizers, especially Jehovah's Witnesses, all classified as social deviants, would be drafted into special military units; they would be given no weapons but would instead be socially "rehabilitated" through national service. Although compulsory military service was claimed not to be primarily for these purposes, that was a not insubstantial side effect.[30]

In November 1965, the army's high command, with the Prime Minister's approval, formed groups called the Military Units to Aid Production (UMAP). These units would be filled by drafting social deviants, that is, everyone whose behavior was not strictly in accordance with the public definition of good citizenship. The first UMAP draftees were treated so brutally that some of their officers were court-martialed and convicted of torture, but the organization was soon brought under control by Ernesto Casilla, who headed the UMAP in its formative months.[31]

The UMAP functioned throughout the sugar harvest of 1965–66 and 1966–67, but it was not universally approved. When many intellectuals and university faculty were sent to the UMAP as alleged homosexuals, the Cuban National Union of Writers and Artists (UNEAC) protested to the Prime Minister. Although Castro had approved the establishment of the UMAP and at first spoke well of it, he agreed that treatment of UMAP draftees was scandalous; the UMAP was disbanded after the 1967 harvest.

This decision was resisted by the army high command, whose journal ran articles in four different issues in the spring of 1967 defending the UMAP's record.[32] Castro's defeat of the military establishment in this case, even though he was himself a civic soldier, demonstrated his power and showed that there were limits to the potential expansion of the military. The military would still recruit and train "good revolutionaries" but its "rehabilitative" and truly repressive mission was thereafter sharply curtailed.

Production

The military was more successful in expanding its role into economic areas. Even from 1962 to 1964, when their strictly military mission was paramount, LCB units in the Escambray mountains were helping the peasants in the fields; this work fit in with their strategy in combatting insurgents who threatened that area and others.[33] But expansion of the military's economic activities came only after foreign and domestic military threats had declined.

Cutting sugar cane requires very limited skill. The principle use of the military in sugar harvests was to guarantee a cheap labor supply in times of labor scarcity. Batista had used the army similarly in the 1930s—though for distribution, not growth of the economy. In 1968, 51,000 soldiers were assigned to the sugar harvest (representing about 46 percent of the regular armed forces and about a fifth of all the armed forces); in 1969, 38,000 were assigned there (35 and 15 percent, respectively); in 1971, 43,000 (39 and 17 percent). In the extraordinary 1970 harvest, however, 70,000 troops were pressed into service, representing about 64 percent of the regular forces and 28 percent of all the armed forces generally.[34]

Unlike Batista's military in the 1930s, which contributed little in terms of technical and managerial skills to economic growth, the Revolutionary Armed Forces in the 1960s took on various nonmilitary technical and managerial jobs to encourage growth. In 1967, the air force operated sixty airplanes used in spraying and fertilizing fields, and the army formed a motorized brigade to run mechanized equipment for tilling new fields for sugar. By the spring of 1969 all farm machinery was under military supervision. Soldiers who had previously served in tank or motorized units were shifted to this new brigade. The Che Guevara Brigade, organized in the fall of 1968 into thirty-six subunits throughout the six provinces, operated entirely in agriculture. Its commander-in-chief, Raúl Guerra Bermejo, was also a member of the party's Central Committee. The brigade retained a strict military organization and chain of command; it took over all the machinery formerly administered by the state farms using civilian personnel.

In 1970 the military cut 20 percent of the giant sugar-cane harvest. They organized and operated the combines that mechanized cane cutting. They coordinated the cane loading at strategic locations and supervised the transportation of cane for the sugar mills in the eastern provinces; they operated all the tractors and cane lifters. They built roads, railroad tracks, and temporary housing. Members of the Luis Turcios Lima Brigade of the Eastern Army won the coveted title, National Heroes of Labor. The harvests in the late 1960s and in 1970 were directed from a national command post linked to the field through provincial, regional, and municipal outposts. The harvest took on all the aspects of a military campaign: it was a battle and a struggle no less essential to the survival of the revolution than the military engagements of earlier years.[35]

The growing economic role of the Cuban military served to blunt criticism that the armed forces were becoming an excessive burden on the Cuban economy, a complaint that was heard even in the early 1960s, when it was clear that the government depended on the armed forces for survival. Dissatisfaction grew in the mid-1960s, as insurrections were defeated. The old military objectives had been achieved; until new ones were found, the military organization needed a new objective for its survival. In 1966 the military agreed to cancel purchases of helicopters and military-transport aircraft and to purchase airplanes suitable for aerial crop spraying instead; they also agreed to transfer 250 pilots on active military service to these agricultural tasks. Both moves were justified on budgetary grounds.[36]

In mid-1967, these reallocations of money and manpower still did not satisfy all the critics. The military responded in two ways. First, they sharply increased their economic activities, and, second, they reasserted the priority of military expenditures in the national budget. Raúl Castro remarked on July 22, 1967, that the country had to "sacrifice even some aspects of its social development in construction work to earmark more of our resources for preparing the country for a war whose outbreak we cannot foresee." In January 1968, when the military had clearly become an active force in the economy, Fidel Castro acknowledged the priority of the military's needs in the allocation of scarce strategic resources such as petroleum.[37]

The armed forces won in the end. In 1968, the defense budget rose by 20 percent, its largest annual increase for the entire decade (see table 1). The proportion of gross national product made up by military expenditures rose to its highest level since 1962; the military budget was growing faster than the economy, even in a good year such as 1968. In return, one-fifth to one-half of military personnel cut sugar cane in 1968. Though the defense budget was retracted in 1969 to its 1967 level, it reached new heights again in 1972. Contrary to expectations, the military's expansion of its economic role continued and became more institutionalized with each subsequent harvest, until it is now routine for soldiers to engage in the annual "battle" of the sugar harvest. They have yet to prove that they are more successful than civilians in rescuing the Cuban economy, but their commitment to participation in it and the acceptance of it by the nation are no longer questioned.

However, the form of this participation has changed as a result of substantive changes in the internal organization of the Cuban armed forces. Because of objective role conflict in the performance of military units, the armed forces were reorganized in 1973 to combat the resulting decline in combat preparedness and the increase in costs. Field officers in units had been unable to cope with role conflict. For the first time in revolutionary history, the armed forces responded by creating new, highly specialized military units. The units within the armed forces that had engaged in production merged with the Centennial Youth Column, the voluntary agricultural work organization called the Followers of Camilo and Che, and the "minibrigades" for production, which had existed in the armed forces, to form the Army of Working Youth under the Ministry of the Armed Forces. This army specializes in production; when these tasks are completed, or if they are only seasonal, the members of the Army of Working Youth are expected to prepare for combat. Officers of the Army of Working Youth are military officers with their own training, ranks, and system of promotion. This organization allows the other military units to concentrate on their strictly military tasks.[38]

In practice, however, the Army of Working Youth has ended up working almost entirely in production, not in combat preparedness. They account for over a fifth of all cane cutters in the 1975, 1976, and 1977 harvests. The first secretary of the Oriente provincial party, Armando Hart, argued in 1975 that the Army of Working Youth had made an indispensable contribution to economic production in that province by providing a permanent agricultural work force stationed in the fields even between harvests, by covering work-force shortages in the least populated areas, and by providing a margin of safety in the number of workers available at peak harvest.[39] But its level of combat readiness remains extraordinarily low. While reservists apparently participate in war games, the Army of Working Youth seems not to do so and is consequently even less well trained than many reserve units. At the first conference of party members in the Army of Working Youth in the fall of 1975, it was noted that the army had sought to "strengthen its infrastructure to increase combat preparedness in the future," but evidently this has not yet occurred.[40] For one thing draftees into the Army of Working Youth are unruly. Reports concerning their performance in the 1976 harvest in Matanzas province—where half of the members were new to the work—suggest that the conscripts were not disciplined enough to be usefully assigned to any task, including farm labor. The officers in command were praised for their "tough, determined, and persistent attitude" in trying to overcome the "difficulties" encountered in shaping up their personnel,[41] but their efforts were apparently not entirely successful. The productivity of armed forces personnel remains below the average of cutters generally and just a shade above that of student volunteers (in spite of the picture presented by the Cuban press, which lauds the efforts of the best military units a good part of the time). Compared with voluntary workers, their productivity is only half as much; since both groups are drawn disproportionately from the working class, class differences cannot explain this disparity. Neither group lives or works regularly in the countryside, and still the voluntary workers do twice as well as the draftees. For the first half of the 1973 harvest in Matanzas (until April 6), military cane cutters can be compared with other groups in terms of their productivity (the national average for all groups had been 176 arrobas per worker) and their representation in the harvest work force:

	Arrobas per cutter	% of provincial cane cutters
Regular workers	290	17
Volunteer workers	264	—
Peasant volunteers	226	41
Army of Working Youth	143	11
Havana student volunteers	128	—

National productivity for the entire harvest per cane cutter was 401 arrobas in 1974, 502 in 1975, 582 in 1976; in the Army of Working Youth, it was about 197 arrobas in 1974 and between 242 and 252 in 1975.[42]

Clearly the application of military conscription to the sugar-cane harvest is at best inefficient, if not grievously coercive as well. The problems of the Cuban economy are too complex for excessive reliance on the armed forces to solve them, and the political costs of maintaining an army for manual labor may well prove to be too high.

The civic-soldier pattern has spread overseas as Cuban military personnel began to operate in other countries. Some Cuban troops who went to Angola as soldiers shifted emphasis within the civic-soldier role to work in normally civilian activities. President Castro told Cubans working in construction in Angola in 1977 that they "must be workers and soldiers at the same time." That is part of the tradition begun by the Cuban health-care personnel, who arrived in Angola in October 1975 and who fought as soldiers in the war. In the 1970s Cuban civic soldiers have built roads and airports in Guinea, hospitals in Peru, and schools in Tanzania, while serving as military trainers and advisors.[43]

The armed forces have not abandoned either their economic or their military missions; they have reorganized to allow both to be pursued simultaneously. Fidel Castro noted that the organizational changes "made possible an increase in the armed forces' defensive power while at the same time maintaining their participation in economic tasks,"[44] further evidence of the institutionalization of a very adaptable military organization.

The development of the Army of Working of Youth has paved the way for a much more drastic future step, namely, the devolution of all productive tasks back to civilians. The reasons for its establishment could also be taken as evidence of conflict within the armed forces. Some officers probably argued that the profession of arms was a full-time occupation and that military preparedness required undivided attention. Others may have argued that the armed forces should remain in production. This is only an inference; the net effect of the creation of the Army of Working Youth has in fact been to increase the power of the armed forces over production and to allow it to grow at the expense of civilian agencies. The consensus in the armed forces is that they ought to contribute directly to production, even if not all of its personnel should do so regularly.[45]

Military Training and Military Service

In the 1970s, the military expanded in two further directions. An experimental program of regular military training as an integral part of the senior high-school and university curricula was inaugurated in 1975 and is being extended to all senior high schools. Courses are conducted in the eleventh and twelfth grades by armed forces officers. The minister of education, himself a former military man, stressed that these would be among the most important courses in senior high schools and universities, not only because of their contribution to the national security, but also because of their educational value, a comment that harks back to the original conception of the socioeconomic mission of the armed forces, which centered on the belief that military training would develop the "Communist personality" by instilling modesty, confidence, honesty, camaraderie, courage, affection and respect for other socialist countries, patriotism, and conscientious discipline. These programs are similar to the Reserve Officers' Training Corps (ROTC) programs in the United States, except that the Cuban program is still compulsory (though at present only for the students in the schools where it was inaugurated); the degree of military control over the educational program also seems to be greater in Cuba than it has been in the United States.[46] When the program becomes universal, the government may be able to use it to require each citizen to have civilian and military roles fused into the civic-soldier pattern. The program, however, has potential problems. Students are faced with conflicting expectations from their superiors in the Ministries of Education and the Armed Forces; they must also decide how to allocate their own time. Thus this program has the potential for generating the same objective role conflicts that are typical of the civic-soldier experience.

Compulsory military service, instituted in 1963, and compulsory social service, instituted in 1973, have contributed to the preservation of Cuban social stratification, at least for the time being. Every young man must serve his country for three years at a place designated by the government; women may become soldiers if they choose to do so. One can enter the regular or the productive units of the armed forces or perform alternative civilian service. Only one-third of the young men of sixteen or seventeen entered the armed forces in 1972; the rest did other things. Since even the least skilled can cut cane, the social-service system includes everyone, but it does lead to the exemption of the best educated from military service in the strict sense. The protection of the well educated on the grounds that they serve the community is the conservative effect of the social-service system and one that benefits the elite, but the requirement that the best educated serve for a specified period where the government wants them to serve is rare among countries; it is the radical aspect of the law. The laws instituting compulsory service might have stipulated that some portion of secondary-school and university graduates must enter military service— or cut cane—but it did not, thus guaranteeing that educated Cubans would be exempted at least from the hardships of military or agricultural life.[47]

In the mid-1970s, even before the Angolan war, the importance of the armed forces was again being proclaimed. On November 22, 1974, Prime Minister Castro asserted that "our country will need . . . greater and greater defense capacity over an indefinite period," because "even if one day there should be economic and even diplomatic relations between [Cuba and the United States] that would not give us the right to weaken our defenses, for our defense can never depend on the good faith of imperialists." Seven months later Raúl Castro stressed the "essential need constantly to increase our military strength . . . despite the fact that the present balance of power favors the socialist camp and despite the positive advances made in international detente."[48] The need for military strength derived first from national security, then from its socioeconomic missions, and, finally, simply from the sense that the armed forces were "good in themselves" and that the survival of the revolution required nothing but the best.

While there is evidence that the military is valued as an institution by its officers, some of the best of whom, though young, have already served in it for many years, there are also indications that military service is un- popular and civilian service regarded as much preferable. This public perception has led to a variety of incentives to lure draftees into the regular forces. They pay more for overtime work and for high quality work, and good service is rewarded with gifts, foreign vacations, and early promotion, as well as with the usual array of banners, certificates, medals, flags, and insignia. Good soldiers are also rewarded with frequent furloughs and reduced terms of service. Punishments include suspension of leaves and extension of tours of duty, as well as demotion and imprison- ment. At least some of these incentives would not be necessary if military service were more popular with draftees.[49]

One basis for dissatisfaction within the regular armed forces is poor pay. Prime Minister Castro reported to the First Party Congress that "so far it has not been possible to provide fair and just compensation" to the military—a particularly touchy point during the Angolan war. He added, however, that salaries for officers were being increased, that steps were being taken to build more military housing, and that new funds would soon improve the standard of living of military personnel more generally.

A much more serious problem was the low regard in which military service was held by the rest of the population. The Prime Minister told the First Party Congress that the "present concept as to who should be drafted" must be changed to eliminate "a situation in which military service, far from appearing and being presented as an honor, is regarded as something with which parents can threaten their sons who do not study, which teachers can use to intimidate their students, and which the agencies use as a threat and as a means to punish breaches of discipline." Although the armed forces were willing to undertake civilian tasks, civilians were not eager for military ones. The Prime Minister's admission that military service was generally unpopular was, rather surprisingly, made at the height of the Angolan war.[50]

The rest of the world has often put the military to peaceful uses, but rarely on the scale of the Cuban military's involvement in social and economic tasks.[51] Among the other Communist countries, the Soviet armed forces provide the greatest contrast. They have stuck strictly to military concerns, arguing that modern technology requires that they give full attention to military pursuits. Even in the early years of the Soviet revolution, there was little of the kind of role expansion into nonmilitary employment practiced by the Cuban armed forces,[52] either because of policy or because of military resistance to the idea. The Chinese come closer to Cuban practice. In the People's Republic of China the "Great Leap Forward" was probably comparable to Cuba's giant harvest of 1970; soldiers were involved in both. But officers in the Chinese army resisted using the military for social and economic tasks much more strongly than their Cuban counterparts have done, arguing along with their Soviet colleagues that the profession of arms is a full-time occupation.[53]

There is no comparable resistance within the Cuban military. On the contrary, soldiers seem to take on nondefense tasks with a great deal of enthusiasm. Although there may have been some resistance to work in the 1970 harvest, the military's participation was nonetheless extraordinary. Still the armed forces reverted quickly enough to their "normal" degree of participation, and there are indications that Fidel Castro wanted even more manpower than he got for the harvest.[54] The formation of the Army of Working Youth also suggested that some officers preferred specialization in military tasks and that they supported creating the Army of Working Youth to free themselves from production tasks. With these exceptions, however, the Cuban military seems willingly involved in social and economic tasks, partly because they have deliberately set about redesigning their mission so that it will appear useful to society in order to protect their budget, and partly to promote expansion of military organizations.

The Political Mission of the Armed Forces

The political mission of the Cuban military has four aspects. One is the absorption of the structure of the Communist party, so that the corporate autonomy of the military institutions is preserved and conflict between the party and the armed forces minimized. Another is the prevention of the cleavages that plagued the armed forces before the revolution, those between commissioned and noncommissioned officers and between professional and nonprofessional commissioned officers. A third is the political indoctrination of recruits and the weeding out of the unreliable. A final aspect is the development of cadres that can be exported to the civilian population, particularly to positions in the civilian elite. It is at this level that the civilian and military tasks of the soldier are fused by placing the civic soldier in the position of highest command in both the party and the military. The military commander is not merely a technician; he is also a political officer. A party leader is not only a politician; he is a technician and a manager competent in military as well as civilian tasks.

The Party in the Armed Forces

In 1961–62 the party's crisis was a result of the confrontation between Fidel Castro and the prerevolutionary Communists, not of friction with the military. In those same years, however, the party sought to control the armed forces through political instructors who were first trained at the Osvaldo Sánchez School for the Revolutionary Armed Forces and then assigned to military units. Because they lacked military training and operational field experience and because they were imposed from outside to erode the chain of command, they were strongly opposed by the professional military commanders. These early political instructors were simply copying the experience of political commissars in the military in other Communist countries; one result of the massive expulsions from the party in 1962 was the abandonment of that system. Beginning in 1963, students at the Osvaldo Sánchez School were drawn directly from the military ranks and were usually already officers; the curriculum was revamped so that 40 percent of the program would be devoted to military topics, reviving the civic-soldier experience from guerrilla days, merging civilian and military responsibilities.[55]

By the end of 1963, party recruitment and party organization in the military had begun in earnest.[56] A trial run was made among the mountain corps (*compañías serranas*) in Oriente, followed by initial party organizations in the regular units of the Eastern Army. The members of each military unit were classified into eight ranks, from soldier to commanding officer. Each had an assembly, directed by a commission of political instructors appointed by the party's political bureau in the armed forces, to elect "exemplary combatants" (in addition to commissioned officers, all of whom were automatically named exemplary combatants). All exemplary combatants were interviewed individually and then met in rank groups with the commissions for criticism and self-criticism. The commission members selected the new Communist party members from these groups, after discussing the candidates both among themselves and with their ranking officers. The new members were presented to the rest of the unit and to the party cell, or *núcleo,* established within the unit; this cell included all party members regardless of military rank. Party officers were elected at the cell level in the unit and progressively upward in battalions and armies. Once a unit had a party cell, it could recruit on its own, without going through the procedure of electing exemplary combatants, but new recruits were still subject to final assembly approval.

Differences between military and civilian party-recruitment procedures were reduced in the 1970s when the party and the Communist Youth Union existed throughout the armed forces. From that time on, prospective members joined the youth union first and passed on into the party—whether a military or a civilian cell—at the appropriate age, provided political and ideological criteria were met.

In the beginning neither military orders nor officers' personal and political conduct could be criticized in the party cell. By the mid-1960s, this rule held only for the first year of party formation in a military unit. By the second year, although military orders and regulations still could not be questioned, the personal and political conduct of the officers could be discussed, regardless of the rank of either officer or critic. Both officers and particular orders could be criticized at all times by higher-ranking officers, however, and by political instructors assigned to higher-ranking military units.

Political work in the armed forces was directed by the national commission of the party in the armed forces, headed by Raúl Castro. Political instructors are not elected; they are appointed and assigned by the national commission upon completion of their training. Two political channels exist within the armed forces. One is the party, organized from the bottom up; the other is the political instructors, organized from the top down in political sections in the military units at all levels. The two channels are not wholly separate, however, but are coordinated in two ways. First, both the political instructors and all party members belong to the party's organization at each military level; second, they are all under the same command.

In contrast to the situation in the early 1960s and possibly in other Communist countries, "there is no separation of activity between military and party obligations."[57] Communist party organization parallels the military hierarchy. Criticism of one's superiors is difficult, but possible; innovation remains a prerogative of the top. Just as the party has penetrated the armed forces, so too the military has penetrated the party. The party within the armed forces is led by the military high command, not by civilian party cells or other agencies outside the military. The party in the armed forces is self-contained; nonmilitary party members have no authority over it. Party criticism within the military is criticism within the party, criticism of the military by the party, and criticism of the party by the military, all at the same time, because party and military are often fused.

The formation of the party in the military was complete by the end of 1966. It had moved geographically from the eastern to the western provinces and hierarchically from the bottom up. The last place to organize party cells was the national headquarters of the Army Chief of Staff. By the fall of 1970, 69.6 percent of all officers in the armed forces belonged to either the party or the Communist Youth Union. By the summer of 1973, the proportion rose to 85 percent; in 1976, it was still 86 percent. Since 1970 the fifteen-member advisory commission of party members of the armed forces to the Political Bureau has been composed entirely of commissioned officers, at least half of whom have the highest ranks in existence at the time in the Cuban military. In the fall of 1970, 69 percent of the members of the party in the military were commissioned officers. At the end of 1975, 48 percent of the entire western fleet (but 92 percent of its officers) belonged to the party or the youth union; 70 percent of the entire Interior Ministry belonged to the party or the youth union by mid-1976. Enlisted soldiers and draftees made up a large, though unspecified, proportion of the membership of the Communist Youth Union.[58] The high overlap between the officer corps and the party and youth union membership helps fuse political and military authority, though alone it is not sufficient for the task.

In the Soviet Union, by contrast, the proportion of military officers who belong to the party has grown over time: 32 percent in 1924, 65 percent in 1928, 86 percent in 1952, 90 percent in the early 1960s, 93 percent in 1966 (when 80 percent of all Soviet armed forces personnel were either in the party or in the Communist Youth Union, mostly the latter).[59] But this high representation has not prevented repeated conflicts between the party and the military throughout Soviet history.[60] In Cuba the militarization of the political instructors; the willing acceptance of political norms, roles, and structures by military officers; the unified leadership that has preserved a single military chain of command; the self-containment of the party within the military to preserve the institutional autonomy of the armed forces; and the presence of the civic soldiers at the core of the ruling elite in charge of civilian and military organizations have combined to prevent similar conflicts. In the Soviet Union, even when political commissars and military commanders agree on specific issues, the central organizations of the party have little contact with either.[61] In the absence of fusion at the top, conflict between Soviet central civilian and party organizations and military leaders will no doubt continue.

The chief problem in the relationship between party and military in Cuba has been the failure to fulfill political programs in military units. Military commanders tend to leave political matters to the political instructors. In the spring of 1968, according to the Army Chief of Staff, the result was not the concentration of power in the hands of the political instructors but the downgrading of political work. At that time, military commanders were urged to take more interest in the political education of their subordinates, even though the daily tasks were attended to by the instructors.[62] Thus there was no evidence of conflict between the party and military tasks at the level of the military unit. Apparently the military commanders ignored the request, because four years later, the quality of political work in the military was still low. Top party leaders complained that political issues were being handled merely as administrative matters within the party, that discussions were superficial, that too little time was allocated to political issues in the party in the armed forces, that issues concerning the internal affairs of the party were often ignored, that ordinary party members did not participate much in discussions and that, when they did, the officers or the political instructors interrupted to clarify or rebut the members' arguments.[63]

In the aftermath of the Angolan war, political problems have continued. The only criticism of the air force and antiaircraft defense units in 1976 dealt with the poor quality of their political work. The work of the Communist Youth Union was said to be particularly bad; "numerous" members of the youth union, who had reached the age of eligibility for party membership, were reported to be unacceptable because of poor political and ideological preparation. Furthermore, youth union procedures for monthly evaluation of its membership were not being enforced.[64]

A second problem of the party within the military was its lack of democracy. An absence of democratic procedures is not surprising in a military organization; given the ideological commitments of the party and the revolution, however, one would expect at least some degree of democracy in the party, even in its military branches. None exists in the military party, first because officers account for over two-thirds of its membership; military chiefs not only monopolize party debate but use their military rank to gain party rank. Although the chairmanship of party meetings is supposed to be elective, the military chief usually assumes the post automatically and uses it to curtail discussion. The second reason for nondemocratic procedures is that voting at the cell level is by acclamation; this method also makes it easy for officers to impose their views on cell members. At the higher levels, balloting is secret and direct, although all nominations for party office are made by the political sections. The election of delegates to the party conference, the governing body of the party in the military, is also by acclamation, and the amount of competition is once again low. In the 1972 elections for the party commission to supervise the work of the political sections, for instance, which were held at the party conference, the political sections nominated fifteen candidates for nine membership and four alternate posts; voting was by secret ballot. Although nominating twice as many people as posts (requiring twenty-six nominations in this case) is proposed now and again, it is rarely acted upon and the situation has not changed.[65]

A third problem of the party in the military is the military party's lack of autonomy from the nonparty military and vice versa, a fact that obscures both the political and the military chain of command. There is no clear boundary between party and technician. For example, a squadron engineer is not able to plan and implement a program for servicing airplanes without coordinating this work with the party cell's secretary and with the principal political officer, called the chief's substitute for political and partisan work. Similarly, the party secretary and the political officer cannot plan and implement their own political work; the squadron engineer also has the authority to tell party members what to do, even though the engineer may not be a party member. The Communist Youth Union in the armed forces is also not autonomous enough from the party; it has no control over the admission of new members. Those who are too young for party recruitment are simply sent to the youth union until they reach the age required to enter the party; the youth union in the military is little more than the party's annex.[66]

The proportion of soldiers and noncommissioned officers in the military party—almost one-third—is fairly high, much higher than in the Soviet military, where the proportion of soldiers and noncommissioned officers fell as low as 3 percent of all military party members in the 1940s.[67] The relatively high proportion of soldiers, corporals and sergeants among party members in Cuba can be explained by the revolution's commitment—qualified, as already noted—to democratic principles even within the armed forces, which is in part a reaction to the cleavage between commissioned and noncommissioned officers in the Cuban military before the revolution. Although this rivalry is at least latent in most military institutions, Cuba is particularly sensitive on the subject because army sergeants and corporals, led by Batista, overthrew the government and the officer corps in 1933. Many officers were arrested or killed. Cuban officers would not like to see another coup like Batista's.[68] The second major cleavage within the military before the revolution had formed between the professional officers, some trained in Cuba, some abroad, and those who owed their rank to their participation in military coups and shrewd politicking. In the 1950s about one-sixth of the officers were nonprofessionals.[69]

The revolutionary government tried to avoid these rivalries by instituting a new promotion policy. No less than three-quarters and more typically nine-tenths of all professional officers promoted and graduating cadets are members of either the Communist Party or the Communist Youth Union. Among commissioned officers promoted in 1968, party and youth union membership was as follows:[70]

		Party and youth union members
	N	%
First captains	35	94.3
Captains	56	100.0
Lieutenants	1,757	78.1

For graduating cadets in the late 1960s and early 1970s the comparable figures are these:[71]

		Party and youth union members
	N	%
1969 (March)	414	97.0
1969 (August)	731	89.0
1970	1,304	87.0
1973	—	95.0
1975	—	82.0

Among the officers promoted through the ranks, party membership is widespread; few belonged to the youth union. In 1968, none of the first captains and captains promoted and only 8.8 percent of the lieutenants promoted belonged to the youth union. Youth union membership, however, is more widespread among the graduating cadets; in March 1969, their numbers were equally divided between the party and the youth union. As the revolution becomes a matter of history, officers or cadets are now rarely promoted on account of their experience in the rebel army. Although all the first captains and captains promoted in 1968 had served in the rebel army, only a third of the lieutenants promoted had done so; only 1.2 percent of the cadets graduating in March 1969 had ever served in the rebel army. Party membership has become a prerequisite of promotion in the upper ranks and youth union membership of promotion from cadet status to the junior ranks. Even in the reserves, 74 percent of the 5,702 reserve officers promoted in 1975 and 80 percent of the five thousand promoted in 1976 belonged to either the party or the youth union.[72]

The conflict between party and military in the early 1960s had occurred in part because so few military men were party members. By the 1970s, promotion policies guaranteed almost total overlap of officers and party members. The political deficiencies within the armed forces, especially in the Communist Youth Union, may explain the decline in the proportion of graduating cadets belonging to the party or the youth union from 1973 to 1975; the decline may result in a sharper line being drawn between military professionals and military politicians if the present pattern continues.

The new promotion policy provides a program of remedial training for officers with little formal military training. Although the Prime Minister had claimed that only officers professionally trained in military schools would be promoted, in fact officers with purely operational experience and no formal training were still going up the ranks in the late 1960s. Professionalizing the armed forces was easier said than done. The Ignacio Agramonte School for Officers in the city of Matanzas theoretically required a fifth-grade education for admission; this rule was frequently broken in the 1960s. It was not until 1967 that all entering students had achieved a sixth-grade education.[73] Nonetheless, the military's educational level was still better than that of the civilian political leadership; in 1969, 79 percent of all party members still did not have a sixth-grade education. Lack of education in the military, however, gradually became grounds for nonpromotion—in 1975 a number of military personnel in the Ministry of the Interior were not promoted because of too little schooling.[74]

A split appeared in 1975 concerning the value of schooling for military officers, notwithstanding its obvious link to promotion. Many officers, perhaps a majority, even in the units with the highest education levels, preferred to emphasize military practice and war games rather than classroom work, which remained the principal way to conduct political-education courses for officers. Although it remains the policy of the high command to insist on booklearning—including political education—a dispute about its value and its content broke out into the open for the first time.[75]

Through these promotion policies the revolutionary government sought to politicize the officer corps, especially the younger officers who had good professional training but little or no combat experience, but it also sought to professionalize and partly to politicize nonprofessional officers with a great deal of practical experience and very little formal training. The common grounds of professionalism and politics, the leaders believed, would reduce the rivalries that had weakened the Cuban military in the past. But resistance to the new policies had become evident by 1975, when fewer graduating cadets joined the party and the youth union and officers questioned the value of schooling.

The main task of the party in the armed forces is to support the authority of the military chain of command and enhance its prestige. Party members are expected to strengthen troop morale in and out of combat through propaganda, political education, and surveillance. They are active in the Angolan war, as they were against counterrevolutionaries in Cuba in the early 1960s. Party work in the military also has a useful byproduct: it yields a great deal of information about troops and officers alike, and this can be helpful in deciding about promotion or forced retirement in their careers. The practice of criticism and self-criticism in party cells has institutionalized the gathering of personal information and led to better discipline in the military; it has also generated support for the government, exposed opposition to it, and introduced political criteria for promotion.[76]

The military party's program is based on a system of *captación* or tutoring. Party and youth union members act as the tutors; each is given several non-party members for supervision and is expected to find out about the anxieties and personal or family problems of their charges, educate them politically, and see to it that they attend political meetings and other party activities. The program is supposed to improve morale, discipline, and the level of education among the troops. Its byproducts, according to Raúl Castro, include the identification of homosexuals and of religious individuals for "rehabilitation." It is further intended to stimulate competition for promotion.

The party runs study groups for officers who are party members in proper ideology; there are less formal sessions with all military party members on all subjects, professional and personal as well; reports to headquarters by party members must describe all this activity as well as ordinary military work. The party tutors also work with members who are "lagging behind" most noticeably. Military party procedure requires an annual evaluation of each member's work, a special evaluation whenever a party member is charged with misbehavior, and another when any member is transferred. Whenever there are serious infractions there may be a court-martial, with a military tribunal made up exclusively of Communist party and Communist Youth Union members. In the fall of 1970, at the second national meeting of the military party, the two criticisms leveled against the party's work in the armed forces were, first, insufficient criticism and self-criticism among members and, second, failure to probe into members' personal affairs; these criticisms suggest that these programs had been rich lodes of information in the past.[77]

Systematic evaluation procedures were not established in the armed forces outside the party until 1966; before that time promotions depended entirely upon a superior officer's opinion of a candidate. The first general evaluation of all officers was completed in 1969, but the process did not become routine until 1975. All officers are now evaluated when they are first commissioned, when they shift assignments, when they complete four years in the same assignment, and when they retire. Although these procedures were modeled after party evaluations, they are less rigorous. At first undertaken by the commanding officer of the appropriate military unit, evaluations were made the responsibility of the immediately superior officer after 1975. The entire process, however, is supervised in each unit by a commission comprised of the chief's substitute for political work, the party's organization secretary, and the officer in charge of personnel; it consequently remained under close political scrutiny.[78]

Exporting Military Models

Up to now the discussion has focused on the political activities within the armed forces. But another, parallel development was the inverse of that endeavor—this is, the export of military models and personnel to the rest of the political system. Party organization in the armed forces by and large ended by 1966; in the civilian central administration, it began mostly in 1967. The party drew on that experience in building the civilian party, particularly the principle of unified command. Said Armando Hart: "There cannot be dual leadership in a central State organization. The maximum authority of the party in each branch of the State apparatus, will be that of the minister or president of the organization, who works under the direction of the Party Central Committee and Political Bureau. If in any case this should turn out to be impossible, we will have to consider the demotion of the executive."[79]

In the military the party had made it a regular practice to hold assemblies for evaluating its work; they were held virtually every year in every unit at different levels. National meetings were held less regularly, but there was one in 1966 and another in 1970.[80] These, too, became models for the civilian party. Although there had been provincial assemblies in the civilian party since the early days,[81] the military version had a seriousness and regularity that were to be carried over into the civilian party.

The military had also developed cadres for assignment to specifically civilian duties, as the proportion of members of the Central Committee with military background indicates. This percentage has always been and still is very high, though it reached a peak in 1965. Since 1965, officers whose tasks within the leadership had been strictly military at that time have come to assume new responsibilities in civilian life. This civic-soldier career pattern predominates in all the leading institutions of party and government. Aside from the members of the top elite discussed earlier, there are many examples lower down on the ladder. Rogelio Acevedo, for instance, who headed the militia in 1960, has been a member of the Central Committee since 1965. From 1969 to 1972 he was the Political Bureau's delegate to Camagüey province; he has since returned to the armed forces as a deputy minister.

Navy Captain Rolando Díaz Astaraín, was minister for the recovery of misappropriated goods from November 1959 to March 1960, then minister of the treasury until June 1962. Back in the navy, he served as its commander-in-chief for four years then joined the merchant marine. Román Alvarez Rodríguez graduated from the naval academy as an officer in 1952, resigned his commission in 1955, and was subsequently imprisoned and exiled by the Batista government. In January 1959 he was made captain of one of Cuba's three frigates, the *Antonio Maceo*. He then switched to the industrialization department of the National Insitute for Agrarian Reform and eventually to the merchant marine. At the beginning of 1964, he rejoined the navy as the second officer in command, in charge of combat preparedness. At the end of 1965, he returned to the merchant marine, again as a ship's captain. Some time in the late 1960s, in *Granma's* cautious phrasing, "the comrade also fulfilled his internationalist duties." He was back as navy second in command of the engineering council when he died in September 1974.

Jesús Reyes García was one of the original expedition that landed in Cuba with Fidel Castro aboard the yacht *Granma* in 1956. In 1960–61, he was the chief of bodyguards in the Ministry of the Interior. He was in charge of the Havana bus lines in 1962, returning to the armed forces as a captain in 1963, attended military school in 1964, and subsequently became a naval machinist in the merchant marine. From the late 1960s until his death in 1974, he was director of an automobile-repair enterprise.[82] The careers of Diaz Astarain, Alvarez Rodríguez, and Reyes García illustrate the frequent interchange of personnel between the navy and the merchant marine.

The 1973 reform of military ranks and titles included the provision that officers on the inactive list could no longer use their military titles. Although the change was primarily symbolic, it did help to disinguish between active and former officers in positions of power, and it may eventually serve to break down the civic-soldier model. When these civilianized officers rejoin the military, however, they immediately recover their titles, so the divorce between the two spheres is by no means complete. The practice of exporting cadres from military to civilian life, begun in the early 1960s, has also been continued. As leaders training in the military ranks matured, their attention was shifted to civilian tasks. In the central ministries as well as at various levels of the civilian party ranks, one encounters inactive soldiers with great frequency.

The Cuban armed forces differ from the military that performs nonmilitary tasks in non-Communist countries in several ways: the party functions within the military, which is thoroughly politicized; the military performs not only managerial and technical but also menial tasks; and there have been no military coups in revolutionary Cuba, as there often have been in other countries where the military element within the government remains strong. The Cuban armed forces differ also from the Soviet armed forces in that they have a much broader perception of their role in society. Unlike the Soviets, they do not retreat behind strict military professionalism to avoid other tasks, and they exercise greater authority in the Central Committee. The Soviet pattern of military membership on the Central Committee—between 7 and 13 percent—was set by the late 1930s; before that time its share of the Central Committee was even smaller (table 2).[83]

The military in the People's Republic of China more closely resembles the Cuban, [84] but the armed forces' participation in central decision making is more stable and better institutionalized in Cuba than in China; moreover, there has been no purge of the Cuban military on the scale of the Lin Piao affair, nor any military coup attempt in Cuba comparable to Lin Piao's. If all Cuban Central Committee members with military titles at the time of their appointments are counted, then the Cuban military share of its party Central Committee easily exceeds that of the Chinese (table 2). If in the Chinese case members designated as military are in fact devoted strictly to military tasks, then the Chinese military representation on the committee has exceeded the Cuban share twice, in comparable situations (1940–50 in China and 1962 in Cuba; the late 1960s in both countries). The Cuban military share exceeded that of the Chinese in the mid-1960s and mid-1970s. The trend in Cuba has been steady; in China it is more erratic.

Professional Chinese officers are known to have resisted becoming involved in nonmilitary tasks even during the Cultural Revolution. The injection of the armed forces into the Cultural Revolution was no military coup; rather, it was the consequence of a political decision made primarily by leaders outside the armed forces. The People's Liberation Army (PLA) did not set out to expand its role, as the Cuban armed forces had done between 1965 and 1968. Power simply gravitated to it, expanding its sphere of influence; the impetus had come from outside the military. During the Cultural Revolution, the rivalry between military professionals and military politicians simmered beneath the surface. Professional commanders who still opposed any large-scale political involvement were important in the anti–Lin Piao coalition. Cuban officers, in contrast, welcomed role expansion as the vehicle for organizational survival. It is possible that the establishment of the Army of Working Youth was a consequence of professional military resistance to nonmilitary tasks and that the new military specialization thus made possible effective fighting in Angola, but there is little real evidence to support the notion, which is inapplicable to the 1960s in any case. The effect of the reorganization in 1973 was not only to permit military specialization but also to increase military responsibilities over production by absorbing many of the civilian duties of the Communist Youth Union. While both the Cuban and the Chinese military have engaged in role expansion, Chinese officers have resisted it far longer and more strenuously than their Cuban counterparts. In China the impetus for role expansion came primarily from outside the armed forces, while in

Table 2. Military representation on Communist Central Committees in the People's Republic of China, Cuba, and the Soviet Union

Country and year	All members (includes alternates)		Full members (excludes alternates)	
	% military	Number	% military	Number
China				
1949–1950	38.1	168	—	—
1962	24.6	171	—	—
1969	—	—	51.2	170
1973	31.3	319	31.8	195
Cuba[a]				
1962				
Total military	—	—	56.0	25
Strictly military	—	—	28.0	25
1965				
Total military	—	—	70.0	100
Strictly military	—	—	58.0	100
1975				
Strictly military (before First Party Congress)	—	—	38.9	90
Strictly military (after First Party Congress)	32.3	124	32.1	112
Soviet Union				
1956	—	—	7.5	122
1966	—	—	8.2	195
1971	—	—	10.2	235

Sources: Donald W. Klein, "The 'Next Generation' of Chinese Communist Leaders," *China Quarterly* no. 12 (October–December 1962): 66; Ellis Joffe, "The Chinese Army after the Cultural Revolution: The Effects of Intervention," ibid., no. 55 (July–September 1973): 457; *China News Summary* no. 483 (September 6, 1973); Robert H. Donaldson, "The 1971 Soviet Central Committee: An Assessment of the New Elite," *World Politics* 24, no. 3 (April 1972): 382–409.

[a]"Total military" members are those with military rank at the time of their appointment; "strictly military" members are those who were engaged primarily in military affairs, including political work within the military; this classification includes internal-security personnel in the Ministry of the Interior. Statistics for 1962, when the Central Committee had not yet been established, are for the national directorate of the United Party of the Socialist Revolution.

Cuba expansion has come about equally as a result of pressures from within and from outside.

In 1964 Chinese were publicly called upon to "learn from the experience of the PLA in political education and ideological work." This appeal made the army a model for the rest of the system for at least a few months. During the Cultural Revolution, however, the export of political models to the rest of the political system was not emphasized; the PLA intervened primarily to restore order. It also exported middle- and low-level cadres to roles as regional or local political leaders through the Revolutionary Committees. In the years since the Cultural Revolution, however, civilian rule has been restored and the export of cadres from the military to the political system has been limited. Although some Maoists may have had a civic-soldier model in mind and although they may even have intended to diffuse this role, they did not in fact succeed to the degree that the leaders with a similar plan have succeeded in Cuba.

Revolutionary Cuba has been governed, in large part, by leaders whose civilian and military roles were fused during the insurgency against Batista and who have intentionally made the civic soldier the norm for all, even in purely civilian organizations. From the early 1960s to the mid 1970s, no alternative civilian elite capable of governing the country appeared in Cuba. There has also been little evidence of conflict between strictly civilian and strictly military leaders, because both types divide among themselves in disputes.

From 1965 to 1975, the survival and growth of the armed forces were achieved by reemphasizing the continuing legitimacy of old military objectives and expanding the roles of the military beyond defense. Military organizations did not fade away, but organizational boundaries became blurred. At the same time, national-defense strategy came to depend on civilian mobilization rather than on a standing armed force. With their strictly military functions fading in importance, the military took on social, economic, and political tasks.

Conflict between military and civilian agencies was reduced, at first, by the decrease in specialization within the military, so that both kinds of organizations undertook similar tasks in nonmilitary areas. The pressures of conflicting roles felt by civic soldiers serving in civilian agencies may also have diminished; they were no longer obliged to lobby for the reduction of their former comrades-in-arms' budgets since the military now performed nonmilitary tasks, diverting some military resources to assist civilians. Civilian party members learned from the military how to shape party structures; civilian party hierarchies filled vacant posts by drawing on civic soldiers.

These changes in the armed forces' definition of their role were generally welcomed by the elite because they reduced disputes within the leadership and made less acute the conflicts felt by civic soldiers administering civilian agencies and by low-ranking personnel in all agencies. However, the new role definitions created new role conflicts within the military. Civilian organizations began to compete with the armed forces for the time and resources of military units, thus creating intersender role conflict. Officers and soldiers also experienced role conflict in allocating their own time, exacerbating intrasender role conflict: should they emphasize military or other tasks? To cope with these new problems, the Army of Working Youth, which has devoted its energies almost entirely to production, was established in 1973. Military units once again became specialized. Some performed ordinarily civilian tasks in production and did little else; others performed almost exclusively military tasks. Role conflicts were reduced for personnel in units with military specialization, but not for the others, who have continued to experience them.

It has become fashionable to write about the militarization of the Cuban revolution, a concept that suggests the late 1960s were drastically different from other years. In fact, the behavior of the armed forces has remained essentially the same, although they did undertake more nondefense tasks in the late 1960s. I believe the concept of militarization is inappropriate to the Cuban situation because it fails to account for the special political quality of civic soldiers, who are important in many areas, from running the government to running farm equipment. These soldiers went to military school after they had fought and won the war against Batista, during which they acquired their extramilitary concerns for the first time. The Cuban civic soldiers have been different from the armed forces both in other Communist and in non-Communist countries because of their eagerness and conviction that military and political personnel and methods cannot be separate but must overlap if revolutionary goals are to be achieved.

Yet the civic soldiers remaining in the armed forces are soldiers still, and Cuba's reliance on them indicates important failures on the part of the revolutionary government. The need to employ the armed forces in the sugar harvests highlights the failure of economic production and the government's inability to handle problems of labor supply. The concept of the civic soldier evolved in Cuba in a context of the failure of economic growth. Nor has the performance of the military in economic production been any more successful than that of civilians. The years of least economic growth, this is, the late 1960s, were also those that saw the greatest degree of military responsibility for the economy and the highest level of political discontent in the civilian population. The use of military techniques in the 1970 harvest contributed to the workers' quasi-strike of that year. The more general adoption of military methods in politics stifled criticism from below and limited the adaptability of the political system.

What, then, is the future of the military in the political and economic life of Cuba? A number of developments in the mid-1970s suggest future trends that may prove to depart sharply from the domination of the civic soldier in the past. First, there is the possibility that military personnel exported to civilian life might at last become totally demilitarized and produce a civilian ruling elite for the first time since the fall of Aníbal Escalante in 1962. During the Angolan war there were already enough influential civilians around to object to the military's demands for personnel and resources. There was also popular dislike of compulsory military service; instances of insubordination occurred within the ranks; lack of discipline in the Army of Working Youth was a serious problem, and its level of combat preparedness was low; and the usefulness of formal military education—including political education—was being challenged. The military share of the Central Committee membership has declined, as has the proportion of graduating military cadets who belong either to the Communist Youth Union or to the Communist party. The time may have come to separate the military clearly from the civilian, so that the profession of arms in Cuba could be considered a full time occupation.[85]

On the other side, the expansion of the armed forces' role continues. The draft is used to force civilians to serve the state for three years, in military, productive, or other tasks designated by the government. Efforts to use military methods to educate Cuban young people have been accelerated. The importance of military skills has been reemphasized as a result of the Angolan war. The Army of Working Youth's very establishment is an example of military role expansion, because it absorbed the productive activities of the Communist Youth Union. The change in military doctrine relies on the mobilization of civilians in time of war and on improving the professional military competence of the very large reserve forces in preparation for war. The active reservists who serve as much as three months each year in the military typify the civic soldier, fusing civilian and military life year round. The militarization of the reserves and the growth of the Army of Working Youth have spread the civic-soldier role to the mass of the population. The military share of the Central Committee, while it may have declined from former days, is nonetheless still the highest in the Communist world, while the proportion of officers who belong to the party and the youth union exceeds four-fifths of the total. A civilian elite, though it now certainly exists, has not yet been well developed. Although pressures have arisen within the Cuban armed forces to put the civic soldier to rest, to stop using the military for civilian tasks, and to concentrate on military professionalism, they are not yet triumphant.

The Armed Forces: Renewed Importance

The armed forces have been essential for the survival of revolutionary rule. They were among the first entities to be professionalized and institutionalized; the rest of the party and government subsequently learned from them. The armed forces have also been very capable over the years of protecting their organizational stakes and expanding their influence.[86] In the second half of the 1970s, Cuba fought two wars abroad (in Angola and in Ethiopia) and came to maintain a large permanent overseas military presence. In the fall of 1980, that amounted to approximately 35,000 troops.[87] To support them, the armed forces undertook new programs that increased their social weight and claimed additional resources. Partly as a result of those commitments, and partly because of deteriorating relations with the United States since 1978, the Cuban Armed Forces induced these policy changes. This section will discuss only the political and organizational aspects of the recent growth of the Cuban Armed Forces.

The Cuban military still accounts for a very high proportion of the party Central Committee. Although their share of the membership has declined, the absolute number of military full and alternate Central Committee members has increased. Military overrepresentation in the Central Committee, compared to the military share of party membership, apparently also increased from 1975 to 1980. It should be assumed that the membership composition of the party Congress reflects the composition of the party membership rather more closely than does the Central Committee. The latter necessarily overrepresents the top elites. Therefore, the ratio of Central Committee membership shares to Congress membership shares (as a proxy for party membership shares) is a measure of the relative strength of representation of a given category of people.

The military accounted for about 19 percent of the First Party Congress but for only 13.7 percent of the Second Party Congress. The party was formed most quickly within the armed forces in the late 1960s and early 1970s; the military share of the entire party probably declined in the late 1970s because the party's civilian sector grew more rapidly. This would also explain the relative decline of the military shares from one party Congress to the next. The military share of Central Committee membership, however, declined more slowly than the military share of the Congress. Relative military overrepresentation thus increased from 1975 to 1980. The ratio of the military's share of the full membership of the Central Committee to its share of the membership of the party Congress was 1.69 in 1975; in 1980, that statistic grew to 1.77. For all members (full and alternate), that statistic grew from 1.70 in 1975 to 1.98 in 1980. The armed forces and the Interior Ministries thus entered the 1980s claiming a rising relative share of party power.[88]

The armed forces have obtained the approval of "veteran's preference" for returning troops in jobs and housing, especially for those left vacant by those who became exiles in 1980. The Society for Patriotic-Military Education (SEPMI) was established in January 1980. It helps to prepare low-skill specialists who might work eventually in the armed forces, and it promotes sports that help to train people in militarily useful activities (target shooting, parachuting, and the like). The SEPMI is also a propaganda organ for the armed forces, building support for the military and its programs. Within a year of its founding, SEPMI had 80,721 affiliates in 671 local associations; its 371 sports clubs had over 13,000 members. By January 1982, SEPMI had 117,363 members in 987 local associations. Given that most of the equipment for these sports is expensive and must be imported, the commitment to this program is all the more remarkable.[89]

Also in 1980, the government established a new Territorial Militia. These units are to be financed largely by the people's donations beyond the formal military budget; the militia's training, which occurs during weekends and vacations, amounts to forty class hours a year. Thus the military have successfully claimed more resources from the rest of the society. The Territorial Militia's creation has been justified publicly as a response to threats from the Reagan administration in the United States. In fact, as Armed Forces Minister Raúl Castro has explained, the armed forces had pushed earlier for the establishment of these units out of their strategic and organizational perspectives:"The organization of these units is necessary in order to round out our defense system." "We have accelerated the process," added General Castro, "to meet the threats hurled by the new U.S. administration."[90] The basic rationale, then, comes from the armed forces' need for organizational growth, now only made politically easier within Cuba by the changing international situation.

The Territorial Militia revives in part the old notion of the militia that had disappeared as the professional military reserves and the civil defense were developed. The Territorial Militia seeks to include students who are not yet in the military or the reserves, women, able-bodied people above military reserve age limits, and workers who cannot leave the factories to serve in the armed forces on a regular basis. The Territorial Militia is to be included in military planning and exercises. It will be used primarily in military construction, rear guard operations, and the protection of factories and farms. The units most closely linked to the regular armed forces are commanded by regular officers.

To implement this organizational innovation, a military officer has been assigned to every municipal and provincial government to coordinate national defense at the grass roots. Never before had the armed forces penetrated subnational government so effectively. The ideological rationale also hearkens to a pattern of role expansion familiar in the Cuban military in earlier years. As General of the Army Raúl Castro put it, "the organization of the militia is also related to a broader concept of national defense, which should be seen as the unity of all factors of defense and production."[91]

The armed forces have also obtained full recognition of their five top schools as equivalents of a university. When the reform of higher education in 1976 established the Ministry of Higher Education, only the Military Technical Institute was designated as a center of higher education. By academic year 1977–78, all five of the top military schools qualified as higher education centers. Finally, in December 1980, the Executive Committee of the Council of Ministers established full equivalency between the engineering degrees granted by these five military schools and the universities. The Armed Forces Ministry retained full control over these schools; they were not turned over to the Ministry of Higher Education, even though the latter is headed by a former general. More importantly, this reflects the continuing upgrading of the professional quality of the Cuban military officer corps. Beginning with the class of 1982, the Cuban Armed Forces will receive only officers who are university graduates. That had not been the norm previously.[92]

The armed forces have also obtained resources to raise the standard of living of officers and troops. Facilities have been improved; housing has been built; social and recreational clubs for officers and troops have been established. Wages, pensions, and other social security benefits have been increased. These benefits maintain differences by rank, so that in each instance the rewards to officers are greater.[93]

The armed forces succeeded as well in changing the draft recruitment policy. Beginning in 1979, they began to draft the male graduates of technological and senior academic secondary schools before they went on to the university, thereby markedly improving the quality of draftees. The terms of service were also changed. Draftees who distinguished themselves militarily and politically could get a reduction of up to one year in the ordinary three-year term of service so that they could continue their university education. While the armed forces were thus allowed for the first time to systematically tap better trained young people, the intention has also been announced of generalizing this practice so that the completion of secondary education (academic or vocational) will become a prerequisite for military service, raising the draft age from 16 to 18. Given the extraordinary expansion of the Cuban educational system, this further policy change should be feasible soon.[94]

The changes in draft policy clarify the motivations for the other policy changes. The Territorial Militia and the SEPMI will reach students not in active military service either before or after they serve in the armed forces. The quality of military personnel will be improved without interrupting the links between the armed forces and the country's youth from age sixteen on. A probable corollary policy (not, however, yet mentioned) is that young people with poor academic records and discipline problems might be excluded from the regular armed forces and channelled to the Army of the Working Youth, devoting their time to burdensome economic tasks (sugar-cane harvest, construction, and so forth) under military discipline for three years.[95]

The armed forces began training regular university students as reserve officers in the 1967–77 school year. As of 1981, over 5,000 new reserve officers were made available by these university programs; the inflow should remain at least at that number through 1985. Indeed, as the program is extended to all universities (and comes to include women) in the early 1980s, General Raúl Castro expects to be receiving 10,000 new reserve officers per year. As a part of the policy of strengthening the armed forces, these regular university students are called up for one month's intensive military training at the end of each school year and for six months' training upon graduation.[96]

Reserve call-ups for training also became more frequent and all-encompassing in the early 1980s. Reservists who had not been called up for military training in a number of years, including many over age 40, were called back for further military training in 1980 and in 1981.[97]

The formal military budget has changed little in the late 1970s (after doubling in real terms from its level in the early 1970s). Military expenditures in the 1981 budget are 842 million pesos, the highest sum ever, but account for only 7.5 percent of the total expenditure budget, the lowest share in recent years.[98] However, the military's economic burden is much higher upon adding the new extrabudgetary costs, such as the financing of the Territorial Militia. But the most important way to assess the military burden is its impact on personnel. More than 100,000 military have been sent to Angola and Ethiopia (original troops, plus replacements) in 1975–80. Thus, the combined effect of past practices (including a large and active military reserve), recent changes, and foreseeable innovations in the military's relations with society have greatly increased the scope and weight of the armed forces' authority and influence in a systematic, organized fashion.[99]

The armed forces have, of course, maintained the most hierarchically strict command relations within their own organization. Systematic politicization by the Communist party has not challenged the military rank structure. The proportion of officers who belonged to either the party or the Communist Youth Union rose from 86 percent in 1976 to over 90 percent in 1981. The persistence of the military hierarchy within the party can be shown in part by an analysis of the ranks of delegates to the Second Party Congress in the leading military units. Combining the three territorial armies (West, Center, and East), the Air Force, and the Rear Guard Forces, the delegates elected through normal processes in these units were: seventeen division and brigade generals, thirty-five colonels and lieutenant colonels, eight other officers, and no one below the rank of first lieutenant (four civilian workers of the armed forces were also elected).

Partly in compensation, the Central Committee developed a procedure (applied generally, not just in the military) to reach into any organization to pick delegates with outstanding work records to the party Congress. The "direct" delegates, thus selected, included no generals, two colonels and lieutenant colonels, seven other officers, and still no one below the rank of first lieutenant (seven civilian workers were also selected). Even after these efforts, the military delegation to the Second Congress remained top-heavy. The navy, too, adhered to this pattern. No one below the rank of ship captain was a Congress delegate (two civilian workers were also sent). In addition, no one below the rank of colonel became a full member of the Central Committee. All division generals but for the head of the Air Force made it as full Central Committee members (the Air Force Chief remained a Central Committee alternate).[100]

The armed forces have shown once again that they are Cuba's most politically skillful bureaucracy. The mixture of a plausible international threat, a considerable weight within the party elite, and extraordinary organizational skills have prepared the armed forces well to continue to succeed in a politically stratified Cuba.

The weight of wars seemingly without end, however, has also led to much greater specialization within the military, and between the armed forces and civil society. The profession of arms—especially when one is under fire, as in Angola and in Ethiopia—is uniquely a full-time profession. This has increased pressure away from the types of activities that might detract from the central mission of making certain that the arms of the revolution are victorious.

Yet this very victory rests as well on one fundamental conception of the civic soldier: the intense politicization of the military as a means to build morale, patriotism, loyalty, and discipline. Cuba's military heroes and military leaders have had career paths that have emphasized both the political and the technical aspects of life in Cuba's armed forces. So long as that happens, much of the civic soldier will endure, although the pressures of overseas wars have certainly been transforming the Cuban military into a more conventional force.

Conclusions

There is much about the "civic soldier" model that continues to explain many activities of the Revolutionary Armed Forces and their relations with the rest of Cuban society. There is still today an Army of the Working Youth. Military officers continue to fill many roles in the party's Central Committee and, more recently, as alternate members of the party's Political Bureau. The armed forces remain one very important pool of talent for leadership in the civilian society upon retirement.

The "civic soldier" model received a new lease on life in the 1980s when doctrine for the defense of the homeland shifted to the "war of the whole people": every Cuban would fight an invading force. The growth of the Territorial Militia has been extraordinary. Training has been substantial— and ordinary life has been disrupted as the entire population goes through war games and air-raid and invasion alerts.

The Cuban Armed Forces continue to rely on the mobilization of reservists, rather than on having a permanent, huge standing army, to meet many internationalist commitments, even the largest ones in Angola and in Ethiopia. Cuban civilians in Angola have also changed roles, when attacked, assuming military reserve posts, as might be expected from the classic civic soldier.

In the only case when Cubans fought directly against the United States armed forces—in Grenada in October 1983—Cuban reservists acquitted themselves better than Cuba's regular army officers. Cuban construction workers in Grenada were, typically, reservists. They fought with courage and determination against U.S. forces. Indeed, they fought so well that U.S. officers at first thought there were many more Cubans on the island than was the case. In contrast, the Cuban commanding officer, Pedro Tortolo, committed fundamental mistakes in organizing the resistance: he was asleep when the invasion began; he did not think the invasion would occupy the whole island; consequently, he did not distribute weapons to all the reservists, nor enough munitions to those who received weapons. Colonel Tortolo gave this testimony in public upon his immediate return to Cuba when he was still being treated as a hero; he was not pressured into making these comments—though they led to the Cuban government's decision to take away his military rank in punishment.

And yet, there have been important changes which in part modify and in part nullify the original civic soldier model. The most important modification is that the civic soldier model had an element of reciprocity, where the Revolutionary Armed Forces gave as much as they took from civil society. Much of what remains of the civic soldier model, however, is the mechanism for the armed forces to penetrate civil society to obtain the resources needed for war. This is much closer to the model of a traditional military establishment, although the Cuban Armed Forces do it in ways consistent with the traditions and practices described in this chapter.

Notes

1. Samuel P. Huntington, *The Soldier and the State* (Cambridge, Mass.: Harvard University Press, 1957), pp. 80–85.
2. The terms are taken from Amos Perlmutter, "The Praetorian State and the Praetorian Army: Toward a Taxonomy of Civil-Military Relations in Developing Politics," in *Political Development and Social Change,* ed. J. L. Finkle and R. W. Gable (New York: Wiley, 1971), pp. 314–324.
3. See, for instance, Gino Germani and Kalman Silvert, "Politics, Social Structure and Military Intervention in Latin America," *European Journal of Sociology* 2 (1961): 62–81; Morris Janowitz, *The Military in the Political Development of New Nations* (Chicago: University of Chicago Press, 1964): Samuel P. Huntington, *Political Order in Changing Societies* (New Haven: Yale University Press, 1968), chap. 4.
4. The role theory described here is based on that of Robert L. Kahn, Donald M. Wolfe, Robert P. Quinn, and J. Diedrick Snoek, *Organizational Stress: Studies in Role Conflict and Ambiguity* (New York: Wiley, 1964), pp. 11–35.

5. H. A. Simon, *Administrative Behavior* (New York: MacMillan, 1961), p. 118. P. M. Blau has argued that the attainment of organizational objectives (such as military security) generates a stress on finding new objectives (such as those in the areas of politics or economics). I think it is likely that organizational growth has been a specific goal of the military organizations or, at the very least, that the prevention of organizational decline has been such a goal. The concept of the civic soldier has legitimized shifts in objectives or missions of the military organization as perceived by the entire elite. In turn, the ability to shift objectives, as Samuel Huntington has argued, adds to the organizational age of the military organization, so that it becomes more fully institutionalized. See P. M. Blau, *The Dynamics of Bureaucracy* (Chicago: University of Chicago Press, 1955), p. 195; Huntington, *Political Order,* pp. 13–17; W. H. Starbuck, "Organizational Growth and Development," in *Handbook of Organizations,* ed. J. G. March (Chicago: Rand McNally, 1965), pp. 451–533.

6. Ricardo Adam y Silva, *La gran mentira* (Havana: Editorial Lex, 1947); Louis A. Pérez, *Army Politics in Cuba, 1898–1958* (Pittsburgh: University of Pittsburgh Press, 1976), chaps. 2–5.

7. Fulgencio Batista, *Revolución social o política reformista* (Havana: Prensa Indoamericana, 1944), pp. 58–59, 62, 82–85, 123–124, 127; *Cuba's Three Year Plan* (Havana: Cultural S.A., 1937); Consejo Corporativo de Educación, Sanidad y Beneficencia, *Militarismo, anti-militarismo, pseudomilitarismo* (Ceiba del Agua, Cuba: Talleres del Instituto Cívico-Militar, 1939), pp. 5–6, 8, 82, 106; Edmund Chester, *A Sergeant Named Batista* (New York: Holt, 1954); Pérez, *Army Politics in Cuba,* chaps. 6–11.

8. José Suárez Amador, "Octavo aniversario de L.C.B.," *Verde olivo* 11, no. 28 (July 12, 1970): 4–5; ibid., 4, no. 47 (November 24, 1963): 5, 10–11; *Granma,* March 5, 1966, p. 8; ibid., March 13, 1966, p. 8; *Granma Weekly Review,* January 4, 1976, p. 8.

9. For a discussion of the various estimates of the numbers of people killed in the 1950s and 1960s, see Jorge I. Domínguez, "The Civic Soldier in Cuba," in *Political-Military Systems: Comparative Perspectives,* ed. Catherine M. Kelleher (Beverly Hills, Calif.: Sage Publications, 1974), pp. 216–218; see also Hugh Thomas, *Cuba: The Pursuit of Freedom* (New York: Harper & Row, 1971), pp. 1024–1025, 1042, 1044; Raúl Castro, "Graduación del III curso de la escuela básica superior 'General Máximo Gómez,'" *Ediciones al orientador revolucionario* no. 17 (1967): 11; *Granma Weekly Review,* June 13, 1971, pp. 2–3; ibid., December 12, 1971, p. 6; ibid., January 4, 1976, p. 7; Julio C. Fernández, "¿Que fue el bandidismo?" *Bohemia* 68, no. 23 (June 4, 1976): 44–49. See Carlos Rivero Collado's *Los sobrinos del tío Sam* (Havana: Instituto Cubano del Libro, 1976) for a fascinating, though obviously partisan, history of Cuban-exile counterrevolutionary activities written by the son of Batista's former prime minister, who became a revolutionary double agent operating in the United States until 1974.

10. *Granma Weekly Review,* January 4, 1976, p. 7.

11. Alfredo Reyes, "Ejército de la tiranía," *Verde olivo* 7, no. 45 (November 12, 1966): 23, 27–28.

12. For Prime Minister Castro's estimates, see *Granma Weekly Review,* December 12, 1971, p. 6; ibid., December 1, 1974, p. 7. See also Osvaldo Dorticós, "El error que no cometeremos jamás es el de no estar alerta," *Cuba socialista* no. 59 (July 1966): 1, 10–12; *Granma,* April 16, 1973, p. 1; ibid., August 9, 1975, p. 2; ibid., June 8, 1976, p. 4; ibid., April 20, 1976, p. 2; *Granma Weekly Review,* September 28, 1975, p. 7; *Verde olivo* 16, no. 43 (October 27, 1974): 17–18; International Institute for Strategic Studies, *The*

Military Balance 1966–67 (London, 1966), p. 11 (hereafter cited as *IISS*); *IISS, 1970–71,* p. 76; *IISS, 1974–75,* p. 65; *IISS, 1975–76,* p. 64; Gabriel García Márquez, "Colombian Author Writes on Cuba's Angola Intervention," *Washington Post,* January 10, 1977, p. A14; T. N. Dupuy and Wendell Blanchard, *Almanac of World Military Power,* 2d ed. (Dunn Loring, Va.: Dupuy, 1972), p. 24; Howard I Blutstein, Lynne Cox Anderson, Elinor C. Betters, Deborah Lane, Jonathan A. Leonard, and Charles Townsend, *Area Handbook for Cuba* (Washington, D.C.: Government Printing Office, 1971), p. 439. For a history of the Frontier Corps and its auxiliary units, see Eliseo Alberto, "De pie en la frontera," *Cuba internacional* 6, no. 61 (September 1974): 20, 23, 25.

13. *IISS, 1975–76,* p. 64; *IISS, 1974–75,* p. 65; *IISS, 1970–71,* p. 76; *IISS, 1968–69,* p. 12; *IISS, 1966–67,* p. 11; Stockholm International Peace Research Institute, *World Armaments and Disarmament Yearbook, 1973* (Stockholm: Almqvist and Wiksell, 1973), pp. 248–249, 337 (hereafter cited as *World Armaments*); *World Armaments, 1972,* p. 141; Dupuy and Blanchard, *Almanac of World Power,* pp. 24–25 and glossary; John Stanley and Maurice Pearton, *International Trade in Arms* (New York: Praeger, 1972), p. 216; *Granma,* April 18, 1972, p. 2 (I am grateful to Carmelo Mesa-Lago for this reference); U.S., Congress, House, Committee on Foreign Affairs, Subcommittee on Inter-American Affairs, "Soviet Activities in Cuba," in *Hearings,* 93rd Cong. (Washington, D.C.: Government Printing Office, 1974), p. 56; *Granma Weekly Review,* December 12, 1976, p. 11.

14. Raúl Castro, "Las FAR rinden profundo y sentido homenaje al vigésimo aniversario," *Bohemia* 65, no. 31 (August 3, 1973): 28; idem, "Graduación del III curso."

15. *Granma Weekly Review,* April 17, 1973, p. 2; *Granma,* April 16, 1973, p. 1; ibid., April 16, 1975, p. 2.

16. "Algunos aspectos relacionados con la ley del servicio militar general y su reglamento," *Verde olivo* 17, no. 4 (January 26, 1975): 54; *Granma,* March 18, 1975, p. 3; ibid., July 11, 1975, p. 2; *Granma Weekly Review,* December 1, 1974, p. 7; ibid., July 3, 1977, p. 3; Raúl Castro, "Sabemos que el imperialismo se debilita," *Verde olivo* 17, no. 29 (July 20, 1975): 4; "Sistema de registro militar," ibid., no. 12 (March 23, 1975): 61.

17. "Sobre el trabajo político en el aseguramiento a los ejercicios de tiro con armas de infantería," *Verde olivo* 16, no. 24 (June 16, 1974): 28–29, 31.

18. On army schools, see González Tosca, "Escuelas," ibid., 13, no. 49 (December 6, 1971): 51, 87–90; on navy schools, Agenar Martí, "A toda máquina," *Cuba internacional* 6, no. 60 (August 1974): 12–13; "Convocatoria," *Verde olivo* 18, no. 7 (February 15, 1976): 36–39; Lisanka, "Escuela de cadetes inter-armas 'General Antonio Maceo,'" ibid., 17, no. 21 (May 25, 1975): 37; "Primer encuentro de egresados del ITM," ibid., no. 27 (July 6, 1975): 52; Eloísa Ballester, "Por una mejor eficiencia económica," ibid., 18, no. 20 (May 16, 1976): 53. See also ibid., 9, no. 17 (April 28, 1968), pp. 5–7, 10; *Granma Weekly Review,* May 30, 1971, p. 6; ibid., January 20, 1974, p. 7; *Granma,* July 24, 1975, p. 3; Raúl Castro, "La emulación socialista," *Verde olivo* 17, no. 5 (February 2, 1975): 11. On military research, see Centro Nacional de Investigaciones Científicas, *Informe, 1969* (Havana: Universidad de La Habana, 1969), p. 12; Comisión Nacional Cubana de la UNESCO, "Los estudiantes investigan," *Boletín* 12, no. 48 (January–February 1973): 14; *Granma,* December 25, 1974, p. 1.

19. *Granma Weekly Review,* December 16, 1973; *Granma,* July 12, 1976, p. 4; ibid., July 15, 1976, p. 3; ibid., November 25, 1976, p. 1.

20. Sergio Canales and Leonel Gil, "La casa central de las FAR," *Verde olivo* 17,

no. 30 (July 27, 1975): 14, 16–17; Héctor de Arturo and Jorge Blanco, "Primera conferencia del partido en el EJT," ibid., no. 46 (November 16, 1975): 17; Lisanka, "Brigada aérea de la guardia 'Playa Girón,'" ibid., 18, no. 17 (April 25, 1976): 43.
21. *Granma Weekly Review,* August 8, 1976, p. 3.
22. R. Castro, "Sabemos," p. 3; Mario Rodríguez, "El estado mayor," *Verde olivo* 17, no. 47 (November 23, 1975): 35; Raúl Castro, "Con la realización de la maniobra," ibid., no. 50 (December 14, 1975): 16–17, 54; Joaquín Quinta, "La maniobra," ibid., p. 55; "Maniobra 'Primer Congreso,'" ibid., 18, no. 1 (January 4, 1976): 38, *Granma,* December 5, 1975, p. 1.
23. García Márquez, "Colombian Author," p. A14; idem, "Cuba en Angola: Operación Carlota," *Proceso* (January 1977): 14; *New York Times,* February 17, 1977, p. 1; *Granma,* June 8, 1976, p. 4. For a mistaken estimate by the United States government, see Drew Middleton, "The Cuban Soldier in Angola," *New York Times,* March 3, 1976, p. 4.
24. For a study of the racial composition of the Cuban armed forces, see Jorge I. Domínguez, "Racial and Ethnic Relations in the Cuban Armed Forces: A Non-Topic," *Armed Forces and Society* 2, no. 2 (February 1976): 273–290; the method described in that article has been applied to January 1976 data for Cuba's three armies drawn from *Verde olivo,* 18, no. 4 (January 25, 1976): 15–16, and ibid., no. 5 (February 1, 1976): 56–57. See also Georgie Anne Geyer, "Cuba in Angola: A New Look," *Boston Globe,* June 20, 1976, p. 56.
25. To establish the dates, compare *Verde olivo* 17, no 34 (August 24, 1975): 12; ibid., no. 35 (August 31, 1975): 60; and ibid., no. 37 (September 14, 1975): 55. President Marien Ngouabi of the Congo, one of Cuba's key allies during the Angolan war, arrived in Cuba on September 13, 1975; he was the only one of eight heads of state visiting Cuba in that year to spend all his public time in military-related activities. Cuban military personnel had been in the Congo as early as mid-August; see E. G. Viamonte, "Impresiones de una visita," in *Verde olivo* 17, no. 38 (September 21, 1975): 10. For other changes in top commands, see ibid., no. 39 (September 28, 1975): 54; ibid., no. 40 (October 5, 1975); ibid., no. 42 (October 19, 1975); ibid., 18, no. 32 (August 8, 1976): 16, 61; *Granma,* July 24, 1976, p. 1; ibid., July 28, 1976, p. 4. For Fidel Castro's acknowledgment of the presence of Cuban forces in Angola in October 1975, see *Granma,* April 20, 1976, p. 2; for an acknowledgment of an even earlier arrival, see Barry A. Sklar, "Cuba: Normalization of Relations," Issue Brief no. IB75030, Congressional Research Service, Library of Congress (March 3, 1976), p. 23.
26. *Granma Weekly Review,* January 4, 1976, p. 7.
27. For a detailed discussion of these costs, see Jorge I. Domínguez, "The Cuban Operation in Angola: Costs and Benefits for the Cuban Armed Forces," *Cuban Studies* 8, no. 1 (January 1978). See also Fiscalía Militar de las FAR, "Los estímulos y las correcciones disciplinarias," *Verde olivo* 17, no. 47 (November 23, 1975): 22–24; idem, "Las reclamaciones en las FAR," ibid., 18, no. 31 (August 1, 1976): 40; "Las resoluciones y acuerdos del primer congreso del partido comunista de Cuba," ibid., no. 18 (May 2, 1976): 30; Sklar, "Cuba: Normalization of Relations," p. 12.
28. For an extended discussion of these activities, see Jorge I. Domínguez, "The Armed Forces and Foreign Relations," in *Cuba in the World,* ed. Cole Blasier and Carmelo Mesa-Lago (Pittsburgh: University of Pittsburgh Press, 1978); see also William J. Durch, "The Cuban Military in Africa and the Middle East: From Algeria to Angola," Center for Naval Analyses, professional paper no. 201 (Arlington, Va., 1977).
29. *Verde olivo* 4, no. 47 (November 24, 1963): 19. For a discussion of the early

development of the civic soldier (although the author does not use that term) in the Cuban armed forces in the late 1950s, during the rebellion, and in the early 1960s, see Louis A. Pérez, Jr., "Army Politics in Socialist Cuba," *Journal of Latin American Studies* 8, no. 2 (November 1976): 251–264.

30. *Verde olivo* 4, no. 47 (November 24, 1963): 19–20, 52; "El proyecto de ley del servicio militar obligatorio," *Cuba socialista* no. 28 (December 1963): 85–87.
31. *Granma,* April 14, 1966, p. 8. I was mistaken in my "Civic Soldier in Cuba," pp. 219–220, 232; Casillas did not become chief of staff, and Castilla was not head of UMAP.
32. *Granma,* April 14, 1966, p. 8; ibid., March 16, 1966, p. 4; *Verde olivo* 7, no. 43 (October 30, 1966): 14–15, supplement; ibid., 8, no. 11 (March 19, 1967): 34–38; ibid., no. 12 (March 26, 1967): 27–30; ibid., no. 18 (May 7, 1967): 19–21; ibid., no. 19 (May 14, 1967): 36–39; see also José Yglesias, *In the First of the Revolution: Life in a Cuban Country Town* (New York: Vintage Books, 1968), pp. 274–302; Lourdes Casal, "Literature and Society," in *Revolutionary Change in Cuba,* ed. Carmelo Mesa-Lago (Pittsburgh: University of Pittsburgh Press, 1971), p. 459.
33. *Verde olivo* 4, no. 47 (November 24, 1963): 10–11; ibid., no. 4 (January 27, 1963): 52–53; ibid., 11, no. 28 (July 12, 1970); 5; *Granma,* March 5, 1966, p. 8.
34. The percentages assume that the size of the military remained stationary in this period at about 110,000 for the regular forces and 250,000 for all forces. The numbers were taken from *Granma Weekly Review,* July 18, 1971, p. 9. This modifies substantially information in my "Civic Soldier in Cuba," p. 221.
35. Fidel Castro, "Brigada invasora Che Guevara," *Verde olivo* 8, no. 44 (November 5, 1967): 6–7; Fidel Vascos, "Brigada invasora Che Guevara: año 1," ibid., 9, no. 45 (November 10, 1968): 6–7; ibid., 10, no. 45 (November 9, 1969): 7–9, 62; ibid., 11, no. 4 (January 25, 1970): 32; "Algunas tareas cumplidas por las FAR en 1970," ibid., no. 52 (December 27, 1970): 14; René Dumont, "The Militarization of Fidelismo," *Dissent* (September–October 1970): 417–420; K. S. Karol, *Guerrillas in Power* (New York: Hill and Wang, 1970), pp. 444–450, 534–544.
36. *Política internacional* 4, no. 16 (1966): 214–215.
37. R. Castro, "Graduación del III curso," p. 22; *Granma Weekly Review* January 7, 1968, p. 3.
38. *Granma Weekly Review,* August 12, 1973, p. 2; *Granma,* April 3, 1975, p. 5; *Juventud rebelde,* January 5, 1975, p. 1.
39. *Granma,* August 5, 1975, p. 3; ibid., April 2, 1977, p. 2.
40. de Arturo and Blanco, "Primera conferencia del partido," p. 18.
41. "Acto de fin de zafra del EJT en Matanzas," *Verde olivo* 18, no. 21 (May 23, 1976): 52.
42. "A paso de victoria se llama Matanzas," *Bohemia* 65, no. 20 (May 18, 1973): 26; *Granma,* January 5, 1976, p. 5; ibid., January 6, 1976, p. 3; ibid., March 24, 1976, p. 1; ibid., July 13, 1976, p. 3, *Bohemia* 68, no. 16 (April 16, 1976): 60.
43. *Granma Weekly Review,* April 3, 1977, p. 1: García Márquez, "Cuba en Angola," pp. 7, 14; Georgie Ann Geyer, "Cuba in Angola," p. 56. For a general discussion, see Domínguez, "Armed Forces and Foreign Relations."
44. *Granma Weekly Review,* January 4, 1976, p. 7.
45. One possibility is that military officers who favored nonmilitary tasks were appointed to civilian posts in the 1970s, while more professional officers who resisted the idea were not. The theory is difficult to prove, though there is some evidence to back it up. Some professional officers have remained within the armed forces, among them Division General Senén Casas Regueiro,

chairman of the Joint Chiefs of Staff, first deputy minister of the armed forces, and a veteran of the Angolan war. Other professional officers, however, have been appointed to major civilian posts. José Ramón Fernández, a leading officer in the 1950s, educated a generation of officers to recognize the need for military competence, but even he favored the civic-soldier role and was himself appointed minister of education in 1973; Diocles Torralba, former chief of the air force and antiaircraft defense, preceded Casas Regueiro as chairman of the Joint Chiefs of Staff and joined the executive committee of the cabinet in 1972. Finally, some officers in charge of some professional military activities in the armed forces are hardly typical of professional officers; such is the case of Division General Regelio Acevedo, deputy minister of the armed forces for technical training and weapons in the mid-1970s, who had led the militia and served in civic-soldier positions in the 1960s.

46. *Granma Weekly Review,* March 23, 1975, p. 4; "Los estudiantes universitarios ven materializado un viejo deseo," *Verde olivo* 17, no. 49 (December 7, 1975); *Granma,* January 30, 1976; ibid., February 22, 1976, p. 1.

47. *Granma Weekly Review,* p. 3; see also "El proyecto de ley del servicio military obligatorio," *Verde olivo* 4, no. 47 (November 24, 1963): 53–54; ibid., 13, no. 32 (August 8, 1971): 9; *Granma Weekly Review,* July 30, 1967, p. 11; ibid., April 16, 1972, p. 7.

48. *Granma Weekly Review,* December 1, 1974, p. 7; *Granma,* July 11, 1975, p. 2.

49. *Granma Weekly Review,* August 12, 1973, p. 2; Fiscalía Militar, "Los estimulos," pp. 22, 24.

50. *Granma Weekly Review,* January 4, 1976, p. 7.

51. Hugh Hanning, *The Peaceful Uses of Military Forces* (New York: Praeger, 1967).

52. Roman Kolkowicz, *The Soviet Military and the Communist Party* (Princeton: Princeton University Press, 1967), pp. 36–79, 309–321.

53. John Gittings, *The Role of the Chinese Army* (New York: Oxford University Press, 1967), pp. 29–32, 176–201; Ellis Joffe, *Party and Army: Professionalism and Political Control in the Chinese Officer Corps, 1949–1964* (Cambridge, Mass.: Harvard University, East Asian Research Center, 1965), pp. 80–87 (hereafter cited as *Party and Army in China*).

54. Karol, *Guerrillas in Power;* Dumont, "Militarization of Fidelismo"; Andrés Suárez, "How the Cuban Regime Works" (unpublished, 1972).

55. *Verde olivo* 4, no. 7 (February 17, 1963): 6–7.

56. José Causse Pérez, "La construcción del partido en las Fuerzas Armadas Revolucionarias de Cuba," *Cuba socialista* no. 47 (July 1965): 51–66; Raúl Castro, "Problemas del funcionamiento del partido en las FAR" *Cuba socialista* no. 55 (March 1966): 45–48; *Verde olivo* 4, no. 44 (November 2, 1963): 35–41; ibid., 4, no. 50 (December 15, 1963): 3, 12; ibid., no. 51 (December 22, 1963): 3–10, 58–59, 66.

57. E. Yasells, "Reseña de una asamblea,' *Verde olivo* 8, no. 51 (December 24, 1967): 11.

58. Ibid., 7, no. 52 (December 13, 1966): 4; ibid., 8, no. 51 (December 24, 1967): 12; ibid., 11, no. 40 (October 4, 1970): 8, 10; *Granma,* March 1, 1966, p. 4; ibid., August 4, 1975, p. 3; ibid., June 8, 1976, p. 4; *Granma Weekly Review,* January 4, 1976, p. 7; ibid., December 12, 1976, p. 12; *Bohemia,* Vol. 65, no. 31 (August 3, 1973), p. 28.

59. Raymond Garthoff, "The Military in Russia, 1861–1965," in *The Armed Forces and Society,* ed. Jacques Van Doorn (The Hague: Mouton, 1968), pp. 247, 253.

60. Kolkowicz, *Soviet Military and Communist Party.*

61. For a fascinating discussion of this behavior, see Timothy Colton, "Army, Party and Development in Soviet Politics" (Ph.D. diss., Harvard University, 1974).
62. Quoted in Rosendo Gutiérrez, "Segunda asamblea de balance," *Verde olivo* 9, no. 9 (March 3, 1968): 11.
63. "Indicaciones sobre el proceso asambleario," ibid., 14, no. 42 (October 15, 1972): 55–59.
64. "Reunión nacional de instructores para el trabajo de la UJC en las FAR," ibid., 18, no. 9 (February 29, 1976): 96; "Tercer activo del Partido en la DAAFAR," ibid., no. 28 (July 11, 1976): 53.
65. "Indicaciones,": 55–59.
66. "Trabajo político partidista para elevar la conciencia técnica," *Verde olivo* 16, no. 22 (June 2, 1974): 31; D. Kindelán, "Décimo aniversario de la U.J.C.-F.A.R.," ibid., no. 25 (June 23, 1974): 54.
67. Kolkowicz, *Soviet Military and Communist Party*, p. 74.
68. Luis Aguilar, *Cuba 1933* (Ithaca: Cornell University Press, 1972), pp. 187–188.
69. José Suárez Júñez, *El gran culpable* (Caracas, 1963), pp. 64, 91–92.
70. Computed from *Política internacional* 6, nos. 22–24 (1968): 93.
71. *Granma Weekly Review,* March 16, 1969, p. 7; ibid., August 31, 1969, p. 1; *Verde olivo* 11, no. 34 (August 23, 1970): 8; *Bohemia* 65, no. 31 (August 3, 1973): 27; Abelardo Colomé, "Continuamos luchando," *Verde olivo* 17, no. 31 (August 3, 1975): 18.
72. *Política internacional* 6, nos. 22–24 (1968): 93; *Granma Weekly Review,* March 16, 1969, p. 7; *Granma* April 17, 1975, p. 2; Juan Escalona, "Las FAR y los reservistas," *Verdo olivo* 18, no. 17 (April 25, 1976): 17–18.
73. *Verde olivo* 9, no. 17 (April 28, 1968): 5–6; ibid., 8, no. 19 (May 14, 1967): 7; ibid., no. 20 (May 21, 1967): 18; *Granma Weekly Review,* July 20, 1969, p. 10.
74. *Granma,* December 3, 1975, p. 2.
75. "Entrenamiento de tiro antiaéreo," *Verde olivo* 17, no. 13 (March 30, 1975); 21.
76. Causse Pérez, "La construcción del partido," pp. 54–55; *Granma Weekly Review,* January 10, 1971, pp. 10–11; ibid., January 24, 1971, pp. 10–11; ibid., March 5, 1966, p. 8.
77. R. Castro, "Problemas del funcionamiento del partido," pp. 56–57; *Verde olivo* 10, no. 2 (January 12, 1969): 29; ibid., 11, no. 40 (October 4, 1970): 8–9; "El trabajo de las organizaciones políticas y las organizaciones del partido y la U.J.C. en aseguramiento de preparación política de oficiales, clases y soldados," ibid., 16, no. 23 (June 9, 1974): 30–31; "Informe central del Vice Ministro Jefe de la Dirección Política," ibid., no. 17 (April 28, 1974): 55; "Sobre el trabajo político en el aseguramineto a los ejercicios de tiro con armas de infantería," ibid., no. 24 (June 16, 1974): 28–29, 31.
78. Venancio Rivas Pérez, "Evaluación de los oficiales de las FAR," *Verde olivo* 17, no. 9 (March 2, 1975): 19, 21, 23.
79. *Granma Weekly Review,* May 14, 1967, p. 11.
80. *Granma,* May 20, 1966, p. 5; Yasells, "Reseña de una asamblea," pp. 11–12; "Primera asamblea de balance del partido," *Verde olivo* 8, no. 51 (December 24, 1967): 61; "Sección política de la marina de guerra revolucionaria," ibid., 9, no. 2 (January 14, 1968): 38; "Primera asamblea de balance del partido comunista de Cuba en el cuerpo blindado," in ibid., no. 7 (February 18, 1968): 13–15; Gutiérrez, "Segunda asamblea de balance," pp. 8–12; "Asamblea de balance del partido en el ejército de Oriente," ibid., 10, no. 5 (February 2, 1969): 52–53; "Balance del partido en el cuerpo ejército de Camagüey," ibid., no. 42 (October 19, 1969): 25; "Segunda asamblea de

balance del partido comunista de Cuba en una unidad en Matanzas," ibid., no. 43 (October 26, 1969): 28; "Segunda asamblea de balance del partido en el ejército del centro," ibid., no. 44 (November 2, 1969): 58; "Segunda asamblea de balance del partido comunista de Cuba en el estado mayor general," in ibid., no. 49 (December 7, 1969): 32–33; "Segunda reunión del partido en las Fuerzas Armadas Revolucionarias," ibid., 11, no. 40 (October 4, 1970): 7–8.

81. Luis Méndez, "La asamblea provincial del PURS en Matanzas," *Cuba socialista* no. 31 (March 1964): 134–135.

82. *Granma*, October 4, 1974, p. 3.

83. Colton, "Army, Party and Development in Soviet Politics."

84. The following comments on China are based mainly on Joffe, *Party and Army in China*, pp. 57–72; Gittings, *Role of the Chinese Army*, chaps. 5, 8, 11, 12; Jürgen Domes, "The Cultural Revolution and the Army," *Asian Survey* 8, no. 5 (May 1968): 349–363; Harvey Nelsen, "Military Forces in the Cultural Revolution," *China Quarterly* no. 51 (July–September 1972): 444–474; Philip Bridgham, "The Fall of Lin Piao," ibid., no. 55 (July–September 1973): 427–449; Jonathan D. Pollack, "The Study of Chinese Military Politics: A Framework for Analysis," in *Political-Military Systems,* ed. Catherine M. Kelleher, pp. 239–270.

85. For further elaboration of this point of view, see two thoughtful pieces by William M. LeoGrande: "The Politics of Revolutionary Development: Civil-Military Relations in Cuba, 1959–1976" (Paper presented at annual meeting, Midwest Political Science Association, Chicago, April 21–23, 1977), pp. 26–32, 41–43; "Party Control and Political Socialization in Communist Civil Military Relations: The Case of Cuba" (Paper presented at ninth national convention, the American Association for the Advancement of Slavic Studies, Washington, D.C., October 13–16, 1977), pp. 27–29.

86. For background, see Domínguez, *Cuba,* Chapter 9.

87. Computed from *Granma Weekly Review,* August 3, 1980, p. 3; and ibid., November 30, 1980, Supplement, p. 3.

88. *Granma Weekly Review,* December 20, 1980, p. 5; Domínguez, *Cuba,* p. 332.

89. *Granma Weekly Review,* June 22, 1980, p. 3; *Granma,* January 5, 1981, p. 1; *Granma,* January 28, 1982, p. 3; *Bohemia* 71, 33 (August 17, 1979), p. 54: Lesmes La Rosa, "Primer aniversario de la SEPMI," *Verde olivo* 22, 5 (February 1, 1981), pp. 14–15.

90. *Granma Weekly Review,* February 8, 1981, p. 12; *Granma,* January 27, 1982, p. 2.

91. Ibid. See also ibid., February 1, 1981, p. 2.

92. Lesmes La Rosa and Jorge Luis Blanco, "Las FAR en el primer quinquenio," *Verde olivo* 21, 51 (December 21, 1980), p. 8; Mario Rodríguez, "Convertirse en oficial-ingeniero," ibid., 21, 46 (November 16, 1980), p. 34; and Concepción Duchesne, "Incremento y desarrollo de la educación superior," *Bohemia* 72, 48 (November 28, 1980), p. 36.

93. For examples, see Jorge L. Blanco, "Casa de Oficiales," *Verde olivo* 20, 16 (April 22, 1979), pp. 35–36; ibid., 20, 30 (July 29, 1979), p. 52; LaRosa and Blanco, "Las FAR en el primer quinquenio," pp. 4, 7–8; and José Cazañas Reyes, "Nace una comunidad," ibid., 21, 49 (December 7, 1980), pp. 11–13.

94. *Verde olivo* 20, 32 (August 12, 1979); "Ejército Occidental: primera década," ibid., 21, 51 (December 21, 1980), pp. 53–55; La Rosa and Blanco, "Las FAR en el primer quinquenio," p. 6; *Granma Weekly Review,* December 28, 1980, p. 10.

95. For an update on the Army of the Working Youth, see Luis López, "Un trienio de intensa labor," *Verde olivo* 21, 44 (October 12, 1980), pp. 48–49.

96. *Granma Weekly Review,* April 19, 1981, p. 2.
97. Jorge Luis Blanco, "Reservistas," *Verde olivo* 22, 5 (February 1, 1981), pp. 38–40.
98. See *Granma Weekly Review,* January 11, 1981, p. 4, for the 1981 budget. For earlier ones, see Dominguez, "Political and military limitations and consequences of Cuban policies in Africa," *Cuban Studies* 10, 2 (July 1980), pp. 23–24.
99. *Granma Weekly Review,* December 28, 1980, p. 10, carries the military section of Fidel Castro's main report to the Second Party Congress.
100. Domínguez, *Cuba,* p. 366; *Granma Weekly Review,* November 29, 1981, Special Supplement, p. 5; José Cazañas Reyes, "IV conferencia del partido en el ejército occidental," *Verde olivo* 21, 41 (October 12, 1980), pp. 50–51; Rubén Fonseca, "VII conferencia del partido en la MGR," ibid., pp. 52–53; Jesús Casal Guerra, "VII conferencia del PCC en la DAAFAR," ibid., 21, 40 (October 5, 1980), pp. 50–51; "Sexta conferencia del Partido-Jefatura de Retaguardia," ibid., pp. 52–53; Lesmes La Rosa, "VI conferencia del partido en el ejército oriental," ibid., pp. 53–55; Pablo Noa, "VIII conferencia del PCC en el ejército central," ibid., pp. 55–56.

IV
The Military
in Power

David Pion-Berlin

The Defiant State: Chile in the Post-Coup Era

During the 1970s Latin American military regimes generally pursued free-market economic strategies.[1] In an apparent backlash against reformist civilian governments, which had relied on public-sector investment and state controls to generate economic growth, these military regimes trusted in market forces. While expanding the state's security apparatus, they also greatly reduced its economic functions. Political repression became the means by which the armed forces could silence popular demands for state-led investment, expenditure, regulation, and distribution.

The purest application of the free-market (also referred to as monetarist) doctrine was that undertaken by the Chilean military from 1975 to 1983. While other regimes waffled, the Chileans were ruthless in their dogmatic adherence to laissez-faire precepts. It has been assumed in the Chilean case (and elsewhere) that such policies were beneficial to the capitalist class.[2] Indeed, there seemed to be little evidence in the Chilean case to challenge that assertion during the first five years of the program; the correlation between state policies and economic rewards to the privileged class seemed nearly perfect. The freeing of prices and contraction in wages (which were 40 percent less in real terms in 1975 than they were in 1970) led to sharp reductions in labor costs and higher profits for owners. These trends were reinforced with restrictive labor legislation. A series of decrees issued in 1978 abolished Chile's largest union organizations, restricted union membership to plant levels, and made political activity by wage earners criminal.[3] All this effectively weakened labor's bargaining power with management.

Of course, correlations tell us nothing about causation. Yet it has been *presumed* by leading scholars that dominant economic groups in Chile had, through concentration of wealth and strong personal ties with public officials, transformed the state into an agent servicing their own economic gain.[4] Further, some writers have argued that the economic model chosen by the regime was merely the "expression of the interests of a small group of entrepreneurs who today control a large part of the private economy."[5] Consequently, the autonomy of state managers was limited and free-market doctrine was merely the ideological underpinning for a profit-driven capitalist class.

However, problems emerged in 1981 that cast doubt on this thesis. The junta's economic program was shaken by speculative practices of Chile's giant financial conglomerates, which together controlled 85 percent of the firms that experienced growth during the post-coup period and which had placed their representatives in key positions within the government.[6] These groups demanded safeguards which required modifications in the economic model. Yet the regime not only refused to comply but finally intervened to break up the two largest financial groups in the country— while leaving the monetarist economic program intact. What would motivate the Pinochet regime to pursue economic policies in defiance of significant capitalist actors? And *if* state managers were not answerable to the dominant class, then what was their principal social base of support?

We will argue that state policymakers during the military government had been less driven by commitments to the private sector and more persuaded by their associations with like-minded economists and financial experts from abroad. Together these individuals comprised a community of peers drawn together by a *common intellectual heritage rather than a uniform set of material interests*. Academic rather than business experiences proved to be more salient in shaping state policies. Ideas took on a value of their own for the Chilean technocrats who managed the monetarist program of the military government.[7] It will be argued that a set of intellectual concerns may help explain both the rigidity of state policy and the emergence of conflicts between the military government and Chile's dominant capitalist class.

Ideas and Communities

Rulers pursue ideas as well as interests. They may subscribe to doctrines that neither emerge from nor serve class interests. Of course the distinction, in traditional Marxian treatments, is irrelevant, since it is said that ideas are nothing more than the expression of material relations of production.[8] Ruling ideas are class-bound in origin and purpose, and thereby strengthen the position of dominant classes with respect to subordinate ones.

Karl Mannheim disagreed with the Marxian position, arguing that while ideas are grounded in social reality, they are not rooted in economic classes. Intellectuals, who are the principal bearers of ideas, form a kind of "freely floating" class, "recruited from an increasingly inclusive area of social life" and united through educational history rather than socioeconomic position, according to Mannheim.[9] He took issue with Antonio Gramsci, who thought the intellectuals were the "dominant group's deputies exercising the subaltern functions of social hegemony and political government." [10] Instead, these individuals were autonomous and thus capable of pursuing ideas independent of class interests.

Mannheim's conceptual schema is useful in the Chilean case. The economic technocrats who dutifully served the military junta also shared a common frame of reference with similarly trained economists abroad. If these specialists were part of a transnational community of peers, such a group could have provided the regime with an alternate social base of support. The monetarist community, like Merton's collectivity, has a "sense of solidarity by virtue of sharing common values and ideas," rather than social or economic position.[11] The greater the extent and intensity with which ideas are shared, the easier it becomes for elites to resist the loss of legitimacy with groups outside the community. What follows is the application of this thesis to the Chilean case.

The Monetarist Community

The monetarists are modern-day economic liberals with a belief in the dictum that governments which govern less govern best. They consider state intervention to set prices or control trade as sins, contending that the capitalist market is inherently stable and fully capable of rationally allocating resources on its own. Secondly, they claim inflation is the primary obstacle to growth. Inflation is precipitated by an excessive expansion of the money supply, which in turn is often fueled by government deficits. Hence they call for drastic cuts in federal spending and investment.

The monetarist "school" has its nucleus in the economics department at the University of Chicago. Notable past members of the department, including Milton Friedman, George Stigler, and Harry Johnson, have made theoretical contributions to the study of inflation and trade using monetary variables. Countless former students from the department have gone on to hold high-ranking governmental positions in the third world. The monetarist school's international linkages grew out of the 1940s with the founding of the International Monetary Fund (IMF) in 1945. The IMF was established to provide a framework for international monetary management and to promote free trade. As a result of contact with developing countries (including Chile) in the 1950s, the fund's research division made the first policy-relevant, theoretical advances in a monetary approach to the balance of payments.[12]

The international monetarist network reaches beyond the confines of Chicago and the IMF to take different forms. Social contacts between these like-minded economists have been intermittently maintained through the Mt. Pelerin Society.[13] Founded in 1947 by Friedrich Von Hayek, a contemporary and critic of Sir John Maynard Keynes, the society combatted what it saw as the erosion of respect for free-market principles. Milton Friedman, the leading spokesman for the monetarist cause, was one of its original members and served as its president in the 1960s. With over six hundred members, the society has spawned institutions worldwide (including the Center of Public Studies in Santiago, Chile) to promote monetarist ideas and influence policymakers. Von Hayek has visited Chile on several occasions, and his views have had a profound impact on the Pinochet regime. For instance, it is alleged that Pinochet borrowed the name for his revised 1980 Constitution from a 1960 book by Von Hayek entitled *The Constitution of Liberty.*

In 1956, under the auspices and funding of the U.S. Agency for International Development, the University of Chicago established an exchange program with the Catholic University of Chile. An eight-year contract was signed bringing Chicago faculty to Chile to teach, and Chilean masters students to the United States to receive their doctorates. The monetarists had a free hand at shaping the Catholic University economics department in their own mold. The program was used to counteract the growing influence of the structuralist school, which advocated state intervention and selective controls. The exchange program served as a mechanism for transfering these economic ideas to a third-world setting.

The economists at Catholic University remained isolated from the main currents of thought during the 1960s and 1970s. They were considered extremists and were shunned by President Frei (1964–70) and opposed by President Allende (1970–73). But even the business community kept their distance from these radical free-marketeers until 1973. At that time, the efforts to unseat the Unidad Popular government brought businessmen and intellectuals from Catholic University together to draw up a proposal for post-Allende economic strategies.[14]

Commissioned by the navy and financed in part by the CIA, the three hundred-page document was pro-capitalist yet eclectic in its prescriptions, reflecting the heterogeneity of its authors. Nonetheless, this provided the "Chicago Boys" with exposure. In 1975, the military called on some of those monetarists who had helped draft the report to head up their economic team. Among them were Jorge Cauas, an influential businessman and former faculty member at Catholic University's economics department, who became minister of finance (the top-ranking economic policy position). Sergio de Castro, a Ph.D. graduate from the University of

Chicago, became minister of economics. The monetarist school's position was consolidated in December of 1976, when de Castro replaced Cauas, and the positions of economics minister, Central Bank president, and vice-president were offered to Pablo Baraona, Alvaro Bardon, and Sergio de la Cuadra respectively—all Chicago University graduates.

Though separated by distance, this transnational community has kept up contacts. Since 1975, members of the Chicago University faculty have made numerous trips to Chile to lecture at the university and to advise the government. Arnold Harberger, for example, has maintained a close personal relationship with Sergio de Castro for over twenty years, having served as his dissertation advisor and long-term mentor. It would be erroneous to suggest that the Chicago faculty has in any way dictated the terms of the Chilean free-market program; the Chileans have set their own course as equal members of this intellectual community. But it is a course that has had the solid support of their North American counterparts.

The International Monetary Fund also maintains contact through its "missions," which periodically visit Chile to discuss loan requests with Central Bank and ministerial officials. These missions (which are comprised of a team of IMF financial experts assigned to specific countries) began their work in 1956, when the IMF provided Chile with its first standby loan in return for compliance with an orthodox monetarist stabilization plan. After a period of strained relations between the fund and Chile during the Allende period, contacts were resumed after the coup with loan agreements signed in January of 1974 and March of 1975. Thereafter, Chile depended less on the fund and more on private bank credit. The IMF, however, paved the way for private assistance by certifying Chile's creditworthiness.

The First Phase: Economic Pragmatism

Few doubted the military's commitment to the capitalist classes in the aftermath of the coup d'état of September 11, 1973. In one bold stroke, General Augusto Pinochet's junta crushed the Unidad Popular experiment in socialism and vowed to restore order, efficiency, and competitiveness to the economy. The business elite were pleased at the junta's apparent dedication to a free-enterprise system. "Chile must become a land of property owners, not a country of proletarians," said the government in its March 1974 Declaration of Principles.[15]

Prices were freed and wages frozen; the peso was devalued, which raised prices and reduced working-class income levels even farther. Peasant holdings were confiscated and returned to wealthy landowners, once Allende's land-reform program was annulled. In pursuing policies favorable to the propertied classes, the junta initially rejected laissez-faire economics, instead calling for an active state role:

> The acceptance of free enterprise, as described, must in no case be taken as a disregard for the active and very important role given to the state in the economic field. The state's mission is not limited to ensuring a healthy competition and exercising a control over private enterprise to avoid abuse or monopoly. A modern economy also requires the state to participate in comprehensive economic planning.[16]

The state maintained public-sector investment to sustain demand and production levels. It retained selective price controls to contain the enormous inflationary pressures imposed by the devaluation and stopped short of fiscal austerity cuts that would jeopardize the economy's productive capacity. Pragmatism in defense of corporate profit was the guiding philosophy during the first year and a half of military rule.

Acting through interest associations called gremios, or guilds, the propertied class exerted strong influence on the development of economic policy. But the regime and not the private sector controlled patterns of influence in accordance with its own interests. The junta solicited advice from the gremios as part of a broader effort to create for itself a civilian base of support. These interest groups would provide a structure for social mobilization in defense of the state. This corporatist-styled solution would (in theory) build a depoliticized movement of intermediary organizations aimed at complementing the political power of the state.[17] Prior to 1975, this political concept was dominant and shaped the military's economic program as well.

The Second Phase: Economic Dogmatism

Beginning in April of 1975, the junta's economic focus shifted in fundamental respects. The pragmatic approach had not produced results: inflation and unemployment and trade and fiscal deficits were rising uncontrollably, while production was declining. Monthly price increases averaged 20 percent from January to March of that year; industrial production was down 15 percent and unemployment up 13.3 percent; reserves had plummeted from $121.6 million in 1973 to $41.1 million by the end of 1974, and the fiscal deficit as a percentage of GDP stood at 10.5 percent. This was considerably lower than Allende's deficit of 24.7 percent, but not low enough to convince the IMF and private banks that Chile was creditworthy.[18]

In March, University of Chicago economists Milton Friedman and Arnold Harberger arrived in Santiago with a formula for economic recovery based on the principles of orthodox monetarism. They argued that inflation was the principal obstacle to economic growth and was driven by the excessive expansion of the money supply. To bring the money supply under control, they tried to convince the junta to adopt a tight fiscal and monetary policy to include cutbacks in public expenditure and investment and credit restrictions. Secondly, they called for the relaxation of trade and currency controls to "open up" the Chilean economy to competitive international forces. Lower tariffs and exchange decontrol would permit the free flow of goods and capital into the domestic market, rationally reallocate the country's resources, and spur economic growth.

The government's economic plan coincided with the principles of the monetarist school. And by 1982 its accomplishments, *within the parameters set by the monetarist school,* were considerable. Government expenditures as a proportion of GDP were halved by 1979. The fiscal deficit was slashed from 24.7 percent of GDP in 1973 to .8 percent in 1978; and from 1979 to 1981 the federal budget showed a surplus. Inflation, which was 374.7 percent in 1975, was reduced to just 19.7 percent in 1981. Credit restrictions raised the cost of money, as interest rates, which were negative in real terms under Allende, became positive. This generated huge influxes of foreign capital, erasing the balance of payments deficit. Even the GDP recovered from its fall in 1975, averaging a growth rate of 7.2 percent from 1976 to 1982.[19] The economic team lowered tariffs to a uniform rate of 10 percent, which left the Chilean market exposed to international competition and a flood of imported goods. The import bill rose, but higher world prices for copper and a devalued peso contributed to larger export revenues and produced a trade surplus through 1977.[20]

The international monetarist community agreed with this positive prognosis. Milton Friedman called the "recovery" an "economic miracle" and cited Chile as a showcase of free-market capitalism. Friedman's receipt of the 1976 Nobel Prize in economics lent prestige to his endorsement of the Chilean model. Arnold Harberger said de Castro's ministry had "done the things the wise old men at the World Bank and the IMF have been saying for twenty-five years," [21] predicting that in ten years Chile's level of economic development would be comparable to Spain's, and that in twenty years it would enjoy the same standard of living as Holland. And for its part, the IMF provided a "seal of approval" that opened the floodgates for foreign credit. Private banks, confident that the Chilean model was the "correct" one, granted 3.3 billion dollars in loans to Pinochet's government between 1975 and 1978.[22]

The cumulative effect of this international praise was to bolster the Chicago Boys' stature in the military regime. The junta appreciated the monetarists' international contacts and prestige, which assured a constant flow of credit for arms purchases and higher military salaries. But as the costs of the liberal plan began to outweigh the benefits, the generals would draw validation from this respected group of international economists and financial advisors. They would be reminded by these economic authorities that despite the grumblings of certain sectors in Chilean society, their assumptions and proposals for economic recovery were fundamentally correct.

Reminders were needed, since all was not healthy with the Chilean economy. Growth was decidedly unbalanced. Productive sectors declined relative to nonproductive sectors. The industrial share of GDP fell from an average of 24.9 percent in 1971–1975 to an average of 22 percent in 1976–1982. Meanwhile, the financial sector expanded at an average annual rate of 12.2 percent in 1975–1982, enlarging its share of the overall economy from 5.3 percent in 1974 to 11.3 percent of GDP in 1982.[23] Capitalist enterprises in textiles, chemicals, plastics, and steel production (to name a few) lost business, while major banks and financial institutions thrived. As winners and losers emerged, the state's relations with each changed. Industrial interest groups such as SOFOFA (Sociedad de Fomento Fabril—Society for Industrial Development, the most important industrial interest group in Chile) repeatedly asked the government to change its exchange-rate policy, provide tariff protection, and offer incentives for domestic producers. At every step they were turned away. As the effects of the liberal policies worsened the lot of important fractions of the industrial sector, channels of communication became vehicles for protest rather than support. For that reason, business commissions previously charged with making recommendations to the president were eliminated, and gremios were taken over by the state and their elected officials removed.

Likewise, large and medium-sized landowners who had greeted the coup with enthusiasm, and who had supported the Pinochet government during the first five or six years, soon discovered their own interests were in conflict with state policies. By the fourth quarter of 1981, the overvalued peso had contributed to a decline in exports of 13.8 percent over the previous year, as Chilean goods became less competitive on the world market. Domestic producers were also hurt by the influx of lower-priced food imports. Carlos Podlech, president of the Wheat Growers Association, said that "as a result of the inflexible application of economic policy, national agriculture is short of finance and in virtual bankruptcy."[24] The junta's response to these concerns was that the theory of comparative advantage would predict that certain sectors would fall by the wayside, as more competitive ones succeeded. Despite the recessionary trends in the economy, fully evident by the middle of 1981, the regime persisted with its liberal policies, and called the downtown a "cost of economic recovery." The junta even turned its back on the complaints of the SNA (Sociedad Nacional de Agricultura—National Organization of Agriculture), an organization of politically conservative large landowners and for years a bulwark of support for the military government.

Structural imbalances in the economy became acute by 1981, with an expanding finance sector resting on a narrowed productive base. Carlos Diaz-Alejandro understates the problem when he says, in reference to the Southern Cone economies (including Chile's) that the "rebirth of a variety of financial instruments offering handsome returns has probably contributed to a sluggish rate of capital formation."[25]

The average annual rate of investment declined from 15.3 percent during the period 1960–1970 to 11.1 percent during 1974–1980.[26] The restructuring of the financial sector produced an impressive inflow of foreign credit used primarily for speculative purposes. Even as businesses closed their doors (bankruptcies increased by 520 percent from 1975 to 1981), investors sought safe havens in commodity markets and housing and realty ventures.

As capital formation declined, capital concentration increased. Financial conglomerates seized the assets of faltering companies with a voracity that earned them names like "Las Piranas," growing through acquisition and not investment. In the short term, these firms profited as a direct result of regime policies. In the longer term, the monetarist model undermined these same companies. The November 1981 collapse of eight major banks and financial companies owned or controlled by Chile's wealthiest economic groups was but the first in a series of crises to beset the private sector. Who were these groups? And how did the regime's practices affect their interests?

The Regime and the Dominant Class: Ideas vs. Interests

An economic group, or "clan" as it is referred to in Chile, is distinct from a corporation because it has controlling interests in numerous firms across diverse sectors of the economy. The name correctly suggests that the groups' principal social links are familial (most but not all clans are family based). Their structure bears out the results of a study done by Maurice Zeitlin of Chilean corporate executives. He found that industrialists and bankers were commonly related to large landowners through immediate and extended kinship ties. Families with the largest number of top investors in business also had the largest number of landed elites. This suggested that significant portions of the industrial and agricultural bourgeoisie comprised one unified social class.[27]

The most powerful clans have interests in manufacturing, construction, mining, commerce, and most especially banking. They have centralized ownership and management in the same hands so as to more rationally administer and control these veritable empires of capital. The largest group, Cruzat-Larrain, controlled nearly 25 percent of the assets of the 250 largest firms in Chile. The second largest group, the BHC (named after its flagship bank, Banco Hipotecario de Chile) had holdings in 65 firms. Combined, these clans had an estimated capital base of 4 billion dollars.[28] By way of their extensive holdings throughout the economy, the clans could be said to have a dominant position within their class.

In 1975 and 1976, the junta sold off its interests in ten major banks and auctioned off an additional 197 firms to the highest bidder. These measures were consistent with the liberal goal of reducing fiscal deficits by eliminating subsidies and transfers to state-owned enterprises. In the process, large firms acquired numerous assets. With control of the banks, coupled with privileged access to foreign credit, these corporations bought out competitors who were struggling to keep afloat in the midst of the 1975 recession. Others barely stayed solvent by borrowing credit from the clans at exorbitant interest rates. As these firms became increasingly indebted to the clans, the latter profited from the differential between the international and domestic cost of borrowing, yet themselves went into debt with U.S. and European banks.

The impressive growth of the domestic financial market provided the dominant groups with the illusion of economic security. With bank deposits at an all-time high, the potential for productive investment and future growth was enormous. The accumulation of obligations to foreign creditors was thought to be inconsequential. As one newspaper editorial succinctly put it, "If the indebtedness serves to increase the country's productive capacity, that indebtedness can pay for itself."[29] In reality, the financial system undermined Chile's productive capacity by shifting resources toward speculative and consumptive activities. These economic clans sustained their industrial, agricultural, and commercial holdings in the short term through intragroup loans. These funds were used to import consumer items, and commercial deficits prompted even more borrowing from abroad. From 1977 to 1981, Chile's external debt grew at 29 percent annually, the highest rate in the world. Central Bank President Pablo Baraona noted in 1981 that during the previous decade Chilean companies had increased their capital by 40 percent and their indebtedness by 1,000 percent (though the bulk of that indebtedness had come in the previous five years).[30]

In 1981, the nation's forty-eighth largest firm, CRAV (Compania Refinería Azucar Vina—Vina Sugar Refining Company), a member of the Cruzat-Larrain Group, went bankrupt. Its demise was attributed to questionable lending practices by its principal creditor banks, themselves controlled by Cruzat-Larrain. Given its size and established position in the private sector, CRAV's fall was completely unexpected. In November of that year, the collapse of a major economic clan, Sahli-Tassara, forced the government to take control of its banks and finance companies and place its owners under arrest. The group had been dragged down through huge losses suffered by its major industrial and agricultural holdings.

The clans' lending policies had finally led a giant agro-industrial conglomerate and a major group past the brink of insolvency. Should a chain of collapses result, Chile would be threatened with default on her external debt (60 percent of which was private).[31] The country needed a steady flow of foreign capital in 1982 to cover annual service payments on its external debt. But given the failure of major financial institutions in Chile, international creditors were wary.

Theoretically, the regime should have come to the clans' defense. These groups had an indisputably powerful position in the Chilean economy, and their personal ties to the government provided them with political clout as well. For instance, Fernando Leniz, the junta's first minister of economics, later left government to run Cruzat-Larrain's forest industries. Jorge Cauas, the former minister of finance, later became head of that clan's main bank, Banco de Santiago. Yet the junta took no steps to shore up the very financial groups which had prospered most as a result of state policies. Instead, the junta increasingly saw their fortunes tied to the retention of the monetarist plan and cooperation of the monetarist community *at the expense of the major economic groups*. The monetarists were not willing to take the blame for the growing economic crisis (which had become a depression by 1982). Instead, they laid it at the doorstep of the clans and their questionable financial practices. The facts were compelling: by June of 1982, bad debts comprised 80 percent of the capital and reserves of Chile's twelve largest banks.[32] Sergio de Castro's blistering attacks on Javier Vial, the president of Grupo BHC, through the medium of *El Mercurio* (the leading mouthpiece of the liberals), symbolized the growing rift between the economic team and its alleged class allies. In July of that year, Pinochet ordered Vial to relinquish the BHC banks' 25 percent holding in Banco de Chile. This was part of a broader effort to delink the financial group's capital from its members and diversify its assets. After handing down his first set of regulations governing bookkeeping practices, Pinochet lamented the fact he had not disciplined the financial elite sooner; saying "I should have deported 100, no, 200 of these paper emperors . . ."[33]

The response of the dominant class was to abandon its previous allegiance to orthodox liberalism and fiscal austerity and lobby for greater state protection and production incentives.[34] In September 1982, the clans seemed to have won a victory in the appointment as finance minister of Rolf Luders, vice-president of the BHC group. However, Luders's practices as finance minister were completely unexpected and pointed up the clear contradictions between the monetarist school and the dominant class.

Unlike most of the others, Chicago graduate Rolf Luders employed his economic training for business pursuits, rather than as a stepping stone to the public sector. He masterminded the takeovers that sparked the rapid growth of the BHC group. As the second largest shareholder in BHC, Luders was universally recognized as an important financial figure. With the economic groups in danger of crumbling under the weight of indebtedness and industrial stagnation, Luders, himself an advocate of monetarist views, understood that modifications in strategy were needed. While defending the free market in philosophical terms, he proposed a pragmatic reactivation strategy that included governmental stimulation of production, employment, and demand. And rather than point to recessionary trends in the international system, he blamed the current crisis primarily on the rigid policies of the past, and called for less dogmatism and greater consultation with the private sector.[35]

Private interests dictated that the state reverse its commitments to austerity. But the monetarists held their ground. In a sharply worded address, Alvaro Bardon, who had been appointed under-secretary to Luders, and who continued to share Sergio de Castro's orthodox views, disputed Luders's analysis. In an effort to exonerate the monetarists, Bardon shifted the cause of Chile's problems back on the external sector, claiming that declining prices for Chilean copper and unusually high interest rates were imposing obstacles to the nation's recovery. His remarks indicated that the hard-line liberals still retained considerable power within the regime. Thereafter, Luders could not carry out his reactivation plan, much to the dismay of the economic groups.

Luders's entrance into the ministry did not precipitate the ideological confrontation that seemed all but certain to develop after his initial proposals. Instead, the finance minister drew himself closer to the monetarists, and farther away from the business establishment. His efforts to secure an $850 million loan from the International Monetary Fund in the fall of 1982 to service the country's annual debt led him to back the fund's proposals for economic stabilization which included tight restrictions on money supply growth, ceilings on the fiscal deficit, and elimination of preferential exchange rates for dollar debtors (enacted earlier that year to minimize the cost of repayment for heavily indebted companies).

The financial minister's final and dramatic break with the dominant class came in January of 1983. Apparently acting on his own (though with the blessings of Pinochet), he intervened in eight major Chilean banks, four of which belonged to the country's two most powerful economic clans.[36] The state took over the administration of two financial institutions belonging to Cruzat-Larrain and liquidated the assets of the BHC bank whose chief executive had been, ironically, Luders himself. In fact, of the five other banks affected, three had been run by past and present members of the monetarist team.[37] Together, these banks accounted for $3.8 billion of Chile's foreign debt. Without them, the clans, who had built their fortunes through indebtedness, could no longer finance their operations. The state froze all withdrawals, guaranteed deposits, and temporarily assumed the burdens of debt repayment to foreign creditors. By 1984, all Cruzat-Larrain's assets had been signed over to a government bankruptcy commission.

The state had dismantled the most powerful economic groups in the country. Moreover, it had done so with the approval of their former representatives. Faced with the choice of rescuing his own company or realigning with the monetarist school, Rolf Luders chose to do the latter.

Though personalities changed during 1982 and the beginning of 1983, the monetarists remained in control before, during, and after the state's seizure of the clan's assets.[38] Said one banker:

"The supporters of the model have triumphed again at the expense of those (the clans) who want a more popular policy." Then commenting on Rolf Luders's predicament, he added:

> He is standing between two fires but has only one bucket of water. For a time the minister promised heterodox solutions in the short term, but he has lost impetus. He has been forced to stick closer to the model and has been unable to help the private sector in the way he initially wanted to.[39]

Acting with considerable independence and power, the military government found a remedy that penalized the clans but pleased the monetarist community. Though the state had to temporarily intervene in the marketplace, this was a small price to pay to secure a program of fiscal and monetary austerity. But it would be erroneous to suggest that the Chileans were buckling under the pressure of the IMF: acting out of conviction, the monetarist team pursued a strategy which they believed to be correct. Luders was eventually replaced by Carlos Caceres, described by one economist as being "more convinced about the Fund policies than the Fund people are themselves." [40] Caceres reached an agreement with the fund which led to the renegotiation of Chile's debt with U.S. creditors. The plan departed only slightly from previous ones by raising tariffs from 10 to 20 percent to protect foreign exchange reserves. In the main, it was orthodox in its call for reduced fiscal deficits and devaluation of the currency.[41]

The Caceres-IMF plan did nothing to lift Chile out of the most severe depression of the century. GDP declined by 14.3 percent in 1982 and by .8 percent the following year. In the first week of April 1984, Pinochet removed the finance minister, and in doing so, ended the monetarists' nine-year grip on policy formation. Finally, a program of economic reactivation was proposed which included easier credit, labor-intensive public work programs, and higher tariffs. However, by early 1985 it appeared the monetarists had reestablished control with the appointment of Hernan Buchi as finance minister. Though a graduate of Columbia University, Buchi shares the Chicago school's preference for tight control on public sector spending.

Conclusion

Given the state of the economy in the spring of 1984, it was not surprising that Pinochet made some adjustments. But why had the change not come sooner? What were the regime's motivations for dogmatically persisting with policies which had become unacceptable to the dominant capitalist class? It is the contention of this paper that an explanation can be found in the military regime's rigid adherence to the norms and values of the monetarist school. The junta's economic team enjoyed a special partnership with international financial and intellectual elites committed to the monetarist doctrine. Their near-religious devotion to the tenets of the monetarist school made them prized members of this community. The junta's "Chicago Boys" found alternative sources of legitimation for policies which had become unpopular at home with powerful business interests. Despite its narrow political base, the regime was reminded by these economic authorities that its assumptions and proposals for economic recovery were fundamentally correct.

This view departs from both dependency and Marxian analyses. The dependency perspective would argue that Chile's policy choices are conditioned by that country's position in the international system. As an indebted third-world country, it must *reluctantly* adhere to economic formulas prescribed by powerful capitalist institutions (like the IMF) which control the supply of credit.[42] Thus the Pinochet regime could do nothing more than comply with these formulas in a world of limited choice.

However, although there were occasional disagreements about the precise targets (i.e., the proposed fiscal deficits or bank credit ceilings), there were no philosophical disputes between Chile's policymakers and fund officials. On the contrary, the Chileans pursued orthodox monetarist solutions with a vigor never before seen on the Latin American continent. There was a *shared* consensus between like-minded economists in Santiago and abroad that the free-market plan would work.

Within a Marxian framework, governmental activities are directed by the interests of a ruling capitalist class. In the *Communist Manifesto,* Marx wrote "The executive of the modern state is but a committee for managing the common affairs of the whole bourgeoisie."[43] The authorities cannot freely initiate policies, but must follow those prescribed by the class which they serve. In turn, policy-relevant ideas are always those of the ruling class. As Marx states, "The class which is the ruling material force of society is at the same time its ruling intellectual force."[44] State doctrines both reflect and serve the interests of those in control of the means of production. State policies, and policy-relevant ideas, it is argued, are always functional to capitalism.

Chile's dominant class, comprised of a network of powerful family-based groups, profited from the privatization of state-owned firms and the freeing of interest rates. They became close associates of state officials and placed top executives in key posts within the economic and finance ministries and the Central Bank. The personal links between the private and public sector, and more particularly between the dominant capitalist class and the economic ministry, should make Chile an ideal test case for class dominance and a least-likely case for state autonomy. Ralph Miliband argues that the state is primarily the "guardian and protector of the economic interests of the capitalist class," as evidenced by the social bonds between state officials and ruling-class elites.[45] Whereas in other systems, influence must be measured indirectly or presumed, in this situation the visibility of ties between capitalists and public officials should be proof in and of itself. Had the state in fact become an instrument of a ruling class?

Our analysis concludes this was not the case. On the contrary, state managers exhibited both independence and flexibility. They could and did align with capital when it was in their interests to do so; they could just as easily renounce their ties when they wanted to. Fully capable of shifting support groups, the regime found sustenance through its association with the liberal economic community.

Rolf Luders, former minister of economy and finance, entered public office with intentions of satisfying the clans' desires for a state-led economic recovery. Instead, he found himself drawn back into the monetarist formulas of austerity and limited state participation. University of Chicago graduate Alvaro Bardon, for example, had served as Central Bank president and economics under-secretary, but also had interests at stake as chief executive for a large private bank. When the clans asked the state to boost demand and production, he stood in the way. And when the interests of the state and those of the dominant class collided and the regime seized the assets of the nation's largest banks, Bardon was supportive, despite the fact that one of those banks was formerly his own. Bardon's loyalties to the private sector were eclipsed by his allegiances to the monetarist school. Moreover, the chief economic advisor to the junta and principal architect of the liberal plan, Sergio de Castro, had no major business interests to speak of. His ideas were shaped through his academic experiences at the University of Chicago and the Catholic University of Chile.

The Chilean regime found sustenance through its association with the monetarist school. State officials who had personal commitments to the private sector overcame these by reinforcing their ties with the intellectual peers. Their zealous dedication to the "cause" dulled their sensitivities toward their former class allies, while heightening their respect for the norms and values of this economic community. Thus, despite significant setbacks to important fractions of the capitalist class, policymakers found justification for their views within the monetarist school rather than abandon them to placate domestic opponents. Only by recognizing the insertion of elites into this community can one explain the military regime's defiance of the dominant class in the post-coup era.

Notes

1. For references to the links between military governments and free-market policies, see David Collier, ed., *The New Authoritarianism in Latin America*

(Princeton: Princeton University Press, 1979); Alejandro Foxley, *Latin American Experiments in Neoconservative Economics* (Berkeley: University of California Press, 1983); William R. Cline and Sidney Weintraub, eds., *Economic Stabilization in Developing Countries* (Washington, D.C.: The Brookings Institution, 1981).

2. Roberto Frenkel and Guillermo O'Donnell argue that although IMF-styled free-market programs benefit only a narrow portion of the business community, they do protect the interests of the capitalists as a class. See Roberto Frenkel and Guillermo O'Donnell, "The Stabilization Programs of the International Monetary Fund and Their Internal Impacts," in Richard R. Fagen, ed., *Capitalism and the State in U.S.—Latin American Relations* (Stanford: Stanford University Press, 1979), p. 171–216.

3. Karen L. Remmer, "Political Demobilization in Chile, 1973–1978," *Comparative Politics* 12 (April 1980): 288–289.

4. An important proponent of this view is Fernando Dahse, who provided the first detailed account of capital concentration by the economic clans, in Fernando Dahse, *Mapa de la Extrema Riqueza: Los Grupos Económicos y el Proceso de Concentración de Capitales* (Santiago: Editorial Aconcagua, 1979).

5. Ibid., p. 14.

6. Ibid., p. 198.

7. The importance of ideas in social science explanation was advanced by Max Weber in his classic study, *The Protestant Ethic and the Spirit of Capitalism*, trans. by Talcott Parsons (London: George Allen and Unwin Ltd., 1930).

8. Robert C. Tucker, ed., *The Marx-Engels Reader* (New York: W. W. Norton & Co., 1972), pp. 136–138.

9. Karl Mannheim, *Ideology and Utopia: An Introduction to the Sociology of Knowledge* (London: Kegan Paul, Trench, Trubner & Co., 1946), p. 139.

10. Quinton Hoare and Geoffrey Newell Smith, eds. and trans., *Selections from the Prison Notebooks of Antonio Gramsci* (New York: International Publishers, 1972), p. 12.

11. Robert K. Merton, *Social Theory and Social Structure* (New York: The Free Press, 1968), pp. 353–354.

12. The most important monetary model for balance of payments adjustment was formulated by an IMF researcher in the mid-1950s. See J. J. Polak, "Monetary Analysis of Income Formation and Payments Problems," *IMF Staff Papers* 6 (November, 1957): 1–50.

13. Latin America Bureau, *Chile: the Pinochet Decade: The Rise and Fall of the Chicago Boys* (London: Latin America Bureau, 1983), pp. 56–57.

14. Pilar Vergara, *Auge y Caída del Neoliberalismo en Chile: Un Estudio Sobre la Evolución Ideológica del Régimen Militar,* Documento de Trabajo Numero 216 (Santiago: Facultad Latinoamericana de Ciencias Sociales, 1984), pp. 65–66.

15. Republic of Chile, *Declaration of Principles of the Chilean Government* (1974), p. 31.

16. Ibid., p. 31.

17. Ibid., p. 36.

18. Statistics on inflation, production, and unemployment for those months cited are found in Vergara, *Auge y Caída,* p. 89; reserve information in International Monetary Fund, *International Financial Statistics Yearbook,* July 1984, p. 228; deficit figures from República de Chile, Banco Central, *Indicadores: 1960–1982* (Santiago: Banco Central, 1984), p. 44.

19. Fiscal and GDP data are from the República de Chile, Banco Central, *Indica-*

dores: 1960–1982; inflation figures from International Monetary Fund: *International Financial Statistics Yearbook, 1984.*

20. Beginning in 1977, the government opted for a declining rate of devaluation, and in 1979 fixed the peso at thirty-nine to the dollar. This was a controversial measure (taken by Sergio de Castro) aimed at reducing the expansionary effects of export surpluses and capital inflows (since a less valuable dollar would buy fewer pesos upon entering the Chilean economy).

21. *Fortune,* 2 November 1981, pp. 138, 140.

22. These figures and a detailed analysis of U.S. bank support for the junta are found in Isabel Letelier and Michael Moffitt, "How the American Banks Keep the Chilean Junta Going," *Business and Society Review* 29 (Spring 1979): 42–51.

23. República de Chile, Banco Central, *Indicadores: 1960–1982,* p. 67.

24. *Latin America Regional Report: Southern Cone,* 18 December, 1981, p. 7.

25. Carlos F. Diaz-Alejandro, "Southern Cone Stabilization Plans," in *Economic Stabilization in Developing Countries,* ed. William R. Cline and Sidney Weintraub (Washington, D.C.: The Brookings Institution, 1981), p. 137.

26. Alejandro Foxley, *Latin American Experiments in Neo-conservative Economics* (Berkeley: University of California Press, 1983), p. 45.

27. Maurice Zeitlin and Richard Earl Ratcliff, "Research Methods for the Analysis of the Internal Structure of Dominant Classes: The Case of Landlords and Capitalists in Chile," *Latin America Research Review* 10 (Fall 1975): 5–61.

28. Fernando Dahse, *Mapa de la Extrema Riqueza,* p. 193; *Latin America Regional Report: Southern Cone,* 4 February 1983, p. 2.

29. *El Mercurio,* 3 November 1979, p. 43.

30. *Forbes,* 7 December 1981, p. 42.

31. External debt figures are found in *Wall Street Journal,* 18 January 1982, p. 1.

32. Latin America Bureau, *Chile: The Pinochet Decade,* p. 101.

33. Ibid., p. 101.

34. Since their fortunes during the first seven years after the coup had been tied to the regime's monetarist practices, it is not surprising that the clans remained ideological allies of the junta in the short term.

35. Rolf Luders's analysis of the economy was made in Republic of Chile, *Towards Economic Recovery in Chile: A Report on the Economy and Public Finances of Chile by the Minister of Economy and Finance, Mr. Rolf Luders,* December 1983, pp. 4–6.

36. That this was Luders's personal choice was confirmed for me in an interview with a former top-ranking official of the Javier Vial Group. In addition, this same official was completely surprised by and could not explain Luders's decision to break up his own company, having expected the economics and finance minister to take less drastic steps.

37. *Latin America Weekly Report,* 21 January 1983, p. 1.

38. Despite Sergio de Castro's resignation in April 1982 in opposition to a proposed devaluation of the peso, the Chicago influence prevailed within the economic and finance ministries. No plans were made for demand stimulation, wage increases, tariff protection, or similar measures which normally signal a break with orthodox monetarist solutions. De Castro's replacement was Sergio de la Cuadra, former Central Bank president and a graduate of the University of Chicago.

39. These statements were made by Hipólito Lagos, head of the Banco O'Higgins, in *Euromoney,* February 1983, p. 62.

40. *Latin America Regional Report: Southern Cone,* 18 November 1983.

41. *New York Times,* 24 March 1983, p. D 13.

42. A dependency approach to international finance and the third world is taken in Cheryl Payer, *The Debt Trap: The IMF and the Third World* (New York: Monthly Review Press, 1975).

43. Karl Marx, "Communist Manifesto," in *The Marx-Engels Reader,* ed. Robert C. Tucker (New York: W. W. Norton & Co., 1972), p. 337.

44. Karl Marx, "The German Ideology," in *The Marx-Engels Reader,* pp. 136–137. In more modern Marxian treatments, the state is granted relative autonomy, meaning it has the independence to occasionally oppose special interests to protect the general and long-term welfare of the capitalist class. But its independence is compromised since the state is thought to be imbedded in a system which by definition guarantees the well-being of the dominant class. The case for relative autonomy is made in Nicos Poulantzas, *Political Power and Social Classes* (London: Humanities Press, 1968).

45. Ralph Miliband, "The Capitalist State: Reply to Nicos Poulantzas," *New Left Review* 59 (January/February 1970), p. 57. For the complete analysis, see Ralph Miliband, *The State in Capitalist Society: The Analysis of the Western System of Power* (London: Quartet Books, 1973).

Peter S. Cleaves
and
Henry Pease García

State Autonomy and Military Policy Making

Policy making in military regimes compared with that in institutional democracies generally takes place within a smaller circle of governing elites and amid greater secrecy. Nevertheless, all leaders, the military executive included, must abide by similar rules when designing policy: they must maintain the governing coalition and mediate pressures from relevant social groups. Military leaders may find it to their advantage to open up the policy-making process, either by calling upon the expertise of state bureaucrats or by soliciting the advice of class spokesmen. These tactics help improve the policies' technical features before promulgation and enhance their chances for popular acceptance afterwards. This chapter examines President Juan Velasco Alvarado's skillful management of a polity that defied the usual limits on state autonomy and produced important changes in Peruvian society. The Velasco regime (1968–1975) utilized an image of unified armed forces and the policy-making process itself to advance social reforms that weakened the dominant class and significantly increased the power of the state apparatus. At the same time, the regime suffered politically from internal disunity, incoherent economic policies, and a lack of popular support. Opposition forces in the society eventually regrouped and succeeded in reducing the regime's autonomy.

To maintain a high degree of policy-making discretion, Velasco sought to insulate the governing elite from interfering pressures. The regime propagated the myth of the unity of the armed forces, repressed unruly groups and radical spokesmen of the dominant class, and co-opted many of Peru's intellectual and technical specialists, while keeping them at a prudent distance from decision centers. After experiencing early defeats, many economic elites, fearful of further change, tried to penetrate the governing group by means of family contacts, well-placed bureaucrats, and editorials and advertisements in the national newspapers. They also advised against international loans and engaged in economic noncooperation locally. Eventually, they succeeded in gaining at least partial representation for their interests, and consequently, a silent political struggle broke out at the summit of power between military leaders committed to reform and their more conservative colleagues. Toward 1974 the unity of the government started to crumble. The regime of Francisco Morales Bermúdez, taking power in August 1975, gave full access to spokesmen from the dominant classes, shifted the ideology of government to the right, and restored government unity after expelling military radicals. State autonomy was notably reduced during "Phase Two" of the military government (1975–1980). The generals prepared to return government to traditional civilian parties after fulfilling their purpose of "reforming the reforms" in order to render them inoffensive to the then most powerful groups in society.

The first section of this chapter presents background on the crisis that preceded the emergence of the Velasco regime. The military's position in the correlation of forces at the time helps explain the degree of autonomy it achieved. Subsequent sections describe the policy-making styles of the Velasco and Morales Bermúdez governments and provide empirical information on the changes in several variables: state power, state unity, the unity of the dominant class, and its relation with other social forces. By way of conclusion, we put forth various observations on the political implications of this overall experience.

The Capitalist State and Relative Autonomy

The relationship between class and state differentiates among theories of the modern state. Some theories have not dismissed simplistic propositions that consider the state a servile instrument of the economic interests of the dominant class. Other theories persist in conceiving the state as an entity that exists *above* social classes or a juridical abstraction that is somehow separate from class interests. Policy-making studies, however, depart from a prior analysis of the function and role of the state in a given social formation. Their value lies not just in understanding the process of policy formulation and decision making but also in clarifying the relationship between the state and dominant classes at certain historical moments.

Recent contributions to Marxist theory have elaborated on the classical works of Marx, Engels, and Gramsci by describing the capitalist state as a cohesive element in the unity of a social formation.[1] The capitalist state distinguishes itself from other types of states (based on the divine right of kings or a hierarchical distinction between citizens and noncitizens) because specific class domination is absent or obscured in the workings of formal institutions. The capitalist state is thus a complex web of class relations, not only ideological but also political. Therefore, the administration of power requires a combination of mechanisms to achieve consensus or apply coercion, joined together in distinct ways depending on each social formation. Gramsci's main contribution was the concept of hegemony, which stressed the importance of the governing class's ideological predominance over subsidiary or allied classes; he also showed how this relationship is maintained by means of coercion.[2] Hegemony (consensus) and coercion (dictatorship) combine to lend consistency to the capitalist state. When the state relies mainly on coercion (such as in typical dictatorships), it is usually entering or leaving a crisis that has brought into question the state's ability to unify the interests of the dominant classes, their fractions, and allies.

As Poulantzas writes, the way to avoid conceiving of the state as a simple instrument of the dominant class is to stress the "self-unity" or the "relative autonomy" of institutionalized political power.[3] This cohesive factor impedes competitive relations among subgroups in the power bloc from leading to extreme fragmentation or repartition of institutionalized power. To achieve this level of cohesion, the state needs and attains a "relative autonomy from the classes or fractions of the power bloc and, by extension, of its allies or support groups."[4]

This theoretical elaboration reaffirms the class character of the modern state but discards the idea of a state totally subject to a dominant class. It also assumes that part of the unifying function allows the state at times to confront directly the interests of bourgeois groups.[5] The political writings of Marx, especially *The Eighteenth Brumaire of Louis Bonaparte,* suggest that the dominant class can be fragmented, particularly when it intervenes in politics. Marx (as well as Gramsci), however, referred to relative autonomy only in certain situations, such as in an equilibrium of social forces or a tumultuous political upheaval, when an impasse in the power bloc leads to extreme cases of state autonomy.[6] Poulantzas goes one step further by proposing that relative autonomy is a characteristic of capitalist states in general, without which they could not achieve self-unity in their institutionalized political power. From this perspective, relative autonomy is understood to be present in all situations, not just in times of equilibrium or impasse. The margin of autonomy varies according to the correlation of social forces and their weight in the political arena. Specific instances of relative autonomy are thus best analyzed in the context of the traits of each social formation, the organization of the state, and the orientations and interplay of its various subunits, including, as in Peru, the armed forces.[7]

An important consideration in studying state autonomy in authoritarian systems is the unity of the state apparatus. A state riddled by disputes over doctrine, policy options, or personal loyalties cannot enjoy high autonomy for two reasons. First, these divisions prevent a consolidation of institutional objectives because the state becomes little more than an amalgam of factions. Second, a fragmented state increases the number of entry points for private sector representatives who can exploit the state's internal disharmony to their own advantage. If these representatives are able to gain allies throughout the state apparatus, the margin of autonomy declines noticeably. Both tendencies were evident in Peru after the midpoint of the Velasco regime.

In normal instances, policy-making styles vary depending upon the degree of state autonomy, the peculiar mixture of formal state institutions that may exist, such as a parliament and a judiciary, and the nature of the crisis that gave rise to the regime. When high relative autonomy exists, the state should be able to formulate and execute measures that are different from, indeed contrary to, those proposed by classes or fractions in the power bloc.[8] Under conditions of low autonomy, state officials would remain accessible to forces from all corners; policy options might spring from any of a number of groups interested in the issue area. Normally, economic interest groups work out their differences in the private arena and join forces to pressure the government toward a specific policy. The situation is reversed when state autonomy is high and the governing nucleus can maintain its distance from other power groups. Leadership makes judgments on the nature of the problem, checks its observations with sympathetic technocrats and ideologues, and dictates orders from the top. To carry out its policies, the state uses the support it has from one of the pillars of the executive branch of government (in Peru's case, the armed forces) and proceeds with the passive acceptance of subordinated groups.

Two interesting aspects of the Velasco government were its high autonomy and its efforts to use that autonomy to increase state power. It is important not to confuse relative autonomy with the power of the state, however, particularly in the economic sphere. The two are obviously interrelated, but the distinction is necessary, because high degrees of autonomy do not always correspond to high degrees of power. Thus, the Brazilian state in 1964 could be powerful and nonetheless display little autonomy. And the Chilean state under Allende could be weak and highly autonomous. In the Peruvian case, the autonomy achieved by Velasco in 1968 was sufficiently high to force a partial reshuffling of the power bloc. At the same time, the state's economic power was quite weak and it strengthened itself, at least in relative terms, through the expropriation of property belonging to the oligarchy. In the context of a new correlation of forces, both nationally and internationally, state autonomy had declined considerably by 1975, despite the fact that the state was manifestly more powerful in the economy.

In considering the Peruvian experiment, it is important to remember that Peru's social formation is peripheral capitalism, and in 1968, neither the state nor civil society was highly institutionalized, which indicates that noncapitalist traits were to be found at the time. The armed services, which throughout the republican period had frequently headed governments, were by far the most stable and consolidated organizations. The prevalence of authoritarianism in the society, the past frequency of dictatorships, and the exclusion of vast sectors of the population from the political system facilitated a high degree of relative autonomy for the state when the power bloc lacked unity of command. Thus, the political characteristics of the pre-1968 state and the situation in which the military regime came to power help explain its possibilities for action.

The Revolutionary Government of the Armed Forces

The 1968 military coup was the culmination of the crisis of Peru's so-called oligarchic state, a form of domination that traces its origins to the nineteenth century and reached its peak in the 1950's.[9] Members of the power bloc during this period were social classes and fractions controlling large plantations on the coast, *latifundistas* in the middle and high sierra (whose local power was based on the persistence of noncapitalist relations of production), and large banking and insurance concerns. These fractions, together with large merchandizers, tended to resist capitalist modernization, although they had begun to diversify into industry. Important foreign investors, particularly from the United States, controlled such natural resources as mining and petroleum, and transnational industries had penetrated the local economy after the Second World War. The hegemonic fraction of the power bloc, however, was made up of the agricultural exporters (denominated "sugar barons" by the APRA in the 1930s). After 1950, the growth and dynamism of modern industrial sectors and the demands of the middle classes posed serious challenges to this hegemony. The crisis of the oligarchic state was characterized by a decline in the cohesiveness of the power bloc and was reflected in successive compromise regimes incapable of articulating a consistent polity.

Tensions in the system also occurred outside the power bloc. Modernization in manufacturing, construction, fishing, and mining concerns increased the size and weight of the working class and generated important sectors of small and middle-sized enterprises. After 1960, the oligarchy was less able to control the working class movement. The decline of the semifeudal latifundia led to a rupture in the rural economy and provoked out-migration, rapid urbanization, and an end to traditional rural isolation. In the 1950's, peasants had a significant impact on the political scene by invading land, forming unions, and demanding more humane working conditions; in response, the state provided social services to divert lower-class pressures. From 1930, faced with the growth of APRA and the socialists, the oligarchy had reverted to repressive military dictatorships to maintain itself in power. Later, it attempted to achieve national con-sensus among the lower and middle classes through the construction of public works and the provision of social services. By the 1960s, such techniques were no longer sufficient to maintain its dominant position.

Great national enthusiasm accompanied the inauguration of President Fernando Belaúnde Terry in 1963. The political alliance between the Acción Popular and Christian Democratic parties was a new attempt to satisfy the most pressing demands of the popular sectors. Agrarian and industrial reform, reorganization of the state bureaucracy, educational reform, and defense of democratic liberties also appealed broadly to the middle classes and were espoused by their political parties. Spokesmen for the modern wing of the dominant class also proposed economic measures favoring its interests, such as a halt to devaluations that preju-diced industry and favored those oligarchic sectors dealing in exports. The emergent industrial bourgeoisie also urged the creation of an activist state that would nurture industrialization. The challenge to oligarchic domina-tion transformed itself into an overt threat when a guerrilla movement appeared in 1965. These insurgents, however, were rapidly eliminated by the armed forces, thus restoring the belief of the dominant class that it could avoid change. Moreover, the ability of the lower class to mobilize was hampered by the state's willingness to make partial concessions to its demands and by close military monitoring of organizing activities of the Aprista party.

Consequently, during the Belaúnde presidency, the oligarchic sectors firmly and systematically resisted reform. In alliance with the old Aprista party and supporters of ex-dictator Manuel Odría, they controlled parlia-ment and were able to turn back Belaúnde's reformist initiatives. By the end of his presidential administration, Belaúnde no longer represented a force for change but sought instead to execute public works projects, a superannuated means of obtaining consensus in light of the seriousness of national problems. In the last months of his government, widespread public discontent was generated by the suspicion that the president had caved in to United States pressure and come to an agreement that favored the International Petroleum Company. The weakness of the political party system impeded a resolution of the crisis through the parliament or judiciary.

Into this scene marched the Revolutionary Government of the Armed Forces, led by General Juan Velasco Alvarado. On October 3, 1968, the event seemed like just another *golpe,* but the regime legitimized itself soon afterward by nationalizing the IPC oil wells, installations, and refinery. Encouraged by acclaim for this move, the government confronted and rapidly displaced those oligarchic fractions occupying the most important seats of power. It undertook a serious agrarian reform, which had been frustrated during the previous regime, and expropriated in one act the large sugar-exporting plantations. Gradually, the government nationalized major components of the banking and commercial sectors and took over the traditional latifundia of the sierra. Their owners, by being "masters of lives and haciendas," had been the local constables for the system of oligarchic domination by controlling the peasant masses. The regime also strengthened the power of the state in the economy by nationalizing many Peruvian and foreign firms involved in natural resource extraction, basic industry, and the provision of services.

The content of Velasco's policies emerged from an interpretation of Peru's socioeconomic problems prevalent in the political community in the 1960s. The analysis, molded by middle-class civilian intellectuals and technocrats who were influenced by dependency theory, was picked up by the military and propagated in part through academic courses at the CAEM. The underlying principles were that Peru's underdevelopment stemmed from disproportionate economic and political power in the hands of an anachronistic upper class, lack of national integration, a weak state, and inordinate dependence on the international market. Moreover, the major reforms undertaken later (in agriculture, industry, education, natural resources, public administration, etc.) had been central elements of the political party platforms on the left, including the Communist party. Some military men adopted these points of view after fighting the 1965 guerrilla movement and observing at close quarters the defects of the traditional order they were supposed to defend. Broader segments of the military justified their new role on the principle of national defense and on the thesis, which gained ascendancy during the Vietnam War, that internal security was precarious as long as a country was underdeveloped.[10] The post-1968 reforms thus derived from an ideological framework that included concepts of national defense and class conciliation, significantly influenced by the middle sectors who made their presence felt in this regime as they had over the previous decades in molding this way of thinking.

The main support for the military regime came from the armed forces themselves. In the beginning, the regime took advantage of the general passiveness of the society, which was a by-product of the longevity of the oligarchic state, and the disenchantment of the majority of the population with Belaúnde's reform program. The 1968 coup, however, cannot be described as a concerted effort by the military as an institution. The initiative for the takeover came from Velasco, who at the time was ranking head of the army and of the joint chiefs of staff, and from a group of colonels who made up the nucleus of the new government. The formal summit of power also consisted of the revolutionary junta, made up of the commanding officers of the three branches of the armed services, who were supposedly endowed with governing authority over regime initiatives.

The military reforms brought about an accelerated reshuffling of the classes and fractions in the power bloc, within a framework of class reconciliation of the groups deemed to have legitimate roles in national development. The result was virtually to exclude the oligarchy (agricultural exporters, traditional landowners and bankers, and large merchants) from power and enhance the relative status of modern industrialists. These changes, however, came about not under the direction of the industrial bourgeoisie, but under military leaders who forged a state that could intervene significantly in the economy. Because of the degree of autonomy achieved during the initial period, the state was able to impose its will on various sectors of the industrial class. By 1975, the state sector controlled agriculture (in that the peasant cooperatives were under the strong influence of state officials and a great number of middle-sized properties had also been expropriated), important manufacturing industries, a large proportion of the country's natural resources in copper (Cerro de Pasco) and iron (Marcona), and the whole of the oil industry (Petroperú). State agencies also managed all essential public services (such as electrical power, telephones, and railroad transport), and the state acted as the principal intermediary for Peruvian exports. The result was a new form of Peruvian state that implied significant changes in the relationship between economics and politics and a different configuration of forces in the power bloc.

Nationalization and property reform were ideological catchwords of the 1960s and were at the core of Velasco's plan to transform Peruvian society. The government expected to move toward a system of modern, state-directed capitalism that reconciled the interests of new economic classes with those of the popular sectors. The regime was not, however, able to devise a program that was acceptable to both groups, for the orthodox economic policies pursued by Velasco's finance minister, Francisco Morales Bermúdez, worked at cross-purposes. The government substantially increased public investment while attempting to provide tax incentives, but private investors were wary. The industrialization policy corresponded to the import-substitution model and was expected to garner support from national and foreign entrepreneurs, but they too were less than cooperative. Although the regime's rhetoric implied a rejection of capitalism, its economic decisions did not replace the prevailing productive structure or alter substantially the logic of capital accumulation. A form of state capitalism was consolidated during "Phase One" of the military regime, but conditions did not exist to assure its stability. Although many observers felt that the economic measures were the next step in a continuing process of capitalist modernization, the Velasco government soon became engaged in serious conflicts with modern fractions of the bourgeoisie that needed to be resolved prior to the inception of a stable form of political domination.

Velasco demonstrated a high degree of state autonomy during his confrontations with modern industrial sectors. At the beginning, the groups most negatively affected by the regime's policies were members of the traditional oligarchy. Later the reforms impinged on the rest of the agrarian bourgeoisie, including middle-sized landowners, and industrial sectors that, although not expropriated, clashed with the regime over the Industrial Community, restrictions on firing of workers, and measures to increase the state's role in the economy. The government offered industrialists a series of generous short-term economic incentives while it continued its reform program, ignored industrialists' complaints, and even deported some outspoken businessmen. From 1970 to 1975, these sectors engaged the government in a succession of tense confrontations that reverberated in the armed forces and eventually eroded the regime's main base of support.[11] The attacks were not carried out in unison because some industrialists appeared to accept conciliatory overtures from the government. The fact was, however, that the protests of the industrial sectors did not cease until the end of Phase One of the military government and the ouster of Velasco. Under Morales, the situation was reversed. These fractions in the power bloc gained ascendancy and were able to obtain considerable satisfaction for their demands during the second phase.

The Velasco government was not an accidental detour in the evolution of Peruvian politics, however, but rather a crucial link between one period and another. It was a natural consequence of a long history of gradual though significant changes in the economy that had not yet had their impact on the makeup of the power bloc. The military reform program reassembled the country's main power contenders and stimulated the emergence of a new dominant class. That the industrial bourgeoisie had no program of its own helps explain the wide autonomy that the Velasco regime enjoyed once it liquidated the traditional agricultural exporters. As we discuss later, the conflicts within the military government after 1972 were suggestive of the contradictory aims of different fractions of this emerging dominant class.

In summary, the Velasco government enjoyed relatively high autonomy soon after its inception, and by 1973 the oligarchic purge was almost complete. Its unity, however, eroded concurrently with the reconstitution of a power bloc that allowed the country's bourgeoisie to take the initiative in designing a new form of political domination. Industrial, commercial, middle-sized agricultural, and professional groups and the Aprista, Acción Popular, and Christian Popular political parties never completely buckled under the military; even popular groups participated in strikes and showed growing opposition to the regime. Velasco's refusal to admit the existence of an impending economic crisis and his reckless disregard of a threatening international situation involving Peru, Chile, and Bolivia contributed to the creation of a new coalition of forces that agreed at least on the need for his overthrow. In Phase Two, faced with pressure from powerful civilian groups, the military government saw its relative autonomy decline as it tried to stay on top of a deteriorating economic situation and a severely split governing elite. To satisfy the insistent demands of the dominant class (particularly local industrialists and foreign capital), the Morales Bermúdez government shifted to the right in 1976 and tried to squash the political protests of popular sectors.[12]

Table 1 illustrates the degree of overlap betweeen state policies and the interests of powerful and weak civilian groups during the two phases of the military government.[13] This table is meant to serve two purposes: it points out the basic positions of groups that participated in the debate over various state initiatives; and it provides an idea of the degree of conflict between powerful groups and Velasco and the more harmonious relationship between these groups and Morales Bermúdez. The table suggests that the state under Velasco was considerably more autonomous than under Morales. Many more of Velasco's policies were detrimental to the dominant class than corresponded to its interests. Under Morales, policies were more likely to benefit the powerful than to counter their interests; only one clearly favored a lower-class group. The table helps clarify why traditional power holders, although not totally enchanted with Morales Bermúdez were considerably more at ease with him in the presidential chair than with his predecesor. In line with the definitions presented earlier in this chapter, we conclude that the state under Velasco enjoyed relatively high autonomy, whereas under Morales Bermúdez it was characterized by moderate autonomy.

Autonomy and Policy Making

Between 1968 and 1977, Peruvian governments passed more than 4,000 laws. The content of these decrees and the style used to formulate them were generally different under Velasco and Morales Bermúdez. Major policy initiatives under Velasco were in the spheres of foreign affairs, agriculture (agrarian reform), economic growth, industrialization, natural resources (including fishing and forestry), the mass media, and property reform. Under Morales Bermúdez, important decrees involved devaluations, economic measures pertaining to wages and prices (the stabilization package), weakening the industrial community requirement, rescinding workers' job security, and military hardware purchases.[14] Despite this multitude of cases, few studies exist of the policy-making process, par-

Table 1. Group Interests and Public Policy, 1968–1980

	Powerful Groups							Weak Groups		
	Importers-Exporters	*Industrialists*	*Military*	*Church*	*Foreign Capitalists*	*Bureaucracy*	*Medium-Sized Farmers*	*Peasants*	*Workers*	*Shantytown Dwellers*
VELASCO PERIOD										
Industrial policies	—	N	—	—	N	Y	—	—	Y	—
Foreign policy	N	N	—	—	N	—	—	—	—	—
Agrarian policies	N	Y	Y	—	N	—	N	Y	Y	Y
Education policy	—	N	—	N	—	—	—	—	Y	Y
SINAMOS activities	N	N	N	—	N	—	N	—	N	Y
State growth	N	N	Y	—	N	Y	—	—	—	—
Press reform	N	N	—	—	N	Y	N	Y	Y	—
Social property	N	N	—	—	N	Y	—	—	Y	Y
Urban land	—	N	—	—	—	—	N	Y	—	Y
MORALES BERMÚDEZ PERIOD										
Devaluations	—	N	—	—	Y	—	N	N	N	N
Foreign policy	Y	Y	—	—	Y	—	—	—	—	—
Social property	—	Y	—	—	Y	N	Y	—	N	N
Industrial policies	Y	Y	—	—	Y	N	—	—	N	—
Labor policies	Y	Y	—	—	—	—	Y	N	N	N
Withdrawal of food subsidies	—	N	—	N	—	—	Y	Y	N	N
Military hardware	N	N	Y	—	—	—	—	—	—	—

Y = group interests generally consistent with policy goals
N = group interests generally inconsistent with policy goals
— = policy goals are irrelevant or ambiguous for group interests

tially because, in the absence of a parliament, most decisions were taken behind closed doors.

Decision making in Peru at this time was centralized in a governing elite. Under Velasco, this elite was comprised of the president, the revolutionary junta, and the heads of ministries, who were grouped together in the cabinet. This governing elite was dependent on a broad consensus within the military establishment, which needed to feel it had a voice in the system. Each of the ministries was designated to one of the three branches of the armed services. All ministers were either generals (including the air force) or admirals in active service appointed by the president from a list of three names provided by the commander of the respective service branch. Until 1975, the cabinet encompassed both the president and the members of the junta and was empowered to debate and vote on all laws, a responsibility that diluted the authority of the junta. Under Morales Bermúdez an important change occurred at the summit of power—the junta was separated from the cabinet and awarded authority over the most important political and military decisions. This move placed the three heads of the armed services on an equal footing at a moment when divisions among military leaders were prevalent. The new distinction between the cabinet and the junta was also a principal cause of the stagnation in the decision-making process during the first months of phase two, and it marked the beginning of the turn to the right. Morales acted more like the president of the junta in this context, as opposed to Velasco, who was clearly the head of the cabinet.

The summit of power retained maximum formal and real power over the direction of government and the state administration. The principal policy-making parties under Velasco were the Comité de Asesoramiento de la Presidencia (COAP), the sectoral ministries within their own domains, ministries advising on the policies in other sectors, and "miscellaneous consultants." The most influential of these consultative groups were the general staffs and intelligence services of each branch of the armed forces. The COAP was made up of about thirteen colonels under the direction of an army general who had the rank of a state minister and the authority to request the floor (but not to vote) in cabinet meetings. COAP acted as the president's staff and was the functional equivalent of a parliamentary commission that coordinated laws before presenting them for a final vote.

Reshaping the state in its own image, the military split the public bureaucracy into a large number of sectoral ministries. In the cabinet meetings, each minister was recognized as the virtual authority in his field and his wishes were generally accepted. When a minister was successfully challenged (mainly by the president, and sometimes by the COAP), he generally resigned and was often replaced by a more malleable personality. The various ministries and principal public offices were permanently assigned to the three armed services, ensuring a certain continuity in the sectoral split but giving the internal conflicts wider effects. The ministry with the greatest influence on policy originating elsewhere was the Economy and Finance (because of the tax, budgetary, and foreign currency implications of each policy). Over time, intersectoral coordination became a problem and new "horizontal" agencies were created, whose directors had the right to attend cabinet meetings. Despite their integrating functions, these agencies did not substantively alter the inertia of sectoral prerogatives.

Miscellaneous individuals were often consulted during policy formulation, especially on complex or momentous issues. These outside individuals helped advise the COAP (which called together ad hoc task forces whose members often served *ad honorem*), ministers, and sometimes the president directly. They were generally professionals in various fields, technocrats, high-level public servants, and, less frequently, class spokesmen, either from the unions or interest groups. It is important to remember that because the regime defined itself strictly as the government of the armed forces (the strength of this sentiment was one of its main props), the government elite always kept these civilian consultants at arm's length.

Behind the scenes, various elements of the armed forces intervened both subtly and more overtly in policy formulation. Out of the public eye, officers made known their preferences on policy alternatives to their comrades-in-arms holding political posts. Ranking military officers on the general staffs and intelligence services participated formally in the policy-making process by submitting their opinions on particular issues or joining special investigative commissions. Each ministry had its own version of a mini-COAP to advise the minister, the most important of which were in the Ministry of Agriculture, the National Planning Institute, and SIN-AMOS. The civilians appointed to these groups had little independent power and needed to rely on well-placed military officers to exert influence. The appointment of civilian ministers of state under Morales Bermú-dez did not substantively alter this power balance, except in the economic sphere and during the last few months of the military government. Class spokesmen and the large newspapers also contributed to the tone and content of policy debate.

The regimes displayed not one, but four main policy-making patterns; these can be classified from the most closed to the most open. In the first, policy decisions originated in COAP on instructions from the president and his closest advisors, and after a cabinet session, the legislation was promulgated as a *fait accompli*. This procedure was characteristic primarily of Velasco; for example, the parties affected by the 1969 press law were not privy to the legislative deliberations and became aware of the government's intentions virtually upon publication of the law.

In the second pattern, policy suggestions originated in the ministries and were submitted to COAP and the president for approval, without consultation with representatives of other governmental and nongovernmental jurisdictions. The laws governing currency and the banks, devaluation, the 1974 press expropriation, urban land reform, and the industrial sector were enacted in this manner. Again, Velasco was more prone than Morales Bermúdez to utilize this more restricted policy-making procedure.

The third pattern of policy making saw initial drafts originate in the ministry and the COAP "coordinate" their circulation among other governmental agencies for suggestions, invite the reserved comments of preselected miscellaneous individuals, and draw up the final legislation.

The coordination procedure—described in Directive 3B of 1969—was recognized as the model policy-making formula, for the large majority of laws abided by it. Most of the Velasco administration's coordinated legislation was of little import, however, with the exception of the Industrial Community Law, the nationalization of the fishing industry, and the founding of SINAMOS.

The fourth method of policy making involved submitting a measure to broader public or private scrutiny. Under Velasco, civic minded individuals sent written observations to the local press (which published some of them), discussing the native communities' jungle law and social property; these critiques appeared in print before the laws were promulgated. The educational reform was also debated more openly, and a constituent assembly was democratically elected to draw up university statutes (which, subsequently, were not ratified by the regime).

These policy-making patterns refer to formal decisions that became public decrees. Often, however, events manipulated prior to the issuance of a decree were equally important. The forced resignation of a leading political figure might pave the way for a new law, as did the departures of Minister José Benavides prior to the Agrarian Reform Law, Minister Luis Vargas Caballero prior to the expropriation of the press, and ministers Jorge Fernández Maldonado, Miguel de la Flor, and Enrique Gallegos just prior to the government's turn to the right. In these cases, powerful members at the summit of power were able to exert their influence on the direction of government without participating in the nuts and bolts of drafting precise legislation. The most significant example of this informal policy-making process took place in the period preceding the overthrow of President Velasco on August 29, 1975. Fervent activity by class spokesmen and other pressure groups set the stage for Velasco's ouster.

High autonomy was most characteristic of the policy-making process during the early years of the Velasco government and was concomitant with closed policy making, the absence of challengers to regime authority, and success of initial reform measures—the expropriation of IPC and the large sugar plantations, for example, which required secrecy to be effective. When the Velasco regime was sufficiently confident of the passivity of potential opposition and quick action was necessary, policy continued to be made in the inner circles of government and implemented rapidly. When legislative initiatives required a great deal of technical expertise and were the exclusive domain of one ministry, they were drafted in the sector and approved by the president on the advice of COAP. The regime followed Directive 3B when potential opposition was of such magnitude that countervailing opinions had to be completely aired, or when the law required the collaboration of a number of ministries or groups for its implementation. By ostensibly sharing authority, the directive allowed the regime to co-opt both bureaucratic representatives and civilian elements whose support (or neutrality) it needed to proceed with its overall plan.

Many observers, however, have commented on the hollow nature of this participation. Over time, the policy-making style moved perceptibly from secrecy toward fuller public debate. The regime showed a trend toward airing its structural reforms more widely before instituting them when it sensed its power and unity were on the decline or when the reform's impact lay far in the future and the regime could score ideological points while minimizing the antagonism of opposing groups.[15]

The early period of the Morales Bermúdez government, dubbed "spring politics," was characterized by a broadside attack by spokesmen of the dominant class on the armed forces and governing elite. This attack placed the government on the defensive and reduced its leeway for negotiation. Morales Bermúdez did not resist the attempt by local and foreign private interests to penetrate decision-making circles. During this second phase of military government, the COAP and the National Planning Institute were downgraded. Although the military retained the prerogative of making and announcing decisions, Morales conferred extensively with industrialists, officials of the International Monetary Fund and World Bank, executives of transnational corporations, and political party leaders, who were much better organized than they had been during Phase One. Government policy soon resembled their list of priorities: for economic elites, the priorities were to repress strikes, permit the firing of workers, enervate the industrial community, and undercut social property; for political leaders of the bourgeoisie, they were the promise of elections and the forced retirement of military radicals; and for the International Monetary Fund, implement an austerity plan or face national bankruptcy. Meanwhile, the government met head-on the organized popular sectors that were angered by regressive economic policies. The state was powerful in the economy, in its repressive capabilities, in its control of almost all forms of mass communication (newspapers, radio, and television), but the relative autonomy of this government vis-á-vis the newly reconstituted dominant classes was clearly reduced. Earlier, state power had helped buffer the regime from the interests of these groups, but eventually, in the absence of popular support, it exacerbated the regime's general isolation, which was fully manifest by 1977.[16]

State Unity

We can now address in more detail the subjects of unity, relative power, state autonomy, and policy making. The first issue, state unity, involves that of the governing elite, the cabinet—which retained legislative and executive functions—the leadership of the armed forces, and the bureaucratic apparatus. The October 1968 coup was promoted by a nucleus of officers close to Velasco that collaborated in the planning and execution of the overthrow of Belaúnde. This nucleus was not a full-fledged government faithfully representing the three service branches, but a team of like-minded army officers who surrounded the president and gradually moved into important jobs in the government.[17]

It soon became apparent, however, that there was no substantive agreement among military officers about the policies the government would undertake. The summit of power was heterogeneous, and most of its members had been weaned on the militant anticommunism of the 1950s; these officers were prepared to be the protectors of the established order and not the promoters of social change. Over time, it was possible to differentiate between those military officers who participated actively in the coup, or accorded the revolution unquestioning loyalty, and those who adjusted to the new situation and sought a position of influence within it. Some members of the armed forces wished to mend fences with the oligarchy and the IPC; others were intransigent about ending their dominant role in the economy. Some military men wished to promote industrial development through a strong state, and others were more attracted to a liberal economic model. A few officers totally rejected capitalism and spoke freely of socialism, whereas officers sympathetic to the private sector beat their breasts furiously whenever investors complained about insufficient guarantees for capital. Some officers, inculcated with elitist and hierarchical principles, were repelled by government rhetoric that exalted the popular sectors. Others, flattered by crowd applause but fearful of lower-class power, preferred to supervise and manipulate popular participation through state-controlled organizations. Over time, some officers sought ways to facilitate popular participation (within the limits posed by the regime's ideology and military base), which would stymie their colleagues' corporatist advances through a rear-guard action. Thus self-management styles of development were widely heralded while the government was imposing bureaucratic, vertical controls on increasingly mobilized popular classes.

The typical behavior of individual state ministers, generals, or admirals included a clear commitment to change, conformism, militant anticommunism, or protection of the established order, all of which existed simultaneously in a swirl of nuances, concealed prejudices, and ideological confusion. These crosscurrents were evident in the society as a whole and also penetrated the summit of power. Although the generals at first tried to keep their disputes hidden, gradually these differences were transformed into definable political tendencies that reared up in moments of crisis.[18] They cannot be considered minor nuances because they help explain the range of government policies and the contradictions that plagued them, especially when military men became spokesmen for class positions while trying to maintain institutional loyalty.

Divisions in the unity of the armed forces were present from the beginning and subtly manifested themselves as early as the IPC nationalization and the agrarian reform. The regime managed the situation fairly easily during the first years of government, however, and outsiders had difficulty identifying the membership of different tendencies. The discrepancies were mitigated by the ministers' or generals' common adherence to military norms, which inhibited them from rushing to join cliques, political parties, or military lodges that would have revealed these splits more clearly. Velasco continually emphasized the regime's military nature. As a result, civilians were not permitted entry into the governing elite. They could advise, support, or implement policies, but they could not claim full membership in the military government. This exclusiveness increased the military's identification with the process.

The original basic nucleus needed to be broadened if only to attract competent officers to fill government positions. The COAP was the primary testing ground for assaying the capabilities and loyalties of military officers who wished to be generals and ministers. These newly recruited military men were used to displace the conservative and liberal officers who participated in the government in the first two years. But as the size of the nucleus grew, so did the resentment and/or ambitions of officers with differing views. Slowly but surely, spokesmen for powerful classes began to map out the contours of political opinion within the regime and achieve representation for their views. More than one military minister became a spokesman for narrow economic interests. Consequently, the defeat of oligarchic sectors during the first years of government also forced the departure of several ministers in uniform. Likewise, when the regime later collided with liberal members of the industrial bourgeoisie, another group of military men left the government. This jostling eventually broke the unity not only of the regime but also of the armed forces.

By the midpoint of the Velasco regime, the state apparatus was also pervaded by internal conflicts among ministries, agencies, and the newspapers (which the government had expropriated and placed under its control). These splits hindered the coherence and effectiveness of the state. For example, the Agriculture Ministry expropriated farms for the agrarian reform; then the Housing Ministry cancelled the expropriations on the excuse that the lands were needed for urban growth. State functionaries carrying out their duties embargoed rural properties; then the navy courts, under pressure from middle-sized farmers, arrested and tried the officials for "sabotaging the agrarian reform." In the economic sphere, food subsidies and price controls impoverished the countryside at the same time that agrarian reform was supposed to be a priority. In social mobilization, SINAMOS struggled initially for influence over popular and union organizations created by the Ministries of Fisheries, Industries, and Education, with the connivance of military intelligence. The battle raged until SINAMOS was reorganized and handed over to the corporatist faction of the army. Other divisions in the state included frequent bureaucratic conflicts between the central government ministries and the public enterprises.

Although at any one time only about three hundred officers served in the civilian bureaucracy, military presence was pervasive among ministerial advisors, vice-ministers, agency heads, heads of state enterprises, and regional directors of SINAMOS. Many generals and colonels, skillful in generating consensus within the ranks for the government program, counted on later appointments to high positions in ministries or public enterprises. The placement of military officers in those posts complicated the political crosscurrents in the regime, because it permitted bureaucratic cleavages to disrupt the armed forces. The divisions were reflected in tense personal relationships between officers, favoritism in promotions and transfers, aspirations to obtain lucrative public sector posts, and a sensation that those who remained in strictly military affairs were not getting ahead.

Those spokesmen of the dominant class who raised the specter of communism and warned about the dangers of "politization and divisions in the armed forces" found fertile ground to cultivate among resentful military officers. The conflict between the group known as "La Misión," which was corporatist-leaning, and the so-called progressive military leaders intensified in the last years of the Velasco regime. "La Misión" had followers among the modern industrialists organized in the Exporters' Association (ADEX), but not in the larger National Industrial Society (SNI), and was opposed by the more radical military men. The dispute involved principally the relationship between the regime and popular groups but was complicated by the fact that only a minority of industrialists felt "La Misión" could serve their interests, for it promised stability even at the cost of repressive measures.[19] An intense ideological struggle ensued, spurred by the fervid anticommunism of "La Misión," whose McCarthyite tactics against the progressive generals caused consternation in military circles. The dispute over policy positions at the summit of power led to political rigidity, an increasing use of authoritarian methods to quiet civilian critics, and an inability to articulate a new form of political domination. This *immobilisme* aggravated the regime's isolation, gave a free hand to "La Misión" in its intimidation tactics, and finally gave rise to the alliances that resulted in the overthrow of Velasco and the installation of Morales Bermúdez.

Morales Bermúdez moved against Velasco on the basis of widespread adverse opinion to the president and the ministers forming "La Misión." Even the progressive generals who had supported Velasco since 1968 felt that he needed to be removed from office in order to thwart the aspirations of "La Misión," whose leader, General Javier Tantaleán, saw himself as the next president. Subsequently, the progressive generals failed to gain influence in the new government and they too were gradually displaced, victims of the antagonism of the dominant class, its international allies, generals who wished to return the army to its original functions, and conservative admirals who wanted to reverse Velasco's policies. Morales Bermúdez sought to strengthen military unity in several ways. The most important change was to upgrade the role of the junta by restoring its ascendancy over the cabinet. Another important change was to invite ranking military generals (for example, heads of regional military districts) to take part in crucial political deliberations, particularly during the regime's weakest period (1976–1978). Meeting the army staff headquarters or in the National Palace, these generals played a decisive role in purging radicals from the government and mapped a strategy for dealing with international tensions.

State Power

In 1968, the public bureaucracy was ripe for reform. The absence of modern budgeting and planning mechanisms, the existence of multifunctional ministries, and disruptive antagonism between the executive and legislative branches made the Peruvian bureaucracy during the last months of Belaúnde's regime perhaps the most chaotic in Latin America. The executive was impotent and faced an irresponsible Congress; the constitutional framework facilitated corruption and blocked policy innovation. The bureaucracy was characterized by overlapping functions, reduced size and economic activity, little executive control (except over the forces of repression), and rampant penetration of private parties into public decision making. The national budget, considered by many specialists the key to rational public policy making, had become a bad joke.[20] After the coup, the military rulers—with strong support from civilian *técnicos*—initiated a series of reforms that transformed the public sector. Practically overnight, the regime implemented a number of administrative measures, widely practiced elsewhere in Latin America, only nascent in Peru, to strengthen the state. Under Velasco, the state reflected relatively high sectoral definition, centralized administrative processes, dynamic growth, and absorption of an ever greater percentage of the GNP.

To facilitate the coordination of the industrial, agrarian, and national resource sectors, the regime considered it absolutely necessary to break up the unwieldy Ministry of Development and Public Works. The structural reform of 1969 initiated a movement toward functional specialization broken only by the creation of SINAMOS. The number of ministries grew from eleven in 1968 to seventeen in early 1975, with several national systems with ministerial rank under the presidency. The administrative reform coincided with the state's assumption of new functions, By 1975, little remained of the image of the state apparatus led by President Belaúnde. The state controlled the greater part of the banking system, important enterprises in the natural resource sector (mining, petroleum, and fishing), and manufacturing industries (paper, cement, steel, naval construction), as well as a large number of public services formerly in private hands.[21] With the disappearance of the large landowners, the state regulated the agrarian cooperatives and foreign commerce and, although with difficulty, began to intervene in internal food marketing.

Simultaneously, the influence of the National Planning Institute (INP) rose significantly. Before 1968, the INP was politically crippled in the cross fire between Belaúnde and the National Congress. Belaúnde had considerable confidence in his own grand design for the country; the Congress, unable to censure the INP director because he was not a cabinet minister, chose instead to reduce the INP's powers and budget. In 1966, many professional planners, completely demoralized, left the institute and were replaced by nonspecialists. With the military government, however, the situation turned around dramatically and the INP became one of the most important agencies in the Peruvian public sector. From 1969 to 1971, its budget increased by a quarter in real terms. It hired staff members with new technical skills, and it established sectoral planning offices in all the large investment ministries. Each year's Annual Operating Plan gave the INP authority to pass on budgetary entries, an important requisite for effective short-term planning. INP officials helped set original budgetary ceilings (in association with the budget bureau), ordered sectoral projects by priority (both at the ministerial level and with Finance's Department of Economic Affairs), and approved all modifications in sectoral investment.

The growth of the state apparatus coincided with the displacement of traditional power groups, the nationalization of foreign enterprises, and the implementation of new industrial legislation. Although the proportion of the gross national product controlled by the state was significant, the regime found that it was enormously difficult to supervise and coordinate all of the activities it absorbed. These changes occurred in such a short period of time that in most cases formal state authority was subject to extensive interference by domestic and international economic forces. The state's learning process in the marketing of minerals and fishmeal was painful and costly, leading to management errors that were picked up by groups in the governing elite skeptical of full state control. The INP, despite its political power, never succeeded in completely overcoming sectoral competition reinforced by divisions in the summit of power. The development plans proved difficult to execute, and many of the large public sector enterprises operated without paying much attention to INP directives.

Although funds from international lending agencies dried up soon after Velasco's ascension to the presidency, after renegotiating the public debt and reaching agreements on partial indemnization for nationalizations, the government was able to obtain large loans from private international banks. These loans were oriented toward long-term development projects in irrigation, mines, and petroleum and toward the expansion of public enterprises. Based on 1970 trends, military and civilian planners projected that from 1971 to 1975 exports of fishmeal, minerals, and sugar would reap $6.8 billion and imports would total $7.5 billion or less. By increasing its foreign debt by $564 million, the government could maintain its balance of payments at a reasonable level while creating the necessary infrastructure in the extractive industries to finance, into the late 1970s and beyond, such other aspects of the polity as educational reform, social property, and gearing up the agrarian cooperatives to full production.[22]

A short period of economic expansion took place until 1973, at which time the first indications appeared that Peru was entering one of the worst periods of economic crisis in its history. By 1973, the government had achieved a modest increase in real wages, but this indicator declined steadily thereafter. The government attempted to compensate for inflation through a policy of food subsidies until 1975; their withdrawal alienated popular groups. The regime refused to recognize the existence of an economic crisis in 1974 and early 1975. The fact was that the Velasco regime was trying to implement a national industrial plan based on import substitution and an agrarian reform that did not increase food productivity, without attempting to modify the rate of population growth and without breaking the country's economic dependency on the international system. These contradictions eventually undermined the viability of any specific reform and exacerbated differences within the governing elite.

Morales Bermúdez, the principal architect and promoter of Velasco's economic policies, led the transition from crisis to stabilization as prime minister in the months prior to the coup. The government confronted the economic crisis of 1975 to 1978 with successive attempts at stabilizing policies, reaching agreements first with United States banks and later with the International Monetary Fund, but found itself incapable of sufficient discipline to apply their provisions. The regime reached its nadir in 1977 and 1978, when it was almost totally isolated, internationally and at home. State power, although objectively much greater than in 1968, was still insufficient to restore the economy or resist international and domestic pressures. Unable to attract a minimum amount of popular support, the government accepted one by one the claims of local entrepreneurial groups and foreign capitalists to cancel social reforms, discard some state industries, eliminate members of the governing elite, repress the unions, and drastically alter the regime's ideological principles. The aimless acquiescence to these political demands, together with the draconian measures imposed by the International Monetary Fund, led to depression and turmoil that, for the military, could be resolved only through incentives for the private sector and a return to electoral politics.

Unity of the Dominant Class

The high relative autonomy of the state in 1968 was due to the lack of unity in the dominant classes and a favorable international situation. When these factors changed, so did the regime's freedom of action. The initial reforms of the Velasco period sounded the death knell for those social groups that were considered oligarchical—the agricultural exporters, traditional sierra landowners, and traditional bankers. Industrial and agrarian bourgeoisies could not be called "oligarchic" because of their clear rejection of the governing model since the late 1950s. But the inability of the military to strike an accord with modern industrialists, which were at the same time the most dynamic element of the dominant class, placed the industrial class in the opposition to the regime and induced it to seek alliances with middle-sized farmers, disenchanted journalists unemployed after the expropriation of the press, and leaders of middle-class political parties. In 1973, entrepreneurs belonging to the National Industrial Society recognized that their error to date was their failure to coordinate their actions with other economically powerful groups that opposed the regime; the alliance set the stage for the eventual redefinition of the power bloc.[23]

Beginning with the General Industrial Law in 1970, the industrialists confronted the government on several fronts, simultaneously negotiating, obstructing, and obtaining short-term benefits. They utilized import privileges (designed to spur industrial growth) to increase the capital base of their industries and freeze the size of the labor force. They took advantage of loopholes in the Industrial Communities Law and the complicity of the minister of industries to slow movement toward worker ownership to a snail's pace. They declined to invest handsome short-term profits to increase productive capacity, preferring to buy government bonds or transfer their monies abroad. They used their contacts with military officers to try to block reform initiatives and sharpened divisions at the summit of power by mounting a consistent ideological campaign, including Mc-Carthyite attacks on progressive military officers, to defend what they called "Western and Christian civilization."

Small and middle-sized farmers, under the leadership of agrarian bourgeoisie, whose interests were threatened by the agrarian reform, became effective allies of the industrialists.[24] After trying to evade the agrarian reform by parcelling large farms, the bourgeoisie waged a consistent newspaper campaign against the government and succeeded in expanding its numbers through the addition of many small landowners who, although not under threat of expropriation, were fearful of the government's intentions. In the end, the land of many middle-sized property owners was expropriated, and the government worked hard to regain the support of small property owners; but the impact of this political mobilization was unsettling to the armed forces.[25]

Industrialists and farmers perceived that the Achilles' heel of the government was the heterogeneity of political positions in the armed forces and the military's inherent anticommunism. Campaigns were thus designed to spread confusion about the government's objectives and portray the country as nearing a social transformation led by communist infiltrators. The major daily newspapers, which remained in the hands of private owners until July 1974, perpetuated these campaigns on a massive scale. An analysis of *La Prensa* and *El Comercio* between 1973 and 1975 indicates a high degree of coordination in the actions of the SNI, small and middle-sized farmers, traditional political spokesmen, and such interest groups as the College of Lawyers. These newspapers' editorials, written principally for a military audience, had their desired effect of sowing uncertainty in the upper levels of the armed forces.

In summary, the deep divisions at the summit of power and throughout the government must be analyzed in the context of systematic opposition by the modern fractions of the dominant class that were not part of the oligarchy. Ironically, because the regime nurtured hopes for eventual reconciliation, the dominant class was gradually able to regroup and gain the strength to undermine state unity. The struggle was not just between the regime and its adversaries but rather permeated all levels of the government and the armed forces. Although the liberal bourgeoisie lost several of its leaders through deportations and its spokesmen inside the regime through forced resignations (such as that of Admiral Vargas Caballero in May 1974), it never lost touch with decision-making circles. Indeed, new spokesmen, such as "La Misión," even won access to the summit of power. The political struggle, therefore, was characterized by the progressive recomposition of the dominant class, which was melded in its opposition to the military government. This two-sided game of shifting alliances had its effect on governmental unity, and on the final definition of the regime.

The world political situation also increased the isolation and rate of decay of the Velasco government. In 1968, the international scene favored the regime. Velasco's confrontation with the United States over the nationalization of the IPC took place at a time when American eyes were turned toward Asia. By 1970, Velasco was hardly the only problem for the American State Department in Latin America and perhaps not even the most important. Salvador Allende was confirmed as the first Marxist president elected in the hemisphere. In Bolivia, a leftist general, J. J. Torres, became head of state. In Argentina, Juan Perón returned from a long exile abroad in the midst of widespread uncertainty about his intentions. In Ecuador, Guillermo Rodríguez Lara deposed José María Velasco Ibarra and promised social reforms *a la peruana*. This series of events bolstered Peru's feelings of military security vis-á-vis her traditional rivals, Chile and Ecuador, which appeared to have like-minded governments, and for three years Velasco was not distracted by issues of national defense.

By 1973, however, the tables had turned. Allende and Torres had been toppled and the Pinochet and Banzer dictatorships were using geopolitical rivalries to distract and unite their repressed citizenries. With the support of some exiled Peruvians, the Inter-American Press Society focused on the expropriation of the daily newspapers, and its members published sensational articles on repression in Peru. After receiving a negative reply from Washington, the Velasco government purchased armaments from the Soviet Union, thus straining relations with the United States, a country that had provided arms to Chile even under the Allende regime. International and geopolitical issues had special relevance for the armed forces, which were, in the last analysis, responsible for national security. Velasco's opponents aggravated worries on this front by claiming that the regime, given its isolation in Latin America and its poor relations with the United States, could even lead Peru to military defeat should hostilities break out with Chile.

The correlation of forces at the summit of power proved to be progressively unfavorable for the continuation of the Velasco government. Until now, we have analyzed the regime's relative autonomy with regard to the dominant class and their international support. The recomposition of the dominant groups and the breakdown of military unity cannot be fully explained, however, without making reference to the popular sectors. The latter have to be included to understand the isolation of the regime, its inability to broaden its social base, and the absence of popular protest when it was finally toppled.

The Regime's Isolation from Popular Groups

Despite its setbacks in the 1950s, the oligarchic state had retained its ability to fragment and demobilize popular organizations, either through official repression or the inertia of the traditional landholding structure. Although by the end of the 1960s, peasant unions had gained some strength and were able to challenge prevailing patterns of domination, there was no centralization in the peasant movement. Moreover, the Belaúnde government, alarmed by the guerrilla insurgency of 1965, strove to neutralize those peasant unions that existed. At the time, there was only one officially recognized workers' confederation, the Confederación de Trabajadores del Perú, which was controlled by the APRA and which lost influence during the Belaúnde period because of membership dissatisfaction with the leadership and because of APRA's connivance with the oligarchy in opposing Belaúnde's reforms.

The political parties were weak in 1968, partially as a consequence of the general disillusionment with the country's democratic institutions and the abstract content of most political discourse. The leftist parties were certainly weaker. Upon the disappearance of the parliament, Velasco found the parties so inoffensive that his regime did not bother to outlaw them. The APRA, the only mass party, did not even attempt to challenge the strength of the military government in 1968.

The government took advantage of the passive consensus of the majority of the population to move forward with the initial reforms. But over time, its actions helped mobilize these groups, often in opposition to the government. In the countryside, the struggle for land took place both inside and outside the limits of the Agrarian Reform Law and crystallized political consciousness in existing peasant unions. The Velasco regime witnessed the first serious attempts to centralize the peasant movement in the Confederación de Campesinos del Perú (led by leftist forces) and the Confederación Nacional Agraria (a creation of government in 1974). In the city, workers' organizations multiplied. The Confederación General de Trabajadores del Perú (CGTP), controlled by the Communist party, obtained legal recognition from the government and became the most influential labor organization. The regime promoted its own central coordinating body for the working class, without much success, but the creation of the industrial communities greatly affected the workers' movement. The campaign by labor leaders against the entrepreneurs' attempt to evade the profit- and ownership-sharing law raised the workers' political consciousness. Other sectors of the popular classes became organized through their participation in social property cooperative enterprises or neighborhood groups in the shantytowns *(pueblos jóvenes)*. From incipient levels in 1968, regional and sectoral popular mobilization increased considerably. Although lacking central coordination, this movement succeeded in socializing a new generation of opposition leaders who would become prominent during the second phase of the military government.

A political plan derived from the ideology of the middle sectors was unlikely to spur mass mobilization. Moreover, the impact of government policy toward popular organizations prevented the regime from gaining any consistent support. Flushed by its early successes, the government felt it could ignore many existing labor leaders and generate its own backing. It recognized that the left was sharply divided between those affiliated with popular groups, those in opposition to the regime at the national level, and those supporting the government. But in trying to take advantage of the situation, the regime overplayed its hand. It created parallel organs of "representation" in industries and in modern plantations, tried to displace traditional union militants, and was stalemated by a prolonged adversary relationship with skillful labor organizers that sapped its energy. Although Velasco's reforms provided many material benefits for workers, its labor policies split the workers into numerous factions. The regime's "representative" organs were received differently. The Confederación Nacional Agraria (CNA), promoted by SINAMOS, managed to win a considerable measure of popular support, while the Sindicato de Educadores de la Revolución Peruana (SERP) and the Central de los Trabajadores de la Revolución Peruana (CTRP) remained bureaucratic. All, however, became targets of opportunity for the progressives and "La Misión" adherents. Government agents became increasingly manipulative in managing these groups and actually dampened their members' enthusiasm for the regime.

The absence of popular support stemmed from the fundamental contradiction between the concept of mass mobilization and the norms of military hierarchy. The regime's ideas on popular participation were authored by civilians close to the regime rather than by the military leaders themselves. Nevertheless, the original members of the basic nucleus were receptive to these innovations and helped give them form and substance in the creation of SINAMOS. SINAMOS was instituted only after two previous attempts to link government with the people (the Committees for the Defense of the Agrarian Reform and the Committees for the Defense of the Revolution) had been accused of communist infiltration. From 1972 onward, SINAMOS was continuously in the eye of the hurricane. Led first by Leonidas Rodríguez Figueroa, who felt perfectly at ease with progressive civilian collaborators, it was later headed by two generals (Rudecindo Zaveleta and Pedro Sala Orosco) who were sympathetic to principles of vertical command and, toward the end of the Velasco regime, actually opposed the progressive officers. As part of "La Misión," and assisted by intelligence operatives, Zavaleta and Sala Orosco took on the responsibility of breaking the back of incipient popular organizations, creating parallel entities, and selectively repressing those they could not control. Even during its heyday, SINAMOS was interpreted by popular groups as an attempt to manage their affairs from the "top down." Its behavior was relatively benign, however, compared with the clandestine operations of the Interior Ministry, the complicity of the ministries of Labor and Industry and the intelligence services in reorganizing the National Confederation of Industrial Communities, and the not-so-subtle police suppression of striking miners and school teachers. SINAMOS' ultimate fate demonstrated that for this regime popular mobilization needed to be accompanied by vertical and bureaucratic controls.

Although the "top down" label was resented by committed civilians in the regime, the interpretation was, on the whole, accurate. In designing a program for participation, the regime could achieve military consensus only by incorporating popular groups under the institutionalized tutelage of the armed forces. The progressive officers could not propose an alliance with popular organizations that the military did not directly control. This aspect of the process represented the ultimate gordian knot, because civilian mobilization created anxieties in the military and Velasco was unwilling to sever his relationship with the armed forces. The government avoided the main issue by choosing to engage in dialogue with only those groups that provided overt support, such as the CGTP, a tactic that failed to secure stable props for its rule. The Velasco regime's inability to deal adequately with the question of participation was perhaps its most significant failing.

This analysis of the regime and its contradictions points out the recurring elusiveness of an alliance between the military and popular organizations. This miscarriage is symptomatic of a regime that by definition is *of* the armed forces. Even Velasco did not foresee that, as the political competition intensified, the regime could not break ranks with the military. Nor could it mount an effective campaign against a capitalist system which had given life to these very same military institutions. The coup of August 29, 1975, which was greeted with applause from the right and absolute silence from the popular sectors, was simply a military act that confirmed the internal bankruptcy of the regime.[26]

The decline of real salaries, which began in 1973, accelerated with the implementation of stabilization policies under the Morales Bermúdez government. The popular sectors joined forces to protest their deteriorating economic situation; the repression by the government simply strengthened their resolve. A general strike in July 1977 paralyzed the country, further isolating the military regime, and helped convince the armed forces to return to an electoral system of government.

Conclusions

Exceptional state autonomy between 1968 and 1972 appeared to coincide with an impasse at the summit of power caused by the collapse of the oligarchic state, the inability of potentially powerful bourgeois groups to act politically to serve their interests, and the institutional coherence of the armed forces (which filled the vacuum). Taking advantage of the crisis, Velasco utilized this high relative autonomy during the first phase of the military government to exclude the traditional classes and fractions from the power bloc and strengthen the state economically. A closed policy-making style prolonged the initial thrust, kept traditional politicians, entrepreneurs, and spokesmen of the dominant class off balance, and postponed their ability to reconsolidate in effective opposition to the regime. Although the class character of the state was inferred from its continuing tolerance of capitalism, the political regime did not express the interests of classes and fractions dominant in the society at large. While Velasco did not institute socialism and promulgated many policies that were in the long-term interests of the industrial class, the regime relied for its support on the military institutions and did not enter into partnership with modern bourgeois groups.

The lack of such an alliance under Velasco can be explained by the liberal ideology of the industrial bourgeoisie (which wished to subordinate the oligarchic classes rather than eliminate them); by the industrial bourgeoisie's relative inexperience in trying to protect its interests through political means; and by the progressive radicalization of key members of the governing military elite, who personally were not at ease with the values of the entrepreneurial class. Although the military government essentially was offering the industrial bourgeoisie a set of reforms based on class reconciliation and state backing for private industrialization, these modern sectors interpreted the government's intentions as an all-out attack on the capitalist order.

The military regime faced the prospect that although they were temporarily scattered, the most dynamic sectors of the dominant class would eventually regroup. Velasco's early political victories contributed to the radicalization of the polity at the summit of power, but they also helped to solidify the coordinated opposition of the industrial interest groups. In 1973, these opponents began to retake the offensive, which together with setbacks on the geopolitical and international economic fronts and a lack of support from the popular classes led to increased internal struggle, receptivity to opposition demands by members of the governing group, and the gradual reduction of the state's initial high relative autonomy.

The second phase of the military government, headed by Morales Bermúdez, displayed less relative autonomy until decisions were made to transfer power back to civilians in 1979. In 1976 and 1977, the bourgeoisie appeared to be united in its attempt to substitute civilians for the military rulers. Nonetheless, Morales was able to control the pace and direction of the turn to the right, including the repression of some bourgeoisie spokesmen in 1976, the imposition of a timetable that included a constituent assembly to precede general elections (against the wishes of important segments of the bourgeoisie), and a contradictory economic plan that gave priority to the demands of international capital and negatively affected companies that produced for the internal market. These events were consistent with a normal level of relative autonomy of the state; the regime could maneuver between fractions of the dominant class and even make concessions to popular pressures. It could not, however, end its isolation until it determined to transfer power from military hands.

Although the return to civilian rule was the principal demand of the dominant class, the position was not accompanied by a definable political program that would bridge the considerable gaps between the bourgeois political parties. For this reason, the Morales Bermúdez government was able to retain some negotiating room in the armed forces and the political community at large.[27] The new civilian president was installed in a situation much different from that in 1963 or 1968, because now the dominant class was relatively homogeneous and there was a military class that was battle-tested during the Velasco period and watchful of the political direction the government would take.

Policy-making styles over this long period appear to be correlated with levels of autonomy and state power. High autonomy is feasible only temporarily and is usually accompanied by a secretive policy-making style. The Velasco regime displayed characteristics of high power and autonomy during the 1968–1972 period, and its policy-making style followed suit. The early years of the regimes of Kemal Ataturk in Turkey and Fidel Castro in Cuba are comparable examples. The state that is weak, whether as a result of severe internal divisions or a low resource base, is susceptible to the bullying of powerful economic or political interests; its low autonomy is manifest in public policies that favor those interests. The first years of the state under Morales Bermúdez had features that were consistent with this description. The state was divided, power was scattered, and representatives of powerful interests had a predominant say in shaping policy. The constraints on each regime, however, are not understood simply through the success or failure of its reforms, but in terms of the social groups which accorded it support, and its evolving relations with the dominant classes and rising popular sectors.

What final evaluation can be made of the unusually high autonomy of the Velasco period? It is evident that closed policy making helped—though it was not essential—to force the decline of the agricultural and financial oligarchy and in a way to assist the regrouping of the power bloc. The hermetic style of the governing elite was essential for designing a polity that could paralyze, momentarily, those economic power holders who, Velasco felt, prevented the popular sectors from improving their social condition.

It appears that the Velasco government did not recognize the inherently temporary nature of high autonomy, especially when it repeatedly claimed in its speeches that the reforms were "irreversible." Disregarding the fundamental interests of powerful economic and institutional participants is a viable strategy as long as those elements are in disarray. Misrepresentation of one's ultimate objectives and high autonomy itself have their own half-life. Velasco and his entourage can claim little credit for the disarray of the upper class and the degree of cohesion of the military in 1968. Notwithstanding, his administration forcefully took advantage of the high state autonomy prevailing at the time to advance several reforms that would have been dead letter in other historical circumstances.

In summary, the Velasco government tried to keep the dominant classes off balance and its military cohorts in line, and it made overtures to the popular sectors. The effort fell short, but it reaffirms the importance of relative autonomy as one means of changing the composition of the governing group. The Velasco experience is also a reminder of several other principles. First, social and economic reforms derived from an ideology of the middle sectors are unlikely to appeal to the authentic interests of popular sectors. Second, a military establishment that owes its existence to the capitalist system will not easily destroy its source. Third, institutions based on the norms of vertical command and discipline—such as the armed forces—are intolerant of spontaneous and autonomous organization of labor unions and popular groups. Fourth, high relative autonomy is a temporary phenomenon; over time, dominant classes will regroup or a new power bloc will emerge. Finally, the armed forces, even when they appear to be leftist leaning and enter government in a situation of high relative autonomy, are, in the last analysis, unreliable leaders of revolutionary movements.

Notes

1. For Marx's and Engels' major statements on the concept, see Karl Marx, *Capital: A Critique of Political Economy* (New York: Random House, 1906), "The Working Day," pp. 255–330; *Grundisse: Foundations of the Critique of Political Economy* (rough draft), trans. by Martin Nicolaus (Harmondsworth, England: Penguin Books, 1973); Marx, *The Eighteenth Brumaire of Louis Bonaparte* (New York: International Publishers, 1963); and Karl Marx and Friedrich Engels, *Correspondence 1846–1895*, trans. by Dona Torr (London: Lawrence and Wishart, 1936), "Letter to Conrad Schmidt," p. 480.
2. See Antonio Gramsci, *Notas sobre Maquiavelo, sobre la Política y sobre el Estado Moderno* (Mexico City: Juan Pablos Editores, 1975).
3. Nicos Poulantzas, *Clases Sociales y Poder Político en el Estado Capitalista* (Mexico City: Siglo XXI, 1969).
4. Ibid., pp. 331–333.
5. Ibid., pp. 394–395. By its nature, Poulantzas argues, the capitalist state is led by a hegemonic class, but this does not deny the state's relative autonomy vis-à-vis the power bloc, or the hegemonic class or fraction within it.
6. Gramsci does not limit high relative autonomy (Caesarism) only to a situation of equilibrium of "fundamental" social forces but urges the analyst to examine the relations between principal groups (socioeconomic and sociotechnical) of the dominant classes and the auxiliary elements that are guided by or subordinated to their hegemonic influence, paying particular attention to peasants and military groups. See Gramsci, *Notas*, p. 88.
7. Poulantzas, *Clases Sociales*, pp. 331–332. (Poulantzas concedes that this notion is not sufficiently developed analytically but argues that it nonetheless has value.)
8. A complete study of relative autonomy should include a qualitative examination of favorable opinion of policies by fractions of the dominant class, the policies' effect on their objective interests, and the policies' impact on the interests of the bourgeoisie in general.
9. Concerning political regimes prior to 1968, see Henry Pease García, *El Ocaso del Poder Oligárquico: Lucha Política en la Escena Oficial, 1968–1975* (Lima: DESCO, 1977), chapters 1 and 5; Julio Cotler, *Clases, Estado, y Nación en el Perú* (Lima: Instituto de Estudios Peruanos, 1978); and Laura Madalengoitia, *Burguesía y Estado Liberal* (Lima: DESCO, 1979). The political regimes from 1930 to 1950 had as one of their primary purposes the control of anti-oligarchic forces, namely, the APRA.
10. This point will not be elaborated upon here. The importance of national defense to military ideology is fundamental but does not displace the other elements mentioned. It served as a factor to join the heterogeneous elements of the armed forces faced with the ideological implications of the socioeconomic reforms. Alfred Stepan discusses the maturation of the military's outlook in *The State and Society: Peru in Comparative Perspective* (Princeton: Princeton University Press, 1978), pp. 127–147.

11. See Pease, *El Ocasò,* for a periodization of the political struggle at the summit of power between 1968 and 1975.
12. The turn to the right is analyzed in Henry Pease García, *Los Caminos del Poder: Tres Años de Crisis en la Escena Política* (Lima: DESCO, 1979).
13. A caution on the methodology utilized in constructing Table 1 is appropriate. Only those policies considered to represent major changes in the respective policy arenas are included in the left-hand column. The indication of whether they were in the interests of the various social and economic groups is judgmental, worked out in consultation with analysts of Peruvian politics of this period. In addition, it should be clear that these are public laws that touched broad segments of the political community. A considerable number of decisions were formulated that influenced the political scene but do not appear here, such as military promotions, the selection of individuals for deportations, the appointment of ministers and military investigative commissions, and so forth. The reader should consider that this figure is intended for illustrative purposes only.
14. For several in-depth articles on programs of the Velasco regime, see Abraham F. Lowenthal, ed., *The Peruvian Experiment: Continuity and Change Under Military Rule* (Princeton: Princeton University Press, 1975). The compendium edited by Henry Pease García and Olga Verve, *Perú, 1968–1976: Cronología Política* (Lima: DESCO, 1974, 1977), contains rich data culled from newspaper files on the progression of events after the military seized power. First-person reports of the Velasco regime are Francisco Moncloa, *Perú: ¿Qué Pasó?* (Lima: Editorial Horizonte, 1977); and Hector Béjar, *La Revolución en la Trampa* (Lima: Ediciones Socialismo y Participación, 1977). For more details on the property reforms, see Peter T. Knight, *Perú, ¿Hacia la Autogestión?* (Buenos Aires: Editorial Proyección, 1974); and on the educational reform, Peter S. Cleaves, "Implementation of the Agrarian and Educational Reforms in Peru," *Technical Papers Series,* no. 8 (Institute of Latin American Studies, University of Texas at Austin, 1977).
15. For information on which of these four styles the military government used for major policy initiatives, see Peter S. Cleaves and Martin J. Scurrah, *Agriculture, Bureaucracy, and Military Government in Peru* (Ithaca, N.Y.: Cornell University Press, 1980), p. 92.
16. This political juncture is treated in Pease, *Los Caminos,* pp. 103–332.
17. The best-known members of the military nucleus in 1968 were Colonels Jorge Fernández Maldonado, Leonidas Rodríguez Figueroa, Enrique Gallegos, and Rafael Hoyos. Later they were joined by Colonels José Graham Hurtado, Miguel de la Flor, Raúl Meneses, Javier Tantaleán, Pedro Richter, and several others. With time, the concept of the nucleus loses its utility because of political differentiation in the governing elite.
18. It is not possible to predict military political behavior simply from the class origins of the military personnel, given the organization and doctrines of the military institutions and the way they are formed in society. The military is clearly part of the capitalist system, but one cannot extrapolate mechanically from that fact the behavior, interests, or objectives of individuals or fractions of the armed services. Nor can the contradictions, conflicts, or public declaration of the period be explained solely on the basis of the ideological beliefs of different goals or their frequent references to issues of national defense. Rather, these outcomes must be analyzed in relation to the ability of dominant social forces to regroup politically and the range of options that were available to economic groups and military officers after each successive crisis.
19. The "La Misión" group promoted the Movimiento Laboral Revolucionario from the Ministry of Fishing, headed by Javier Tantaleán, to splinter unions.

20. See Pedro-Pablo Kuczynski, *Peruvian Democracy under Economic Stress: An Account of the Belaúnde Administration, 1963–1968* (Princeton: Princeton University Press, 1977); Jane S. Jaquette, *The Politics of Development in Peru*, Latin American Dissertation Series, no. 33 (Ithaca, N.Y.: Cornell University, 1971); and Naomi J. Caiden and Aaron Wildavsky, *Planning and Budgeting in Poor Countries* (New York: John Wiley, 1973).
21. Actually, a state steel company and shipyards existed previously, but they were relatively small enterprises. For the growth of the state's presence in the economy, see E. V. K. FitzGerald, *The State and Economic Development: Peru since 1968* (Cambridge: Cambridge University Press, 1976).
22. See *Plan Nacional de Desarrollo, 1971–1975* (Lima: Instituto Nacional de Planificación, 1971).
23. See the declarations of the president of the SNI on July 19, 1973, in response to a homage to him by industrialists, farmers, the College of Lawyers, and other interest associations, cited in Pease, *El Ocaso*, p. 112.
24. See Henry Pease García, "La Reforma Agraria en la Crisis del Estado Oligárquico," in Pease, et al., *Estado y Política Agraria* (Lima: DESCO, 1977).
25. For a broad treatment of agrarian policies during this period, see Cleaves and Scurrah, *Agriculture, Bureaucracy, and Military Government in Peru.* Also, Cynthia McClintock, *Peasant Cooperatives and Political Change in Peru, 1969–1977* (Princeton: Princeton University Press, 1981); and Mariano Valderrama, *Site Años de Reforma Agraria* (Lima: Pontificia Universidad Católica, 1975).
26. The deterioration in the health of the regime and of Velasco himself led to a consensus among military leaders that Velasco needed to be replaced. The original recommendation to force his voluntary retirement was overruled by Morales Bermúdez. The ouster is treated in Pease, *Los Caminos*, pp. 55–76, and in Carlos Urrutia, et al., *Autogestión en el Perú, 1968–1979* (Lima: CIDIAG, 1980), which also includes comments by General Arturo Valdéz, who was subdirector of the COAP and secretary of the cabinet, on political events at the time.
27. The best example was the economic policy of Minister Javier Silva Ruete, which provided tangible benefits to entrepreneurs and helped assure approval of the government's approach to transferring power to civilians. At the time, these measures increased the level of state autonomy, which was nonetheless quantitatively much less than the extraordinary situation in 1968.

Karen L. Remmer

Evaluating the Policy Impact of Military Regimes in Latin America

A central issue in the analysis of military regimes in Latin America is their policy impact. How successful are military governments in promoting economic development? How do their policies and performances compare with those of civilian governments? The sheer volume of research on the causes of military takeovers in Latin America implies that regime changes have important consequences. Yet to date we are far from having satisfactory answers to the questions posed above. As a recent study of public policy in Latin America noted, "If students of Latin American politics were to inventory verified propositions regarding the performance of Latin American regimes, the resulting list might not exceed zero" (Ames and Goff 1975, p. 175).

The purpose of this essay is to explore the reasons for this state of affairs. It reviews some of the basic theoretical arguments linking regime type to public policy in Latin America, examines the manner in which these have been tested by recent empirical studies, and underlines basic methodological and conceptual problems in the evaluation of regime performance. It will attempt to show that our current ignorance about the policy consequences of military rule is related not only to a paucity of research and/or data, but to the use of inappropriate research strategies.

From Karen L. Remmer, "Evaluating the Policy Impact of Military Regimes in Latin America," *Latin American Research Review* 13, no. 2 (1978), pp. 39–54. Copyright © 1978 by the *Latin American Research Review* and reprinted by the permission of the author and the *Latin American Research Review*.

Finally, an attempt will be made to offer suggestions for recasting future research.

Theoretical Relationships

Highly plausible arguments have been advanced to support the proposition that military governments tend to pursue distinctive public policies. To date most of this discussion has centered around the relationship between military rule and general developmental outcomes, with one group of scholars arguing that military governments tend to promote socioeconomic development and a second arguing just the opposite.

The first position was clearly delineated some fifteen years ago by the historian John J. Johnson, who pointed to the social class and professional backgrounds of officers and argued that concern for national defense and prestige, technical proficiency, and middle-class orientations create a tendency for the military actively to support economic development (1962, pp. 121–27). Thus, Johnson noted that in the more developed countries, such as Argentina, where professionalism was well advanced, "the armed forces are in the forefront of those most concerned with the desirability of industrial growth" (1962, p. 138). More recently, the propensity of the military to pursue economic development has been related to a variety of other factors: a concern for institutional survival and internal security (Einaudi and Stepan 1974); linkages with incumbents of other technocratic roles who perceive popular demands on civilian regimes as an obstacle to further development (O'Donnell 1973); the cohesiveness, efficiency, and coercive capability of the military as a political institution (Fidel 1975, pp. 6–7; Lissak 1975, p. 48); and the insulation of the military from the demands of particularistic interests that may compromise national development efforts (Fidel 1975, p. 10).

Although the military-as-economic-modernizer position never engendered more than limited support among Latin Americanists, it gained a new respectability in the aftermath of the Brazilian and Peruvian corps of the 1960s. Analyses of these regimes lent concrete support to the view that corporate self-interest might lead military officers to be more concerned than civilians with basic developmental problems (Einaudi and Stepan 1974; Stepan 1973; Clinton 1971). Although their policies have differed considerably, the Peruvian and Brazilian cases have also illustrated that the centralized power structures and coercive capabilities of military regimes may prove useful in carrying out basic structural reforms, imposing austerity, creating internal stability, and, in general, pursuing a focused and determined developmental effort.

In this connection it is argued that developmental success in the Latin American context of late development is likely to demand not only a determined effort, but also the ability to ignore or repress both the resistance to reform of entrenched interests and the pressures from below for immediate gains in consumption. Especially in the Brazilian case, where relatively high economic growth rates have been linked with coercive limitation of consumption (Fishlow 1973), the experience of the past decade could be cited in favor of the view that "if there is to be development, the military institution and military personnel are most likely to be its handmaidens" (Fidel 1975, p. 11).

Despite, and even in some cases because of, the developmental efforts of the Peruvian and Brazilian militaries, most Latin Americanists remain skeptical about the willingness and capacity of military regimes to promote economic development. This negative perspective on the relationship between military government and economic development was also presented in the early 1960s by an historian, Edwin Lieuwen (1961). The military was pictured as a conservative and even reactionary force, preoccupied mainly with preserving its corporate self-interest and generally lacking the political and administrative resources necessary for the pursuit of a successful developmental effort (1961, p. 145). A more recent examination of the Latin American military arrives at a similar position: "It is clear that, if one has to generalize about the role of the Latin American military as a whole, one must consider their role, on balance, still to be a conservative or reactionary one" (Needler 1972, p. 45).

Other arguments advanced to support this second general position include the following: (1) characteristics of military institutions, such as discipline and internal cohesion, are not retained in a nonmilitary context of action (Willner 1970, p. 263); (2) the professional expertise of the military is not readily transferred to civilian politics, which requires skill in communication, compromise, and bargaining (Lissak 1975, p. 49; Willner 1970, p. 263); and (3) the developmental programs of military regimes are undermined by propensities towards corruption, waste, excessive military spending, and alliances with reactionary civilian groups (Lieuwen 1961, pp. 148–51; Needler 1969, pp. 242–43). The implication of these arguments is that civilian governments are more likely to possess the political skills, experience, and resources necessary to check abuses of power, encourage rational planning, and engender public support for developmental efforts.

It should be noted that there is a third perspective on the relationship between military regimes and economic development that dismisses both the negative and the positive arguments outlined above on the grounds that regime type is irrelevant. One version of this position stresses ecological constraints and suggests that socioeconomic variables are more important in explaining policy differences than political variables. Although this argument has wide applicability, it appears particularly plausible in the Latin American context. As the dependency literature (Bonilla and Girling 1973; Cardoso and Faletto 1969; Bodenheimer 1971; Cockcroft et al. 1972; Frank 1971, 1972) has emphasized, the dynamics and

structure of economic development in Latin America cannot be understood without taking into account factors such as imperial domination,
foreign investment and technology, foreign aid, and export demand—
factors that domestic policymakers cannot control directly. A major variant on this argument suggests that civilian and military regimes do not
even have different policy orientations, either because the civilian-military
dichotomy is totally artificial (Ronfeldt 1974), or because the same class,
sectoral, or status group interests control the government no matter who
occupies the top positions (Nun 1967). Finally, the policy relevance of
system-level characteristics has been questioned on the grounds that
factors such as operational style and formal institutional arrangements,
which may account for policy variations, are not systematically related to
regime type or regime orientation (Ayres 1975).

In short, the literature is deeply divided on the basic theoretical question. Do the policies and performance records of military regimes differ
from those of civilian regimes? Much of the literature suggests that they
do, but disagrees on how, and much suggests that they do not. In such a
situation empirical studies play a key role in choosing between theories.

Empirical Studies

The empirical studies of regime type, public policy, and policy outcomes
conducted so far, whether focused on Latin America or including other
areas as well, tend to support the conclusion that regime differences have
little or no impact on public policy. As Philippe Schmitter (1975, p. 37)
comments in summarizing this research:

> The conclusions have tended to be similar whether arrived at by statistical
> inference from synchronic correlations across units, or descriptive evalua-
> tion based on diachronic counter-factual assumptions within units. We have
> been led to believe that the relatively constant features of ecological setting
> and underlying class interests and/or the persistence of subtle machinations
> by informal cliques and patron-client dyads impose such narrow and fixed
> parameters upon performance that it makes no "real" difference if political
> structures are more or less centralized, more or less competitive, or more or
> less participatory. Such an overdetermined system (provided the three layers
> of determinism are self-reinforcing) will produce the same outputs and
> outcomes—i.e., benefit the same interests—in any case short of violent
> revolution.

To determine whether or not to accept this conclusion, it is necessary to
examine how recent research has approached the study of regime differences. Rather than undertake an extensive review of the literature on
the Latin American military, which has already been surveyed (e.g.,
McAlister 1966; Rankin 1974), the subsequent discussion will focus on

recent comparative studies that have explicitly and systematically investigated the relationship between regime type and policy.

To begin with the most ambitious efforts, several cross-national aggregate studies have examined the relationship between military rule and economic development throughout the Third World. The earliest of these studies, conducted by Eric Nordlinger (1970), was based on a population of seventy-four countries and attempted to test the relationship between military strength and seven indicators of economic and social change. These indicators included relatively standard measures of economic change such as the rate of growth of per capita GNP as well as somewhat more unusual and subjective indices such as "leadership commitment to economic development." Finding relatively weak correlations between military strength and indicators of socioeconomic development, except for the least developed countries in his sample, Nordlinger concluded that "within a particular social and political context (when there is hardly a middle class to speak of, and when workers and peasants have not been politically mobilized), soldiers in mufti sometimes allow or even encourage economic modernization." However, in other contexts (i.e., outside sub-Saharan Africa) "officer-politicians are commonly unconcerned with the realization of economic change and reform" (p. 1134). It should be noted that Nordlinger explicitly ruled out the claim that civilian regimes are necessarily more successful in carrying out modernizing changes (p. 1134).

Nordlinger's conclusions have been reconsidered in a recent study by Robert W. Jackman (1976), who applies a covariance analysis model to Nordlinger's data as well as a new set of data covering the decade 1960 to 1970 for seventy-seven Third World countries. The use of a more sophisticated statistical model leads Jackman to conclude, in contrast to Nordlinger, that "military intervention in the politics of the Third World has no unique effects on social change, regardless of either the level of economic development or geographic region" (p. 1096).

Two recent cross-national aggregate data studies by McKinlay and Cohan (1975, 1976), based on an initial sample of 115 countries, reach conclusions that are very similar to Jackman's. In the first of these studies, McKinlay and Cohan compare the performance of military and civilian regimes over the 1951–70 period, using indicators of annual change in per capita GNP, cost of living, food production, exports, primary education, military spending, and military size. Like Nordlinger, they find that military regimes perform significantly better than civilian regimes in the poorest countries (p. 21), although their evidence also suggests that in Latin America military regimes perform somewhat better than civilian ones (pp. 21–22). However, McKinlay and Cohan conclude that "military regimes do not in aggregate form a distinctive regime type in terms of performance" (p. 23). They find that the rate of growth of primary education was the only overall significant performance difference between military and civilian governments.

The second study by McKinlay and Cohan (1976), covering the 1961–70 period, uses different data and statistical techniques to arrive at the same basic conclusion. In this study, McKinlay and Cohan found evidence that military regimes tend to occupy a weaker international trading position than their civilian counterparts, but that their economic performance rates, measured in terms of the rate of growth of per capita GNP, cost of living, and exports, compared favorably with nonmilitary regimes (p. 863). Military regimes were clearly distinguished from civilian regimes only by their lower levels of political activity and higher levels of political change.

The most extensive study to date of the consequences of regime differences in Latin America, a study by Philippe Schmitter (1971), partially confirms the findings of these cross-regional studies. Using both cross-sectional and longitudinal data, Schmitter concluded that no regime type was exclusively linked with developmental success as measured by such indicators of performance as average annual percentage increases in inflation, exports, industrial production, and per capita GNP. Military and noncompetitive regimes were slightly more successful in curtailing inflation, increasing foreign exchange earnings, and promoting economic growth, especially in industry; however, environmental factors, particularly dependence on foreign capital, aid, and trade, were more important in understanding performance variations than regime type. Regime type only appeared relevant for understanding variations in governmental allocations (outputs) as distinct from system performance (outcomes). In particular, Schmitter found that military regimes in Latin America tend to spend less on social welfare, rely more heavily on indirect taxation as a source of government revenue, and extract fewer resources for the pursuit of public policies than civilian governments. However, most correlations between regime type and policy outputs were weak, supporting the view that regime differences are relatively unimportant for understanding policy differences in Latin America.

Other recent studies of public policy in Latin America have also cast doubt on the relevance of regime differences. Margaret Daly Hayes' detailed work (1973, 1975) on longitudinal changes in Brazilian national expenditures, for example, indicates that military and civilian regimes in Brazil have not differed extensively in their economic goals and policy outputs. Compared to their military counterparts, civilian governments in the 1950–67 period were more likely to spend money on social development and the civilian bureaucracy and less likely to spend funds on military equipment; but all regimes in this period gave priority to national development with an emphasis on infrastructure development (1975). Moreover, ecological constraints, particularly GDP, political conflict, primary export earnings, inflation, and debt service, explain a high proportion of the variation in expenditure patterns over time (Hayes 1973).

In summary, recent research clearly suggests that underlying socioeconomic conditions impose such basic constraints on political actors that it makes little difference whether they are civilian or military. Similar conclusions have been reached by studies employing very different units of analysis and research strategies. However, before concluding that Latin Americanists, who have expended considerable time and effort explaining the causes of regime variations, have been totally misguided, some of the weaknesses of these studies should be underlined.

Central Research Problems

To begin at the most basic level, serious problems of data availability, comparability, reliability, and validity impose definite restrictions on the generalizations that can be derived from the public policy studies described above. The problem of data availability alone has produced some rather unorthodox and questionable research procedures. Nordlinger (1970), for example, correlated indicators of regime type measured at one period of time (1957–62) with indicators of policy measured over an earlier time period (1950–63). While various leaps may be necessary in drawing causal inferences about policy outcomes, simple logic excludes attributing responsibility for policy outcomes at $Time_1$ to regimes and policy outputs at $Time_2$.

To mention some other data problems, national ministry expenditures have been used as indicators of policy commitment to basic areas such as education and defense, despite tremendous cross-national variations in accounting procedures. In some Latin American countries education is funded by autonomous agencies and state governments as well as the national ministry; similarly, defense expenditures funded by outside aid or other ministries go unreported in defense ministry totals. Data on policy outcomes, although often more readily available, are not necessarily better. Governments do manipulate data for political purposes, and different standards are used in different countries for measuring everything from school enrollments to inflation.

Even more serious, the search for comparable indicators has restricted policy analysis to crude and readily quantifiable variables. As studies of public policy in Latin America have routinely noted (Schmitter 1971, p. 20; Hayes 1975, p. 50; Ames and Goff 1975, p. 195; Baloyra 1974, p. 9), the assumption that allocative policies provide an adequate inventory of policy outputs is theoretically unsound, particularly since common sense suggests that some of the major differences between military and civilian governments have to do with regulatory and symbolic policies. The right of workers to organize and strike, price and wage controls, the regulation of foreign investment, land reform, expropriation of private industry, control of the media—all these are policies that involve tremendous political conflict and affect economic development; yet none of them is likely to be directly reflected in government budgets. Enrique Baloyra's longitudinal study of public policy in Venezuela (1974) underlines this point. Baloyra found major contrasts between the oil policies of military and civilian regimes, but these contrasts were not reflected in the expenditures of the Ministry of Mining and Hydrocarbons. In short, government allocations provide, at best, a very partial guide to public policy.

In addition, it should be emphasized that indicators such as the proportion of the budget derived from indirect taxation or spent on education provide very little information even about allocative policies. For example, it makes a difference whether government revenues are derived from import or export taxes, although both are indirect forms of taxation. It also makes a difference whether import taxes are levied on luxury goods, raw materials, or industrial equipment. If indicators are too insensitive to monitor such differences, it is questionable whether we can draw any conclusions about the impact of political variables.

Problems also develop in drawing inferences about either the causes or the consequences of allocative policies. High levels of spending on education, for example, do not necessarily reflect a reformist orientation or even a regime priority. As Robert G. Drysdale and Robert G. Myers (1975, p. 257) point out in a perceptive essay on Peruvian education, government expenditures over time have been strongly influenced by factors such as growth in the school-age population, rapidly rising aspirations for education, previous regime commitments, relative and absolute increases in teachers' salaries, and the level of external financing from international development agencies. In short, simple contrasts between current spending levels and those of the previous regime may tell us little about regime priorities.

Education policy also illustrates a basic difficulty in drawing conclusions about the consequences of government allocations. High levels of educational expenditure may retard or promote growth, encourage or discourage income redistribution, and break down or maintain social privilege (Drysdale and Myers 1975, p. 254). Hence it may be misleading to assume that "compared to other areas of the federal budget, education is relatively beneficial to the lower classes" (Ames and Goff 1975, p. 179). By themselves, rough indicators of government expenditures and revenues just do not tell us enough about public policy. Complicating this problem, of course, is the fact that our general knowledge of the impact of alternative policies is limited.

The use of indicators of policy outcomes such as the rate of growth in GNP also raises numerous difficulties. First, policy outcomes are a very indirect reflection of regime preferences and policy decisions. While some studies have assumed that "extraneous factors" such as foreign investment, foreign aid, and export prices are distributed randomly (see especially Nordlinger 1970, p. 1138), it is necessary to control for a whole host of environmental factors to draw conclusions about the impact of regime type on system performance. The difficulty is that we have no neat list of such variables; moreover, serious statistical problems arise in analyzing the impact of a very large number of variables with a limited case base. The large gap that exists between regime type and policy outcomes also points to the importance of treating policy outputs as intervening variables—something that few studies have attempted to do.

A second major problem in using outcome indicators is that time lags occur between policy decisions and policy outcomes. High rates of investment under civilian regimes may not be reflected in indices of economic growth or energy consumption until another government is in office. To cite another example, an indicator of policy outcomes such as the annual percentage change in the number of physicians per 1,000 population, one of the four measures of social change used by Jackman (1976), will be very unresponsive to policy change in the short run.

The erratic growth pattern of Latin American countries also raises questions about the findings of cross-national studies of regime impact. A "snapshot" approach or examination at a single point in time may provide very misleading evidence. Table 1 illustrates the difficulty. Whereas in 1969 and 1970 the average per capita increase in GNP was higher for the civilian regimes in Latin America, in 1971 and 1972 the reverse was true. It should be noted that only one country shifted regime categories during these four years.

Finally, as the recent debate over the Brazilian regime has indicated, there are no established criteria for evaluating regime performance. Data that are available, such as GNP increase per capita, say very little about other less available monitors of performance such as the growth of income inequality. To date studies have taken a very narrow and selective view of system performance.

Diachronic studies evaluating the impact of regime changes within a single country, such as Hayes's work on Brazil (1973, 1975), offer solutions to some of the problems mentioned above, particularly problems in the comparability of data, selection of operational indicators, and instability of system performance. But these gains entail certain costs. Sample size is sharply limited, reducing the possibility of controlling for independent variables. Moreover, the consequences of regime changes can only be evaluated against necessarily counter-factual assumptions. As Schmitter (1975, p. 38) has persuasively argued, regime changes often occur to *prevent* policy changes. To demonstrate that a military regime's policy performance is identical to that of its civilian predecessor may miss the point. In short, problems in the operationalization of dependent variables, whether policy outputs or outcomes, plague both cross-national and diachronic studies.

But perhaps the most fundamental weakness of studies analyzing the relationship between regime type and public policy performance has to do

Table 1. Average Annual Rates of Growth in Per Capita GNP by Regime Type

Regime Type	1969	1970	1971	1972
Civilian	3.1	4.3	1.8	2.1
Military	2.4	3.3	3.3	3.3

Source: Statistics and Reports Division, Office of Financial Management, Bureau for Program and Management Service, Agency for International Development, Gross National Product: Growth Rates and Trend Data by Region and Country 1973:2.

with the independent variable. By assuming that regime type has the same meaning across political units, time periods, and even cultural regions, existing studies of public policy have built their conclusions into their questions. Obviously, military regimes do not form a homogeneous group. Military governments are reformist as well as conservative, populist as well as authoritarian, and personalist as well as corporatist. By aggregating all types of military regimes together, research to date has ensured that differences in regime type will appear irrelevant. Moreover, the use of the civilian-military dichotomy has obscured possible overlaps between civilian and military governments (Weaver 1973, pp. 94–95). Officers may exercise substantial influence even if civilians are in top positions and vice versa.

Recasting the Issues

The preceding discussion of conceptual and empirical problems found in recent research suggests that it is premature to conclude that regime type is not important for understanding public policy in Latin America. Rather, what can be concluded is that comparative studies of the relationship between regime type and public policy have defined policy outputs and policy outcomes too narrowly and/or too crudely in operational terms to demonstrate that regime type is not a significant independent variable. In addition, regime type has been so broadly defined, using the civilian-military dichotomy, that it is questionable whether the independent variable has been operationally specified in a manner sufficient to uncover policy consequences. The major contribution of the empirical studies conducted so far may simply be to demonstrate that the relationship between regime type and public policy is not easily studied using readily available aggregate data.

The manner in which the theoretical issues have been conceptualized for research may be part of the problem. An appropriate strategy in such a situation is to step back and reconceptualize those issues. One way to do this is to reconsider, one by one, the questions raised by the original arguments over regime type and public policy. At least three questions present themselves: (1) What is the nature of regime type (how can the independent variables be specified)?; (2) What is the nature of policy outputs (how can the intervening variables be specified)?; and (3) What is the nature of policy outcomes (how can the dependent variable be specified)?

The first issue, that of regime type, raises questions about the nature of military regimes and the extent to which they differ from civilian regimes. Military regimes are assumed to share certain characteristics (such as cohesion, ability to ignore popular pressures for consumption, etc.) that make them different from civilian regimes, supposedly leading to different policy outputs. The real thrust of this argument has to do with the characteristics imputed to military regimes, not the fact that they are military. Therefore, it may be suggested that the civilian-military dichotomy leads to the use of spurious variables. The relevant variables are those qualities attributed, very possibly incorrectly, to military or civilian regimes.

If we avoid the assumption that military regimes share certain characteristics and civilian regimes share others, we can reopen the question of what is the best way to arrive at a typology of regimes that is relevant for the explanation of policy consequences. Indeed, avoiding this assumption would seem fully justified in view of the accumulation of studies that have appeared since the Johnson-Lieuwen debate first began. The many case studies of military, and for that matter civilian, regimes show that Johnson, Lieuwen, and those that followed them were both wrong, or from another perspective, both right. Some military regimes are cohesive, some are not; some are developmentalist, some are not; some mobilize the population, some demobilize it; and so on.

The fact that military regimes need not share the characteristics attributed to them does not mean that those attributes are unimportant. On the contrary, it is precisely in terms of such attributes that a meaningful typology of regimes might be specified. Such a typology could be based, for example, on the following attributes that have been the subject of attention in the literature discussed: regime cohesiveness, degree of pluralism and/or interest-group autonomy, extent of developmentalist orientation, degree of popular support, control of mass media, extent of monopoly over the instruments of coercion, level of citizen participation in politics, and professional training and expertise of administrators. Such a list is hardly comprehensive, nor is it intended to be. It does serve to illustrate, however, the type of regime characteristics that appear and reappear in the discussion of military versus civilian regimes and that could be used as the basis for deriving a more theoretically meaningful typology of regimes for predicting public policy outputs.

Operationalizing regime characteristics such as those listed above certainly presents difficulties. Numerous studies of political development have provided us with measures of formal democracy and political stability, such as the degree of party competitiveness, degree of popular participation in elections, degree of press freedom, level of civil strife, and regularity of constitutional succession (see, for example, Banks 1971; Russett et al. 1964; Taylor and Hudson 1972; Collier 1975; Feierabend, Feierabend, and Nesvold 1973; Cutwright 1963; Bwy 1968; Adelman and Morris 1967; Johnson 1976; Elkins 1974). There have been fewer attempts to operationalize other theoretically relevant regime variables; nevertheless, the possibility of investigating them should not be excluded. The first item of the tentative list presented above, for example, has been plausibly operationalized in a recent study by means of a simple dichotomy between "senior leadership-headquarters planned coups" and "nonsenior leadership-headquarters planned coups" (Thompson 1976). Another recent study presents some imaginative suggestions for constructing nominal and ordinal scales of interest representation in Latin America (Collier and Collier 1977).

Turning to the second question, that of policy outputs, it might fairly be concluded that such outputs have been too narrowly construed. Most studies have utilized data on public expenditures and revenues as indicators of policy outputs. For the reasons discussed above, such data fail to provide an adequate picture of the policies followed by a regime.

What types of variables should be examined? This question should be answered in terms of the characteristics that are presumed to be important for distinguishing between types of public policy, rather than in terms of the convenience of data collection. In the case of Latin America, debate centers around issues such as government policy towards foreign investment, the degree of state involvement in the economy, allocations between the export sector and the internal market, the importance of agricultural versus raw materials and/or industrial development, interest group organization, distribution versus concentration of income, and land reform. The importance attached to such policies is easily seen in the extent to which the discussion of them dominates the recent literature analyzing controversial regimes such as those of Peru, Mexico, Brazil, and Chile (Lowenthal 1975; Chaplin 1976; Hansen 1974; Stepan 1973; Loveman 1976; Steenland 1974).

A more theoretically meaningful analysis of public policy might not lead to interval-scale indices of a type preferred in comparative studies, but it should be possible to arrive at ordinal-scale descriptions that would serve a similar purpose. One such technique, which has not been applied to the analysis of policy outputs in Latin America, would be developmental scaling (Leik and Matthews 1974), of which the Guttman scale is a special case. For example, land reform efforts might form the following scale: (1) no land reform; (2) a land reform that has not been seriously administered; (3) an active land reform limited to colonization; (4) an active land reform limited to colonization, public lands, and the expropriation of unused private lands; (5) an active land reform with some expropriation of private land but limited distributive results; (6) a land reform with a major redistributive impact; (7) a land reform of such an extent that the private sector is virtually eliminated. Similar scales could be derived to describe policy towards foreign investment, sectoral favoritism, income redistribution, and so on. Their use might entail some loss in the sophistication of data analysis, but they would permit systematic comparison and theoretical relevance in policy research.

The situation with respect to policy outcomes or overall system performance is far more complex. Insofar as system performance is treated in economic terms, it could be argued that the analysis of policy outcomes is a question for economists rather than students of government. As is evident from any perusal of the economic literature on Latin America, economists themselves disagree on the impact of particular public policies such as inflation or import substitution. Moreover, as small economic units linked to the world market, Latin American nations are extremely vulnerable to shifts in commodity prices, investment flows, and lending policies of rich nations and multilateral agencies. To take a single, but not farfetched, example, the performance of the Cuban economy depends in the short run far more on the price of sugar in the world market than on the economic policies of the Cuban government. Any attempt to evaluate system performance in Latin America must therefore attempt to factor out a host of exogenous variables, including influences as difficult to assess as maneuvers by multinational corporations or destabilization efforts by foreign governments.

For such reasons, it may be premature to attempt to assess system performance in Latin America, at least in economic terms. Similar problems, perhaps even more acute in data terms, attend efforts to assess system performance in political or social terms. Given our inability to analyze policy outcomes in any manner not open to serious theoretical and empirical question, the wisest course may well be to "bracket" efforts to assess system performance and concentrate research efforts on the relationship between regime type and policy outputs.

Conclusion

In summary, empirical studies have failed to establish any strong relationship between regime type and public policy in Latin America. The limitations of such studies, however, are so great that the relationship is still not clear. Nevertheless, analysis of these limitations does suggest some basic directions for future investigation.

It is recommended that the study of this issue should sidestep, for the immediate future, the analysis of system performance or outcomes, focusing instead on government policies or outputs. The impact of regime type on public policy should not be investigated in terms of civilian-military dichotomy, but rather in terms of the characteristics that have been imputed to civilian and military regimes. The analysis of policy outputs should be expanded beyond the study of gross categories of expenditures and revenue to include specific policies followed in key areas of state intervention, defined in more qualitative terms that can be categorized in a manner allowing systematic comparative analysis.

Such a research strategy will require far more detailed and conceptually relevant data than are currently available in cross-national data banks. Collecting such data necessitates greater recourse to case studies of individual countries, planning documents, and expert assessments. While cross-national comparisons will continue to be important, time-series data of the sort already emphasized in case studies deserve greater attention. In short, if we are to answer basic questions about the relationship of regime type to policy impact, a considerable effort to generate appropriate data remains before us.

References

Adelman, Irma and Cynthia Taft Morris
   1967   *Society, Politics and Economic Development: A Quantitative Approach.* Baltimore, Md.: Johns Hopkins University Press.

Ames, Barry
   1973   "Rhetoric and Reality in a Militarized Regime: Brazil Since 1964." *Sage Professional Paper in Comparative Politics,* 4, 01–042. Beverly Hills and London: Sage Publications.

Ames, Barry and Ed Goff
   1975   "Education and Defense Expenditures in Latin America: 1948–1968." In *Comparative Public Policy: Issues, Theories, and Methods,* edited by Craig Liske, William Loehr, and John McCamant, pp. 175–97. Beverly Hills and London: Sage Publications.

Anderson, Charles W.
   1967   *Politics and Economic Change in Latin America.* New York: Van Nostrand.

Ayres, Robert L.
   1975   "Political Regimes, Explanatory Variables, and Public Policy in Latin America." *The Journal of Developing Areas* 10 (October):15–36.

Baloyra, Enrique A.
   1974   "Oil Policies and Budgets in Venezuela, 1938–1968," *Latin American Research Review* (henceforth LARR) 9, no. 2 (Summer):28–72.

Banks, Arthur S.
   1971   *Cross-Polity Time Series Data.* Cambridge, Mass.: The MIT Press.

Bodenheimer, Susanne

1971   "Dependency and Imperialism: The Roots of Latin American Underdevelopment." *Politics and Society* 1 (May):327–57.

Bonilla, Frank and Robert Girling (eds.)
1973   *Structures of Dependency.* Stanford, Calif.: n.p.

Bwy, Douglas P.
1968   "Political Instability in Latin America: The Cross-Cultural Test of a Causal Model." LARR 3, no. 1 (Spring):17–66.

Cardoso, Fernando Henrique and Enzo Faletto
1969   *Dependencia y desarrollo en América Latina.* México: Siglo Veintiuno.

Chaplin, David (ed.)
1976   *Peruvian Nationalism: A Corporatist Revolution.* New Brunswick, N.J.: Transaction Books.

Clinton, Richard L.
1971   "The Modernizing Military: The Case of Peru." *Inter-American Economic Affairs* 24 (Spring):43–66.

Cockcroft, James D. et al. (eds.)
1972   *Dependence and Underdevelopment: Latin America's Political Economy.* Garden City, N.Y.: Doubleday Anchor Books.

Collier, David
1975   "Timing of Economic Growth and Regime Characteristics in Latin America." *Comparative Politics* 7 (April):331–59.

Collier, David and Ruth Berins Collier
1977   "Who Does What, to Whom, and How: Toward a Comparative Analysis of Latin American Corporatism." In *Authoritarianism and Corporatism in Latin America,* edited by James M. Malloy, pp. 489–512, Pittsburgh, Pa.: University of Pittsburgh Press.

Cutwright, Phillips
1963   "National Political Development: Measurement and Analysis." *American Sociological Review* 28 (April):253–64.

Drysdale, Robert S. and Robert G. Myers
1975   "Continuity and Change: Peruvian Education." In *The Peruvian Experiment,* edited by Abraham F. Lowenthal, pp. 254–301. Princeton, N.J.: Princeton University Press.

Einaudi, Luigi and Alfred C. Stepan
1974   "Changing Military Perspectives in Peru and Brazil." In *Beyond Cuba: Latin America Takes Charge of Its Future,* edited by Luigi R. Einaudi, pp. 97–105. New York: Crane, Russak & Co., Inc.

Elkins, David J.
1974   "The Measurement of Party Competition." *American Political Science Review* 68 (June):682–700.

Feierabend, Ivo K., Rosalind L. Feierabend, and Betty A. Nesvold
   1973   "The Comparative Study of Revolution and Violence." *Comparative Politics* 5 (April):393–424.

Fidel, Kenneth
   1975   "Militarism and Development: An Introduction." In *Militarism in Developing Countries,* edited by Kenneth Fidel, pp. 1–31. New Brunswick, N.J.: Transaction Books.

Fishlow, Albert
   1973   "Some Reflections on Post-1964 Brazilian Economic Policy." In *Authoritarian Brazil,* edited by Alfred C. Stepan, pp. 69–118. New Haven, Conn.: Yale University Press.

Frank, Andre Gunder
   1971   *Capitalism and Underdevelopment in Latin America.* London: Penguin Books.
   1972   *Lumpenbourgeoisie: Lumpendevelopment,* translated by Marion Davis Berdecio. New York: Monthly Review Press.

Hansen, Roger D.
   1974   *The Politics of Mexican Development.* Baltimore, Md.: The Johns Hopkins University Press.

Hayes, Margaret Daly
   1973   "Ecological Constraints and Policy Outputs in Brazil: An Examination of Federal Spending Patterns." Paper presented at the Annual Meeting of the American Political Science Association.
   1975   "Policy Consequences of Military Participation in Politics: An Analysis of Tradeoffs in Brazilian Federal Expenditures." In *Comparative Public Policy: Issues, Theories, and Methods,* edited by Craig Liske, William Loehr, and John McCamant, pp. 21–52. Beverly Hills and London: Sage Publications.

Jackman, Robert W.
   1976   "Politicians in Uniform: Military Governments and Social Change in the Third World." *American Political Science Review* 70 (December):1078–97.

Johnson, John J.
   1964   *The Military and Society in Latin America.* Stanford, Calif.: Stanford University Press.

Johnson, John J. (ed.)
   1962   *The Role of the Military in Underdeveloped Countries.* Princeton, N.J.: Princeton University Press.

Johnson, Kenneth F.
   1976   "Scholarly Images of Latin American Political Democracy in 1975." LARR 11, no. 2 (Summer):129–40.

Leik, Robert K. and Merlyn Matthews
1974   "A Scale for Developmental Processes." In *Scaling: A Sourcebook for Behavioral Scientists,* edited by Gary M. Maranell, pp. 365–87. Chicago, Ill.: Aldine Publishing Company.

Lieuwen, Edwin
1961   *Arms and Politics in Latin America.* Rev. ed. New York: Frederick A. Praeger.

Lissak, Moshe
1975   "Center and Periphery in Developing Countries and Prototypes of Military Elites." In *Militarism in Developing Countries,* edited by Kenneth Fidel, pp. 33–57. New Brunswick, N.J.: Transaction Books.

Loveman, Brian
1974   "Unidad Popular in the Countryside: Ni Razón, Ni Fuerza." *Latin American Perspectives* 1 (Summer):147–55.
1976   "The Transformation of the Chilean Countryside." In *Chile: Politics and Society,* edited by Arturo Valenzuela and J. Samuel Valenzuela, pp. 238–96. New Brunswick, N.J.: Transaction Books.

Lowenthal, Abraham F.
1974   "Armies and Politics in Latin America." *World Politics* 27 (October):107–30.

Lowenthal, Abraham F. (ed.)
1975   *The Peruvian Experiment: Continuity and Change under Military Rule.* Princeton, N.J.: Princeton University Press.

McAlister, Lyle N.
1966   "Recent Research and Writing on the Role of the Military in Latin America." LARR 2, no. 3 (Fall):5–36.

McKinlay, R. D. and A. S. Cohan
1975   "A Comparative Analysis of the Political and Economic Performance of Military and Civilian Regimes." *Comparative Politics* 8 (October):1–30.
1976   "Performance and Instability in Military and Nonmilitary Regime Systems." *American Political Science Review* 70 (September):850–64.

Needler, Martin C.
1969   "The Latin American Military: Predatory Reactionaries or Modernizing Patriots?" *Journal of Inter-American Studies* 11 (April):237–44.
1972   *The United States and the Latin American Revolution.* Boston, Mass.: Allyn and Bacon, Inc.

Nordlinger, Eric A.
1970   "Soldiers in Mufti: The Impact of Military Rule upon Eco-

nomic and Social Change in the Non-Western States."
American Political Science Review 64 (December):1131–48.

Nun, José
   1967   "The Middle-Class Military Coup." In *The Politics of Con-formity in Latin America,* edited by Claudio Veliz, pp. 68–118. London: Oxford University Press.

O'Donnell, Guillermo A.
   1973   *Modernization and Bureaucratic-Authoritarianism.* Berkeley, Calif.: Institute of International Studies.

Rankin, Richard C.
   1974   "The Expanding Institutional Concerns of the Latin American Military Establishments: A Review Article." LARR 9, no. 1 (Spring):81–108.

Ronfeldt, David F.
   1974   "Patterns of Civil-Military Rule." In *Beyond Cuba: Latin America Takes Charge of Its Future,* edited by Luigi R. Einaudi, pp. 107–26. New York: Crane, Russak & Co., Inc.

Russett, Bruce M. et al. (eds.)
   1964   *World Handbook of Political and Social Indicators.* New Haven, Conn.: Yale University Press.

Schmitter, Philippe C.
   1971   "Military Intervention, Political Competitiveness and Public Policy in Latin America: 1950–1967." In *On Military Interven-tion,* edited by Morris Janowitz and J. van Doorn, pp. 425–506. Rotterdam: Rotterdam University Press.

   1975   "Corporatism and Public Policy in Authoritarian Portugal." *Sage Professional Paper in Contemporary Sociology,* 1, 06–011. Beverly Hills and London: Sage Publications.

Steenland, Kyle
   1974   "Rural Strategy under Allende." *Latin American Perspectives* 1 (Summer):129–46.

Stepan, Alfred C.
   1973   "The New Professionalism of Internal Warfare and Military Role Expansion." In *Authoritarian Brazil,* edited by Alfred C. Stepan, pp. 47–65. New Haven, Conn.: Yale University Press.

Taylor, Charles Lewis and Michael C. Hudson
   1972   *World Handbook of Political and Social Indicators.* 2 ed. New Haven, Conn.: Yale University Press.

Thompson, William R.
   1976   "Organizational Cohesion and Military Coup Outcomes." *Comparative Political Studies* 9 (October):255–76.

Weaver, Jerry L.
   1973   "Assessing the Impact of Military Rule: Alternative Ap-

proaches." In *Military Rule in Latin America: Function, Consequences, and Perspectives,* edited by Philippe C. Schmitter, pp. 58–116. Beverly Hills and London: Sage Publications.

Willner, Ann Ruth
   1970   "Perspectives on Military Elites as Rulers and Wielders of Power." *Journal of Comparative Administration* 2 (November):261–76.

V
Democratization and Extrication from Military Rule

Douglas A. Chalmers
and
Craig H. Robinson

Why Power Contenders Choose Liberalization: Perspectives from South America

Many nations in South America have again begun the process of reshaping the regimes under which they live. Leaders are modifying or dismantling the military-authoritarian regimes which became widespread in the 1960s and 1970s to experiment with more liberal institutions and practices. Much is at stake in these changes. The history of terror, repression, and the violations of human rights which formed part of the military-authoritarian pattern has received ample documentation in the world press. The liberalization of South American regimes (for such we shall call the change that is in process) has already reduced the use of arbitrary coercion in Brazil and Uruguay.

There is another, more direct stake in these changes. A regime is essentially a pattern of policy-making, and the form of regime shapes the way political demands and visions become the policy that guides state action. As the state plays a larger and larger role in the lives of South Americans, the direction and quality of its policy are more important. Designing a regime—the institutions and practices through which policy is made—is therefore an act with great and ramifying consequences.[1]

We wish to propose a way of looking at these changes, offering tentative ideas about what is and is not changing, and what the crucial determinants are. We tend to be optimistic about the outcome in most countries, but we are not in a position to make hard predictions. Our point, however, is to provide a focusing lens for analysis of what will be a fast-moving and complex process occurring in many places at the same time.

The installation of authoritarian regimes in the 1960s and 1970s can be understood as the action of certain groups, principally the military, domestic and foreign businessmen, and high-level civil servants, to reshape (often forcibly) regimes to create order and promote economic growth according to a specified model. In a parallel fashion, the current wave of liberalization represents the beginnings of another attempt to "fashion a tool," to shape political institutions so the major groups can achieve a variety of goals under new conditions.

There are many questions which need to be asked about the current efforts at liberalization. How far will it go? Will the reforms introduced last? In whose interest will the state operate once the reforms have been made? What conditions will these reforms create for the mobilization of class energies to transform the social system toward socialism, or to complete the transformation of these societies into modern industrial ones? All these need answers, but it is our contention that a prior step must be to ask why a liberal form of regime is being considered in the first place.

Dynamics Behind Liberalization

We do not believe that liberal regimes are emerging by accident nor that they are the "natural" outcomes of underlying processes. Nor are they the result of work by advocates of human rights, no matter how sincere, well organized, and supported internationally. Liberalization is taking place, and will only go further, because influential groups in these countries find a liberal regime to be the most appropriate and useful manner of organizing political life under the present circumstances. The first task, before predicting its future or its consequences, must be to understand why and for whom liberal regimes have now become more attractive than authoritarian ones.

We emphasize the regime preferences of major groups not because we think *all* regime changes are determined by a collective decision based on such preferences, but because the particular characteristics of the current process make these preferences especially important. Today there is a protracted political confrontation, or "debate," concerning the manner in which the national state policy-making process will be structured. It is not, to be sure, a debate in a parliamentary style such as one might find in a constitutional convention (although such a convention was part of the process in Peru). It is more open and fluid and subject to the political capacities of groups for shaping agendas, building support, and forcing compliance.

It is, however, similar to a debate in that it is aimed at a collective decision, in this case a decision regarding how the nation will do its business. The outcome of this "debate" will depend on the resources and resourcefulness with which the participants act (and in an authoritarian situation, resources and the opportunities to use them are very unequally distributed). Chance occurrences are also important in an uninstitu- tionalized, freewheeling, and always potentially violent political engage- ment. But the first important step in analyzing such a debate is to identify who the major actors are and what they see their interests to be in the outcome of the "debate."

At other times, both in Latin America and elsewhere, regimes have taken shape under circumstances which precluded the possibility of a protracted debate, eliminated some potential actors, or forced the issue away from that of building a decision-making process. The fall of au- thoritarian regimes is often marked by conflict and disorder which leaves no time for serious political debate about the shape of the regime which replaces it. Some situations are revolutionary in the sense that old rulers become more intransigent and their opposition more insistent until an explosion occurs. Either the power holders hang on, precipitating a revolu- tionary battle (as in China or Vietnam) or, seeing their power fade, they suddenly collapse or depart, leaving a military scramble (as in Mexico and Russia).

Another sort of transition with violent diversions from concern for the niceties of regime formation takes place when authoritarian regimes are overthrown as part of a military conquest from outside. The process of shaping the new regime takes second place to winning power, imposing order, and establishing the legal right to rule. Crafting the state apparatus in line with the interests of the major power blocs is never the task at the time of the struggle, but only after the basic type of regime has been established.

In contrast to the more classic revolutionary situations in Nicaragua, and perhaps currently in El Salvador and Guatemala, there is little evi- dence now that the authoritarian regimes in the major South American countries will yield to a military struggle, either because of the rulers' intransigence or their sudden collapse. The broad conditions for turmoil, as they are conventionally understood, still exist. Social change has not slowed, and the gap between the rich and the poor is apparently still growing. However, for many reasons (some of which we shall review later in considering particular calculations), the chances of the process going out of control seem remote. The opposition seems willing to work within the system and the ability of governments to apply controls strongly and flexibly seems great.

Even in those cases where initial steps toward liberalization were perceived to be getting out of hand, control was established, or reestablished. In Brazil, for example, relatively minor groundswells of opposition after the 1978 elections were quickly channeled. In Peru, opposition to the economic austerity program of the Morales Bermúdez government in 1977–1978 was channeled into the electoral politics of 1979–1980. Much more severely, the Argentine military reestablished controls after the fiasco which followed Perón's death and ended that particular effort at liberalization. This latter case shows clearly that reestablishing control is not always an ideal nor necessarily a sign of health. It does suggest that regimes may be shaped from the top. The choice, as always, is constrained by circumstances but not preempted by disruptions nor overtaken by events.

The absence of breakdown means that the power holders of the authoritarian regime (the military and state bureaucrats) will not be deposed forcibly and will play a critical role in the "debate" over the new regime. The opposition plays a role as well, and the new regime will be the product of struggle and conflict. The opposition operates under disabilities ranging from the rather mild repression (now) in Brazil to the massive force periodically used in Argentina. Nevertheless, the opposition, through demands, example, demonstrations, and negotiations, not only struggles against the restraints of authoritarianism, but shares in shaping the new regime. In other words, the "debate" is carried on with a wide range of participants with little chance of an exclusive imposition from any side.

Moreover, the "debate" is not short-circuited by becoming only a division of the spoils between mutually isolated blocs engaged in a long-term political confrontation. Such a "deal" took place in Colombia in 1958, for example, as the National Front Agreement between the warring Liberal and Conservative blocs divided power in a "consociational" system (Wilde, 1978; Dix, 1980).[2] A liberal regime was created whose main characteristics were a rigid formula for allocating offices and no design for policy making. Although there is class conflict, conflict between domestic and foreign interests, and other major cleavages in South America, there are no countries where one can speak of longstanding confrontations between well-established ethnic, regional, or partisan blocs. The question of liberalization can no longer be resolved merely by parity and alternation in some form of party pact.

Calculated choice plays an important role in regime change in Latin America because cultural preferences for one or another kind of regime are weak or divided. This allows a few degrees of freedom for constitution makers. Much of the interesting work on democracy explores the cultural patterns (either in the sense of beliefs and values or of social practices) which underlie stable democracies (Almond and Verba, 1965; Dahl, 1971). There has also been considerable interest in the cultural roots of authoritarianism in Latin America and elsewhere (Wiarda, 1974). Such patterns of beliefs and practices in society do represent a constraint on the authors of constitutions; but for two reasons, operating with different force in different countries, and however important for many aspects of political behavior, we believe that this constraint of culture is minimal in shaping regimes. First, in many countries such as Brazil, Peru, and Argentina, several regimes have succeeded one another. What predispositions might exist toward one or another type of regime are never reinforced for very long and, even more, are not only confronted constantly with alternatives but also with past failures. The second factor is the presence of multiple tendencies in each country. Support for the exclusive legitimacy of one type of regime is rarely strong among very large segments of the population.[3]

In sum, the current process of liberalization is not like those processes of regime formation where circumstances impose outcomes and minimize debate. There is no major disruption and overthrow which would make order the overriding imperative and involve the physical elimination of major groups. There is no grand division between blocs which would reduce regime formation to a division of spoils. And there is no strong, unified political tradition which would give exceptional legitimacy to a single type of regime.

Regime formation, in other words, is a collective political decision. Under such conditions, the new regime will be shaped by powerful groups' interests in the structure of decision-making. This structure will be viewed in terms of its specific effect on the policies to be made and the relationship among the crucial participants (Chalmers, 1978). In such a process, every group will identify a regime interest, that is a preference for a particular structuring of the policy-making process. Occasionally groups define their permanent interests in terms of a preferred regime form, as in the case of monarchists or political liberals. Most politically articulate groups will have some ideal form of regime (usually "democracy") to be achieved "someday." In practice, however, regimes are almost always preferred on the basis of their utility in achieving other goals, and shift according to circumstances. The regime interests of businessmen, for example, may at one time be liberalizing to free them from regulation and at other times authoritarian to free them from disorder or challenges from other social groups. In the same manner, a party of the left may at one time have an interest in liberalization to enable it to achieve a wide base of support and at other times authoritarianism as a means of strengthening its internal cohesion, or when they are in power, of implementing their programs.

In a political confrontation among these regime interests, the institutions considered will be evaluated in terms of experience with the institutions of the existing regime, previous regimes, and relevant foreign ones. The debate will concern the medium range, not "forever," and will reflect efforts to solve problems that have arisen under the existing regime while aiming at a new solution to serve for about the same period as the last one, perhaps ten to twenty years. This implies that support for any new regime is likely to be conditional, just as support for the current regimes has been, but this should not be surprising in areas such as Latin America where regimes change often and social and economic change has been rapid. Since choices are not guided principally by widely and strongly held attachments to particular regimes, they are subject to change. Expectations are that a new regime will have to be reevaluated as circumstances change and new problems arise. It is quite likely, too, that the least change possible and necessary will be preferred, since they are not working out an ideal, but fashioning a tool. This is not a matter of incrementalism for its own sake, but of selecting the means appropriate to the end, and no more.

Regime interests are shaped for some groups, such as the military, by their prominent position and the special requirements of their institution as a corporate entity. Other groups, such as foreign businessmen, will have their perceptions shaped by the way in which they see the changes affecting their narrow material interest. Groups will judge their regime interest in terms of their relationship to the current authoritarian regimes. A simple relevant typology would include the ruling groups, which are those currently exercising power; the "accepting" groups, which are those who supported the regime, at least initially (either on the grounds of the direct benefits it would bring them, or the lack of any alternative), but who do not actively participate politically; and, finally, those who are in opposition.

Although the action of the ruling groups is critical, and that of the opposition most directly at stake, it appears to be the accepting groups, often a large segment of the middle class, professional, managerial and skilled strata, which provide the dynamic element in regime changes. They are the ones to whom the authoritarian rulers appeal for support in the first days of the regime, and the ones the rulers must at least minimally satisfy to stay in power. More than the opposition itself, their demands for liberalization are likely to be the most effective in convincing the rulers of the need for a change.

Liberalization versus Democratization

The choice that we are concerned with is the choice of regime, the norms which govern the procedures and practices for making policy, implementing it, and for selecting the people who play the appropriate roles. For understanding the nature of the choice being made, it is important to view a regime as a pattern of policy-making, rather than simply a set of rules or institutions. The choice before South Americans now is not what formalities to observe, but what shape to give the process which converts demands and ideas into state action.

The structure of norms which comprise the regime exists at several different levels. There are those which describe actual practice. There are legal norms meant to regulate practice which we often associate with a constitution. And there are symbolized norms which provide general guidance and meanings, such as the labels adopted (for example, "revolutionary" or "democratic"), and the clusters of "official" ideological rationalizations. A regime awards influence to some and not to others, makes some kinds of policy possible and others "out of the question." A regime by itself does not change social relationships nor the basic resources of major groups. But it shapes state action, which is called on more and more to direct, guide, and alter those relationships and resources. The regime is a form, but it is not a mere formality.

To change a regime, then, means to change the configuration of these norms. Regimes change constantly. The weakening of municipal autonomy, the introduction of primaries in an electoral process, or the weakening of cabinet responsibility to the parliament are all changes in the regime. What is at stake in these countries, however, is the change *of* a regime, that is, one which alters the principles on which the regime is ordered.

Using the conventional language, it would be usual to consider the opposite of an authoritarian regime a democratic one, and therefore to call the process of change we are considering "democratization." We have referred to it as "liberalization," however, in order to make clear a very important distinction which "democratization" tends to blur. The latter term embraces both a process of inclusion in the political process and the establishment of an open, competitive relationship among those who are already participating (Dahl, 1971). We use "liberalization" to denote only the second aspect of democracy, that which concerns contestation, competitiveness, openness. The reason for doing so is to emphasize the fact that the inclusionary aspects of democratization are unlikely in the process of regime change taking place in South America in the 1980s.

That the two processes occur independently is clear. The inclusion of substantial new segments of the population into the political process often takes place at a time when competition is being severely restricted. Perón's incorporation of large segments of organized labor in the 1940s in Argentina is an obvious example. But it is also true that increased competitiveness (liberalization) can take place without new inclusions.

Although it seems logical, many will not accept the distinction because "inclusion" (and "exclusion") is ambiguous. Here we use it to mean bringing a social group into the political system so that its interests become part of the calculus of policy-making, and its relationship to the state, conscious and explicit. Such was the case with the entry of labor under Perón. The other meaning of "inclusion" (which we shall not use) is that of giving such a group an independent and autonomous voice in the policy-making process. This does not describe what happened under Perón. This latter aspect is conceptually identical with increasing competitiveness.

Perceiving liberalization without inclusion requires that one understand groups to be "in" the political system, but not competing. It requires seeing the process of establishing the authoritarian regimes in South America not as "exclusion" of the working class, for example, but as the transformation of the relationships between the state and the workers by limiting their organizations and expression so that they no longer effectively compete. Rather than being excluded from the system, they are more tightly controlled, and, in fact, brought more closely into relationship with the state.

We dwell on this distinction because the pressures for inclusion have been so strong in South America over the last century that observers tend to assume that any relaxation of controls will result in such inclusion (and that no change without it is important). Highly oligarchic societies have been under attack for a long time in the region, as social changes have redefined the interests of provincial and professional hangers-on into "middle sectors," "marginals" into workers, and individually dependent peons into peasants. The recognition of parties representing these groups singly or in combination has been symbolic of this process of inclusion, and so has the evolution of various forms of corporatist institutions.

This process is no doubt far from over, but it does not appear to be at issue now in the major countries where liberalization is taking place. Few political actors, in the ruling groups or the opposition, are suggesting new self-definitions of groups in terms of their national importance as was being done in the *concientizaca·* of the 1960s.

In part, this is the result of the continuing control by relatively conservative military rulers in most countries. Opposition parties have little to gain by announcing radical new definitions of the political public when it would probably earn them deprivation of the slender rights of political mobilization that are becoming available. In addition, in most countries this redefinition of the political public has already proceeded far beyond what the parties, even in conditions of relative organizational freedom, have been able to mobilize successfully. For the moment, one might argue that there is no one available to include. This is, of course, not to argue that every citizen has an established right to participate in the political system. But the issue is now a question of numbers, the extension of mobilization to the rest of the peasants, workers, service employees, and others who are already partially mobilized. The important task now is that of making the nominal participation that is available through corporatist institutions or official parties more meaningful. This brings us back to the question of liberalization, that is, structuring the regime so that there is more meaningful participation in a regime formed on the principle of an open, competitive policy process.[4]

Principles of a Liberal Regime

In order to see what might be found useful and desirable about a liberal regime, it is necessary to break down this principle of "open, competitive regime" into those elements which distinguish it from the type of authoritarian regime which has predominated in the region.[5] Liberal democratic theory provides us with a wide variety of characteristics to choose from at various levels of specificity. Free elections are often thought to be the hallmark of liberal regimes. For our purposes, though, this is too specific an institution, and in itself, not clearly a shaping device for policy. Respect for individual civil and political rights is clearly a hallmark of liberal regimes, but as we have indicated before, the drive toward human rights has a limited value in indicating the choices of elites, except in a fairly restricted sense of the desire of the rulers to satisfy international standards on this subject.

We identify four principles of liberal regimes which might play an important role in a calculation of advantages and costs for elites:

1. Liberal regimes formally assign responsibility for making decisions to a series of institutions operating together through some formal policy-making procedure. Authoritarian ones concentrate such responsibility in the hands of the authoritarian ruler(s).
2. To control political dissidence, liberal regimes depend on consensus-backed legal procedures (or perhaps "hegemonic" institutions, to use a phrase from the neo-Marxist tradition with some relevance) while authoritarian regimes employ repression emanating from the "will of the ruler(s)."
3. Liberal regimes are pluralistic, with the participation and consultation of more, and more diverse, interests and groups than the "limited pluralism" of the authoritarian regime.
4. Liberal regimes encourage the articulation of many points of view, injecting diverse and conflicting information into the policy process, whereas authoritarian regimes sharply restrict the information flow, particularly its public form.[6]

We shall organize the rest of our discussion around the way groups view each of the four "principles" characterizing the liberal regime.

The Deconcentration of Formal Responsibility

Every regime vests ultimate responsibility for decisions somewhere, and indicates how and to whom accountability is enforced. This is not a question of describing actual patterns of influence and debate, but of establishing a regulating procedure. The placing of all responsibility on the authoritarian ruler obviously does not mean that the president-general makes all the decisions. But the authority and incentive to intervene throughout the policy process which it provides obviously affects the way decisions are made.

The military-authoritarian regimes in South America typically vested the broadest possible authority in a president or revolutionary council made up of the top military leaders. Accountability through elections was eliminated and, although it rarely was stated in a constitutional document, a very narrow pattern of formal accountability to the senior officer corps of the military services was substituted, enforced either by the threat of a "coup within the coup" (as in Peru), or through some form of regular selection of the president or controlled elections (as in Brazil).[7]

If authoritarian regimes are established in the midst of civil war, as in the case of the installation of Franco's rule in Spain, the basis of the supreme authority of the *caudillo* may be exceedingly difficult to view objectively as a grant of authority. In most cases over the last two decades, however, the concentration of authority and responsibility can be described as the abandonment of that responsibility by the established elite and its award to the military under a vague, implicit contract. Chile's military coup in 1973 might be an exception to this, in part because of the intensity of the conflicts which preceded it, but also because of the forceful and rather reckless assertion of power by the military, that is, the violation of the "contract" which many of the more moderate opponents of Allende thought they had in supporting the coup.

The choice to liberalize involves a choice to deconcentrate that authority. One historically significant way has been the devolution of authority to provincial (state) or local units in a federal system. Despite some symbolic identification with federalism, however, this sort of deconcentration has had very few roots in Latin America (Veliz, 1979) and seems more and more remote in all modern complex societies. Much more important will be that form of deconcentration which vests authority in a set of procedures through which responsibility is shared by the legislature, the executive and, probably, various forms of "autonomous" agencies. Accountability is enforced through the complex set of elections and formal requirements for hearings familiar in Western Europe and the United States.

Two aspects of the deconcentration of formal responsibility are noteworthy. Responsibility is diffused away from one identifiable point to many, acting through an impersonal process. In addition, restrictions are set on arbitrary action through accountability mechanisms, "checks and balances," and legal controls.

A very important aspect of the founding of authoritarian regimes in South America concerns the particular repository of supreme authority and responsibility, the military as an institution. The constitutions and public opinion of Latin American countries often granted the military a guardian role to act in times of crisis. For many years this meant either a temporary holding action by the military high command (until new elections could be held, for example) or the emergence from the military of a leader who took over the presidential role. This "last promotion" of a military officer was often merely an irregular means of selecting a chief executive who differed in his political behavior and structure of support only marginally from the civilian rulers he replaced. The earlier caudillos, such as Gómez in Venezuela or Díaz in Mexico, built political machines of regional commanders. The Mexican revolutionary generals were politicians who could use force. Carlos Ibáñez in Chile, and Perón in Argentina, were military men who virtually abandoned their military ties as they became more active politically. The significance of their military status was that they could come in without the usual party commitments. But they soon developed their own.

The recent military takeovers, however, went much further in actually installing the military hierarchy, command system, and system of promotions, not merely some military man. The attraction of the military was not merely that of a new face with few prior commitments, but of an entirely new and very different set of procedures and principles. Not just a man, but an institution "above politics" was taking over. Except for the brief caretaker juntas, this was not possible before because only in the 1960s did the professionalization of the military high command assume the strength and self-confidence sufficient to be a viable alternative (Einaudi and Stepan, 1971; Stepan, 1973). Although the military is often referred to as the "only party" in the authoritarian regimes, it is there in part because it is so very different from a political party or political machine in structure. This aspect facilitates a clear and rapid assignment of authority and responsibility in the authoritarian regime, but it also generates more clearly and rapidly the tensions and pressures that lead to a reversal of the grant, and thus to liberalization.

The pressures that bring about a choice for liberalization come both from within the military institution and from those who are subordinated to it. On the part of the military, the political strains of governing become increasingly difficult to insulate from the military-as-institution. When the mandate is clear, as it is in the crisis days of installation, political differences within the military can be minimized and the command character of military organization finds a rough parallel in the "needs" of governing (at least as seen by those who support the model adopted by the coup coalition). As time passes, the issues become more complex and crosscutting. In place of the panicked consensus on reestablishing order and, in the more conservative countries, carrying out "orthodox" economic policies, divisions emerge. The "hard line" versus the "soft line" within the military reflects division on the extent of repression. There are also differences concerning the role of the state in the economy and status of the multinational corporations. The competing developmental models clash with the need for unity within the military. The system of accountability within the high command, with its emphasis on seniority and defined career patterns based on military experience, conflicts with the needs of political management. Either the chain of command breaks down as the military becomes highly politicized, or the military as an institution draws back from politics.[8]

A variety of ways out of this situation short of liberalization have been tried or discussed. Dissident factions within the military have sought to solve the problem by an even firmer hard line (as in Brazil in 1969). Frequent efforts to build a dominant official party (as with the ARENA in Brazil and talk of a Mexican solution) or a corporatist political structure (as with SINAMOS in Peru) have all failed. To oversimplify, one might say that once the military's status "above politics" was exhausted, there were no other similar institutions, groups, or individuals which could merge with the military or create a new form of authoritarian regime in the military's image.

We suggest, therefore, that pressure toward liberalization comes from the military itself, which wishes to withdraw in order to preserve "good order and discipline." It seeks to avoid the opprobrium which goes with taking responsibility for complex and not always successful policies and the political divisions within the officer corps which might tear it apart.

From the standpoint of the ruling and accepting groups, the dangers of living with an absolute and arbitrary power vested in the hands of an institution which rules neither because of its technical skills nor its political stature are more obvious. When there is no dispute over the direction of the government's policy, the risk is minimal; but, from the moment that alternative possibilities exist, the power in the hands of the military becomes an increasingly uncertain affair. The dangers of a dramatically populist turn on the part of the military, not uncommon in the past, seems remote in the 1980s. But the danger of incompetence, of "reckless nationalism," or any other strong choice when there is uncertainty about the solution to pressing problems, is great.

Having suffered at the hands of the military, opposition groups are clearly not likely to be strong proponents of maintaining the generals' arbitrary power. There are many on the left who would like to install their own version of an authoritarian regime if given the chance, but with the passing of the crisis atmosphere, their chances of seizing power in this absolute fashion are very slight. In the manner of all oppositions, they are likely to settle for conflating demands for radical action and liberalizing the regime in order to build support for future actions. They, like the other groups in society, have much to gain from transferring ultimate responsibility to an open set of procedures, rather than vesting it in a particular person or institution.

Controls over Political Dissidence

The second dimension distinguishing liberal and authoritarian regimes concerns the manner in which antisystem political actions are prevented, channeled, or otherwise controlled. Totalitarianism differs from both liberal and authoritarian regimes by its very broad definition of what is considered disruptive. But the aspect which distinguishes the liberal from the authoritarian regimes, and plays a role in the elite calculation of costs and benefits, concerns the *means* used for control.

The hallmark of the authoritarian regime is the importance given to the arbitrary use of coercion, while in liberal regimes the emphasis is on the enforcement of commonly held norms through the courts. Both types of regimes are marked with coercion, but the authoritarian ones use it arbitrarily to stimulate fear and uncertainty, while the liberal ones strive to link it with stable expectations and legal norms. Both types of regime encourage large elements of passivity (for example, among the deprived, who might be tempted to rebel) and cooptation (among the most ambitious, who might be tempted to lead such rebellion).

The installation of the authoritarian regimes takes place at a time in each country when the controls are perceived to be breaking down. In a liberal regime, the effectiveness of the controls depends on agreement on the importance of order compared with goals achieved through disorder, and the effectiveness of enforcement institutions (courts, police, and so on). In varying degrees, from the relatively minor disturbances in Peru to the prolonged and intense breakdown of order in Allende's Chile, these elements began to decay in the 1960s. Conservative forces began to fear subversion more than disorder. Forces on the left began to reject the norms which formed the basis of behavior as being part of "capitalist hegemony." The agencies of enforcement (often including the army itself) became divided, politicized, and less effective in promoting order than in conducting "struggle."[9]

From the standpoint of the ruling groups of the authoritarian regime, the new system of arbitrary coercion had many advantages. It did not depend on consensus but rather relied on unilateral action. The shift from courts to police as enforcement devices allowed for much stricter control, more easily turned to political ends. By means ranging from intimidation to murder, the influence of opposition groups could be sharply curtailed. The accepting groups, the prospering middle class which came to accept the authoritarian controls, traded off their liberties for protection from the threat of disorder and subversion from below.

Several changes have come about in the past few years which have altered the calculations of the elites; the most dramatic have concerned the left. The leadership of radical movements has been decimated by murder, exile, and internal divisions. Reflecting a worldwide trend, radical movements have given new attention to the possibilities or necessities of working within the system. Throughout the 1960s and 1970s, there were segments on the left, often the communist parties, which advocated a more inside strategy, and sometimes cooperated with military rulers, as in Peru and Panama. The international models which appeared a decade ago to justify the disruptive, revolutionary road have lost their appeal as countries like Cuba and China have put a much more moderate face to the world. Chile's failure with the "peaceful road to socialism" appears not to have led, as one might expect, to a renewed commitment to violent change, but to a commitment to building a much stronger internal political base within the country than the Allende UP coalition had. Whatever its coherence and viability, Eurocommunism also served to emphasize strategies which involve accepting norms of political behavior in order to get on with the work of building an overwhelming majority (Carrillo, 1978).

For the accepting groups, particularly the middle sectors, the arbitrary use of repression, arrest, torture, and coercion increasingly came to touch their own lives, and for many, must seem less a guarantee against subversion than a direct threat to their own interests. Just who was the "enemy" of the government became less clear and less subject to the panicked consensus of the early days of the regime. From the standpoint of the ruling groups, the costs of arbitrary coercion begin to outrun the benefits when the instruments that are created to exercise this arbitrary force begin to escape the control of governmental leadership. This appears to have occurred in several countries, for example, in Brazil and Argentina. The very arbitrariness to the exercise of coercion against dissidents necessary to achieve the state of terror among large groups of people has led to severe difficulties in controlling the secret police entrusted with the task.

The international criticism of human rights violations is at least harrassing to governing elites. In addition, foreign businessmen, however they might have liked direct action taken against antiforeign movements in the early days of the regime, much prefer a system of controlling dissidents which is more predictable and, in a profound sense, more orderly.

The ruling groups in the region have before them many experiences in which arbitrary coercion used to maintain order has turned into disorder. There are a few cases where coercion stimulated more revolutionary action. Cuba in the 1950s is an example, as Batista's ever increasing use of terror made the revolutionary groups stronger. And there are other cases where the use of repression has led to a state of open war in the countryside, not immediately threatening the government, but nevertheless, exceedingly costly. The most prominent examples of the past few decades are the *Violencia* in Colombia, which decimated the countryside for more than a decade, and the continuing civil war in Guatemala.

Ruling groups, therefore, have a very strong self-interest in promoting a liberal form of regime, both because the chastened left may be more easily controlled, and because repression is a monster which can often get out of their hands.

Increased Pluralism

The adoption of a liberal regime will have the consequence of changing the criteria which determine whose views will help to shape policy. The military-authoritarian regimes set narrow limits. None ever publicly announced that they would rely on the opinions and desires of only a few, but all limited access. Under the rhetoric of defending the nation from subversive and corrupt politicians, conservative military rulers in Brazil, Argentina, Chile, and Uruguay moved to prevent radical political parties, labor unions, peasant organizations, and a wide variety of cultural and educational institutions from playing an active role by lobbying, agitating, suggesting, protesting, or otherwise participating in shaping policy. They were proscribed or converted into passive channels for the dissemination and implementation of government polity. In effect, this left the field dominated by the military, the foreigners, and the *tecnicos.*

Liberalization of the regime would reverse this process and those with the interest and the resources to do so, and who meet the formal requirements of the law, would presumably participate at will. The circumstances which would make this reopening of the system more desirable include the changing status of the opposition, the demand for strengthening nationalist influence on policy, and the complexity of the policy process in the rapidly expanding state. A few words about each are in order.

The most obvious gainers from liberalization will be the groups in the opposition, since they have not only lost their right to a say in policy-making, but have also borne the brunt of repressive policies affecting their interests. The most obviously affected groups, however, will probably be the least effective in ending authoritarianism. The political parties and revolutionary organizations which were the targets of direct attacks by the military governments are probably the least likely to be able to regroup and muster their strength. Organized labor, on the other hand, may be more effective. Its interests, and often its organizations, were, in many cases, the explicit targets of government policies aimed at controlling wage rates and the turmoil associated with the periodic demands for raises.[10]

Labor is often divided as a political force. Particularly in the cases of Argentina and Brazil (in very different ways), the corporate interests of labor leaders, frequently placed in office by the patronage of direct appointment by the government in power, will often suggest great caution in liberal reforms which might expose them to challenge from below. With that qualification, however, it is certain that labor will be on the side of liberalization if only to increase its influence. It may be effective episodically (as in the general strikes in Peru) or later in the process of change, when its resource of numbers for votes and demonstrations is more useful.

Labor's influence in a more liberal regime is likely to be tolerated by business, state planners, and economists because of their greater receptivity to the increased wages and other benefits which labor would demand. After a period of enforced austerity to accumulate capital for investment, many are seeking a stronger consumer demand. In addition, shortages of skilled labor may have the same effect, since skilled workers are likely to be the strongest participants in a newly liberalized regime, particularly through the organized unions.

A second area in which pressures for liberalization are emerging is more problematic, but perhaps more important and interesting. It concerns the impact that liberalization is likely to have on the influence of foreign interests in the decision-making process. The basic facts of economic dependency are not likely to change for these countries, but the capacity of the national communities to shape their own policies within that framework has changed and will continue to change. Opportunities emerge from the diversification of dependency, with the development of new exports, new sources of capital, and new trading partners, and with the proliferation of multinational corporations and international agencies.

Seizing these opportunities depends on the increasing sophistication of policymakers and in making nationalist interests more influential in policy-making. Liberalization is likely to strengthen this influence. It will thus be seen as a useful instrument by those with an interest in curbing the foreigner, both domestic businessmen anxious for protection and state officials seeking to extract the best possible deal in the expanding range of international contracts.

Liberalization can be seen not as simply freeing participation in the policy process to all comers, but as shifting the criteria for participation. Liberal institutions are built around participation by citizens. Its formal requirements are built around citizenship. Votes are for citizens, political office-holding is for citizens, and the formal right of access to the executive is for citizens.

Such formal requirements under the conditions holding in Latin America for many years have rather little impact on actual practice, although we believe that the situation is changing. Liberal regimes, from national independence through the middle of the twentieth century, have often been exceptionally penetrable by foreign embassies and businessmen. The great disparity of resources, the respect foreigners were given by many Latin Americans, and the overpowering dominance of a single outside nation (Britain in the nineteenth century and the United States more recently), opened liberal and authoritarian regimes to foreign influence, whatever the constitution said.

In the 1930s and 1940s, nationalist resistance to the foreigner often seemed to require purposeful exclusion by an authoritarian regime. Perón in his early period, Cárdenas in Mexico, and more recently, Castro in Cuba used authoritarian regimes to shape a nationalist policy. But things have changed. The old style of corrupting the legislators and buying the press is less effective with tighter supervision, more exposure, and much greater skepticism of the benefits of subservience to the foreigner.[11] The preferred habitat of the international executive, business or governmental, in this age of highly technical decision-making and high public exposure, is in the conference rooms of the presidency and the ministries of trade, finance, and planning, not in the halls of Congress or party election headquarters.

With very few exceptions, the authoritarian regimes in the 1960s and 1970s were open to international penetration far more than the liberal regimes that preceded them. The current liberalization will reaffirm the nationalist character of policy-making, not necessarily as an aggressive ideological nationalism, but through creating more opportunities for domestic businessmen to influence economic policy, more watchdog committees with subpoena powers to examine the practices of multinational corporations, and more elections to promote nationalist definitions of policy problems.[12]

Yet another set of conditions which promotes liberalization in the form of pluralization of influence is the increasingly diversified clientele of the state. The years of authoritarian rule have been ones in which the state apparatus in every country has expanded rapidly in size, functions, and responsibilities. The capacity of the state to collect taxes, to regulate the economy in both its domestic and international aspects, to administer expanding welfare and health programs, and to manage productive enterprises, has grown enormously. Ironically, in several cases, this growth has taken place under regimes which have rhetorically identified themselves with antistate symbols, reflecting the generally antisocialist mood of most military regimes. The expansion has taken place nevertheless.

The state's functions have multiplied and the impact on citizens has become complex and increasingly difficult to handle by the team of tecnicos assembled by the authoritarian rulers. Considerable pressure for liberalization comes from the middle sectors, heretofore content to remain passive acceptors of the authoritarian regime. They are drawn into active involvement with the ramifying state activity because of their range of specialized interests and concerns. The many demands to participate in particular issue areas have built up to more general demands for liberalization. The responsible state administrators as well will find it increasingly useful to provide some means of flexible sounding of opinion, some procedures which will take special, complex, and ever-changing decisions out of their hands, or at least have a way of validating their decisions through participation of those most affected.

Counteracting this will be the reaction to the inevitable erosion of the power of governments to plan comprehensively, and thus liberalization may be resisted by the top level technocrats.[13] The rationality and comprehensiveness of plans may be impossible, however, in the face of such complexity, since planners are unable to comprehend all aspects of policy. The wisest of planners may see liberalization as a way to avoid unreasonable demands for comprehensive plans that they cannot provide.

More Open to New Information

The policy process is not just a competition of interests, but is also a dialog or debate in which information, proposals, and problem-definitions interact to define the agenda, inform the choices, and supply the technical knowledge necessary for implementation. In an ideal policy process, information flows freely and decisions flow smoothly from it. A thorough exploration of problems for state action is accompanied by clarification of values and identification of available instruments for action. The process then moves expeditiously to a decision that reflects fairly the information and a reasonable accounting of interests, and finally, to implementation. The conscious distortion introduced under authoritarian regimes restricts the first steps in this process. Liberal regimes emphasize precisely those steps (at the risk of disrupting the later ones).

In the strongly mobilizational revolutionary regimes which have been called totalitarian, this flow of information is strongly shaped around the ruling ideology. Contemporary military-authoritarian regimes have not had anything as strongly structured as an ideology. The occasional efforts to propagate a unique vision of the world such as the "national security doctrine" of the Brazilian military, or the corporatist ideas in Argentina or Peru, have generally been haphazard and inconsistent. But restrictions on information have been severe. Press censorship, purges of the universities, control of the electronic media, and the sharp limitation of public debate in parliamentary institutions have been common.

Like other authoritarian regimes, those in South America have consciously distorted the information flow to guard policy-making from "distractions." They have restricted the open public arenas of discussion, sharply limited the flow of information about the values and attitudes of citizens, and shifted debate on policy away from the early stages of problem-definition to questions of implementation. The advantages lie in the concentration of effort on chosen policies. The costs lie in potential error and failure to adapt.

Since most South American elites have experience with the liberal regimes, their evaluation will measure the authoritarian system not against an ideal of free information, but against the potential deformations in a liberal regime. From the standpoint of ruling groups, at least two possible dangers exist in the more open liberal regime. The first is that critics may seize on divisions to polarize opinion and to mobilize a revolutionary force. Second, and usually more realistically, uncertainty may prevent making any decision whatever, or lead to hasty and ill-considered ones. The two fears are intertwined since immobilism may lead to revolution, and both fears played an important role in the overthrow of liberal regimes in the 1960s.

The behavior of these regime types is not inherent in their structure, but depends on the conditions under which they operate. The conditions which made the authoritarian distortion of the informational flow rational (from the point of view of the ruling groups) was the conviction that, at least in the short run, there were very few options for policy makers to follow. The choices were thought clear and implementation has to be harsh and thorough. In Brazil, Chile, Argentina, and Uruguay, among others, these measures included austerity (particularly for working-class consumption), infusions of foreign capital to further industrialization and revive exports, and measures to clean out subversion and corruption from public administration. In Peru, dedication to these goals was supplemented with a commitment to implementing the modernizing reforms that had been stalled in a deadlocked Congress.

In the early sixties, with the Cuban revolution much in their minds, the revolutionary and democratic left also advocated strong policies of structural change. The challenge from the left was not one cast in a manner to question and clarify goals and means. It was given and accepted as an alternative set of goals held with equal certainty and supported by a theory of basic, structural conflicts which rejected the possibility of serious political debate.

For the left and the right, politics became the process of seizing or increasing power to implement policies already thought to be clear. The right saw political debate as merely a subversive means of mobilization. The left saw political debate as superfluous (except as a tactical maneuver) in an age when the content and irreconcilability of interests were obvious.[14]

In the past ten years, both the left opposition and the ruling groups have lost that certainty about the agenda. The left has turned toward a complex and many-sided internal debate as guerrilla and other strategies to attain power failed. The assumption that the use of that power would have been clear has been questioned with the fading of the belief that Cuba or China have proven programs of action.

The military governments and their allies have carried out parts of their programs, changed other parts, and moved on to other problems. The complication of their agenda has come with the problem of defining "success" in the light of serious income inequalities and such issues as the environmental problems associated with rapid growth. The worldwide energy crisis has created a new set of problems which cannot be handled by merely pushing legislation through and implementing it forcefully. Dramatic shifts in the international balance of power have made foreign linkages a question of choice rather than a simple acceptance of a tie with an ascendant United States. Managing an enormous international debt might appear to demand authoritarian enforcement of austerity, but it also demands a more fluid and subtle strategy backed by a larger degree of public support. The question is no longer simply how determined a government is in implementing the obvious, tough decisions, but how well it decides what decisions to take.

Opening the debate to diverse sources of opinion and analysis will increase the amount of information and insight about problems and their solutions. Decision makers will be able to use this broad range of ideas to establish a more appropriate agenda of politics. The more sensitive members of the ruling groups will see the desirability of trading a measure of arbitrary power for the greater informational resources available under a liberalized regime.

From the opposition's point of view, liberalizing the information flow is an obvious *desideratum* to put their case before the public. The accepting groups, decreasingly confident that they understand or are fully convinced by the drastic policies of the authoritarian regimes, seek a fuller debate. In so far as these accepting groups are the better-educated middle sectors in the professional, university, and communications fields, the desire to open up the process of decision-making also becomes of direct personal concern. It is precisely in the sphere of debate and discussion that their resources and skills become highly valued.

The free flow of information can, and perhaps has, become not simply an ideal of liberal theorists, but an instrument for dealing with complex problems.

Summary

Liberal regimes are often treated by analysts as desirable on moral and philosophical grounds, but as impractical luxuries. In contrast, authoritarian regimes are seen as potentially evil, but effective. We believe that this is a dangerous point of departure. It overestimates the potency of liberal values and underestimates the utility of liberal institutions. There are, to be sure, many Latin Americans genuinely committed to political liberalism, and, as in most Western societies, there is no doubt a general preference for democratic values over authoritarian ones. But we believe that the driving force for liberalization lies in the fact that important groups believe liberal procedures and institutions are more effective and efficient *under existing conditions.*

We have tried to show some of the more powerful arguments which might persuade groups with totally instrumental views that liberalization was desirable. We cannot, in this sort of presentation, demonstrate conclusively that the groups do in fact see things this way, but we hope to have illustrated a line of argument which is uncommon in discussions of liberalization and bears further exploration.

We go one step further. Liberalization seems to us to be on the agenda in the major South American authoritarian systems because certain basic circumstances have changed which have increased the utility of liberal institutions. These rather basic "structural" changes increase the probability of liberalization. They do not, of course, determine it. Even if we are right about the general direction of structural change, such changes are not irreversible. Further they must be perceived, and the political responses, confrontations, and debates must successfully produce the desired liberalization. But there is room for optimism.

Rather than repeating all the particular trends which encourage optimism, it may be useful to summarize by indicating three aspects of change which appear to be crucial for the swings between authoritarian and liberal regimes by virtue of their effect on calculations of utility.

The agenda of politics: Liberal regimes become rational choices when the issues facing a country are diffuse and complex, requiring procedures for identifying problems, clarifying goals, and ordering priorities. Authoritarian regimes become more likely when some process has focused this agenda on a small range of crucial, basic issues and the major task concerns mobilizing energies and ensuring forceful implementation.

The level and type of conflict: The institutions of a liberal regime are by far the most effective in serving the interests of groups seeking to win the commitment of the state and society toward achieving broad goals. They fade in those situations in which a substantial and powerful group subjectively defines its own interest as fundamentally irreconcilable with those of the existing society, or of some particular group within society. Authoritarian regimes, in other words, emerge when some group has defined its interest in "zero-sum" terms. This happens when a traditional elite, or perhaps a threatened bourgeoisie, reacts against what it perceives to be a fundamental threat from new forces, whether it be international forces of modernization working to extinguish traditional institutions or a socialist revolutionary group. Such a self-definition of irreconcilable hostility also characterizes some revolutionary left organizations, which cut off all debate in order to use the clashes and potentially violent conflict to radicalize.

State expansion: The growth of state services, bureaucracy, and assumption of responsibility for social and economic functions is a persistent and dominant trend, marked by periods of administrative centralization and decentralization. The manner in which that rhythm is related to the political control of administration in authoritarian or liberal regimes is by no means simple, but appears to us fundamental. Without pretending to identify a simple theoretical proposition, we believe this relationship is important in the transitions going on in South America. The tremendous expansion in the state apparatus which took place under the authoritarian regimes (especially including the growth of strong bureaucratic "fiefdoms" in financial, development, and defense areas) seems to demand the adoption of a pluralistic political process to establish accountability. Authoritarian procedures may be necessary at other phases, in order to push an aggressive expansion of state control over segments of civil society, or to back up a vigorous administrative centralization.

We must emphasize that liberalization if it is carried to completion, will not bring the end of capitalism, transform traditional isolated backlands into functioning parts of modern society, or drastically alter the international dependency of these countries. Nor will it dramatically democratize these societies, in the sense in which we have defined that term. In short, liberalization is not a revolutionary process.[15] It is, nonetheless, a very significant one. First, it will directly affect the lives of millions of South Americans who have suffered under the authoritarian regimes. Second, liberalization is significant because it creates the conditions necessary for political dialog, debate, and confrontation. The return to public politics will not solve the basic structural questions facing South American societies, but it is probably a prerequisite to the specification of those questions. Although some seem to believe that what needs to be done is obvious, it is our belief that an open political process of identifying those needs is an important first step.

This phase of liberalization may well be as fragile as the last. In other words, the wheel may turn once again. To the modern mind schooled either in the virtues of political stability or of revolutionary finality, this may seem to make the game not worth playing. We would suggest that there is another model, which provides a different perspective. An ideal as attractive as that of stability would be a nation which is able to adapt its regime form to changing conditions. Assuming that the costs of changing regimes do not exceed the benefits of the change, such a political system of adaptive regime changes would have much to recommend it. No doubt this ideal is as utopian as one which posits some perfect regime which can endure forever, but the emphasis that we have placed on the utilities and values of adaptation (in this case, toward a liberal regime) might suggest that an approximation of such adaptation is at least as plausible and reasonable to strive for as the goal of perfect stability.

Choice implies different responses to variable conditions. It also implies the possibility of mistakes, failure, and the breakdown of the constituent process of liberal regimes themselves. But the reasons for liberalization seem strong enough to suggest that liberalization will be the wave of the immediate future.

Notes

1. The act of shaping a regime and forming a constitution has often been singled out as a special and especially important political act (Arendt, 1963). Behavioralists and Marxists have led us away from such "formalism," but with increasingly less justification as the state expands its role and makes the political process more important, and its structure more significant.
2. See Rustow (1970), in which he argues that stable democracies often, perhaps always, go through such a standoff phase. His concern is with *stable* democracies, and not the immediate turn to a liberal regime.
3. This is the phenomenon that Anderson (1967) had in mind in referring to the "living museum" of political ideas in Latin American societies. It is unclear whether it is more appropriate to think of these diverse legitimizing cultures as dividing the people, as in the image of competing parties in Chile, for example, or whether it is not more appropriate to see for most countries a repertoire of traditions available. Stepan (1978) treats the "organic state" tradition, stemming from Catholic thought and underlying the experiments with corporatism in Peru, as an "available option" showing a model and suggesting grounds for its adoption. In this case, of course, the *constraining* quality of political culture disappears. Also, Wiarda, while arguing that the corporatist tradition may well give different meaning to what is "democratic" and what is not, recognizes the existence of both "corporatist-organicist-patrimonialist" features and "liberal-republican-representative ones based on the Anglo-American model" (1980: 240). The emphasis must return to decision.
4. To be more accurate, one should probably refer to this process as a "republicanization" rather than "liberalization" since the latter term is associated with laissez-faire economic policies, as well as the political reforms of the nineteenth century that went with them. The role of the state is so great that "liberalization" in that complete sense probably is no longer possible. "Republicanization" would fit better, too, with the classical notion of creating a *res publica* which would allow for realization of citizenship rights in guiding the state. Unfortunately, "republicanization" would rightly be considered, now, to be hopelessly confusing, anachronistically carrying notions of overturning monarchies.
5. It is tempting to turn to the definition of an authoritarian regime, such as that offered by Linz (1970), and "work backwards" toward the liberal regime. Of the four main characteristics that Linz offers, however, two—"mentalities," rather than ideologies, and demobilization—are essentially distinctions between the authoritarian regime he is concerned with (Spain under Franco) and the "totalitarian" regimes. Only "limited pluralism" and "rule by an individual or small group" are clearly relevant here.
6. The emphasis on information freedom is an old theme in liberal thought, although it has often, recently, been treated as an individual right to information and expression, rather than as an element of the policy process. See, however, such earlier theorists as Mill (1859) and, among the modern writers, Apter's (1965, 1968) use of information as a key part of the definition of "reconciliation system," his word for more liberal regimes.
7. Brazil's military leaders originally thought after the 1964 coup, sufficient power could be concentrated by purging Congress, the press, and the courts, but retaining a formally liberal assignment of responsibility to a congress, courts, and elections. By 1968–1969, they concluded that formal responsibility would have to be concentrated in the hands of the President through declaration of much wider decree powers and a severely weakened Congress.

8. This notion parallels the common one that the military has no means of legitimation, no institutional support to provide political backing, and thus rules only by coercion (O'Donnell, 1979). But this carries the point too far. Legitimacy comes not only from the "mediations" of guaranteed individual rights and popular access to decision-making, as O'Donnell implies, but from a generalized belief that the leaders are making appropriate policy. Some authoritarian rulers (for example, Franco in Spain) were able to maintain political support for a very long time on the basis of such a basic appeal, despite the viciously divided society at the beginning of his regime. Authoritarian regimes are not inherently devoid of legitimation; their ability to maintain legitimacy depends on the generally accepted definition of "what needs to be done" and their effectiveness in doing it. In this they share characteristics with liberal regimes, of course, as they do in using coercion when all else fails.

9. The abandonment of order in this fashion is the subject of many analyses (for example, Linz and Stepan, 1978) of the collapse of liberal regimes, a central theme of political analyses after the horrifying experiences of the period from the 1920s through 1945 in Europe.

10. Among the most convincing analyses of the argument that there was a structural source leading to the installation of authoritarian regimes is that of O'Donnell (1973), who emphasized the economic crisis (of "import substitution") and the need for an explicit set of controls on labor in order to continue the capitalist development model then holding sway. But see also Collier (1979), which is largely devoted to reviewing, refining, and modifying parts of this thesis.

11. It may be suggested that Chile, where the CIA funneled money to influence elections in 1964 and 1970, is an exception. We believe, however, that the "old-fashioned" efforts of corruption and influence were of relatively less importance, perhaps even negative, and that in so far as outside influence helped an Allende's overthrow, it was through the international economic measures that were taken.

12. In this regard see Flynn's discussions of the Parliamentary Inquiry into the role of the multinational corporations in Brazil (1978: 488–492) for an example of the kind of activities which may have more impact under a liberalized regime than this did under an authoritarian one.

13. The tendency of liberal regimes to parcel out decision-making has been a long-standing theme of a certain group of critics of American politics (for example, Schattschneider, 1960; McConnell, 1970; and Lowi, 1969). The same point is made by conservative critics such as Huntington (Crozier et al., 1975).

14. Hirschman (1963) has long emphasized correctly the importance for politics in the region of the way in which problems are perceived as requiring basic structural change for their solution. He has recently (1979) returned to this theme, noting that an "autonomous increase in problem-and-solution proposing" and "ideological escalation" preceded the rise of authoritarianism. We are inclined to give considerable weight to such factors for the specific task of explaining the shaping of regimes, although perhaps more than he, we emphasize the variability of this mood of certainty about major, structural changes.

15. In this sense, Cardoso's (1979) distinction between a regime, which may be changing, and a state, which is not, is pertinent, although he uses a very formalistic definition of regime.

References

Almond, G. A. and S. Verba (1965) *The Civic Culture: Political Attitudes and Democracy in Five Nations.* Boston: Little, Brown.

Anderson, C. (1967) *Politics and Economic Change in Latin America: The Governing of Restless Nations.* New York: Litton.

Apter, D. A. (1968) "Why political systems change." *Government and Opposition* 3 (Autumn): 411–427.

———(1965) *The Politics of Modernization.* Chicago: Univ. of Chicago Press.

Arendt, H. (1963) *On Revolution.* New York: Viking.

Cardoso, F. H. (1979) "On the Characterization of Authoritarian Regimes in Latin America," in D. Collier (ed.), *The New Authoritarianism in Latin America.* Princeton, N.J.: Princeton Univ. Press.

Carrillo, S. (1978) *Eurocommunism and the State.* Westport, Conn.: Lawrence Hill.

Chalmers, D. A. (1978) "The politicized state in Latin America," in J. M. Malloy (ed.), *Authoritarianism and Corporatism in Latin America.* Pittsburgh: Univ. of Pittsburgh Press.

Collier, D. [ed]. (1979) *The New Authoritarianism in Latin America.* Princeton, N.J.: Princeton Univ. Press.

Crozier, M., S. P. Huntington, and J. Watanuki (1975) *The Crisis of Democracy.* New York: New York Univ. Press.

Dahl, R. A. (1971) *Polyarchy: Participation and Opposition.* New Haven, Conn.: Yale Univ. Press.

Dix, R. H. (1980) "Consociational Democracy: The Case of Colombia." *Comparative Politics* 12 (April): 303–321.

Einaudi, L. and A. Stepan (1971) *Latin American Institutional Development: Changing Military Perspectives in Peru and Brazil.* Santa Monica, Cal.: Rand Corporation.

Flynn, P. (1978) *Brazil: A Political Analysis.* Boulder, Col.: Westview.

Hirschman, A. (1979) "The Turn to Authoritarianism in Latin America and the Search for Its Economic Determinants," in D. Collier (ed.), *The New Authoritarianism in Latin America.* Princeton, N.J.: Princeton Univ. Press.

———(1963) *Journeys Towards Progress: Studies of Economic Policy-Making in Latin America.* New York: Twentieth Century Fund.

Linz, J. (1970) "An Authoritarian Regime: Spain," in E. Allardt and S. Rokkan (eds.), *Mass Politics: Studies in Political Sociology.* New York: Macmillan.

———and A. Stepan [eds.] *The Breakdown of Democratic Regimes.* Baltimore: Johns Hopkins Univ. Press.

Lowi, T. (1969) *The End of Liberalism.* New York: Norton.

McConnell, G. (1970) *Private Power and American Democracy.* New York: Vintage.

Mill, J. S. (1975) [1859] *On Liberty.* New York: Norton.

O'Donnell, G. (1979) "Tensions in the Bureaucratic-Authoritarian State and the Question of Democracy," in D. Collier (ed.), *The New Authoritarianism in Latin America.* Princeton, N.J.: Princeton Univ. Press.

———(1973) *Modernization and Bureaucratic-Authoritarianism: Studies in South American Politics.* Berkeley: Institute of International Studies, University of California.

Rustow, D. (1970) "Transitions to Democracy: Toward a Dynamic Model." *Comparative Politics* 2 (April): 337–363.

Schattschneider, E. E. (1960) *The Semi-Sovereign People.* New York: Holt, Rinehart & Winston.

Stepan, A. (1978) *The State and Society: Peru in Comparative Perspective.* Princeton, N.J.: Princeton Univ. Press.

———(1973) "The New Professionalism of Internal Warfare and Military Role Expansion," in A. Stepan (ed.), *Authoritarian Brazil: Origins, Policies and Future.* New Haven, Conn.: Yale Univ. Press.

Veliz, C. (1979) *The Centralist Tradition in Latin America.* Princeton, N.J.: Princeton Univ. Press.

Wiarda, H. J. (1980) "The Struggle for Democracy and Human Rights in Latin America: Toward a New Conceptualization," in H. Wiarda (ed.), *The Continuing Struggle for Democracy in Latin America.* Boulder, Col.: Westview.

———[ed.] (1974) *Politics and Social Change in Latin America: The Distinct Tradition.* Amherst: Univ. of Massachusetts Press.

Wilde, A. (1978) "Conversations among Gentlemen: Oligarchical Democracy in Colombia," in J. Linz and A. Stepan (eds.) *The Breakdown of Democratic Regimes.* Baltimore: Johns Hopkins Univ. Press.

Jonathan Hartlyn

Military Governments and the Transition to Civilian Rule: The Colombian Experience of 1957–1958

In the 1980s, a number of the countries in Latin America whose civilian political regimes were overthrown by military regimes are undergoing or attempting to consolidate processes of democratization or redemocratization. In this context, the reexamination of earlier examples of durable transitions from authoritarian military regimes to civilian regimes may shed light on the relative importance of different factors in determining particular outcomes. The study of such transitions can usefully occur at three levels of analysis: the impact of the international environment and external actors; the role of national actors, events, and political arenas; and the role of key individuals and political statecraft, voluntaristic actions, and circumstance (Middlebrook, 1981). This paper considers the interaction of both international and domestic factors and employs elements from all three levels of analysis in focusing on why the regime of General Gustavo Rojas Pinilla (1953–57) in Colombia was unable to consolidate itself and on the major predicaments faced by the interim military junta during its fifteen-month period in power (1957–58), the period of the transition process to the consociational National Front.[1]

This chapter examines the three major predicaments that such transi-

From Jonathan Hartlyn, "Military Governments and the Transition to Civilian Rule: The Colombian Experience of 1957–1958," *Journal of Interamerican Studies and World Affairs* 26, no. 2 (1984), pp. 245–281. "Revised and reprinted by permission of the author and the *Journal of Interamerican Studies and World Affairs.*

tion processes confront. One predicament relates to the transition coalition, which is the coalition of political, social, and economic groups dedicated to a return to democratic rule. Given the inevitable differences among the various groups, how can the transition coalition prevent divisions from opening up the way for a return to the old authoritarian regime, or to the creation of a new one? Can guarantees be provided to the central actors in the transition processs to retain their loyalty and support? One point of stress within the coalition may well be treatment of the military. Thus, a second predicament in any transition process is the management of the armed forces who have stated their willingness to return to the barracks. If we assume the military continues to hold the monopoly of force in a country, then what is required is to convince the military that their best interests continue to be served by their decision to withdraw from power. There is a constant need to defuse the potential threat of a counter-coup to stop the process of transition.

Logically, these two predicaments subsume most others, whose importance would be reflected by their impact on either the military or the transition coalition. Yet, one predicament is so frequently a significant accompanying factor that it warrants separate analysis: the economy. Questions regarding the management of the economy may threaten the coherence of the transition coalition or re-create opposition within the military to the transition process.

The central theme of this analysis is that the ultimate success of the transition process in Colombia is best understood in terms of two mutually reinforcing factors: a skillful political leadership confronting a weak opposition, and particularly favorable domestic structural conditions (along with less favorable international ones). During the period of the military junta, the transition process was seriously challenged by each predicament. The transition to civilian rule was spearheaded by leaders of the country's two major political parties, the Liberal and the Conservative, who had committed themselves by a series of pacts eventually approved by a national plebiscite to govern the country jointly. Just a few years earlier, political conflict between the two parties paved the way for one of the bloodiest chapters in Colombian history, known as *la violencia* (the violence).

The parties' National Front agreement limited majoritarian representative democracy in the country, while assuring each party it would not be excluded from power. The agreement in its final form stipulated that from 1958 to 1974 the presidency would alternate between members of the two parties; all Cabinet offices, legislative and judicial posts, and government employment positions were to be divided equally (and exclusively) between the two parties. In addition, most measures would require a two-thirds vote in Congress for approval. The consociational nature of the political regime thus established is evident from the unique strength and nature of the two major political parties in Colombia, the fact that a return to civilian rule in 1958 was inconceivable without extensive mutual guarantees between the two parties and from the characteristics of the National Front agreement negotiated by the party leaders.[2] Yet at times consociational pact-making succeeded almost in spite of these leaders. This indicates how important various political, economic, and social conditions were in providing a structural space and opportunity for the negotations to be successful. It also shows how weak the challenges were to the success of the transition process. Subsequent events would demonstrate the conservative nature of the consociational solution: it promoted the defense of organized minority rights over majority rights, thwarted reform, and produced governments with strong immobilist tendencies (for a similar point regarding the Venezuelan case, see Karl, 1981; see also Levine, 1978).

The Rojas Regime: How It Rose, Why It Fell

General Gustavo Rojas Pinilla came to power in the midst of *la violencia* at the behest of a segment of the Conservative party and elements of the military, and with the approval of the Liberals, many of whose leaders were in exile. His only opposition came from the president he had deposed, the Conservative Laureano Gómez, and from the small Communist party.

This was the first military government in Colombia during this century. The history of the country has been one of hegemonic one-party rule, violent civil wars, and coalition governments, assuring that the two political parties formed in the mid-nineteenth century would be the vehicles through which political demands could be channeled. The last of the country's civil wars had begun as a result of the 1946 elections by means of which the minority Conservatives had gained the presidency because of a split within the Liberal party. Violence accelerated following the assassination in 1948 of the populist Liberal Jorge Eliécer Gaitán in the streets of Bogotá resulting in days of rioting, the *bogotazo* (Oquist, 1980: 118–121). After a complex series of maneuvers, including several failed attempts at compromise between Liberal and Conservative leaders, the political regime collapsed in November 1949. Facing impeachment proceedings in the Liberal-dominated Congress, the Conservative president Mariano Ospina (1946–50) declared a state of siege, closed Congress, banned public meetings, and imposed censorship of the press and radio (Wilde, 1978: 51–58).

Following these actions, Gómez, unopposed, was elected president. By this time, large areas of the country were submerged in violence.[3] Under Gómez, censorship intensified, repression against labor increased, and violence against Liberals and Protestants, sometimes with the cooperation of local clergy, intensified. As Gómez moved toward imposing a new falangist-corporatist constitution on the country that would vastly strengthen his powers, and as violence continued unabated, Conservative leaders, particularly former President Ospina, began to conspire with the military against him, eventually leading to Gómez's overthrow in June 1953.

The Colombian military did not have the capability or the inclination to govern the country without civilian assistance. General Rojas, like much of the military officer corps by this time, identified with the Conservative party. Rojas also desired Church support and approval. Initially, his goal appeared to be to broaden and improve the Conservative party (Dix, 1967: 116). To provide a veneer of legitimacy to his rule, Rojas had the National Constituent Assembly (ANAC—*Asamblea Nacional Constituyente*) elect him to fill the remainder of Gómez's term. The ANAC had been established upon Gómez's request in order to approve his constitutional reform. Subsequently, with Ospina presiding, the ANAC "elected" Rojas president for the 1954–58 term. Rojas' government was heavily staffed with Conservatives, particularly Ospinistas, and his major economic and political advisers were civilians. Yet, as it became clearer that he was seeking to consolidate and probably prolong his stay in office, civilian opposition began to intensify.

The weakness of Rojas' challenge to the traditional parties was a reflection of their continued centrality to Colombia's political life. As he moved ambiguously and ultimately unsuccessfully toward attempting to build his own political base within labor as well as his own political organization, he alienated the Church and the political actors who had initially supported him. Other factors also contributed to his weakening base of support: he alienated broad sectors of the population by government brutality, incompetence, and corruption and by continued press censorship; in late 1954 and 1955, government troops clashed with Liberal and Communist peasant groups, as other modalities of violence continued, leading political and economic leaders to fear an incipient social revolution in the making; his Peronist leanings and economic policies gained him U.S. opposition; and Rojas lost the support of powerful domestic economic actors by his statist and populist economic policies even as economic transformations during his period in office strengthened their organization and coherence (for general descriptions of this period, see Martz, 1962; Dix, 1967; Williams, 1976; and Tirado, 1978).

By late 1956, Rojas' hold on power had eroded considerably. A central cause of that erosion was the consociational alternative created by political party leaders to oppose him. In early 1956, the former Liberal president, Alfonso López Pumarejo (1934–38; 1942–45) suggested that Liberals agree to support a previously agreed-upon Conservative candidate for the 1958–62 presidential period and seek an agreement with the Conservative party by means of which the parties would be represented in the executive branch in a manner proportional to their legislative representation. Alberto Lleras was chosen to direct the party in order to seek agreement with the Conservatives.

Much as interparty violence has had extensive historical antecedents in Colombia, so bipartisan coalitions also have occurred frequently in Colombian history. Prior examples include the *Concordia Nacional* immediately following the turn of the century civil war known as the War of the Thousand Days, the *Unión Republicana* a few years later, the *Concentración Nacional* government that ushered the Liberals into power in 1930, and the essentially unsuccessful *Unión Nacional* governments of Alberto Lleras (President, 1945–46) and of Mariano Ospina (in 1946–48 and for a brief period in 1948–49). Remarkably, the components of the National Front agreement had all been suggested or implemented at some point in the 1946–49 period (Wilde, 1978).

Why would the Liberal party, which had received an electoral majority in the country since the 1930s, agree to support a candidate of the opposing party for the presidency? There appear to have been two major reasons. Conservatives were to a significant extent already in power and were unlikely to sign an agreement that would require substantially relinquishing it. And, it was even less likely that Rojas, a "Conservative in uniform," would ever agree to hand power over to a Liberal (retired military officer, interview with author, 1982; see also *El Tiempo*, 1957f).

Yet, with whom should the Liberals seek an agreement? The Conservatives remained bitterly divided. Gómez was unforgiving of all who played a role in his overthrow, especially within his own party. The Liberals approached Ospina first, but he was reluctant to negotiate with them. He feared that if he reached an agreement with the Liberals, the wrath of Gómez would descend upon him, further diminishing his standing within the party—which was already affected by his links to Rojas (Lleras, García and a prominent Conservative politician, interviews with Pinilla, 1979; Villareal, interview with the author, 1982). Numerous Ospinistas also retained high positions in the government, although by 1956 Ospina personally had distanced himself from the Rojas regime (Tirado, 1978: 183).

Thus, Lleras sought out Gómez in exile in Spain in July 1956. Discussions between the two leaders led to the Declaration of Benidorm, which called for a return to republican rule by means of one or more coalition governments (the text of this and subsequent documents are in Colombia, Cámara de Representantes, 1959). A "Civic Front" of opposition began to grow within the country. By January 1957, after the minister of war declared that the armed forces had "irrevocably" decided that Rojas would remain as president until 1962, Ospina indicated his full support for the bipartisan alternative with a Conservative presidential candidate. Guillermo León Valencia became that candidate and a symbol of the parties' opposition to Rojas. His Conservative credentials, bravery, and fiery rhetoric were requirements for a candidacy with an uncertain future (Liberal and Conservative politicians, interviews with author, 1982).

The next stage in the creation of the political alternative to Rojas was the Pact of March ("Joint Manifesto of the Liberal and Conservative Parties"). The extensive document called for free elections for the presidency, in which the two parties would present jointly a single candidate of the Conservative party, and guarantees of parity. Furthermore, it reaffirmed the privileged position of the Catholic Church in Colombia (see Levine and Wilde, 1977). Gómez opposed parts of the pact, and most members of the Laureanista Directorate ended up not signing the joint manifesto (Vázquez, n.d.: 232; Betancur, interview with Luis Pinilla, 1979). To place additional pressure on the Rojas government, Valencia's candidacy was officially launched in April.

As the succession crisis brought increasing numbers of political leaders into the transition coalition, the country's growing economic crisis further convinced businessmen of their need to support the party alternative. Forced to choose between potential future presidential ambitions of his civilian and military advisers, Rojas opted for the military, thus losing the counsel of his major strategist and minister of government, Lucio Pabón Núñez, in April.

The crisis came to its resolution during the "days of May." On May 1, Rojas unsuccessfully tried to place the parties' candidate, Valencia, under arrest. Student demonstrations erupted in the country's major cities. On May 5, police tear-gassed the Bogotá church of an antigovernment priest. Two days later, a nationwide civic strike led by the country's bankers, industrialists, and merchants shut down the country's major cities. On May 8, Rojas desperately convened the Constituent Assembly, which quickly approved his reelection for the subsequent presidential term. Rojas also nationalized a major bank and decreed that banks could not charge interest on outstanding loans while they were closed, although deposits would continue to earn interest. (See Ediciones Documentos Colombianos, 1957: 178–80; the decrees were annulled by the Junta on May 11 [226]). The next day, the Church hierarchy strongly attacked the regime. Businesses continued closed and massive demonstrations against the government continued. On May 10, a five-man military junta was placed in charge of government and Rojas flew into exile.

The only bulwark of support for the regime remained the armed forces, which retained extreme loyalty to Rojas. Yet, the armed forces feared for their institutional cohesion and possessed serious doubts about their "mission" in the context of the Rojas government. Some military officers had been displeased by the corruption within the regime. Toward the end, most objected to the sudden turn to socialism indicated by the nationalization of the banks. Within the senior ranks, there was little desire to battle the unarmed middle-class civilian demonstrators in the streets and concern that significant public opinion mobilized by the "Civic Front" was anti-military. Elements of the air force appeared prepared to take violent action to force Rojas' downfall.[4]

Finally, Rojas asked Antonio Alvarez Restrepo to convene a group of Conservatives to study formulas for his withdrawal from office. Valencia and other opposition leaders demanded that the Liberals be included in any transition government. The military, through their intermediary, General Rafael Navas Pardo, insisted on a military junta so they could dismantle the military government themselves. Finally, the civilians agreed to a junta in which the Cabinet would have equal numbers of Liberals and Conservatives (see Ediciones Documentos Colombianos, 1957: 197–200; also, Alvarez, Navas, Lleras, and others, interviews with author, 1982).

The military junta consisted of high-ranking military officers, though seniority was not strictly respected. General Gabriel París, Rojas' former minister of war, became head of the junta. Probably the two most active and ambitious members of the junta were General Navas, former commander of the army, and General Luis Ordóñez, former head of the intelligence service. The fourth and fifth members were Vice-Admiral Rubén Piedrahita and General Deogracias Fonseca. It is unlikely Rojas was totally free in selecting the junta (confidential interviews with author, 1982; see Martz, 1962: 249–50; Dix, 1967: 120–28; and Rojas' explanation in Colombia, Senado de la República, Comisión Instructora, 1960: 758–74).

Many players harbored secret plans: Rojas expected the junta, which had several members who had been deeply loyal to him, would soon invite him to return; some Conservatives hoped the transition would allow them to continue governing, largely excluding Liberals; a few military officers probably possessed presidential ambitions of their own. Yet the strength of the alternative, the Civic Front, was immense as was reflected in the junta's program announced the day of its formation: formation of a bipartisan Cabinet, temporary closing of the Constituent Assembly, reestablishment of freedom of the press, and elections to replace the junta at the end of Rojas' presidential term in August 1958 (Junta Militar de Gobierno, 1957).

Consociational Pact-Making During the Transition Process

Continued violence in the countryside, spreading in some instances to the cities, and serious economic problems confronted the junta and its bipartisan Cabinet. Yet, party leaders also had a continuing political problem. They needed to decide how they would provide mutual guarantees to each other, and the process by which power would be transferred to them from the military junta. The major problem, apparent even before the fall of Rojas, was the split within the Conservative party. The concrete issues the parties faced were the specific mechanisms by which mutual guarantees would be provided and the presidential candidacy of Guillermo León Valencia.

The negotiations by means of which these two issues were settled were complex; different actors' intransigence and last-minute crises fostered the hope of opposition movements. Yet, in spite of their differences, *all* the major political leaders were firmly opposed to any alternative political regime that did not comprise extensive mutual guarantees to the two parties—of that much *la violencia* and the Rojas government had convinced them. Thus, even as the difficulties mounted, none of the disgruntled actors were available as allies to forces opposed to the transition process. Furthermore, they did not have other significant differences relating to the socioeconomic order or central political procedures and constitutionalism.

The Liberals continued to identify with the presidential candidacy of Valencia. Yet Gómez continued to communicate from Spain his total opposition to Valencia. He appeared to have several motives: a desire to punish those Conservatives who had conspired to overthrow his government; a fear that a weak, divided Conservative party in the presidency would provide a bad government from which the Liberals could derive advantage; and, personal antipathy to Valencia. At the same time, Valencia made several negative comments about the armed forces that further fueled opposition to his candidacy within the military.[5] Furthermore, there was no agreement on how coalition rule would work. Faced with these problems, Alberto Lleras traveled once again to visit Laureano Gómez in Spain.

The Plebiscite and Mutual Guarantees

What form were the mutual guarantees between the parties to take? Confronted with a divided Conservative party and fearful of the alternatives of extended military rule, renewed partisan violence or class-oriented conflict, Liberals and Conservatives alike were inclined toward a rigid agreement between the two parties. Thus, in the Pact of Sitges, Lleras and Gómez agreed to parity in Congress and in the Cabinet for a period of twelve years. They concurred that the most practical method of instituting this agreement was by means of a national plebiscite. If congressional elections were held first and one party received a significant majority, that could complicate successful passage of a constitutional reform imposing parity. An extraconstitutional agreement to present joint Liberal-Conservative congressional lists would not necessarily solve the problem, since nothing could prevent those opposed to the National Front plan from presenting dissident lists (see the discussion by Lleras in *El Tiempo*, 1957p). Lleras was wildly acclaimed upon his return from Sitges and the military junta enthusiastically backed the new pact. The Pact of

March disappeared from public discourse and the new agreement made no mention of presidential candidacies.

Because of the Conservative divisions, elaboration of the constitutional reform to be approved by the plebiscite required a complex three-month process. The text was finally approved by the military junta and its bipartisan Council of Ministers in October and elections were set for December 1, 1957. The Liberals agreed to a special preamble affirming the centrality of the Catholic Church in the country. The core of the agreement as it emerged was the consociational measures of parity in Congress and a mandatory two-thirds majority vote until 1968 with certain exceptions, parity in the executive and judicial branches[6] and a number of measures to depoliticize public administration. These measures included the creation of a civil service, restrictions on political activities of government employees, and prohibitions against political discrimination in hiring and promoting public officials. Other measures granted women the right to vote (a measure initially approved by Rojas), required that legislators be paid a daily wage rather than a salary (to prevent absenteeism), declared that all future constitutional amendments would have to be approved by Congress, stated that presidential and congressional elections would be held on the same day, and decreed that at least 10 percent of the national budget should be spent on education. The confidence of the military in the transition process increased, as it was specified that members of the armed forces could serve in government independent of the requirements of parity. This measure promised them autonomy in managing their own affairs. Since 1958 the Ministry of Defense has always been occupied by a military officer.

Presidential Candidates

The issue that still threatened to torpedo the carefully constructed agreement remained Valencia's presidential candidacy. Gómez returned to Colombia in October 1957 to excoriate Valencia who had just been acclaimed as candidate in an Ospinista Convention. Soon after, Valencia's candidacy was rejected at the Laureanista Convention. In November, Gómez wrote the junta requesting that the plebiscite be postponed and threatening to pull out of the National Front agreement if congressional elections were not held first so that the Conservative faction with the majority could present its presidential candidate (Navas interview with author, 1982). The junta called together the major political leaders at the Presidential Palace. The Liberals leaned on Valencia to concede to Gómez, and an agreement was reached *just nine days* before the scheduled date for the plebiscite election. The "Pact of San Carlos" established that congressional elections would be held prior to the presidential ones, and that Valencia's candidacy would have to be ratified by the newly elected members of Congress of both parties (text of accord in Colombia, Cámara de Representantes, 1959: 89–91; Navas, Lleras and Jaramillo interviews with the author, 1982).

Although these last-minute complications accentuated conspiratorial opposition (discussed below), the plebiscite was approved by 95 percent of the voters in a high turnout election. Given the complexity of the agreement, it is likely that many voters were not certain for what they were voting. However, major organized groups in society endorsed the plebiscite: the parties, the Church, industrial, commercial, financial, and labor organizations. Only Gilberto Alzate and Jorge Leyva, from the right wing of the Conservative party, opposed the constitutional reform.[7] In the March congressional elections Gómez's adherents received 59 percent of the Conservative vote (which in turn represented 42 percent of the total vote). Most of the remaining Conservative vote went to supporters of Valencia, although backers of Gilberto Alzate, pro-Rojista, and anti-National Front, did win a few seats (*El Tiempo*, 1958a and 1958b; *Semana*, 1957a).

Now that a Valencia candidacy was ruled out by the Laureanista victory, the central question shifted: who would be the National Front candidate for the May 4 elections? Incredibly, the issue was resolved *just ten days* prior to the elections, when Alberto Lleras accepted the nomination. In accepting, Lleras agreed to present a constitutional amendment to Congress providing for alternation of the presidency between the two parties for the following three terms, and extending the agreement on parity in Congress an additional four years. In that way, in the period 1958–74 each party would hold the presidency for two terms, and the last National Front president would be a conservative. As with the previous negotiations, the steps preceding this determination were fraught with obstacles (Vazquez, n.d.: 312–20; Martz, 1962: 268–69). They fueled considerable Conservative dissatisfaction and a coup attempt two days before the presidential elections.[8]

Lleras had been the public figure most identified with the bipartisan National Front effort and the opposition to Rojas. Yet, given the fact his candidacy was defined only days before the May 4 election, his margin of victory highlights both the dominance of the National Front actors and the weakness of their opposition. Lleras was opposed by Jorge Leyva, whose sectarian Conservative campaign supported by Alzate garnered only 20 percent of the total vote and won a majority only in the department of Norte de Santander. On August 7, 1958, Lleras was given the oath of office by the new president of the Senate, Laureano Gómez.

The Armed Forces and the Transition Process

The difficulties surrounding final negotiation of the plebiscite and determination of who would be the first National Front president offered opportunities to disgruntled Rojista military and sectarian Conservatives to try to overthrow the junta. Part of the mobilization against the Rojas regime resulted from opposition to the favoritism and corruption of the regime. Continued press about the "crimes" committed during the Rojas government could serve to mobilize support for the civilian alternative. Yet, the country was now governed by military officers who had occupied central positions in the previous government whose continued support was essential for the success of the transition process. In addition, vigorous investigation could also implicate civilians who were now defenders of the transition process. Thus, the central strategy pursued by the party leaders was the de-linking of the Rojas regime from the armed forces, suggesting that the attempts to create an independent political movement, his government's economic policies, and most of the financial irregularities were committed by members of the "presidential family" and a few civilians closely tied to Rojas, not by the military.[9]

This strategy of de-linking was greatly facilitated by the fact that Rojas' dictatorship was relatively benign, even by 1950s standards (cf. accounts in Szulc, 1959). An official investigating committee was established to explore charges of alleged irregularities regarding coffee contraband, double-invoicing of imports, selling of import licenses, livestock transactions, land purchases, use of public agencies for private gain, and bank loans for the Rojas family. However, the committee complained of official obstructionism and changed personnel several times and few arrests were made.[10]

The junta sought to prevent counter-coup movements. Because of the strong pro-Rojas sentiment within the army's intelligence branch, a separate intelligence organization charged with keeping track of conspiracies to overthrow the government was established under General Navas (Matallana and Forero, interviews with author, 1982). Counter-coup movements found support within arch-Conservative and pro-Rojista groups. Some Conservatives were upset by the presence of Liberals in the Cabinet and the fact that Liberals were slowly being appointed as mayors and governors. Some military officers felt a sense of betrayal against Rojas and the armed forces, as well as a loss of status. Following the fall of Rojas, mysterious explosions rocked the homes of anti-Rojista newspaper columnists. Partisan violence in rural areas and assassinations in urban areas, particularly of amnestied guerrillas, continued.

In the second half of 1957, coup conspiracies sought to bring Rojas back to the country. Four months after his fall from power, Rojas was stopped in the Dominican Republic. The junta threatened to suspend the license of any airline that brought Rojas to Colombia. Another plan called for Rojas to enter Colombia from Venezuela (Cúcuta) and lead a march to Bogotá. Rojas apparently lost his nerve and did not appear. The uprising by the regional Police Battalion was quickly controlled by loyal troops. In November, as the politicians argued over elections, the junta foiled another coup attempt, arresting and eventually purging many pro-Rojista officers (see *El Tiempo*, 1957n; 1957m; and 1957c; Navas and Forero, interviews with author, 1982).

The most serious challenge to the regime came only two days before the presidential elections. On May 2, 1958, four of the five members of the junta, and Alberto Lleras (the presidential candidate), were apprehended in the early morning by elements of the military police and the national police in Bogotá. The fifth, Piedrahita, avoided capture, and by a fluke, Lleras, was released by troops not involved in the plot. Lleras and Piedrahita rallied loyalist forces from the Presidential Palace, and the support the coup leaders had expected did not emerge. The leaders of the coup, of whom the most important was Lieutenant Colonel Hernando Forero, commander of the Bogotá Military Police Battalion, were allowed to seek diplomatic asylum in return for the safe release of the junta members.

Additional facts about the failed coup remain in dispute (the following details are from Forero, interview with author, 1982). Two Conservative leaders knew at least the outlines of the coup plot. One, Gilberto Alzate, wrote a draft proclamation which he subsequently withdrew after it appeared the coup attempt was failing. Many members of the Constituent Assembly that had reelected Rojas in May 1957 and had been dissolved by the junta were prepared to reconvene to provide some legitimacy for the coup. Furthermore, Forero noted that the coup was discussed with two members of the junta who never openly rejected it, and that one had expressed interest in serving in a subsequent government if the coup were successful. In addition, the commanders of both the army and the air force were also involved in coup discussions. At the time, Forero accepted most of the blame for the coup, and no attempt was made to investigate his allegations that higher officials were involved. The junta members denied any involvement, and Lleras absolved them of any responsibility (see also Dix, 1967: 127–28; Leal, 1970; and Revista de Historia, 1977). One plausible interpretation is that the coup was essentially the idea of ambitious middle-level officers in conjunction with a few arch-Conservatives, and that senior officers may have listened to their plots, and in some cases acquiesced to them, without seeking direct involvement. Indeed, officers in only four of the seven battalions in Bogotá were directly involved in planning the attempted coup.

Could the coup have succeeded if the entire junta and Lleras had been captured? The post-coup plan of the plotters, their "mission," was vague. They had shelved the idea of calling for the immediate return of Rojas. There was, moreover, no significant economic or social plan (Forero, interview with author, 1982). If the coup plot had progressed, violence could have rapidly escalated within the country as civilian opposition expressed itself and the armed forces divided. Liberals had strengthened their organizations and only a minority of the Conservatives would have given their support; Laureanistas, in particular, would have rejected overtures from the military.

Senior military officers, impressed by the support for return to party rule by financial, industrial, and commercial elites, fearful of the loss of prestige of the armed forces and the divisive currents within it, and confronted by civilians who appeared sensitive to their major fears, stood by their pledge to withdraw from power. As they perceived the country's situation, probably correctly, the other major alternative was a chaotic period of unstable governments with uncertain domestic and international support. The National Front did not threaten them personally or the armed forces as an institution. It would permit them to focus their attention on what they perceived as a growing guerrilla threat in the countryside and place responsibility for management of the economy on the civilians.

The Economy

As Rojas left office in May 1957, the country faced numerous economic problems. As one economist has written:

> The bad news included growing payment arrears, capital flight, tightening import restrictions, increasing use of bank credit to finance public deficits, as well as a generally expansive credit policy, growing inflationary pressures, a rising black-market peso rate, stagnant real output, and, last but not least, a falling dollar coffee price (Diaz-Alejandro, 1976: 19).

In its fifteen months in office, the new government imposed a stabilization plan that cleared away many of the short-term economic problems they inherited, permitting the first civilian government to inherit a more positive economic picture. One of the country's central problems remained the external sector, because of low coffee prices. As Table 1 indicates, the country's total exports dropped significantly in the period the junta was in office. The effects of the stabilization plan imposed by the junta are reflected in Table 2. During the period in which the junta was in office, economic growth declined, industry went into a recession, inflation climbed upward, and public expenditures were cut back. Real wages, after a brief upsurge due to a decreed wage increase, soon fell due to inflation. Yet, when compared to other countries, the drops in growth rates resulting from the stabilization plan do not appear as sharp in Colombia during these years (Diaz-Alejandro, 1976: 20–21, 24).

Transition leaders viewed recovering Colombia's external credit as esential for economic recovery (see the analysis by the outgoing ANDI president, *El Tiempo*, 1957t). Two weeks after the May coup, the International Monetary Fund was invited to visit the country. The most serious problem

Table 1. Colombia: External Sector

	Coffee Prices (lb. New York) 1	60 kg. Sack Exported (thousands) 2	Total Exports (Current U.S. $Millions) 3	Total Imports cif (Current U.S. $Millions) 4
1952	57¢	3,032	514.6	415.4
1953	60¢	6,632	670.9	546.7
1954	80¢	5,754	763.0	671.8
1955	64¢	5,867	657.3	669.3
1956	73¢	5,070	738.4	657.2
1957	64¢	4,824	667.3	482.6
1958	52¢	5,440	607.8	399.9
1959	45¢	6,413	635.9	415.5

Sources: Columns 1, 2, and 3, Zuleta, 1975; column 4, Nelson et al., 1971:157.

Table 2. Colombia: Economic Indicators

	Growth in GDP (% Change from Previous Year, 1970 Constant Dollars) 1	Inflation Index (Bogota composite) (% Change from Previous Year) 2	Industrial Production (% Change from Previous Year) 3	Public Investment (Millions 1970 pesos) 4
1953	6.0	7.5	6.5	2,146
1954	7.2	9.0	14.4	2,646
1955	4.0	0.0	12.9	3,710
1956	3.9	6.4	2.9	3,519
1957	1.5	14.6	− 1.0	3,102
1958	2.3	15.0	− 1.1	2,739
1959	7.8	7.2	5.6	2,788

Sources: Columns 1 and 2, Wilkie, 1974:393, 227; column 3, Poveda, 1976; column 4, Amézquita and Fernández, 1977:6.

consisted of the backlog of unpaid short-term commercial loans taken out principally in 1955 and 1956. In June the government devalued the peso significantly and reduced the differential between the import and export rates, cut public expenditures (including a reduction in the size of the armed forces by ten thousand men) and established a new agency to review import requests. The junta was able to acquire significant external support for the country, including a $60 million credit from the U.S. Export-Import Bank as well as a $27 million private bank loan. However, as coffee prices continued to drop, reserves also fell and the pressure on the peso continued to be excessive. This led, in March 1958, to a second devaluation as well as to the establishment of a new coffee retention tax (Wiesner, 1978: 72–74).

As it became apparent that the country would need further external assistance, a commission led by Alfonso López Pumarejo and Mariano Ospina, ex-presidents from different parties with extensive financial experience, was sent to Washington, D.C., just weeks before the presidential election. The composition of the commission was intended to reassure international creditors of bipartisan support for a continued stabilization effort, especially important given the uncertainties regarding which party would be in the presidency.[11] Simultaneously, Colombia followed Brazil's lead in seeking cooperation from the United States for a coffee producers association that would prevent prices from falling even more sharply by voluntarily keeping stocks off the world market (see Zuleta, 1975; Delfim Netto and Andrade Pinto, 1973).

The junta's economic stabilization program provided Alberto Lleras with the opportunity to initiate his government in August 1958 with a more expansive economic program. Future Colombian presidents were not to be so fortunate at their inauguration.

Concluding Reflections

The military withdrawal from power in Colombia in favor of the civilian National Front in 1958 was not inevitable. However, the structural conditions for its occurrence in the late 1950s were highly favorable. Certain factors at the international level militated against the successful institutionalization of the Rojas regime and operated in favor of the consociational alternative. These included U.S. opposition to the Rojas regime in part due to its Peronist trappings, reflected in the withdrawal of credit by the United States as well as international financial institutions and the extension of credit and diplomatic support to the interim military junta and its civilian backers. However, the overall international economic picture for Colombia during the Rojas government *and* the period of transition was clouded by continued dependency on a single principal export, coffee, and its low world price.

More significant factors of explanation for the success of the transition must be sought at the national level. International actors supported initiatives sponsored by domestic political and economic actors. The political parties, though weak institutionally, completely dominated the political landscape. The experience of *la violencia* was devastating to the Church and to party leaders. The idea of bipartisan coalition rule was strongly rooted in historical antecedents and compelling given the *continuismo* of Rojas and the fear of incipient radical movements in the countryside. A more organized and diversified industry had reasons beyond the ties of traditional party loyalties to oppose Rojas' statist and populist policies and to favor the consociational alternative which promised greater stability and economic policies more consonant with their interests. Urban, and especially rural, masses, the primary victims of the bloodshed, were largely acquiescent toward an agreement that promised peace.

In the end, however, it was the actions of specific individuals that finally created the specific pacts and agreements facilitated by these conditions. And, as we saw above, at a number of points, the process appeared to be near a total impasse. These critical junctures—the Pact of Sitges and the national plebiscite, the Pact of San Carlos regarding congressional elections and the Valencia candidacy, the last-minute presidential candidacy of Alberto Lleras—reflected neither institutional or ideological problems nor problems with social mobilization, but the continued domination of the political landscape by party leaders in control of collectivities with entrenched loyalties. The solutions reached indicated the creativity of the country's political leaders and their considerable capacity to reach agreements with opposing party leaders and carry their party followers along. Gómez's imposition of the Lleras candidacy, even if at eventual personal political cost, is an excellent example of that capacity. Yet, that countermovements were unable to take advantage of these moments of near paralysis in the process—e.g., the unraveling of the conspirational movement prior to the plebiscite, the dismal failure of the May 2, 1958, coup, the small percentage of votes for the Conservative Leyva in spite of the sudden switch to a Liberal presidential candidate—underscores how favorable the structural conditions were, and how weak the challenges.

A number of alternative scenarios can be imagined. *If* coffee prices had remained high, and *if* Rojas had been a more daring and imaginative ruler, e.g., willing to risk gaining a new term by means of elections, conceivably he would not have been replaced in 1957. However, how much longer could his movement have lasted? For, in the final analysis, Rojas was forced to rely on a part of the Conservative party that was unwilling to subsume its identity within a new movement, even as Rojas had shown himself incapable of developing an independent support base. Furthermore, if he moved in a radical populist or socialist direction to seek that support, as suggested by his nationalization of banks, he would have lost support within the largely Conservative armed forces.

Indeed, examination of each of the predicaments of the transition process shows the relative weakness of their challenge to the success of the civilian alternative. In terms of the coherence of the transition coalition, once the two parties were willing to provide mutual guarantees that neither would be excluded from power, *the* major conflict area between them was resolved. Both shared a commitment to the socioeconomic order, and the range of issues on which they differed was narrow. The National Front period would show that major policy issues cut across the parties rather than between them. The key events of this period—the fall of Rojas, the party pacts and their approval, the choice of president—point to the fact that the most difficult problems revolved around reaching interelite agreement, not "selling" the solutions that were reached to the parties' mass following. In both these ways, current regime transitions in Latin America are likely to face much more severe challenges: parties are less likely to share as broad a consensus on social and economic issues, and new parties are likely to develop or old ones are more likely to possess a more organized and less acquiescent following.

The military predicament was resolved in large part by de-linking the Rojas regime from the armed forces as an institution and blaming all excesses on him and his immediate advisers. The levels of professionalism within the Colombian military at the time and its involvement and penetration into state activities were both low. De-linking was also facilitated by the fact that the Rojas dictatorship was comparatively benign. Transition negotiations were neither very formal nor very protracted, and the military's central concerns of institutional autonomy and of regaining prestige were respected by the party leaders who recognized they would need to rely on the armed forces in the future. Notwithstanding, there were significant coup movements within the armed forces. None had any chance of long-term permanence, although under different circumstances one of the coup attempts may have had momentary success. In sum, the problems of military withdrawal for contemporary cases is far more complex than it was for Colombia in 1957–58. Current military governments are much more likely to involve the military as an institution in power, eliminating de-linking as a possible strategy, and the question of institutional or personal culpability in human rights violations becomes a core issue requiring resolution in any transition process.

Finally, even Colombia's economic problems in that period, in comparative perspective, do not appear that serious. Although the relative success of the country's stabilization plan is notable, compared to contemporary rates of inflation, debt-service ratios, balance of payments deficits, and budgetary shortfalls in Latin America, Colombia's economic problems in those years appear more manageable. This was particularly true since the central political and economic actors did not differ significantly in terms of their desire to stabilize the economy, improve the country's balance of payments, and take other domestic policy measures necessary to regain international credit.

To date Colombia has had extremely modest success in translating its limited political democracy into social or economic democracy. Thus, if this example suggests that contemporary processes of transition will be far more difficult to implement, it also underscores the continuing chal-

lenge social actors and potential civilian political regimes in those countries will face in using political democracy to implement social and
economic justice.

Notes

1. For the purposes of this paper, and in somewhat arbitrary fashion, the transition process is defined as occurring in the period of time between when the
   armed forces authoritatively state their desire to withdraw from power and the
   first civilian regime is inaugurated. The activities of the major elements of the
   transition coalition prior to the period of the transition process revolve around
   the creation of a democratic alternative.
2. Arend Lijphart introduced the term "consociational democracy" to describe a
   pattern of democratic politics in countries marked by actual or potential
   violent conflict across the major segments of their societies. This conflict is
   avoided within an open political regime by means of overarching elite cooperation. One central means by which this cooperation can be implemented is
   government by a grand coalition of political leaders of the country's major
   conflict groups (see Lijphart, 1977). On applications to Colombia, see Dix
   (1980) and Wilde (1978).
3. This complex phenomenon constitutes an essential backdrop to this entire
   period. Although the intense rivalry between the two parties, fearful of permanent exclusion from the state even as access to the state was growing in
   importance, and the inability of party leaders to compromise were the primary
   causes of *la violencia* in my view, it rapidly took on various modalities in
   different regions of the country. Following the *bogotazo* and its aftermath, the
   greatest concern to the Ospina government and particularly the Gómez government was the guerrilla bands, predominantly Liberal, which began forming
   in the country's eastern plains and elsewhere by late 1949. Conservatives
   formed counter-guerrillas, employed the openly partisan police force in brutal
   fashion, and increasingly relied upon the army. Other kinds of violence—land
   feuds, village rivalries, banditry, assassinations, mob violence, pillaging—
   predominated elsewhere or gradually developed. See Oquist, 1980; the initial
   landmark study is Guzmán, et al., 1962; for bibliographical references, see
   also Ramsey, 1973; a useful recent study on the violence in a coffee-growing
   area of the country is Arocha, 1979.
4. Interviews with high military officers from that period, Summer, 1982. Some
   suggested that a talk with Monsignor Builes was important in convincing an
   ambivalent Rojas to step down (confidential interviews with author, 1982). See
   also the letter to the armed forces by three former civilian ministers of war,
   dated May 7, 1957, and the statement by Alberto Lleras and Guillermo León
   Valencia promising guarantees and asking the military's help in finding a
   solution to the country's crisis without bloodshed in Ediciones Documentos
   Colombianos (1957: 161–67).
5. The concerns of the military were noted by Navas and Jaramillo in interviews
   with the author, 1982. Navas stressed he thought it would have been difficult
   for the junta to turn over power to Valencia. See also Vázquez (n. d.: 265–66)
   and Pinilla (1980: 47–50).
6. Alfonso López Pumarejo was fearful of a Conservative ploy to keep Liberals
   out of local office by keeping parity only in the Cabinet; he insisted parity be
   extended to the entire executive branch (see *El Tiempo*, 1957k and 1957j). The
   junta extended parity to the judicial branch (Villareal, interview with author,
   1982; see *El Tiempo*, 1957i; and 1957h).

7. The Communist party was in a quandary. The plebiscite, by nullifying certain of Rojas' decrees, would return legal status to the party; at the same time, the measures on parity would reduce the party's future role in politics. In the end, the party called for its adherents to cast blank ballots. See Partido Comunista de Colombia, 1980: 138–39.

8. Belisario Betancur noted there had been "general panic" among Conservative congressmen as a result of Gómez's suggestion (interview with Pinilla, 1979). Many claimed that as a result of this maneuver Gómez lost his standing within the Conservative party, permitting the Ospinistas to regain majority status in the next elections (Emiliano, Jaramillo Ocampo and another prominent Conservative politician, interviews with author, 1982).

9. See in particular the editorial by an "anonymous military officer" in *El Tiempo,* 1957r and the speech by Alberto Lleras to military officers in February 1958, reprinted in Junta Militar de Gobierno, 1958. Upon the request of the junta, the transition coalition changed its name from "Civic Front" to "National Front."

10. Regarding complaints of obstructionism, see *El Tiempo,* 1957t; 1957r; 1957q; 1957f; 1957e; 1957d and 1957a.

11. *Semana,* 1958; Alvarez and Jaramillo, interviews with author, 1982. Soon after assuming the Ministry of Finance, Alvarez noted there were no significant differences in economic policy between the two parties (*Semana,* 1957d). As a result of IMF drawings, World Bank loans, and U.S. assistance, foreign aid to Colombia in 1958 totaled $108.2 million, significantly higher than previous years: 1953, $25.1M; 1954, $42.7M; 1955, $18.2M; 1956, $30.7M, and 1957, $39.0M (Wilkie and Haber, 1981: 518 ("all drawings"), 514 ("actual loans"), 371 ("gross actual assistance")).

References

Alvarez Restrepo, A., interview with author (1982) Bogotá.

Amézquita, S. and J. Fernández (1977) "La economía colombiana, 1950–1975," *Revista de Planeación y Desarrollo* 9 (Oct.–Dec.)

Arocha, J. (1979) *La violencia en el Quindío.* Bogotá: Ediciones Tercer Mundo.

Betancur, B., interview with Luis Pinilla (1979) Bogotá, taped.

Cepeda, F. and C. Mitchell (1980) "The Trend Toward Technocracy," in A. Berry, R. Hellman, and M. Solaún (eds.), *Politics of Compromise: Coalition Government in Colombia.* New Brunswick: Transaction Books.

Colombia, Cámara de Representantes, Secretaría (1959) *Por Qué y Cómo Se Forjó el Frente Nacional.* Bogotá: Imprenta Nacional.

Colombia, Departamento Administrativo Nacional de Estadística (1972) *Colombia Política.* Bogotá.

Colombia, Senado del la República, Comisión Instructora (1960) *El Proceso contra Gustavo Rojas Pinilla ante el Congreso de Colombia,* Tomo II. Bogotá: Imprenta Nacional.

Delfim Netto, A. and C. A. de Andrade Pinto (1973) "The Brazilian

Coffee: Twenty Years of Set-backs in the Competition on the World Market, 1945/1965," in C. M. Pelaez (ed.), *Essays on coffee and development*. Rio de Janeiro: Instituto Brasileiro de Café.

Diaz-Alejandro, C. (1976) *Foreign Trade Regimes and Economic Development: Colombia.* New York: Columbia University Press.

Dix, R. H. (1980) "Consociational Democracy: The Case of Colombia." *Comparative Politics* 12 (April): 303–21.

———— (1967) *Colombia: The Political Dimensions of Change.* New Haven: Yale University Press.

Ediciones Documentos Colombianos (1957) *Las Jornadas de Mayo.* Bogotá: Editorial Antares.

El Catolicismo (1957) May 17.

El Tiempo (1958a) March 18.

———— (1958b) March 13.

———— (1957a) Dec. 20.

———— (1957b) Dec. 7.

———— (1957c) Nov. 18.

———— (1957d) Nov. 17.

———— (1957e) Nof. 16.

———— (1957f) Nov. 13.

———— (1957g) Oct. 31.

———— (1957h) Oct. 5.

———— (1957i) Sept. 20.

———— (1957j) Sept. 12.

———— (1957k) Sept. 11.

———— (1957l) Sept. 9.

———— (1957m) Sept. 3.

———— (1957n) Sept. 1.

———— (1957o) Aug. 28.

———— (1957p) Aug. 20.

———— (1957q) July 2.

———— (1957r) June 29.

———— (1957s) June 12.

———— (1957t) May 22.

Emiliano Román, R., interview with author (1982) Bogotá.

Forero, Col. (r) H., interview with author (1982) Bogotá.

García Herrera, A., interview with Luis Pinilla (1979) Bogotá, taped.

Gutiérrez Gómez, J., interview with author (1982) Medellín.

Guzman, G., O. Fals Borda and E. Umaña Lima (1963–64) *La violencia en Colombia,* 2 vols. Bogotá: Ediciones Tercer Mundo.

Jaramillo Ocampo, H., interview with author (1982) Bogotá.

Junta Militar de Gobierno (1957). *Itinerario Histórico:* Tomo I. Bogotá: Secretaría General de Gobierno.

—— (1958) *Itinerario Histórico:* Tomo II. Bogotá: Secretaría General de la Junta.

Kalmánovitz, S. (1978) *Desarrollo de la agricultura en Colombia.* Bogotá: Editorial La Careta.

Karl, T. (1981) "Petroleum and Political Pacts: The Transition to Democracy in Venezuela." Washington, D.C.: The Wilson Center, Latin American Program, Working Papers No. 107.

Leal B., F. (1970) "Política e intervención militar en Colombia," in R. Parra S. (ed.), *La dependencia externa y el desarrollo político en Colombia.* Bogotá: Universidad Nacional de Colombia.

Levine, D. H. (1978) "Venezuela since 1958: The Consolidation of Democratic Politics," in J. Linz and A. Stepan (eds.), *The Breakdown of Democratic Regimes: Latin America.* Baltimore: The Johns Hopkins University Press.

—— and A. W. Wilde (1977) "The Catholic Church, 'Politics,' and Violence: The Colombian Case," *Review of Politics* 39 (April): 220–49.

Lijphart, A. (1977) *Democracy in Plural Societies: A Comparative Exploration.* New Haven: Yale University Press.

Lleras, R., C., interview with author (1982) Bogotá.

——, interview with Luis Pinilla (1979) Bogotá, taped.

—— (1963) *Hacia la restauración democrática y el cambio social:* Tomo I, 1955–61. Bogotá: n.p.

Martz, J. D. (1962) *Colombia: A Contemporary Political Survey.* Chapel Hill: University of North Carolina Press.

Matallana, Gen. (r) J. J., interview with author (1982) Bogotá.

Middlebrook, K. J. (1981) "Notes on Transitions from Authoritarian Rule in Latin America and Latin Europe." Washington, D.C.: The Wilson Center, Latin American Program, Working Papers Number 82.

Navas Pardo, Gen. (r) R., interview with author (1982) Bogotá.

Nelson, R. R., T. P. Schultz and R. L. Slighton (1971) *Structural Change in a Developing Economy: Colombia's Problems and Prospects.* Princeton: Princeton University Press.

Olson, M. (1971) *The Logic of Collective Action.* Cambridge: Harvard University Press.

Oquist, P. (1980) *Violence, Conflict and Politics in Colombia.* New York: Academic Press.

Partido Comunista de Colombia (1980) *Treinta Años de Lucha del Partido Comunista de Colombia.* Bogotá: Ediciones Paz y Socialismo.

Pinilla, L. (1980) "Cómo Se Ejerce El Poder En Colombia?" Master's thesis. Bogotá: Universidad Javeriana.

Posada Angel, J., interview with author (1982) Medellín.

Poveda R., G. (1976) *Políticas económicas, desarrollo industrial y tecnología en Colombia, 1925–1976.* Bogotá: Colciencias.

Premo, D. L. (1972) "Alianza Nacional Popular: Populism and the Politics of Social Class in Colombia, 1961–1970." Ph.D. dissertation. Austin: University of Texas.

Ramsey, R. W. (1973) "Critical Bibliography on La Violencia in Colombia," *Latin American Research Review* 8 (Spring).

Revista de Historia (1977) "El 2 de mayo de 1958 [Interview with Hernando Forero]," *Bogotá,* Volume 1 (August): 4–11.

Semana (1958) April 19–25.

—— (1957a) Sept. 6–13.

—— (1957b) Aug. 23–30.

—— (1957c) Aug. 2–9.

—— (1957d) May 24–31.

Szulc, T. (1959) *The Twilight of Tyrants.* New York: Henry Holt and Co.

Tirado M., A. (1978) "Colombia: siglo y medio de bipartidismo," in *Colombia Hoy.* Bogotá: Siglo XXI.

Tobón V., J., interview with author (1982) Medellín.

Vázquez C., C. (n.d.) *El Frente Nacional: Su Origen y desarrollo.* Cali: Carvajal y Cia.

Villareal, J. M., interview with author (1982) Bogotá.

Wiesner, E. (1978) "Devaluación y mecanismo de ajuste," *Banca y Finanzas* (Bogotá) No. 159 (March): 43–123.

Wilde, A. W. (1978) "Conversations among Gentlemen: Oligarchical Democracy in Colombia," in J. Linz and A. Stepan (eds.), *The Breakdown of Democratic Regimes: Latin America.* Baltimore: The Johns Hopkins University Press.

Wilkie, J. W. (1974) *Statistics and National Policy.* Supplement 3, *UCLA Statistical Abstracts of Latin America.* Los Angeles: University of California at Los Angeles.

—— and S. Haber (eds.) (1981) *Statistical Abstract of Latin America,* Vol. 21. Los Angeles: UCLA Latin American Center Publication.

Williams, M. (1976) "El Frente Nacional: Colombia's Experiment in Controlled Democracy," Ph.D. dissertation. Nashville: Vanderbilt University.

Zuleta, L. A. (1975) "El sector cafetero y los fenomenos inflacionarios," *Cuadernos Colombianos* (Bogotá) No. 7: 431–519.

Alexandre de S.C. Barros
and
Edmundo C. Coelho

Military Intervention and Withdrawal in South America

Irrespective of the peculiarities of the several military interventions in internal politics which took place roughly from 1960 to 1975, it seems clear that there was, during this period, a wave of authoritarianism sweeping many countries of the world. Nowadays, it seems that we are witnessing a new "wave" sweeping the world, this time in the opposite direction, that is, toward "liberalization" and the withdrawal of the military from power.

This article will deal with one aspect of liberalization in one region of the world, namely, with military withdrawal from governing positions in South America. This examination takes place in the context of an argument outlining the differing nature of what we call "structural" interventions in contrast to "conjunctural" interventions. Until recently, Colombia and Venezuela were considered to be the only South American countries where the military did not have a preeminent position in the running of government. In all the other countries of the continent the role of the military was very important, although the styles, rhetoric, and cosmetics of regimes were different. Thus, from the officially bloodthirsty Chilean regime established in late 1973 to the "tolerant to rightist violence"

From Alexandre de S. C. Barros and Edmundo C. Coelho, "Military Intervention and Withdrawal in South America," *International Political Science Review* 2, no. 3 (1981), pp. 341–349. Copyright © International Political Science Association 1981. Reprinted by permission of the authors and Sage Publications Inc.

Argentinian government, passing through civilian-de-jure-but-military-de-facto government of Uruguay, and the economically successful but tor-ture-lenient Brazilian regime, from left-speaking Peru to right-screaming Bolivia, all countries in South America experienced a brand of military authoritarianism which, now that the smoke is clearing, proves to have been quite similar, despite the conspicuous peculiarities. Just as all these countries set out on the authoritarian road more or less at the same time, they are now experiencing liberalization trends in a way which is so similar that it seems to be orchestrated.

One hypothesis which has been extensively used to explain the "au-thoritarianization" of these countries during the 1960s and early 1970s has been that of the active role of the United States in sponsoring the setting up of such regimes (especially in Brazil and Chile). The degree to which the role of the United States has been emphasized reaches the highest degrees of paranoia. Although it is clear that, in virtually all cases, the participation of the United States has been a necessary condition, it was hardly a sufficient explanation. Nowadays, the same hypothesis—that of U.S. participation—is being used in a reverse way. It seems that the U.S. attitude did have some impact upon the recent liberalization of regimes. However, like the previous converse hypothesis, this one does not seem to us to provide sufficient explanation of the liberalization of regimes in South American countries, which have to cope with several forms of U.S. presence in the continent.

Although we do not deny the direct role in the politics of South Amer-ican countries which the United States played, still plays, and will con-tinue to play for the foreseeable future, we have instead opted for alternative hypotheses based on organizational characteristics which we will discuss more extensively in this article.

Professionalization

The explanation of the probabilities of military intervention in politics has been, in the recent past, based upon the hypothesis of "professionaliza-tion." The correlation between intervention and professionalization has a positive or negative sign depending on whether one adopts the "Hunt-ingtonian" or the "Janowitzian" versions for the explanation of military intervention. In both cases the prestige of the hypotheses seems to rest more on the authority of their authors than in the explanatory power of the hypotheses themselves.

The analysis of the process of professionalization has been developed in sociology to explain changes which have occurred—or are occurring—in several *occupations*.

In the case of the military, it does not make sense to dissociate the military *occupation* from a military *organization*. In contrast with other professionalized occupations, it seems that, historically, some form of organization, although rudimentary and temporary, preceded the emergence of the military occupation as a permanent and exclusive activity of individuals. The historical evolution of national armies tells us more about their present behavior than the use of the general hypothesis related to the process of professionalization of the military occupation. We refer to the historically indissoluble association between the state organization and the military organization and posit that the pace of professionalization of the military occupation depends on, and responds to, organizational requirements, especially the adaptation needs of the military organization in its national and international contexts.

Once we accept this premise, it becomes appropriate to take from organization theory the hypothesis of a strong impulse towards autonomization underlying the process of evolution of any organization. This impulse gains momentum once the initial stage is overcome, that is, once the major organizational preoccupation ceases to be one with survival of the organization. It is possible to think, then, particularly in the case of military organizations, of *degrees of autonomy* of the organization, rather than of *levels of professionalization* of the military occupation. It is possible to think of scales in which the military organization acquires higher and higher degrees of autonomy within the state apparatus, combined with different degrees of autonomy of the state itself, vis-à-vis civil society. We can thus consider the wave of military governments in South America as part of a process of autonomization of the state vis-à-vis civil society, in which the armed forces are its bureaucratic vanguard.

It is not difficult to find examples of interventions in politics on the part of the armed forces in different stages of the process of professionalization, whether in different countries or within the same country at different periods. What actually happens is that in the measure that a given military establishment advances in the scale of autonomization, its intervention in politics becomes qualitatively different because it is aimed at solving qualitatively different organizational problems. Of course, this may require higher degrees of professionalization, but it does not make of this factor a causal or determinant variable in the explanation of interventionism. One possible way of posing the above problem is to suggest a correlation between degrees of autonomy and degrees of "openness" of the armed forces to the influences which come from civil society. The higher the degree of autonomy, the lower the degree of openness to civil society. The military's standing vis-à-vis the problems of society in general is increasingly less dependent on taking into consideration the political standing and preferences of other groups in society. This implies and expresses a high degree of corporate consciousness, but it also implies a high degree of institutional alienation. This state of alienation from the rest of society is one of the characteristics of the recent interventions which makes them qualitatively different.

The expression of institutional alienation takes place not only because of the existence of different values, specific competencies, or different mentalities which cause a high degree of estrangement of the armed forces with respect to civil society, but mainly because the armed forces do not find a role to perform in society. The equation is a familiar one: On the one hand, we have military organizations with a monopoly on the instruments of legitimate physical coercion and a considerable degree of institutional autonomy within the state; on the other, we find these powerful organizations attached to the classical functions of external defense which they will seldom be called upon to perform. In sum, we are dealing with a situation of "structural unemployment" for the armed forces.

In this situation—and in the context of "mass praetorianism"—the armed forces actually face a wide "offer" of roles which are different and incompatible among themselves, ill-defined (or ambiguously defined) by the several civilian groups which are interested in using them for private purposes. The consequences of the performance of any of these ambiguous roles will be lack of confidence and hostility on the part of those groups which perceive themselves as losers. This situation strengthens the military's feeling of always being at odds with important groups in society, and reinforces their political disorientation. The alienation also results from the different "instrumentalities" attributed to the armed forces by different social groups which do not manage to agree on common rules for the legitimate use of military force.

For a long time, the armed forces accepted and played this game, as their institutional needs and demands were also at stake. In particular, at this stage there was a constant attempt on the part of the armed forces to protect or strengthen their internal autonomy by means of rebellions or interventions and to affirm their rights to the state monopoly on legitimate physical coercion. These attempts were primarily aimed at preventing interference on the part of civilian governments or politicians in internal questions such as pay scales, promotion systems, criteria and pace of reequipment or modernization, and appointments to command positions.

Besides that, by intervening in politics, the military attempted to stabilize and make predictable a turbulent and fragmented political environment which threatened the military principles of hierarchy, discipline, and internal cohesion by appealing to groups of individual officers or military factions. At an early stage, and in the context of a lack of common rules on the use of organized military coercion, it becomes very easy to "politicize" institutional questions. It is this kind of politicization which has resulted in military interventions generally characterized by their brevity and by a quick return to the barracks. These could be called almost "conjunctural" interventions.

In Search of a Role

In spite, or perhaps because, of this, the structural question remained latent, namely: Which is the role of the armed forces in society? In the case of South American countries—and with the help of the French *doctrine de la guèrre révolutionaire* and the U.S. emphasis on internal security—the answer came wrapped in a package labeled *internal security doctrines*. These doctrines allowed for the establishment of a "functional" relationship between the so-called classical tasks of armed forces— namely, external defense—and the problem of economic development. Internal security became a development production factor like capital or labor. The result was that all aspects and problems related to development became an area of concern to the military institution. The presence of the military was therefore justified in all sectors of national life, and all of them could be labeled—when necessary *as defined by the military*—as national security issues, questions, or areas. In this way, the role of the military organization was framed in terms of *production* of internal security, which becomes by doctrinal definition a socially valuable "commodity" in the context of a developing society. (Actually, this scheme, although justifying a presence, does not really define a role because the doctrine gives the military organization too wide a scope and lacks behavioral specificity and functional focus).

Thus, it can be seen that the military answer to its feeling of alienation from society is a demand for a growingly extensive participation. This expansion of military activities on the basis of the doctrine of internal security coincides in some countries of the continent with the maximum level of expansion of the functions of the state, and with an unprecedented effort on the part of the military to liberate the state from the various class interests. In other words, the autonomization of the armed forces within the state apparatus expressed by means of the transformation of the military elite into a ruling elite has paralleled the autonomization of the state from civil society, in the sense that it makes it possible to distinguish clearly state power from class power. Although the policies of these relatively autonomous states differ greatly from country to country, one can see the emergence of a common general structural pattern in the design of the relationships between state and civil society. Some label these emerging regimes as "state corporatist," but the goal pursued in various degrees by these military rulers is to reshape society into a nonconflictual, functional unit, with the state mediating and adjudicating the claims of social classes. Under military rule, these regimes open a new "public space" based on internal security, the exclusive domain of the armed forces. Within this "statutory space," the armed forces are expected to find their new and definitive identity.

In the case of conjunctural interventions, operation of military withdrawal from politics is relatively easy. Once the more immediate institutional demands are satisfied—or, alternatively, once the circumstantial factors which threaten the basic organizational principles of the armed forces are removed or corrected—the armed forces lose both the reason and justification for military rule.

The exact reverse takes place with the recent structural interventions. On the one hand, the military have to deal with critical situations which affect the integrity of the military organization and/or its basic operational procedures. In their dual status as institution and as rulers, the military have not been able to solve the problematic relationship between the political apparatus of the state and the armed forces. In some countries of the continent, the difficulty may be the absence of formal provisions for rotating officers appointed to the presidency by the military elite. The absence of formal criteria for succession becomes a real threat to the discipline, hierarchy, and internal cohesion of the armed forces, since it very frequently leads to confrontation between military factions. Usually, however, the question is one of choice between military principles (i.e., rank and seniority) and political expediency. Occasionally, as soon as an officer is invested with the symbols of the presidency, he demands the subordination of the armed forces to his authority—as if he was not the "delegate" of the military organization in a "routine military assignment." Such situations operate as centrifugal forces pushing the military to get out of the political scene in the name of the integrity of the institution. On the other hand, there is the bureaucratic feeling—inspired by the sacredness of "standard operational procedures—that "not enough has been done." This is especially true in military organizations, which are accustomed to a totally (or at least as totally as possible) controlled environment out of the situation of war. In any event, once the military make the choice of following this track, usually the only possible outcome is escalation.

There is also the serious question of the definition of a role for the military once they withdraw from politics. It is impossible for the military to get out and return to their "old" (i.e., previous to the intervention) role because their role has actually changed. However, society also does not yet seem able to offer an alternative role for the military. Stating the question in terms of military jargon, it is necessary to find or create another "doctrine" which is capable either of supporting and legitimizing the military in a situation of "underemployment" or "unemployment" vis-à-vis the role they played when they were in the seats of power or alternatively, of providing the military with "full employment," of a nature different from the one which was in force while they were in power.

The prospects of creating such conditions have been worsened by the failure of the military to institutionalize new regimes. Their goal of a nonconflictual, harmonic, organic society in which the armed forces would find the right niche for themselves has been eroded as time passed.

In addition to a closed decisional structure reflecting the disposition of the military to retain complete autonomy vis-à-vis civil society (and their fear of "contagion"), the doctrine of internal security has not provided the military with goals of a more flexible nature which could accommodate those of other elites. Just as the autonomy of the military is an asset in the stage of regime installation, it becomes a handicap in the phase of institutionalization.

If we consider "professionalization" as a loose and purely chronological concept (i.e., the longer time passes, the more the military get trained and become "professionalized"), we can expect that they will become more different from their own societies and more autonomous. However, they also become more similar to other military establishments across national lines. We are suggesting that autonomization and professionalization imply a shift of reference groups from societal groups to professional ones. If this hypothesis is true, then it becomes possible to reconcile the notion of the "liberalization" which is taking place in South America with the growing process of professionalization in the several armed forces of the continent.

Once they take over political power and remain in this role for a relatively long time, the military go through a dual process of role performance. Their performance as professionals and rulers gives them the opportunity to interact with one another across international borders in a much more systematic way than was the case when they were solely performing the role of professional soldiers. Under normal circumstances, as the military professionalize, they interact in a growingly more limited fashion with society, becoming more similar internally and more different from their civilian compatriots. The peculiar brand of parochialism-internationalism which is exhibited by the military tends to shift toward internationalism. This process allows for the forging of more relevant alliances among sword-bearers across national boundaries at the expense of solidarity with their own populations.

These conditions are not totally inescapable, but students of military sociology have generally disregarded the problem of withdrawal of the military and, more importantly, have disregarded the study of the military themselves at the moment of transition to civilian government. If we consider that the military *function* will have to continue to be performed in society, then it becomes more urgent to study the military *qua* organization. We shall thus be able to project the role of this group if and when the society returns to a situation which, although desirable from the point of view of political values, is in Latin America statistically infrequent and deviant: namely, that of a democratic government marked by civilian control.

Alain Rouquié

Demilitarization and the Institutionalization of Military-Dominated Polities in Latin America

Any assessment of the possible evolution of military-dominated polities in Latin America depends on the perspective used to explain their recurrent emergence in the past. If one believes that contemporary militarism is merely a culturally determined anachronism offering transitory resistance to the ultimate political good—i.e., representative democracy—one assumes a unilinear evolution which is predictable and practically inevitable. Infrastructural interpretations of the appearance of modern authoritarian regimes likewise underline the latters' transitory nature. Functionalist determinism, by establishing a more or less instrumental correspondence between dominant economic actors and regime types, foresees an end to the authoritarian system when its supposed "objectives" have been fulfilled. The "necessary" or indispensable character of authoritarian rule for peripheral capitalism in its present phase will therefore assure with equal inevitability the disappearance of authoritarian regimes once they complete their historic role. These two contradictory perspectives have in common a facile and dogmatic certainty concerning the "exceptional" nature of authoritarian regimes. In effect, those who interpret Latin American history in terms of a protracted "struggle for democracy," like those who perceive the political arena as directly subordinated to the episodic necessities of capital, take for granted an inevitable outcome of liberalization.

The partisans of both of these theses generally ignore the strictly *military* dimension of the great majority of Latin American authoritarian regimes. The "liberal" perspective does so because its adherents have decided that armies as political forces are only an atavistic legacy of the past. Since modern politics is based exclusively on representative government and rational procedures of administrative specialization, obstacles to attaining this ultimate good must stem from some hangover from the past. Starting from these premises, one cannot envisage professionalized military institutions in terms of bureaucratic modernity, nor analyze the political implications of this development. The "economicist" perspective is equally neglectful of the martial component. Its mode of analysis omits the institution which is at the center of power since this is merely supposed to be the expression or instrument of exogenous socioeconomic factors. In short, the specific manifestations and particular processes of military organizations are treated as epiphenomenal by both approaches.

A less reductionist approach would focus the analysis on the real power holders in political systems dominated by the military, take into account the specificity of the military corporation and of its pattern of alliances and civil support, and locate its extra-institutional political resources in the framework of structural constraints derived from each national society. It would not assume that the nature of post-authoritarian outcomes is known in advance. This is not to assume that military power is ineradicable, but that it has its own logic. The successive waves of militarization and demilitarization which the continent has experienced since 1945 should be enough to inspire caution on the part of those who would make predictions in this realm.

In effect, whereas in 1954 twelve out of twenty republics were being governed by military leaders who had come to power by force, by the middle of 1961, only one such leader was left: Stroessner in Paraguay. In seven years, revolutions and assassinations terminated ten military presidencies, whereas in Peru another withdrew "legally."[1] It is true that these military leaders headed very diverse regimes, including some virtual democracies, and that the disappearance of the leader did not always change the regime's character, as demonstrated by the situation in Nicaragua after the assassination of the not-very-military dictator Somoza in 1956. These regimes were often military only in the sense of the president's profession and by virtue of their origin, but they evolved in quite different directions. Should one attribute to a burst of anti-militarism the deposing of Perón, who was a legally reelected constitutional president, or the overthrow of the personal tyranny of Pérez Jiménez in Venezuela, of General Magloire of Haiti, or of Colonel J. M. Lemus in El Salvador, even if all these military leaders, like Batista in Cuba and Rojas Pinilla in Colombia, had been at least at a certain point the army's choice to occupy executive office? What should one say, after this ebbing of the tide, about the military wave which from March 1962 (Argentina) to November 1964 (Bolivia) and June 1966 (Argentina, again) put an end to civil regimes in nine of the continent's countries? Was it a prolongation or a phenomenon of another kind when, at the beginning of 1970s, a series of coups d'état hit countries with solid traditions of civil government that some had estimated to have been "definitively" demilitarized (Chile and Uruguay), while in Argentina a new military intervention assumed a violent nature unprecedented in that nation's history?

As of 1976–77, democracy seemed to be making some headway once again. The time was apparently ripe for some liberalization of military rule and, even, the return of civilians to power. If one judges merely on the basis of figures, in 1978 twelve electoral consultations took place on the continent. This intense electoral activity seemed to augur a return to representative procedures. In fact, it ranged from authoritarian plebiscites to competitive elections, and included some ambiguous cases in between. The Chilean referendum and the fifth reelection of President Stroessner are far from indicating the termination of despotic systems. In Venezuela and Colombia, elections occur regularly and hardly constitute remarkable events. In Brazil, legislative elections took place in a framework of conditions and restrictions designed to assure regime continuity, but they were nevertheless unfavorable to the government. In Peru, Ecuador, and Bolivia, elections had the principal aim of preparing for the return of civilians to power, the free play of democratic institutions, and an orderly retreat of the military to their barracks.

This historical survey provides little support for unilineal and synchronic interpretations of military power, such as those described above. Nor do we believe that these movements in opposing directions condemn the states of the continent to an indefinite alternation between civil and military regimes. They indicate rather that the forms of demilitarization are complex and diverse, and that they may have their limits. Such an ebb and flow invites us to examine, without *a priori* assumptions and reassuring generalizations, the realities of demilitarization and, thus, the real impact of the militarization of the state. Does the latter phenomenon constitute a simple parenthesis without institutional consequences, after which, once the army returns to barracks, countries return to their previous regimes? Or, on the contrary, is it the case that the military do not withdraw until they judge that they have removed the political obstacles to a civil regime and created socioeconomic conditions favorable to the normal functioning of democratic institutions? We are inclined to be rather doubtful about either of these scenarios, and feel it necessary to examine empirically the outcome of postmilitarism in all its ambiguity.

The Exception and the Rule

Reference has often been made to the instability of concentrated power. Institutionally, military regimes—even when they appear to be the most common form of domination in a country—nevertheless remain "exceptional," paradoxical though this may seem. In effect, the official and dominant ideology throughout the continent is liberal and democratic. The incessant transformation of military regimes and the limited duration of noncivilian governments derive in part from their illegitimacy as perceived by the principal actors involved. In the Latin American normative and cultural context, those who hold military power know that, whatever they say, there still exists above them a superior legitimacy, that of the constitutional order. Not only can they not claim its support, but they also must ultimately pay lip service to it.[2] In fact, military regimes are only really legitimized by their future. If elected governments have legitimacy by virtue of their origin, *de facto* governments have legitimacy only by the way they exercise power, and almost, one might say, by the performance they ultimately accomplish. The past may be used to justify the arrival of the military in power, but customary references to political and social chaos, to the vacuum of power, and to menaces of every kind, still reflect objectives that must eventually be attained or outcomes that must finally be avoided. The military regime, therefore, always lives for the future. It is, in its essence, transitory. A permanent system of military rule is almost a contradiction in terms.[3] The army cannot govern directly and durably without ceasing to be an army. And it is precisely the subsequent government, the successor regime, that legitimates the prior military usurpation.

Even if one makes a relatively arbitrary distinction between *provisional* (or caretaker) governments and constituent military regimes, in neither case has the historical experience been based on an explicitly avowed intention to create a new type of state, a definitive and durable mode of exercising political power. The democratic regime has been and still remains more legitimate in Latin America than this omnipresent state of exception. Contemporary Latin American military regimes differ notably in regard from the dictatorships that Europe or other continents have known in modern times, precisely because of their constitutional precariousness. They do not pretend to create a new legitimacy, to construct a new system of political values on the ruins of the old. The European authoritarian regimes between 1920 and 1945 had the ambition of founding a "new order" in opposition to liberalism and democracy, of creating a "thousand-year Reich." The Latin American military dictatorships of today are first of all regimes without a stable justifying ideology. The "doctrine of national security" which in one form or another is shared by these institutionalized military governments provides a discourse or language which serves temporarily to disguise their illegitimacy, but it is incapable of generating a new and permanent source of legitimacy. Moreover, the doctrine has above all performed the internal function of forging and mobilizing a consensus within the military institution, around the alarmist image inherent to the profession of arms. Its hypotheses concerning internal war, by enlarging the specter of threats and by situating them inside national society, provide an institutional basis for the army's intervention, but they do not explain it. Such hypotheses may justify a more or less enduring occupancy of the posts of national leadership, but they do not establish a new basis of power. Briefly, the theory of national security cannot substitute for a legitimating ideology. Neither the consistency of the theory, nor the extent of its diffusion, nor the constitutive nature of its functions permits such a substitution.

Representative democracy always remains on the horizon for these regimes. They must invoke it for their own legitimation and in their own policy objectives, while at the same time proposing to improve, reinforce, amend, and even protect it, but never to annihilate or destroy it as has been the case elsewhere. Such an observation holds for the Brazilian "sistema," which has always preserved (under careful supervision) parties, elections, and a legislative assembly—not to mention the archaic militarism of Stroessner, who, like all the classic dictators on the continent, has himself regularly reelected to the presidency, and tolerates (under strict surveillance) a decorative multiparty system. In Uruguay and Argentina also, the proclamations, declarations, projects, and maneuvers of the ruling military refer to no other political system and no other source of legitimacy than those identified with representative democracy. The justification is certainly superficial—a facade behind which quite different practices are promoted—but for all that, it serves to contradict martial messianism and undermine any idea of permanent military rule. No matter how central their position in the political system and how great their autonomy of decision-making, the governing military are constrained by the political culture of the dominant internal or external classes, whose self-interested liberalism constitutes a restraint on the organicist tendencies of the men in uniform. It is as if the dominant classes believe that the reestablishment of the market in economic matters cannot really be legitimized unless accompanied by a certain restoration of the market in political affairs.

Thus, in Argentina, all the corporatist and antiliberal overtones of the military in power—from Uriburu in 1930 to Onganía in 1966–70—have only provoked a defensive rallying of the economic and social establishment, and the replacement of the "anti-constitutionalist" generals by more liberal members of the military.[4] In Uruguay, Bordaberry, the civilian president of a military dictatorship imposed by the "slow-motion" coup d'état of 1973, was dismissed by the high command in June 1976 for advocating "new institutions" in opposition to "the most cherished democratic traditions of the country." He had in effect pushed the logic of "military sovereignty" to the limit by proposing in a memo the suppression of the party system, and the introduction of a new authoritarian state in which the armed forces alone would assure legitimacy. Although they have militarized power, and have promoted the hypertrophy of the nation's defense institutions and an unlimited expansion of their responsibilities, Uruguay's generals will not for one moment renounce the fiction of a civil executive. Uruguay, the garrison state, has a nonmilitary president and a government from which officers are practically absent. The parties are only suspended, and the text of the constitutional referendum of November 30, 1980, although it made the participation of the armed forces in executive power official, also anticipated the legalization of the two traditional parties and a return to limited and purified representative procedures. The rejection by the electorate of this plan after the pretense of a campaign had the merit of showing that the military had been correct not to underestimate the vigor and appeal of the party system—even after seven years of prohibition and adverse propaganda. This was also demonstrated by the Peruvian elections of May 1980 and the Argentine elections of 1973, after twelve and seven years, respectively, of suspension of institutionalized political competition.[5]

The government presided over by General Pinochet since September 1973 in Chile figures among the most antiliberal military regimes in Latin America, and among those which concede the least to even the rhetoric of democracy. Indeed, the authoritarian discourse of the Chilean military—their insistence on the need for new institutions—is very reminiscent of Franco's Spain. Corporatist inclinations are expressed without concealment by advisers and those responsible for the "hard" line of the regime—the "renovators," as they call themselves—who reject absolutely the parliamentary and partisan institutions in force until 1973. Immediately after the coup d'état, General Pinochet himself promised a new constitution which would "dispense forever with politicians, sectarianism, and demagogy."[6] The minister of the interior declared in September 1975 that "all political parties . . . act only to divide citizens, to favor demagogically their adherents and to cause the soul of the nation to deteriorate." The influential newpaper *Mercurio,* spokesman for the moderates (*blandos*) and partisan of a limited opening, commented on these remarks in the following way: "The government desires the annihilation or progressive disappearance of parties."[7] But although the constitutional debate on the aims and timetables of the Plan of Chacarillas (July 1977) may have encouraged the hopes of the "hard-liners" for the establishment of an "authoritarian democracy," the constitution submitted to a plebiscite on September 11, 1980, apart from the gradualism and the restriction of liberties which it imposes, nevertheless anticipates in the relatively distant future (1989) the establishment of a representative system, including parties, a congress, and a president elected by universal suffrage. Needless to say, this juridical structure is intended above all to justify the permanence in power of General Pinochet himself. But the reliance upon a constitutional text of noncorporatist inspiration and the fixing of a time limit to exceptional rule are sufficient to prove that, even in the Chilean case, the antiliberal temptation and the wish definitively to exclude the "vanquished" politicians of 1973 must be accommodated within the dominant democratic ideology.

These attempts to place representative practices under strong surveillance differ fundamentally from the ways and means adopted by dictatorships outside the continent to achieve the same objectives. If one compares the regime of General Franco with that of General Pinochet, the similarities may catch one's attention at first, but the differences are nonetheless important. These two counterrevolutionary systems both sought to break with the previous political situation, to deny open expression to political dissidents,[8] and to exclude the "defeated" from power forever, by prolonging the victorious coalition (of the coup d'état or civil war) via the unlimited personal authority of the leader of the successful military operation. But in the case of Franco, antipluralism made no concessions for forty years, except at the summit of state power and within his technocratic-bourgeois coalition. Liberal democracy was perpetually condemned without regard for internal developments or the international context. Franco, *caudillo* of Spain "by the grace of God," never tolerated even incidental questioning of his permanence in power. Neither the referendum of 1947 nor that of 1966 posed the question of choosing the chief of state, or of setting the length of his mandate. Furthermore, the opposition eventually accepted the idea that the dictatorship was lifelong and that a change of regime could take place only after the *caudillo*'s death.[9] General Pinochet, for his part, has stipulated the duration of his provisional regime (only after four years in power, it is true)—whatever may be his real intentions for the future—and he has not excluded the revival of parties and of competitive elections, although tempering the possibility of such developments by diverse prohibitions designed "to protect democracy." This is proof, in my view, that one cannot create a new legitimacy just as one wishes in an environment which is hostile to such ideological adventures. With this awareness of the limits of state militarization in Latin America, let us now examine the extent to which demilitarization is being accomplished, at what level, with what scope, and the kinds of regimes being established when the state is demilitarized.

The Postmilitary State and the Forms of Institutionalization

An analysis of the retreat of the army from power discloses diverse phenomena. Civilianization of the military state, however extensive, is by no means the same as a return to "democratic normality." For purposes of comparative equivalence, we will only examine the transformation of systems of extensive military domination—that is, regimes initiated by force in which the sovereignty of military institutions is exercised collectively and controls not only the selection of the executive but the making of all major policy decisions. We will therefore leave aside authoritarian regimes of other kinds, patrimonial or partisan, even though coercion and officer participation play large parts in them.

We can also set aside, almost from the start, a first type of demilitarization—that brought about by force through a civilian *pronunciamiento*. In general, it is the military who overthrow regimes of their peers by violence (or sometimes, and indeed most frequently, by the *threat* of violence). Some personal dictatorships, patrimonial autocracies, and postmilitary tyrannies have been driven out by uprisings of civilians, occasionally allied with factions of the armed forces. Without going back to Peru in the nineteenth century or to the civilian *montoneras* of Piérola, it was a combined civil and military revolution that overthrew General Ubico and his brief successor in Guatemala in 1944. That same year, in El Salvador, students and soldiers put an end to the dictatorship of Hernández Martínez. It was guerrillas and, therefore, civilians who fought Somoza's National Guard in 1979 and put an end to the dynasty in Nicaragua, repeating in different circumstances the Cuban precedent. But among institutionalized military governments, only that of Bolivia in 1952 was overthrown by civilians. The military junta which annulled the electoral victory of Paz Estenssoro's *Movimiento Nacionalista Revolucionario* (MNR) was in effect routed in the streets of La Paz. In this case, the relatively low level of effective militarization of power was followed by a drastic demilitarization. The Bolivian army was largely dismantled. Its officers were violently purged and, hence, rendered harmless to the new revolutionary civilian government.

The most common form of demilitarization, however, consists of leaving military structures in place while attempting to remove the armed forces from power. For reasons both external and internal to the institutions of the armed forces, direct military government cannot be made permanent, so that the continuity of martial power requires additional developments. We can group these into two dominant tendencies: *personalization* and *legalization*. Both of these models may, but need not necessarily, be linked to a democratic opening, which itself may be either real or a facade.

The transfer of power to a military leader who personally dominates the established hierarchy constitutes one means of subordinating the armed institutions to the executive and of returning the army to its professional tasks. The transition from the impersonal power of an institution to the personal power of a man, even a general, is never accomplished very easily. This personalization of power is naturally less difficult the less bureaucratized the military institution. Somoza, *jefe director* of the National Guard of Nicaragua, and Trujillo, *generalíssimo* of the Dominican army, "personalized" the neocolonial military institutions which had been placed in their hands. This had occurred before they assumed power. It was an act performed in their own name and not in the name of the military as such. Personalization occurred quite differently in Bolivia in 1964, when Barrientos had to prevail over his rivals by ratifying his power as "first among equals" through an electoral mobilization in which he appropriated a specific historico-military legitimacy (the Chaco tradition) and created a basis of popular support that was partly personal in character (the military-peasant pact). The eventual establishment of Barrientos as constitutional president served to prolong the military junta at the same time that it represented an extension of the preceding legal regime in which the putschist general had served as vice president. General Banzer had less success than his predecessor when he attempted to repeat the operation. Having come to power as a result of a coup d'état in 1971, he governed until 1974 with a section of the political class at the head of a conservative coalition. When, in 1974, he reshuffled his government and replaced the civilian politicians of the MNR and the Falange with military officers, he seemed to have emerged with enhanced personal power, but in practice the army had once again taken over the state apparatus.[10] After having announced presidential elections at various intervals from 1974 onward, General Banzer had to resign in 1978 when the army insisted that he not be a candidate in the election he was organizing. He then supported Juan Pereda, his former minister of interior, and the hopelessly divided armed forces proclaimed their neutrality. The ensuing elections of July 1978 were immediately followed by a coup d'état led by the "official" winner, a weakly legitimated and fraudulently elected successor of a military power structure that had been incompetently institutionalized.

Democratic procedures may also enable a military regime which has fallen into an impasse to find a legal means for self-perpetuation in power. In Argentina in 1945, the regime born of a coup d'état in 1943 was caught in an apparently fatal crossfire between internal and external oppositions strengthened by the defeat of the Axis powers. Nevertheless, one officer among their ranks, the "workers' colonel," was at the height of his personal popularity. Ill-regarded by one part of the army, which rejected his pro-labor stance and opposed his political ambitions, Perón still presented his candidacy for the presidency in free elections, and thereby offered an honorable way out to the institution which had brought him to power and which he sought to represent. The "revolutionary" officers of 1943, even though hostile to Perón, had no choice but to accept the return of the traditional parties and the candidacy of the man who had used the vice presidency in the military government as a stepping stone to elected office. Moreover, Perón, throughout his first presidency, took great care to draw attention to his military investiture, and sought to appear as the successor to the "Revolution of June 4, 1943." Thus, by an electoral sanction favorable to the candidate of the army or to one who presents himself as such, the military institution can recover its coherence and cease in principle to be directly responsible for policy. Vertical discipline can impose itself once again, reestablishing internal unity after a period of deterioration. Demilitarization may stop here, or it may, on the contrary, be pursued and extended as a result of alternative political resources which become available to the elected military leader, to the point that he can sometimes end up cutting himself off dangerously from his support in the armed forces. This is what happened to Perón after 1951.

The transfer of power to a military head of state may permit demilitarization without immediately leading to dangerous and uncertain electoral procedures. Usurpation by the military institution can culminate in the dictatorship of one man. This is what seems to be evolving today in Chile. Since 1977, there has been a prolongation of the military regime, reflecting the tutelary role in which the armed forces have found themselves, and confirming the absolute power of General Pinochet. His irresistible ascension, which has relegated the junta to a merely legislative and constituent role, was skillfully promoted by the success of the January 1978 referendum, whose text, imposed on the other members of the junta, stipulated: "I support General Pinochet."

In the Chilean case, it may be argued that the high level of professionalization and the limited political experience of the armed forces are not unrelated to this process of personalized institutionalization of the military regime. Hierarchical discipline has substituted for political consensus. Fear of a return of the "vanquished" has cemented cohesion around a single leader who symbolizes a counterrevolutionary policy questioned by no one in the army. This may explain the feeble response to the criticisms made by General Leigh, the air force representative in the junta, with regard to General Pinochet's political projects, and the subsequent lack of response to Leigh's dismissal in 1978, which was accompanied by the early retirement or resignation of eighteen of the twenty-one air force generals. The slowness of the "constitutional itinerary" and the persistence of international isolation have had the effect of reinforcing military support for an "institutionalization without opening" that, nevertheless, gives the army essential guarantees. The army may no longer govern Chile, but it is still not very far from power, and above all it continues to regard itself as an integral part of the power structure.

Most often, what is called the institutionalization of a military regime involves its legalization within the constitutional framework. This transformation, which has certain features in common with a return to democracy and which may be associated with a certain liberalization of political practices, signifies that the political power of the military is embedded purely and simply within an institutional framework which is presumed to be legitimate. The military then uses that framework to dispose of the major sources of uncertainty inherent in the democratic process. These processes may lead—as, for example, in Guatemala—to "military governments which are at the same time elected, constitutional, and anti-democratic."[11] This legalization generally takes place according to two modalities: either a controlled and coercive multiparty system, or the creation of a dominant military party.

This last formula is well illustrated by the system in operation in El Salvador from 1950 to October 1979, the date of General Carlos Humberto Romero's overthrow by a civil and military junta. The military in power in 1948 attempted to imitate the Mexican Institutionalized Revolutionary Party (PRI), but without its popular base, by creating an official party, the PRUD (Revolutionary Party of Democratic Unification),[12] a true party of colonels. The Party of National Conciliation (PCN) which succeeded it was both the partisan expression of the military institution[13] and its electoral prolongation. But it was also the party of the state, in which, under the aegis of the army, transactions between civilian or military bureaucracies and the dominant class were carried out. With alternations between political openings and restrictions on political competition, notably whenever the PCN lost ground, this "military party" subsequently controlled political life, obtained a parliamentary majority, and caused a colonel or a general to be elected to the presidency—although not without occasional resort to visible fraud, as in 1972. The PCN's defeat by the opposition in 1972 revealed the decline of this partially open electoral system. The resort to fraud, repression, and limitation of electoral competition which followed revealed the importance and decay of the machinery created to assure the legal continuity of the military-controlled state.

The institutionalization of General Torrijos's nationalist military regime in Panama seems to have followed a parallel path to that of the Salvadorean colonels—despite differences in political orientation. The Democratic Revolutionary party (PRD) launched by its partisans nearly ten years after the national guard's 1968 coup d'état against the traditional oligarchic parties seemed also to aspire to transform itself into a Mexican-style institutionalized party. Its success in the legislative elections of 1978 permitted the new civilian president, elected by the Assembly, to democratize the regime without taking great risks.[14] Will the renaissance of competitive political life eventually take place at the expense of the PRD, and will the process of democratization extend to acceptance of an eventual defeat of the official party? By retaining personal command of the national guard, General Torrijos remained the strong man of Panama in the classic Central American tradition of military *caudillismo* and *continuismo,* and such outcomes seemed quite unlikely. It was whispered in Panama that the new president, Aristides Royos, was no more than the transitory occupant of a six-year term conceded by Torrijos.[15] The latter's unexpected death in 1981, of course, may have upset these calculations.

The very fluid politico-military situation in Honduras offers us a singular case of an attempt at institutionalization within a traditional two-party arrangement. As in Peru, the reformist military officers who came to power in December 1972 found themselves confronted by conservative demands for a return to normal political practices. After the eviction of General López Arellano, and then of his successor, Melgar Castro, in August 1978 the government of the armed forces entered a third stage which put an end to the cycle of reforms. The conservative National party which supported the new government offered to play the role of a "military party, that is to say, a civilian organization through which the military could continue to exercise power."[16] For this, elections were necessary. They took place on April 20, 1980, but gave an unexpected victory to the traditional Liberal adversaries of the National party. Thanks to Liberal goodwill and international circumstances, this vote of protest against the military did not have the predictable consequence of provoking a coup d'état to annul the "unwelcome" results. Liberal and Conservative deputies joined forces to elect General Paz García, head of the military junta, to the provisional presidency of the republic until subsequent elections could be held after the drafting of a new constitution,[17] and the winning party accepted a minority position in the intervening government.

In Guatemala, the state has been profoundly militarized. The army not only occupies power but also fulfills numerous civilian functions, and constitutes a veritable bureaucratic bourgeoisie. The military high command supervises nominations to all posts of responsibility.[18] In spite of more or less regular competitive elections, there is no single and distinctive military party. But in 1974 all three presidential candidates were generals. Since the overthrow of Arbenz, the progressive civilian president, by Castillo Armas in 1954, "anticommunist" governments supported by the army have occupied power with or without popular ratification. Since 1970—in a climate of increasing violence—generals have regularly acceded to the presidency as a result of elections which the army always manages to win. The same scenario is repeated with variations: the armed forces choose a candidate who will necessarily become the chief executive. They then negotiate with one or two parties on the right or extreme right which provide the incumbent with his label and his electoral base. Pluralist competition is limited to a "constitutional arc" from which the parties of the left are banished by definition.[19] In 1970 General Carlos Arana Osorio was elected president with the support of the Movement of National Liberation (MLN), "the party of organized violence" and of counter-terrorism; in 1974 General Kjell Laugerud was the candidate of a coalition of the MLN and the Institutional Democratic party (PID); in 1978, the ironically named Revolutionary party allied itself with the PID in order to elect General Romeo Lucas García. It seems that only Arana Osorio really won any of these elections. His successors owed their accession to power to fraud or to strong-arm measures by the previous government. For example, in 1974 General Laugerud certainly obtained fewer votes than General Ríos Montt, but the government had his election ratified by the Congress.[20] Ríos Montt, having insufficient support in the army, had to leave the country. These legal and constitutional governments are therefore really the expression of an institutionalized military state in its "controlled and coercive multiparty" mode. But simultaneously they represent a type of demilitarization which may alternatively close or open in the direction of establishing less exclusionary systems.

The evolution of Brazil illustrates both the ambiguities and the opportunities of a redemocratization controlled by military power in which the military have not suppressed formal democratic procedures, even if they have emptied them of much of their content. The policy of "decompression" and "opening" undertaken since 1974 by General Geisel and pursued by his successor, General Figueiredo, has provoked an undeniable liberalization, involving the suppression of dictatorial powers given to the president by Institutional Act No. 5, the suppression of censorship, an amnesty, a return of political exiles, and the reestablishment of direct elections for governors and senators. These were all stages of a "gradual" democratization managed by the government at a rhythm of their own choosing. The reactivation of civil society and the enlargement of the arena of political tolerance (as demonstrated by the proliferation of extreme left publications which now circulate legally) may nevertheless be perceived as forming a new strategy of institutionalization following the failure of the compulsory two-party system installed after 1965. The continual electoral progress of the tolerated opposition (the Brazilian Democratic Movement—MDB) and the poor showing since the legislative elections of 1974 of the official party, ARENA, created a delicate and potentially uncontrollable situation for those in power. It was thought by some strategists of the regime that a well-regulated opening could assure continuity by limiting from the outset the "plebiscitary deadlock"[21] which the regime had created for itself because of its identification with ARENA and the existence of a clear two-party choice offered to the electorate. Some observers have argued that the return of the pre-1964 leaders to political activity and the restoration of a multiparty system are measures calculated to split the MDB and, thus, to weaken the opposition while ostensibly freeing it.[22] Although the new law on parties has not succeeded for the moment in completely isolating the left by provoking profound political regroupings, it has favored the formation of two more conservative parties—the Social Democratic party (PDS), party of the president, and a moderate, centrist opposition, the Brazilian Popular party (PPB). This new range of parties could make possible an alternation in power without risks, acceptable to the military on condition that the more militant opposition was divided or, even better, atomized. But the prohibition of "electoral alliances" designed to prevent the formation of a united opposition compelled the PPB to merge with the MDB, thus complicating the regime's calculations. The continued good showing of the MDB (now transformed into the PMDB), was not part of the plan, while the rise of an unexpected "Workers' party" (PT) complicated the intended opening even more.

Such an opening of the electoral arena constitutes a novel legitimation tactic by an isolated regime which is in crisis, and which is looking for an enlarged base of support. According to this scenario, "slow and gradual" democratization would in no way be the prelude to a transformation of the "system," but would prolong the existing practice of changing the rules of the game when the previous ones had become disadvantageous. This new manifestation of *casuismo* and flexibility by a regime which is a past master in elections at the game of "whoever loses, wins," could produce—in spite of all its built-in safeguards—certain unexpected consequences which could in the longer run affect its very nature.[23] As Fernando Henrique Cardoso so rightly points out, until now "it was the system which legitimized the parties."[24] Now the parties have become essential elements in the functioning of the regime, to the point where the head of state is regarded as a party leader. Within this framework, liberalization could have its own dynamic. The utilization of authoritarian measures to contain a tolerated democracy could become unfeasible—it is only by playing the electoral game that the project can result in something, and bring the regime what it needs: legitimation. An eventual authoritarian regression would cause the political dividends of the strategy to be lost. Restricted political liberalization may not remain compatible with a potentially uncontrollable social opening now that long repressed and delayed popular demands have burst spontaneously into view. The repression of major strikes in April–May 1980 and of free trade unions seems to indicate that the regime does not intend to modify its control over the "dangerous classes" bequeathed by Vargas's *Estado novo,* which had hardly been modified during the "democratic experience" of 1946 to 1964. Will this authoritarian resource remain in reserve, and does it indicate the limits beyond which liberalization will not be allowed to go? Is this, indeed, the social price to be paid in order to make the political opening irreversible? Whatever the case, it would seem that the regime does not intend to hold back, or to lose the initiative. It holds all the trump cards in its own hands, and seems to assume that democracy will work in its favor. What is being created, then, is not so much a restricted democracy but rather a democracy in which those in power cannot lose.[25] The key test evidently remains the presidential succession. The renaissance of civil society and the reactivation of the parties and of parliamentary life, by reducing the scope of authoritarianism, also reduce the space for military sovereignty. The regime is changing its nature, but to whom will power ultimately belong?

Civil Government and Military Power

While one can see the ambiguous character of controlled liberalization without rupture, one must also be aware of the opportunities provided by the conservation of even a democratic facade. Both imply a certain degree and form of demilitarization. In the recent history of Latin America, noninstitutionalized military governments have generally agreed to withdraw from power only in the context of certain guarantees. They have endeavored, to the best of their ability, to fix the subsequent rules of the game. What is more, they have not hesitated, when the situation permitted it, to demand a place for the military institutions in the constitutional structure of the emergent democracy and, hence, a permanent right to supervise ensuing political decisions. The plan for a constitution proposed by the Uruguayan military in the referendum of November 30, 1980 was intended to provide just such a juridical basis to their *de facto* power, by stipulating that the National Security Council (COSENA), made up of senior officers, would have the right to challenge the conduct of members of both the executive and legislative branches of power, without itself being responsible to any higher authority, and that it could intervene in "matters relating to national security" and even (with the president) declare a "state of emergency" without reference to Parliament—except *a posteriori*.[26] As we know, this tutelary democracy was rejected by the electorate after having been condemned by a spectrum of parties ranging from the *Frente Amplio* on the left to the traditional *Blanco* and *Colorado* organizations.[27]

In 1972, the Argentine military, in power since 1966, faced a climate of crisis. In order to avoid an uncontrollable social explosion, it was decided to organize elections without proscriptions for the first time since 1955. But the military wanted to avoid an electoral "leap in the dark," which, according to them, could allow a return to the "disastrous errors of the past." To this end, General Lanusse, president of the government of the armed forces, sought to obtain a series of guarantees from civilian political forces which would have given the army the upper hand. The military, in search of an honorable outcome, even made the holding of elections conditional on a "Grand National Accord" of all the political groups under its aegis. A military candidate of transition and national unity would have nicely suited the high command. When the political groups rejected any institutionalization of military participation in the reestablished democracy, and the attempts at generating an official candidate had failed, the military, *in extremis*, insisted on a double guarantee. They reformed the electoral law to institute two rounds of voting for the presidential election if a majority was not obtained the first time, and imposed a residence clause which effectively would have prevented Perón from becoming a candidate. This accumulation of safeguards and stratagems imposed by the *de facto* regime hardly elicited much support from the political forces. Finally, the junta of the commanders-in-chief issued a declaration, in the absence of an agreement, which recorded the principles that the military wanted to have respected. This text foresaw that the armed forces would oppose, among other things, an "indiscriminate amnesty" of subversives, and it anticipated that the armed forces would have to "share governmental responsibilities."[28]

In reality, the regime had already lost the initiative. The massive electoral victory of the Peronist candidate swept away the restraints placed by the departing government. The slogan "Cámpora to government, Perón to power" rendered ridiculous the proscriptive clause imposed by the generals. In spite of their own electoral law, the military declared the Peronist candidate, Cámpora, elected, even though he had received only 49.5 percent of the votes, in order to avoid the humiliation they would have faced in a second presidential round, in all likelihood even more agitated and more massively hostile to the holders of power. The two political parties against which the coup d'état of 1966 had been directed (the Peronists and the Radicals) together received 70 percent of the suffrage. The semiofficial candidate of the armed forces did not even get 3 percent of the votes! The group of candidates who collectively represented continuity scarcely surpassed 18 percent.[29] What is more, the new government promulgated an immediate general amnesty, and the elected president refused all institutional suggestions regarding the choice of men charged with representing the armed forces. Command over the army was even disrupted by the nomination of a commander in chief who did not come from the cavalry, the branch which had dominated it since 1960.

In Ecuador, *mutatis mutandis,* the military (which had come to power in 1972) withdrew while trying to impose conditions analogous to those of the Argentine army. The Ecuadorian military, having decided to return to the government to civilians after a palace revolution in 1976 which removed General Guillermo Rodríguez Lara from office, announced their wish to give the country a truly representative democracy. Nevertheless, the junta took its own precautions, or rather tried to establish a democratic system which would conform to the military's image and interests. The transition process was thus marked by a stately slowness: it would last not less than three years and began by excluding from the election the three most representative candidates considered by the army to be dangerous demagogues. As an added precaution, a electoral law was promulgated in February 1978 providing that the future president must not be a previous incumbent. This deprived both Velasco Ibarra, an eternal *caudillo* who had already been elected president five times, and Carlos Julio Arosamena of any future. Yet another *ad hoc* clause stipulated that the future president must be an Ecuadorian and the child of an Ecuadorian. This requirement was specifically directed against Assad Bucarám, head of the Concentration of Popular Forces and one of the leading potential candidates, who was the son of a Lebanese. This populist leader, who enjoyed great support among the subproletariat of Guayaquil, was the heavy favorite in the election, as he had previously been in 1972 at the time of the coup d'état.

This use of the veto and control over candidacies, contrary to democratic norms, augured poorly for the reestablishment of a legitimate and constitutional regime. The imposition of voting in two rounds, on the French model, leaving only the two leading candidates in the competition at the second stage, was apparently intended to promote a united front of conservatives. The interlude of nearly ten months between the two rounds, and the numerous incidents which accompanied the campaign, hardly gave much grounds for hoping that the results would be respected if they did not correspond to the wishes of the military. More especially, the military's support for Sixto Durán, the conservative candidate, was almost visible, while Bucarám, excluded, was represented by proxy, through his nephew by marriage, Jaime Roldós. Eventually, after an obstacle-ridden process as difficult as it was uncertain, it was Roldós who won the election and who became the constitutional president of Ecuador in August 1979, without the military attempting to question the result of the vote.

It does not always work out like this. The military appear not to accept withdrawal unless the civil government which replaces them is very similar to their own policies or preferences, or unless the elections produce a victory for their own candidate. In any other cases, the result may be invalidated either immediately or eventually, after a period of observation, when circumstances are more propitious. According to the formulation of François Bourricaud, the multiplication of "contentious elections" expresses this *continuista* behavior. The agitated political life of Bolivia from 1978 to 1980 illustrates this tendency well. General Banzer's official candidate in the election of July 9, 1978, General Pereda, was the author of a coup d'état on July 21 designed to assure his "victory"—a victory whose legality was strongly contested, notably by the moderate left wing candidate, Siles Suazo. In November 1978, the constitutionalist sector of the army, led by General Padilla, overthrew General Pereda and organized new elections, which were held in June 1979. Since these elections did not yield a clear majority, the president of the Senate became head of state. The process of constitutionalization pursued its course until November 1, 1979, when Colonel Natusch Busch seized power but was compelled to resign after a fortnight. He was replaced by the president of the Chamber of Deputies, Mrs. Lydia Gueiler. New elections were held on June 29, 1980, and marked a clear shift to the left. Siles Suazo, who was ahead with a center-left coalition, would have been ratified by Congress as head of state on August 4. General Banzer, who had presented himself as a candidate in these elections, had obtained only 15 percent of the votes. However, of July 17, 1980, a bloody and overpowering coup d'état installed General García Meza as president of the republic. The putschists no longer speak of elections. Their primary stated objective, to "extirpate the Marxist cancer," postpones any form of institutionalization to a very nebulous future.

Unable to impose their preferred form of government and prolong their ascendancy, the armed forces may qualify their withdrawal by insisting on corporative defense measures which would impede the reestablishment of civilian supremacy in all domains. Thus the "postmilitary" civilian regime may rule only if elected authorities agree not to exercise control over military appointments. Such an affirmation of military autonomy is a frequent legacy of the militarization of power, and a standard price paid for the return of the military to their barracks. In Peru, President Belaúnde, elected after the military interlude of 1962, was required in 1963 to designate as commander in chief of each branch of the army the highest ranking officer and to nominate military ministers, in accord with the wishes of the high command. In Ecuador, shortly before the first round of presidential elections in July 1978, the military reformed the organic law of the armed forces and decreed that the future president would have to name as minister of defense the officer occupying the highest position in the hierarchy.[30]

Even a military defeat at the polls accompanied by a veritable rout in the face of exasperated public opinion, such as occurred in Argentina in March–May 1973, may not guarantee a return to full representative democracy, even if the army respects the results of the elections. The demilitarization of government need not signify demilitarization of power where the military have entrenched themselves as quasi-legitimate actors in the political game. Thus from 1973 to 1976, Argentine military leaders, apparently routed by Peronism and swept aside by the electoral landslide, in fact "accompanied" the evolution of the political situation step by step. It was only after the high command restored Perón to his rank of general and gave him the green light that Perón deposed his proxy, Cámpora. Under subsequent commanders in chief, the army was still a force in public life—regardless of its more or less strong inclination toward neutrality when faced with a regime which rapidly fell apart after the death of the "leader." The effort by Mrs. Perón's government to attract military participation and, therefore, legitimacy, provoked a very serious crisis in August 1975 and was a prelude to the eventual collapse of civilian power. The ostentatious political neutrality of the Argentine high command was revealed in March 1976 to have been a mere facade behind which they were preparing the way for a subtle form of putschist intervention. Their theory of the "ripe fruit" and the military's complacency about allowing the situation to worsen contradict any suggestion that the uprising of 1976 was either accidental or spontaneous.

These mock withdrawals from government by the Argentine army[31] in no way signify that countries which have once known military power in the contemporary period are condemned to inevitable repetitions of it. With its half century of martial domination, Argentina is without doubt the extreme case of a militarized political system. Nevertheless, who would deny that the return to barracks is never definitive, and that the postmilitary state, whatever its degree of democracy, continues to live in the shadow of the barracks? This reality conditions the conduct of civilian actors. They always face the alternatives of discouraging a putsch or attempting to provoke one. No one knocks on the barracks doors who is not sure there is some chance of being asked to enter. But there is nothing inevitable about the outcome. To not defer to military intervention is to affirm civilian power and to make militarist usurpation more and more difficult, thereby serving to demilitarize the political system. On the other hand, the permanent menace or fear of a putsch is a real form of intervention, as has been evident recently in Spain. Since Franco's death, allusions to military "tolerance" continue to fill political life, while the specter of Pavia's horse still haunts the Parliament.[32]

Demilitarization therefore has its degrees. The return of civilians to power is not automatically equivalent to the "civilianization" of power, even after free and representative elections. One may ask why, under what influences, and in what conditions the military hand over office to civilians, but one may also inquire as to what explains the limitations on the process of "extricating" militarism from politics. We will first of all consider the reasons for the formal opening of systems dominated by the military, and then the causes of recurrent "praetorian" militarism.

The Moment of Civilian Politicians

The multiplicity of hypotheses that one might put forward with regard to the causes of transition from military authoritarian rule to civilian representative regimes in Latin America complicates all attempts at explanation. The political, social, and economic conditions generally listed as explanatory factors apply in fact to all sorts of authoritarianism—not just to the martial variety. Besides, a certain number of them seem of little explanatory value by reason of their reversibility, and even their "mythological" nature. It is by this latter term that Wanderley Guilherme dos Santos critically evaluates the contradictory economic interpretations of authoritarianism:

> It is thus that economic recessions are presented sometimes as an explanation of the erosion of authoritarianism, given that it would be impossible for these regimes—according to these theories—to coopt the masses and/or the elites via the distribution of advantages; sometimes the same recession is presented as an explanation of the survival of authoritarianism, given that only authoritarian procedures may be possible if one has to suppress popular demands, in a context of acute penury. Inversely, high rates of economic growth and accumulation have been used both to explain the continuation of authoritarianism, since the regimes can thus anesthetize the population, and particularly the masses, via the distribution of new advantages, *and* to explain the erosion of authoritarian systems; on the argument that the social groups benefitting selectively from the growth will begin to demand a greater

political participation. The erosion, just as the permanence of authoritarianism—political phenomena—are thus "inferred" as much from economic growth as from economic recession. When contrary processes simultaneously explain inverse results, they belong to the mythology of conventional classification.[33]

Deterministic hypotheses of closer and more immediate bearing seem at the same time both convincing and of little operational use. This is true of those interpretations of the recent "hesitations" of Latin American military regimes and of their tendencies toward liberalization and institutionalization which rely on the assumption that they have accomplished the process of "authoritarian restructuring of capitalism" which necessarily gave rise to them.[34] If one considers that Pinochet's Chile is the most accomplished example of such a transformation, to the point where it has been possible to speak of a veritable "capitalist revolution," the recent evolution of the Chilean situation would seem to contradict the validity of this thesis. Both officials of the regime and a number of its more crucial civilian supporters have stated that there are still "objectives" to be attained rather than a timetable to be followed, even if in practice some not very restrictive timetable has been adopted. But the future prospect of the "seven modernizations," concerning the privatizing and "modernizing" of the essential sectors of national activity by denationalizing them (so as to establish the ascendancy of the market and to change mentalities), has not prevented the fixing of a calendar for the progressive construction of an institutionalized and representative polity.[35]

If it is evident that such factors as the behavior and expectations of the different actors, the range of political resources at the disposal of martial power, the duration of its ascendancy, and the initial justification for its emergence should be taken into consideration, the international hemispheric conjuncture and the processes internal to the military institutions also seem to merit serious consideration in any explanation of political changes occurring within systems of martial domination. Two sequences which appear contradictory, but are most often complementary, help to illuminate these transformations. One concerns the voluntarism and intentionality of the military actors, and relates to the overarching question of legitimacy which we have already discussed, as well as to the necessity of avoiding or obviating the risk of democratic uncertainty. The other, involving multiple social determinants as well as the particular functioning of "factions" and "parties" within the military, underlies the difficult, unprogrammed and undetermined nature of the demilitarization process, the result of a whole series of perverse and accidental influences, of misunderstandings or errors by the protagonists.

It does not require much argument to demonstrate the importance of the hemispheric conjuncture as a factor affecting the diffusion and fluctuation, as well as the orientation, of martial power.[36] The hemispheric policy of the United States—the alternation after 1945 between anticommunist

vigilance and democratizing preoccupations of successive U.S. administrations—imparts a rhythm to the phases of autocracy and the waves of
demilitarization which follow with only short time lags. This does not
diminish the role of internal dynamics in the more autonomous Latin
American states, but does imply formal and other "cosmetic" adaptations
in their case. If the overthrow of President Frondizi in Argentina in March
1962 was a response to strictly national conflicts dating back to 1955, the
military putschists borrowed their justification from the defensive perspective outlined by the Pentagon in the framework of post-Cuban-revolu-
tion strategic objective, but disguised their illegitimacy with a legal
cloak—by making Vice President Guido the president—in order to satisfy
the criteria of respectability inherent in the Alliance for Progress. In this
case, the contract between the civilian reformism of Kennedy and the
counter-insurrectionary antireformism of the hemispheric defense inspired by the Pentagon permitted a double reading of the politico-military
process and resulted in a policy operating at two levels.

More recently in Bolivia, the failure of the November 1 1979, putsch and
the success of the July 17, 1980 coup d'état are not unrelated to the
continental conjuncture and, hence, to U. S. policy. Colonel Natusch
Busch was compelled to resign after a fortnight under pressure from the
Carter administration, which was supporting the process of democratization. The member countries of the Andean Pact, forming a veritable
democratic bloc,[37] reinforced the stand of Washington by not recognizing
the usurpers. In July 1980 President Carter, at the end of his term and in
mid-electoral campaign, could condemn only morally and feebly a determined and brutal military intervention which, itself, was anticipating the
victory of his opponent. Observers have in fact remarked that General
García Meza's coup took place the day after the Republican convention's
nomination of Ronald Reagan, who was (and remains) the hope of all
conservative forces on the continent.

More generally, it is appropriate for a martial regime to demilitarize and
legalize itself somewhat—both by reason of the global ideology we alluded
to earlier and by virtue of the specific nature of the military apparatus in
its relationship to power. Not only do the internal tensions brought about
by the tasks of government weaken corporative cohesion and thus the
defensive capacities which provide the foundation for the (provisional)
legitimacy of the military's usurpation of power, but they also reduce the
political resources of the institution. In power, the military suffer a dangerous "desacralization." Furthermore, the overt, unconstitutional form
of military governance is neither a necessity nor even a good solution for
military power and those who support it. Such direct rule corresponds
rather to a stage, to a moment of political domination. Legalization is the
next stage. In terms of a cost-benefit analysis, the choice for the military
involves a difficult equilibrium between the political costs deriving from
the risks of democracy and the institutional costs required by martial

authoritarianism. This is why institutionalization only rarely implies the withdrawal of the military from power, and why legalization does not often have complete and unrestricted democracy as its objective. On the contrary, the military withdrawal contains an element of continuity, and represents the accomplishment of the mission invoked to justify the initial intervention. The calling of elections, even if pluralism is not limited by the authorities, does not *ipso facto* entail the restoration or installation of an authentic democracy. If one adopts the definition of *democratic procedures* proposed by Schumpeter, according to which "it means only that the people have the opportunity of accepting or refusing the men who are to rule them,"[38] the postmilitary state is more likely to organize elections without surprises and without effects. The true holders of power are not affected by them.

Moreover, the key figures in conservative military systems and their ideologues and allies very explicitly reject the uncertainties of the democratic game. Their avowed ideal, of "protected democracy," reflects the search for an absolute guarantee against the risk of a legal advent to power by the adversaries of the status quo. One of the ideologues most listened to by successive Argentine military regimes wrote, after the overthrow of the civilian government in 1976, that the new governments of the Southern Cone were in the process of founding "future democracies on a bedrock of order and development."[39] The "hard-liners" of the Chilean regime aspire, for their part, to put in place definite remedies against democratic subversion since, in the words of one of them, "one cannot always live on one's guard."[40] But the best "protection" of democracy is in fact the use—perverted, denatured, controlled—of democratic procedures to legitimize authoritarian rule. The well-established and stable postmilitary state gives rise, like all durable authoritarian regimes in Latin America, to semicompetitive political systems—that is, to systems in which open and uncontrolled competition is restricted to the periphery of power, while the real holders of power keep out of the way of the electoral contest.[41] This system presents its users with the legitimizing advantages of representative regimes without the risks of alternation or massive shifts in coalitional strength. It is clearly in this direction that military-dominated systems move when they have the opportunity and when they have not lost the initiative. The conservative military do not have a monopoly on this strategy, as demonstrated by the experience of Panama, which under populist Torrijos moved smoothly toward an exemplary semicompetitive system.

General Figueiredo's Brazil, with its gestures toward "decompression," seems to be tending toward such an outcome. Certainly the development of forces favorable to the liberalization of the regime, as well as the convergence of the tolerated political opposition with the industrial bourgeoisie and of the new middle class with the old political class, have played a role, but the system controlled the choice of instruments and the timing of initiatives. Moreover, Geisel's project not only consisted of splintering the opposition front by abolishing the two-party system, but also of rendering the army politically autonomous. General Figueiredo was chosen by Geisel as a successor against the wishes of the military apparatus. The army lost its role as decisive elector. With the legitimacy of the military presence being contested by civil society,[42] as illustrated by the electoral results, it was undoubtedly opportune to provide a legal base for the system without recourse to the army. Demilitarization without risk is also evident in the care subsequently taken by General Geisel and the "palace group" surrounding him to separate within the army those with institutional responsibilities from those with military leadership roles (*chefia* against *liderança*, to apply Rizzo de Oliveira's distinction[43]), in order to impose a bureaucratic hegemony on the armed forces and, most notably, in order to prevent the appearance of politico-military leaders possessing their own legitimacy and following.[44] This nondemocratic plan could, of course, escape the control of those who put it into operation. The "perfect political crime," in the words of an opposition deputy, could fail to be consummated. There is a narrow margin between risk and legitimacy. The maximum of uncertainty—and thus of electoral *fair play*—produces a maximum of legitimacy. Thus in Brazil the outcome is still uncertain despite the precautions taken by the regime. The direct election of state governors for the first time in November 1982 took place within the framework of liberalization as promised, but it did nothing to increase the legitimacy of those in power. The undeniable victory of the opposition in the richest and most populous states of the country's center and south made even more ridiculous the pretence of a presidential election based on an *ad hoc* electoral college where the regime is guaranteed a majority if its official party does not split under the pressure of public opinion massively demanding direct elections and substantially disaffected by the growing economic crisis. If the opposition obtains a majority in this rigged electoral college and defeats the government's candidate, then the *democradura* will have been defeated. If not, what sort of legitimacy would such a badly elected president have to govern such a crisis-ridden country? In this case, tensions within the military establishment in the face of a revived civil society so buffeted by policies of economic austerity could provoke rather unexpected reactions.

In fact it is frequently the case that processes internal to the military apparatus shape the phases of demilitarization and open the way to eventual democratic alternation. A failure in the martial apparatus, a grave conflict with the officer corps, can condemn the project of institutionalization. An appeal may then be made to civilians and to democratic sanctions in order to escape from the impasse or to overcome further destabilizing splits. We do not wish to imply by this that the behavior of other actors is unimportant, nor that the outcome of the processes of demilitarization-institutionalization is unaffected by other factors such as the duration of the noncivilian government, the circumstances of its installation, and the level of violence which it introduces into the society. But the return of the military to barracks is above all a military problem, and it would be somewhat paradoxical to study it without considering this decisive angle. It is evident that the erosion accompanying the exercise of power is more demoralizing for the military establishment as a state institution than for a political party,[45] and that economic and social crises amplify its internal conflicts around military issues.

A civilian restoration, accomplished by unconditional elections and without proscriptions, frequently comes about as the result of a change in the inner circle produced by a palace revolution. The project of the military which initially justified their seizure of power is thus over-whelmed after several years of uncertainty and indirection (three years in Argentina after 1970, three years, too, in Ecuador after 1976, but five years in Peru from 1975–80). Then, the military have only to prepare their retreat in good order and with "honor." Military refusal to sustain a political orientation or to endorse a *caudillista* attempt often gives rise to intervals marked by multiple coups. Thus, in Peru and Honduras in 1975, and in Ecuador in 1976, the conservative sector of the army opposed the military reformists in power, provoking the fall respectively of Velasco Alvarado, Rodríguez Lara, and López Arellano. But a second factor was the refusal, in the name of the corporative functioning of military power, to give a blank check to a man brought into government by the army. This factor has the same consequences. The two courses sometimes coincide, as in Peru. In the name of institutional rotation of the members of the executive—such as occurred in Brazil after 1964, and in Argentina after 1976—the Peruvian high command deposed Velasco Alvarado, who wanted to hold onto power beyond the time prescribed by military regulations and who had attempted to acquire a personal following. The changed alignment of the "military party," explicable according to certain observers in terms of the economic crisis and the urgency of negotiating with resurgent social forces,[46] led to the restoration of democracy. In the absence of charismatic resources and given the refusal to attempt any partisan mobilization, a bureaucratic system without support or project could only retreat or collapse. The regime of General Morales Bermúdez, bereft of partisan support and of the will to obtain it, nevertheless lasted five years, certainly representing an unprecedented case of "political levitation," but also illustrating the difficulties inherent in an orderly transfer of power when the internal military situation is so lacking in consensus.

In Argentina, after the overthrow of General Onganía, who had not fixed any limit on his power and who intended to place the army outside the government, General Lanusse, commander in chief and kingmaker, brought to power the ephemeral General Levingston. The latter broke with the liberal economic policy of his predecessor without having the means to do so and without specifying alternative goals for his government. It only remained for the high command to acknowledge the failure of the "Argentine revolution" by preparing the withdrawal of the army. The acute internal cleavages and the intensity of social tensions hardly permitted them anything other than to transfer the government to civilians or to throw themselves into a repressive assault, which internal conflicts within their ranks would scarcely allow.

In such cases, the resort to civilians and the opening up of free democratic competition without guarantees for the incumbents of government seems like the only outcome that would reconstitute the internal cohesion of the armed forces. Faced with the danger of the splintering and decomposition of their institution, an electoral consultation eases tensions and reunifies a military apparatus torn between contradictory tendencies. It is not out of a taste for the paradoxical that, parodying the martial rhetoric, one may say that on such occasions, civil intervention puts a limit on military dissension. In the absence of a minimal consensus, let alone a coherent program within the armed forces, formal demilitarization by the democratic route comes to seem inescapable. But in order for the tactical withdrawal to be effective, it is still necessary to have a minimum of agreement on the neutrality to be observed, if the military politicization is not to lead to a cascade of coups and counter-coups in the Bolivian style. Furthermore, since the military disagreements are not unrelated to civilian conflicts, such an outcome is only possible if the majority of the political forces have accepted the need for a demilitarization, and if the military do not perceive any direct peril or intention of seeking revenge on the part of returning civilians.

The Future of Military Rule— or How to Keep Them in Their Barracks

There are numerous obstacles to the departure of the military from the political scene—that is, from command over government—which slow down or prevent the return of freely elected civilians to public affairs. They derive for the most part from a logic internal to the military corporation. The permanence of the threat which justified the army's coming to power obviously represents the most frequently mentioned obstacle. A blaze of urban terrorism or an incompletely extinguished focus of rural guerrilla activity will engender militarist twitching scarcely propitious for a democratic relaxation. The abstract invocation of the "communist danger" or the "Marxist cancer" which must be extirpated before returning to normal institutional functioning only has validity insofar as the specter of subversion remains a concrete threat for significant sectors of opinion. The counterrevolutionary logic cannot but nourish itself on the memory of the revolutionary menace. The recollection of three years of Popular Unity government is still the surest foundation of the Chilean dictatorship. But in Brazil, sixteen years after the overthrow of the Goulart regime and the rout of the populist forces, those responsible for the "system," although they are the authors of the manichean doctrine of "ideological frontiers," have played down this worn-out and, henceforth, ineffective legitimation. In Argentina, on the contrary, the chaotic condition of Isabelita's government and "subversive aggression" so undermined the value of democratic coexistence that the counter-terrorist regime installed in 1976 has acquired a far-from-negligible stock of political capital.

The level of official violence constitutes another decisive variable. A weakly repressive military regime enjoys much greater freedom of maneuver. A terrorist government, on the contrary, risks being eventually called to account by the people. Violations of human rights, the problem of those who have "disappeared" in the course of the antisubversive fight, will require at least illumination, if not the establishment of penal responsibilities when the situation becomes normalized. In Argentina, the specter of Nuremberg haunts the barracks and explains the *fuite en avant* into the Malvinas/Falklands adventure, as well as the uncertainties that attended the surrender of power to civilians until the last moment on December 10, 1983. "Argentina does not confess except before God,"[47] proclaimed General Videla's minister of the interior only recently. The demoralization and defensive reflex of an army that has carried out the "dirty work" of a revolutionary war explains the multiple and feeble guarantees promulgated by the military in power before their return to barracks (e.g., the Self-Amnesty Law, the Anti-Subversive Law). This situation makes more understandable the "prudent audacity" of the newly elected President Alfonsín in dealing with the military question. He has sought to reestablish the sovereignty of law and of civilian authority, and to avoid all measures which could provoke a corporative reflex that might unite all officers against the democratic government. In Brazil, despite a skillful amnesty which whitewashed the "dark moments" of the repression, public revelations and the denunciations of the officers' responsibilities in the assassination of opponents provoked a very vigorous response by the military ministers in February 1981. They warned against any "revanchist" attempt, saying that it might put brakes on the process of decompression. "The honor of the barracks is above the rights of man" was the headline of an opposition weekly.[48] The liberalization seemed at least to be hostage to that necessity.

It is with regard to this question in particular that the strategies of the civilians enter into play. Their margin of maneuver is narrow. The search for compromise and their acceptance of the "law of silence" imposed by the military may permit the political forces and supporters of democracy to make some gains.[49] Avoiding direct confrontation, dissipating any personal or institutional disquiet among the officers most compromised in the repression, can, curiously, facilitate progress toward the rule of law and representative procedures. But this also means restoring legitimacy by an act of weakness, underwriting the impunity of the usurpation—in a word—placing the military apparatus in an arbitrary and irresponsible position, thus demilitarizing the government while maintaining the militarization of the political system. This is the eternal dilemma of the skillful and the pure—foxes and lions, Machiavelli would say—of accommodation and intransigence. But it is also a fundamental difference between a conceded transition and democratic rupture, which perhaps takes into account the evolution of the balance of forces.

The nature and the duration of the military government, tied to the preceding characteristic, condition the processes of eventual demilitarization. If democracy restores both the competitive procedures for the choice of rulers, and that substratum of freedoms which makes them possible and regular, certain Latin American military systems only suppress the former while but feebly restricting the latter. The restriction of party or union freedoms, and even to a certain extent restrictions on the freedom of expression, were not in fact major features of the Peruvian or Panamanian military regimes after 1968, or of the Ecuadorian between 1972 and 1979. The Argentina of Generals Onganía, Levingston, and Lanusse, in comparison with other neighboring or subsequent authoritarian regimes, allowed a remarkable level of tolerance *vis-á-vis* the opposition. The sustained vitality of civil society no doubt facilitated the diverse forms of demilitarization undertaken by these regimes.

By contrast, the persistence of noninstitutionalized military power and the corruption caused by an absolutist exercise of authority make political alternation more improbable. The case of Bolivia, and of an army highly fractionalized into cliques, in which the accession to officer grade seems like a path to social advancement, perhaps best exemplifies this phenomenon. It has even been possible to venture the hypothesis that the refusal on several occasions in 1979–80 to recognize the results of elections which did not assure military continuity had to do both with the fears of numerous officers that they would have to reveal, before public opinion or the tribunals, the origin of their enrichment, and with the wish of more junior officers of the army to take part in the feast of the corrupted. But it is true that besides these psychologistic and anecdotal explanations,[50] one can find a deeper significance in the Bolivian case which touches on the militarization of the whole political system.

If in Bolivia the defense of the institution which thought itself to be threatened by the return of civilians, and notably by the victory of a moderate left, blocked the transition, it was also and above all because in this case the army has provided the terrain and the arena in which all political struggles occur. In this "praetorianized" system, civilian political sectors have always been implicated in the military interventions. A military clique rarely launches a putschist adventure without a sectional endorsement or without an alliance with civilian groups. The civilian-military overlap, the permanent articulation of the two spheres, makes the "extrication" of militarism and the "civilianization" of power difficult. Contrary to a view marked by liberal ethnocentrism, in a system so militarized, there do not exist two worlds entrenched like two camps prepared for battle, with civilians on one side and the military on the other. Far from provoking a sacred union of the political class or of the social forces organized to defend democratic institutions in danger, any military uprising will enlist the public support of certain civilian forces competing with their rivals. It seems that in Bolivia this "praetorianization" of political life is not unrelated to the absence of a political majority, as indicated at the last elections. Also in Argentina, where the army has dominated political life for fifty years, the demilitarization of government does not necessarily change the system for all that, and sets no real limit on the likelihood of a "praetorian inversion." Elections are not synonymous with democracy. The disengagement of the armed forces from executive power and the lasting return to a liberal-constitutional model of civil-military relations is a difficult and lengthy task. It must confront models of behavior which have been strongly internalized. This sort of blockage cannot be overcome in Argentina without a profound societal and cultural transformation.[51] The choices and behaviors of political actors are not insignificant or inconsequential, but attitudes and tactics are not programmable and are themselves conditioned by social and cultural reality that recurrent military intervention contributes to forming and deforming.

By Way of Conclusion

Without doubt, it is easier to demilitarize the government than the centers of power. Many instances of opening up or of legal institutionalization represent merely tactical withdrawals that will allow subsequent interventions once the military apparatus has reconstituted its political resources. If not that, withdrawal may only be a question of assuring the juridical bases for the continuity of a system established by force. The objection can be raised that there have indeed been successful cases of demilitarization. Without having the cruelty to recall the precedents of Chile or Uruguay, let us examine these illustrative democracies of today, sheltered for twenty years or more from the military storms which have periodically or consistently shaken their neighbors. If one examines the civil-military relations of Mexico, Costa Rica, Venezuela, or Colombia, leaving aside what might happen in any of these countries tomorrow, one may inquire into the means adopted for establishing civilian preponderance and the steps required. The initial question, however, is whether these countries hitherto experienced protracted phases of militarization and, if so, how they overcame it. In fact, only Venezuela and Colombia emerged from a military dictatorship to a restoration of civilian power. But in the Colombian case, the brief interlude of General Rojas Pinilla in 1953 was based on the support of almost all political groups,[52] which called him to power in order to put an end to the *violencia* tearing the country apart. The *rapprochement* of the two traditional parties in 1957 sounded the death knell of the military government, just as their dissension had presided over its birth. In Venezuela, which had only recently emerged from decades of *caudillo* dictatorship, the army in 1948 ousted from government the civilian reformists whom they had previously helped install, but the ascension of General Pérez Jiménez to supreme and absolute power drew together the dispossessed officers and the democratic opposition. The putsches by opposing factions which punctuated the presidency of Rómulo Betancourt after 1958 underline the difficulties of civilian supremacy. Nevertheless, the Acción Democrática party's influence within the military helped to reinforce the democratic party all the more surely since Pérez Jiménez had so discredited army intervention in political life.

In Mexico, the generals of the revolutionary armies formed part of the power elite, and then of the dominant party. The stabilization of the revolutionary order in their collective interest facilitated the containment of spontaneous and predatory forms of military *caudillismo*. The "generals" had in some sense to recognize the civilian power in which they participated in order to assure their political preeminence. In Costa Rica, which has not experienced true military intervention since 1917, the army was suppressed in 1948. Even before its legal abolition, the permanent military apparatus was already on the road to institutional decline.[53] Thus, there has not been a transition from military domination to civilian preponderance there either.

Does this mean that the extirpation of militarism can only occur by some miracle, or under exceptional historical conditions? Could it be, as certain sympathizers with the Cuban or Sandinista revolutions think, that only "the total politicization of the military . . . will in future exclude all militarization of politics?"[54] Certainly, an army emerging from and guarantor of a revolutionary process and staffed with political commissars, selecting their cadres on the basis of extramilitary merits,[55] presents few risks for established power. The maximization of civilian power imposes a sort of "subjective control"—according to Huntington's distinction—which is very secure. But one should not confuse contexts, for we are not here considering the prospects for liberal democracy marked by pluralism and alternation. Thus suppressing the civilian/military distinction can and often does result in militarizing the whole of social life. The civil/military fusion in the ruling elite of Cuba seems to have overridden the distinction, in a way that has tipped the balance toward military preoccupations. Even there, the model of the "civic soldier" which, according to Jorge I. Domínguez, results from this fusion is not without its own forms of role conflict.[56]

Reverting to the capitalist societies of the continent and to outcomes framed within the pluralist constitutional context, it is evident that there are no preestablished scenarios for democratic reconstruction. Outside the revolutionary scheme which we have just mentioned, which is founded on the liquidation of the state army, there are only limited precedents that can give us merely a first approximation to a possibilistic model of demilitarization. We should, however, observe that the path to "civilianization" through armed struggle is not identical with the repudiation of capitalism in the short or medium term. Civilian supremacy in Mexico has its origin in the dissolution of the Porfirista army and its replacement by revolutionary armies, closely linked with the emergence of the new regime. But the same schema applied in Bolivia in another international context was a failure. The 1952 revolution purged the army to the point of practically annihilating it, but instead of creating a popularly based and politicized army, the government of the MNR, alarmed by social agitation and the workers' militias that they did not control, strove to reconstitute the classical army with the help of a U.S. military mission.[57] In Bolivia, far from favoring demilitarization, the specter of the dissolution of the military institution is today one of the unifying sources of military intervention.

The liberalization of military regimes often gives the impression of a stratagem, of bending to the wind in order to survive. Underlining the provisional nature of power may serve to disarm the opposition. The latter is often faced with a difficult choice: accepting the marked cards of the regime and thereby legitimizing its activities, or refusing to participate and thereby paralyzing the institutional process. In fact, the distinction between an electoral farce and an opening which would be usable by civilian forces does not depend upon the degree of competitiveness of the elections. Elections without surprises, or won in advance by those in power, may advance the process of subsequent demilitarization—first, by sanctioning the competitive system without the aid of the military, and above all, by giving the right of self-expression to the forces of opposition. But the decisive test occurs not at the level of the electoral competition, but at that of consitutional liberties. Organizing apparently pluralistic elections may procure a facade of legality, which does not modify the authoritarian nature of power. Accepting the political game requires opening up a space of freedom which may, in turn entail a "qualitative jump." The logic of these two outcomes is different; the risks are not the same. In the latter case, if the opening has a content, and even though it may not lead immediately to a "democratic rupture," the tactic of adopting a "low profile" by forces which are politically moderate (but not moderately democratic) and which are capable of temporary compromises, can be effective. This may allow them to ameliorate the balance of forces.

In this case, the precarious character of the civilian regime under close military surveillance implies first constructing democracy *before* changing society.[58] It means limiting the stakes in order to permit a political agreement on noninvolvement of the military so as to resolve subsequent political conflicts. This is the accord to which Venezuelan and Colombian parties subscribed in the 1950s. It is also what has underlain the behavior of the parliamentary political forces of both right and left in Spain since 1976.[59] From here, several stages may be envisaged without prejudging their order. One of them consists of democratizing the institutions and notably the apparatus of the state (army, police, tribunals), and another, virtually contradictory with the first, consists of creating, in a less dramatic climate, the condition of alternation which is the very expression of real pluralism, and which thus constitutes, without any fireworks, the true "democratic rupture."[60] This long and uncertain path to democracy involves a gamble: one has to accept the game proposed by those in power, in order to beat them at their own game. For this to happen, it helps if the whole of the political class and the majority of social sectors participating favor democratic values and procedures, and accept the uncertainties of the polls, and if the civilian, social, and political forces can say a definitive farewell to arms—before their military brethren have.

Notes

1. The reference is to General Odría, who left power in July 1956 and organized free elections in which his candidate was defeated. For the waves of militarism, see Edwin Lieuwen, *Generals versus Presidents, Neo-Militarism in Latin America* (London, 1964).
2. See Adam Przeworski, "Some Problems in the Study of the Transition to Democracy," Latin American Program Working Paper No. 61 (Washington, D.C.: Woodrow Wilson International Center for Scholars, 1979), pp. 5–8.
3. The idea of a "permanent military government" seems as transitory and dated as that of the irresistible rise of democracy. Cf. Mario Esteban Carranza, *Fuerzas armadas y estado de excepción en América Latina* (Mexico, 1978), chap. 5.
4. See Alain Rouquié, *Pouvoir militaire et société politique dans la Republique Argentine* (Paris, 1978), passim.
5. Cf. Alain Rouquié, "L'Uruguay, de l'Etat providence a l'Etat garnison," *Etudes* (Paris), (June 1979): p 750.
6. Speech by General Pinochet on September 11, 1973, cited by Cristina Hurtado-Beca, "Le processus d'institutionnalisation au Chili," *Problèmes d'Amérique Latine* (Paris), LVIII (December 1980): 78.
7. See *El Mercurio*, September 26 and 28, 1975.
8. Jorge de Esteban and Luis López Guerra, *La crisis del estado franquista* (Madrid, 1977), pp. 28–29.
9. Cf. Carlos Semprun Maura, *Franco est mort dans son lit* (Paris, 1978).
10. Cf. Yves Le Bot, "Bolivie: les militaires, l'Etat, la dépendance: une décennie de pillage," *Amérique Latine* (Paris) (July–September 1980): 8.
11. According to Edelberto Torres Rivas, "Vie et mort au Guatemala, réflexions sur la crise et la violence politique," *Amérique Latine* (April–June 1980): 5.
12. See "El Salvador: The Process of Political Development and Modernization"

in Ronald McDonald, *Party Systems and Elections in Latin America* (Chicago, 1971, pp. 260–63.

13. He is not alone; one may read in *El Salvador, Election Factbook, 1967,* Institute for the Comparative Study of Political Systems, p. 13: "Ninety percent of the dozen political parties which have functioned since 1944 have been in reality military cliques or factions in disguise."

14. Cf. "Mixed Blessings for Government in Panamanian Poll Result," *Latin America Weekly Report* (London) (October 3, 1980).

15. "La visite à Paris du président Royo," *Le Monde,* May 3, 1979.

16. Víctor Meza, "Honduras; crisis del reformismo military y coyuntura política," *Boletín el Instituto de Investigaciones Económicas y Sociales,* Universidad Autónoma Nacional de Honduras (Tegucigalpa), no. 98 (September 1980).

17. Ibid., and *Latin American Weekly Report* (August 22, 1980).

18. Cf. Salvador Sánchez Estrada, "La repressión des indiens dans la frange transversale nord du Guatemala," *Amérique Latine* (April–June 1980): 73–77.

19. The anticommunist right consists of six parties. In 1979 the legal opposition included the Christian Democratic party, the Social Democratic party, and the United Front of the Revolution. These legal opposition parties have lost a great number of cadres assassinated by paramilitary forces.

20. Cf. Susan Jonas and David Tobias, *Guatemala, una historia inmediata* (Mexico, 1976), p. 318.

21. According to the formulation of José Alvaro Moises, "Crise política e democracia: a transicao dificil," *Revista de Cultura e Política* (São Paulo), no. 2 (August 1980): 13.

22. Cf. Luciano Martins, "La réorganisation des partis politiques et la crise économique au Brésil," *Problèmes d'Amérique Latine* (Paris), LV (March 1980): 23.

23. See Alain Rouquié, "Le modèle brésilien a l'épreuve," *Etudes* (May 1977): 628–32.

24. F. H. Cardoso, "Les impasses du régime autoritaire: le cas brésilien," *Problèmes d'Amérique Latine* LIV (December 1979): 104.

25. The plans for electoral reform designed to give an advantage to those in power and to conservative parties would thus be associated with sophisticated forms of "gerrymandering," assuring a comfortable majority to the "system." But even in the bosom of the PDS there is no agreement on the use of such strategies. Cf. "Golbery Plots on Strategy for the Rest of the Year," *Latin American Regional Report* (Brazil).

26. Cf. *Le Monde,* November 29, 1980, and *La Prensa* (Buenos Aires), (December 3, 1980).

27. Cf. Luis Rico Ortiz, "Uruguay, un análisis del plebisciot" (Paris, 1981) (multigr.), p. 37.

28. Cf. Alain Rouquié, "Le retour du general Perón au pouvoir," "Les élections generales du 11 mars 1973 et l'élection présidentielle du 23 septembre," *Problèmes d'Amérique Latine* XXXIII (September 1974): 20.

29. Ibid., p. 31.

30. *Le Monde,* July 14, 1978.

31. See my article "Argentine: Les fausses sorties de l'armée et l'institutionnalisation du pouvoir militaire," *Problèmes d'Amérique Latine* LIV (December 1979): 109–29.

32. General Pavia, in 1874, at the head of an infantry battalion dissolved the Cortes and put an end to the ephemeral republic before delivering power to Serrano, who governed dictatorially. Cf. F. G. Bruguera, *Histoire contemporaine d'Espagne, 1789–1950* (1953), p. 286, and Manuel Tunon de Lara, *La España del siglo XIX, 1808–1914* (Paris, 1961), p. 194.

33. Wanderley Guilherme Dos Santos, "A ciência política na América Latina (notas preliminares de autocritica)," *Dados* (Rio de Janeiro) 23, no. 1 (1980): 24.
34. Cf. Sergio Spoerer, *América Latina, los desafíos del tiempo fecundo* (Mexico, 1980).
35. Thus, retirement will henceforth be established on a system of individual "capitalization," and not as a function of the principle of national solidarity; cf. "Reforma provisional. Compare su futuro," *Ercilla* (Santiago) (November 26, 1980).
36. On this subject the reader should look at my article, "Révolutions militaires et indépendance nationale en Amérique Latine (1968–1971)," *Revue Française de Science Politique* XXI, nos. 5–6 (October and December 1971).
37. Cf. "Declaración del Pacto Andino contra el golpe militar," *El País,* (Madrid) (November 14, 1979).
38. J. Schumpeter, *Capitalisme, socialisme et démocratie* (Paris, 1965), p. 368.
39. Mariano Grondona, *Visión* (Mexico) (May 1, 1976). See the discussion of this point of view by Daniel Waksman Schinca in *El Día* (Mexico) (May 11, 1976) ("Algo más que simples dictaduras").
40. According to Lucía Pinochet, the president's daughter, *Hoy,* no. 151 (June 11, 1980), quoted by C. Hurtado Beca, "Le processus d'institutionnalisation . . . ," op. cit., p. 89.
41. Cf. Alain Rouquié, "La hipótesis bonapartista y el surgimiento de sistemas políticos semi-competitivos," *Revista Mexicana de Sociología,* no. E (1978): 164–65.
42. Cf. on this point Eliezer Rizzo de Oliveira, "Conflits militaires et décisions sous la présidence du général Geisel," in Alain Rouquié et al., *Les partis militaires au Brésil* (Paris, 1980), pp. 134–39.
43. Eliezer Rizzo de Oliveira, ibid., and *As forças armadas: política e ideología no Brasil* (1964–69) (Petropolis), pp. 10–11.
44. As Goes Monteiro, Dutra, Teixeira Lott, or Albuquerque Lima all had been in their time.
45. This is what General Morales Bermúdez stated in an interview in April 1979, "Un entretien avec le président du Pérou," *Le Monde,* April 13, 1979.
46. According to Hugo Neira, "Au Pérou le retour de l'oligarchie," *Etudes* (Paris) (October 1980): 304.
47. "Posición oficial ante la Comisión fue expuesta anoche al pais por Harguindeguy," *La Nación,* September 24, 1979.
48. *Movimento,* February 23, 1981.
49. According to the formulation of Ricardo Balbín, leader of the Argentine Radical party, who would accept the imposition of this "law."
50. The relations with the narcotics mafia and the self-interested protection given by the present leaders of the country to the drug traffickers (see *Newsweek,* February 2 and March 9, 1981, and *Le Matin-Magazine* (Paris) October 18), in fact cover over structural, permanent phenomena that one might characterize as "privatization of the state" or "patrimonialization of the bureaucracy" and that Laurence Whitehead has analyzed as an "absence of relations of legitimate authority" and of "group domination" in his article "El estado y los intereses seccionales: el caso boliviano," *Estudios Andinos,* no. 10 (1974–75).
51. See the conclusion of my book *Pouvoir militaire et société politique,* op. cit.
52. Gerard Fenoy, "L'armée en Colombie," *Cahiers du monde hispanique el luso-brésilien* (Toulouse), 26 (1976): 86–87. Only supporters of the conservative Laureano Gómez were opposed to the military solution to the crisis.
53. See Constantino Urcuyo Fournier, "Les forces de sécurité publiques et al politique au Costa Rica, 1960–78," (Thesis, Paris, September 1978), chap. 1.

54. Régis Debray, "Nicaragua, une modération radicale," *Le Monde Diplomatique,* September 1979, p. 8.
55. This is what appeared on reading the military program of the Sandinista government; see "Organización de un nuevo ejército nacional," in Programa de la Junta de Gobierno de Reconstrucción Nacional de Nicaragua, published in *Bohemia* (Cuba), August 3, 1979.
56. Jorge I. Domínguez, "The Civic Soldier in Cuba," in Catherine Mardle Kelleher, ed., *Political-Military Systems, Comparative Perspectives* (Beverly Hills, 1971), pp. 209–37.
57. See Alfonso Camacho, "Bolivia: militares en la política," *Aportes* (October 1971): 7376.
58. This is the position defended by the leadership of the Spanish Socialist Worker's party (PSOE) against its left wing. This position was reinforced by the failed putsch of February 23, 1981. See the interview of Felipe González, general secretary of the PSOE, in *L'Unité,* March 7, 1981.
59. Where one has been able to witness joint action at the time of the great demonstration for democracy which followed the antiparliamentary putsch, by former high officials of the Franco regime like Fraga Iribarne and the communist, socialist, and syndicated leaders of the oppositon.
60. Post-Kemalist Turkey offers this type of scenario in the framework of an elected regime set up by the postmilitary state. But with a coup d'état every ten years since 1960, one can scarcely offer it as an example of demilitarization of the political system.

Contributors

Alexandre de S.C. Barros is Associate Professor and Researcher at IUPERJ in Rio de Janeiro. His 1978 dissertation for the University of Chicago analyzed the impact of professionalization on the Brazilian military. His publications include articles and papers on international conflict and civil-military relations.

Douglas A. Chalmers is Professor of Political Science at Columbia University. His publications include *Changing Latin America* (New York Academy of Political Science, 1972) and numerous articles and chapters on Latin American politics, parties, and the state.

Peter S. Cleaves is currently working for the First National Bank of Chicago. From 1977 to 1982 he was a Ford Foundation representative in Mexico. His publications include *Bureaucratic Politics and Administration in Chile* (Berkeley, Calif., 1974) and *Agriculture, Bureaucracy, and Military Government in Peru* (Cornell, 1980).

Edmundo C. Coelho is Associate Professor and Researcher at IUPERJ in Rio. His publications include *Em Busca de Identidade: O Exécito e a Política na Sociedad Brasileira* and other works on organization theory and military sociology.

Jorge Domínguez is Professor of Politics at Harvard University. His publications include *Cuba: Order and Revolution* (Belknap, 1978), *Insurrection or Loyalty* (Cambridge: Harvard University Press, 1980), *Cuba: Internal and International Affairs* (Beverly Hills, Calif.: Sage Publications, 1982), and *Central America: Current Crisis and Future Prospects* (Foreign Policy Association, 1984).

J. Samuel Fitch is Associate Professor of Political Science at the University of Colorado in Boulder. His publications include *The Coup d'Etat as a Political Process* (The Johns Hopkins Press, 1977) and articles on

civil-military relations, U.S. military assistance, and human rights in
Latin America.

Jonathan Hartlyn is Assistant Professor of Political Science at Vanderbilt
University. His publications include articles on politics and policy
processes in Colombia.

Abraham F. Lowenthal is Professor of International Relations at the Univer-
sity of Southern California, Executive Director of the Inter-American
Dialogue, and former Director of the Latin American Program at the
Woodrow Wilson International Center for Scholars. His publications
include *The Dominican Intervention* (Harvard, 1972), *The Peruvian
Experiment* (Princeton: Princeton University Press, 1975), and *The
Peruvian Experiment Reconsidered* (Princeton: Princeton University
Press, 1983).

Richard Millett is Professor of History at Southern Illinois University at
Edwardsville. His publications include, *Guardians of the Dynasty*
(Maryknoll, N.Y.: Orbis, 1977), *The Restless Caribbean* (New York:
Praeger, 1979), and other works on the military and U.S. policy in
Central America.

Liisa North is Professor of the Faculty of Arts and Fellow of the Centre for
Research on Latin America and the Caribbean at York University.
Her publications include *Civil-Military Relations in Argentina, Chile,
and Peru* (California-Berkeley, 1973), *Bitter Ground: The Roots of
Revolt in El Salvador* (Westport, Conn.: Lawrence Hill, 1981), and
articles on the military and politics in Latin America.

José Nun is Professor of Political Science at the University of Toronto and
Director of CLADE in Buenos Aires. His publications include works
on Latin American society and politics. His current research focuses
on the consolidation and institutionalization of democratic regimes.

Guillermo O'Donnell is Academic Director of the Helen Kellogg Institute
for International Studies at the University of Notre Dame where he
holds the Kellogg Chair in International Studies. He is also a Fellow
of IUPERJ in Rio de Janeiro. His publications include *Modernization
and Bureaucratic Authoritarianism* (California-Berkeley, 1973), *El Estado Burocrático Autoritario, 1966–1973* (Ed. Belgrano, 1982), and
Transitions From Authoritarianism (The Johns Hopkins Press, forthcoming).

Henry Pease García is Director of the Center for the Study and Promotion
of Development (DESCO) in Lima and Professor in the Catholic

University of Peru. His publications include *El Ocaso del Poder Oligárquico* (DESCO, 1977), *Los Caminos del Poder* (DESCO, 1979), and other works on military governments and politics in Peru.

David Pion-Berlin is Assistant Professor of Political Science at Ohio State University. His publications include articles on military regimes and political repression in Argentina and Chile. His research interests include the role of ideas in social science inquiry.

Karen L. Remmer is Associate Professor of Political Science at the University of New Mexico and Associate Editor of the *Latin American Research Review*. Her publications include *Party Competition in Argentina and Chile* (Nebraska, 1984) and articles and papers on military government, the impact of military rule, and economic stabilization.

Craig H. Robinson is currently a researcher at American University. His dissertation for Columbia University analyzed the process of liberalization of the military regime in Peru.

David Ronfeldt is a member of the permanent staff of The Rand Corporation. His publications include *Atencingo: The Politics of Struggle in a Mexican Village* (Stanford, 1973), *The Modern Mexican Military* (San Diego, Calif., 1984), and articles and monographs on international politics and U.S. policy in Latin America.

Alain Rouquié is a member of the Centre d'Etudes et de Recherches Internationales in Paris. His publications include *Poder Militar y Sociedad Política en Argentina* (EMECE Editores, 1981), *Argentina, Hoy* (Siglo XXI, 1982), and *Cómo Renacen las Democracias* (EMECE Editores, 1985).

Alfred Stepan is Professor of Political Science and Dean of the School of International and Public Affairs at Columbia University. His publications include *The Military in Politics: Changing Patterns in Brazil* (Princeton, 1971), *Authoritarian Brazil* (New Haven: Yale University Press, 1973), and *The State and Society: Peru in Comparative Perspective* (Princeton: Princeton University Press, 1978).

Index